SO-AMO-858

POPE PIUS XII LIB., ST. JOSEPH COLLEGE
3 2528 01303 0491

341

DATE DUE   61772

INTERNATIONAL LAW: CURRENT AND CLASSIC

INTERNATIONAL LAW

Current and Classic

RICHARD N. SWIFT

New York University

John Wiley & Sons, Inc.

NEW YORK • LONDON • SYDNEY • TORONTO

Copyright © 1969 by John Wiley & Sons, Inc.

All rights reserved. No part of this book may
be reproduced by any means, nor transmitted,
nor translated into a machine language without
the written permission of the publisher.
10   9   8   7   6   5   4   3   2   1

Library of Congress Catalog Card Number: 68-23928
SBN   471   83980   9
Printed in the United States of America

To my father
and to the memory of my mother

Preface

This book has been prepared to help liberal arts students and, particularly, students of international relations understand the role that law plays in international affairs. It will serve equally well to introduce international law to future law students who can, with guidance from their instructors, use it to acquire basic techniques, which are important for every lawyer.

Casebooks on international law often appear formidable to the beginner, and textbooks on the subject are sometimes so removed from litigation that they deny most students access to the exciting controversy that is one of the law's most interesting features. By concentrating on principal issues in international law and by eliminating legal minutiae, I have tried to present here illustrative materials and commentary, which teachers and students can use as a basis for discussions. The book should, moreover, help communicate the essentials of international law to the ordinary citizens upon whom, in the last analysis, any better world depends.

RICHARD N. SWIFT

Contents

Cases and Documents Quoted or Cited*

* Grateful acknowledgement is made to the American Society of International Law for permission to reproduce those cases and documents taken from the *American Journal of International Law* and *International Legal Materials*.

List of Abbreviations

A.J.I.L.	*American Journal of International Law*
Annual Digest	*Annual Digest of Public International Law Cases* (1919–1949); from 1950, entitled *International Law Reports;* London
Butler and Jacoby	Geoffrey Butler and Simon Maccoby, *The Development of International Law* (London: Longmans Green, 1928)
B.Y.B.I.L.	*British Year Book of International Law*
Clunet	*Journal du Droit International Privé et de la Jurisprudence Comparée* (founded 1874 by Edouard Clunet; from 1915, entitled *Journal du Droit International* (Paris)
de Visscher	*Théories et Réalités en Droit International* (1952; 2d ed., 1955), translated by Percy E. Corbett as *Theory and Reality in Public International Law* (Princeton: Princeton University Press, 1957)
D.S.B.	United States *Department of State Bulletin*
F. Supp.	Federal Supplement, containing decisions of U.S. District Courts
F. 2d	Federal Reporter, 2nd series, containing decisions of U.S. Circuit Courts
G.A.	United Nations General Assembly
Hackworth	Green Haywood Hackworth, *Digest of International Law* (8 vols., Washington: Government Printing Office, 1940–1944)
Harvard Research	Research in International Law under the auspices of the Law School of Harvard University, directed by Manley O. Hudson, published as supplements to *A.J.I.L.*

Hudson, *International Legislation*	Manley O. Hudson, *International Legislation* (9 vols., Washington: Carnegie Endowment for International Peace, 1931–1937)
Hyde	Charles Cheney Hyde, *International Law, Chiefly as Interpreted and Applied by the United States* (2d ed. rev., 3 vols., Boston: Little, Brown and Company, 1947)
I.C.J.	*Publications of the International Court of Justice*
I.L.M.	*International Legal Materials*
International Law Reports	See *Annual Digest, supra*
J.D.I.	See Clunet, *supra*
K.B.	King's Bench Division, Great Britain, High Court of Justice
Moore, *Digest*	John Bassett Moore, *Digest of International Law* (8 vols., Washington: Government Printing Office, 1906).
P.C.I.J.	*Publications of the Permanent Court of International Justice*
O.R.	*Official Records* of the General Assembly (G.A.) or Security Council (S.C.)
R.S.	Revised Statutes of the United States
Ralston's Report	*Venezuelan Arbitrations of 1903*, prepared by Jackson H. Ralston, assisted by W. T. Sherman Doyle (Washington: Government Printing Office, 1904)
Rec. A.D.I.	*Recueil des Cours de l'Academie de Droit International de la Haye*
R.D.I.L.C.	*Revue de Droit International et de Législation Comparée* (Brussels)
S.C.	Security Council of the United Nations
Schwarzenberger	Georg Schwarzenberger, *International Law* (2d ed., London: Stevens and Sons, 1949)
Sirey	*Recueil General des Lois et des Arrets* (founded by J.-B. Sirey)
Sørensen	Max Sørensen, "Law of the Sea," *International Conciliation* No. 520 (New York:

	Carnegie Endowment for International Peace, 1958)
Stat.	United States *Statutes-at-Large*
T.I.A.S.	U.S. Treaties and Other International Acts Series
T.S.	U.S. Treaty Series
U.N.C.I.O. Docs.	*Documents of the United Nations Conference on International Organization, San Francisco, 1945* (16 vols., 1945–1946)
U.N. Doc.	United Nations Document
U.N.T.S.	United Nations Treaty Series
U.S.	United States or *U.S. Supreme Court Reports*
U.S. For. Rel.	*Papers Relating to the Foreign Relations of the United States*
Whiteman	Marjorie M. Whiteman, *Digest of International Law* (Washington: Government Printing Office, 1963 ff.)

INTERNATIONAL LAW: CURRENT AND CLASSIC

CHAPTER I

Introduction to International Law

The Nature of International Law

Law is everywhere. Rigid laws govern the lives of all plants and animals on earth; and above the earth:

> The heavens themselves, the planets and this centre
> Observe degree, priority, and place,
> Insisture, course, proportion, season, form
> Office and custom, in all line of order.[1]

The more scientists investigate, the more evidence of natural orderliness they find. Nature mercilessly requires each of us to respect her laws and, although she creates an infinite variety of species, she makes each member of the genus basically alike. History has shown us, furthermore, that when men live in groups and form societies, they require an order that goes beyond the one nature has imposed upon them. For this additional regime they usually look to time-honored customs, or they establish reasonable rules to make life manageable and comfortable. Many such codes of law exist, of course, in a world of many peoples.

Small, weak, or primitive societies traditionally had simple codes of conduct, but strong centralized societies, like the modern nation-states, have had to develop an intricate network of laws and a complex machinery to interpret and enforce their rules. Many tensions in new states arise, in fact, from the effort governments are making to move from one type of society to another.

Still another level of human activity that men have recognized exists in the "Society of Nations." This society has never been strong; it has never developed a formal constitution; and it has never had a central government. The institutions that it has created, like the League of Nations and the United Nations, have been weak. Nonetheless, the mod-

[1] Shakespeare, *Troilus and Cressida*, I, iii, l. 85.

1

ern nation-state could not develop apart from the Society of Nations, since from the very start, men neither could nor would live in isolated national communities. Men have always wanted and needed to trade, visit, and communicate with their neighbors, near and far, and to do so in an orderly fashion they had to agree upon the rules they believed they should observe in meeting and treating with each other. These rules are known collectively as international law.

Some students of international relations deny that there is any such thing as international *law*, because to them the essence of law is the force that designated agents use to compel members of society to obey rules, and no such force exists in the Society of Nations. Those who argue that international law does in fact exist justify their use of the word *law* in various ways. Some point out that many legal systems have lacked sanctions, that is to say, means of enforcing the rules, in the early stages of their development; others say that war and reprisals may be considered crude sanctions of international law; and a third group talks of systems of "pure" law, insisting that the law exists whether or not states abide by it or enforce it. Actually the reasons why law binds its subjects are manifold and complex, and all the theories are valid to some degree.

The problem of why subjects obey the law appears in a more familiar guise when one asks himself why one obeys the laws of his own state. Why, for instance, do most people refrain from stealing? True, every community has laws against robbery and enforces them. But the laws and their enforcement do not by any means account for the extent to which people respect one another's property. Fear of punishment obviously deters some would-be criminals. But states—at least free states—cannot depend entirely on fear of sanctions to enforce the law. When a state leans too heavily on fear or force, it is too likely to fall into violence and revolution to be an ideal legal order. In most cases, the laws against stealing are easy to enforce because the average person is honest. He refrains from stealing not merely because criminal law forbids it or because he fears punishment, but because stealing violates a sense of moral law inculcated by parents and teachers. He obeys the law because it coincides with his own moral values, and faced with temptation, he is restrained more by moral than criminal sanctions.

On the other hand, when the civil or criminal law violates man's sense of what is right and proper, he is likely to ignore the law even as many Americans flouted the Eighteenth Amendment to their Constitution, prohibiting traffic in intoxicating liquors, which until its repeal was probably honored more in the breach than in the observance. The laws of a nation-state bind the citizen most securely when they correspond to his feeling that they are "right." That is why communities attempting to establish new laws against such offenses as littering or jaywalking are usually successful not at the moment when they pass the laws, but only when, with educational campaigns, they win the support of citizens. Likewise, the passage of the U.S. Voting Rights Act of 1965[2] will not create binding law everywhere until an overwhelming majority of citizens are determined to enforce it.

Obviously states do not depend only upon the consciences of their citizens to get people to observe the law. They rely upon their legislative, executive, and judicial authorities, and they provide sanctions which are, ideally, just and swift. It is in these institutional devices that everyone, regardless of his theories, agrees that international law in its present form is inadequate: it does not have the legislative, executive, or judicial machinery of the nation-state. And although sincere observers have put forward radical proposals for world federation and world law to fill the gaps that now exist, history suggests that any lasting remedies for the law's defects will come not by suddenly transforming existing institutions, but only by helping new law to evolve. In international society, as Philip Jessup has pointed out, we have learned to speak of developing rather than undeveloped or even underdeveloped nations; international law, too, may be regarded not as undeveloped or underdeveloped law, but as developing law.[3] To move into a better world tomorrow, man must start with the imperfect tools at his disposal today. One of these tools is an international law that is not administered by a central agency, not a complete code of law, not always clear, and to which states subject themselves in varying degrees on different occasions.

The Lotus Case below illustrates the shortcomings of international law, which students should bear in mind at the outset.

[2] Public Law, 79 Stat. 437, 89–110.
[3] Philip C. Jessup, "Diversity and Uniformity in the Law of Nations," *A.J.I.L.*, LVIII (1964), 343.

THE S. S. LOTUS

Permanent Court of International Justice, 1927

Series A, No. 10

THE FACTS[4]

. . . .

On August 2nd, 1926, just before midnight, a collision occurred between the French mail steamer *Lotus*, proceeding to Constantinople, and the Turkish collier *Boz-Kourt*, between five and six nautical miles to the north of Cape Sigri (Mitylene). The *Boz-Kourt*, which was cut in two, sank, and eight Turkish nationals who were on board perished. After having done everything possible to succour the shipwrecked persons, of whom ten were able to be saved, the *Lotus* continued on its course to Constantinople, where it arrived on August 3rd.

At the time of the collision, the officer of the watch on board the Lotus was Monsieur Demons, a French citizen, lieutenant in the merchant service and first officer of the ship, whilst the movements of the *Boz-Kourt* were directed by its captain, Hassan Bey, who was one of those saved from the wreck.

As early as August 3rd the Turkish police proceeded to hold an enquiry into the collision on board the Lotus; and on the following day, August 4th, the captain of the *Lotus* handed in his master's report at the French Consulate-General, transmitting a copy to the harbour master.

On August 5th, Lieutenant Demons was requested by the Turkish authorities to go ashore to give evidence. The examination, the length of which incidentally resulted in delaying the departure of the *Lotus*, led to the placing under arrest of Lieutenant Demons—without previous notice being given to the French Consul-General—and Hassan Bey, amongst others. This arrest, which has been characterized by the Turkish Agent as arrest pending trial (*arrestation preventive*), was effected in order to ensure that the criminal prosecution instituted against the two officers, on a charge of manslaughter, by the Public Prosecutor of Stamboul, on the complaint of the families of the victims of the collision, should follow its normal course.

The case was first heard by the Criminal Court of Stamboul on August 28th. On that occasion, Lieutenant Demons submitted that the Turkish Courts had no jurisdiction; the Court, however, overruled his objection. When the proceedings were resumed on September 11th, Lieutenant Demons demanded his release on bail: this request was complied with on September 13th, the bail being fixed at 6,000 Turkish pounds.

On September 15th the Criminal Court delivered its judgment, the terms of which have not been communicated to the Court by the Parties. It is, however, common ground, that it sentenced Lieutenant Demons to eighty days' imprisonment and a fine of twenty-two pounds, Hassan Bey being sentenced to a slightly more severe penalty.

[4] [1927] *P.C.I.J.*, Ser. A, No. 10, pp. 10–12.

It is also common ground between the Parties that the Public Prosecutor of the Turkish Republic entered an appeal against this decision, which had the effect of suspending its execution until a decision upon the appeal had been given; that such decision has not yet been given; but that the special agreement of October 12th, 1926, did not have the effect of suspending "the criminal proceedings . . . now in progress in Turkey."

The action of the Turkish judicial authorities with regard to Lieutenant Demons at once gave rise to many diplomatic representations and other steps on the part of the French Government or its representatives in Turkey, either protesting against the arrest of Lieutenant Demons or demanding his release, or with a view to obtaining the transfer of the case from the Turkish Courts to the French Courts.

As a result of these representations, the Government of the Turkish Republic declared on September 2nd, 1926, that "it would have no objection to the rerference of the conflict of jurisdiction to the Court at The Hague."

The French Government having, on the 6th of the same month, given "its full consent to the proposed solution," the two Governments appointed their plenipotentiaries with a view to the drawing up of the special agreement to be submitted to the Court; this special agreement was signed at Geneva on October 12th, 1926, and the ratifications were deposited on December 27th, 1926.

[THE ISSUES][5]

According to the special agreement, the Court has to decide the following questions:

(1) Has Turkey, contrary to Article 15 of the Convention of Lausanne of July 24th, 1923, respecting conditions of residence and business and jurisdiction, acted in conflict with the principles of international law—and if so, what principles— . . . as well as against the captain of the Turkish steamship—[by instituting] joint criminal proceedings in pursuance of Turkish law against M. Demons, officer of the watch on board the *Lotus* at the time of the collision, in consequence of the loss of the *Boz-Kourt* having involved the death of eight Turkish sailors and passengers?

(2) Should the reply be in the affirmative, what pecuniary reparation is due to M. Demons, provided, according to the principles of international law, reparation should be made in similar cases?

THE LAW[6]

I

. . . The prosecution was instituted because the loss of the *Boz-Kourt* involved the death of eight Turkish sailors and passengers. It is clear, in the first place, that this result of the collision constitutes a factor essential for the institution of the criminal proceedings in question; secondly, it follows

[5] The material in this section has been transposed from its original position in the Court's decision, *ibid.*, p. 5.
[6] *Ibid.*, pp. 13, 14, 16–32.

from the statements of the two Parties that no criminal intention has been imputed to either of the officers responsible for navigating the two vessels; it is therefore a case of prosecution for involuntary manslaughter. . . .

Lieutenant Demons and the captain of the Turkish steamship were prosecuted jointly and simultaneously. . . . [T]he proceedings against the captain of the Turkish vessel in regard to which the jurisdiction of the Turkish Courts is not disputed, and the proceedings against Lieutenant Demons, have been regarded by the Turkish authorities as one and the same prosecution, since the collision of the two steamers constitutes a complex of facts the consideration of which should, from the standpoint of Turkish criminal law, be entrusted to the same court. . . .

II

Having determined the position resulting from the terms of the special agreement, the Court must now ascertain which were the principles of international law that the prosecution of Lieutenant Demons could conceivably be said to contravene.

It is Article 15 of the Convention of Lausanne of July 24th, 1923, respecting conditions of residence and business and jurisdiction, which refers the contracting Parties to the principles of international law as regards the delimitation of their respective jurisdiction.

This clause is as follows:

Subject to the provisions of Article 16, all questions of jurisdiction shall, as between Turkey and the other contracting Powers, be decided in accordance with the principles of international law.

. . . .

Now the Court considers that the words "principles of international law," as ordinarily used, can only mean international law as it is applied between all nations belonging to the community of States. . . . . In these circumstances, it is impossible—except in pursuance of a definite stipulation—to construe the expression "principles of international law" otherwise than as meaning the principles which are in force between all independent nations and which therefore apply equally to all the contracting Parties. . . .

III

The Court, having to consider whether there are any rules of international law which may have been violated by the prosecution in pursuance of Turkish law of Lieutenant Demons, is confronted in the first place by a question of principle which . . . has proved to be a fundamental one. The French Government contends that the Turkish Courts, in order to have jurisdiction, should be able to point to some title to jurisdiction recognized by international law in favour of Turkey. On the other hand, the Turkish Government takes the view that Article 15 allows Turkey jurisdiction whenever such jurisdiction does not come into conflict with a principle of international law.

The latter view seems to be in conformity with the special agreement itself, No. 1 of which asks the Court to say whether Turkey has acted contrary to the principles of international law and, if so, what principles. According to the special agreement, therefore, it is not a question of stating principles which would permit Turkey to take criminal proceedings, but of formulating the principles, if any, which might have been violated by such proceedings.

This way of stating the question is also dictated by the very nature and existing conditions of international law.

International law governs relations between independent States. The rules of law binding upon States therefore emanate from their own free will as expressed in conventions or by usages generally accepted as expressing principles of law and established in order to regulate the relations between these co-existing independent communities or with a view to the achievement of common aims. Restrictions upon the independence of States cannot therefore be presumed.

Now the first and foremost restriction imposed by international law upon a State is that—failing the existence of a permissive rule to the contrary—it may not exercise its power in any form in the territory of another State. In this sense jurisdiction is certainly territorial; it cannot be exercised by a State outside its territory except by virtue of a permissive rule derived from international custom or from a convention.

It does not, however, follow that international law prohibits a State from exercising jurisdiction in its own territory, in respect of any case which relates to acts which have taken place abroad, and in which it cannot rely on some permissive rule of international law. Such a view would only be tenable if international law contained a general prohibition to States to extend the application of their laws and the jurisdiction of their courts to persons, property and acts outside their territory, and if, as an exception to this general prohibition, it allowed States to do so in certain specific cases. But this is certainly not the case under international law as it stands at present. Far from laying down a general prohibition to the effect that States may not extend the application of their laws and the jurisdiction of their courts to persons, property and acts outside their territory, it leaves them in this respect a wide measure of discretion which is only limited in certain cases by prohibitive rules; as regards other cases, every State remains free to adopt the principles which it regards as best and most suitable.

This discretion left to States by international law explains the great variety of rules which they have been able to adopt without objections or complaints on the part of other States; it is in order to remedy the difficulties resulting from such variety that efforts have been made for many years past, both in Europe and America, to prepare conventions the effect of which would be precisely to limit the discretion at present left to States in this respect by international law, thus making good the existing lacunæ in respect of jurisdiction or removing the conflicting jurisdictions arising from the diversity of the principles adopted by the various States.

In these circumstances, all that can be required of a State is that it should not overstep the limits which international law places upon its jurisdiction; within these limits, its title to exercise jurisdiction rests in its sovereignty.

It follows from the foregoing that the contention of the French Government to the effect that Turkey must in each case be able to cite a rule of international law authorizing her to exercise jurisdiction, is opposed to the generally accepted international law to which Article 15 of the Convention of Lausanne refers. Having regard to the terms of Article 15 and to the construction which the Court has just placed upon it, this contention would apply in regard to civil as well as to criminal cases, and would be applicable on conditions of absolute reciprocity as between Turkey and the other contracting Parties; in practice, it would therefore in many cases result in paralyzing the action of the courts, owing to the impossibility of citing a universally accepted rule on which to support the exercise of their jurisdiction.

*　*　*

Nevertheless, it has to be seen whether the foregoing considerations really apply as regards criminal jurisdiction, or whether this jurisdiction is governed by a different principle: this might be the outcome of the close connection which for a long time existed between the conception of supreme criminal jurisdiction and that of a State, and also by the especial importance of criminal jurisdiction from the point of view of the individual.

Though it is true that in all systems of law the principle of the territorial character of criminal law is fundamental, it is equally true that all or nearly all these systems of law extend their action to offences committed outside the territory of the State which adopts them, and they do so in ways which vary from State to State. The territoriality of criminal law, therefore, is not an absolute principle of international law and by no means coincides with territorial sovereignty.

This situation may be considered from two different standpoints corresponding to the points of view respectively taken up by the Parties. According to one of these standpoints, the principle of freedom, in virtue of which each State may regulate its legislation at its discretion, provided that in so doing it does not come in conflict with a restriction imposed by international law, would also apply as regards law governing the scope of jurisdiction in criminal cases. According to the other standpoint, the exclusively territorial character of law relating to this domain constitutes a principle which, except as otherwise expressly provided, would, *ipso facto,* prevent States from extending the criminal jurisdiction of their courts beyond their frontiers; the exceptions in question, which include for instance extraterritorial jurisdiction over nationals and over crimes directed against public safety, would therefore rest on special permissive rules forming part of international law.

Adopting, for the purposes of the argument, the standpoint of the latter of these two systems, it must be recognized that, in the absence of a treaty provision, its correctness depends upon whether there is a custom having the force of law etablishing it. The same is true as regards the applicability of this system—assuming it to have been recognized as sound—in the particular case. It follows that, even from this point of view, before ascertaining whether there may be a rule of international law expressly allowing Turkey to prosecute a foreigner for an offence committed by him outside Turkey, it is necessary to begin by establishing both that the system is well-founded and that it is applicable in the particular case. Now, in order to establish the first of these points, one must, as has just been seen, prove the existence of a principle of international law restricting the discretion of States as regards criminal legislation.

Consequently, whichever of the two systems described above be adopted, the same result will be arrived at in this particular case: the necessity of ascertaining whether or not under international law there is a principle which would have prohibited Turkey, in the circumstances of the case before the Court, from prosecuting Lieutenant Demons. And moreover, on either hypothesis, this must be ascertained by examining precedents offering a close analogy to the case under consideration; for it is only from precedents of this nature that the existence of a general principle applicable to the particular case may appear. For if it were found, for example, that, according to the practice of States, the jurisdiction of the State whose flag was flown was not established by international law as exclusive with regard to collision cases on the high seas, it would not be necessary to ascertain whether there were a more general restriction; since, as regards that restriction—supposing that it existed—the fact that it had been established that there was no prohibition in respect of collision on the high seas would be tantamount to a special permissive rule.

The Court therefore must, in any event, ascertain whether or not there exists a rule of international law limiting the freedom of States to extend the criminal jurisdiction of their courts to a situation uniting the circumstances of the present case.

IV

The Court will now proceed to ascertain whether general international law, to which Article 15 of the Convention of Lausanne refers, contains a rule prohibiting Turkey from prosecuting Lieutenant Demons.

For this purpose, it will in the first place examine the value of the arguments advanced by the French Government, without however omitting to take into account other possible aspects of the problem, which might show the existence of a restrictive rule applicable in this case.

The arguments advanced by the French Government . . . are, in substance, the three following:

(1) International law does not allow a State to take proceedings with regard to offences committed by foreigners abroad, simply by reason of the nationality of the victim; and such is the situation in the present case because the offence must be regarded as having been committed on board the French vessel.

(2) International law recognizes the exclusive jurisdiction of the State

whose flag is flown as regards everything which occurs on board a ship on the high seas.

(3) Lastly, this principle is especially applicable in a collision case.

❉   ❉   ❉

As regards the first argument, the Court feels obliged in the first place to recall that its examination is strictly confined to the specific situation in the present case, for it is only in regard to this situation that its decision is asked for.

As has already been observed, the characteristic features of the situation of fact are as follows: there has been a collision on the high seas between two vessels flying different flags, on one of which was one of the persons alleged to be guilty of the offence, whilst the victims were on board the other.

This being so, the Court does not think it necessary to consider the contention that a State cannot punish offences committed abroad by a foreigner simply by reason of the nationality of the victim. For this contention only relates to the case where the nationality of the victim is the only criterion on which the criminal jurisdiction of the State is based. Even if that argument were correct generally speaking—and in regard to this the Court reserves its opinion—it could only be used in the present case if international law forbade Turkey to take into consideration the fact that the offence produced its effects on the Turkish vessel and consequently in a place assimilated to Turkish territory in which the application of Turkish criminal law cannot be challenged, even in regard to offences committed there by foreigners. But no such rule of international law exists. No argument has come to the knowledge of the Court from which it could be deduced that States recognize themselves to be under an obligation towards each other only to have regard to the place where the author of the offence happens to be at the time of the offence. On the contrary, it is certain that the courts of many countries, even of countries which have given their criminal legislation a strictly territorial character, interpret criminal law in the sense that offences, the authors of which at the moment of commission are in the territory of another State, are nevertheless to be regarded as having been committed in the national territory, if one of the constituent elements of the offence, and more especially its effects, have taken place there. French courts have, in regard to a variety of situations, given decisions sanctioning this way of interpreting the territorial principles. Again, the Court does not know of any cases in which governments have protested against the fact that the criminal law of some country contained a rule to this effect or that the courts of a country construed their criminal law in this sense. Consequently, once it is admitted that the effects of the offence were produced on the Turkish vessel, it becomes impossible to hold that there is a rule of international law which prohibits Turkey from prosecuting Lieutenant Demons because of the fact that the author of the offence was on board the French ship. Since, as has already been observed, the special agreement does not deal with the provision of Turkish law under which the prosecution was instituted, but only with the question whether the prosecution should be regarded as contrary to the principles of international law, there is no reason preventing the Court from confining itself to observing that, in this case, a prosecution may also be justified from the point of view of the so-called territorial principle. . . .

It has been sought to argue that the offence of manslaughter cannot be localized at the spot where the mortal effect is felt; for the effect is not intentional and it cannot be said that there is, in the mind of the delinquent, any culpable intent directed towards the territory where the mortal effect is produced. In reply to this argument it might be observed that the effect is a factor of outstanding importance in offences such as manslaughter, which are punished precisely in consideration of their effects rather than of the subjective intention of the delinquent. But the Court does not feel called upon to consider this question, which is one of interpretation of Turkish criminal law. It will suffice to observe that no argument has been put forward and nothing has been found from which it would follow that international law has established a rule imposing on States this reading of the conception of the offence of manslaughter.

                                ✲   ✲   ✲

The second argument put forward by the French Government is the principle that the State whose flag is flown has exclusive jurisdiction over everything which occurs on board a merchant ship on the high seas.

It is certainly true that—apart from certain special cases which are defined by international law—vessels on the high seas are subject to no authority except that of the State whose flag they fly. In virtue of the principle of the freedom of the seas, that is to say, the absence of any territorial sovereignty upon the high seas, no State may exercise any kind of jurisdiction over foreign vessels upon them. Thus, if a war vessel, happening to be at the spot where a collision occurs between a vessel flying its flag and a foreign vessel, were to send on board the latter an officer to make investigations or to take evidence, such an act would undoubtedly be contrary to international law.

But it by no means follows that a State can never in its own territory exercise jurisdiction over acts which have occurred on board a foreign ship on the high seas.[7] A corollary of the principle of the freedom of the seas

---

[7] Article 11 of the Convention on the High Seas, adopted in 1958 by the United Nations Conference on the Law of the Sea, provides that:

1. In the event of a collision or of any other incident of navigation concerning a ship on the high seas, involving the penal or disciplinary responsibility of the master or of any other person in the service of the ship, no penal or disciplinary proceedings may be instituted against such persons except before the judicial or administrative authorities either of the flag state or of the state of which such person is a national.

2. In disciplinary matters, the state which has issued a master's certificate or a certificate of competence or license shall alone be competent after due legal process, to pronounce the withdrawal of such certificates, even if the holder is

is that a ship on the high seas is assimilated to the territory of the State the flag of which it flies, for, just as in its own territory, that State exercises its authority upon it, and no other State may do so. All that can be said is that by virtue of the principle of the freedom of the seas, a ship is placed in the same position as national territory; but there is nothing to support the claim according to which the rights of the State under whose flag the vessel sails may go farther than the rights which it exercises within its territory properly so called. It follows that what occurs on board a vessel on the high seas must be regarded as if it occurred on the territory of the State whose flag the ship flies. If, therefore, a guilty act committed on the high seas produces its effects on a vessel flying another flag or in foreign territory, the same principles must be applied as if the territories of two different States were concerned, and the conclusion must therefore be drawn that there is no rule of international law prohibiting the State to which the ship on which the effects of the offence have taken place belongs, from regarding the offence as having been committed in its territory and prosecuting, accordingly, the delinquent.

This conclusion could only be overcome if it were shown that there was a rule of customary international law which, going further than the principle stated above, established the exclusive jurisdiction of the State whose flag

---

not a national of the state which issued them.

3. No arrest or detention of the ship, even as a measure of investigation, shall be ordered by any authorities other than those of the flag state.

As of the end of 1967, 40 states had ratified this Convention.

United Nations Conference . . . , *OR*, IV, Second Committee

[In the material below, "article 35" in a draft treaty (U.N. Doc. A/Conf. 13/L. 17/Add. 1, at p. 150 in the above *OR*) is identical with Article 11 of the Convention on the High Seas, as finally adopted.]

[p. 77] 28. Mr. Lütem (Turkey) explained that he had voted against article 35 because it was contrary to a well-known judgement of the Permanent Court of International Justice . . . and to the municipal legislation of his own country, and would adversely affect the exercise of penal jurisdiction. His government earnestly hoped that the United Nations would establish a single international organ to settle disputes about competence in regard to cases arising from collisions or other incidents of navigation on the high seas. . . .

[pp. 58–59] 50. Mr. Lütem (Turkey) regretted that article 35, which dealt with collision and other incidents of navigation on the high seas, stipulated that jurisdiction in such cases could be exercised solely by the flag State—a principle borrowed from the Brussels Convention of 10 May 1952—or by the State of which the accused person was a national. The International Law Commission had stated that the purpose of its proposal was to protect ships and their crews from the risks of penal proceedings before foreign courts, since such proceedings might constitute an intolerable interference with international navigation. Even if those views were accepted—and they seemed to be essentially the views of Powers with large merchant fleets—the Turkish delegation believed that the text proposed by the Commission failed to provide for all the difficulties that might arise.

51. The Turkish delegation's position was based on several considerations. First, the proposed text conflicted with the judgment of the Permanent Court of Interna-

was flown. The French Government has endeavoured to prove the existence of such a rule, having recourse for this purpose to the teachings of publicists, to decisions of municipal and international tribunals, and especially to conventions which, whilst creating exceptions to the principle of the freedom of the seas by permitting the war and police vessels of a State to exercise a more or less extensive control over the merchant vessels of another State, reserve jurisdiction to the courts of the country whose flag is flown by the vessel proceeded against.

In the Court's opinion, the existence of such a rule has not been conclusively proved.

In the first place, as regards teaching of publicists, and apart from the question as to what their value may be from the point of view of establishing the existence of a rule of customary law, it is no doubt true that all or nearly all writers teach that ships on the high seas are subject exclusively to the jurisdiction of the State whose flag they fly. But the important point is the significance attached by them to this principle; now it does not appear that in general, writers bestow upon this principle a scope differing from or wider than that explained above and which is equivalent to saying that

---

tional Justice in the *Lotus* case to which his government had been a party. The Court's decision on that occasion clearly represented the only applicable rule of positive international law, for the 1952 Convention had only been ratified by very few States. Secondly, Turkish legislation contained provisions—the most important being article 6 of the Penal Code—which could not be reconciled with the principles contained in the article. And thirdly, collisions and similar incidents of navigation on the high seas raised other issues besides conflicts of jurisdiction. The most important consideration was in fact the speedy and just punishment of the culprits, which could only be achieved if the case was disposed of by a single authority. Article 35, however, seemed to imply that, in certain circumstances, a case might be investigated by one State and tried by another. The article thus seemed to lay undue stress on the prevention of conflicts of jurisdiction and failed to make adequate provision for the effective prosecution of justice.

52. The problem could only be resolved if it was clearly established that one body alone would be competent. That purpose could be achieved in two ways: jurisdiction might be vested not in several States but in one State only, to be designated by some international committee; or a special international judicial organ might be set up, with full powers to deal with all proceedings arising out of collisions and similar incidents. Which of those alternatives to adopt was a matter solely for the Conference. The Turkish delegation would not insist on its amendment (A/CONF.13/C.2/L.73), but hoped that the article would be reshaped so as to provide a truer reflection of the accepted law in the matter.

[Mr. Gidel (France)]

56. The fears voiced by the Turkish representative regarding article 35 seemed somewhat exaggerated. The Turkish Government's view had been upheld by the Permanent Court of International Justice in the *Lotus* case, and it would accordingly be fully within its rights in formulating an express reservation to the article, stating that it would adhere to the provisions of its own penal code. That, however, was no reason why the provision should not be accepted by the Conference as a whole, especially since the principle of "passive jurisdiction" had in more recent years been the subject of much adverse comment and the signatories to the Brussels Convention of 1952 had agreed that continued adherence to that principle would cause unreasonable interference with international shipping.

the jurisdiction of a State over vessels on the high seas is the same in extent as its jurisdiction in its own territory. On the other hand, there is no lack of writers who, upon a close study of the special question whether a State can prosecute for offences committed on board a foreign ship on the high seas, definitely come to the conclusion that such offences must be regarded as if they had been committed in the territory of the State whose flag the ship flies, and that consequently the general rules of each legal system in regard to offences committed abroad are applicable.

In regard to precedents . . . there is no lack of cases in which a State has claimed a right to prosecute for an offence, committed on board a foreign ship, which it regarded as punishable under its legislation. Thus Great Britain refused the request of the United States for the extradition of John Anderson, a British seaman who had committed homicide on board an American vessel, stating that she did not dispute the jurisdiction of the United States but that she was entitled to exercise hers concurrently. This case, to which others might be added, is relevant in spite of Anderson's British nationality, in order to show that the principle of the exclusive jurisdiction of the country whose flag the vessel flies is not universally accepted.

The cases in which the exclusive jurisdiction of the State whose flag was flown has been recognized would seem rather to have been cases in which the foreign State was interested only by reason of the nationality of the victim, and in which, according to the legislation of that State itself or the practice of its courts, that ground was not regarded as sufficient to authorize prosecution for an offence committed abroad by a foreigner.

Finally, as regards conventions expressly reserving jurisdiction exclusively to the State whose flag is flown, it is not absolutely certain that this stipulation is to be regarded as expressing a general principle of law rather than as corresponding to the extraordinary jurisdiction which these conventions confer on the state-owned ships of a particular country in respect of ships of another country on the high seas. Apart from that, it should be observed that these conventions relate to matters of a particular kind, closely connected with the policing of the seas, such as the slave trade, damage to submarine cables, fisheries, etc., and not to common-law offences. Above all it should be pointed out that the offences contemplated by the conventions in question only concern a single ship; it is impossible therefore to make any deduction from them in regard to matters which concern two ships and consequently the jursidiction of two different States.

The Court therefore has arrived at the conclusion that the second argument put forward by the French Government does not, any more than the first, establish the existence of a rule of international law prohibiting Turkey from prosecuting Lieutenant Demons.

✻　✻　✻

It only remains to examine the third argument advanced by the French Government and to ascertain whether a rule specially applying to collision cases has grown up, according to which criminal proceedings regarding such cases come exclusively within the jursidiction of the State whose flag is flown.

In this connection, the Agent for the French Government has drawn the Court's attention to the fact that questions of jurisdiction in collision cases, which frequently arise before civil courts, are but rarely encountered in the practice of criminal courts. He deduces from this that, in practice, prosecutions only occur before the courts of the State whose flag is flown and that that circumstance is proof of a tacit consent on the part of States and, consequently, shows what positive international law is in collision cases.

In the Court's opinion, this conclusion is not warranted. Even if the rarity of the judicial decisions to be found among the reported cases were sufficient to prove in point of fact the circumstance alleged by the Agent for the French Government, it would merely show that States had often, in practice, abstained from instituting criminal proceedings, and not that they recognized themselves as being obliged to do so; for only if such abstention were based on their being conscious of having a duty to abstain would it be possible to speak of an international custom. The alleged fact does not allow one to infer that States have been conscious of having such a duty; on the other hand, as will presently be seen, there are other circumstances calculated to show that the contrary is true.

So far as the Court is aware there are no decisions of international tribunals in this matter; but some decisions of municipal courts have been cited. Without pausing to consider the value to be attributed to the judgments of municipal courts in connection with the establishment of the existence of a rule of international law, it will suffice to observe that the decisions quoted sometimes support one view and sometimes the other. . . . [As] municipal jurisprudence is thus divided, it is hardly possible to see in it an indication of the existence of the restrictive rule of international law which alone could serve as a basis for the contention of the French Government.

On the other hand, the Court feels called upon to lay stress upon the fact that it does not appear that the States concerned have objected to criminal proceedings in respect of collision cases before the courts of a country other than that the flag of which was flown, or that they have made protests: their conduct does not appear to have differed appreciably from that observed by them in all cases of concurrent jurisdiction. This fact is directly opposed to the existence of a tacit consent on the part of States to the exclusive jurisdiction of the State whose flag is flown, such as the Agent for the French Government has thought it possible to deduce from the infrequency of questions of jurisdiction before criminal courts. It seems hardly probable, and it would not be in accordance with international practice, that [Governments] . . . would have omitted to protest against the exercise of criminal jurisdiction . . . if they had really thought that this was a violation of international law. . . .

The conclusion at which the Court has therefore arrived is that there is no rule of international law in regard to collision cases to the effect that criminal proceedings are exclusively within the jurisdiction of the State whose flag is flown.

The offence for which Lieutenant Demons appears to have been prosecuted was an act—of negligence or imprudence—having its origin on board the

Lotus, whilst its effects made themselves felt on board the *Boz-Kourt*. These two elements are, legally, entirely inseparable, so much so that their separation renders the offence non-existent. Neither the exclusive jurisdiction of either State, nor the limitations of the jurisdiction of each to the occurrences which took place on the respective ships would appear calculated to satisfy the requirements of justice and effectively to protect the interests of the two States. It is only natural that each should be able to exercise jurisdiction and to do so in respect of the incident as a whole. It is therefore a case of concurrent jurisdiction.

* * *

The Court, having arrived at the conclusion that the arguments advanced by the French Government either are irrelevant to the issue or do not establish the existence of a principle of international law precluding Turkey from instituting the prosecution which was in fact brought against Lieutenant Demons, observes that in the fulfilment of its task of itself ascertaining what the international law is, it has not confined itself to a consideration of the arguments put forward, but has included in its researches all precedents, teachings and facts to which it had access and which might possibly have revealed the existence of one of the principles of international law contemplated in the special agreement. The result of these researches has not been to establish the existence of any such principle. It must therefore be held that there is no principle of international law, within the meaning of Article 15 of the Convention of Lausanne of July 24th, 1923, which precludes the institution of the criminal proceedings under consideration. Consequently, Turkey, by instituting, in virtue of the discretion which international law leaves to every sovereign State, the criminal proceedings in question, has not, in the absence of such principles, acted in a manner contrary to the principles of international law within the meaning of the special agreement. . . .

V

Having thus answered the first question submitted by the special agreement in the negative, the Court need not consider the second question, regarding the pecuniary reparation which might have been due to Lieutenant Demons.

FOR THESE REASONS, the Court, having heard both Parties, gives, by the President's casting vote—the votes being equally divided—judgment to the effect

(1) that, following the collision which occurred on August 2nd, 1926, on the high seas between the French steamship *Lotus* and the Turkish steamship *Boz-Kourt*, and upon the arrival of the French ship at Stamboul, and in consequence of the loss of the *Boz-Kourt* having involved the death of eight Turkish nationals, Turkey, by instituting criminal proceedings in pursuance of Turkish law against Lieutenant Demons, officer of the watch on board the *Lotus* at the time of the collision, has not acted in conflict with the principles of international law, contrary to Article 15 of the Convention

of Lausanne of July 24th, 1923, respecting conditions of residence and business
and jurisdiction;

(2) that, consequently, there is no occasion to give judgment on the question of the pecuniary reparation which might have been due to Lieutenant
Demons if Turkey, by prosecuting him as above stated, had acted in a manner
contrary to the principles of international law. . . .

The Basis and Sources of International Law

In *The Lotus Case* the Court advances reasons why it believes international law binds states, and it alludes to the sources of the law when
it observes that the "rules of law binding upon States . . . emanate
from their own free will as expressed in conventions or by usages generally accepted as expressing principles of law. . . ."[8] It should be obvious, however, that a system of law which rests on the consent of those
who are subject to its rules might be undesirably elastic,[9] and theorists
have developed other ways of explaining why states might consider
themselves bound by international law. One theory finds the roots of
international law in natural law, universally applicable rules derived
from "right reason." The Stoic philosophers originally developed the
idea of natural law in Greece of the third century B.C., and their ideas
were transmitted in modified form through Roman and medieval times
to the 16th and 17th century writers on international law.[10] In succeeding
centuries, when exactly what "right reason" stood for seemed less clear
than it had been to people closer to the Middle Ages, natural law came
to seem increasingly unsatisfactory as a basis for the law of nations.
In the nineteenth century, the theory that international law rested in
large part on universal moral principles (naturalism) gave way to theories which based the law entirely on the will and practice of states
(positivism). The ultimate logic of positivism, however, embraces the
idea that whatever is is right, and robs the law of any ethical standards
by which to judge state behavior. Modern writers recognize inadequacies
in both naturalism and positivism, and many scholars and practitioners
now believe that the basis of obligation in law lies outside the law
itself in unprovable premises, for example, in *pacta sunt servanda*
("treaties must be observed") or in *voluntas civitatis maximae est
servanda* ("the will of the international community must be obeyed").[11]

[8] Supra, p. 7.
[9] Charles De Visscher, "Contribution à l'étude des sources de droit international,"
R.D.I.L.C., XIV (3rd ser., 1933), 395–420.
[10] Arthur Nussbaum, *The Concise History of the Law of Nations* (New York: The
Macmillan Company, 1947), pp. 20–21.
[11] D. Anzilotti, *Cours de Droit International*, I, 42–43 (Gidel, transl., 1929); and
H. Lauterpacht, *The Function of Law in the International Community* (Oxford:
Clarendon Press, 1933), pp. 418–423.

Axioms may seem to be flimsy foundations for law, but they are the basis not only of international law but of domestic law as well. Every society rests upon the implicit agreement of the members to abide by certain fundamentals. Up to the 19th century, for instance, many people believed that monarchs derived their right to command from the "Divine Right of Kings." Despite many political tracts on the subject, no one could prove that there was in fact a Divine Right, or that, even if it did exist, it was an adequate basis for government. Both king and subject had to assume that it was a valid theory and, as long as they both believed in it, they could base their political society upon it. When enough subjects began to doubt that the assumption of Divine Right was valid and became dissatisfied with it, the revolutions of the 17th, 18th, and 19th centuries took place. Divine Right was discarded in favor of the theory that governments, in the words of the American Declaration of Independence, "are instituted among Men, deriving their just powers from the consent of the governed." But the adherents of this theory of consent, the democrats, can no more prove their theory than the absolutists could prove theirs; they too assume that they have an adequate basis of government. And as long as the people believe the theory, they have. When it no longer seems reasonable to the people, democracy perishes as it did in fascist Italy and Nazi Germany, or fails to establish itself firmly, as in many new states. As a practical matter, then, a theory of government and law must satisfy the citizens, and if it does, they need no further proof of its validity.

What is true about the law in the nation-state is also true about international law: it rests on certain axioms, but different theorists subscribe to different axioms. Jurists consequently find it necessary to fortify their decisions by speculating on the premises at the base of international law, as in the cases of *The United States v. The Schooner La Jeune Eugénie* and *The Antelope*. Both these cases have to do with the slave trade which flourished in the 18th and 19th centuries until international humanitarian movements brought pressure on governments to bring it to an end. The United States could not act on the matter for more than two decades because according to the United States Constitution, Congress might not interfere with the "Importation of Such Persons as any of the States . . . shall think proper to admit . . . prior to the Year one thousand eight hundred and eight" (Art. I, Section 9). In that year, Congress did prohibit further importation of slaves. Great Britain had outlawed the slave trade in 1807; Sweden followed suit in 1813; Holland in 1814; and the United States Congress went further in 1820 by denouncing as a pirate any person within the jurisdiction of the United States who engaged in the slave trade.

The illicit trade persisted, however, under the flags of nations which had not declared the traffic illegal. Great Britain at first attempted to fight it singlehanded by ordering her cruisers to visit suspected vessels, and at the Congress of Vienna, the British proposed an economic boycott against countries which refused to abolish the slave trade. Since the British fleet would have had to enforce the boycott, and since the other European nations did not desire to support measures to strengthen Britain's maritime supremacy, the governments merely adopted a general declaration

. . . that, regarding the universal abolition of the trade in negroes as a measure particularly worthy of their attention. . . . they are animated by a sincere desire to co-operate in a most prompt and a most effective execution of this measure by all the means at their disposition and to act in the employment of these means with all the zeal and all the perseverence which they owe to so great and admirable a cause.

No effective multilateral action followed this declaration, however, and for the next thirty years states merely made bilateral treaties by which certain states granted each other the right to visit and search vessels suspected of engaging in the slave traffic. France, Denmark, Sardinia, and Sweden made such bilateral arrangements, but other states, including Spain, and (for a long time) Brazil and the United States, refused to permit foreign ships to search their merchant vessels. Slave traders could therefore fly the Spanish flag, for instance, and operate without much interference. Curtailing the trade was also very difficult because the slaves had to be found on board before a vessel could be detained; moreover, the owners of ships condemned in national prize courts for engaging in the trade could sell them and in this way avoid any financial loss to themselves.[12]

The United States attempted to prohibit the slave trade by using its own Navy to intercept ships transporting slaves. In the case of the *United States v. The Schooner La Jeune Eugénie*, for example, a libel[13] was brought by the United States against the schooner *La Jeune Eugénie*, seized on the coast of Africa for being employed in the slave trade. The government alleged that the schooner was offending against the slave trade acts of the United States and against the general law

[12] H. G. Soulsby, *The Right of Search and the Slave Trade in Anglo-American Relations, 1814–1862* (Baltimore: Johns Hopkins Press, 1933), p. 13 and W. L. Mathieson, *Great Britain and the Slave Trade, 1839–1864* (London: Longmans, Green and Co., 1929), p. 27, cited in Linden Mander, *Foundations of Modern World Society*, (Stanford: Stanford University Press, 1947), pp. 259–260; see Act of May 14, 1820, 3 Stat. 600 for U.S. law referred to.
[13] A "libel" in law is the plaintiff's written statement of his cause of action and of the relief he seeks.

of nations. The French consul made a claim on behalf of the schooner's owners, who were subjects of France living in Basseterre, Guadaloupe. The consul challenged the jurisdiction of the United States Circuit Court, First Circuit, arguing that *La Jeune Eugénie* was a French vessel, owned by French subjects, and as such was exclusively under the jurisdiction of French courts.

The facts in *The Antelope* case[14] are more complicated. A privateer, the *Colombia,* sailing under a Venezuelan commission, entered Baltimore in 1819. It clandestinely shipped a crew of thirty or forty men, proceeded to sea, hoisted the Artegan flag, assumed the name *Arraganta,* and continued its voyage along the coast of Africa. Her officers and most of her crew were citizens of the United States. Off the coast of Africa, she captured an American vessel from Bristol, Rhode Island, from which she took 25 Africans; she captured several Portuguese vessels from which she took more Africans; and she captured a Spanish vessel, the *Antelope,* from which she also took a considerable number of Africans. The *Arraganta* and the *Antelope* sailed together to the coast of Brazil where the *Arraganta* was wrecked, and her master, Metcalf, and a great part of his crew, were made prisoners. The rest of the crew, with the armament of the *Arraganta,* were transferred to the *Antelope* which, thus armed, assumed the name of the *General Ramirez,* commanded by John Smith, a citizen of the United States. The U.S. revenue cutter *Dallas* under the command of Captain Jackson, found the *General Ramirez* hovering near the United States coast, and finally brought it into the port of Savannah. At the time, the *General Ramirez* had on board more than 280 Africans, all captured in the course of the voyage. In port, the ship and the Africans were libelled and claimed by both the Portuguese and Spanish vice-consuls. They were also claimed by the United States as having been transported from foreign parts by American citizens, contrary to the laws of the United States. The United States Government maintained that the Africans were entitled to their freedom by American law and the law of nations.

In both these cases, the Courts had to discuss the nature of the slave trade. Justice Story, in the case of *La Jeune Eugénie* put the issue this way:

. . . The first question naturally arising out of the asserted facts is, whether the African slave trade be prohibited by the law of nations; for if it be so, it will not, I presume, be denied, that confiscation of the property ought to follow; for that is the proper penalty denounced by that law for any violation of its precepts; and the same reasons, which enforce that penalty ordinarily, apply with equal force to employment in this trade.[15]

[14] 23 U.S. (10 Wheat.) 66 (1825).
[15] 2 Mason [U.S.] 409 (1st Cir. 1822).

Chief Justice Marshall in *The Antelope* also asked whether the slave trade was prohibited by the law of nations. Interestingly enough, the two jurists came to opposite conclusions on this question. Justice Story concluded that the trade was prohibited by asserting that natural law was a sufficient basis for international law; Justice Marshall found the trade legal by denying the force of natural law and relying upon the practice of states. It is interesting to compare their reasoning.

Justice Story in the *United States v. The Schooner La Jeune Eugénie* stated:

I shall take up no time in the examination of the history of slavery, or of the question, how far it is consistent with the natural rights of mankind. That it may have a lawful existence, at least by the way of punishment for crimes, will not be doubted by any persons, who admit the general right of society to enforce the observance of its laws by adequate penalties. That it has existed in all ages of the world, and has been tolerated by some, encouraged by others, and sanctioned by most, of the enlightened and civilized nations of the earth in former ages, admits of no reasonable question. That it has interwoven itself into the municipal institutions of some countries and forms the foundations of large masses of property in a portion of our own country, is known to all of us. Sitting, therefore, in an American court of judicature, I am not permitted to deny that under some circumstances it may have a lawful existence; and that the practice may be justified by the condition, or wants, of society, or may form a part of the domestic policy of a nation. It would be unbecoming in me here to assert, that the state of slavery cannot have a legitimate existence, or that it stands condemned by the unequivocal testimony of the law of nations.

But this concession carries us but a very short distance towards the decision of this cause. It is not, as the learned counsel for the government have justly stated, on account of the simple fact, that the traffic necessarily involves the enslavement of human beings, that it stands reprehended by the present sense of nations; but that it necessarily carries with it a breach of all the moral duties, of all the maxims of justice, mercy and humanity, and of the admitted rights, which independent christian nations now hold sacred in their intercourse with each other. What is the fact as to the ordinary, nay, necessary course, of this trade? It begins in corruption, and plunder, and kidnapping. It creates and stimulates unholy wars for the purpose of making captives. It desolates whole villages and provinces for the purpose of seizing the young, the feeble, the defenceless, and the innocent. It breaks down all the ties of parent, and children, and family, and country. It shuts up all sympathy for human suffering and sorrows. It manacles the inoffensive females and the starving infants. It forces the brave to untimely death in defence of their humble homes and firesides, or drives them to despair and self-immolation. It stirs up the worst passions of the human soul, darkening the spirit of revenge, . . . envenoming the cruel, famishing the weak, and crushing to death the broken hearted. This is but the beginning of the evils. Before the unhappy captives arrive at the destined market, where the traffic ends, one quarter part at least in the ordinary course of events perish in cold blood under the inhuman, or thoughtless treatment of their oppressors.

Strong as these expressions may seem, and dark as is the coloring of this statement, it is short of the real calamities inflicted by this traffic. All the wars, that have desolated Africa for the last three centuries, have had their origin in the slave trade. The blood of thousands of her miserable children has stained her shores, or quenched the dying embers of her desolated towns, to glut, the appetite of slave dealers. The ocean has received in its deep and silent bosom thousands more, who have perished from disease and want during their passage from their native homes to the foreign colonies. I speak not from vague rumours, or idle tales, but from authentic documents, and the known historical details of the traffic—a traffic, that carries away at least 50,000 persons annually from their homes and their families, and breaks the hearts, and buries the hopes, and extinguishes the happiness of more than double that number. "There is," as one of the greatest of modern statesmen has declared [William Pitt, the Younger, 1792], "something of horror in it, that surpasses all the bounds of imagination."

It is of this traffic, thus carried on, and necessarily carried on, beginning in lawless wars, and rapine, and kidnapping, and ending in disease and death, and slavery—it is of this traffic in the aggregate of its accumulated wrongs, that I would speak, if it be consistent with the law of nations? It is not by breaking up the elements of the case into fragments, and detaching them one from another, that we are to be asked of each separately, if the law of nations prohibits it. We are not to be told, that war is lawful, and slavery lawful, and plunder lawful, and the taking away of life is lawful, and the selling of human beings is lawful. Assuming that they are so under circumstances, it establishes nothing. It does not advance one jot to the support of the proposition, that a traffic, that involves them all, that is unnecessary, unjust, and inhuman, is countenanced by the eternal law of nature, on which rests the law of nations.

Now the law of nations may be deduced, first, from the general principles of right and justice, applied to the concerns of individuals, and thence to the relations and duties of nations; or, secondly, in things indifferent or questionable, from the customary observances and recognitions of civilized nations; or, lastly, from the conventional or positive law, that regulates the intercourse between states. What, therefore, the law of nations is, does not rest upon mere theory, but may be considered as modified by practice, or ascertained by the treaties of nations at different periods. It does not follow, therefore, that because a principle cannot be found settled by the consent or practice of nations at one time, it is to be concluded, that at no subsequent period the principle can be considered as incorporated into the public code of nations. Nor is it to be admitted, that no principle belongs to the law of nations, which is not universally recognized, as such, by all civilized communities, or even by those constituting, what may be called, the christian states of Europe. Some doctrines, which we, as well as Great Britain, admit to belong to the law of nations, are of but recent origin and application, and have not, as yet, received any public or general sanction in other nations; and yet they are founded in such a just view of the duties and rights of nations, belligerent and neutral, that we have not hesitated to enforce them by the penalty of confiscation. There are other doctrines, again, which have met the decided hostility of some of the European states, enlightened as well as powerful, such as the right of search, and the rule that free ships do not make free goods, which, nevertheless, both Great Britain and the United States maintain, and in my judgment with unanswerable arguments, as settled rules in the Law of Prize, and scruple not to apply them to the ships of all other nations. And yet, if the general custom of nations in modern times, or even in the present age, recognized an opposite doctrine, it could not, perhaps, be affirmed, that that practice did not constitute a part, or, at least, a modification, of the law of nations.

But I think it may be unequivocally affirmed, that every doctrine, that may be fairly deduced by correct reasoning from the rights and duties of nations, and the nature of moral obligation, may theoretically be said to exist in the law of nations; and unless it be relaxed or waived by the consent of nations, which may be evidenced by their general practice and customs, it may be enforced by a court of justice, whenever it arises in judgment. And I may go farther and say, that no practice whatsoever can obliterate the fundamental distinction between right and wrong, and that every nation is at liberty to apply to another the correct principle, whenever both nations by their public acts recede from such practice, and admit the injustice or cruelty of it.

Now in respect to the African slave trade, such as it has been described to be, and in fact is, in its origin, progress, and consummation, it cannot admit of serious question, that it is founded in a violation of some of the first principles, which ought to govern nations. It is repugnant to the great principles of christian duty, the dictates of natural religion, the obligations of good faith and morality, and the external maxims of social justice. When any trade can be truly said to have these ingredients, it is impossible, that it can be consistent with any system of law, that purports to rest on the authority of reason or revelation. And it is sufficient to stamp any trade as interdicted by public law, when it can be justly affirmed, that it is repugnant to the general principles of justice and humanity.

Justice Marshall in *The Antelope* gave short shrift to a similar line of argument in his decision:

In examining claims of this momentous importance; claims in which the sacred rights of liberty and of property come in conflict with each other; which have drawn from the bar a degree of talent and of eloquence, worthy of the questions that have been discussed; this Court must not yield to feelings which might seduce it from the path of duty, and must obey the mandate of the law.

That the course of opinion on the slave trade should be unsettled, ought to excite no surprise. The Christian and civilized nations of the world, with whom we have most intercourse, have all been engaged in it. However abhorrent this traffic may be to a mind whose original feelings are not blunted by familiarity with the practice, it has been sanctioned in modern times by the laws of all nations who possess distant colonies, each of whom has engaged in it as a common commercial business which no other could rightfully interrupt. It has claimed all the sanction which could be derived from long usage, and the general acquiescence. That trade could not be considered as contrary to the law of nations which was authorized and protected by the laws of all commercial nations; the right to carry on which was claimed by each, and allowed by each.

The course of unexamined opinion, which was founded on this inveterate usage, received its first check in America; and, as soon as these States acquired the right of self-government, the traffic was forbidden by most of them. In the beginning of this century, several humane and enlightened individuals of Great Britain devoted themselves to the cause of the Africans; and, by frequent appeals to the nation, in which the enormity of this commerce was unveiled, and exposed to the public eye, the general sentiment was at length roused against it, and the feelings of justice and humanity, regaining their long lost ascendency, prevailed so far in the British Parliament as to obtain an act for its abolition. The utmost efforts of the British government, as well as that of the United States have since been assiduously employed in its suppression. It has been denounced by both in terms of great severity, and those concerned in these measures operating on their own people, they have used all their influence to bring other nations into the same system, and to interdict this trade by the consent of all.

Public sentiment has, in both countries, kept pace with the measures of government; and the opinion is extensively, if not universally entertained, that this unnatural traffic ought to be suppressed. While its illegality is asserted by some governments, but not admitted by all; while the destestation in which it is held is growing daily, and even those nations who tolerate it in fact, almost disavow their own conduct, and rather connive at, than legalize, the acts of their subjects; it is not wonderful that public feeling should march somewhat in advance of strict law, and that opposite opinions should be entertained on the precise cases in which our own laws may control and limit the practice of others. Indeed, we ought not to be surprised, if, on this novel series of cases, even Courts of justice should, in some instances, have carried the principle of suppression farther than a more deliberate consideration of the subject would justify. . . .

In the United States, different opinions have been entertained in the different Circuits and Districts; and the subject is now, for the first time, before this Court.

The question, whether the slave trade is prohibited by the law of nations has been seriously propounded, and both the affirmative and negative of the proposition have been maintained with equal earnestness.

That it is contrary to the law of nature will scarcely be denied. That every man has a natural right to the fruits of his own labour, is generally admitted; and that no other person can rightfully deprive him of those fruits; and appropriate them against his will, seems to be the necessary result of this admission. But from the earliest times war has existed, and war confers rights in which all have acquiesced. Among the most enlightened nations of antiquity, one of these was, that the victor might enslave the vanquished. This, which was the usage of all, could not be pronounced repugnant to the law of nations, which is certainly to be tried by the test of general usage. That which has received the assent of all, must be the law of all.

Slavery, then, has its origin in force; but as the world has agreed that it is a legitimate result of force, the state of things which is thus produced by general consent, cannot be pronounced unlawful.

Throughout Christendom, this harsh rule has been exploded, and war is no longer considered as giving a right to enslave captives. But this triumph of humanity has not been universal. The parties to the modern law of nations do not propagate their principles by force; and Africa has not yet adopted them. Throughout the whole extent of that immense continent, so far as we know its history, it is still the law of nations that prisoners are slaves. Can those who have themselves renounced this law, be permitted to participate in it effects by purchasing the beings who are its victims?

Whatever might be the answer of a moralist to this question, a jurist must search for its legal solution, in those principles of action which are sanctioned by the usages, the national acts, and the general assent of that portion of the world of which he considers himself as a part, and to whose law the appeal is made. If we resort to this standard as the test of international law, the question as had already been observed, is decided in favor of the legality of the trade. Both Europe and America embarked in it; and for nearly two centuries, it was carried on without opposition, and without censure. A jurist could not say, that a practice thus supported was illegal, and that those engaged in it might be punished, either personally, or by deprivation of property.

Justice Story was, of course, aware of the practice of states, and in *La Jeune Eugénie*, he dealt with it as follows:

Now there is scarcely a single maritime nation of Europe, that has not in the most significant terms, in the most deliberate and solemn conferences, acts, or treaties, acknowledged the injustice and inhumanity of this trade; and pledged itself to promote its abolition. I need scarcely advert to the conferences at Vienna, at Aix-la-Chapelle, and at London, on this interesting subject, as they have been cited at the argument of this cause, and authenticated by our own government, to show what may be emphatically called the sense of Europe upon this point. France, in particular, at the conference at Vienna, in 1815, engaged to use "all the means at her disposal and to act in the employment of these means with a cause." (The abolition of the slave trade.) And accordingly, in the treaty of peace between her and Great Britain, France expressing her concurrence without reserve in the sentiments of his Britannic majesty with respect to this traffic, admits it to be "repugnant to the principles of natural justice, and of the enlightened age, in which we live"; and, at a short period afterwards, the government of France informed the British government, that it had "issued directions in order, that on the part of France the traffic in slaves may cease from the present time everywhere and forever." The conduct and opinions of Great Britain, honourably and zealously, and, I may add, honestly, as she has been engaged in promoting the universal abolition of the trade, are too notorious to require a pointed enumeration. She has through her Parliament expressed her abhorrence of the trade in the most marked terms, as repugnant to justice and humanity; she has punished it as a felony, when carried on by her subjects; and she has recognized through her judicial tribunals the doctrine, that it is repugnant to the law of nations. Our own country, too, has firmly and earnestly pressed forward in the same career. The trade has been reprobated and punished, as far as our authority extended, from a very early period of the government; and by a very recent statute, to mark at once its infamy and repugnance to the law of nations, it has been raised in the catalogue of public crimes to the bad eminence of piracy. I think, therefore, that I am justified in saying, that at the present moment the traffic is vindicated by no nation, and is admitted by almost all commercial nations as incurably unjust and inhuman. It appears to me, therefore that in an American Court of Judicature, I am bound to consider the trade an offence against the universal law of society and in all cases, where it is not protected by a foreign government, to deal with it as an offence carrying with it the penalty of confiscation.

And I cannot but think, notwithstanding the assertion at the bar to the contrary, that this doctrine is neither novel nor alarming. That it stands on principles of sound sense and general policy, and, above all, of moral justice, and I confess, that I should be somewhat startled, if any nation, sincerely anxious for the abolition, and earnest in its duty, should interpose its influence to arrest its universal adoption.

Both jurists agreed, however, that regardless of the status of the slave trade, the sovereign rights of nations to make their own rules to regulate it had to be respected.

Justice Story in *La Jeune Eugénie* put it this way:

There is an objection urged against the doctrine which is here asserted, that ought not to be passed over in silence; and that is, if the African slave trade is repugnant to the law of nations, no nation can rightfully permit its subjects to carry it on, or exempt them from obedience to that law; for it is said, that no nation can privilege itself to commit a crime against the law of nations, so as thereby to produce an injury to any other nation. But if it does, this is understood to be an injury, not against all nations, which all are bound or permitted to redress; but which concerns alone the nation injured. The independence of nations guarantees to each the right of guarding its own honour, and the morals and interest of its own subjects. No one has a right to sit in judgment generally upon the actions of another;

at least to the extent of compelling its adherence to all the principles of justice and humanity in its domestic concerns. If a nation were to violate as to its own subjects in its domestic regulation the clearest principles of public law, I do not know, that the law has ever held them amenable to the tribunals of other nations for such conduct. It would be inconsistent with the equality and sovereignty of nations, which admit no common superior. No nation has ever yet pretended to be the *custos morum* of the whole world; and though abstractedly a particular regulation may violate the law of nations, it may sometimes, in the case of nations, be a wrong without a remedy. . . .

And Justice Marshall in *The Antelope* wrote as follows:

In this commerce, thus sanctioned by universal assent, every nation had an equal right to engage. How is this right to be lost? Each may renounce it for its own people; but can this renunciation affect others?

No principle of general law is more universally acknowledged, than the perfect equality of nations. Russia and Geneva have equal rights. It results from this equality, that no one can rightfully impose a rule on another. Each legislates for itself, but its legislation can operate on itself alone. A right, then, which is vested in all by the consent of all, can be devested only by consent; and this trade, in which all have participated, must remain lawful to those who cannot be induced to relinquish it. As no nation can prescribe a rule for others, none can make a law of nations; and this traffic remains lawful to those whose governments have not forbidden it.

But both jurists came essentially to the same conclusions about the disposition of the slaves, allowing, of course, for the differences in the facts of the case. Justice Story said in *La Jeune Eugénie:*

Thus far I have proceeded in the cause without reference to any other claims, but those asserted in the original libel and answer. But at a late period in this cause, by direction of the president, a suggestion has been filed by the District Attorney, expressing a willingness to yield up the vessel to the French government, or its consular agent, for the purpose of remitting the cause for ultimate adjudication to the domestic forum of the sovereign of the owners. To a suggestion of this nature this court is bound to listen with the most respectful attention. It is understood to be, not a direction to the court, for that is beyond the reach of executive authority, but an intimation of the wishes of the government, so far as its own rights are concerned, to spare the court any farther investigation. If it had seemed fit to all the parties, whose interests are before the court, to agree to the course held out by this suggestion, it would have relieved my mind from a weight of responsibility, which has most heavily pressed upon it. But the French claimants resist this course, and require, that the property should be delivered over to their personal possession and not to the possession of their sovereign. Under such circumstance this court must follow the duty prescribed to it by law, independently of any wishes of our own government or of France. I have been compelled, therefore, reluctantly to travel over the whole merits of the cause, and to decide it with reference to the French owners upon the great principles, on which it has been argued.

After listening to the very able, eloquent, and learned arguments delivered at the bar on this occasion—after weighing the authorities, which bear on the case, with mature deliberation—after reflecting anxiously and carefully upon the general principles, which may be drawn from the law of nations to illustrate or confirm them, I have come to the conclusion, that the slave trade is a trade prohibited by universal law, and by the law of France, and that, therefore, the claim of the asserted French owners must be rejected. That claim being rejected, I feel myself at perfect liberty, with the express consent of our own government, to decree, that the property be delivered over to the consular agent of the King of France, to be dealt with according to his own sense of duty and right. . . .

And Justice Marshall stated in *The Antelope:*

If it is consistent with the law of nations, it cannot in itself be piracy. It can be made so only by statute; and the obligation of the statute cannot transcend the legislative power of the state which may enact it.

If it be neither repugnant to the law of nations, nor piracy, it is almost superfluous to say in this Court, that the right of bringing in for adjudication in time of peace, even where the vessel belongs to a nation which has prohibited the trade, cannot exist. The Courts of no country execute the penal laws of another; and the course of the American government on the subject of visitation and search, would decide any case in which that right had been exercised by an American cruiser, on the vessel of a foreign nation, not violating our municipal laws, against the captors.

It follows, that a foreign vessel engaged in the African slave trade, captured on the high seas in time of peace, by an American cruiser, and brought in for adjudication, would be restored.

The general question being disposed of, it remains to examine the circumstances of the particular case.

. . . .

Had the *Arraganta* been a regularly commissioned cruiser, which had committed no infraction of the neutrality of the United States, her capture of the *Antelope* must have been considered as lawful, and no question could have arisen respecting the rights of the original claimants. The question of prize or no prize belongs solely to the Courts of the captor. But having violated the neutrality of the United States, and having entered our ports, not voluntarily, but under coercion, some difficulty exists respecting the extent of the obligation to restore, on the mere proof of former possession, which is imposed on this government.

If, as is charged in the libels of both the Spanish and Portuguese Consuls, as well as of the United States, she was a pirate, hovering on the coast with intent to introduce slaves in violation of the laws of the United States, our treaty requires that property rescued from pirates shall be restored to the Spanish owner on his making proof of his property.

Whether the *General Ramirez,* originally the *Antelope,* is to be considered as the prize of a commissioned belligerent ship of war unlawfully equipped in the United States, or as a pirate, it seems proper to make some inquiry into the title of the claimants.

In support of the Spanish claim, testimony is produced, showing the documents under which the *Antelope* sailed from Havana on the voyage on which she was captured; that she was owned by a Spanish house of trade in that place; that she was employed in the business of purchasing slaves, and had purchased and taken on board a considerable number, when she was seized as prize by the *Arraganta.*

Whether, on this proof, Africans brought into the United States, under the various circumstances belonging to this case ought to be restored or not is a question on which much difficulty has been felt. It is unnecessary to state the reasons in support of the affirmative or negative answer to it because the Court is divided on it, and, consequently, no principle is settled. So much of the decree of the Circuit Court as directs restitution to the Spanish claimant of the Africans found on board the *Antelope* when she was captured by the *Arraganta,* is affirmed. . . .

[The Court then awarded ninety-three Africans to the Spanish claimants, rejected the Portuguese claim, and concluded:]

We think, then, that all the Africans, now in possession of the Marshal for the District of Georgia and under the control of the Circuit Court of the United States for that District, which were brought in with the *Antelope,* otherwise called the *General Ramirez,* except those which may be designated as the property of the Spanish claimants, ought to be delivered up to the United States, to be disposed of according to law. So much of the sentence of the Circuit Court as is contrary to this opinion, is to be reversed, and the residue affirmed.

As indicated in several cases above, courts often look to treaties as one of the sources of international law. Custom is another principal source, and its importance is well illustrated by the case of *The Paquete Habana, The Lola,*[16] two fishing smacks, which at the beginning of the Spanish-American War were regularly engaged in fishing off the coast of Cuba, sailing under the Spanish flag, each owned by a Spanish subject residing in Havana. The crew received shares of the proceeds from the catch of fish, which were sold alive. Both vessels left Havana and fished in the territorial waters of Spain. The *Lola* also fished in a wider area. On their return, both boats were captured near Havana by one of the ships in a United States blockading squadron. Neither fishing vessel had any arms or ammunition on board, and neither crew had any knowledge of the blockade, or even of the war, until the boats

[16] 175 U.S. 677 (1900).

were stopped by the blockading vessel. Neither made any attempt to run the blockade or offered any resistance at the time of her capture, nor was there any evidence that either ship or crew was likely to aid the enemy. Both boats were condemned as prizes of war and sold by auction on order of the District Court of the United States for the Southern District of Florida, "the Court not being satisfied that as a matter of law, without any ordinance, treaty, or proclamation, fishing vessels of this class are exempt from seizure."[17]

On receiving the case, the United States Supreme Court first disposed of a question of jurisdiction and then went back to the year 1403 to trace the long history of the customs which gave immunity to fishing vessels in time of war.

THE PAQUETE HABANA, THE LOLA

UNITED STATES SUPREME COURT, 1900

175 U.S. 677

By an ancient usage among civilized nations, beginning centuries ago, and gradually ripening into a rule of international law, coast fishing vessels, pursuing their vocation of catching and bringing in fresh fish, have been recognized as exempt, with their cargoes and crews, from capture as prize of war.

This doctrine, however, has been earnestly contested at the bar; and no complete collection of the instances illustrating it is to be found, so far as we are aware, in a single published work, although many are referred to and discussed by the writers on international law . . . It is therefore worth the while to trace the history of the rule, from the earliest accessible sources, through the increasing recognition of it, with occasional setbacks, to what we may now justly consider as its final establishment in our own country and generally throughout the civilized world. . . .

In 1403 and 1406, Henry IV issued orders to his admirals and other officers, entitled "Concerning Safety for Fishermen—*De Securitate pro Piscatoribus.*" By an order of October 26, 1403, reciting that it was made pursuant to a treaty between himself and the King of France; and for the greater safety of the fishermen of either country, and so that they could be, and carry on their industry, the more safely on the sea, and deal with each other in peace; and that the French King had consented that English fishermen should be treated likewise; it was ordained that French fishermen might during the then pending season for the herring fishery, safely fish for herrings and all other fish, from the harbor of Gravelines and the island of Thanet to the mouth of the Seine and the harbor of Hautoune. And by an order

[17] *Ibid.,* p. 679.

of October 5, 1406, he took into his safe conduct, and under his special protection, guardianship and defence, all and singular the fishermen of France, Flanders and Brittany, with their fishing vessels, everywhere on the sea . . . and it was therefore ordered that such fishermen should not be interfered with, provided they should comport themselves well and properly, and should not, by color of these presents, do . . . anything that could prejudice the King, or his kingdom of England, or his subjects. . . .

[France, Spain, Holland, England, Prussia, the United States, Japan, and other states have exempted enemy fishing vessels from capture, even in the absence of treaties, although there have sometimes been exceptions to this custom, *e.g.*, in The Young Jacob and Johanna (1798), 1 C. Rob. 20.] Lord Stowell, in delivering judgment [in that case], said: "In former wars, it has not been usual to make captures of these small fishing vessels; but this rule was a rule of comity only, and not of legal decision." . . . [I]t is true that, so far as appears, there has been no such [judicial] decision on the point in England. The word "comity" was apparently used by Lord Stowell as synonymous with courtesy or good will. But the period of a hundred years which has since elapsed is amply sufficient to have enabled what originally may have rested in custom or comity, courtesy or concession, to grow, by the general assent of civilized nations, into a settled rule of international law. . . .

International law is part of our law, and must be ascertained and administered by the courts of justice of appropriate jurisdiction, as often as questions of right depending upon it are duly presented for their determination. For this purpose, where there is no treaty, and no controlling executive or legislative act or judicial decision, resort must be had to the customs and usages of civilized nations; and, as evidence of these, to the works of jurists and commentators, who by years of labor, research and experience, have made themselves peculiarly well acquainted with the subjects of which they treat. Such works are resorted to by judicial tribunals, not for the speculations of their authors concerning what the law ought to be, but for trustworthy evidence of what the law really is. Hilton v. Guyot, 159 U.S. 113, 163, 164, 214, 215.

Wheaton places, among the principal sources of international law, "Text-writers of authority, showing what is the approved usage of nations, or the general opinion respecting their mutual conduct, with the definitions and modifications introduced by general consent." As to these he forcibly observes: "Without wishing to exaggerate the importance of these writers, or to substitute, in any case, their authority for the principles of reason, it may be affirmed that they are generally impartial in their judgment. They are witnesses of the sentiments and usages of civilized nations, and the weight of their testimony increases every time that their authority is invoked by statesmen, and every year that passes without the rules laid down in their works being impugned by the avowal of contrary principles." Wheaton's International Law (8th ed.), 15.

Chancellor Kent says: "In the absence of higher and more authoritative sanctions, the ordinances of foreign states, the opinions of eminent statesmen, and the writings of distinguished jurists, are regarded as of great consideration on questions not settled by conventional law. In cases where the principal jurists agree, the presumption will be very great in favor of the solidity of their maxims; and no civilized nation, that does not arrogantly set all ordinary law and justice at defiance, will venture to disregard the uniform sense of the established writers on international law." I Kent Com. 18. . . .

[The Court then surveys the opinions of many writers on international law from Argentina, Austria, England, France, Germany, Netherlands, Portugal, Spain, and Switzerland, and continues:]

This review of the precedents and authorities on the subject appears to us abundantly to demonstrate that at the present day, by the general consent of the civilized nations of the world, and independently of any express treaty or other public act, it is an established rule of international law, founded on considerations of humanity to a poor and industrious order of men, and of the mutual convenience of belligerent States, that coast fishing vessels, with their implements and supplies, cargoes and crews, unarmed, and honestly pursuing their peaceful calling of catching and bringing in fresh fish, are exempt from capture as prize of war. . . .

This rule of international law is one which prize courts, administering the law of nations, are bound to take judicial notice of, and to give effect to, in the absence of any treaty or other public act of their own government in relation to the matter. . . .

Upon the facts proved in either case, it is the duty of this court, sitting as the highest prize court of the United States, and administering the law of nations, to declare and adjudge that the capture was unlawful, and without probable cause; and it is therefore, in each case,

Ordered, that the decree of the District Court be reversed, and proceeds of the sale of the vessel, together with the proceeds of any sale of her cargo, be restored to the claimant, with damages and costs.

[Fuller, C. J., and Harlan and McKenna, J. J., dissenting, echoed Lord Stowell's views that the practice of exempting enemy fishing vessels from capture was not a customary rule of international law, but only a rule of comity or courtesy, and that, furthermore, the President had not authorized the practice.]

Fishing, of course, is an age-old occupation, and one might well ask whether custom has any role to play in areas of human activity which are more recent in origin. Some idea of the way new "customs" play a role in international law can be had by considering the case of *The Scotia*.[18] On January 9, 1863, the British government established certain "Regulations for preventing collisions at sea," which included "Rules concerning lights." The United States Congress adopted similar rules

[18] 81 U.S. (14 Wall.) 170 (1871).

on April 29, 1864, and over thirty other countries accepted similar rules for their ships at about the same time.

On April 8, 1867, a British steamer of the Cunard line, the *Scotia,* was sailing near mid-ocean, on her way from Liverpool to New York. She was displaying the proper lights: white at the masthead, green on starboard, red on port. The American sailing ship *Berkshire,* in about the same position, was proceeding from New Orleans to Le Havre. The *Berkshire,* as a sailing ship, was supposed under the rules to carry the colored lights, but no white masthead lights. However, she showed no colored lights and did display a white light at her bow, about four feet about the level of the deck. The officers of the *Scotia* saw this light close to the water, assumed that it was on the masthead, and concluded that the *Berkshire* was a steamship far off. Not seeing any colored lights confirmed their opinion because the regulations specified the white lights were to be visible for five miles, the colored for but two.

Because of these misapprehensions, the *Scotia* and the *Berkshire* collided, and the *Berkshire* was sunk with her cargo. Her owners then attempted to recover their losses in legal proceedings. The District Court at New York decided, however, that courts of admiralty were required to take judicial notice that the British regulations existed and that numerous maritime states had accepted them. The Court said that, because so many states had adopted the rule, it had become a rule and usage of the sea; and "that by this rule and usage—in other words, by the law of the sea as it existed at the time of the collision—the *Berkshire* was bound to exhibit colored lights and colored lights alone. . . ."[19] Because the *Berkshire* had not done so, she had no remedy.

The Circuit Court confirmed this decree, and the matter was appealed to the Supreme Court.

THE SCOTIA

UNITED STATES SUPREME COURT, 1871

81 U.S. (14 WALL.) 170

[The lawyer for the *Berkshire* argued:]

There can be no reasonable doubt that this case is to be governed, not by the municipal laws of either the United States or Great Britain, but by the maritime law. The main question is, what is that law? It is conceded that, at least until a recent period, it imposed no obligation upon either

[19] *Ibid.,* p. 176.

of the vessels to carry colored lights, or precluded either from carrying a white light. Now, has this law been changed? . . . . [C]onceding that any number of municipal ordinances were proved, they do not make any change in the maritime law. The high seas are outside of the territory of municipal powers, and their laws have no force there. Nor can any force be derived from them when taken together. It cannot be maintained when the laws of Great Britain, the United States, and France have, neither separately nor collectively, any effect whatever on the sea, that still if the concurring status of substantially all other maritime states were added, the combined effect would be to give them effect there. How many nations must join? Who is to determine what is a maritime state, in order to know whether all have joined? Who or what is to appraise the unlettered mariner that the municipal statutes of all nations have at last been brought into harmony? . . . .

Mr. Justice Strong delivered the opinion of the court:

. . . .

. . . We think the Scotia had a right to conclude that the Berkshire was a steamer rather than a sailing vessel, and that, when first seen, she was at the distance of four or five miles, instead of being near at hand. Such was the information given her by the ship's white light, fastened as it was to the anchor-stock on deck, and no watchfulness could have enabled her to detect the misrepresentation until it was too late. Both vessels were moving under similar regulations. The Berkshire was an American ship, belonging to the mercantile marine, and she was required by the act of Congress of April 29th, 1864, to carry green and red lights, which she did not carry, and she was forbidden to carry the white light, which she did carry. By exhibiting a white light, she, therefore, held herself forth as a steamer, and by exhibiting it from her deck, instead of from her masthead, she misrepresented her distance from approaching vessels. It is clear the Scotia would have been justified in taking her for a steamer had she been known to be an American ship. But it is insisted on behalf of the appellants that, inasmuch as the act of Congress is a mere municipal regulation, obligatory as a statute only upon American vessels, the Scotia, a British steamer, cannot avail herself of it to fault an American ship, or to justify her own conduct. Waiving for the moment consideration of the question whether this position is well taken, it is yet true that the Berkshire was under the statute, though on the high seas, and that the Scotia was subject to and sailing under similar regulations (the British orders in council of January 9th, 1863); that the collision happened in the known path of vessels navigating between the United States and Great Britain, and that there was a reasonable probability that vessels in that path would be either American or British, and would, therefore, carry the lights prescribed by the laws of those countries. The steamer might well, therefore, in the absence of knowledge, act upon that probability, and in the emergency into which she had been brought might, without fault, apply the rule of navigation common to the ships of both countries.

But . . . we think that independently of the act of Congress, considered as a mere municipal regulation, the Berkshire was bound to show a green light on her starboard, and a red light on her port side, without exhibiting any white light; and that the Scotia may set up in defence her failure to carry such green and red lights, as also the fact that she did improperly show a white light. And we think that her breach of duty in these respects misled the officers of the steamer, and caused them to act on the assumption that she was a steamer, and therefore under obligation to pass on the port side. If so, the collision was solely due to the fault of the ship. We rest this conclusion not solely, or mainly, upon the ground that the navigation laws of the United States control the conduct of foreign vessels, or that they have, as such, any extra-territorial authority, except over American shipping. Doubtless they are municipal regulations, yet binding upon American vessels, either in American waters or on the high seas. Nor can the British orders in council control our vessels, though they may their own. We concede also that whether an act is tortious or not must generally be determined by the laws of the place where the act was committed. But every American vessel, outside of the jurisdiction of a foreign power, is, for some purposes at least, a part of the American territory, and our laws are the rules for its guidance. Equally true is it that a British vessel is controlled by British rules of navigation. If it were that the rules of the two nations conflicted, which would the British vessel, and which would the American, be bound to obey? Undoubtedly the rule prescribed by the government to which it belonged. And if, in consequence, collision should ensue between an American and a British vessel, shall the latter be condemned in an American court of admiralty? If so, then our law is given an extra-territorial effect, and is held obligatory upon British ships not within our jurisdiction. Or might an American vessel be faulted in a British court of admiralty for having done what our statute required? Then Britain is truly not only mistress of the seas, but of all who traverse the great waters. It is difficult to see how a ship can be condemned for doing that which by the laws of its origin, or ownership, it was required to do, or how, on the other hand, it can secure an advantage by violation of those laws, unless it is beyond their domain when upon the high seas. But our navigation laws were intended to secure the safety of life and property, as well as the convenience of commerce. They are not in terms confined to the regulation of shipping in our own waters. They attempt to govern a business that is conducted on every sea. If they do not reach the conduct of mariners in its relation to the ships and people of other nations, they are at least designed for the security of the lives and property of our own people. For that purpose they are as useful and as necessary on the ocean as they are upon inland waters. How, then, can our courts ignore them in any case? Why should it ever be held that what is a wrong when done to an American citizen, is right if the injured party be an Englishman?

. . . .

The question still remains, what was the law of the place where the collision occurred, and at the time when it occurred. Conceding that it was not the law of the United States, nor that of Great Britain, nor the concurrent regulations of the two governments, but that it was the law of the sea, was it the ancient maritime law, that which existed before the commercial nations of the world adopted the regulations of 1863 and 1864, or the law changed after those regulations were adopted? Undoubtedly, no single nation can change the law of the sea. That law is of universal obligation, and no statute of one or two nations can create obligations for the world. Like all the laws of nations, it rests upon the common consent of civilized communities. It is of force, not because it was prescribed by any superior power, but because it has been generally accepted as a rule of conduct. Whatever may have been its origin, whether in the usages of navigation or in the ordinances of maritime states, or in both, it has become the law of the sea only by the concurrent sanction of those nations who may be said to constitute the commercial world. Many usages which prevail, and which have the force of law, doubtless originated in the positive prescriptions of some single state, which were at first of limited effect, but which when generally accepted became of universal obligation. The Rhodian law is supposed to have been the earliest system of marine rules. It was a code for Rhodians only, but it soon became of general authority because accepted and assented to as a wise and desirable system by other maritime nations. The same may be said of the Amalphitan table, of the ordinances of the Hanseatic League, and of parts of the marine ordinances of Louis XIV. They all became the law of the sea, not on account of their origin, but by reason of their acceptance as such. And it is evident that unless general assent is efficacious to give sanction to international law, there never can be that growth and development of maritime rules which the constant changes, in the instruments and necessities of navigation require. Changes in nautical rules have taken place. How have they been accomplished, if not by the concurrent assent, express or understood, of maritime nations? When, therefore, we find such rules of navigation as are mentioned in the British orders in council of January 9th, 1863, and in our act of Congress of 1864, accepted as obligatory rules by more than thirty of the principal commercial states of the world, including almost all which have any shipping on the Atlantic Ocean, we are constrained to regard them as in part at least, and so far as relates to these vessels, the laws of the sea, and as having been the law at the time when the collision of which the libellants complain took place.

This is not giving to the statutes of any nation extra-territorial effect. It is not treating them as general maritime laws, but it is recognition of the historical fact that by common consent of mankind, these rules have been acquiesced in as of general notice. Foreign municipal laws must indeed be proved as facts, but it is not so with the law of nations.

The consequences of this ruling are decisive of the case before us. The violation of maritime law by the Berkshire in carrying a white light (to say nothing of her neglect to carry colored lights), and her carrying it on deck instead of at her masthead, were false representations to the Scotia.

They proclaimed that the Berkshire was a steamer, and such she was manifestly taken to be. The movements of the Scotia were therefore entirely proper, and she was without fault.

As the cases above indicate, it is much easier to determine that a treaty exists than to determine that a custom exists. Nonetheless, custom is an important source of law—and not just of international law. As Justice Cardozo wrote, in fixing a boundary line between the states of Delaware and New Jersey, "International law, or the law that governs between states, has at times, like the common law within states, a twilight existence during which it is hardly distinguishable from morality or justice, till at length the *imprimatur* of a court attests its jural quality."[20]

Relation of Municipal to International Law

Although the preceding cases deal with international questions, it is evident that the courts refer frequently in their decisions to "municipal" law, or the laws of the individual nation-states. Theorists differ about the relation between municipal and international law. Some, the "Dualists," believe that the law of nations and municipal law are essentially different in sources, in the relations they regulate, and in substance, and that consequently municipal law functions independently of international law. The "Monists," on the other hand, argue that both laws are essentially one because they ultimately regulate the conduct of individuals and bind them independently of their will. The Monists maintain, moreover, that the two law systems are inseparable because without an international law which posits the equality and independence of a number of sovereign states, it would be logically impossible to have any municipal law.[21]

In practice, since most states regard international law as part of their own law, it makes little practical difference whether jurists consider municipal law subordinate, equal, or superior to international law. Both *The Scotia* and *The Paquete Habana,* for instance, demonstrate how the courts generally try to harmonize municipal and international law. Only occasionally do the courts assert that municipal law is incompatible with international law. But because it helps clarify the consequences of the Monist and Dualist positions, the cases illustrating the Dualist approach are worth looking at. One such case, where a court declared the supremacy of municipal law, is *Mortensen v. Peters.*[22]

[20] New Jersey v. Delaware, 291 U.S. 361 (1934).
[21] See L. Oppenheim, *International Law: A Treatise* (7th ed., H. Lauterpacht, ed., London: Longman's Green and Co., 1948), I, 35–37.
[22] Great Britain, High Court of Justiciary of Scotland, 1906, 8 Sess. Cas. (5th ser.), p. 93.

In this case a Danish sea captain, Emmanuel Mortensen, was arrested on British territory for having violated the Herring Fishery Act, passed by Parliament in 1889, and the bylaws of the Fishery Board set up by that act. The law forbade fishing within the Moray Firth, where Mortensen had engaged in otter-trawling. Mortensen maintained, however, that although he had fished in the Moray Firth, he was fishing outside the waters that international law regarded as subject to the territorial jurisdiction of Great Britain—namely, outside an imaginary straight line drawn across the Firth "in the part nearest the entrance at the first point where the width does not exceed ten miles."[23] Consequently, Mortensen argued that the prohibitions he was accused of violating did not actually apply to him because he was not within British territory.

The Lord Justice-General dealt with the matter in this way:

I apprehend that the question is one of construction, and of construction only. In this Court we have nothing to do with the question of whether the Legislature has or has not done what foreign powers may consider a usurpation in a question with them. Neither are we a tribunal sitting to decide whether an Act of the Legislature is *ultra vires* as in contravention of generally acknowledged principles of international law. For us an Act of Parliament duly passed by Lords and Commons and assented to by the King, is supreme, and we are bound to give effect to its terms. The counsel for the appellant advanced the proposition that statutes creating offences must be presumed to apply only (1) to British subjects; and (2) to foreign subjects in British territory; and that short of express enactment their application should not be further extended. The appellant is admittedly not a British subject, which excludes (1); and he further argued that the *locus delicti*, being in the sea beyond the three-mile limit, was not within British territory; and that consequently the appellant was not included in the prohibition of the statute. Viewed as general propositions the two presumptions put forward by the appellant may be taken as correct. This, however, advances the matter but little, for like all presumptions they may be redargued, and the question remains whether they have been redargued on this occasion.

The first thing to be noted is that the prohibition here, a breach of which constitutes the offence, is not an absolute prohibition against doing a certain thing, but against doing it in a certain place. Now, when the Legislature, using words of admitted generality—"It shall not be lawful," &c., "Every person who," &c.—conditions an offence by territorial limits, it creates, I think, a very strong inference that it is, for the purposes specified, assuming a right to legislate for that territory against all persons whomsoever. This inference seems to me still further strengthened when it is obvious that the remedy

---

[23] This dividing line between territorial and international waters in bays was embodied in a number of international treaties and widely accepted as a principle of international law.

to the mischief sought to be obtained by the prohibition would be either defeated or rendered less effective if all persons whosoever were not affected by the enactment. It is obvious that the latter consideration applies in the present case. Whatever may be the views of anyone as to the propriety or expediency of stopping trawling, the enactment shews on the face of it that it contemplates such stopping; and it would be most clearly ineffective to debar trawling by English subjects while the subjects of other nations were allowed so to fish.

It is said by the appellant that all this must give way to the consideration that international law has firmly fixed that a *locus* such as this is beyond the limits of territorial sovereignty, and that consequently it is not to be thought that into such a place the Legislature could seek to affect any but the King's subjects.

It is a trite observation that there is no such thing as a standard of international law extraneous to the domestic law of a kingdom, to which appeal may be made. International law, so far as this Court is concerned, is the body of doctrine regarding the international rights and duties of states which has been adopted and made a part of the law of Scotland. Now, can it be said to be clear by the law of Scotland that the *locus* here is beyond what the Legislature may assert right to affect by legislation against all whomsoever for the purpose of regulating methods of fishing?

I do not think I need say anything about what is known as the three-mile limit. It may be assumed that within the three miles the territorial sovereignty would be sufficient to cover any such legislation as the present. It is enough to say that that is not a proof of the counter proposition that outside the three miles no such result could be looked for. The *locus* although outside the three-mile limit, is within the bay known as the Moray Firth, and the Moray Firth, says the respondent, is *intra fauces terrae*. Now, I cannot say that there is any definition of what *fauces terrae* exactly are. But there are at least three points which go far to shew that this spot might be considered as lying therein.

1st. The *dicta* of the Scottish institutional writers seem to show that it would be no usurpation, according to the law of Scotland, so to consider it.

. . . .

2d. The same statute puts forward claims to what are at least analogous places. If attention is paid to the schedule appended to section 6, many places will be found far beyond the three-mile limit—*e.g.*, the Firth of Clyde near its mouth. I am not ignoring that it may be said that this in one sense is proving *idem per idem*, but none the less I do not think the fact can be ignored.

3d. There are many instances to be found in decided cases where the right of a nation to legislate for waters more or less landlocked or landembraced, although beyond the three-mile limit, has been admitted. . . .

It seems to me therefore, without laying down the proposition that the

Moray Firth is for every purpose within the territorial sovereignty, it can at least be clearly said that the appellant cannot make out his proposition that it is inconceivable that the British Legislature should attempt for fishery regulation to legislate against all and sundry in such a place. And if that is so, then I revert to the considerations already stated which as a matter of construction made me think that it did so legislate.

. . . .

I am therefore of opinion that the conviction was right, that both questions should be answered in the affirmative, and that the appeal should be dismissed.

In *Mortensen v. Peters,* the Lord Justice-General made clear his view that the courts of Great Britain should give priority to Acts of Parliament over any other evidence of law. On the other hand, many scholars and statesmen who wish to develop both a stronger international law and a more orderly international community believe that people must be willing to give the needs of the international community priority over the needs of the nation-state. Some of the newer constitutions of nations, the Constitution of the Netherlands, for instance, recognize that it is desirable for states to strengthen the society of nations.[24]

EXCERPTS FROM THE CONSTITUTION OF THE NETHERLANDS
(as amended in 1956)

Article 58. The King shall have the supreme direction of foreign relations. He shall promote the development of the international legal order.

Article 59. The King shall not declare the Kingdom to be at war with another Power except with the previous consent of the States-General. This consent shall not be required when as a result of an actual state of war consultation with the States-General has appeared to be impossible.

The States-General shall discuss and decide on these matters in united assembly.

The King shall not declare a war between the Kingdom and another Power to be terminated except with the previous consent of the States-General.

Article 60. Agreements with other Powers and with organizations based on international law shall be concluded by or by authority of the King. If required by such agreements they shall be ratified by the King.

The agreements shall be communicated to the States-General as soon as possible; they shall not be ratified and they shall not enter into force until they have received the approval of the States-General.

The Courts shall not be competent to judge the constitutionality of agreements.

[24] See J. H. F. van Panhuys, "The Netherlands Constitution and International Law," *A.J.I.L.,* XXXXVII (1953), 537 and *A.J.I.L.,* LVIII (1964), 88. The Articles of the Constitution printed here appear as an annex to the second of these articles, pp. 107–108.

Article 61. Approval shall be given either expressly or tacitly.

Express approval shall be given by an act.

Tacit approval shall be regarded as having been given, unless, within thirty days after a submission pertaining thereto of an agreement to both Chambers of the States-General, the wish is expressed by or in the name of one of the Chambers or by at least one fifth of the constitutional membership of one of the Chambers that the agreement should be subjected to express approval.

The period referred to in the previous paragraph shall be suspended for the time of adjournment of the States-General.

Article 62. Except in the case referred to in Article 63, approval shall not be required:

(a) if the agreement is one with respect to which this has been laid down by law;

(b) if the agreement is exclusively concerned with the implementation of an approved agreement, in so far as the Act of Approval did not otherwise stipulate;

(c) if the agreement does not impose any considerable pecuniary obligation on the Kingdom and if it has been concluded for a period not exceeding one year;

(d) if in exceptional cases of a cogent nature it would definitely conflict with the interests of the Kingdom that the agreement shall not enter into force until approval has been given.

An agreement within the terms of (d) shall as yet be submitted as soon as possible to the States-General for approval. In this case Article 61 shall apply. If approval of the agreement is withheld, the agreement shall be terminated as quickly as legally possible.

Unless it would manifestly conflict with the interest of the Kingdom, the agreement shall not be entered into except subject to the reservation that it shall be terminated in case of approval being withheld.

Article 63. If the development of the international legal order requires this, the contents of an agreement may deviate from certain provisions of the Constitution. In any such case approval can only be given expressly. The Chambers of the State-General can adopt a Bill pertaining thereto only by a two-thirds majority of the votes cast.

Article 64. The provisions of the four preceding Articles shall apply, *mutatis mutandis,* to adherence to and denunciation of agreements.

Article 65. Provisions of agreements which, according to their terms, can be binding on anyone shall have such binding force after having been published.

Rules with regard to the publication of agreements shall be laid down in the law.

Article 66. Legislation in force within the Kingdom shall not apply if this application would be incompatible with provisions of agreements which are binding upon anyone and which have been entered into either before or after the enactment of such legislation.

Article 67. With due observance, if necessary, of Article 63, legislative, administrative, and judicial powers may be conferred on organizations based on international law by, or in virtue of, an agreement.

With regard to decisions made by organizations based on international law Articles 65 and 66 shall similarly apply.

There are, however, strong forces in other states that oppose any moves that seem to contravene state sovereignty. One of the most important of these movements was led by former Senator John W. Bricker (Republican, Ohio), who once proposed restricting the treaty-making power of the United States by amending the Constitution.

CONSTITUTION OF THE UNITED STATES: Article VI, Par. 2.

This Constitution, and the Laws of the United States which shall be made in Pursuance thereof; and all Treaties made, or which shall be made, under the Authority of the United States, shall be the supreme Law of the Land; and the Judges in every State shall be bound thereby, any Thing in the Constitution or the Laws of any State to the Contrary notwithstanding.

BRICKER AMENDMENT PROPOSAL
(January 1957)

Sec. 1.   A provision of a treaty or other international agreement not made in pursuance of this Constitution shall have no force or effect. This section shall not apply to treaties made prior to the effective date of this Constitution.

Sec. 2.   A treaty or other international agreement shall have legislative effect within the United States as a law thereof only through legislation, except to the extent that the Senate shall provide affirmatively, in its resolution advising and consenting to a treaty, that a treaty shall have legislative effect.

Sec. 3.   An international agreement to other than a treaty shall have legislative effect within the United States as a law thereof only through legislation valid in the absence of such an international agreement.

Sec. 4.   On the question of advising and consenting to a treaty, the vote shall be determined by yeas and nays, and the names of the Senators voting for and against shall be entered on the journal of the Senate.

The conflict in spirit between the Netherlands constitutional amendment of 1956 and the Bricker amendment proposal of 1957 is clear and strikes at the heart of the nation-state system. States can obviously continue asserting the primacy of their own national interests or replace the standard of national interest with that of international interest and abandon the shibboleths of national sovereignty. For the moment, as the report below indicates, states seem most interested in formulating principles that will fortify their present position.

"REPORT OF THE SPECIAL COMMITTEE ON PRINCIPLES OF INTERNATIONAL LAW
CONCERNING FRIENDLY RELATIONS AND CO-OPERATION AMONG STATES,"
16 NOVEMBER 1964, PP. 163, 166–168 (U.N. DOC. A/5746)

PRINCIPLE D [*i.e.* the principle of sovereign equality of States]

I. *The points of consensus*
1. All States enjoy sovereign equality. As subjects of international law they have equal rights and duties.
2. In particular, sovereign equality includes the following elements:
    (a) States are juridically equal.
    (b) Each State enjoys the rights inherent in full sovereignty.
    (c) Each State has the duty to respect the personality of other States.
    (d) The territorial integrity and political independence of the State are inviolable.
    (e) Each State has the right freely to choose and develop its political, social, economic and cultural systems.
    (f) Each States has the duty to comply fully and in good faith with its international obligations, and to live in peace with other States.

ANNEX B

Views expressed in the discussion, concerning which no consensus was reached

1. *The question whether or not reasons of a political, social, economic, geographical or other nature can restrict the capacity of a State to act or assume obligations as an equal member of the international community*

   Czechoslovakia . . . , *Romania* . . . and *Poland* . . . favoured a provision that the capacity of a State could not be so restricted.

   United Kingdom . . . : no objection to the concept, but as formulated it would give rise to political controversy.

2. *The question whether States have the right to take part in the solution of international questions affecting their legitimate interests, including the right to join international organizations and to become parties to multilateral treaties dealing with or governing such interests*

   Czechoslovakia . . . , *Romania* . . . , *Poland* . . . , *USSR* and *Ghana* favoured a provision recognizing such a right.

   Mexico . . . : difficult to speak of such a right at the present time. *France* . . . : the Special Committee should not deal with the problem. *United Kingdom* . . . and *Australia* . . . : difficulties in view of Article 4 of the Charter and United Nations practice in regard to multilateral conventions.

3. *The question whether States have the right to dispose freely of their natural wealth and resources*

   Czechoslovakia . . . , *Mexico* . . . , *Yugoslavia* . . . , *Romania* . . . , *UAR* . . . , *India* . . . , *USSR* . . . and *Nigeria* favoured a provision recognizing such a right; *Ghana* . . . believed States had such a right, subject only to their liability at law to make compensation.

United Kingdom . . . : agree in principle, but should be balanced by a reference to General Assembly resolution 1803 (XVII). *United States* . . . redraft: "the right, subject to international law and to the terms of agreements entered into by the State, to the free disposal of its natural wealth and resources." *Japan* . . . : reference unnecessary and inappropriate. *Australia* . . . : wondered whether there were exceptions to the principle.

4. *The question whether territories which, in contravention of the principle of self-determination, are still under colonial domination can be considered as integral parts of the territory of the colonial Power*

Czechoslovakia . . . and *UAR* . . . , favoured a provision that such territories cannot be so considered.

United Kingdom . . . and *Australia* . . . : such a provision would be acceptable.

5. *The question whether every State has a duty to conduct its relations with other States in conformity with the principle that the sovereignty of each State is subject to the supremacy of international law*

Netherlands . . . , *France* . . . , *United Kingdom* . . . , and *Japan* . . . favoured a provision to that effect.

Mexico . . . : great difficulty in accepting such a provision. *Romania* . . . , *UAR* . . . , *USSR* . . . and *Ghana* . . . : opposed to such a provision.

6. *The questions whether the jurisdiction of a State is exercised equally over all inhabitants, whether nationals or aliens, and whether aliens can claim rights superior to those of nationals*

Mexico . . . expressed the view that aliens could not claim rights superior to those of nationals.

7. *The principle that the fundamental rights of States may not be impaired in any manner whatsoever*

Mexico . . . suggested the inclusion of the principle.

8. *The principle that the right of each State to protect itself and to live its own life does not authorize it to commit unjust acts against another State*

Mexico . . . suggested the inclusion of the principle.

9. *The question whether economically advanced countries have the obligation to do what they can to narrow the gap between themselves and the less developed countries*

UAR . . . stated that there was such an obligation.

10. *The question whether a State has the right to remove any foreign troops or military bases from its territory*

UAR . . . stated that there was such a right.

11. *The question whether a State has the right to conduct any experiment or resort to any action which is capable of having harmful effects on other States or endangering their security*

UAR . . . and *India* . . . favoured a provision that States have no such rights.

12. *Reference to the objective (in the Preamble of the Charter) of establishing conditions under which justice and respect for obligations under international law can be maintained*
    Australia . . . suggested such a reference.

Whether international law can in fact ever govern international relations without changing these basic principles is one of the critical issues of our time.

Subjects of International Law

Statesmen and theorists traditionally have believed that international law gives rights to and imposes obligations on states rather than individuals; that is, they consider states to be the "subjects" of international law and individual human beings mere "objects" whom the law affects only indirectly through state action.

The historical roots of this view of international law are clear enough. The law applied originally to sovereign rulers. In theory and practice they were personally immune from punishment, but because they were responsible for conducting the foreign affairs of their realms, it was, in theory at least, possible to hold them responsible for violating international (and even domestic) law.

As personal rulers were forced to yield more and more to impersonal states, however, neither sovereignty nor the responsibility for a state's obeying the law rested any longer with the individual ruler. Paradoxically, the more democratic a government became and the more "responsible" to the citizens at home, the more dispersed its powers were and the harder it became to assign responsibility for violating international law. In any case, the impersonal state (unlike the earlier sovereigns) was not flesh and blood. It was therefore ineducable and in itself impervious to reason, pain, or pleasure. It obviously could not respond like an individual to the sanctions of the law or to any other external stimuli. International law, as a result, found itself in a blind alley. Enforcing the law had always been difficult in practice, because no one could guarantee that an absolute sovereign would respond to the pressures of public opinion and the moral sanctions of international law or that he would abide by the law because he personally feared the consequences of war. Nor could anyone be sure that war, if it occurred, would serve the ends of justice. But although the devices for enforcing the law against an absolute sovereign had been imperfect, an individual monarch was, at least, a tangible object against whom to apply the sanctions of international law—in theory, anyway. It was impossible, however, even in theory, to direct sanctions against the dispersed bureaucracy and authority of the more modern states.

The consequences of this dilemma were formidable. After World War I, for instance, the Allies attempted to prosecute and punish persons charged with offenses against the laws of war. One of the most serious problems they had to resolve was whether, and if so, how, to punish Kaiser Wilhelm II, who had received sanctuary in the Netherlands. The American government held that the Kaiser, as the head of a state, was not responsible for his conduct to any authorities other than those of Germany. The United States considered the Kaiser's acts the political acts of a state and therefore maintained that the Allies could not try him before a foreign tribunal. Offenses against international morality were admittedly deplorable, but the United States believed that they might not be tried before a judicial tribunal unless they were also offenses against existing international law. Overruling the United States' view, the Council of the Conference of Paris of 1919 demanded that the Kaiser be tried "for a supreme offense against international morality and the sanctity of treaties." The Netherlands Government declined to honor this request, however, even though the Allies incorporated it in the Treaty of Versailles.[25] The Dutch and United States views were entirely consonant with traditional international law, even though there were some who may have questioned the justice of the law.

After World War II a similar problem arose, and Robert H. Jackson, Chief of Counsel for the United States in prosecuting the war criminals at Nuremberg, took account of some interwar developments and dealt with the same issue in quite a different way:

International Law is more than a scholarly collection of abstract and immutable principles. It is an outgrowth of treaties or agreements between nations and of accepted customs. But every custom has its origin in some single act, and every agreement has to be initiated by the action of some state. Unless we are prepared to abandon every principle of growth for International Law, we cannot deny that our own day has its right to institute customs and to conclude agreements that will themselves become sources of a newer and strengthened International Law. International Law is not capable of development by legislation, for there is no continuously sitting international legislature. Innovations and revisions in International Law are brought about by the action of governments designed to meet a change in circumstances. It grows, as did the Common Law, through decisions reached from time to time in adapting settled principles to new situations. Hence, I am not disturbed by the lack of precedent for the inquiry we propose

[25] Hyde, III, 2409–2455.

to conduct. After the shock to civilization of . . . World War [I], however, a marked reversion to the earlier and sounder doctrines of International Law took place. By the time the Nazis came to power it was thoroughly established that launching an aggressive war or the institution of war by treachery was illegal and that the defense of legitimate warfare was no longer available to those who engaged in such an enterprise. It is high time that we act on the juridical principle that aggressive war-making is illegal and criminal.

. . . .

The United States is vitally interested in recognizing the principle that treaties renouncing war have juridical as well as political meaning. We relied upon the Briand-Kellogg Pact and made it the cornerstone of our national policy. We neglected our armaments and our war machine in reliance upon it. All violations of it, wherever started, menace our peace as we now have good reason to know. An attack on the foundations of international relations cannot be regarded as anything less than a crime against the international community, which may properly vindicate the integrity of its fundamental compacts by punishing aggressors. We therefore propose to charge that a war of aggression is a crime, and that modern International Law has abolished the defense that those who incite or wage it are engaged in legitimate business. Thus may the force of the law be mobilized on the side of peace.

Any legal position asserted on behalf of the United States will have considerable significance in the future evolution of International Law. In untroubled times progress toward an ineffective rule of law in the international community is slow indeed. Inertia rests more heavily upon the society of nations than upon any other society. Now we stand at one of those rare moments when the thought and institutions and habits of the world have been shaken by the impact of world war on the lives of countless millions. Such occasions rarely come and quickly pass. We are put under a heavy responsibility to see that our behavior during this unsettled period will direct the world's thought toward a firmer enforcement of the laws of international conduct, so as to make war less attractive to those who have governments and the destinies of people in their power.

—Report to the President of the United States by
Robert H. Jackson, June 7, 1945.

The Nuremberg trials have generated considerable controversy, in part because of the assumption implicit in the proceedings that the international community can apply international law directly to individuals.[26] Whether those trials (and the war crimes trials in the Far East) have actually extended the jurisdiction of the law cannot be established conclusively, because the trials may not in fact suffice to establish the

[26] Philip C. Jessup, *A Modern Law of Nations* (New York: The Macmillan Company, 1948), pp. 161–162; Quincy Wright, *Contemporary International Law: A Balance Sheet* (New York: Doubleday and Co., 1945), pp. 19–23.

new customs to which Jackson alluded in his report. In any case, one would not wish to (and cannot) depend on advances in international law to result solely from major holocausts like world wars. Making international law apply to individuals remains therefore a continuing problem. States can be expected to resist with great vigor any peacetime moves to make the law apply directly to individuals because to do so is to cut wide swaths through the sacred fields of national authority. Few national officials have, until recently, been willing to move beyond the traditional position that, aside from states, international law applies directly only to pirates, who may be tried by any state which captures them.

Changes in the law come slowly, of course, for law is essentially (and properly) conservative. It is consequently quite difficult for new ideas of law to prevail, and those who attempt to move too fast are often disappointed. New conditions and institutions like the League of Nations, the United Nations, the Permanent Court of International Justice (and its successor, the International Court of Justice), and the institutions of the European Community, do nonetheless introduce into international society new ideas and new ways of dealing with legal problems.

One significant change in the law can be seen in the status granted to the United Nations by the International Court of Justice in its Advisory Opinion on "Reparation for injuries suffered in the service of the United Nations."[27] Count Folke Bernadotte, a Swedish national, was assassinated September 17, 1948, while serving as United Nations Mediator in Palestine. The General Assembly subsequently asked the International Court whether "in the event of an agent of the United Nations in the performance of his duties suffering injury in circumstances involving the responsibility of a State, . . . the United Nations, as an Organization, [has] the capacity to bring an international claim against the responsible *de jure* or *de facto* government with a view to obtaining the reparation due in respect of the damage caused (a) to the United Nations, (b) to the victim or to persons entitled through him?" (General Assembly Resolution 258 [III], December 3, 1948.)

[27] *Advisory Opinion*, [1949] *I.C.J. Rep.* 174.

REPARATION FOR INJURIES SUFFERED IN THE SERVICE OF THE UNITED NATIONS

International Court of Justice, Advisory Opinion, 1949

[1949] I.C.J. Rep. 174

The questions asked of the Court relate to the "capacity to bring an international claim"; accordingly, we must begin by defining what is meant by that capacity, and consider the characteristics of the Organization, so as to determine whether, in general, these characteristics do, or do not, include for the Organization a right to present an international claim.

Competence to bring an international claim is, for those possessing it, the capacity to resort to the customary methods recognized by international law for the establishment, the presentation and the settlement of claims. Among these methods may be mentioned protest, request for an enquiry, negotiation, and request for submission to an arbitral tribunal or to the Court in so far as this may be authorized by the Statute.

This capacity certainly belongs to the State; a State can bring an international claim against another State. Such a claim takes the form of a claim between two political entities, equal in law, similar in form, and both the direct subjects of international law. It is dealt with by means of negotiation, and cannot, in the present state of the law as to international jurisdiction, be submitted to a tribunal, except with the consent of the States concerned.

When the Organization brings a claim against one of its Members, this claim will be presented in the same manner, and regulated by the same procedure. It may, when necessary, be supported by the political means at the disposal of the Organization. In these ways the Organization would find a method for securing the observance of its rights by the Member against which it has a claim.

But, in the international sphere, has the Organization such a nature as involves the capacity to bring an international claim? In order to answer this question, the Court must first enquire whether the Charter has given the Organization such a position that it possesses, in regard to its Members rights which it is entitled to ask them to respect. In other words, does the Organization possess international personality? This is no doubt a doctrinal expression, which has sometimes given rise to controversy. But it will be used here to mean that if the Organization is recognized as having that personality, it is an entity capable of availing itself of obligation incumbent upon its Members.

To answer this question, which is not settled by the actual terms of the Charter, we must consider what characteristics it was intended thereby to give to the Organization.

The subjects of law in any legal system are not necessarily identical in their nature or in the extent of their rights, and their nature depends upon the needs of the community. Throughout its history, the development of international law has been influenced by the requirements of international life, and the progressive increase in the collective activities of States has already given rise to instances of action upon the international plane by certain entities which are not States. This development culminated in the establishment in June 1945 of an international organization whose purposes and principles are specified in the Charter of the United Nations. But to achieve these ends the attribution of international personality is indispensable.

The Charter has not been content to make the Organization created by it merely a centre "for harmonizing the actions of nations in the attainment of these common ends" (Article I, para. 4.). It has equipped that centre with organs, and has given it special tasks. It has defined the position of the Members in relation to the Organization by requiring them to give it every assistance in any action undertaken by it (Article 2, para. 5.), and to accept and carry out the decisions of the Security Council; by authorizing the General Assembly to make recommendations to the Members; by giving the Organization legal capacity and privileges and immunities in the territory of each of its Members; and by providing for the conclusion of agreements between the Organization and its Members. Practice—in particular the conclusion of conventions to which the Organization is a party—has confirmed this character of the Organization, which occupies a position in certain respects in detachment from its Members, and which is under a duty to remind them, if need be, of certain obligations. It must be added that the Organization is a political body, charged with political tasks of an important character, and covering a wide field namely, the maintenance of international peace and security, the development of friendly relations among nations, and the achievement of international co-operation in the solution of problems of an economic, social, cultural or humanitarian character (Article I); and in dealing with its Members it employs political means. The "Convention on the Privileges and Immunities of the United Nations" of 1946 creates rights and duties between each of the signatories and the Organization (see, in particular, Section 35). It is difficult to see how such a convention could operate except upon the international plane and as between parties possessing international personality.

In the opinion of the Court, the Organization was intended to exercise and enjoy, and is in fact exercising and enjoying, functions and rights which can only be explained on the basis of the possession of a large measure of international personality and the capacity to operate upon an international plane. It is at present the supreme type of international organization, and it could not carry out the intentions of its founders if it was devoid of international personality. It must be acknowledged that its Members, by entrusting certain functions to it, with the attendant duties and responsibilities, have clothed it with the competence required to enable those functions to be effectively discharged.

Accordingly, the Court has come to the conclusion that the Organization is an international person. That is not the same thing as saying that it is a State, which it certainly is not, or that its legal personality and rights and duties are the same as those of a State. Still less is it the same thing as saying that it is "a super-State," whatever that expression may mean. It does not even imply that all its rights and duties must be upon the international plane, any more than all the rights and duties of a State must be upon that plane. What it does mean is that it is a subject of international law and capable of possessing international rights and duties, and that it has capacity to maintain its rights by bringing international claims.

The next question is whether the sum of the international rights of the Organization comprises the right to bring the kind of international claim described in the Request for this Opinion. That is a claim against a State to obtain reparation in respect of the damage caused by the injury of an agent of the Organization in the course of the performance of his duties. Whereas a State possesses the totality of international rights and duties recognized by international law, the rights and duties of an entity such as the Organization must depend upon its purposes and functions as specified or implied in its constituent documents and developed in practice. The functions of the Organization are of such a character that they could not be effectively discharged if they involved the concurrent action, on the international plane, of fifty-eight or more Foreign Offices, and the Court concludes that the Members have endowed the Organization with capacity to bring international claims when necessitated by the discharge of its functions.

. . . .

The question [I(a)] is concerned solely with the reparation of damage caused to the Organization when one of its agents suffers injury at the same time. It cannot be doubted that the Organization has the capacity to bring an international claim against one of its Members which has caused injury to it by a breach of its international obligations towards it. The damage specified in Question I (a) means exclusively damage caused to the interests of the Organization itself, to its administrative machine, to its property and assets, and to the interests of which it is the guardian. It is clear that the Organization has the capacity to bring a claim for this damage. As the claim is based on the breach of an international obligation on the part of the Member held responsible by the Organization, the Member cannot contend that this obligation is governed by municipal law, and the Organization is justified in giving its claim the character of an international claim.

When the Organization has sustained damage resulting from a breach by a Member of its international obligations, it is impossible to see how it can obtain reparation unless it possesses capacity to bring an international claim. It cannot be supposed that in such an event all the Members of the Organization, save the defendant State, must combine to bring a claim against the defendant for the damage suffered by the Organization.

The Court is not called upon to determine the precise extent of the reparation which the Organization would be entitled to recover. It may, however, be said that the measure of the reparation should depend upon the amount of the damage which the Organization has suffered as the result of the wrongful act or omission of the defendant State and should be calculated in accordance with the rules of international law. Amongst other things, this damage would include the reimbursement of any reasonable compensation which the Organization had to pay to its agent or to persons entitled through him. Again, the death or disablement of one of its agents engaged upon a distant mission might involve very considerable expenditure in replacing him. These are mere illustrations, and the Court cannot pretend to forecast all the kinds of damage which the Organization itself might sustain.

. . . .

[As for Question I (b)], it is unnecessary to repeat the considerations which led to an affirmative answer being given to Question I (a). It can now be assumed that the Organization has the capacity to bring a claim on the international plane, to negotiate, to conclude a special agreement and to prosecute a claim before an international tribunal. The only legal question which remains to be considered is whether, in the course of bringing an international claim of this kind, the Organization can recover "the reparation due in respect of the damage caused . . . to the victim. . . ."

The traditional rule that diplomatic protection is exercised by the national State does not involve the giving of a negative answer to Question I (b).

In the first place, this rule applies to claims brought by a State. But here we have the different and new case of a claim that would be brought by the Organization.

In the second place, even in inter-State relations, there are important exceptions to the rule, for there are cases in which protection may be exercised by a State on behalf of persons not having its nationality.

In the third place, the rule rests on two bases. The first is that the defendant State has broken an obligation towards the national State in respect of its nationals. The second is that only the party to whom an international obligation is due can bring a claim in respect of its breach. This is precisely what happens when the Organization, in bringing a claim for damage suffered by its agent, does so by invoking the breach of an obligation towards itself. Thus, the rule of the nationality of claims affords no reason against recognizing that the Organization has the right to bring a claim for the damage referred to in Question I (b). On the contrary, the principle underlying this rule leads to the recognition of this capacity as belonging to the Organization, when the Organization invokes, as the ground of its claim, a breach of an obligation towards itself.

Nor does the analogy of the traditional rule of diplomatic protection of nationals abroad justify in itself an affirmative reply. It is not possible, by a strained use of the concept of allegiance, to assimilate the legal bond which exists, under Article 100 of the Charter, between the Organization on the one hand, and the Secretary-General and the staff on the other, to the bond of nationality existing between a State and its nationals.

The Court is here faced with a new situation. The questions to which it gives rise can only be solved by realizing that the situation is dominated by the provisions of the Charter considered in the light of the principles of international law.

The question lies within the limits already established; that is to say it presupposes that the injury for which the reparation is demanded arises from a breach of obligation designed to help an agent of the Organization in the performance of his duties. It is not a case in which the wrongful act or omission would merely constitute a breach of the general obligations of a State concerning the positions of aliens; claims made under this head would be within the competence of the national State and not, as a general rule, within that of the Organization.

The Charter does not expressly confer upon the Organization the capacity to include, in its claim for reparation, damage caused to the victim or to persons entitled through him. The Court must therefore begin by enquiring whether the provisions of the Charter concerning the functions of the Organization, and the part played by its agents in the performance of those functions, imply for the Organization power to afford its agents the limited protection that would consist in the bringing of a claim on their behalf for reparation for damage suffered in such circumstances. Under international law the Organization must be deemed to have those powers which, though not expressly provided in the Charter, are conferred upon it by necessary implication as being essential to the performance of its duties. This principle of law was applied by the Permanent Court of International Justice to the International Labour Organisation in its Advisory Opinion No. 13 of July 23, 1926 (Series B, No. 13, p. 18), and must be applied to the United Nations.

Having regard to its purposes and functions already referred to, the Organization may find it necessary, and has in fact found it necessary, to entrust its agents with important missions to be performed in disturbed parts of the world. Many missions, from their very nature, involve the agents in unusual dangers to which ordinary persons are not exposed. For the same reason, the injuries suffered by its agents in these circumstances will sometimes have occurred in such a manner that their national State would not be justified in bringing a claim for reparation on the ground of diplomatic protection, or, at any rate, would not feel disposed to do so. Both to ensure the efficient and independent performance of these missions and to afford effective support to its agents, the Organization must provide them with adequate protection.

This need of protection for the agents of the Organization, as a condition of the performance of its functions, has already been realized, and the Preamble to the Resolution of December 3rd, 1948 . . . shows that this was the unanimous view of the General Assembly.

For this purpose, the Members of the Organization have entered into certain undertakings, some of which are in the Charter and others in complementary agreements. The content of these undertakings need not be described here; but the Court must stress the importance of the duty to render to the Organization "every assistance" which is accepted by the Members in Article 2, paragraph 5, of the Charter. It must be noted that the effective working of the Organization—the accomplishment of its task, and the independence and effectiveness of the work of its agents—require that these undertakings should be strictly observed. For that purpose, it is necessary that, when an infringement occurs, the Organization should be able to call upon the responsible State to remedy its default, and, in particular, to obtain from the State reparation for the damage that the default may have caused to its agent.

In order that the agent may perform his duties satisfactorily, he must feel that this protection is assured to him by the Organization, and that he may count on it. To ensure the independence of the agent, and, consequently, the independent action of the Organization itself, it is essential that in performing his duties he need not have to rely on any other protection than that of the Organization (save of course for the more direct and immediate protection due from the State in whose territory he may be). In particular, he should not have to rely on the protection of his own State. If he had to rely on that State, his independence might well be compromised, contrary to the principle applied by Article 100 of the Charter. And lastly, it is essential that—whether the agent belongs to a powerful or to a weak State; to one more affected or less affected by the complications of international life; to one in sympathy or not in sympathy with the mission of the agent—he should know that in the performance of his duties he is under the protection of the Organization. This assurance is even more necessary when the agent is stateless.

Upon examination of the character of the functions entrusted to the Organization and of the nature of the missions of its agents, it becomes clear that the capacity of the Organization to exercise a measure of functional protection of its agents arises by necessary intendment out of the Charter.

The obligation entered into by States to enable the agents of the Organization to perform their duties are undertaken not in the interest of the agents, but in that of the Organization. When it claims redress for a breach of these obligations, the Organization is invoking its own right, the right that the obligations due to it should be respected. On this ground, it asks for reparation of the injury suffered, for "it is a principle of international law that the breach of an engagement involves an obligation to make reparation in an adequate form"; as was stated by the Permanent Court in its Judgment No. 8 of July 26th, 1927 (Series A, No. 9, p. 21). In claiming reparation based on the injury suffered by its agent, the Organization does not represent the agent, but is asserting its own right, the right to secure respect for undertakings entered into towards the Organization.

Having regard to the foregoing considerations, and to the undeniable right of the Organization to demand that its Members shall fulfil the obligations entered into by them in the interest of the good working of the Organization, the Court is of the opinion that, in the case of a breach of these obligations, the Organization has the capacity to claim adequate reparation, and that in assessing this reparation it is authorized to include the damage suffered by the victim or by persons entitled through him.

The question remains whether the Organization has "the capacity to bring an international claim against the responsible *de jure* or *de facto* government with a view to obtaining the reparation due in respect of the damage caused

(a) to the United Nations, (b) to the victim or to persons entitled through him" when the defendant State is not a member of the Organization.

In considering this aspect of Question I (a) and (b), it is necessary to keep in mind the reasons which have led the Court to give an affirmative answer to it when the defendant State is a Member of the Organization. It has now been established that the Organization has capacity to bring claims on the international plane, and that it possesses a right of functional protection in respect of its agents. Here again the Court is authorized to assume that the damage suffered involves the responsibility of a State, and it is not called upon to express an opinion upon the various ways in which that responsibility might be engaged. Accordingly the question is whether the Organization has capacity to bring a claim against the defendant State to recover reparation in respect of that damage or whether, on the contrary, the defendant State, not being a member, is justified in raising the objection that the Organization lacks the capacity to bring an international claim. On this point, the Court's opinion is that fifty States, representing the vast majority of the members of the international community, had the power, in conformity with international law, to bring into being an entity possessing objective international personality, and not merely personality recognized by them alone, together with capacity to bring international claims.

Accordingly, the Court arrives at the conclusion that an affirmative answer should be given to Question I (a) and (b) whether or not the defendant State is a Member of the United Nations. . . .

Despite the willingness of the International Court to grant the United Nations an "international personality" and the agreement of states generally with the Advisory Opinion, ardent reformers cannot suddenly change international law to make it apply directly to individuals. The case of *Sei Fujii v. California* illustrates the problem very well. Fujii, a Japanese national ineligible for United States citizenship, purchased land in Los Angeles County despite the Alien Land Law of California, which forbade aliens ineligible for citizenship to acquire real estate. Fujii then brought an action against the State to determine the validity of his title, contending that the Alien Land Law was invalid because it denied him equal protection of the laws by arbitrarily discriminating against him solely because of race, thereby violating the Fourteenth Amendment of the United States Constitution. He also stated in passing that the Land Law was contrary to the "declared principles and spirit of the United Nations Charter." The Superior Court of Los Angeles County upheld the Land Law. Fujii then carried his case to the District Court of Appeal, which supported him and declared the relevant portions of the Land Law unenforceable. The District Court rested its decision, not upon the United States Constitution, but entirely on the United Nations Charter and the Universal Declaration of Human Rights:

The Charter has become "the supreme law of the land; and the judges in every State shall be bound thereby, anything in the constitution or laws of any State to the contrary notwithstanding." (United States Constitution, art. VI, sec. 2.) The position of this country in the family of nations forbids trafficking in innocuous generalities, but demands that every State in the Union accept and act upon the Charter according to its plain language and its unmistakable purpose and intent.

. . . .

A perusal of the Charter renders it manifest that restrictions contained in the alien land law are in direct conflict with the plain terms of the Charter . . . [referring to the Preamble, and to articles 1, 2, 55, and 56] and with the purposes announced therein by its framers. It is incompatible with article 17 of the Declaration of Human Rights which proclaims the right of everyone to own property. We have shown that the expansion by the Congress of the classes of nationals eligible to citizenship has correspondingly shrunk the group ineligible under the provisions of the alien land law to own or lease land in California until the latter now consists in reality of a very small number of Japanese. The other Asiatics who still remain on the proscribed list are so few that they need not be considered.

Clearly such a discrimination against a people of one race is contrary both to the letter and to the spirit of the Charter which, as a treaty, is paramount to every law of every State in conflict with it. The alien land law must therefore yield to the treaty as the superior authority. The restrictions of the statute based on eligibility to citizenship, but which ultimately and actually are referable to race or color must be and are therefore declared untenable and unenforceable.

The decision attracted much attention in legal circles throughout the country, primarily because it relied so heavily on the United Nations Charter. The Court implied that the Charter was a "self-executing" treaty; that is, it operated to create justiciable rights in private persons immediately after it was ratified. Most lawyers, jurists, and scholars, on the other hand, had previously regarded the Charter as "non-self-executing," as merely stipulating that the members of the United Nations would sometime enact such laws as they believed necessary and desirable to fulfill the standards adumbrated in the Charter. The State of California so contended, and after being denied a rehearing in the District Court, brought the case to the California Supreme Court, which in April 1952 decided that although the Land Law was indeed unconstitutional, it was invalid under the Fourteenth Amendment to the Constitution and not because of provisions of the Charter.[28]

---

[28] For decisions of the California Court of Appeals, see 217 P. 2d 481 and 218 P. 2d 595 (1950); for decision of the Supreme Court of California, see 38 Cal. 2d 718, 242 P. 2d 617 (1952). See also *A.J.I.L.*, XXXXIV (1950) 543–548, 590–591, and *A.J.I.L.*, XXXXVI (1952), 682–690 for notes by Manley O. Hudson and Charles Fairman.

States are obviously reluctant to concede the jurisdiction over their own nationals to any other authority. Nonetheless, in a number of instances states have authorized international organizations and even other governments to exercise jurisdiction over their nationals. The United States, for instance, has agreed to allow foreign governments to try its soldiers stationed abroad for certain crimes, and the states in the European Coal and Steel Community have granted to the Community's Court the power to adjudicate disputes among coal and steel producers in Belgium, France, Germany, Italy, Luxemburg, and the Netherlands. These practices have given rise to suggestions that a new "transnational law" may be evolving, which treats questions of jurisdiction as procedural matters not involving national honor or sovereignty.[29] These practices may represent a very important germinal element in strengthening international institutions.

[29] See Philip C. Jessup, *Transnational Law* (New Haven: Yale University Press, 1956).

CHAPTER II

Members of the International Community

The day when international law will become fully effective and apply directly to individuals still seems quite far off. In the meantime, states remain the principal subjects of the law. One must, therefore, know what a state is. At first, defining a state seems easy enough. Webster's Dictionary calls it "any body of people occupying a definite territory and politically organized under one government, especially one that is not subject to external control." This definition accommodates states differing greatly from one another in size, population, resources, and type of government. The United States and the Soviet Union, for instance, are Brobdingnagian; Switzerland and Luxembourg, Lilliputian; but they are all established states. On the other hand, Byelorussia and the Ukraine, although they have no real independence, are members of the United Nations, even though the Charter (Art. 4) restricts membership to states. Other anomalies exist in the instances of Monaco, Andorra, and Vatican City, which exercise political authority, issue postage stamps, and send and receive ambassadors, as states customarily do, and yet are not members of the United Nations.

Even if one could decide today which of the world's political entities are states, it would be impossible, short of stopping history in its tracks, to resolve the question for all time because states disappear completely (Estonia, 1940), are transformed (Austria, 1919), or are born anew (Israel, 1948). The African continent since World War II provides the most striking examples of political transformation. What is more, in cases of coups, civil wars, or revolutions, questions of legitimacy arise, and there may even be rival claimants to power within a state (as was the case after the Russian Revolution in 1917, in the Spanish Civil War [1936–1939], and in China after the Communist victory of 1949).

58

All these events require other states to decide whether and how to conduct their relations with rival "governments."

International law at present does not satisfactorily resolve conflicts among pretenders to power. The international law of "recognition" establishes procedures by which states and governments may regularize their relations with one another, and certain legal consequences, some of which we shall examine later, flow from recognition. But historically, politics and force, more often than law, have confirmed states and governments in their claims to authority, and politics more than law governs the act of recognition. Without any impartial agents to determine decisively the merits of states and governments, the international community relies on the executive agencies in each state to recognize other states and governments. Recognition is therefore a step that national political authorities take at their pleasure, often with a bow, but sometimes without any regard at all to international law.

Attempts to develop objective legal criteria for recognition have not been very successful. The traditional attributes of statehood as the dictionary gives them, for instance, are themselves only objective in part. Merely to state the four criteria—people, territory, government, and independence—does not tell us *how many* people a state must have, *how much* territory, *what kind* of government, or *what degree* of independence. A United Nations committee once drew up a list of criteria of self-government. The list was not very useful, however, because the criteria were not precise. The General Assembly concluded that particular circumstances in each case would have to determine whether or not territories were in fact self-governing. Since 1960, when the Assembly adopted the Declaration on the Granting of Independence to Colonial Countries and Peoples, and since 1961, when the Assembly established a Special Committee of 17 (enlarged in 1962 to 24)[1] to implement the Declaration, the United Nations has continued to decide empirically when colonies were qualified for independence.

Without objective criteria, recognition remains subjective, a matter of choice with the recognizing state. States often interpret the same data in different ways and, in the past, they did not all agree, for example, about recognizing the United States of America in 1776, Brazil in 1822, the Soviet Union in 1917, Manchukuo in 1932, or Israel in 1948. States face similar problems in deciding whether to continue recognizing governments or states which disappear, as in the case of the governments in exile in World War II or the Baltic republics in 1940.

[1] See U.N. Doc. A/2428, "Report of the Ad Hoc Committee on Factors" (1953); GA Res. 742 (VIII), 1514 (XV), 1654 (XVI), and 1810 (XVII); and reports of the Special Committee.

The subjective elements in recognition are clear in United States practice, for the United States has always wanted to determine whether a new state or government is able and willing to fulfill its obligations under international law. How the United States determines whether a state or government exhibits this quality, however, varies considerably according to the politics of the situation. In the case of the U.S.S.R., the United States did not determine it for sixteen years; on the other hand, in the case of Israel, President Truman apparently determined it intuitively and instantaneously in 1948.

The existing law of recognition is clearly quite unsatisfactory. States differ with one another about the political bodies that deserve recognition; unrecognized states or their allies are often exacerbated by the policies of states which do not recognize them; and states often distinguish unrealistically between recognition *de jure* and *de facto*. What is more, the hard facts of international life often require states to enter into "unofficial relations" with states they do not recognize; attitudes towards representation in the United Nations and recognition do not always coincide; and the extent to which unrecognized states are bound by international law is unclear. Finally, in the minds of laymen, and apparently in the minds of some statesmen as well, granting and withholding recognition are equated with approval or disapproval. There are no legal grounds for this confusion and, for that matter, no logical ones either, because no one maintains that states approve of the policies of all the states that they recognize.

Two proposals have been advanced to remedy these problems. One, made by Senor Don Genaro Estrada, Secretary of Foreign Relations in Mexico in 1930, would entirely abolish formal recognition and merely have governmental officials deal with whatever authorities happen to control the governmental machinery of a state. This "Estrada Doctrine" still does not help the official who must decide when which of two contending groups of authorities does in fact control the administration. A second approach is to make recognition a collective process through the United Nations or some similar international body.[2]

The Consequences of Recognition

There are those who maintain that the act of recognition creates a state, that recognition is, in other words, a "constitutive" act. But such a theory conflicts with many important facts. For instance, even though

[2] See Herbert W. Briggs, "Community Interest in the Emergence of New States: The Problem of Recognition," 1951 Proceedings, *Am. Soc'y. Int'l Law*, 169–181; S. Rosenne, "Recognition of States by the United Nations," *B.Y.I.L.*, 437–447 (1949). See, however, U.N. Doc. S/1466, "Legal Aspects of Problems of Representation in the United Nations" (1950).

one state may refuse to recognize another, as Russia refused to recognize the United States before 1809 and the United States refused to recognize the U.S.S.R. before 1933, the unrecognized state is objectively no different before or after tardy recognition. What is more, a political entity, not recognized as a state, can still exercise control over its territory regardless of the views of other states. To hold that recognition creates a state, therefore, is to founder in logical impossibilities. For instance, where governments differ in their attitudes toward a new government, as in the case of western attitudes towards Communist China after 1949, the new entity would obviously exist for some states, but not for all. Finally, states often expect other states, which they do not recognize, to behave as though they were subject to international law; but if they did not exist, they could not possibly comply with the law.

Governments that do not hold to the constitutive theory maintain that recognition is "declaratory," that it acknowledges as a fact "something which has hitherto been uncertain, namely, the independence of the body claiming to be a state," and that it thus serves to declare the "state's readiness to accept the normal consequences of that fact. . . ."[3] The declaratory theory, by contrast with the constitutive, corresponds more closely to reality.

Even though international law does not prescribe the conditions regulating the act of recognition, it does specify certain legal consequences that follow once recognition takes place. Once states have declared their intention to regularize their relations with one another, the legal consequences are manifold. For instance, sovereign states enjoy the right both to sue and to enjoy immunity from suit in one another's courts. Moreover, in matters that arise within their jurisdiction, courts generally consider the acts of recognized governments valid. Recognition itself plays a role in establishing these rights, as shown by a number of cases which arose in the United Kingdom between 1917 and 1921 and in the United States between 1917 and 1933, when neither government recognized the Union of Soviet Socialist Republics. The problem has more recently been important in those countries which, since 1949, have not recognized the People's Government of [Communist] China.

The case of *A. M. Luther v. James Sagor and Co.*[4] provides a very clear example of the effect a British Court gave to the act of recognition by His Majesty's Government. A. M. Luther, the plaintiffs, were a manufacturing company incorporated in 1898 in the Empire of Russia and confiscated in 1918 by what was then called the Russian Socialist Feder-

[3] J. L. Brierly, *The Law of Nations*, (6th ed., Oxford: Clarendon Press, 1963), p. 139.
[4] Great Britain, Court of Appeal [1921] 3 K.B. 532.

ative Republic (R.S.F.R.). In 1920, the James Sagor Company of England purchased 1500 cubic meters of plywood boards from the nationalized company and imported them into England. The plaintiffs asked the Court to award them the boards which had arrived in London, claiming that the wood was their property. The Sagor Company, the defendants, argued that the Russian's 1918 confiscation decrees were valid and that their contract with the R.S.F.R. had been made in good faith. A lower court agreed with Luther in 1920. The British Government had not at that time recognized the Russian Government and, since the property was physically within the Court's jurisdiction, it refused to give effect in England to the actions of the unrecognized R.S.F.R. government. Recognition took place in April 1921, however, and on appeal the judgment of the lower court was reversed. Because the Crown now recognized the R.S.F.R., the Court no longer questioned the right of the Russian government to pass title to the goods to the Sagor Company. As the Court of Appeals put it,

> The [British] Government . . . having recognized the Soviet Government as the Government really in possession of the powers of sovereignty in Russia, the acts of that Government must be treated by the Courts of this country with all the respect due to the acts of a duly recognized foreign sovereign State.

In the United States, recognition of the Soviet regime did not take place until 1933. Acting on the theory that an unrecognized state was not entitled to immunity in court, M. Wulfsohn and Company (in the case of *Wulfsohn v. Russian Socialist Federated Soviet Republic*[5] [1923]) sued the R.S.F.S.R. for confiscating a quantity of furs it owned. The furs were not in the United States, so the Court's problem was different from that which the British courts faced in *Luther v. Sagor*. It did not have to decide what effect it should give in its own territory to the action of a foreign government, but whether it could do anything about an action taken by the R.S.F.S.R. inside its own territory. The Wulfsohn Company had to admit that the R.S.F.S.R. was the existing *de facto* government in Russia, and the Court said that because the government did exist, it was:

> . . . clothed with the power to enforce its authority within its own territory, obeyed by the people over whom it rules, capable of performing the duties and fulfilling the obligations of an independent power, able to enforce its claims by military force. . . .

The Court asserted that these were matters of fact, not theory, and that there was no doubt that the act of recognition alone automatically

[5] 234 N.Y. 372, 138 N.E. 24 (1923).

answered a number of questions. For instance, recognition determined for the courts whether a particular government existed; it also determined in time of war, among other matters, how the courts applied neutrality laws. Nonetheless, the Court observed that the actions of a sovereign within his own territories could not be reviewed by a foreign court because "he has not submitted himself to our laws [and without] his consent he is not subject to them." The main reason for observing this immunity was to avoid vexing the peace of nations; without it, the Department of State would be involved in disputes it might feel that it was unwise to pursue. Consequently courts, by tradition, left such matters for the political branches of the government to determine. Therefore, the Court ruled, the R.S.F.S.R., though unrecognized by the United States, nonetheless enjoyed one of the prerogatives of a sovereign and could not be sued in United States courts.

In the same year, and in the same court, the R.S.F.S.R. brought suit in the case of *Russian Socialist Federated Soviet Republic v. Cibrario.*[6] The Court had decided in the Wulfsohn case that the R.S.F.S.R. could not be a defendant; would it now permit the R.S.F.S.R. to be a plaintiff? The Court conceded that if the Russian Government were recognized, it certainly might bring an action in an American court either under a treaty or, more generally, because of "comity," defined as:

. . . that reciprocal courtesy which one member of the family of nations owes to the others. It presupposes friendship. It assumes the prevalence of equity and justice. Experience points to the expediency of recognizing the legislative, executive and judicial acts of other powers. We do justice that justice may be done in return.

Comity is, however, a favor and not a right, the Court observed. Moreover, it is a favor of the nation itself, not an arbitrary favor to be extended or withheld at the pleasure of the Court. Comity always governs where it is consistent with public policy. But since the courts may interpret public policy, the real issue was whether any rule of comity required the Court to permit an unrecognized power to sue: since the United States did not recognize the R.S.F.S.R., should the Court permit the R.S.F.S.R. to bring an action? The Court said no.

Acting according to a different theory—namely, that the rights of a sovereign are vested in the state and not in any particular government which may purport to represent it, courts have on occasion permitted foreign states not recognized by the United States to sue. Thus Mexico asked the Superior Court of Essex County, Massachusetts, to seize certain funds Mexico claimed that Mariono Viamonte y Fernandez, a former

[6] 235 N.Y. 255, 139 N.E. 259 (1923).

Chief Clerk of the Department of Special Taxes in Mexico City, had taken from the country. Because the United States of America recognized the United States of Mexico, even though it did not recognize the existing administration of that State, the Court permitted Mexico to maintain its suit.[7]

Courts have not always been content merely to look to the acts of the political branches of the government for guides to their decisions even though they have never questioned the right of those branches to determine what governments should be recognized. In *Sokoloff v. National City Bank*[8] Justice Benjamin Cardozo considered the case of Boris N. Sokoloff, who, having paid the National City Bank of New York over $30,000, asked it to open an account in his name in its Petrograd (later Leningrad) branch. Subsequent withdrawals reduced the account to $28,000. When the Russian Revolution occurred in November 1917, the R.S.F.S.R. took over these assets, and the Bank argued that the Russian expropriation had not only liquidated its funds in Petrograd, but cancelled its obligation to Sokoloff. Sokoloff thereupon sued the Bank to recover his money. In deciding the case, Cardozo noted that "Courts of high repute have held that confiscation by a government to which recognition has been refused has no other effect in law than seizure by bandits or by other lawless bodies." He observed, however, that after the United States Civil War, acts or decrees of the rebellious states that were just and consistent with public policy were frequently sustained, just as if the governments had been lawful. It seemed, therefore, that "effect may at times be due to the ordinances of foreign governments which, though formally unrecognized, have notoriously an existence as governments, de facto." To Cardozo, these events suggested that "a body or group . . . may gain for its acts and decrees a validity quasi-governmental, if violence to fundamental principles of justice or to our own public policy might otherwise be done."

The general rule remained, nonetheless, that acts or decrees, "to be ranked as governmental, must proceed from some authority recognized as a government de facto." Exceptions to the rule obviously could be made if enforcing it worked an injustice on the parties. He found no injustice, however, in enforcing liability on the National City Bank because the dollars paid by Sokoloff were not physical objects committed to the Bank's keeping, and the Bank did not maintain that it had increased its assets in rubles in Petrograd after Sokoloff deposited his dollars in New York. Sokoloff's deposit was instead an intangible right to receive rubles. The Bank's liability was therefore not affected by

[7] Mexico v. Viamonte y Fernandez, U.S. For. Rel., II, 573.
[8] 239 N.Y. 158, 145 N.E. 917 (1924).

the expropriation because, even though the R.S.F.S.R. could and did deprive the Bank of the privilege of doing business on Russian soil, the R.S.F.S.R. could not, by any action it took, terminate the liability of a corporation formed under United States laws. The Court, therefore, decided that recognition could control its decision, that the decrees of the R.S.F.S.R. were unrecognized, and that the Bank had to restore the funds due to Sokoloff.

Justice Cardozo's decision made it clear that under some conditions the courts had in the past and might again have to admit the validity of the acts of unrecognized governments. This doctrine reappeared in full force in the case of *Salimoff and Co. v. Standard Oil Co. of New York.*[9] This case dealt with actions of the Soviet government in confiscating all oil lands in Russia and selling oil to a number of customers—among them, the Standard Oil Company of New York. Former owners of the property asked for an accounting on the ground that the confiscatory decrees of the unrecognized Soviet government and its seizure of oil lands had no other effect in law on the rights of the parties than "seizure by bandits." Justice Pound implied his opinion by asking a rhetorical question: "Does title pass or is the Soviet government no better than a thief, stealing the property of its nationals and giving only a robber's title to stolen property?" Since the United States refused to recognize the Soviet regime, not because it did not exercise control but for other reasons, Pound felt that "the question as to the validity of acts and decrees of a regime, not the subject of diplomatic recognition, becomes a matter to be decided by the courts in an appropriate case." He noted that the courts of New York had concluded that confiscation decrees had no extraterritorial effect and had sustained the right of certain corporations, whose Russian assets had been confiscated, to continue their operations outside of Russia.

The consequence has been that corporations non-existent in Soviet Russia have been, like fugitive ghosts endowed with extraterritorial immortality, recognized as existing outside its boundaries. The juristic person, the Russian corporation, dead in the country which created it, has received juridical vivification elsewhere. . . . The United States government recognizes that the Soviet government has functioned as a *de facto* or *quasi* government since 1917, ruling within its borders. It has recognized its existence as a fact although it has refused diplomatic recognition as one might refuse to recognize an objectionable relative although his actual existence could not be denied. It tells us that it has no disposition to ignore the fact that such government is exercising control and power in territory of the former Russian empire. . . .

[9] 262 N.Y. 220 (1933).

As a juristic conception what is Soviet Russia? A band of robbers or a government? We all know that it is a government. The State Department knows it, the courts, the nations and the man on the street. If it is a government in fact, its decrees have force within its borders and over its nationals. "Recognition does not create the state. . . ." It simply gives to a *de facto* state international status. To refuse to recognize that Soviet Russia is a government regulating the internal affairs of the country, is to give to fictions an air of reality which they do not deserve.

A careful examination of the New York cases reveals some expressions from which it might be inferred that the Soviet government is still to be regarded as a band of thieves, exercising power without authority, but the basic fact of all the cases is stated as follows: "The State of Russia is now governed by the Russian Socialist Federated Soviet Republic. Such government there exists, clothed with power to enforce its authority within its own territory, obeyed by the people over whom it rules, capable of performing the duties and fulfilling the obligations of an independent power and able to enforce its claims by military force."[10]

Pound concluded, therefore, that the Standard Oil Co. was not in error in assuming that the Soviet government, whether recognized or not, could pass title to the soil.

Similar problems have continued to plague the courts more recently in the case of the Nationalist and Communist Chinese governments. One such case is *Bank of China v. Wells Fargo Bank and Union Trust Co.*[11]

The Bank of China was organized under Chinese law in 1912. The Chinese Government owned two thirds of its stock, and the Bank had a substantial deposit with the Wells Fargo Bank. After Chinese Communist forces gained control of most of the Chinese mainland, the Bank of China moved its main office to Hong Kong. Chinese Communist authorities took over the old main office and named new persons to conduct the Bank. Later the emigré (Hong Kong) directors and management of the Bank brought an action to recover their deposit with the Wells Fargo Bank. The District Court authorized the Wells Fargo Bank to deposit the moneys with the court or to place it in a separate trust account approved by the court.

The emigré directors of the Bank are now scattered. . . . Some of these directors represent a government which is not now, and may never again be, in a position to speak for the Chinese people in respect to the manner in which the corporation shall function in China. The others may or may not be the directors whom the private stockholders now desire to speak for them. It is difficult to perceive how the interests of the corporation, its stock-

[10] Russian Reinsurance Co. v. Stoddard, 240 N.Y., 149, 157 (1925).
[11] 92 F. Supp. 920 (N.D. Calif., 1950).

holders, and its depositors will be protected by placing the *res* in dispute at the disposal of a group of these directors.

To deny the emigré directors control of these funds is not to deprive a government, still recognized by the United States, of funds to carry on its fight for survival. For these are corporate funds which should not be dissipated for purposes other than those of the corporation.

On the other hand, the new management in China is not yet so established as to warrant placing these funds in its hands. Who the private stockholders wish to represent them is at present unknown. The new government directors represent a government, which although in control of the Chinese mainland, has not yet put down all organized resistance. Only time will tell whether this government will become a stable government.

Furthermore, recent international developments bar any decision of this Court which would place these funds in the control of the new management of the bank in China. For this Court to recognize the acts of the so-called "People's Government," in so far as they relate merely to a Chinese corporation which must function under that government, might not necessarily run counter to a merely negative policy of non-recognition on the part of the United States. But, since the announcement of the President on June 27, 1950, that the United States will defend Formosa (the present seat of the *de jure* Chinese government) the policy of the United States appears to be one of active intervention against the aims of the "Peoples Government." Although the Bank of China is a private corporation, the Court must realistically recognize that if the $626,860.07 in controversy were placed in the hands of the new management of the Bank of China, the "Peoples Government" would be aided and abetted.

The only solution which gives promise of affording protection to the Bank of China, its stockholders, and depositors, and at the same time supporting the foreign policy of the United States, is to leave these funds where they are for the present.

The District Court then continued the case *sine die* rather than decide in favor of either group purporting to represent the Bank of China. The Court of Appeals for the Ninth Circuit, on July 30, 1951, dismissed an appeal by the Bank of China without prejudice and remanded the case to the District Court, suggesting that the District Court "may deem it expedient to reexamine the case in the light of changing world conditions and such additional evidence as may be made available to it." [190 F. (2d) 1010, 1012.] At a later stage of litigation, in 1952, the District Court did reconsider the case and, stating that "world conditions have materially changed" since its 1950 decision, awarded the funds to the Bank of China as controlled by the recognized Nationalist Government.[12]

[12] Bank of China v. Wells Fargo Bank and Union Trust Co., 104 F. Supp. 59 (N.D. Cal., 1952).

BANK OF CHINA v. WELLS FARGO BANK
AND UNION TRUST CO.

104 F. Supp. 59 (N.D. Cal., 1952)

If whenever this court is called upon to determine whether there is a government justly entitled to act on behalf of a foreign state in respect to a particular matter, the court is bound to say, without regard to the facts before it, that the government recognized by our executive is that government, then nothing more need be said here. To permit this expression of executive policy to usurp entirely the judicial judgment would relieve the court of a burdensome duty, but it is doubtful that the ends of justice would thus be met. It has been argued that such is the accepted practice. But the authorities do not support this view.

. . . Public policy, rather than the unrecognized status of the Soviet Government, shaped the decisions in the Russian nationalization cases. . . .

Some more recent decisions of the federal courts, involving Soviet nationalization of corporations of the Baltic states, give great weight to the executive policy of non-recognition. But it cannot be said that these decisions establish an all-embracing rule that no extra-territorial effect may ever be given the acts of an unrecognized government.

Nor . . . does the decision of the Supreme Court in the United States v. Pink, 1942, 315 U.S. 203, 62 S.Ct. 552, 86 L.Ed. 796, impose upon this court a duty to give conclusive effect to every act of a recognized government. Pink requires that full faith and credit be accorded those acts which our executive has expressly sanctioned. But such executive sanction is not expressed by governmental recognition per se.

The decisions just set forth, as well as others in this field, reveal no rule of law obliging the courts to give conclusive effect to the acts of a recognized government to the exclusion of all consideration of the acts of an opposing unrecognized government. Nor does it appear that such a sweeping rule would be a sound one.

Even were the court solely concerned with the implementation of our executive foreign policy, it would be presumptuous to blindly effectuate every act of a recognized government or to treat every act of an unrecognized government as entirely fictional. Early in our national history, our recognition policy was generally based on the executive's view of the stability and effectiveness of the government in question. More recently recognition has been granted and withheld at the diplomatic bargaining table. Our policy has thus become equivocal. Conflicting considerations are balanced in the executive decision. Moreover, an act of recognition does not necessarily mark a sudden reversal in executive policy. It may come as a culmination of a gradual change in attitude. Thus the import of recognition or non-recognition may vary with time and circumstance.

Recognition is not intended to sanctify every act, past and future, of a foreign government. The withholding of recognition may cast a mantle of disfavor over a government. But, it does not necessarily stamp all of its acts with disapproval or brand them unworthy of judicial notice. Our executive, on occasion, has even entered into a treaty with an unrecognized government.[13]

This is not to suggest that the courts should regard executive policy in respect to recognition and non-recognition of foreign governments as meaningless or of little consequence. In any particular situation, executive policy may be crucial, as indeed it appears to be in the present case. But, it is a fact which properly should be considered and weighed along with the other facts before the court.

Turning to the record in this case, it appears that two governments are governments in fact of portions of the territory of the State of China. The "Peoples" Government has supplanted the "Nationalist" Government in dominion over the entire Chinese Mainland with an area of more than 3,700,000 square miles, and a population of more than 460,000,000. The "Nationalist'" Government controls one of the 35 provinces of China, the Island of Formosa, which has an area of 13,885 square miles and a population in excess of 6,000,000. It is obvious that the "Peoples" Government is now the government in fact of by far the greater part of the territory of the Chinese State. Nevertheless the "Nationalist" Government controls substantial territory, exceeding in area that of either Belgium or the Netherlands, and in population that of Denmark or Switzerland.

Each government, in its respective sphere, functions effectively. Each is recognized by a significant number of the nations of the world. Each maintains normal diplomatic intercourse with those nations which extend recognition. This has been the status quo for more than two years.

. . . .

This factual situation is without analogous precedent in any reported case. The resulting legal problem, arising as it does out of sweeping historical changes and the claims of rival governments, cannot be met by the application of technical rules of corporation law.

From a practical standpoint, neither of the rival Banks of China is a true embodiment of the corporate entity which made the deposit in the Wells Fargo Bank. The present Nationalist Bank of China is more nearly equivalent in the sense of continuity of management. The Peoples Bank is more representative in ability to deal with the greater number of private stockholders and established depositors and creditors. . . . Were there only one government, in fact, of the Chinese State, or only one government in a position to act effectively for the State in respect to the matter before the Court, the Court might be justified in accepting such a government as the proper

---

[13] The United States and Russia, along with 52 other nations, entered into the Kellogg Pact renouncing war as an instrument of national policy in 1929 when the Soviet Government was as yet unrecognized by our executive. 46 Stat. 2343.

representative of the State, even though our executive declined to deal with it. Here, there co-exist two governments, in fact, each attempting to further, in its own way, the interests of the State of China, in the Bank of China. It is not a proper function of a domestic court of the United States to attempt to judge which government best represents the interests of the Chinese State in the Bank of China. In this situation, the Court should justly accept, as the representative of the Chinese State, that government which our executive deems best able to the further the mutual interests of China and the United States.

Since the Court is of the opinion that it should recognize the Nationalist Government of China as legally entitled to exercise the controlling corporate authority of the Bank of China in respect to the deposit in suit, the motion for summary judgment in favor of the Bank of China, as controlled by the Nationalist Government, is granted. . . .

LATVIAN STATE CARGO & PASSENGER S.S. LINE v. McGRATH, ATTORNEY GENERAL

No. 10131

UNITED STATES COURT OF APPEALS DISTRICT OF COLUMBIA CIRCUIT

188 F. 2d 1000 (1951)

The three vessels were originally owned by citizens and residents of the Republic of Latvia. In June, 1940, armies of the Union of Soviet Socialist Republics occupied Latvia, and pursuant to that occupation a new government, the Latvian Soviet Socialist Republic, was set up. . . . Plaintiff-appellant is a public corporation organized under the laws of the Union of Soviet Socialist Republics. Its claim of title to the funds here involved rests upon the effect and operation of the nationalization decrees.

None of the three vessels was in Latvian waters subsequent to 1939. In 1941 they were in New York, and libels were filed against them on behalf of the prenationalization owners. The present appellant intervened. Trustees were appointed for the vessels. Earnings derived from the operation of the vessels came into the hands of the trustees, and in 1942, the vessels having been sunk, the proceeds of the insurance came into their hands. In 1943, Germany having invaded Latvia, the Alien Property Custodian issued his vesting orders against the property and interest in the hands of the trustees. Germany having been defeated and Latvia having been reoccupied by the Union of Soviet Socialist Republics, the Latvian Soviet Socialist Republic was reestablished and the nationalization decrees were restored to effect.

Appellee says that the incorporation of Latvia into the Union of Soviet Socialist Republics and the nationalization decrees of the Latvian Soviet Socialist Republic have not been recognized by the United States, that the executive policy of nonrecognition is binding upon the federal courts, and that therefore appellant has no title enforceable in those courts.

. . . .

[1,2] The conduct of foreign affairs is, of course, a function of the executive branch of the Government, and the judicial branch has no part in it or control over it.[14] It is settled by United States v. Belmont[15] and United States v. Pink[16] that if there is a formal act by the executive department, either of recognition or of compact, the courts must give full effect to the terms of such act. Our problem, however, does not deal with such an affirmative act.

Moreover we do not have before us a mere failure to recognize in the absence of a strong executive policy against condoning in any way the Soviet occupation of Latvia. It might well be that in the absence of such a policy the usual rules applicable under the established doctrines of conflicts of laws would apply. Thus, in . . . [the *Salimoff Case,* above][17] the State Department refused to certify a policy of hostility to decrees of the unrecognized governments, and the courts accordingly applied those doctrines in arriving at their decisions. Even granting the application of such doctrines, however, there is no assurance that appellant should prevail here. There is, for example, the view suggested by Judge Goodrich, concurring in The Maret,[18] that in the absence of recognition of a foreign government the courts might deny effect to an act of that government which purports to change the ownership of a chattel absent from its borders. In a similar vein is the statement in Compania Espanola v. Navemar[19] to the effect that, where confiscatory decrees are *in invitum,* actual possession by some act of physical dominion or control in behalf of the confiscating government is necessary. No such showing was made in the case at bar. And, furthermore, there is the possible view that, since the nationalization decrees here involved were confiscatory and thus contrary to the public policy of this country, our courts would in no event give them effect.[20] In the view we take, however, it is unnecessary to consider those possibly applicable rules.

In the case at bar it appears that the non-recognition of the nationalization decrees was the result of a deliberate policy of the executive branch of the

[14] United States v. Curtiss-Wright Export Corp., 1936, 299 U.S. 304, 57 S.Ct. 216, 81 L.Ed. 255.
[15] 1937, 301 U.S. 324, 57 S.Ct. 758, 81 L.Ed. 1134.
[16] 1942, 315 U.S. 203, 62 S.Ct. 522, 86 L.Ed. 796.
[17] 1933, 262 N.Y. 220, 186 N.E. 679, 89 A.L.R. 345.
[18] 3 Cir., 1944, 145 F. 2d 431, 444.
[19] 303 U.S. 68 at 75, 58 S.Ct. 432.
[20] Fred S. James & Co. v. Second Russian Ins. Co., 1925, 239 N.Y. 248, 146 N.E. 369, 37 A.L.R. 720; Petrogradsky Mejdunarodny Kommerchesky Bank v. Nat. City Bk., 1930, 253 N.Y. 23, 170 N.E. 479; Sokoloff v. National City Bank, 1924, 239 N.Y. 158, 145 N.E. 917, 37 A.L.R. 712; Laane and Baltser v. Estonian State Cargo and Passenger Steamship Line, [1949] 2 D.L.R. 641 (Can.Sup.Ct.). Compare also the results reached in litigation subsequent to the Civil War involving acts of Confederate state legislatures, where the courts inclined to a public policy view in according or denying validity to such acts.

Government. The record contains three affidavits of the Secretary of State. In pertinent parts they read as follows:

"I Certify That the legal existence of the Treaty of Friendship, Commerce and Consular Rights, as well as of all other treaties between the United States and the Republic of Latvia has not been affected by any of the acts of the Soviet regime which assumed power in Latvia in 1940, or of any subsequent regime in that country."

"I Certify That the incorporation of Latvia by the Union of Soviet Socialist Republics is not recognized by the Government of the United States."

"I Certify That the legality of the so-called 'nationalization' laws and decrees, or of any of the acts of the Soviet regime which assumed power in Latvia in 1940, or of any subsequent regime in that country has not been recognized by the Government of the United States." These affidavits are consistent with the announced foreign policy of this Government.[21]

[3,4] We are of opinion that when the executive branch of the Government has determined upon a foreign policy, which can be and is ascertained, and the non-recognition of specific foreign decree is deliberate and is shown to be part of that policy, such non-recognition must be given effect by the courts. The rule applicable in such circumstances is the same rule applicable to an act of recognition. Any other treatment of a deliberate policy and act of non-recognition would reduce the effective control over foreign affairs by the executive branch to a mere effectiveness of acts of recognition. The control of the executive branch over foreign affairs must necessarily be broader than that.

. . . .

We find ourselves in agreement with other courts which have either implicitly or explicitly recognized the policies of their governments in refusing to countenance the confiscation of vessels by Soviet regimes subsequent to the occupation of those countries by the Union of Soviet Socialist Republics and so have refused to effectuate those confiscations, regardless of the results which would normally be reached under the rules governing conflicts of laws.[22]

The judgment of the District Court is Affirmed.

STEPHENS, Chief Judge, concurs in the result.

[21] Letter of Feb. 23, 1932, from Secretary of State Stimson, Dept. of State Press Releases, weekly issue 126, p. 205, Feb. 24, 1932, 1 Hackworth, Digest of International Law 334–335 (1940); Statement by the Acting Secretary of State, July 23, 1940, Press Release No. 354, N.Y. Times, July 24, 1940, pp. 1, 8; Letters from State Department to Governors of the States, N.Y. Times, March 30, 1948, p. 12; Art. 17 of the Charter of the Organization of American States, signed at Bogota, March 30–May 2, 1948; Department of State Press Release No. 119, Feb. 15, 1951.
[22] The Maret, 3 Cir., 1944, 145 F.2d 431; The Kotkas, D.C.E.D.N.Y., 1940, 35 F. Supp. 983; In re Graud's Estate, Sur., 1943, 43 N.Y.S.2d 803; Laane and Baltser v. Estonian State Cargo and Passenger Steamship Line, [1949] 2 D.L.R. 641 (Can.Sup.Ct.); Zarine v. Owners of SS Ramava, [1942] Ir.R. 148 (Ir.Sup.Ct.); Boguslawski v. Gdynia Ameryka Linie, [1950] 2 All Eng. 355 (C.A.). See also Bernstein v. Van Heyghen Freres Societe Anonyme, 2 Cir., 1947, 163 F. 2d 246, and Bank of China v. Wells Fargo Bank & U. T. Co., D.C.N.D.Cal., 1950, 92 F.Supp. 920, 39 Geo.L.J. 337.

CARL-ZEISS-STIFTUNG v. RAYNER AND KEELER, LTD. AND OTHERS

GREAT BRITAIN, COURT OF APPEAL, 1964

[1965] 1 ALL E.R. 300

Note on Background of Case[23]

This suit was brought by Carl-Zeiss-Stiftung, a charitable foundation with its registered office at Jena in East Germany.[24] The defendants were Carl-Zeiss-Stiftung of Heidenheim in the (Western) Federal Republic of Germany and two English companies who sold optical goods made by the West German "Carl-Zeiss" firm. The relief sought in the action was an injunction to restrain all the defendants from selling optical instruments under the name "Zeiss" unless the goods were those of the plaintiff. The defendants moved to stay the proceedings on the ground that the attorneys for the plaintiff, Courts & Co., were not authorized by the plaintiff to bring the suit. In the Court below, Cross, J., denied the defendant's motion. The decision was appealed by the defendants to the Court of Appeal.

The suit had been instituted pursuant to instructions given by a Dr. Schrade to Courts & Co., a firm of English solicitors. Dr. Schrade had been appointed by the Council (Rat) of Gera to undertake all legal transactions on behalf of the foundation. The Rat is a governmental entity in East Germany that was created by laws of the German Democratic Republic in July 1952.

The charter of the plaintiff foundation, adopted in 1896, provided that the foundation would be represented in legal matters by a "special board" and that the rights and duties of the board were to be vested in the department of the state service of the Grand Duchy of Saxe-Weimar under which the affairs of the University of Jena were placed (the Minister of Education of the Grand Duchy, initially). Rule 113 of the foundation's charter provided for representation of the foundation in the event of political changes:

113. Representation of the Stiftung in case of cessation of present special board.

Should, in consequence of political changes in the State, the provision according to r. 5 of this statute with reference to the representation of the Stiftung become untenable, this representation, including the appointment of the deputy of the Stiftung within the meaning of r. 5 and the statutory administration of the Carl-Zeiss-Stiftung, shall be made over to that department of state, which with regard to the University of Jena occupies the place of the state department of the Grand Duchy of Saxe-Weimar acting as the special board, providing that its seat is in Thuringia, otherwise to the highest administrative authorities in Thuringia.

Plaintiffs argued that the Council of Gera was at the time the suit was instituted and now the highest administrative authority in Thuringia, and its appointment of Dr. Schrade to undertake all legal transactions on behalf

---

[23] This note is reprinted from *International Legal Materials*, IV (1965), 551.

[24] Carl-Zeiss-Stiftung is a charitable foundation that had owned an optical works. The optical works was nationalized by the Russian authorities in 1948. The Court accepted for purposes of argument the foundation's contention that the nationalization did not touch the "Zeiss" trademarks.

of the foundation should be effective to permit Dr. Schrade to retain English lawyers and institute this suit in the English courts.

Defendants argued that the Court should hold that Dr. Schrade acted without authority in instituting the law suit, because to hold that he had authority would be to recognize the German Democratic Republic—a government not recognized by the United Kingdom. This point was not argued in the lower court before Cross, J. There, it had been assumed by both sides that the acts of the German Democratic Republic would be treated as acts of, or under the aegis of, the Soviet Union, a government recognized by the United Kingdom as having authority in East Germany.

In the Court of Appeal, defendants raised the question of recognition and moved the Court to submit certain questions to the Secretary of State for Foreign Affairs. The Court of Appeal held that although the matter had not been raised in the court below, the Court was bound on its own motion to seek proper information. In reply to questions from the Court of Appeal, the Secretary of State for Foreign Affairs on September 16, 1964, stated, "Her Majesty's Government have not granted any recognition de jure or de facto to (a) the German Democratic Republic or (b) its government." The Secretary of State on November 6, 1964, in response to a further inquiry stated to the Court:

Since that time [June, 1945] and up to the present date Her Majesty's government have recognised the state and government of the Union of Soviet Socialist Republics as de jure entitled to exercise governing authority in respect of that zone [area of Germany allocated to the U.S.S.R. by the Potsdam Agreement]. In matters affecting Germany as a whole, the states and governments of the French Republic, the United Kingdom of Great Britain and Northern Ireland, the United States of America and the Union of Soviet Socialist Republics were jointly entitled to exercise governing authority. In the period from Aug. 30, 1945, to Mar. 20, 1948, they did exercise such joint authority through the Control Council for Germany. Apart from the states, governments and control council aforementioned, Her Majesty's government have not recognised either de jure or de facto any other authority purporting to exercise governing authority in or in respect to the zone.

The Court held unanimously that the appeal should be allowed and the plaintiff's writ and all subsequent proceedings struck out. Leave to appeal to the House of Lords was granted. Excerpts from the opinions of Harman and Diplock, L.JJ., follow. Danckwerts, L. J., did not write an opinion.

Excerpt from Opinion of Harman, L. J.[25]

Coming down to modern times, the decision of Roche, J., in *Aksionairnoye Obschestvo A. M. Luther v. James Sagor & Co.* [(1921) 1 K.B. 456] was cited. In that case the Soviet authority had confiscated certain timber and sold it to the defendants in this country. The plaintiff, a Russian company, claimed that no property had passed to the defendants and the judge of first instance assented to that proposition on the ground that the Soviet government had not been recognised by His Majesty's government. It was held,

[25] [1965] 1 All. E.R. 314–316.

that if a foreign government or its sovereignty is not recognised by His Majesty's government the courts of this country will not recognise such foreign government or its sovereignty: that on the facts the Russian Soviet government had not been recognised by His Majesty's government as the government of a Russian Federative Republic or of any sovereign state or power: that accordingly the court was unable to recognise any such Russian government or to hold that it had sovereignty or was able by its decree to deprive the plaintiff company of their property. Roche, J., read Lord Curzon's statement on the subject and said [(1921) 1 K.B. at p. 477]:

It was said on behalf of the defendants that these communications were vague and ambiguous. I should rather say that they were guarded, but as [p. 315] clear as the indeterminate position of affairs in connexion with the subject matter of the communication enabled them to be; but lest it should be deemed that ampler or further information might now be available, I caused communication to be made by a master of the Crown Office to His Majesty's Secretary of State for Foreign Affairs, asking whether there was in addition to the letters to the parties or their solicitors further matter or information which should be placed before me. The reply of the Secretary of State was that he had no further information which he desired to place before me. On these materials I am not satisfied that His Majesty's government has recognised the Soviet government as the government of a Russian Federative Republic or of any sovereign state or power. I therefore am unable to recognise it, or to hold it has sovereignty, or is able by decree to deprive the plaintiff company of its property. Accordingly I decide this point against the defendants.

The case went to the Court of Appeal [(1921) All E.R.Rep. 138; (1921) 3 K.B. 532]. By the time it reached that court the situation had altered in that His Majesty's government had recognised the Soviet government as the de facto government of Russia and existing at a date before the decree of confiscation. The court, therefore, held that the decree and the sale to the defendants could not be attacked. The court also held that Roche, J., had been quite right in the result he reached at the time, there having then been no recognition.

Now there can be no doubt that no recognition has been accorded to the German Democratic Republic. It is said to follow that that body and its laws must be ignored in an English court. On that footing its creature, the Rat, must also be ignored and can have no authority to authorise the start of proceedings here. The plaintiff started its argument by submitting that the defendants ought not to be allowed to argue a case inconsistent with that made below except in so far as the Foreign Office certificates have brought about a change. So far I agree. Starting from here, the plaintiff pointed out that the case had been argued in the court below on the footing that all governmental decrees on the east side of the curtain were either those of the German Democratic Republic or of the Russian occupying power and that it was immaterial which was the true authority. This was well enough so long as East German laws were accepted as valid by both sides, as they then were. In this court the position is quite altered, for we know

now that Her Majesty's government recognises no authority in the Eastern zone but that of Russia. The plaintiff then submits that all laws made by the German Democratic Republic must be taken to have been so made as agents of the Russians and are to be accepted accordingly as the acts of the de jure sovereign. This I am unable to accept. It is in fact notorious that the U.S.S.R. has recognised the German Democratic Republic as a sovereign state and treats its law-making capacity accordingly. The court offered counsel for the plaintiff an opportunity to adduce evidence to the contrary, but he did not avail himself of it.

The plaintiff's second point was that on the footing that there was only one sovereign power in East Germany, namely, the U.S.S.R., the laws which that sovereign regarded as valid must be respected under international law. This I reject: it would entail the consequence that no state could ever disagree with another on a question of recognition of a third.

The plaintiff next argued that in a commercial document, such as the articles, words ought to be given the meaning which commercial people would give them and that the "highest administrative authorities" are what would be meant by those words by commercial people. In support of this proposition two cases were cited, first, a decision of GODDARD, J.[26] and the Court of Appeal in a case called *Kawasaki Kisen Kabushiki Kaisha of Kobe* v. *Bantham Steamship Co., Ltd.*[27] Here the learned judge was construing a charterparty which could be cancelled "if war breaks out involving Japan." The Foreign Office in response to a question were not prepared to say that in their view a state of war existed. GODDARD, J., and the Court of Appeal held that this was not conclusive and that it was open to the umpire on the facts to find as he did that war had broken out. In effect it was held that the word "war" in that charterparty was used in the sense in which the ordinary commercial man would use it. Similar is a decision of SELLERS, J., in *Luigi Monta of Genoa* v. *Cechofracht Co., Ltd.*[28] where the question was whether freight was payable having regard to orders given by "any other government." This was a commercial document again between an Italian and a Czecho-Slovak. The so-called government was the Chinese government of Formosa and was not recognised by Her Majesty's government. Nevertheless the judge as a matter of construction held that it was not essential that it should be so recognised and that in a commercial document it was enough to conclude on the facts that those who gave the order were in control of the country. These decisions in my judgment merely turn on questions of the true construction of the meaning of the commercial documents in question. Contracting parties are at liberty to express their meaning in such terms as they choose. This meaning is not controlled by the attitude of governments.

Apart from this, the plaintiff argues that the proper law of the articles is the law of Germany and that any German, whether in West Germany or in Eastern Germany, as indeed the cases between these parties show,

[26] [1938] 3 All E.R. 80.
[27] [1939] 1 All E.R. 819; [1939] 2 K.B. 544.
[28] [1956] 2 All E.R. 769; [1956] 2 Q.B. 552.

would recognise the Rat as being the authority. Cf. *Banco de Bilbao* v. *Rey. Banco de Bilbao* v. *Sancha*[29] where CLAUSEN, L. J., giving the judgment of the court, said this[30]:

> The question of what body of directors has the legal right of representing the Banco de Bilbao, a commercial entity organised under the laws prevailing in Bilbao, and having its corporate home in Bilbao, must depend in the first place on the articles under which it is constituted. The interpretation of those articles and the operation of them, having regard to the general law, must be governed by the lex loci contractus (see per LORD WRENBURY in *Russian Commercial and Industrial Bank* v. *Le Comptoir d'Escompte de Mulhouse*[31]) i.e., by the law from time to time prevailing at the place where the corporate home (domicilio social) was set up. It seems clear that, for example, a law of the French legislature cannot have—at all events, outside France—any operation in regard to the relations between an English company established in England under English law, and its shareholders, on the one hand, and persons claiming as a board of directors to have control over the affairs of that company on the other. The question accordingly resolves itself into this: What is the government whose laws govern in such a matter the Banco de Bilbao? The answer would seem necessarily to be: the laws of the government of the territory in which Bilbao is situate. Should the question arise as to what government must be recognised in this court as the government of the territory in which Bilbao is situate, the question must, in case of doubt, be resolved by a statement made by His Majesty to this court through the appropriate channel.

Moreover, says the plaintiff, it is absurd to read into this contract, even if the word "lawful" be properly employed, a reference to recognition by Her Majesty's government.

I feel the force of these arguments, but I do not think that they can prevail. The plaintiff through the Rat is seeking to sue in the English courts, and, therefore, it seems to me the English law as to recognition must prevail and in our courts the Rat is not a body which can be recognised as competent to set the wheels of justice in motion.

Excerpts from Opinion of Diplock, L. J.[32]

DIPLOCK, L. J.: The Carl-Zeiss-Stiftung, which both parties to this appeal assert is still in existence, is an artificial person; its legal personality is the creation of the law of a foreign sovereign State. It can act only through the agency of natural persons. The sole issue in this appeal is whether or not any of those natural persons who purported to give or to ratify instructions to Messrs. Courts, a firm of English solicitors, to issue a writ in the name of Carl-Zeiss-Stiftung were entitled according to English law to give such instructions on its behalf. I say "according to English law" because that is the only law which we are entitled to apply—"the law and customs of this realm" of our judicial oaths. English courts are concerned only with the legal

---

[29] [1938] 2 All E.R. 253; [1938] 2 K.B. 176.
[30] [1938] 2 All E.R. at p. 260; [1938] 2 K.B. at p. 194.
[31] [1924] All E.R. Rep. at p. 399; [1925] A.C. at p. 149.
[32] [1965] 1 All E.R. 318, 322–324.

consequences in England of things that happen, whether they happen in England or out of England. That is the limit of our jurisdiction. When it is claimed that things which have happened outside England have legal consequences in England, to which an English court ought to give effect, we ascertain those consequences by applying rules of English law, in particular those rules which are called indifferently "conflict of laws" or "private international law"; but because, despite this latter name, the rules are rules of English law, it by no means follows that the legal consequences in England of a thing which happened abroad will be the same as the legal consequences of that happening in the state in which it happened, or as its legal consequences in any other state.

. . . .

The Council of Gera owes its existence, its constitution, and whatever powers it possesses, to the purported exercise of sovereign powers by persons claiming to be the "government" of the "German Democratic Republic," to wit, a law passed by the peoples chamber or legislature of that "government" and an order made by the Cabinet or executive of that "government." Her Majesty's government does not recognise the "German Democratic Republic" as a sovereign, nor its "government" as a sovereign government. It recognises the government of the U.S.S.R. alone as entitled de jure to exercise governing authority in the area in which Jena is situated.

It follows that in applying the lex loci actus for the purpose of deciding what natural persons were qualified under the statutes of the Carl-Zeiss-Stiftung in 1955 or thereafter to authorise or to ratify the issue of a writ in England in its name, we, as an English court, must ignore any laws passed or orders made by persons purporting to act as the government of the German Democratic Republic. The English cases which established this rule, in particular *Aksionairnoye Obschestvo A. M. Luther* v. *James Sagor & Co.*[33] have already been cited by HARMAN, L. J. I will content myself by adopting the succinct expression of the consequences of non-recognition by STOREY, J., in the United States case of *Gelston* v. *Hoyt* in 1818,[34]:

> No doctrine is better established than that it belongs exclusively to governments to recognise new states in the revolutions which may occur in the world: and until such recognition either by our own government or the government to which the new state belonged *Courts of Justice are bound to consider the ancient state of things as remaining unaltered;*

although as the law has developed in England by 1964, recognition by our own government alone is the decisive factor.

※   ※   ※

Counsel for the plaintiff has argued that in view of Her Majesty's government's recognition of the government of the U.S.S.R. as entitled de jure to exercise governing authority in the area in which Jena is situate, any law, by whomever it purports to be made, which is in fact acted on and

[33] [1921] 1 K.B. 456.
[34] (1818), 3 Wheat. 246 at p. 324.

enforced in that area, must be presumed by an English court to have been made by persons who were authorised to make it by the government of the U.S.S.R. This contention thus baldly stated seems to me to be in flat contradiction of the rule of English law, for it would involve treating the recognition of a new sovereign state by the government of the U.S.S.R. as binding on the English courts instead of recognition of such new state by the government of the United Kingdom. Furthermore, in this particular case it is not as if the Eastern zone of Germany ever "belonged," in STOREY, J.'s phrase, to the U.S.S.R.; the carving out of a new state, the "German Democratic Republic," affected Germany as a whole and the Foreign Office certificate makes it clear that Her Majesty's government does not recognise the authority of the government of the U.S.S.R. to do that. Counsel further asked us to assume—as I am prepared to do—that the government of the U.S.S.R. would recognise the validity of laws made by the "government of the German Democratic Republic." If, he said, a law is for any reason recognised as valid by the government which is itself recognised by Her Majesty's government as entitled to exercise governing authority in the geographical area to which the law purports to apply, the English court must also recognise it as a valid law. For my part I cannot accept this contention either. It is, I think, merely another way of formulating the contention just discussed. If the government of the U.S.S.R. recognised the "government of the German Democratic Republic" as a subordinate government deriving its powers from the government of the U.S.S.R. and exercising them on its behalf in an area in respect of which the government of the U.S.S.R. is recognised by the United Kingdom government as entitled to make laws—as was the case with the provincial government of the Land of Thuringia before 1949—such recognition would be relevant; but there is no evidence, and counsel for the plaintiff does not seek to adduce it, that the government of the U.S.S.R. does so recognise the "government of the German Democratic Republic." All that I am prepared to assume—and I think it is a matter of which I can take judicial notice—is that the government of the U.S.S.R. recognises the "government of the German Democratic Republic" as the independent sovereign government of an independent sovereign state for whose territory the government of the U.S.S.R. claims no power to make laws. It recognises the laws of the "government of the German Democratic Republic" as valid under its own rules of private international law for the purpose of determining the legal consequences in the U.S.S.R. of things which happen in another independent sovereign state. This kind of recognition by the U.S.S.R. of the validity of the laws of the "German Democratic Republic" is irrelevant to the issues which we have to decide in this case.

We are thus compelled to approach the question whether the "Council of Gera" was the special board of the Carl-Zeiss-Stiftung under r. 113 of its statutes on the basis that the purported laws and order of July 23–25, 1952, had never been passed. The Council of Gera owes its very existence to that legislation and order. So far as English courts are concerned it is not merely *not* a "department of state," it is nothing, and the natural persons who purport to act as the "Council of Gera" have no powers in that capacity which we are entitled to recognise.

Counsel for the plaintiff has, however, argued that if the "Council of Gera" is not a "department of state," then there was no longer in existence after 1952 any department of state which with regard to the University of Jena occupied the position of the state department of the Grand Duchy of Saxe-Weimar. Accordingly, he contended, the second part of r. 113 applies; and the Council of Gera is in fact exercising the highest administrative functions in Thuringia whether or not it is recognised by Her Majesty's government. In construing r. 113 of the statutes it would be absurd to construe them so as to limit the "highest administrative authorities in Thuringia" to the highest administrative authorities in Thuringia who are recognised as such by the government of the United Kingdom. The draftsman of the statutes in 1896 cannot have intended this.

Like HARMAN, L. J., I recognise the force of this argument, but I think that it is fallacious. Its fallacy lies in confusing the question of construction with the question of application. I agree that when construing the statutes of the Stiftung the question whether Her Majesty's government has recognised any body of persons as the "highest administrative authorities in Thuringia" is wholly irrelevant; but the question of application is one of fact—who were the highest administrative authorities in Thuringia in 1956? This is a fact which, so far as an English court is concerned, is determined conclusively by the certificate of the Foreign Office. That certificate states specifically that apart from the states and governments of the French Republic, the United Kingdom, the United States of America and the U.S.S.R. and the control council, Her Majesty's government have not recognised "either de jure or de facto any other authority purporting to exercise governing authority in or in respect of the zone," *i.e.*, the area which includes Thuringia. We, therefore, as an English court are precluded from holding that the Council of Gera was in fact in 1956 exercising any governmental powers in the district in which Jena is situate.

There is an air of unreality about this, because there was before this court evidence which was admitted in the court below before the certificate of the Foreign Office was obtained and this contradicts the conclusive evidence which has now been obtained. Evidence to show that the Council of Gera was de facto exercising administrative powers in Gera would not have been admissible if the certificate of the Foreign Office had been obtained earlier. The unreality would have been kept behind the curtain. We, who have a certificate in the terms quoted above, are bound to disregard this evidence which contradicts it.

Finally it was argued that this court would not be precluded by the Foreign Office certificate from finding as a fact that the natural persons who call themselves the Council of Gera were in fact doing acts of administration in the district in which Jena is situated, and that even if the court was bound to hold that they had no authority to do so, nevertheless on the true construction of r. 113 they fell within the description "the highest administrative authorities in Thuringia." I think that this is merely another way of inviting us to say that the Foreign Office certificate is not conclusive as to the relevant factual situation in Thuringia. The certificate is, of course, not conclusive as to the actual things which natural persons are doing in a foreign state, but it is conclusive as to whether those things are being done as acts of government. The question of application does not depend on what actual things natural persons are doing in Thuringia but on who are "the highest administrative authorities," *i.e.*, who are entitled to do or are in fact performing acts of government. We are precluded by the Foreign Office certificate from holding that the natural persons who call themselves the "Council of Gera" are performing any acts of government; and it is not, I think, arguable on the construction of r. 113 that "the highest administrative authorities in Thuringia" means persons who are not performing and are not entitled to perform any acts of government.

Act of State Doctrine

The "act of state doctrine" precludes courts of one country from inquiring into the validity of the public acts that a recognized foreign sovereign power commits within its own territory. Significant cases dealing with this doctrine are referred to in the more recent case below.

BANCO NACIONAL DE CUBA, PETITIONER, v. PETER L. F. SABBATINO ET AL.

United States Supreme Court, 1964

376 U.S. 398

[Sugar owned by C.A.V., an American-owned corporation nationalized by Cuba in August 1960, was bought before nationalization by Farr, Whitlock, a commodity broker in the U.S. The dispute over title to the sugar led New York courts to place the funds paid for it in the hands of Sabbatino as Temporary Receiver. Banco Nacional, an agency of the Cuban government, sought possession of the funds after the District Court for the Southern District of New York and the Court of Appeals both decided that Cuba's expropriation violated international law because it was motivated by a retaliatory and not a public purpose; because it discriminated against U.S. nationals; and because it failed to provide adequate compensation (193 F. Supp. 375, 307 F. 2d 845). The Supreme Court granted certiorari "because the issues involved bear importantly on the conduct of the country's foreign relations and more particularly on the proper role of the Judicial Branch in this sensitive area." (372 U.S. 905.)]

It is first contended that this petitioner, an instrumentality of the Cuban Government, should be denied access to American courts because Cuba is an unfriendly power and does not permit nationals of this country to obtain relief in its courts. . . .

Under principles of comity governing this country's relations with other nations, sovereign states are allowed to sue in the courts of the United States. . . . Although comity is often associated with the existence of friendly relations between States . . . the privilege of suit has been denied only to governments at war with the United States. . . . We do not agree [that the courts should be closed to the Cuban Government]. This Court would hardly be competent to undertake assessment of varying degrees of friendliness or its absence, and, lacking some definite touchstone for determination, we are constrained to consider any relationship, short of war, with a recognized sovereign power as embracing the privilege of resorting to United States courts. Although the severance of diplomatic relations is an overt act with objective significance in the dealings of sovereign states, we are unwilling to say that it should inevitably result in the withdrawal of the privilege of bringing suit. Severance may take place for any number of political reasons, its duration is unpredictable, and whatever expression of animosity it may imply does not approach that implicit in a declaration of war.

It is perhaps true that nonrecognition of a government in certain circumstances may reflect no greater unfriendliness than the severance of diplomatic relations with a recognized government, but the refusal to recognize has a unique legal aspect. It signifies this country's unwillingness to acknowledge that the government in question speaks as the sovereign authority for the territory it purports to control. . . . Political recognition is exclusively a function of the Executive. The possible incongruity of judicial "recognition," by permitting suit, of a government not recognized by the Executive is completely absent when merely diplomatic relations are broken. . . .

We hold that this petitioner is not barred from access to the federal courts.

IV

The classic American statement of the act of state doctrine . . . is found in *Underhill v. Hernandez,* 168 U.S. 250, where Chief Justice Fuller said for a unanimous court (p. 252):

> Every sovereign State is bound to respect the independence of every other sovereign State, and the courts of one country will not sit in judgment on the acts of the government of another done within its own territory. Redress of grievances by reason of such acts must be obtained through the means open to be availed of by sovereign powers as between themselves.

Following this precept the Court in that case refused to inquire into acts of Hernandez, a revolutionary Venezuelan military commander whose government had been later recognized by the United States, which were made the basis of a damage action in this country by Underhill, an American citizen, who claimed that he had been unlawfully assaulted, coerced, and detained in Venezuela by Hernandez.

None of this Court's subsequent cases in which the act of state doctrine was directly or peripherally involved manifest any retreat from *Underhill.*

. . . On the contrary in two of these cases, *Oetjen* [v. Central Leather Co., 246 U.S. 297] and Ricaud [v. American Metal Co., 246 U.S. 304], the doctrine as announced in *Underhill* was reaffirmed in unequivocal terms.

Oetjen involved a seizure of hides from a Mexican citizen as a military levy by General Villa, acting for the forces of General Carranza, whose government was recognized by this country subsequent to the trial but prior to decision by this Court. The hides were sold to a Texas corporation which shipped them to the United States and assigned them to defendant. As assignee of the original owner, plaintiff replevied the hides, claiming that they had been seized in violation of the Hague Conventions. In affirming a judgment for defendant, the Court . . . described the designation of the sovereign as a political question to be determined by the legislative and executive departments rather than judicial, invoked the established rule that such recognition operates retroactively to validate past acts, and found the basic tenet of *Underhill* to be applicable to the case before it.

The principle that the conduct of one independent government cannot be successfully questioned in the courts of another is as applicable to a case involving the title to property brought within the custody of a court, such as we have here, as it was held to be to the cases cited, in which claims for damages were based upon acts done in a foreign country, for it rests at last upon the highest considerations of international comity and expediency. To permit the validity of the acts of one sovereign State to be reëxamined and perhaps condemned by the courts of another would very certainly "imperil the amicable relations between governments and vex the peace of nations." (*Id.*, at 303–304.)

In *Ricaud* the facts were similar—another general of the Carranza forces seized lead bullion as a military levy—except that the property taken belonged to an American citizen. The Court found *Underhill, American Banana,* and *Oetjen* controlling. Commenting on the nature of the principle established by those cases, the opinion stated that the rule

. . . does not deprive the courts of jurisdiction once acquired over a case. It requires only that, when it is made to appear that the foreign government has acted in a given way on the subject-matter of the litigation, the details of such action or the merit of the result cannot be questioned but must be accepted by our courts as a rule for their decision. To accept a ruling authority and to decide accordingly is not a surrender or abandonment of jurisdiction but is an exercise of it. It results that the title to the property in this case must be determined by the result of the action taken by the military authorities of Mexico . . . . (246 U.S., at 309.)

In deciding the present case the Court of Appeals relied in part upon an exception to the unqualified teachings of *Underhill, Oetjen,* and *Ricaud* which that court had earlier indicated. In *Bernstein* v. *Van Heyghen Freres Societe Anonyme,* 163 F. 2d 246, suit was brought to recover from an assignee property allegedly taken, in effect, by the Nazi Government because plaintiff was Jewish. Recognizing the odious nature of this act of state, the court, through Judge Learned Hand, nonetheless refused to consider it invalid on that ground. Rather, it looked to see if the Executive had acted in any manner that would indicate that United States Courts should refuse to give effect to such a foreign decree. Finding no such evidence, the court sustained dismissal of the complaint. In a later case involving similar facts the same court again assumed examination of the German acts improper, *Bernstein v. N. V. Nederlandsche-Amerikaansche Stoomvaart-Maatschappij,* 173 F. 2d 71, but, quite evidently following the implications of Judge Hand's opinion in the earlier case, amended its mandate to permit evidence of alleged invalidity, 210 F. 2d 375, subsequent to receipt by plaintiff's attorney of a letter from the Acting Legal Adviser to the State Department written for the purpose of relieving the court from any constraint upon the exercise of its jurisdiction to pass on that question.[35]

This Court has never had occasion to pass upon the so-called *Bernstein* exception, nor need it do so now. For whatever ambiguity may be thought to exist in the two letters from State Department officials on which the Court of Appeals relied,[36] 307 F. 2d, at 858, is now removed by the position which the Executive has taken in this Court on the act of state claim; respondents do not indeed contest the view that these letters were intended to reflect no more than the Department's then wish not to make any statement bearing on this litigation.

[35] The letter stated:

"1. This government has consistently opposed the forcible acts of dispossession of a discriminatory and confiscatory nature practiced by the Germans on the countries or peoples subject to their controls.

. . . .

"3. The policy of the Executive, with respect to claims asserted in the United States for the restitution of identifiable property (or compensation in lieu thereof) lost through force, coercion, or duress as a result of Nazi persecution in Germany, is to relieve American courts from any restraint upon the exercise of their jurisdiction to pass on the validity of the acts of Nazi officials." (State Department Press Release 296, April 27, 1949, 20 State Dept. Bull. 592.)

[36] Abram Chayes, the Legal Adviser to the State Department, wrote on October 18, 1961, in answer to an inquiry regarding the position of the Department by Mr. John Laylin, attorney for *amici:*

"The Department of State has not, in the *Bahia de Nipe* case or elsewhere, done anything inconsistent with the position taken on the Cuban nationalization by Secretary Herter. Whether or not these nationalizations will in the future be given effect in the United States is, of course, for the courts to determine. Since the *Sabbatino* case and other similar cases are at present before the courts, any comments on this question by the Department of State would be out of place at this time. As you yourself point out, statements by the executive branch are highly susceptible of misconstruction."

A letter dated November 14, 1961, from George Ball, Under Secretary for Economic Affairs, responded to a similar inquiry by the same attorney:

"I have carefully considered your letter and have discussed it with the Legal Adviser. Our conclusion, in which the Secretary concurs, is that the Department should not comment on matters pending before the courts."

The outcome of this case, therefore, turns upon whether any of the contentions urged by respondents against the application of the act of state doctrine in the premises is acceptable: (1) that the doctrine does not apply to acts of state which violate international law, as is claimed to be the case here; (2) that the doctrine is inapplicable unless the Executive specifically interposes it in a particular case; and (3) that in any event, the doctrine may not be invoked by a foreign government plaintiff in our courts.

V

Preliminarily, we discuss the foundations on which we deem the act of state doctrine to rest, and more particularly the question of whether state or federal law governs its application in a federal diversity case.[37]

We do not believe that this doctrine is compelled either by the inherent nature of sovereign authority, as some of the earlier decisions seem to imply [see *Underhill, supra; American Banana Co.* v. *United Fruit Co.*, 213 U.S. 347; *Oetjen, supra,* at 303], or by some principle of international law. If a transaction takes place in one jurisdiction and the forum is in another, the forum does not by dismissing an action or by applying its own law purport to divest the first jurisdiction of its territorial sovereignty; it merely declines to adjudicate or makes applicable its own law to parties or property before it. The refusal of one country to enforce the penal laws of another is a typical example of an instance when a court will not entertain a cause of action arising in another jurisdiction. While historic notions of sovereign authority do bear upon the wisdom of employing the act of state doctrine, they do not dictate its existence.

That international law does not require application of the doctrine is evidenced by the practice of nations. Most of the countries rendering decisions on the subject fail to follow the rule rigidly.[38] No international arbitral or judicial decision discovered suggests that international law prescribes recognition of sovereign acts of foreign governments [see 1 Oppenheim's International Law § 115aa (Lauterpacht, 8th ed., 1955)], and apparently no claim has ever been raised before an international tribunal that failure to apply the act of state doctrine constitutes a breach of international obligation. If international law does not prescribe use of the doctrine, neither does it forbid application of the rule even if it is claimed that the act of state in question violated international law. The traditional view of international law is that it establishes substantive principles for determining whether one country has wronged another. Because of its peculiar nation-to-nation character the usual method

[37] Although the complaint in this case alleged both diversity and federal question jurisdiction, the Court of Appeals reached jurisdiction only on the former ground, 307 F. 2d, at 852. We need not decide, for reasons appearing hereafter, whether federal question jurisdiction also existed. [*Diversity* refers to the difference in nationality between the plaintiff bank (Cuban) and the defendants (U.S.).]
[38] In English jurisprudence, in the classic case of *Luther* v. *James Sagor & Co.*, [1921] 3 K. B. 532, the act of state doctrine is articulated in terms not unlike those of the United States cases. . . .

for an individual to seek relief is to exhaust local remedies and then repair to the executive authorities of his own state to persuade them to champion his claim in diplomacy or before an international tribunal. [See *United States v. Diekelman,* 92 U.S. 520, 524.] Although it is, of course, true that United States courts apply international law as a part of our own in appropriate circumstances [*Ware v. Hylton,* 3 Dall. 199, 281; *The Nereide,* 9 Cranch, 388, 423; *The Paquete Habana,* 175 U.S. 677, 700], the public law of nations can hardly dictate to a country which is in theory wronged how to treat that wrong within its domestic borders.

Despite the broad statement in *Oetjen* that "The conduct of the foreign relations of our Government is committed by the Constitution to the Executive and Legislative . . . Departments," 246 U.S., at 302, it cannot of course be thought that "every case or controversy which touches foreign relations lies beyond judicial cognizance." [*Baker v. Carr,* 369 U.S. 186, 211.] The text of the Constitution does not require the act of state doctrine; it does not irrevocably remove from the judiciary the capacity to review the validity of foreign acts of state.

The act of state doctrine does, however, have "constitutional" underpinnings. It arises out of the basic relationships between branches of government in a system of separation of powers. It concerns the competency of dissimilar institutions to make and implement particular kinds of decisions in the area of international relations. The doctrine as formulated in past decisions expresses the strong sense of the Judicial Branch that its engagement in the task of passing on the validity of foreign acts of state may hinder rather than further this country's pursuit of goals both for itself and for the community of nations as a whole in the international sphere. . . . We could perhaps in this diversity action avoid the question of deciding whether federal or state law is applicable to this aspect of the litigation. New York has enunciated the act of state doctrine in terms that echo those of federal decisions. . . . "The courts of one independent government will not sit in judgment upon the validity of the acts of another done within its own territory, even when such government seizes and sells the property of an American citizen within its boundaries." [*Salimoff & Co. v. Standard Oil Co.,* 262 N.Y. 220, 224, 186 N.E. 679, 681]. . . .

However, we are constrained to make it clear that an issue concerned with a basic choice regarding the competence and function of the Judiciary and the National Executive in ordering our relationships with other members of the international community must be treated exclusively as an aspect of federal law . . . rules of international law should not be left to divergent and perhaps parochial state interpretations. . . . We conclude that the scope of the act of state doctrine must be determined according to federal law.

VI

If the act of state doctrine is a principle of decision binding on federal and state courts alike but compelled by neither international law nor the Constitution its continuing vitality depends on its capacity to reflect the proper distribution of functions between the judicial and political branches of the Government on matters bearing upon foreign affairs. It should be apparent that the greater the degree of codification or consensus concerning a particular area of international law, the more appropriate it is for the judiciary to render decisions regarding it, since the courts can then focus on the application of an agreed principle to circumstances of fact rather than on the sensitive task of establishing a principle not inconsistent with the national interest or with international justice. It is also evident that some aspects of international law touch much more sharply on national nerves than do others; the less important the implications of an issue are for our foreign relations, the weaker the justification for exclusivity in the political branches. The balance of relevant considerations may also be shifted if the government which perpetrated the challenged act of state is no longer in existence, as in the *Bernstein* case, for the political interest of this country may, as a result, be measurably altered. Therefore, rather than laying down or reaffirming an inflexible and all-encompassing rule in this case, we decide only that the Judicial Branch will not examine the validity of a taking of property within its own territory by a foreign sovereign government, extant and recognized by this country at the time of suit, in the absence of a treaty or other unambiguous agreement regarding controlling legal principles, even if the complaint alleges that the taking violates customary international law.

There are few if any issues in international law today on which opinion seems to be so decided as the limitations on a State's power to expropriate the property of aliens.[39] There is, of course, authority, in international judicial[40] and arbitral[41] decisions, in the expressions of national governments,[42] and among commentators[43] for the view that a taking is improper under international law if it is not for a public purpose, is discriminatory, or is without provision

---

[39] Compare, *e.g.*, Friedman, Expropriation in International Law 206–211 (1953); Dawson and Weston, Prompt, Adequate and Effective: A Universal Standard of Compensation? 30 Fordham L. Rev. 727 (1962), with Note from Secretary of State Hull to Mexican Ambassador, August 22, 1938, V Foreign Relations of the United States 685 (1938); Doman, Postwar Nationalization of Foreign Property in Europe, 48 Col. L. Rev. 1125, 1127 (1948). We do not, of course, mean to say that there is no international standard in this area; we conclude only that the matter is not meet for adjudication by domestic tribunals.

[40] See *Oscar Chinn Case*, P.C.I.J., ser. A/B, No. 63, at 87 (1934); *Chorzow Factory Case*, P.C.I.J., ser. A., No. 17, at 46, 47 (1928).

[41] See, *e.g.*, *Norwegian Shipowners' Case* (Norway/United States) (Perm. Ct. Arb.) (1922), 1 U.N. Rep. Int'l Arb. Awards 307, 334, 339 (1948), Hague Court Reports, 2d Series, 39, 69, 74 (1932); *Marguerite de Joly de Sabla*, American and Panamanian General Claims Arbitration 379, 447, 6 U.N. Rep. Int'l Arb. Awards 358, 366 (1955).

[42] See, *e.g.*, Dispatch from Lord Palmerston to British Envoy at Athens, Aug. 7, 1846, 39 British and Foreign State Papers 1849–1850, 431–432. Note from Secretary of State Hull to Mexican Ambassador, July 21, 1938, V Foreign Relations of the United States 674 (1938); Note to the Cuban Government, July 16, 1960, 43 Dept. State Bull. 171 (1960).

[43] See, *e.g.*, McNair, The Seizure of Property and Enterprises in Indonesia, 6 Netherlands Int'l L. Rev. 218, 243–253 (1959); Restatement, Foreign Relations Law of the United States (Proposed Official Draft 1962), §§ 190–195.

for prompt, adequate, and effective compensation. However, Communist countries, although they have in fact provided a degree of compensation after diplomatic efforts, commonly recognize no obligation on the part of the taking country.[44] Certain representatives of the newly independent and underdeveloped countries have questioned whether rules of state responsibility toward aliens can bind nations that have not consented to them[45] and it is argued that the traditionally articulated standards governing expropriation of property reflect "imperialist" interests and are inappropriate to the circumstances of emergent states.[46]

The disagreement as to relevant international law standards reflects an even more basic divergence between the national interests of capital importing and capital exporting nations and between the social ideologies of those countries that favor state control of a considerable portion of the means of production and those that adhere to a free enterprise system. It is difficult to imagine the courts of this country embarking on adjudication in an area which touches more sensitively the practical and ideological goals of the various members of the community of nations.[47]

When we consider the prospect of the courts characterizing foreign expropriations, however justifiably, as invalid under international law and ineffective to pass title, the wisdom of the precedents is confirmed. While each of the leading cases in this Court may be argued to be distinguishable on its facts from this one—*Underhill* because sovereign immunity provided an independent ground and *Oetjen, Ricaud,* and *Shapleigh* because there was actually no violation of international law—the plain implication of all these opinions, and the import of express statements in *Oetjen,* 246 U.S., at 304, and *Shapleigh,* 299 U.S., at 471, is that the act of state doctrine is applicable even if international law has been violated.

. . . .

The possible adverse consequences of a conclusion to the contrary of that implicit in these cases is highlighted by contrasting the practices of the political branch with the limitations of the judicial process in matters of this kind. Following an expropriation of any significance, the Executive engages in di-

[44] See Doman, *supra,* note 39, at 1143–1158; Fleming, States, Contracts and Progress, 62–63 (1960); Bystricky, Notes on Certain International Legal Problems Relating to Socialist Nationalization, in International Assn. of Democratic Lawyers, Proceedings of the Commission on Private International Law, Sixth Congress (1956), 15.

[45] See Anand, Role of the "New" Asian-African Countries in the Present International Legal Order, 56 Am. J. Int'l L. 383 (1962); Roy, Is the Law of Responsibility of States for Injuries to Aliens a Part of Universal International Law? 55 Am. J. Int'l L. 863 (1961).

[46] See 1957 Yb. U.N. Int'l L. Comm'n (Vol. 1) 155, 158 (statements of Mr. Padilla Nervo (Mexico) and Mr. Pal (India)).

[47] There are, of course, areas of international law in which consensus as to standards is greater and which do not represent a battleground for conflicting ideologies. This decision in no way intimates that the courts of this country are broadly foreclosed from considering questions of international law.

plomacy aimed to assure that United States citizens who are harmed are compensated fairly. Representing all claimants of this country, it will often be able, either by bilateral or multilateral talks, by submission to the United Nations, or by the employment of economic and political sanctions, to achieve some degree of general redress. Judicial determinations of invalidity of title can, on the other hand, have only an occasional impact, since they depend on the fortuitous circumstance of the property in question being brought into this country.[48] Such decisions would, if the acts involved were declared invalid, often be likely to give offense to the expropriating country; since the concept of territorial sovereignty is so deep seated, any State may resent the refusal of the courts of another sovereign to accord validity to acts within its territorial borders. Piecemeal dispositions of this sort involving the probability of affront to another State could seriously interfere with negotiations being carried on by the Executive Branch and might prevent or render less favorable the terms of an agreement that could otherwise be reached. Relations with third countries who have engaged in similar expropriations would not be immune from effect.

The dangers of such adjudication are present regardless of whether the State Department has, as it did in this case, asserted that the relevant act violated international law. If the Executive Branch has undertaken negotiations with an expropriating country, but has refrained from claims of violation of the law of nations, a determination to that effect by a court might be regarded as a serious insult, while a finding of compliance with international law would greatly strengthen the bargaining hand of the other State with consequent detriment to American interests.

Even if the State Department has proclaimed the impropriety of the expropriation, the stamp of approval of its view by a judicial tribunal, however impartial, might increase any affront and the judicial decision might occur at a time, almost always well after the taking, when such an impact would be contrary to our national interest. Considerably more serious and far-reaching consequences would flow from a judicial finding that international law standards had been met if that determination flew in the face of a State Department proclamation to the contrary. When articulating principles of international law in its relations with other States, the Executive Branch speaks not only as an interpreter of generally accepted and traditional rules, as would the courts, but also as an advocate of standards it believes desirable for the community of nations and protective of national concerns. In short, whatever way the matter is cut, the possibility of conflict between the Judicial and Executive Branches could hardly be avoided.

Respondents contend that, even if there is not agreement regarding general standards for determining the validity of expropriations, the alleged combination of retaliation, discrimination, and inadequate compensation makes it patently

[48] It is, of course, true that such determinations might influence others not to bring expropriated property into the country, . . . so their indirect impact might extend beyond the actual invalidations of title.

clear that this particular expropriation was in violation of international law.[49] If this view is accurate, it would still be unwise for the courts so to determine. Such a decision now would require the drawing of more difficult lines in subsequent cases and these would involve the possibility of conflict with the Executive view. Even if the courts avoided this course, either by presuming the validity of an act of state whenever the international law standard was thought unclear or by following the State Department declaration in such a situation, the very expression of judicial uncertainty might provide embarrassment to the Executive Branch.

Another serious consequence of the exception pressed by respondents would be to render uncertain titles in foreign commerce, with the possible consequence of altering the flow of international trade.[50] If the attitude of the United States courts were unclear, one buying expropriated goods would not know if he could safely import them into this country. Even were takings known to be invalid, one would have difficulty determining after goods had changed hands several times whether the particular articles in question were the product of an ineffective state act.[51]

Against the force of such considerations, we find respondents' countervailing arguments quite unpersuasive. Their basic contention is that United States courts could make a significant contribution to the growth of international law, a contribution whose importance, it is said, would be magnified by the relative paucity of decisional law by international bodies. But given the fluidity of present world conditions, the effectiveness of such a patchwork approach towards the formulation of an acceptable body of law concerning state responsibility for expropriations is, to say the least, highly conjectural. Moreover, it rests upon the sanguine presupposition that the decisions of

[49] Of course, to assist respondents in this suit such a determination would have to include a decision that for the purpose of judging this expropriation under international law C. A. V. is not to be regarded as Cuban and an acceptance of the principle that international law provides other remedies for breaches of international standards of expropriation than suits for damages before international tribunals. See 307 F. 2d, at 861, 868 for discussion of these questions by the Court of Appeals.

[50] This possibility is consistent with the view that the deterrent effect of court invalidations would not ordinarily be great. If the expropriating country could find other buyers for its products at roughly the same price, the deterrent effect might be minimal although patterns of trade would be significantly changed.

[51] Were respondents' position adopted, the courts might be engaged in the difficult tasks of ascertaining the origin of fungible goods, of considering the effect of improvements made in a third country on expropriated raw materials, and of determining the title to commodities subsequently grown on expropriated land or produced with expropriated machinery.

By discouraging import to this country by traders certain or apprehensive of nonrecognition of ownership, judicial findings of invalidity of title might limit competition among sellers; did the excluded goods constitute a significant portion of the market, prices for United States purchasers might rise with a consequent economic burden on United States consumers. Balancing the undesirability of such a result against the likelihood of furthering other national concerns is plainly a function best left in the hands of the political branches.

the courts of the world's major capital exporting country and principal exponent of the free enterprise system would be accepted as disinterested expressions of sound legal principle by those adhering to widely different ideologies.

It is contended that regardless of the fortuitous circumstances necessary for United States jurisdiction over a case involving a foreign act of state and the resultant isolated application to any expropriation program taken as a whole, it is the function of the courts to justly decide individual disputes before them. Perhaps the most typical act of state case involves the original owner or his assignee suing one not in association with the expropriating state who has had "title" transferred to him. But it is difficult to regard the claim of the original owner, who otherwise may be recompensed through diplomatic channels, as more demanding of judicial cognizance than the claim of title by the innocent third party purchaser, who, if the property is taken from him, is without any remedy.

Respondents claim that the economic pressure resulting from the proposed exception to the act of state doctrine will materially add to the protection of United States investors. We are not convinced, even assuming the relevance of this contention. Expropriations take place for a variety of reasons, political and ideological as well as economic. When one considers the variety of means possessed by this country to make secure foreign investment, the persuasive or coercive effect of judicial invalidation of acts of expropriation dwindles in comparison. The newly independent states are in need of continuing foreign investment; the creation of a climate unfavorable to such investment by wholesale confiscations may well work to their long-run economic disadvantage. Foreign aid given to many of these countries provides a powerful lever in the hands of the political branches to ensure fair treatment of United States nationals. Ultimately the sanctions of economic embargo and the freezing of assets in this country may be employed. Any country willing to brave any or all of these consequences is unlikely to be deterred by sporadic judicial decisions directly affecting only property brought to our shores. If the political branches are unwilling to exercise their ample powers to effect compensation, this reflects a judgment of the national interest which the judiciary would be ill advised to undermine indirectly.

It is suggested that if the act of state doctrine is applicable to violations of international law, it should only be so when the Executive Branch expressly stipulates that it does not wish the courts to pass on the question of validity. See Association of the Bar of the City of New York, Committee on International Law, A Reconsideration of the Act of State Doctrine in United States Courts (1959). We should be slow to reject the representations of the Government that such a reversal of the *Bernstein* principle would work serious inroads on the maximum effectiveness of United States diplomacy. Often the State Department will wish to refrain from taking an official position, particularly at a moment that would be dictated by the development of private litigation but might be inopportune diplomatically. Adverse domestic consequences might flow from an official stand which could be assuaged, if at all, only by revealing matters best kept secret. Of course, a relevant consideration for the State Department would be the position contemplated in the court to hear the case. It is highly questionable whether the examination of validity by the judiciary should depend on an educated guess by the Executive as to probable result and, at any rate, should a prediction be wrong, the Executive might be embarrassed in its dealings with other countries. We do not now pass on the *Bernstein* exception, but even if it were deemed valid, its suggested extension is unwarranted.

However offensive to the public policy of this country and its constituent states an expropriation of this kind may be, we conclude that both the national interest and progress towards the goal of establishing the rule of law among nations are best served by maintaining intact the act of state doctrine in this realm of its application.

In a vigorous dissent to the Sabbatino Case, Mr. Justice White expressed his disappointment at "the Court's declaration that the acts of a sovereign state with regard to the property of aliens within its borders are beyond the reach of international law in the courts of this country. However clearly established that law may be, a sovereign may violate it with impunity, except insofar as the political branches of the government may provide a remedy. This backward-looking doctrine, never before declared in this Court, is carried a disconcerting step further: not only are the courts powerless to question acts of state proscribed by international law but they are likewise powerless to refuse to adjudicate the claim founded upon a foreign law; they must render judgment and thereby validate the lawless act." He makes clear his view that the act of state doctrine should not prevent a court from inquiring into the validity of acts of a foreign government where it believes that those acts may have violated international law. The Supreme Court, however, did not say that it would uphold a clear violation of international law; it argued (and here Justice White disagreed) that international law on the subject of expropriation was not clear and did not clearly oppose the Cuban nationalization. Moreover, the Court said, questions of compensation were matters with which the executive branch should deal.

Outraged by the majority position in the Sabbatino case, the U.S. Congress amended the Foreign Assistance Act of 1961 by adding a new paragraph (2) to the existing Section 620 (e). The revised Section of Public Law 88-633, 88th Congress, 2d Session, approved October 7, 1964, follows:

The President shall suspend assistance to the government of any country to which assistance is provided under this or any other Act when the government of such country or any government agency or subdivision within such country on or after January 1, 1962—

(A)   has nationalized or expropriated or seized ownership or control of property owned by any United States citizen or by any corporation, partnership, or association not less than 50 per centum beneficially owned by United States citizens, or

(B) has taken steps to repudiate or nullify existing contracts or agreements with any United States citizen or any corporation, partnership, or association not less than 50 per centum beneficially owned by United States citizens, or

(C) has imposed or enforced discriminatory taxes or other exactions, or restrictive maintenance or operational conditions, or has taken other actions, which have the effect of nationalizing, expropriating, or otherwise seizing ownership or control of property so owned,

and such country, government agency, or government subdivision fails within a reasonable time (not more than six months after such action, or in the event of a referral to the Foreign Claims Settlement Commission of the United States within such period as provided herein, not more than twenty days after the report of the Commission is received) to take appropriate steps, which may include arbitration, to discharge its obligations under international law toward such citizens or entity, including speedy compensation for such property in convertible foreign exchange, equivalent to the full value thereof, as required by international law, or fails to take steps designed to provide relief from such taxes, exactions, or conditions, as the case may be; and such suspension shall continue until the President is satisfied that appropriate steps are being taken, and no other provision of this Act shall be construed to authorize the President to waive the provisions of this subsection.

(2) Notwithstanding any other provision of law, no court in the United States shall decline on the ground of the federal act of state doctrine to make a determination on the merits giving effect to the principles of international law in a case in which a claim of title or other right is asserted by any party including a foreign state (or a party claiming through such state) based upon (or traced through) a confiscation or other taking after January 1, 1959, by an act of that state in violation of the principles of international law, including the principles of compensation and the other standards set out in this subsection: *Provided,* That this subparagraph shall not be applicable (1) in any case in which an act of a foreign state is not contrary to international law or with respect to a claim of title or other right acquired pursuant to an irrevocable letter of credit of not more than 180 days duration issued in good faith prior to the time of the confiscation or other taking, or (2) in any case with respect to which the President determines that application of the act of state doctrine is required in that particular case by the foreign policy interests of the United States and a suggestion to this effect is filed on his behalf in that case with the court, or (3) in any case in which the proceedings are commenced after January 1, 1966.[52]

[52] In the Foreign Assistance Act of 1965 (Public Law 89-171, 79 Stat. 653), which became law on September 6, 1965, Sec. 301(d) of the 1964 Act was further amended by striking out the provision to the effect that it did not apply "in any case in which the proceedings are commenced after January 1, 1966."

The executive branch opposed the amendment, designed to overturn the Sabbatino decision, for the following reasons:

1. The amendment would mean that, unless the President interposed an objection, U.S. courts would be required to pass on the validity under international law of any act of a foreign state relevant to the case before it. This exposes the foreign policy interests of the United States to embarrassment on two counts.

(*a*) The President's choice of whether or not to object is not as a practical matter a real one. If the President were to decide to object in one case and not to object in another, he would only invite charges of discrimination by the country involved in the latter case and would run an unacceptable risk of an adverse effect on U.S. relations with that country. Moreover, failure to object would raise a question of U.S. adherence to its nondiscrimination pledges under international agreements, both bilateral and multilateral.

(*b*) The President is forced to decide whether a court ruling on the act of a foreign state was prejudicial to U.S. foreign policy at a time and in a manner chosen by private parties to a court case and not at the time and in the manner chosen by the President. This would be unwise. The Executive may be involved in sensitive negotiations on another subject with the Government whose act is being questioned. This means that the President would be forced to decide whether it is better for the court to pass on the validity of the act of the foreign state and risk a breakdown of the negotiations, or to foreclose a court decision on the merits of the case.

2. The decision in the *Sabbatino* case was not a victory for Castro. The Court did not recognize the validity under international law of the Cuban Government's decree. The State Department has taken the position that the decree was not valid under international law. Moreover, all the assets of the Cuban Government in this country, including the property involved in the *Sabbatino* case, are frozen by U.S. Treasury Department regulations and cannot be used for any purpose without the consent of this Government. The property withheld from one American company in that case is blocked against disposition until the Cuban situation changes or the Congress enacts legislation dealing with the matter of Cuban assets in general.

3. The soundness of the *Sabbatino* decision to the national interest is further demonstrated by the following considerations cited by the Supreme Court:

(*a*) There is a wide divergence of views in the world today regarding the limitations on a state's power to expropriate the property of aliens and the sensitivity of this issue in international relations today. As the Supreme Court stated: "It is difficult to imagine the courts of this country embarking on adjudication in an area which touches more sensitively the practical and ideological goals of the various members of the community of nations." It would be most unwise for the Congress to reverse this rule of judicial restraint and force the courts of the United States to pass on issues which are politically sensitive and on which there is little consensus and few guiding precedents.

(*b*) Acts of foreign sovereigns, particularly seizures of property, normally affect a much larger group of U.S. citizens than those that are parties to a court case. As the Supreme Court pointed out, the executive branch is charged with seeking redress for all U.S. citizens affected by the act of the foreign state. To this end the executive branch has available the regular processes of diplomacy, submission to the U.N. and, ultimately, political and economic sanctions such as provided for in section 620(e) of the Foreign Assistance Act. These are the techniques, and frequently the only techniques, available to assure redress for all U.S. citizens affected by the act of the foreign state, and the success of these efforts in behalf of all citizens should not be prejudiced by judicial action on behalf of the few whose claims go to litigation. That any court action adverse to the act of the foreign state would prejudice the other efforts by the executive branch is clear in view of the highly political atmosphere that normally surrounds seizures of alien property by foreign governments.

4. Finally, the result in the *Sabbatino* case was not a setback for international law. It was merely an exercise of judicial restraint in a highly complex and volatile area. Realistically, international law in the most important cases cannot be enforced in private litigation by local courts but should be applied through the practice of states. Like our own Federal-State relations, international relations are governed as much by political adjustments and compromises as by application of rules embodied in conventions or other formal documents. This is a traditional area of judicial restraint and it would be unwise for Congress to foreclose such restraint.[53]

June 25, 1964.

As ordered by the Supreme Court, the U.S. District Court, Southern District of New York, reconsidered the Sabbatino Case. In fact, the Court found it necessary to consider it in two stages, and it rendered two opinions—on July 30, 1965, and November 15, 1965.[54] In its first decision, the District Court had to determine whether the amended Foreign Assistance Act applied to pending cases generally, whether it applied to the Sabbatino Case, whether it was unconstitutional in any way, and what the effect of the amendment was on the Sabbatino Case. The Court concluded that the Amendment plainly included pending cases, under the general principle that "when a statute is to be retroactively applied to past transactions, it is applied to those involved in pending litigation as well."[55]

District Judge Bryan also found that the Amendment applied specifically to the Sabbatino decision, not only because of the plain language of the Amendment, but because of such supporting statements as the

[53] U.S. Senate Committee on Foreign Relations, Hearings on . . . "Foreign Assistance 1964," 88th Congress, 2d Session, p. 619.
[54] 243 F. Supp. 957 (1965) and Memorandum Opinion of November 15, 1965.
[55] C. J. Marshall, U.S. v. Schooner Peggy, 5 U.S. (1 Cranch) 103, 109 (1801).

one in the report of the Senate Committee, which stated flatly that "the amendment is intended to reverse in part the recent decision of the Supreme Court" in the Sabbatino Case. Moreover, the Court pointed out that, if the Sabbatino Case were excluded from the effect of the Amendment, the defendants in that case would be the only victims of the confiscations to be denied the Amendment's benefits; forty pending cases, delayed until the Supreme Court decided the Sabbatino Case, would, however, benefit from the decision. The lower Court held, in addition, that although, as a general rule, "the mandate of an appellate court forecloses the lower court from reconsidering the matters determined above," the new amendment was the supreme law of the land and would have to be applied despite the Supreme Court's earlier decision. Judge Bryan deemed himself "therefore required to make a determination on the merits giving effect to the principles of international law as the Amendment provides."

He also found no constitutional bar to the amendment. Congress was, in his view, exercising its power to regulate commerce; it was not overriding the President's power over foreign relations because the President had signed the amendment and because the amendment itself provided for the President to suggest to the courts when to apply the act of state doctrine; the Constitution does not require courts to apply the act of state doctrine; nor was "the legislative direction to the courts in the amendment not to apply the doctrine . . . an unconstitutional interference with the judicial power." It was not for the courts to say "No" to Congress in determining where the interests of the United States lay in foreign relations. Moreover, Congress had the power to limit the appellate jurisdiction of the Supreme Court and other courts.

Judge Bryan found entirely proper the amendment's provision giving the President the power to invoke the act of state doctrine in cases where national foreign policy interests required. Congress had given similar power to the Executive in other instances, and that power did not interfere with the judicial function. The President "does not attempt to decide the merits. . . . He is merely given the power to determine whether the courts should abstain from deciding one aspect of the merits." The amendment, he pointed out, establishes a presumption that adjudicating the merits would not embarrass the government in conducting foreign policy, but allowed the President to indicate instances where such embarrassment might occur. Judge Bryan found this procedure entirely in keeping with the doctrine of the separation of powers.

Finally, the Court denied that the retroactive provision of the amendment deprived anyone of vested property rights without due process of law, which the Fifth Amendment forbids. "What the Amendment accomplishes is closely analogous to what a legislature does when it extends a statute of limitations. In such cases retroactivity poses no constitutional infirmity . . . even though the extension of the limitations period is applied to pending cases."

Judge Bryan hesitated to reaffirm the position of the Court of Appeals, however, until the President had had an opportunity, under the amendment, to indicate that the foreign policy interests of the United States required or did not require the Court to apply the act of state doctrine. He therefore withheld judgment for sixty days to determine the views of the Executive Branch.

On September 29, the U.S. Attorney for the Southern District of New York, advised the Court "that no determination has been made that application of the act of state doctrine is required in this case by the foreign policy interests of the United States . . . [and] that no such determination is contemplated." Judge Bryan therefore found that the Supreme Court's holding that the act of state doctrine barred determination on the merits no longer applied. In accordance with the decision of the Court of Appeals, he then reaffirmed his original decision that because the Cuban decree of expropriation violated international law, the plantiff's title was invalid and the complaint was dismissed.

Summary. These cases indicate that, in general, courts will not credit the effect of acts of an unrecognized states outside its own borders; that, after recognition, they will validate all decrees of the newly recognized state insofar as their internal effects are concerned; that no decrees in any state, before or after recognition, can compel courts to proceed contrary to the laws of their own forum insofar as assets within the court's control are concerned; but that international law is changing so rapidly that it is not easy to determine what acts of state should be regarded as contravening the law.

CHAPTER III

Continuity of States and State Succession

Continuity of States

Every four years in the United States, at least every five in the United Kingdom, and at diverse intervals elsewhere, elections may constitutionally bring to power new custodians of government. Changes of government moreover occur by revolution. Obviously, if after every change of administration, a state had to reestablish orderly relations with other states, international affairs would be completely chaotic, and statesmen would never know from one minute to the next what treaties were valid or what obligations bound which governments. Governments and business, governmental and private, would suffer beyond measure.

To introduce some order into the constantly changing international scene, international law recognizes the principle of state continuity, which provides that "once a state has come into existence, it continues until . . . extinguished by absorption or dissolution."[1] The government, the instrument through which a state functions, may change from time to time both in form (as in 1961 when the Union of South Africa became a Republic, after having been a self-governing member of the Commonwealth) and in personnel (as after an American presidential election), but the state's international personality continues. "No principle of international law can be more clearly established than this," wrote United States Secretary of State John Quincy Adams on August 10, 1818, "That the *rights* and *obligations* of a nation in regard to other States are independent of its internal revolutions of government. It extends even to the case of conquest. The conqueror who reduces a nation to his subjection receives it subject to all its engagements and duties toward others, the fulfillment of which then becomes his own duty."[2]

[1] Hackworth, I, 127.
[2] Moore, *Digest*, I, Sec. 96.

98

One of the clearest illustration of this doctrine was given by the Supreme Court of the United States in 1870, in the case of *The Sapphire,* an American ship which, in 1867 in San Francisco harbor, collided with and seriously damaged a French ship, the *Euryale.* Napoleon III, then Emperor of the French, as owner of the *Euryale,* filed a libel against the *Sapphire,* and the District Court awarded Napoleon the $15,000 he claimed. The Circuit Court for California later confirmed this decree. But the owners of the *Sapphire* appealed to the Supreme Court in 1869, alleging that the *Euryale* had itself caused the accident. The Supreme Court decided that both ships were partly to blame and ordered the two owners to share the damages. Napoleon had been deposed in the summer of 1870, but the Court made it quite clear that this change in government did not in the least affect the suit. Answering the question of "whether the suit has become abated by the recent deposition of the Emperor," the Court stated:

We think it has not. The reigning sovereign represents the national sovereignty, and that sovereignty is continuous and perpetual, residing in the proper successors of the sovereign for the time being. Napoleon was the owner of the Euryale, not as an individual, but as sovereign of France. . . . On his deposition the sovereignty does not change, but merely the person or persons in whom it resides. The foreign state is the true and real owner of its public vessels of war. The reigning Emperor, or National Assembly, or other actual person or party in power, is but the agent and representative of the national sovereignty. A change in such representative works no change in the national sovereignty or its rights. The next successor recognized by our Government is competent to carry on a suit already commenced and receive the fruits of it. A deed to or treaty with a sovereign as such inures to his successor in the government of the country. If a substitution of names is necessary or proper it is a formal matter, and can be made by the court under its general power to preserve due symmetry in its forms of proceeding. No allegation has been made that any change in the real and substantial ownership of the Euryale has occurred by the recent devolution of the sovereign power. The vessel has always belonged and still belongs to the French nation.[3]

The Sapphire decision was cited again in 1927, when the United States Circuit Court of Appeals, Second Circuit, had to decide the case of the *Lehigh Valley Railroad Company v. State of Russia.* The case originally involved an award by the District Court of the United States for the Southern District of New York to the "State of Russia" to compensate them for a loss of explosives and ammunition being shipped from the United States to Russia, which were at the time in the Jersey City, New Jersey, freight yards of the Lehigh Valley Railroad Co. The

[3] 78 U.S. (11 Wall.) 164 (1870).

Court described the situation and then made it clear that the Bolshevik Revolution of 1917 had not jeopardized the right of the Russian State to have its day in court.

LEHIGH VALLEY RAILROAD CO. v. STATE OF RUSSIA

UNITED STATES, CIRCUIT COURT OF APPEALS, SECOND CIRCUIT, 1927
21 F. 2D 396

Eight carloads of high explosives were on the same railroad siding, and, separated by a single car, on the same siding were several cars of benzol and wet nitro-cellulose; on an adjoining track were several cars of ammunition of cannon. In the same vicinity were eight other cars of ammunition of cannon, two cars of combination fuses, and another car of benzol. A fire started in a car of ammunition prior to the first explosion, which occurred on a barge in the North River, which barge was also loaded with explosives, and then another explosion occurred in a car in the terminal. The barge was owned and operated by the Johnson Lighterage Company. After the fire started, no one, because of fear of the result that might follow from the explosive materials, attempted to put out the fire. Neither the railroad men, private detectives, nor the city firemen attempted to apply water or otherwise combat the fire, with one exception, a crew of the railroad men, who succeeded in removing some cars to a place of safety. Some lost their lives in this act. The railroad company failed to maintain a locomotive at the Black Tom Terminal, and the engine used in removing these cars was brought 2½ miles from Communipaw yards. At the same time there was in force regulation No. 1906, which provided that in case of fire, to protect cars marked by placards "Inflammable," they should be quickly isolated. But in any case the explosions occurred before the engines arrived. Liability was imposed [by the court] below because of the breach of the railroad's obligations as a common carrier. . . .

At the outset the railroad company attacks the right of the defendant in error to maintain the suit, and to do so in the courts of the United States. The right to recover damages for breach of this carrier's obligation became the property of the state of Russia on July 30, 1916, when the loss occurred. The government was then the Russian Imperial Government. . . . On July 5, 1917, Mr. Boris Bakhemeteff was recognized by our State Department as the accredited representative of the Russian government—the provisional Russian Government—as successor to the Imperial Russian Government. He continued as such until July 30, 1922. At that date he retired, and the custody of the property of the Russian government, for which Bakhemeteff was responsible, was recognized by the State Department to vest in Mr. Ughet, the financial attaché of the Russian embassy. The Soviet government, which later secured control of the Russian government, was never recognized by our State Department, and ever since the diplomatic status with our govern-

ment was never altered by the termination of the ambassador's duties. Therefore the provisional Russian Government is the last that had been recognized,
and after its ambassador retired its property was considered by the State
Department to vest in its financial attaché. Prior to his retirement, and while
the accredited ambassador, Mr. Bakhemeteff authorized the suits here considered, which were commenced July 23, 1918.

. . . Mr. Ughet, by the State Department's determination, is entitled to
the custody in the United States of the property of Russia, and as part
of that duty he was authorized to continue the suits for the state of Russia. . . . We must judicially recognize that the state of Russia survives.

Abatement of the action or a dismissal could only be sustained by reason
of the nonexistence of the state, or the action of our government to no longer
recognize the agency once accredited and never revoked. The action was
started by an unquestioned agency. The attorneys and the agency thus employed were obliged to continue until some other government was recognized. . . . Proof of the agency or of the diplomat is dependent entirely
upon the political fact of the recognition by the political department of the
government. The courts may not independently make inquiry as to who should
or should not be recognized. . . . If it be a fact that there is a Russian
Socialist Federated Republic now in charge of the government of Russia,
it would bring no different result here. . . .
The granting or refusal of recognition has nothing to do with the recognition
of the state itself. If a foreign state refuses the recognition of a change
in the form of government of an old state, this latter does not thereby lose
its recognition as an international person. . . . The suit did not abate by
the change in the form of government in Russia; the state is perpetual,
and survives the form of government. . . . . The recognized government
may carry on the suit at least until the new government becomes accredited
here by recognition. . . . .

Incidentally, the Court dismissed the argument that the Lehigh Valley
Railroad might have to compensate a new government again if it paid
agents of the provisional government. It cited cases to show that "It
is only the acts performed in its own territory that can be validated
by the retroactive effect of recognition. Acts theretofore performed outside its own territory cannot be validated by recognition." The Court
consequently authorized the state of Russia to continue prosecuting its
case through Mr. Ughet, and protected the railroad against claims by
any Russian government which the United States might recognize at
some later date.

Most authorities agree that "The principle of the continuity of states
has important results. The state is bound by engagements entered into
by governments that have ceased to exist."[4] Moreover, "Changes of a

[4] Moore, *Digest,* I, 249. See also the Tinoco Arbitration below.

constitutional or, for that matter, of an unconstitutional character within a State do not affect its international personality . . . no government that has overthrown another government by force or succeeds to it in a more normal fashion, can refuse responsibility for the acts of its predecessor. . . ."[5]

In keeping with these principles, a United States-Mexican General Claims Commission decided in the *United States (George W. Hopkins Claim) v. United Mexican States*[6] that postal money orders issued by the usurper, Huerta, were still legal obligations of the Mexican government after Huerta had been deposed. The Commission said:

The greater part of governmental machinery in every modern country is not affected by changes in the higher administrative officers. The sale of postage stamps, the registration of letters, the acceptance of money orders and telegrams (where post and telegraph are government services), the sale of railroad tickets (where railroads are operated by the government), the registration of births, deaths, and marriages, even the rulings by the police and the collection of several types of taxes, go on, and must go on, without being affected by new elections, government crises, dissolutions of parliament, and even state strokes. A resident in Mexico who cleans the government bureaus or pays his school fee to the administration does not and cannot take into consideration the regularity or even legality of the present administration and the present congress; his business is not one with personal rulers, not one with a specific administration, but one with the government itself in its unpersonal aspect.

The Commissioners distinguished "voluntary dealings . . . between the individual and the government agencies," *e.g.*, supplying a revolutionary administration with money, arms, or munitions, which they indicated might be invalid, from ordinary, everyday governmental transactions, which were valid regardless of the administration.

A similar distinction arises in the field of international law [they continued]. There are, on one side, agreements and understandings between one nation and another changing or even subverting its rulers, which are clothed with the character of a free choice, a preference, an approval, and which obviously undertake to bear the risks of such a choice. There are, on the other hand, many transactions to which this character is alien. Embassies, legations, and consulates of a nation in unrest will practically continue their work in behalf of the men who are in control of the capital, the treasury, and the foreign office—whatsoever the relation of these men to the country at large may be. Embassies, legations, and consulates of foreign nations in such capital will practically discharge their routine duties as theretofore, without implying

[5] Schwarzenberger, I (2d ed.), 80.
[6] *Opinions of Commissioners,* 42 (1927).

thereby a preference in favor of any of the contesting groups or parties. International payments (for a postal union, etc.) will be received from such government; delegates to an international conference will often be accepted from such government. Between the two extremes here also there is a large doubtful zone, in which each case must be judged on its merits.

Because purchasing postal money orders was clearly a routine matter, the Commisioners felt Mexico must honor the purchases. And even if the postal money orders were to be considered as contracts of a personal nature with Huerta, the Commissioners reiterated that the acts of a usurper may bind a nation as long as the regime is "in fact the master in the administration of the affairs of the Government . . . ; its illegal origin [would] . . . not defeat the binding force of its executive acts." Whether the United States recognized the Huerta regime—in fact, it did not—the Commissioners found irrelevant. Recognition might affect the ability of the United States to intervene in behalf of its nationals, but would not affect the rights of an American citizen in Mexico or the obligations of the Mexican government under international law.

Perhaps the best statement of the liability of a government for the acts of a usurper are to be found in the Tinoco Arbitration, decided by former United States Chief Justice William Howard Taft.

THE TINOCO ARBITRATION

GREAT BRITAIN—COSTA RICA, 1923

18 *A.J.I.L.* 147 (1924)

[While in office, from January 1917 to August 1919, the Tinoco government of Costa Rica issued currency notes and made contracts, as a result of which actions two British corporations, the Royal Bank of Canada, and the Central Costa Rica Petroleum Company came to possess 998,000 colones,[7] and the Petroleum Company received a grant to explore for and to exploit oil deposits in Costa Rica. On August 22, 1917, the Constitutional Congress of the restored Costa Rican Government passed the Law of Nullities No. 41, invalidating all contracts made by the Tinoco government as well as the legislative decree which had authorized the currency. The British government] asks an award that she is entitled on behalf of her subjects to have the claim of the bank paid, and the concession recognized and given effect by the Costa Rican Government.

The Government of Costa Rica denies its liability for the acts or obligations of the Tinoco government and maintains that the Law of Nullities was a legitimate exercise of its legislative governing power. It further denies the

[7] The Costa Rican gold *colon* was, at this time, worth 46½¢ (U.S.).

validity of such claims on the merits, unaffected by the Law of Nullities. . . .

Coming now to the general issues applicable to both claims, Great Britain contends, first, that the Tinoco government was the only government of Costa Rica *de facto* and *de jure* for two years and nine months; that during that time there is no other government disputing its sovereignty, that it was in peaceful administration of the whole country, with the acquiescence of its people.

Second, that the succeeding government could not by legislative decree avoid responsibility for acts of that government affecting British subjects, or appropriate or confiscate rights and property by that government except in violation of international law; that the act of Nullities is as to British interests, therefore itself a nullity, and is to be disregarded, with the consequence that the contracts validly made with the Tinoco government must be performed by the present Costa Rican Government, and that the property which has been invaded or the rights nullified must be restored.

To these contentions the Costa Rican Government answers: First, that the Tinoco government was not a *de facto* or *de jure* government according to the rules of international law. This raises an issue of fact.

Second, that the contracts and obligations of the Tinoco government, set up by Great Britain on behalf of its subjects, are void, and do not create a legal obligation, because the government of Tinoco and its acts were in violation of the constitution of Costa Rica of 1871.

Third, that Great Britain is stopped by the fact that it did not recognize the Tinoco government during its incumbency, to claim on behalf of its subjects that Tinoco's was a government which could confer rights binding on its successor.

Fourth, that the subjects of Great Britain, whose claims are here in controversy, were either by contract or the law of Costa Rica bound to pursue their remedies before the courts of Costa Rica and not to seek diplomatic intereference on the part of their home government.

Dr. John Bassett Moore. . . in his *Digest of International Law*, Volume I, p. 249, announces the general principle which has had such universal acquiescence as to become well settled international law:

Changes in the government or the internal policy of a state do not as a rule affect its position in international law. A monarchy may be transformed into a republic or a republic into a monarchy; absolute principles may be substituted for constitutional, or the reverse; but though the government changes, the nation remains, with rights and obligations unimpaired. . . .

The principle of the continuity of states has important results. The state is bound by engagements entered into by governments that have ceased to exist; the restored government is generally liable for the acts of the usurper. . . . The origin and organization of government are questions generally of internal discussion and decision. Foreign powers deal with the existing *de facto* government, when sufficiently established to give reasonable assurance of its permanence, and of the acquiescence of those who constitute the state in its ability to maintain itself, and discharge its internal duties and its external obligations.

The same principle is announced by Professor Borchard's . . . *Diplomatic Protection of Citizens Abroad:*[8]

Considering the characteristics and attributes of the *de facto* government, a general government *de facto* having completely taken the place of the regularly constituted authorities in the state binds the nation. So far as its international obligations are concerned, it represents the state. It succeeds to the debts of the regular government it has displaced, and transmits its own obligations to succeeding titular governments. Its loans and contracts bind the state, and the state is responsible for the governmental acts of the *de facto* authorities. In general, its treaties are valid obligations of the state. It may alienate the national territory, and the judgments of its courts are admitted to be effective after its authority has ceased. An exception to these rules has occasionally been noted in the practice of some of the states of Latin America, which declare null and void the acts of a usurping *de facto* intermediary government when the regular government it has displaced succeeds in restoring its control. Nevertheless, acts validly undertaken in the name of the state and having an international character cannot lightly be repudiated, and foreign governments generally insist on their binding force. The legality or constitutional legitimacy of a *de facto* government is without importance internationally so far as the matter of representing the state is concerned. . . .

First, what are the facts to be gathered from the documents and evidence submitted by the two parties as to the *de facto* character of the Tinoco government?

In January, 1917, Frederico A. Tinoco was Secretary of War under Alfredo Gonzalez, the then President of Costa Rica. On the ground that Gonzalez was seeking reelection as President in violation of a constitutional limitation, Tinoco used the army and navy to seize the government, assume the provisional headship of the Republic and become Commander-in-Chief of the army. Gonzalez took refuge in the American Legation, thence escaping to the United States. Tinoco constituted a provisional government at once and summoned the people to an election for deputies to a constituent assembly on the first of May, 1917. At the same time he directed an election to take place for the Presidency and himself became a candidate. An election was held. Some 61,000 votes were cast for Tinoco and 259 for another candidate. Tinoco then was inaugurated as the President to administer his powers under the former constitution until the creation of a new one. A new constitution was adopted June 8, 1917, supplanting the constitution of 1871. For a full two years Tinoco and the legislative assembly under him peaceably administered the affairs of the Government of Costa Rica, and there was no disorder of a revolutionary character during that interval. No other government of any kind asserted power in the country. The courts sat, Congress legislated, and the government was duly administered. Its power was fully established and peaceably exercised. The people seemed to have accepted Tinoco's government with great good will when it came in, and to have welcomed the change. . . .

Though Tinoco came in with popular approval, the result of his two years'

[8] Edwin M. Borchard, *The Diplomatic Protection of Citizens Abroad or The Law of International Claims* (New York: The Banks Law Publishing Co., 1915), pp. 206–207.

administration of the law was to rouse opposition to him. Conspiracies outside of the country were projected to organize a force to attack him. But this did not result in any substantial conflict or even a nominal provisional government on the soil until considerably more than two years after the inauguration of his government, and did not result in the establishment of any other real government until September of that year, he having renounced his Presidency in August preceding, on the score of his ill health, and withdrawn to Europe. The truth is that throughout the record as made by the case and counter case, there is no substantial evidence that Tinoco was not in actual and peaceable administration without resistance or conflict or contest by anyone until a few months before the time when he retired and resigned.

Speaking of the resumption of the present government, this passage occurs in the argument on behalf of Costa Rica:

> Powerful forces in Costa Rica were opposed to Tinoco from the outset, but his overthrow by ballot or unarmed opposition was impossible and it was equally impossible to organize armed opposition against him in Costa Rican territory.

It is true that action of the supporters of those seeking to restore the former government was somewhat delayed by the influence of the United States with Gonzalez and his friends against armed action, on the ground that military disturbances in Central America during the World War would be prejudicial to the interests of the Allied Powers. It is not important, however, what were the causes that enabled Tinoco to carry on his government effectively and peaceably. The question is, must his government be considered a link in the continuity of the Government of Costa Rica? I must hold that from the evidence that the Tinoco government was an actual sovereign government.

But it is urged that many leading Powers refused to recognize the Tinoco government, and that recognition by other nations is the chief and best evidence of the birth, existence and continuity of succession of a government. Undoubtedly recognition by other Powers is an important evidential factor in establishing proof of the existence of a government in the society of nations. What are the facts as to this? The Tinoco government was recognized by [twenty states in 1917]. . . . .

What were the circumstances as to the other nations?

The United States, on February 9, 1917, two weeks after Tinoco had assumed power, took this action:

> . . . In view of its policy in regard to the assumption of power through illegal methods, clearly enunciated by it on several occasions during the past four years, the Government of the United States desires to set forth in an emphatic and distinct manner its present position in regard to the actual situation in Costa Rica which is that it will not give recognition or support to any government which may be established unless it is clearly proven that it is elected by legal and constitutional means.

And again on February 24, 1917:

In order that citizens of the United States may have definite information as to the position of this Government in regard to any financial aid which they may give to, or any business transaction which they may have with those persons who overthrew the constitutional Government of Costa Rica by an act of armed rebellion, the Government of the United States desires to advise them that it will not consider any claims which may in the future arise from such dealings, worthy of its diplomatic support.

. . . .

Probably because of the leadership of the United States in respect to a matter of this kind, her then Allies in the war, Great Britain, France and Italy, declined to recognize the Tinoco government. Costa Rica was, therefore, not permitted to sign the Treaty of Peace at Versailles, although the Tinoco government had declared war against Germany.

The merits of the policy of the United States in this non-recognition it is not for the arbitrator to discuss, for the reason that in his consideration of this case, he is necessarily controlled by principles of international law, and however justified as a national policy non-recognition on such a ground may be, it certainly has not been acquiesced in by all the nations of the world, which is a condition precedent to considering it as a postulate of international law.

The non-recognition by other nations of a government claiming to be a national personality, is usually appropriate evidence that it has not attained the independence and control entitling it by international law to be classed as such. But when recognition *vel non* of a government is by such nations determined by inquiry, not into its *de facto* sovereignty and complete governmental control, but into its illegitimacy or irregularity of origin, their non-recognition loses something of evidential weight on the issue with which those applying the rules of international law are alone concerned. . . . Such non-recognition for any reason, however, cannot outweigh the evidence disclosed by this record before me as to the *de facto* character of Tinoco's government, according to the standard set by international law.

Second. It is ably and earnestly argued on behalf of Costa Rica that the Tinoco government cannot be considered a *de facto* government, because it was not established and maintained in accord with the constitution of Costa Rica of 1871. To hold that a government which establishes itself and maintains a peaceful administration, with the acquiescence of the people for a substantial period of time, does not become a *de facto* government unless it conforms to a previous constitution would be to hold that within the rules of international law a revolution contrary to the fundamental law of the existing government cannot establish a new government. This cannot be, and is not, true. The change by revolution upsets the rule of the authorities in power under the then existing fundamental law, and sets aside the fundamental law in so far as the change of rule makes it necessary. To speak of a revolution creating a *de facto* government, which conforms to the limitations of the old constitution is to use a contradiction in terms. The same government continues internationally, but not the internal law of its being. The issue is not whether the new government assumes power or conducts its administration under constitutional limitations established by the people during the incumbency of the government it has overthrown. The question is, has it really established itself in such a way that all within its influence recognize its control, and that there is no opposing force assuming to be a government in its place? Is it discharging its functions as a government usually does, respected within its own jurisdiction?

. . . .

[Although Costa Rica has cited the Treaty of Washington (1907) among the five Republics of Central America, which barred recognition to states inaugurated by *coups d'état* or revolutions, that treaty provided for recognition after free elections, and all the signatories except Nicaragua did recognize the Tinoco government after it adopted the constitution of 1917 and the people elected Tinoco. Moreover that treaty could not affect the rights of subjects of a non-signatory or change any rules of international law.]

Third. . . . Costa Rica [argues] that Great Britain by her failure to recognize the Tinoco government is estopped now to urge claims of her subjects dependent upon the acts and contracts of the Tinoco government. . . . The contention here . . . precludes a government which did not recognize a *de facto* government from appearing in an international tribunal in behalf of its nationals to claim any rights based on the acts of such government. . . .

I do not understand the arguments on which an equitable estoppel in such case can rest. The failure to recognize the *de facto* government did not lead the succeeding government to change its position in any way upon the faith of it. Non-recognition may have aided the succeeding government to come into power; but subsequent presentation of claims based on the *de facto* existence of the previous government and its dealings does not work an injury to the succeeding government in the nature of a fraud or breach of faith. An equitable estoppel to prove the truth must rest on previous conduct of the person to be estopped, which has led the person claiming the estoppel into a position in which the truth will injury him. There is no such case here.

. . . It may be urged that it would be in the interest of the stability of governments and the orderly adjustment of international relations, and so a proper rule of international law, that a government in recognizing or refusing to recognize a government claiming admission to the society of nations should thereafter be held to an attitude consistent with its deliberate conclusion on this issue. Arguments for and against such a rule occur to me; but it suffices to say that I have not been cited to text writers of authority or to decisions of significance indicating a general acquiescence of nations in such a rule. Without this, it cannot be applied here as a principle of international law.

It is urged that the subjects of Great Britain knew of the policy of their home government in refusing to recognize the Tinoco regime and cannot now rely on protection by Great Britain. This is a question solely between the home government and its subjects. That government may take the course which the United States has done and refuse to use any diplomatic offices to promote such claims and thus to leave its nationals to depend upon the sense of justice of the existing Costa Rican Government, as they were warned in advance would be its policy, or it may change its conclusion as to the *de facto* existence of the Tinoco government and offer its subjects the protection of its diplomatic intervention. It is entirely a question between the claimants and their own government. It should be noted that Great Britain issued no such warning to its subjects as did the United States to its citizens in this matter. . . .

The fourth point made on behalf of Costa Rica . . . is that both claimants are bound either by their own contractual obligation entered into with the Government of Costa Rica, or by the laws of Costa Rica, to which they subscribed, not to present their claims by way of diplomatic intervention of their home government, but to submit their claims to the courts of Costa Rica. . . .

It is doubtful whether these restrictions [to operate according to local laws and not to invoke its status as a foreign corporation with respect to operations] upon the bank . . . go so far as to forbid its appeal for diplomatic intervention in protection of its rights. They show clearly that the powers conferred by the government of its origin cannot enlarge its banking powers in Costa Rica and that its rights are to be decided by Costa Rican courts and according to Costa Rican law. But to carry this to a denial of the right to a diplomatic intervention by its own government to avoid legislative nullification of its rights without a hearing would be going far.

It has been held in a number of important arbitrations, and by several foreign secretaries, that such restrictions are not binding upon a home government and will not prevent it from exercising its diplomatic functions to protect its nationals against the annulment of the rights secured to them by the laws of the country in force when the obligations arose. . . .

It is true that the bank might then have continued its litigation and have contested the validity of the Law of Nullities before the courts of Costa Rica, but it would have had to do so before a court that was elected by the same Congress which passed the Law of Nullities, the previous court having been reorganized by the Congress. Without in any way implying a criticism of the new court, or a doubt as to its spirit of judicial inquiry, I think the previous course of the provisional government, the enactment of the Law of Nullities, and the constitutional limitation upon the scope of the decision of Costa Rican courts, already referred to, so changed the situation with respect to the rights of the bank when it began its suit that the restored government must be held to have waived the enforcement of any limitation upon the right of the bank to invoke the protection of its home government under the circumstances.

[The arbitrator ultimately held that the petroleum concession was invalid even by the Tinoco constitution of 1917. Costa Rica's successor government did not, therefore, have to honor it. On the other hand, Justice Taft did require Costa Rica to assign certain sums to the Royal Bank of Canada to compensate it for the currency issued by the Tinoco government and invalidated by the Law of Nullities.]

When on February 8, 1918, the Soviet Government repudiated, as from December 1, 1917, the public debts of Russia incurred by previous Russian Governments,[9] it angered most of the civilized nations of the world. Britain and France issued a communiqué stating in part:

The Imperial Russian Government, when it contracted, incontestably represented Russia and obligated it definitely. . . . No principle is better established than that according to which a nation is responsible for the acts of its government, no change of authority affecting obligations incurred.[10]

The Soviet Union defended its action by alleging that

. . . revolutions which are a violent rupture with the past carry with them new juridical relations in the foreign and domestic affairs of States. Governments and systems that spring from revolution are not bound to respect the obligations of fallen governments . . . revolution . . . being akin to *force majeure*, does not confer any title to indemnity upon those who have suffered from it. . . . Russia is in no wise obliged to pay the debts of the past, to restore property, or to compensate their former owners, nor is she obliged to pay indemnities for other damages suffered by foreign nationals, whether as a result of legislation adopted by Russia in the exercise of her sovereignty, or as a result of revolutionary events. . . .[11]

The Soviet Union seems in effect to have repudiated its own principle, however, in its subsequent efforts to gain recognition. Thus, in the Litvinoff-Roosevelt Memorandum (November 15, 1933), the U.S.S.R. agreed to "pay to the Government of the United States on account of the Kerensky debt or otherwise a sum to be not less than $75,000,000." The principles set forth by the Soviet Union seem somewhat compromised also by negotiations between the Soviet government and other powers to settle outstanding debts. The negotiations were largely unsuccessful but, to be consistent, the Soviet government would have had to refuse to negotiate at all.[12]

State Succession

The life of states is affected by more than just a change in government. As noted in Chapter II, a new state may be created out of the territory

[9] *J.D.I.*, XXXV (1918), 601, 889, 952, 987.
[10] *Ibid.*, p. 861.
[11] Great Britain, *Accounts and Papers*, XXIII (1922); *State Papers*, XIII, XXXXII, XXXXIII.
[12] *Foreign Relations of the United States, The Soviet Union, 1933–1939*, pp. 119–121, 178–180, 573–582.

of an old one. A colony may become a state, as many territories did in Africa and Southeast Asia after World War II. Or states may lose their identity during war, as did Latvia, Lithuania, and Estonia. War may increase or decrease the territory of states, as the second World War did in the case of the Soviet Union, Germany, Poland, and Japan. Or old names may be attached to new entities, as in the cases of Austria and Hungary, which were created after World War I from the former Austro-Hungarian empire. Each of these instances involves what is known as "state succession," and each one raises the question of the rights and obligations of the states concerned.

In general, a state that acquires authority over land and people from another state succeeds to the rights and obligations of that state. The rights and obligations are not completely taken over, however, because some of them rest on treaties, and a state's treaties die when it is extinguished and do not automatically pass to the successor state. Some treaties are so closely tied to the signatory, that the idea of another state's succeeding to the obligation would be unthinkable as, for instance, political treaties, military alliances, or tariff arrangements. On the other hand, states do succeed to the obligations of "law-making" treaties, at least when these documents declare rather than create legal rules. They also succeed to legal obligations closely connected with the territory if it is in the nature of a servitude—that is, a right of another party to use the land or to benefit from it in some way. So it was that a Commission of Jurists appointed by the Council of the League of Nations held that Finland, even though not a party to the arrangement, was bound to keep the Aland Islands demilitarized, as the Russian Czar had agreed in 1856.[13] Similarly, the International Court of Justice held that the obligations of the Union of South Africa with regard to its Mandate over South West Africa had not changed even though the League of Nations itself had disappeared. Rather, the Court said, the United Nations had automatically succeeded as the international agency to which the Union Government was accountable for its administration.[14]

In cases of partial state succession, *i.e.*, when a state acquires a portion of another state or a new state comes into being on land formerly belonging to another, the treaty rights and obligations of both states remain unaffected.[15] The new states do succeed to the public property of an annexed or ceding state, and they automatically acquire the right to collect taxes and other moneys due the former state. However, private property relations remain unchanged. Thus the title of individuals to

[13] *League of Nations, Official Journal* (Special Supplement No. 3), pp. 17–19 (1920).
[14] International Court of Justice, *Advisory Opinion on the International Status of South-West Africa,* 1950.
[15] Brierly (6th ed.), p. 153.

their own land and contracts among individuals remain intact in cases of state succession, and old laws continue in effect until changed. New states can change old laws and old rights, of course, once territory has changed hands. Therefore, private rights rest in effect upon the will of the new state. When the United States acquired Florida from Spain, the acts of the Spanish king in granting land to persons who later became citizens of the United States remained intact, even though the United States acquired full jurisdiction over the territories His Majesty controlled. The United States Supreme Court made this point in 1833 in the case of *U.S. v. Percheman*, (32 U.S. [7 Pet.] 51):

> It is very unusual [wrote Chief Justice Marshall], even in cases of conquest, for the conqueror to do more than to displace the sovereign and assume dominion over the country. The modern usage of nations, which has become law, would be violated; that sense of justice and of right which is acknowledged and felt by the whole civilized world would be outraged, if private property should be generally confiscated, and private rights annulled. The people change their allegiance; their relation to their ancient sovereign is dissolved; but their relations to each other, and their rights of property, remain undisturbed. If this be the modern rule, even in cases of conquest, who can doubt its application to the case of an amicable cession of territory. Had Florida changed its sovereign by an act containing no stipulation respecting the property of individuals, the right of property in all those who become subjects or citizens of the new government would have been unaffected by the change; it would have remained the same as under the ancient sovereign. . . . A cession of territory is never understood to be a cession of the property belonging to its inhabitants. The king cedes that only which belongs to him; lands he had previously granted, were not his to cede.

States logically are eager not to disorganize private-law relations in the territories they acquire. They naturally prefer not to alienate people living in transferred territory whenever possible. Nor do they wish to arouse "third" states to intervene to protect any of their nationals who might be offended by a successor state's violating existing private law.[16]

Often, at a time a state ceases to exist, citizens of other countries may have legal actions pending against it; just what the obligations of the successor state are in such a case is not clear. The United States found that it could not help an American citizen, Robert E. Brown, whose legal rights seem quite clearly to have been denied by the South African Republic, which Great Britain extinguished in the Boer War in 1900. The United States could not recover damages from Great Britain in his behalf, when it attempted to do so in 1923.[17] On the other hand,

---

[16] On this point, see de Visscher, p. 192.

[17] Robert E. Brown Claim, U.S.-Great Britain, Claims Arbitration, Nielsen's Report, p. 187 (1923). Hawaiian Claims, U.S.-Great Britain Claims Arbitration, *ibid.*, p. 60 (1925).

states frequently assume some or all of the public debts of states whose land they acquire, and they generally continue to acknowledge the validity of contracts made by their predecessors. Lawyers disagree, however, whether the law requires them to do so or whether they do so voluntarily to establish the credit of their regimes. Whether a state will assume a debt often depends on the relation between the territory in question and the former sovereign. If it is a minor part of the former sovereign's territory, it is often held that very little or no part of the former sovereign's debt attaches to it; if a whole state is extinguished, on the other hand, the succeeding state is generally assumed to have acquired the full national debt. The purposes for which former states have incurred particular debts is also relevant: if a debt has no particular relation to the territory in question, it is likely not to be assumed.[18] The matter is clearly quite complex, and has been dealt with at great length in negotiations where the problem arises. Thus, in the peace treaties of 1919, elaborate provisions were made for passing on the public debts of Austria and Hungary to the Succession States which acquired territory from the Austro-Hungarian Monarchy.[19] When a state cedes territory, but continues to exist, the matter becomes even more complicated.

Some jurists believe that multilateral treaties should always survive the disappearance of particular states and bind their successors, but the belief is not universal.[20]

If a state is completely annexed or dismembered, that is, if complete state succession occurs, its rights and obligations do not survive it. When, for instance, Italy overran and annexed Ethiopia in 1936, Haile Selassie, the temporarily deposed emperor, lost his right to maintain a suit in a British court, and the King of Italy, as his successor, acquired this right.[21] More recently, on April 5, 1951, the Civil Tribunal of Brussels held, in granting a divorce to persons of Latvian origin and former Latvian nationality, that the Court should apply the law of the Soviet Union. It was, said the Court, irrelevant whether Belgium had, or had not, publicly commented on the disappearance of Latvia as an independent state.

In public international law [it added] modifications in the structure of states and the distribution of governmental competence may still be executed

---

[18] Hyde, I, 401.

[19] See the Treaty of St. Germain of September 10, 1919, Art. 203; B. and F.S.P., CXII, 317, 405.

[20] C. Wilfred Jenks, "State Succession in Respect of Law-Making Treaties," *B.Y.B.I.L.*, 105 (1952). On this subject, see also, Henri Rolin, "Principes de droit international public," *Rec. A.D.I.*, LXXVIII, 338–339 (1950), and comments by de Visscher, p. 170.

[21] Haile Selassie v. Cable and Wireless, Ltd., No. 23, England, Court of Appeal Chap. 182, 195 (1939).

by force . . . ; . . . the annexation of the entire territory of a state deprives, by force and in a unilateral manner, the former governments of the annexed state which thereby ceases to exist.

Since there was no government of the Latvian Republic and no diplomatic representation between Belgium and Latvia, there was in effect no state of Latvia nor a Latvian nationality. Annexation and incorporation resulted in change of nationality, so the parties became Soviet nationals.[22]

Despite the seeming independence of this Belgian court, it is noteworthy that Belgium and Latvia were not maintaining diplomatic relations at the time, and that in deciding legal questions relating to state succession, as in deciding questions relating to recognition, courts tend to be guided by the executive branches of government. A few years before, for instance, the French Court of Cassation held that a Latvian state did exist, and that a treaty of 1937 made with France applied.[23] And, as we have already seen, in 1951, an American court refused to recognize a Soviet decree nationalizing Latvian ships. Where the courts have to take judicial note of acts the executive has not yet acknowledged, they do; where they do not, they tend to follow the lead of the political branch of their governments.[24]

Problems of state and governmental succession are often highly technical, but the technicalities should not obscure the genuine, human difficulties which these political and legal changes cause. When succession occurs, many important questions hang upon determining exactly when sovereignty passes from one authority to another; what laws or system of laws apply in a transitional period in matters of nationality, crime, or civil actions; whether or not treaties survive; the effects upon private rights and concessions, civil servants, public property, public debts, and contracts.

The classic case in many of these issues is *West Rand Gold Mining Company v. The King,* [1905] 2 K.B. 391. In this case, an English company alleged that before the war (declared 11 October 1899) between the South African Republic and Great Britain, gold owned by the company was taken over by Republican officials. British forces conquered the Republic and annexed all its territories on 1 September 1900. The company claimed that, because of the annexation, the British government was liable for the former Republic's debts.

The Court stated, however, that no principle of international law made

---

[22] Pulenckis v. Augustovskis, 80 Clunet 381.
[23] Gerbaud v. de Meden, 78 Clunet 169.
[24] In The Denny, 127 F. 2d 404, the Court acknowledged Soviet decrees affecting Lithuania, and only Letts were involved.

a conquering state liable, in the absence of express stipulation to the contrary, for financial liabilities of the conquered state incurred before the outbreak of war, unless an agreement expressly provided for the conqueror to discharge them. The Court said that if, by public proclamation or convention, the conquering state promised that it did not plan to repudiate particular liabilities, good faith should prevent such repudiation. But silence was not the equivalent of a promise to honor existing contracts with the government of the conquered state.

On the question of the jurisdiction of municipal courts to adjudicate claims of this type, the Court relied upon authorities from 1793 to 1905, who held that matters which fell properly to be determined by the Crown by treaty or Act of State are not subject to municipal court jurisdiction, and that rights supposed to be acquired thereunder cannot be enforced by such courts.

More recent cases[25] have not departed much from these basic doctrines, although variations on the main themes abound. The establishment of the state of Israel, for instance, raised a wide range of succession problems touching on nationality, criminal jurisdiction, and contracts. One question related to the nationality of people, formerly Palestinians, who became resident in Israel between 1948, when Israel came into being, and 1952, when the Israeli parliament (the Knesset) passed the Israeli Nationality Law. Israeli courts actually differed over these questions, some deciding that such persons were stateless,[26] while others held, contrary to international law, the view that there were no Israeli nationals until the nationality law was enacted. Citing the prevailing view that every inhabitant of a ceded state automatically became a national of the receiving state, the judge held that everyone who lived in land designated *Israel* automatically became a national of Israel unless a law to the contrary had been adopted. Any other view, he pointed out, would lead to the absurd result of a state without nationals.[27]

A question of criminal jurisdiction arose in a case where an Israeli court was to try a man in 1949 for a murder committed in April 1948, about a month before Israel came into being. The alleged murderer

[25] For a convenient summary of these and other cases, see "Succession of States and Governments," [Agenda Item 4], U.N. Doc. A/CN.4/157, "Digest of Decisions of National Courts Relating to Succession of States and Governments: Study . . . by the Secretariat," 18 April 1963, in *Yearbook of the International Law Commission, 1963,* II, 95–170.
[26] In re Goods of Shiphris, Tel Aviv District Court, 13 August 1950, Pesakim Mehoziim, III, 222 (1950–1951); Oseri v. Oseri, Tel Aviv District Court, 7 August 1952, Pesakim Mehoziim, VIII, 76 (1953); Hussein v. Governor of Acre Prison, Supreme Court of Israel, Piskei-Din, 6 November 1952, VI, 897 (1952).
[27] A. B. v. M. B., 6 April 1951, Tel Aviv District Court, Pesakiim Mohoziim, III, 263 (1950–1951).

challenged the court's right to try him, arguing that an Israeli court could not try a person for an offense allegedly committed before the state of Israel came into being. The Court held, however, that Israeli authorities could bring criminal acts to trial even if committed before the change of sovereignty. The power to punish, maintained the Court, continued without lapse from authority to authority, according to "the golden rule" that law continued despite changes of sovereignty, the only exception being in the case of laws incompatible with the constitution and laws of the new sovereign.[28] The same problem arose for Israel in the case of Adolf Eichmann, when Israeli courts dismissed Eichmann's plea that they were incompetent to try him for offenses he had allegedly committed abroad before Israel was established.[29]

In another case, the Israeli Supreme Court had occasion to rule on a contractual matter, and maintained that Israeli authorities were not bound to renew a concession for newspaper kiosks and bookstalls granted in 1938 to Pales Ltd. by the General Manager of the Palestine Railways. The justices argued that Israel was not the successor of the Government of Palestine. A new legal personality had come into being without relation to the one that had disappeared, as May 14, 1948, came to a close and the Mandate to an end. The Court pointed out that there was some doubt about how far a successor state was bound by contracts and concessions made by its predecessor, and that there was even more doubt with regard to a state which was not a successor. Even more than in a case of pure state succession, the Court concluded, the Israeli government was encumbered only by its own volition. Theoretically, the Knesset might have denied all rights acquired by persons under the Mandate; actually, it had recognized certain rights, but the basic question for the Court in each case was what the legislature intended: "Every new State . . . arranges these matters according to its needs and objective capability."[30]

Treaties often determine obligations in cases of succession, as illustrated in many cases, including some relating to Eire, the United States, France, Indonesia, and Austria. In general, these cases show how successor states are free to regard themselves bound by or freed from obligations of their predecessors. For instance, the rights of certain Irish plain-

[28] Katz-Cohen v. Attorney-General of Israel (1949), Supreme Court of Israel, Pesakim Elyonim, II (1949), 216; *Annual Digest*, Case 26 (1949). See also Hyde, I, 394, 397.
[29] Attorney-General v. Eichmann (1961), Israel District Court of Jerusalem, Criminal Case No. 40/61 and Eichmann v. Attorney-General, Supreme Court of Israel, Criminal Appeal No. 336/61, 29 May 1962.
[30] Pales Ltd. v. Ministry of Transport (1955), Supreme Court of Israel, Piskei-Din, IX, 436 (1955); Pasakim Elyonim, 18 (1955), 304; *International Law Reports*, p. 113 (1955).

tiffs to real property in New Hampshire depended in 1948 on whether or not a convention relating to the tenure and disposition of real and personal property, which the United States and the United Kingdom had signed in 1899 was effective between the United States and the Irish Free State (later Eire), created in 1921–1922. Eire had not repudiated the treaty after independence, and the Court accepted writers' views that "on the creation of a new state, by a division of territory, the new State has a sovereign right to enter into new treaties and engagements with other nations, but until it actually does, the treaties by which it was bound as part of the whole State will remain binding on the new State and its subjects" and that "a State formed by separation from another . . . succeeds to such treaty burdens of the parent State as are permanent and attached to the territory embraced in the new State." The Court also referred to *Techt v. Hughes*, 229 N.Y. 222, where the Court maintained that "until the political departments have acted, the courts, in refusing to give effect to treaties, should limit their refusal to the needs of the occasion and in determining whether a treaty survives, reach their conclusions in the light of such broad consideration as 'the dictates of fair dealing, and the honour of the nation.' "[31]

The existence of a treaty was also decisive in the case of two residents of Oregon who died intestate in 1953 and whose heirs and next of kin were residents and nationals of Yugoslavia. The Court had to decide whether the United States and Yugoslavia acknowledged reciprocity in matters of inheritance laws. Without reciprocity, the estates would have gone to the State of Oregon; reciprocity could exist, however, only if the Treaty of 1881, concluded between the United States and the then Prince of Serbia, was still in effect. The Supreme Court of Oregon, and later the Supreme Court of the United States found that the treaty was still in effect, despite state succession.[32] By similar reasoning, United States courts have held that treaties concluded with the Hanseatic cities in 1827 and 1828, regulating tonnage duties on ships, survived the changes of 1871, by which the once sovereign states became constituent parts of the German Empire.[33]

Continuity does not automatically follow, as implied above, every change in sovereignty. For instance, when the Virgin Islands (formerly the Danish West Indies) were ceded to the United States in 1917, "The Organic Act," passed by Congress on March 3, 1917, provided that all local laws in effect on January 17, 1917, would remain in force insofar as was compatible with the change in sovereignty. A Circuit Court of

[31] Hanafin v. McCarthy (1948), Supreme Court of New Hampshire, *A.J.I.L.*, XXXXII (1948), 499.
[32] Kolovrat et al. v. Oregon, 366 U.S. 187 (1961).
[33] Sophie Rickmers Case, 45 F. 2d. 413 (1930).

Appeals latter concluded that this Act had changed local Danish law and had given the islanders the right to be confronted by their accusers and the right not to be deprived of life, liberty, or property without due process of law. As a result, certain criminal trials conducted contrary to these principles were invalidated.[34]

Another example of the law of the successor state prevailing occurred when French courts held that French regulations regarding the dispensation of drugs invalidated licenses issued to hospitals in Savoy and Nice by the King of Sardinia, ruler of the area before 1860. The King had granted these hospitals the right to dispense drugs to the public, and the hospitals argued that France could not abrogate these rights. The French Council of State held, however, that, in the absence of any intervening treaties, the change of sovereignty had placed the hospitals under French law and administration, and that France could legally close the dispensaries without violating the treaty of 1860.[35]

Similarly, where the rights and obligations of a part of a legal person were passed to a successor by express agreement (as when the Republic of the United States of Indonesia succeeded the Netherlands Indies), courts held that all obligations of the Indies (such as possible claims for pay owed a schoolmaster when the Japanese occupied the Indies during the second World War) passed to the successor state and did not inhere in any way in the Kingdom of the Netherlands.[36]

Treaties may also determine the laws to be applied in given cases. When, for instance, under Article 51 of the Treaty of Versailles, Alsace-Lorraine became part of France on November 11, 1918 (the date of the armistice), a contract, made in October 1919 to transport goods from a city in Alsace-Lorraine, was still held subject to German commercial and currency law because, despite the earlier Armistice, the legal system did not change until the Treaty itself came into effect on January 10, 1920.[37]

Like treaties, financial obligations may either survive succession or not, depending on the circumstances. In one case, the Polish Supreme Court denied Poland's obligation in an accident that had occurred before World War I through the fault of Russian railway authorities. Instead of upholding a lower court ruling that the Polish State Treasury, which had taken over the whole Russian Vistula Railway, assumed its obliga-

[34] Soto et al. v. U.S., 273 F. 628 (1921).
[35] In re Hospices Civils de Chambéry et al. (1947); France, Conseil d'Etat; Sirey, III, 39 (1948); *Annual Digest*, Case 20 (1948).
[36] Poldermans v. State of the Netherlands (1956), Holland Court of Appeal of the Hague (December 1955, N.J. 56, 120); Supreme Court, June 1956, N.J., No. 7 (1959).
[37] Application of German Law in Alsace-Lorraine Case (1924), German Reichsgericht (Supreme Court of the German Reich), Fontes Juris Gentium, A, II, No. 309 (1899–1929).

tions, the Supreme Court affirmed that Polish obligations were limited
to those specifically assumed.[38] On the other hand, Austria was held
liable for an action to pay for work commissioned by German State
Railways while Austria was incorporated in Nazi Germany, since the
work related exclusively to, and had been executed for, the benefit of
Austrian State Railways, which continued to benefit from it despite
governmental succession.[39]

Property matters can also be affected by changes in sovereignty. Thus,
according to Turkish law in Samothrace, which applied before Samothrace was ceded to Greece, certain medicinal springs belonged to the
State. Under Greek law, however, the rights inhered in the owner of
the land. Because of the change of sovereignty, Greek law became effective in the island, and the property passed to the private owner.[40] Actually, real property rights of individuals are usually protected in cases
of state succession, as indicated in those instances where the U.S. Supreme Court upheld the property rights of claimants to land in Florida
ceded by Spain to the United States, on the grounds that it was civilized
usage to honor such arrangements despite succession.[41]

The jurisdiction of courts and the standing of parties before them
may also be affected in instances of succession. Thus, in 1927, in the
Indian Province of Bombay, a court ruled against one Damappa and
a partnership of his for certain moneys owed. Damappa did not submit
to the Court's jurisdiction because he was a resident of the then independent State of Jamkhandi, and in 1948 a Jamkhandi Court dismissed
a request for execution of the 1927 judgment as unenforceable in a
foreign state. On appeal, however, the High Court of Bombay held
that it could enforce the judgment because Jamkhandi State had acceded
to India, which made the lower court no longer foreign. The alteration
in the status of the judgment debtor and in the character and authority
of the Court were held to be the decisive elements in the case.[42]

In general, one may say that in matters of governmental and state
succession, courts make every effort to maintain continuity. Obligations
repugnant to the nature of the successor state may not be honored,
however, and therefore the particular circumstances in each case are
scrutinized carefully when issues arise.

[38] Dzierzbicki v. District Electric Association of Vzestochowa (1934), Supreme Court
of Poland, O.S.P. (1934), 288; *Annual Digest,* Case 38 (1933–1934).
[39] Kleihs v. Austria (1948), Supreme Court of Austria, *Annual Digest,* Case 18
(1948).
[40] Springs of Samothrace Case [1932], Greece, Court of Thrace, Thémis, Vol. 43,
p. 426.
[41] U.S. v. Arredondo, 31 U.S. [6 Pet.] 691 (1832); see also above, p. 112.
[42] Chunilal Kasturchand Marwadi and another v. Dundappa Damappa Navalgi
(1950), India, High Court of Bombay (1950), *Indian Law Reports,* Bombay, 640;
International Law Reports, Case 23 (1950).

CHAPTER IV

Jurisdiction: Land, Air, and Rivers

States do not exist in a vacuum. All of them are concerned with the land within their boundaries, with the rivers and seas to which they have access, and with the air and space above them. Their rights to exercise authority over these elements compose their *jurisdiction*. Because jurisdiction is a measure of power, states are naturally much preoccupied with it, and international law must necessarily pay it considerable attention.

Having jurisdiction over an element does not necessarily give a state the right of possession, for it is possible to exercise authority over an object without owning it or having the right to dispose of it. If a state does own an element, however, it is said to have *title* to it.

Land

Territory. States exist upon territory; without it, they would not exist at all. Exercising legal authority over a particular territory is therefore a matter of prime importance for statesmen, who are extremely sensitive to threats to territory.

States usually hold title to their land, but they may exercise jurisdiction over it without having title. The United States, for instance, acquired jurisdiction over certain British naval and air bases by leasing them at the outset of World War II. The jurisdiction did not convey title and ended as the United States surrendered its leases.[1] The requirements for acquiring jurisdiction over territory have changed over the years and may change further now that man is probing outer space, but the traditional modes of acquiring jurisdiction, besides leasing, are cession

[1] See *D.S.B.*, III (September 7, 1940), 199–200, for text of Notes exchanged between the British Ambassador to the United States and the American Secretary of State, and XLIV (March 6, 1961), 350–351 for agreements surrendering leases on West Indian bases.

(after purchase or conquest), avulsion or accretion, gift, prescription and, oldest of all, discovery and occupation.

Discovery and occupation were the most important ways of acquiring jurisdiction during the fifteenth and sixteenth centuries, when Europeans were busy laying claims to the new world. These claims rested in part on ancient Roman legal theories, asserting that to obtain a right of possession required both "a bodily act and a mental attitude." The mental attitude was the intent to possess; the bodily act was prehensile.[2] How these provisions were met by Columbus (in the Bahamas at San Salvador), he tells us in his own journal:[3]

The Admiral took the royal standard, and the captains with the two banners of the green cross, which the Admiral took in all the ships as a sign, with an F and a Y and a crown over each letter one on one side of the cross and the other on the other. Having landed, they saw trees very green, and much water, and fruits of diverse kinds. The Admiral called to the two captains and to the others who leaped on shore . . . and said that they should bear faithful testimony that he, in the presence of all, had taken, as he now took, possession of the said island for the King and for the Queen . . . making the declarations that are required, as is now largely set forth in the testimonies which were made in writing.

In this instance, the intent to possess was clear, and the act of possession was landing, placing the flags, and proclaiming the significance of these acts. These ceremonies were generally regarded as being wholly sufficient in themselves to establish sovereignty to territory,[4] and sovereigns did not refrain even from claiming land that, for reasons of climate, geography, or resources, they could not in fact control. But as different sovereigns became interested in the same lands, they found it necessary to distinguish their claims by some means less evanescent than merely alleging that a subject had been the first to ascertain that a particular territory, previously unknown to European civilization, did in fact exist. As time passed, physical possession became more and more important, as Chief Justice Marshall noted in 1823, in commenting on the title to land which the European sovereigns acquired in the new world:

On the discovery of this immense continent, the great nations of Europe were eager to appropriate to themselves so much of it as they could respectively acquire. . . . But, as they were all in pursuit of nearly the same object, it was necessary, in order to avoid conflicting settlements, and conse-

[2] John Westlake, *International Law* (2 vols., Cambridge: The University Press, 1904), I, 97–98.
[3] Julies E. Olson and Edward Gaylord Bourne, eds., *Original Narratives of Early American History: The Northmen, Columbus and Cabot* (New York: Charles Scribner's Sons, 1906), p. 110.
[4] Arthur S. Keller, Oliver J. Lissitzyn, and Frederick J. Mann, *Creation of Rights of Sovereignty through Symbolic Acts (1400–1800)* (New York: Columbia University Press, 1938), pp. 148–149.

quent war with each other, to establish a principle, which all should acknowledge as the law by which the right of acquisition, which they all asserted, would be regulated as between themselves. This principle was, that discovery gave title to the government by whose subjects, or by whose authority, it was made, against all other European governments, which title might be consummated by possession.[5]

Eventually, as it became possible to sustain life in newly discovered areas, international society insisted not just that states take possession and proclaim their sovereignty, but that they exercise substantial control over the lands whose title they claimed. States incorporated these principles in Articles 34 and 35 of the General Act of the Conference of Berlin, signed on February 26, 1885:[6]

ARTICLE 34

Any Power which henceforth takes possession of a tract of land on the coasts of the African Continent outside of its present possessions, or which, being hitherto with such possessions, shall acquire them, as well as the Power which assumes a Protectorate there, shall accompany the respective act with a notification thereof, addressed to the other Signatory Powers of the present Act, in order to enable them, if need be, to make good any claims of their own.

ARTICLE 35

The Signatory Powers of the present Act recognize the obligation to insure the establishment of authority in the regions occupied by them on the coasts of the African Continent sufficient to protect existing rights, and, as the case may be, freedom of trade and of transit under the conditions agreed upon.

[5] Johnson v. McIntosh, 21 U.S. (8 Wheat.) 543 (1823). This decision concerned title to land in Illinois, and the Supreme Court dismissed the plaintiff's claim, based upon purchase under conveyance from the Piankeshaw Indians. Thus, Marshall indicated (by passing over lightly the claim that logically, at any rate, the Indians enjoyed) the considerable extent to which international law itself was a Western European creation: "In the establishment of these relations, the rights of the original inhabitants were, in no instance, entirely disregarded, but were, necessarily, to a considerable extent, impaired. They were admitted to be the rightful occupants of the soil, with a legal as well as just claim to retain possession of it, and to use it according to their own discretion; but their rights to complete sovereignty, as independent nations, were necessarily diminished, and their power to dispose of the soil, at their own will, to whomsoever they pleased, was denied by the original fundamental principle that discovery gave exclusive title to those who made it. While the different nations of Europe respected the right of the natives, as occupants, they asserted ultimate dominion to be in themselves, and claimed and exercised, as a consequence of this ultimate dominion, a power to grant the soil, while yet in the possession of the natives. These grants have been understood by all, to convey title to the grantees, subject only to the Indian right of occupancy." *Ibid.*, p. 574.
[6] British Sessional Papers, House of Commons, XLVII (1886), 97–117; Hyde, I, 329.

The control states need to have to establish title still varies with the physical environment; states tend to ease the requirements, for instance, as the climate becomes worse. The Permanent Court of Justice made this considerate requirement clear in 1933, when it ruled on rival claims advanced by Norway and Denmark to Eastern Greenland. The Court suggested that "effective occupation" was not necessary to establish title in that harsh climate; it insisted merely on manifestations of state activity. And since it found that the Danish government had been more active in the area than the Norwegian, it confirmed the Danish title.[7]

There being no undiscovered land left on earth, the opportunities to assert claims based on discovery and occupation have disappeared. The doctrines remain important, nonetheless, in current disputes over territory. As recently as 1953, the International Court of Justice traced the title of the Minquiers and Ecrehos Islands back to the year 1066, and confirmed the United Kingdom's title on the evidence of direct possession. The Court attached probative value to the acts of the local authorities on the nearby island of Jersey, who had conducted criminal proceedings concerning the Ecrehos, levied taxes on habitable houses or huts built on the islets since 1889, and registered contracts dealing with real estate there. Similar rights which Jersey authorities had exercised over the Minquiers, *e.g.*, conducting inquests on corpses found on the Minquiers, demonstrated to the Court that the British claims were superior to the French, who offered no comparable evidence of possession.[8]

THE MINQUIERS AND ECREHOS CASE

INTERNATIONAL COURT OF JUSTICE 1953

[1953] I.C.J. 47

. . . .

Both Parties contend that they have respectively an ancient or original title to the Ecrehos and the Minquiers, and that their title has always been maintained and was never lost. The present case does not therefore present the characteristics of a dispute concerning the acquisition of sovereignty over *terra nullius*.

The United Kingdom Government derives the ancient title invoked by it from the conquest of England in 1066 by William, Duke of Normandy.

[7] Permanent Court of International Justice, *Publications*, Series A/B, No. 53, p. 46.
[8] The Minquiers and Ecrehos, [1953] I.C.J. 47.

By this conquest England became united with the Duchy of Normandy, including the Channel Islands, and this union lasted until 1204 when King Philip Augustus of France drove the Anglo-Norman forces out of Continental Normandy. But his attempts to occupy also the Islands were not successful, except for brief periods when some of them were taken by French forces. On this ground the United Kingdom Government submits the view that all of the Channel Islands, including the Ecrehos and the Minquiers, remained, as before, united with England and that this situation of fact was placed on a legal basis by subsequent Treaties concluded between the English and French Kings.

The French Government does not dispute that the Islands of Jersey, Guernsey, Alderney, Sark, Herm and Jethou continued to be held by the King of England; but it denies that the Ecrehos and Minquiers groups were held by him after the dismemberment of the Duchy of Normandy in 1204. After that event, these two groups were, it is asserted, held by the King of France together with some other islands close to the continent, and reference is made to the same medieval Treaties as those which are invoked by the United Kingdom Government.

In such circumstances it must be examined whether these Treaties, invoked by both Parties, contain anything which might throw light upon the status of the Ecrehos and the Minquiers.

. . . Of the manifold facts invoked by the United Kingdom Government, the Court attaches, in particular, probative value to the acts which relate to the exercise of jurisdiction and local administration and to legislation.

In 1826 criminal proceedings were instituted before the Royal Court of Jersey against a Jerseyman for having shot at a person on the Ecrehos. Similar judicial proceedings in Jersey in respect of criminal offences committed on the Ecrehos took place in 1881, 1883, 1891, 1913 and 1921. On the evidence produced the Court is satisfied that the Courts of Jersey, in criminal cases such as these, have no jurisdiction in the matter of a criminal offence committed outside the Bailiwick of Jersey, even though the offence be committed by a British subject resident in Jersey, and that Jersey authorities took action in these cases because the Ecrehos were considered to be within the Bailiwick. These facts show therefore that Jersey courts have exercised criminal jurisdiction in respect of the Ecrehos during nearly a hundred years.

Evidence produced shows that the law of Jersey has for centuries required the holding of an inquest on corpses found within the Bailiwick where it was not clear that death was due to natural causes. Such inquests on corpses found that the Ecrehos were held in 1859, 1917 and 1948 and are additional evidence of the exercise of jurisdiction in respect of these islets.

Since about 1820, and probably earlier, persons from Jersey have erected and maintained some habitable houses or huts on the islets of the Ecrehos, where they have stayed during the fishing season. Some of these houses or huts have, for the purpose of parochial rates, been included in the records of the Parish of St. Martin in Jersey, which have been kept since 1889, and they have been assessed for the levying of local taxes. Rating schedules for 1889 and 1950 were produced in evidence.

A register of fishing boats for the port of Jersey shows that the fishing boat belonging to a Jersey fisherman, who lived permanently on an islet of the Ecrehos for more than forty years, was entered in that register in 1872, the port or place of the boat being indicated as "Ecrehos Rocks," and that the licence of that boat was cancelled in 1882. According to a letter of June, 1876, from the Principal Customs Officer of Jersey, an official of that Island visited occasionally the Ecrehos for the purpose of endorsing the licence of that boat.

It is established that contracts of sale relating to real property on the Ecrehos islets have been passed before the competent authorities of Jersey and registered in the public registry of deeds of that island. Examples of such registration of contracts are produced for 1863, 1881, 1884 and some later years.

In 1884, a custom-house was established in the Ecrehos by Jersey customs authorities. The islets have been included by Jersey authorities within the scope of their census enumerations, and in 1901 an official enumerator visited the islets for the purpose of taking the census.

These various facts show that Jersey authorities have in several ways exercised ordinary local administration in respect of the Ecrehos during a long period of time.

By a British Treasury Warrant of 1875, constituting Jersey as a Port of the Channel Islands, the "Ecrehou Rocks" were included within the limits of that port. This legislative Act was a clear manifestation of British sovereignty over the Ecrehos at a time when a dispute as to such sovereignty had not yet arisen. The French Government protested in 1876 on the ground that this Act derogated from the Fishery Convention of 1839. But this protest could not deprive the Act of its character as a manifestation of sovereignty.

Of other facts which throw light upon the dispute, it should be mentioned that Jersey authorities have made periodical official visits to the Ecrehos since 1885, and that they have carried out various works and constructions there, such as a slipway in 1895, a signal post in 1910 and the placing of a mooring buoy in 1939.

. . . .

The Court, being now called upon to appraise the relative strength of the opposing claims to sovereignty over the Ecrehos in the light of the facts considered above, finds that the Ecrehos group in the beginning of the thirteenth century was considered and treated as an integral part of the fief of the Channel Islands which were held by the English King, and that the group continued to be under the dominion of that King, who in the beginning of the fourteenth century exercised jurisdiction in respect thereof. The Court further finds that British authorities during the greater part of the nineteenth century and in the twentieth century have exercised State functions in respect of the group. The French Government, on the other hand, has not produced evidence showing that it has any valid title to the group. In such circumstances it must be concluded that the sovereignty over the Ecrehos belongs to the United Kingdom.

. . . .

The further evidence produced by the United Kingdom Government in respect of the Minquiers is of the same character as that considered above in connection with its claim to the Ecrehos. As already mentioned, the law of Jersey has for centuries required the holding of an inquest on corpses found within the Bailiwick. Such inquests on corpses found at the Minquiers were held in 1850, 1938 and 1948 and show that jurisdiction was exercised in respect of these islets.

Since about 1815, and perhaps earlier, persons from Jersey have erected and maintained some habitable houses or huts also on the islets of the Minquiers, where they have stayed during the fishing season. Some of these houses or huts have, for the purpose of parochial rates, been included in the records of the Parish of Grouville in Jersey, and property taxes have been paid by the owners. Rating schedules for 1939 and 1950 are produced.

It is established that contracts of sale relating to real property in the Minquiers have, as in the case of the Ecrehos, been passed before the competent authorities of Jersey and registered in the public registry of deeds of the Island. Examples of such registration of contracts are given for 1896, 1909 and some later years.

In 1909 Jersey customs authorities established in the Minquiers a custom-house with the arms of Jersey. The islets have been included by Jersey authorities within the scope of their census enumerations, and in 1921 an official enumerator visited the islets for the purpose of taking the census.

These various facts show that Jersey authorities have in several ways exercised ordinary local administration in respect of the Minquiers during a long period of time.

. . . .

The Court does not find that the facts, invoked by the French Government, are sufficient to show that France has a valid title to the Minquiers. As to the above-mentioned acts from the ninteenth and twentieth centuries in particular, including the buoying outside the reefs of the group, such acts can hardly be considered as sufficient evidence of the intention of that Government to act as sovereign over the islets; nor are those acts of such a character that they can be considered as involving a manifestation of State authority in respect of the islets.

The last remaining land of any size to which states assert conflicting title is in Antarctica. As the chart opposite shows,[9] claims to land there

[9] Reproduced by permission of the *American Journal of International Law*. The chart originally appeared in *A.J.I.L.*, LIV (1960) 348, in connection with Robert D. Hayton, "The Antarctic Settlement of 1959," from which the material on Antarctica is drawn.

ANTARCTICA
NATIONAL CLAIMS

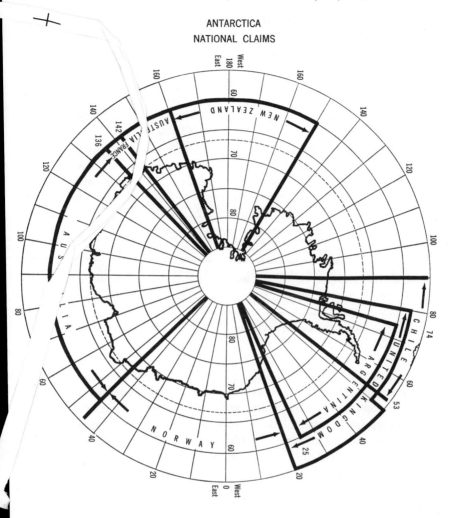

have been advanced since 1821, on the basis of landings and explorations by seven states: Australia, Argentina, Chile, France, New Zealand, Norway, and the United Kingdom. The claims of Argentina, Chile, and the United Kingdom overlap and, since 1949, these three countries have tried to avoid friction by barring naval demonstrations and maneuvers below the 60th parallel. Five other states have also explored in the Antarctic: Belgium, Germany, Japan, Sweden, and the United States, but none of them has formally claimed territory. In 1948, the United States actually took the lead in proposing that the seven claimant countries meet to discuss the possibilities of internationalizing the area. No other government was enthusiastic about this idea, however, and nothing more was done until the eighteen-month International Geophysical Year (IGY) of 1957–1958, when scientists conducted an international research program on the understanding that their work was to be nonpolitical and would not affect territorial claims one way or another.

The Soviet Union, which objected in 1948 to its having been omitted from the list of states concerned about the Antarctic, engaged very actively in the IGY, and fears that the political cold war might extend to the South Pole revived states' interest in coming to some international understanding affecting the Antarctic. The Australian government was particularly apprehensive because Soviet scientists had been assigned to work in an area within the Australian sector.

The United States again took the initiative and, in the spring of 1958, President Eisenhower called for an international conference to perpetuate the era of good feeling that had existed during the IGY. Specifically, he proposed that "Antarctica . . . be open to all nations to conduct scientific or other peaceful activities there."[10] As a result, twelve states (the seven claimants, together with Belgium, Japan, the Union of South Africa, the Soviet Union, and the United States) signed a treaty in 1959, which outlaws military activity and nuclear explosions and bars new territorial claims in the region, and neither confirms nor denies earlier claims. The treaty holds all these claims in abeyance, where they will probably remain until someone discovers some very valuable raw material. Such a discovery would renew pressure on all governments to acquire definite rights in Antarctica. Although the treaty did not go so far as to establish an international administration for Antarctica, some observers hoped that the provisions, allowing a representative of each of the twelve signatories to name inspectors to go anywhere in the Antarctic at any time to inspect installations and activity there, would become useful precedents for regulating armaments and controlling outer space.[11]

Cession usually takes place by purchase or, more frequently, after conquest. Purchases are rare, but students of American history will recall the Gadsden Purchase of 1853 when the United States paid Mexico $10 million for a tract of land in the Southwest, and the purchase of Alaska from Russia in 1867 for $7.2 million. The title passes in these cases with the treaties concluded at the time of purchase. Cession by

---

[10] *D.S.B.*, XXXVIII (1958) 910.
[11] For text, see *U.N.T.S.*, I. No. 5778, vol. 402 (1959) 71.

conquest, *e.g.*, the acquisition from Mexico by cession after war in 1848 of about one quarter of the continental United States, also rests upon treaties concluded after the military action and not upon the act of conquest itself.

Accretion is the gradual increase of land on coasts or shores.

Avulsion is a sudden removal of land from the estate of one party to that of another, as in a sudden change in the course of water. When either accretion or avulsion occurs on an ocean coast because of natural phenomena or human engineering, no international problems arise. Thus, the Dutch need not formally appropriate the land they are constantly redeeming from the sea. But when new land comes into being along the banks of a river, marking an international border, the legal problems may became quite complex. Lands formed by accretion generally belong to the state on whose side of the boundary line the formation occurs. But new land formed by avulsion does not cause a change in boundary.[12] How complex the problems of avulsion can be is well illustrated in the Chamizal arbitration case between the United States and Mexico.

THE CHAMIZAL ARBITRATION

UNITED STATES—MEXICO, INTERNATIONAL BOUNDARY
COMMISSION, CONSTITUTED BY THE TREATY OF
JUNE 24, 1910. 1911

5 *A.J.I.L.* (1911), 782

. . . The Chamizal tract consists of about six hundred acres, and lies between the old bed of the Rio Grande, as it was surveyed in 1852, and the present bed of the river. . . . It is the result of changes which have taken place through the action of the water upon the banks of the river causing the river to move southward into Mexican territory.

With the progressive movement of the river to the south, the American city of El Paso has been extending on the accretions formed by the action of the river on its north bank, while the Mexican city of Juarez to the south has suffered a corresponding loss of territory.

By the Treaties of 1848 and 1853 the Rio Grande, from a point a little higher than the present City of El Paso to its mouth in the Gulf of Mexico, was constituted the boundary line between the United States and Mexico.

The contention on behalf of the United States of Mexico is that this dividing line was fixed, under those treaties, in a permanent and invariable manner, and consequently that the changes which have taken place in the river have not affected the boundary line which was established and marked in 1852.

[12] Hyde, I, 355–356 and Hackworth, I, 409.

On behalf of the United States of America it is contended that according to the true intent and meaning of the Treaties of 1848 and 1853, if the channel of the river changes by gradual accretion the boundary follows the channel, and that it is only in case of a sudden change of bed that the river ceases to be the boundary, which then remains in the abandoned bed of the river.

It is further contended on behalf of the United States of America that by the terms of a subsequent boundary convention in 1884, rules of interpretation were adopted which became applicable to all changes in the Rio Grande, which have occurred since the river became the international boundary, and that the changes which determined the formation of the Chamizal tract are changes resulting from slow and gradual erosion and deposit of alluvion within the meaning of that convention, and consequently changes which left the channel of the river as the international boundary line.

The Mexican Government, on the other hand, contends that the Chamizal tract having been formed before the coming in force of the Convention of 1884, that convention was not retroactive and could not affect the title to the tract, and further contends that even assuming the case to be governed by the Convention of 1884 the changes in the channel have not been the result of slow and gradual erosion and deposit of alluvion.

Finally the United States of America have set up a claim to the Chamizal tract by prescription, alleged to result from the undisturbed, uninterrupted, and unchallanged possession of the territory since the Treaty of 1848.

. . . .

FIXED LINE THEORY

. . . .

The Treaty of Guadalupe Hidalgo, signed on the 2nd February, 1848, provides that the boundary line between the two republics from the Gulf of Mexico shall be the middle of the Rio Grande, following the deepest channel where it has more than one, to the point where it strikes the southern boundary of New Mexico. It is conceded, on both sides, that if this provision stood alone it would undoubtedly constitute a natural, or arcifinious, boundary between the two nations and that according to well-known principles of international law, this fluvial boundary would continue, notwithstanding modifications of the course of the river caused by gradual accretion on the one bank or degradation of the other bank; whereas if the river deserted its original bed and forced for itself a new channel in another direction the boundary would remain in the middle of the deserted river bed. It is contended, however, on behalf of Mexico, that the provisions in the treaty providing for a designation of the boundary line with due precision, upon authoritative maps, and for establishing upon the grounds landmarks showing the limits of both republics, and the direction to commissioners and surveyors to run and mark the boundary in its full course to the mouth of the Rio Grande, coupled with the final stipulation that the boundary line thus established should be religiously respected by the two republics, and no change should ever be made therein, except by the express and free consent of both nations, takes this case out of the ordinary rules of international law, and by a conventional agreement converts a natural, or arcifinious, boundary into an artificial and invariable one. In support of this contention copious references have been made to the Civil Law, distinguishing between lands whose limits were established by fixed measurements (*agri limitati*) and arcifinious lands, which were not so limited (*agri arcifinii*). These two classes of lands were sometimes contrasted by saying that arcifinious lands were those which had natural boundaries, such as mountains and rivers, while limited estates were those which had fixed measurements. As a consequence of this distinction the Roman Law denied the existence of the right of alluvion in favor of the limited estates which it was the custom to distribute among the Roman generals, and subsequently to the Legionaries, out of conquered territory. This restriction of the ordinary rights appurtenant to riparian ownership is however considered, by the best authorities, to have been an exceptional provision applicable only to the case above mentioned, and one of the principal authorities relied on by the Mexican counsel . . . clearly establishes that the mere fact that a riparian proprietor holds under a title which gives him a specified number of acres of land does not prevent him from profiting by alluvion. The difficulty in this case does not arise from the fact that the territories in question are established by any measurement, but because the boundary is ordered to be run and marked along the fluvial portion as well as on the land, and on account of the further stipulation that no change shall ever be made therein. Do these provisions and expression, in so far as they refer to the fluvial portion of the boundary, convert it into an artificial boundary which will persist notwithstanding all changes in the course of the river? In one sense it may be said that the adoption of a fixed and invariable line, so far as the river is concerned, would not be a perpetual retaining of the river boundary provided for by the treaty, and would be at variance with the agreement of the parties that the boundary should forever run in the middle of the river. The direction as to marking the course of the river as it existed at the time of the Treaty of 1848 is not inconsistent with a fluvial line varying only in accordance with the general rules of international law, by erosion on one bank and alluvial deposits on the other bank, for this marking of the boundary may serve the purpose of preserving a record of the old river bed to serve as a boundary in cases in which it cuts a new channel.

Numerous treaties containing provisions as to river boundaries have been referred to by the two parties, showing that in some cases conventional arrangements are made that the river *simpliciter* shall be the boundary, or that the boundary shall run along the middle of the river, or along the thalweg or center or thread of the channel, while a small number of treaties contain elaborate disposition for a fixed line boundary, notwithstanding the alterations which may take place in the river, with provision, however, for periodical readjustments in certain specified cases. The difficulty with these instances is that no cases appear to have arisen upon the treaties in question and their provisions throw little, if any, light upon the present controversy. In one case only among those cited there appears to have been a decision by the Court of Cassation in France (Dalloz, 1858, Part 1, p. 401) holding that when a river separates two departments or two districts, the boundary is fixed in an irrevocable manner along the middle of the bed of the river as it existed at the time of the establishment of the boundary and that it is not subject to any subsequent variation, notwithstanding the changes in the river. Whatever authority this decision may have in the delimitation of departmental boundaries in France, it does not seem to be in accordance with recognized principles of international law, if, as appears from the report, it holds that the mere designation of a river as a boundary establishes a fixed and invariable line.

The above observation as to the Treaty of 1848 would seem to apply to the Gadsden Treaty of 1853, taken by itself, for it provides, in similar language, that the boundary shall follow the middle of the Rio Grande, that the boundary line shall be established and marked, and that the dividing line shall in all time be faithfully respected by the two governments without any variation therein.

While, however, the Treaty of 1848 standing alone, or the Treaty of 1853, standing alone, might seem to be more consistent with the idea of a fixed boundary than one which would vary by reason of alluvial processes, the language of the Treaty of 1853, taken in conjunction with the existing circumstances, renders it difficult to accept the idea of a fixed and invariable boundary. During the five years which elapsed between the two treaties, notable variations of the course of the Rio Grande took place, to such an extent that surveys made in the early part of 1853, at intervals of six months, revealed discrepancies which are accounted for only by reason of the changes which the river had undergone in the meantime. Notwithstanding the existence of such changes, the Treaty of 1853 reiterates the provision that the boundary line runs up the middle of the river, which could not have been an accurate statement upon the fixed line theory.

Some stress has been laid upon the observations contained in the records of the Boundary Commissioners that the line they were fixing would be thenceforth invariable, but apart from the inconclusive character of this conversation, it seems clear that in making any remarks of this nature, the Boundary Commissioners were exceeding their mandate, and that their views as to the proper construction of the treaties under which they were working could not in any way bind their respective governments.

In November, 1856, the draft for the proposed report of the Boundary Commissioners for determining the boundary between Mexico and the United States under the Treaty of 1853 was submitted by the Secretary of the Interior of the United States to the Honorable Caleb Cushing for his opinion as to whether the boundary line under the treaty shifted with changes taking place in the bed of the river, or whether the line remained constant where the main course of the river ran as represented by the maps accompanying the report of the Commissioners. The opinion of Mr. Cushing is a valuable contribution to the subject by an authority on international law. After consideration of the provisions of the treaty, and an examination of a great number of authorities upon the subject, Mr. Cushing reported that the Rio Grande retained its function of an international boundary, notwithstanding changes brought about by accretion to one bank and the degradation of the other bank, but that, on the other hand, if the river deserted its original bed and forced for itself a new channel in another direction, then the nation through whose territory the river thus broke its way did not lose the land so separated; the international boundary in that case remaining in the middle of the deserted river bed.

This opinion was transmitted to the Mexican Legation at Washington and acknowledged by Senor Romero, then Mexican Ambassador at Washington, who, without in any way committing his government, stated his own personal acquiescence in the principles enunciated as being equitable and founded upon the teachings of the most accredited expositors of international law. He further stated that he was transmitting a copy of the opinion to his government. There does not appear to have been any expression of opinion by the Mexican Government at that time as to the soundness of the views expressed by the Hon. Mr. Cushing.

. . . .

It is in consequence of this legitimate doubt as to the true construction of the boundary treaties of 1848 and 1853 that the subsequent course of conduct of the parties, and their formal conventions, may be resorted to as aids to construction. In the opinion of the majority of this Commission the language of the subsequent conventions, and the consistent course of conduct of the high contracting parties, is wholly incompatible with the existence of a fixed line boundary.

In 1884, the following boundary convention was concluded between the two republics:

. . . .

ARTICLE I

The dividing line shall forever be that described in the aforesaid Treaty and follow the centre of the normal channel of the rivers named, notwithstanding any alterations in the banks or in the course of those rivers, provided that such alterations be effected by natural causes through the slow and gradual erosion and deposit of alluvium and not by the abandonment of an existing river bed and the opening of a new one.

. . . .

ARTICLE II

Any other change, wrought by the force of the current, whether by the cutting of a new bed, or when there is more than one channel by the deepening of another channel than that which marked the boundary at the time of the survey made under the aforesaid Treaty, shall produce no change in the dividing line as fixed by the surveys of the International Boundary Commissions in 1852; but the line then fixed shall continue to follow the middle of the original channel bed, even though this should become wholly dry or be obstructed by deposits.

. . . .

On behalf of Mexico it has been strenuously contended that this convention was intended to operate in the future only, and that it should not be given a retroactive effect so as to apply to any changes which had previously occurred. Reference was made to a number of well-known authorities establishing the proposition that laws and treaties are not usually deemed to be retrospective in their effect. An equally well-known exception to this rule is that of laws or treaties which are intended to be declaratory, and which evidence the intention of putting an end to controversies by adopting a rule of construction applicable to laws or conventions which have been subject to dispute. The internal evidence contained in the Convention of 1884 appears to be sufficient to show an intention to apply the rules laid down for the determination of difficulties which might arise through the changes in the river Rio Grande, whether these changes had occurred prior to or after the convention, and they appear to have been intended to codify the rules for the interpretation of the previous Treaties of 1848 and 1853 which had formed the subject of diplomatic correspondence between the parties. While it is perfectly true that the convention was to be applied to *disputes* which might arise in future, it nowhere restricts these difficulties to future changes in the river. It expressly declares that by the Treaties of 1848 and 1853, the dividing line had followed the middle of the river, and that henceforth the same rule was to apply.

. . . .

On the whole, it appears to be impossible to come to any other conclusion than that the two nations have, by their subsequent treaties and their consistent course of conduct in connection with all cases arising thereunder, put such an authoritative interpretation upon the language of the Treaties of 1848 and 1853 as to preclude them from now contending that the fluvial portion of the boundary created by those treaties is a fixed line boundary.

The Presiding Commissioner and the American Commissioner therefore hold that the Treaties of 1848 and 1853, as interpreted by subsequent conventions between the parties and by their course of conduct, created an arcifinious boundary, and that the Convention of 1884 was intended to be and was made retroactive by the high contracting parties.

. . . .

PRESCRIPTION

. . . .

In one of the affidavits filed by the United States to prove their possession and control over the Chamizal district (that of Mr. Coldwell) we find the following significant statement:

In 1874 or 1875 I was present at an interview between my father and Mr. Jesus Necobar Y. Armendariz, then Mexican Collector of Customs at Paso del Norte, now Ciudad Juarez, which meeting took place at my father's office on this side of the river.

Mr. Necobar asked my father for permission to station a Mexican Custom House officer on the road leading from El Paso to Juarez, about 200 or 300 yards north of the river. My father replied in substance that he had no authority to grant any such permission, and even if he had, and granted permission, it would not be safe for a Mexican Customs officer to attempt to exercise any authority on this side of the river.

It is quite clear from the circumstances related in this affidavit that however much the Mexicans may have desired to take physical possession of the district, the result of any attempt to do so would have provoked scenes of violence and the Republic of Mexico can not be blamed for resorting to the milder forms of protest contained in its diplomatic correspondence.

In private law, the interruption of prescription is effected by a suit, but in dealings between nations this is of course impossible, unless and until an international tribunal is established for such purpose. In the present case, the Mexican claim was asserted before the International Boundary Commission within a reasonable time after it commenced to exercise its functions, and prior to that date the Mexican Government had done all that could be reasonably required of it by way of protest against the alleged encroachment.

Under these circumstances the Commissioners have no difficulty in coming to the conclusion that the plea of prescription should be dismissed.

APPLICATION OF THE CONVENTION OF 1884

Upon the application of the Convention of 1884 to the facts of this case the commissioners are unable to agree.

The Presiding Commissioner and the Mexican Commissioner are of the opinion that the evidence establishes that from 1852 to 1864 the changes in the river, which during that interval formed a portion of the Chamizal tract, were caused by slow and gradual erosion and deposit of alluvium within the meaning of Article I of the Convention of 1884.

They are further of opinion that all the changes which have taken place in the Chamizal district from 1852 up to the present date have not resulted from any change of bed of the river. It is sufficiently shown that the Mexican bank opposite the Chamizal tract was at all times high and that it was never overflowed, and there is no evidence tending to show that the Rio Grande in that vicinity ever abandoned its existing bed and opened a new one. The changes, such as they were, resulted from the degradation of the Mexican bank, and the alluvial deposits formed on the American bank, and as has been said, up to 1864 this erosion and deposit appears to come within Article I of the Convention of 1884.

With respect to the nature of the changes which occurred in 1864, and during the four succeeding years, the Presiding Commissioner and the Mexican Commissioner are of opinion that the phenomena described by the witnesses

as having occurred during that period can not properly be described as alterations in the river effected through the slow and gradual erosion and deposit
of alluvium.

The following extracts from the evidence are quoted by the Presiding Commissioner and the Mexican Commissioner in support of their views:

Jesus Serna—Q. When the change took place was it slow or violent?
A. The change was violent, and destroyed the trees, crops and houses.
Ynocente Ochoa—Q. When the change took place was it slow or violent?
A. As I said before, it was sometimes slow and sometimes violent, and with
such force that the noise of the banks falling seemed like the boom of cannon,
and it was frightful.
E. Provincio—Q. Explain how you know what you have stated.
A. Because the violent changes of the river in 1864 caused considerable alarm
to the city, and the people went to the banks of the river and pulled down
trees and tried to check the advance of the waters. I was there sometimes to help
and sometimes simply to observe. I helped to take out furniture from houses in
danger and to remove beams of houses, etc.
Q. When the change took place was it slow or violent?
A. I cannot appreciate what is meant by slow or violent, but sometimes as
much as fifty yards would be washed away at certain points in a day.

. . . .

Q. Please describe the destruction of the bank on the Mexican side that you
spoke of in your former testimony. Describe the size of the pieces of earth that
you saw fall into the river.
A. When the river made the alarming change it carried away pieces of earth
one yard, two yards, etc., constantly, in intervals of a few minutes. At the time
of these changes the people would be standing on the banks watching a piece
going down, and somebody would call "look out, there is more going to fall"
and they would have to jump back to keep from falling into the river.

. . . .

Q. Do you think that those works were constructed to protect against the slow
and gradual work of the river or against the floods?
A. They were made to protect the town from being carried away in the event
of another flood like that of '64, because the curve that the river had made was
dangerous to the town.
Jose M. Flores—Q. Did the current come with such violence between 1864
and 1868 that houses and fields were destroyed?
A. Yes, sir.

. . . .

Q. Please describe the manner of the tearing away of the Mexican bank by the
current when these changes were taking place.
A. The current carried the sand from the bank and cut in under, and then
these pieces would fall into the water. If the bank was very high it took larger
pieces; say two yards, never more than three yards wide, and where the banks
were low it took smaller pieces.

Doctor Mariano Samanieco describes the violence of the change as follows:

The changes were to such a degree that at times during the night the river would wear away from fifty to one hundred yards. There were instances in which people living in houses distant fifty yards from the banks on one evening had to fly in the morning from the place on account of the encroachments of the river, and on many occasions they had no time to cut down their wheat or other crops. It carried away forests without giving time to the people to cut the trees down.

Q. Of the changes of the river that you have mentioned, were they all perceptible to the eye?

A. Yes, sir.

The Presiding Commissioner and the Mexican Commissioner consider that the changes referred to in this testimony can not by any stretch of the imagination, or elasticity of language, be characterized as slow and gradual erosion.

The case of *Nebraska* v. *Iowa* (143 U.S. 359), decided by the Supreme Court of the United States in 1892, is clearly distinguishable from the present case. In *Nebraska* v. *Iowa* the court, applying the ordinary rules of international law to a fluvial boundary between two States, hold that while there might be an instantaneous and obvious dropping into the Missouri River of quite a portion of its banks, and while the disappearance, by reason of this process, of a mass of bank might be sudden and obvious, the accretion to the other side was always gradual and by the imperceptible deposit of floating particles of earth. The conclusion was, therefore, that notwithstanding the rapidity of the changes in the course of the channel, and the washing from the one side onto the other, the law of accretion controlled on the Missouri River, as elsewhere.

· ·

In the present case, however, while the accretion may have been slow and gradual, the parties have expressly contracted that not only the accretion, but the erosion, must be slow and gradual. The Convention of 1884 expressly adopts a rule of construction which is to be applied to the fluvial boundary created by the Treaties of 1848 and 1853, and this rule is manifestly different from that which was applied in the case of *Nebraska* v. *Iowa,* in which the court was not dealing with a special contract. If it had been called upon, in the case just cited, to decide whether the degradation of the bank of the Missouri River had occurred through a slow and gradual process the answer would undoubtedly have been in the negative.

· ·

It has been suggested, and the American Commissioner is of opinion, that the bed of the Rio Grande as it existed in 1864, before the flood, can not be located, and moreover that the present Commissioners are not authorized by the Convention of the 5th December, 1910, to divide the Chamizal tract and attribute a portion thereof to the United States and another portion to Mexico. The Presiding Commissioner and the Mexican Commissioner can not assent to this view and conceive that in dividing the tract in question between the parties, according to the evidence as they appreciate it, they are following the precedent laid down by the Supreme Court of the United States in *Nebraska* v. *Iowa*. . . . In that case the court found that up to the year 1877 the changes in the Missouri River were due to accretion, and that, in that year, the river made for itself a new channel. Upon these findings it was held that the boundary between Iowa and Nebraska was a varying line in so far as affected by accretion, but that from and after 1877 the boundary was not changed, and remained as it was before the cutting of a new channel. Applying this principle, *mutatis mutandis,* to the present case, the Presiding Commissioner and Mexican Commissioner are of opinion that the accretions which occurred in the Chamizal tract up to the time of the great flood in 1864 should be awarded to the United States of America, and that inasmuch as the changes which occurred in that year did not constitute slow and gradual erosion within the meaning of the Convention of 1884, the balance of the tract should be awarded to Mexico.

They also conceive that it is not within their province to relocate that line, inasmuch as the parties have offered no evidence to enable the Commissioners to do so. In the case of *Nebraska v. Iowa* the court contented itself with indicating, as above stated, the boundary between the two States and invited the parties to agree to a designation of the boundary upon the principles enunciated in the decision.

. . . .

Wherefore the Presiding Commissioner and the Mexican Commissioner, constituting a majority of the said Commission, hereby award and declare that the international title to the portion of the Chamizal tract lying between the middle of the bed of the Rio Grande, as surveyed by Emory and Salazar in 1852, and the middle of the bed of the said river as it existed before the flood of 1864, is in the United States of America, and the international title to the balance of the said Chamizal tract is in the United States of Mexico.

The American Commissioner dissents from the above award.

E. LaFleur
Anson Mills
F. B. Puga
[Commissioners]

DEPARTMENT OF STATE PRESS RELEASE NO. 448,
Aug. 29, 1963; 49 *D.S.B.* 480 (1963)

A Convention between the United States of America and the United Mexican States for the Solution of the Problem of The Chamizal was concluded today in Mexico City. . . .

This convention comprises essentially the proposed terms of settlement announced by the Department of State and the Mexican Ministry of Foreign Relations on July 18 (Department of State Press Release No. 375), and approved by the Presidents of the two countries.

The convention will now be submitted to the respective Senates of the two countries for advice and consent to ratification. If it meets with the approval of the two Senates, the Department will seek enabling legislation and appropriations from the United States Congress to provide for execution of its terms so far as the United States is concerned. Thereafter, in accordance with the convention, the United States Section of the International Boundary and Water Commission would proceed to acquire the lands and structures to be transferred to Mexico, and when the lands have been evacuated, and the structures passing intact to Mexico have been paid for by a Mexican banking institution, these lands and structures would be transferred to Mexico. The Mexican Government would at the same time transfer to the United States approximately one half of Cordova Island, a Mexican enclave north of the present channel of the Rio Grande. The International Commission would then relocate the Rio Grande at El Paso so that all Mexican territory in that area would be south of the new river channel.

This is the first bilateral treaty concluded with the Government of Mexico since 1949 and the first major boundary agreement reached since 1933. The Department of State looks upon the Chamizal convention as a notable achievement in inter-American relations and as a major contribution in the peaceful settlement of boundary disputes.

[The Senate consented to the Treaty on December 17, 1963, and it has been in force since January 14, 1964.]

CONVENTION BETWEEN THE UNITED STATES OF AMERICA AND THE UNITED MEXICAN STATES FOR THE SOLUTION OF THE PROBLEM OF THE CHAMIZAL

The United States of America and the United Mexican States: animated by the spirit of good neighborliness which has made possible the amicable solution of various problems which have arisen between them; desiring to arrive at a complete solution of the problem concerning El Chamizal, an area of land situated to the north of the Rio Grande, in the El Paso-Ciudad Juarez region; considering that the recommendations of the Department of State of the United States and the Ministry of Foreign Relations of Mexico of July 17, 1963, have been approved by the Presidents of the two Republics; desiring to give effect to the 1911 arbitration award in today's circumstances and in keeping with the joint communique of the Presidents of the United States and of Mexico issued on June 30, 1962; and convinced of the need for continuing the program of rectification and stabilization of the Rio Grande which has been carried out under the terms of the Convention of February 1, 1933, by improving the channel in the El Paso-Ciudad Juarez region, have resolved to conclude a Convention and for this purpose have named as their plenipotentiaries:

The President of the United States of America:

His Excellency Thomas C. Mann, Ambassador of the United States of America to Mexico, and

The President of the United Mexican States:

His Excellency Manuel Tello, Minister of Foreign Relations,

who, having communicated to each other their respective Full Powers, found to be in good and due form, have agreed as follows:

ARTICLE 1

In the El Paso-Ciudad Juarez Sector, the Rio Grande shall be relocated into a new channel in accordance with the engineering plan recommended in Minute No. 214 of the International Boundary and Water Commission, United States and Mexico. Authentic copies of the Minute and of the map attached thereto, on which the new channel is shown, are annexed to this Convention and made a part hereof. [For map, see p. 143.]

ARTICLE 2

The river channel shall be relocated so as to transfer from the north to the south of the Rio Grande a tract of 823.50 acres composed of 366.00 acres in the Chamizal tract, 193.16 acres in the southern part of Cordova Island, and 264.34 acres to the east of Cordova Island. A tract of 193.16 acres in the northern part of Cordova Island will remain to the north of the river.

ARTICLE 3

The center line of the new river channel shall be the international boundary. The lands that, as a result of the relocation of the river channel, shall be to the north of the center line of the new channel shall be the territory of the United States of America and the lands that shall be to the south of the center line of the new channel shall be the territory of the United Mexican States.

ARTICLE 4

No payments will be made, as between the two Governments, for the value of the lands that pass from one country to the other as a result of the relocation of the international boundary. The lands that, upon relocation of the international boundary, pass from one country to the other shall pass to the respective Governments in absolute ownership, free of any private titles or encumbrances of any kind.

ARTICLE 5

The Government of Mexico shall convey to the Banco Nacional Hipotecario Urbano y de Obras Publicas, S.A., titles to the properties comprised of the structures which pass intact to Mexico and the lands on which they stand. The Bank shall pay the Government of Mexico for the value of the lands on which such structures are situated and the Government of the United States for the estimated value to Mexico of the said structures.

ARTICLE 6

After this Convention has entered into force and the necessary legislation has been enacted for carrying it out, the two Governments shall, on the basis of a recommendation by the International Boundary and Water Commission, determine the period of time appropriate for the Government of the United States to complete the following:

(a) The acquisition, in conformity with its laws, of the lands to be transferred to Mexico and for the rights of way for that portion of the new river channel in the territory of the United States;

(b) The orderly evacuation of the occupants of the lands referred to in paragraph (a).

ARTICLE 7

As soon as the operations provided in the preceding article have been completed, and the payment made by the Banco Nacional Hipotecario Urbano y de Obras Publicas, S.A., to the Government of the United States as provided in Article 5, the Government of the United States shall so inform the Government of Mexico. The International Boundary and Water Commission shall then proceed to demarcate the new international boundary, recording the demarcation in a Minute. The relocation of the international boundary and the transfer of lands provided for in this Convention shall take place upon express approval of that Minute by both Governments in accordance with the procedure established in the second paragraph of Article 25 of the Treaty of February 3, 1944.

ARTICLE 8

The costs of constructing the new river channel shall be borne in equal parts by the two Governments. However, each Government shall bear the costs of compensation for the value of the structures or improvements which must be destroyed, within the territory under its jurisdiction prior to the relocation of the international boundary, in the process of constructing the new channel.

ARTICLE 9

The International Boundary and Water Commission is charged with the relocation of the river channel, the construction of the bridges herein provided for, and the maintenance, preservation and improvement of the new channel. The Commission's jurisdiction and responsibilities, set forth in Article XI of the 1933 Convention for the maintenance and preservation of the Rio Grande Rectification Project, are extended upstream from that part of the river included in the Project to the point where the Rio Grande meets the land boundary between the two countries.

ARTICLE 10

The six existing bridges shall, as a part of the relocation of the river channel, be replaced by new bridges. The cost of constructing the new bridges shall be borne in equal parts by the two Governments. The bridges which replace those on Stanton-Lerdo and Santa Fe-Juarez streets shall be located on the same streets. The location of the bridge or bridges which replace the two Cordova Island bridges shall be determined by the International Boundary and Water Commission. The agreements now in force which relate to the four existing bridges between El Paso and Ciudad Juarez shall apply to the new international bridges which replace them. The international bridge or bridges which replace the two Cordova Island bridges shall be toll free unless both Governments agree to the contrary.

ARTICLE 11

The relocation of the international boundary and the transfer of portions of territory resulting therefrom shall not affect in any way:

(a) The legal status, with respect to citizenship laws, of those persons who are present or former residents of the portions of territory transferred;

(b) The jurisdiction over legal proceedings of either a civil or criminal character which are pending at the time of, or which were decided prior to, such relocation;

(c) The jurisdiction over acts or omissions occurring within or with respect to the said portions of territory prior to their transfer;

(d) The law or laws applicable to the acts or omissions referred to in paragraph (c).

ARTICLE 12

The present Convention shall be ratified and the instruments of ratification shall be exchanged at Mexico City as soon as possible.

The present Convention shall enter into force upon the exchange of instruments of ratification.

DONE at Mexico City the 29th day of August, 1963, in the English and Spanish languages, each text being equally authentic.

/s/ Thomas C. Mann

FOR THE GOVERNMENT OF
THE UNITED STATES OF AMERICA

/s/ Manuel Tello

FOR THE GOVERNMENT OF
THE UNITED MEXICAN STATES

Gifts of land give title to the recipient and, considering the nature of interstate relations, no one will be surprised if instances of gifts are rather rare. Nonetheless, there are a few: the British, for instance, gave

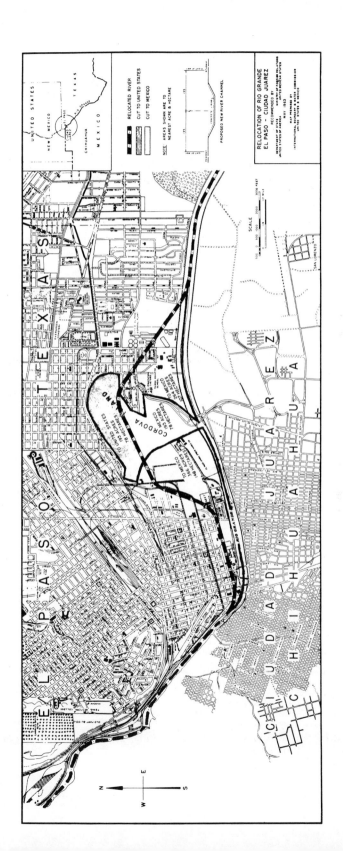

RELOCATION OF RIO GRANDE
EL PASO – CIUDAD JUAREZ

RECOMMENDED BY
DEPARTMENT OF STATE
MINISTRY OF FOREIGN RELATIONS
UNITED STATES OF AMERICA

MAY 1963

MAP PREPARED BY
INTERNATIONAL BOUNDARY & WATER COMMISSION
UNITED STATES & MEXICO

RELOCATED RIVER
CUT TO UNITED STATES
CUT TO MEXICO

NOTE: AREAS SHOWN ARE TO
NEAREST ACRE 8 HECTARE

PROPOSED NEW RIVER CHANNEL

SCALE

UNITED STATES
NEW MEXICO   TEXAS
            EL PASO
            CD. JUAREZ
CHIHUAHUA   MEXICO

the United States Horseshoe Reef in Lake Erie in 1851 on condition that the United States put up a lighthouse, which it did.[13]

Besides these arrangements for title and jurisdiction, there are legal arrangements, by which states enjoy jurisdiction, which do not fall into any established category. In the Canal Zone, for instance, the United States exercises jurisdiction without title, but it has all the rights that go with title. By Article 3 of the Isthmian Canal Convention (1903), Panama granted to the United States:

> . . . all the rights, power and authority within the [Panama Canal] Zone . . . which the United States would possess and exercise if it were the sovereign of the territory . . . to the entire exclusion of the exercise by the Republic of Panama of any such sovereign rights, power or authority.

At the same time, the United States pays Panama $400,000 annually, which, whatever it is, is not rent. This arrangement has no precedent or parallel and, since World War II, has been challenged by the Panamanian government as inconsistent with its national dignity. As a result, the United States announced in late 1964 that it planned to negotiate with Panama "an entirely new treaty" to replace that of 1903 and its amendments. In actual fact, the two states completed drafting three new treaties in mid-1967. One ends exclusive U.S. control over the Canal by establishing a nine-man commission (five U.S. nationals, four Panamanians) to operate it; increases the U.S. annual payment to Panama to $17.1 million; and provides for Panama eventually to have full control over the Canal. The second treaty gives the U.S. the right to build a new sea-level canal in Panama; and the third allows the U.S. to maintain military bases in Panama to defend the waterway. The drafts have encountered opposition in both countries and were not ratified by mid-1968.[14]

Also, there are *trusteeships* under the United Nations, by which states exercise jurisdiction over certain territories. This jurisdiction is exercised under authority of the United Nations Charter and special subsidiary agreements, but it affects few areas. Of the eleven trusteeships in 1949, only two remained after 1967, New Guinea and the Pacific Islands.

One final mode of acquiring jurisdiction is *prescription*, an undisturbed and continuous exercise of dominion by states over territory, which eventually gives title to it. The theory operating here is that, after considerable time, an unchallenged title is a good title. It is noteworthy that the United States unsuccessfully invoked prescription in the Chamizal

[13] Moore, *Digest*, I, 554 and V, 215.
[14] See the *New York Times*, September 14, 1967, p. 12; November 7, 1967, p. 35; December 2, 1967, p. 29.

Arbitration and fought the prescriptive claims of the Netherlands in the Las Palmas case. More recently, in 1959, the principle was unsuccessfully invoked before the International Court of Justice by the Netherlands in a frontier dispute with Belgium. The Court gave precedence to treaties, which several of the dissenting justices believed invalid for various technical reasons. Just how long a state must exercise its authority over a territory before acquiring a prescriptive right is not clear. Grotius spoke about "possession beyond memory,"[15] which is not, of course, a precise delineation. When title to land is in dispute, states not actually in possession guard against prescriptive claims by protesting the occupation of the disputed territory by their opponents. Thus, in 1961, President Frondizi of Argentina made a speech, stressing Argentinian claims to certain British dependencies in the Falkland Islands, which Argentina claims for herself. Disturbed by these remarks, and responding to them, the British Embassy in Buenos Aires delivered a note to the Argentine Foreign Office, reminding Argentina that Britain regarded the Falkland Islands Dependencies as British territory and that Britain preserved title to them. The government of Chile also reaffirmed her claims to the Islands in similar protests.[16]

CASE CONCERNING SOVEREIGNTY OVER CERTAIN FRONTIER LAND

INTERNATIONAL COURT OF JUSTICE, 1959

JUDGMENT OF 20 JUNE 1959

[1959] I.C.J. 209

The final contention of the Netherlands is that if sovereignty over the disputed plots was vested in Belgium by virtue of the Boundary Convention, acts of sovereignty exercised by the Netherlands since 1843 have established sovereignty in the Netherlands.

The weight to be attached to the acts relied upon by the Netherlands must be determined against the background of the complex system of intermingled enclaves which existed. The difficulties confronting Belgium in detecting encroachments upon, and in exercising, its sovereignty over these two plots, surrounded as they were by Netherlands territory, are manifest. The acts relied upon are largely of a routine and administrative character performed by local officials and a consequence of the inclusion by the Netherlands of the disputed plots in its Survey, contrary to the Boundary Convention.

---

[15] *De Jure Belli ac Pacis*, Lib. II, Cap. IV, 9.
[16] *New York Times*, March 15, 1961, p. 15; March 18, 1961, p. 2; and March 19, 1961, p. 26.

They are insufficient to displace Belgian sovereignty established by that Convention.

Having examined the situation which has obtained in respect of the disputed plots and the facts relied upon by the two Governments, the Court reaches the conclusion that Belgian sovereignty established in 1843 over the disputed plots has not been extinguished.

For these reasons,

THE COURT,

by ten votes to four,

finds that sovereignty over the plots shown in the survey and known from 1836 to 1843 as Nos. 91 and 92, Section A, Zondereygen, belongs to the Kingdom of Belgium.

Judge Sir Hersch LAUTERPACHT makes the following Declaration:

I have voted in favour of a decision determining that the sovereignty over the plots in dispute belongs to the Netherlands.

I am of the opinion that the relevant provisions of the Convention must be considered as void and inapplicable on account of uncertainty and unresolved discrepancy.

The Special Agreement of 26 November, 1957, submitting the dispute to the Court is by design so phrased as not to confine its function to giving a decision based exclusively on the Convention of 1843. By the generality of its terms it leaves it open to the Court to determine the question of sovereignty by reference to all relevant considerations—whether based on the Convention or not. Accordingly, in the circumstances, it seems proper that a decision be rendered by reference to the fact, which is not disputed, that at least during the fifty years following the adoption of the Convention there has been no challenge to the exercise, by the Government of the Netherlands and its officials, of normal administrative authority with regard to the plots in question. In my opinion, there is no room here for applying the exacting rules of prescription in relation to a title acquired by a clear and unequivocal treaty; there is no such treaty. It has been contended that the uninterrupted administrative activity of the Netherlands was due not to any recognition of Netherlands sovereignty on the part of Belgium but to the fact that the plots in question are an enclave within Netherlands territory and that, therefore, it was natural that Netherlands administrative acts should have been performed there in the ordinary course of affairs. However, the fact that local conditions have necessitated the normal and unchallenged exercise of Netherlands administrative activity provides an additional reason why, in the absence of clear provisions of a treaty, there is no necessity to disturb the existing state of affairs and to perpetuate a geographical anomaly.

DISSENTING OPINION OF JUDGE ARMAND-UGON

In all the foregoing cases, the Netherlands Government has exercised preponderant governmental functions in respect of the disputed plots, without these having given rise on the part of the Belgian Government to any protest or any opposition. This prolonged tolerance of the Belgian Government in this respect has created an indisputable right of sovereignty in favour the the Netherlands Government. There is no evidence that Belgium claimed restitution of the parcels before 1921, or that any Belgian activities occurred thereon. Reference may here be made to the importance which the Court gave, in the Fisheries case, to the absence of protests by a government in the consolidation of a right (*I.C.J. Report 1951*, p. 138). In the Eastern Greenland case the Permanent Court did not consider that it could neglect governmental acts, even when the Norwegian Government had made certain protests or reservations (*P.C.I.J., Series A/B, No. 53*, pp. 62–63), for it recognized the existence of two elements required to establish a valid title to sovereignty, namely, the intention and the will to exercise such sovereignty, and the manifestation of State activity. Sovereignty over the Minquiers and Ecrehos was decided by this Court exclusively on the basis of facts similar to those relied upon by the Netherlands Government in the present case (*I.C.J. Reports 1953*, pp. 67–70).

Such an intention to exercise sovereignty is particularly notable after the Convention of 1843 and after the draft Convention of 1892. The Netherlands Government has continued to regard these plots as belonging to it, and to exercise there governmental functions in a public and peaceable way. These facts have established Netherlands sovereignty over the disputed plots.

✤　✤　✤

In the final analysis, Article 90 of the Descriptive Minute which is annexed to the Convention of 1843 and which is a part of that Convention provides in the first part that the Communal Minute signed on 22 March 1841 shall be inserted "word for word" as a second part of Article 90. But the Minute which is reproduced is not a literal copy of the Communal Minute signed on 22 March 1841. What is involved is a provision of the Convention of 1843 which is not legally valid. Such a provision cannot constitute a valid title of sovereignty.

On the other hand, the title which is based on the effective, peaceable and public exercise of State functions by the Netherlands over the disputed plots must be given preference over the title of sovereignty relied upon by Belgium, which has never really exercised the State competence which it regards itself as holding.

(*Signed*) ARMAND-UGON.

ARBITRAL AWARD

THE ISLAND OF PALMAS (OR MIANGAS)

April 4, 1928

Reports of International Arbitral Awards, II, 829; 22 A.J.I.L. (1928), 867

If in a dispute as to sovereignty over a portion of territory, one party's claim is based on the fact of the actual exercise of sovereignty, it cannot be sufficient for the other party to establish the title by which the territory was validly acquired at a certain moment; it must also be shown that the territorial sovereignty has continued to exist and did exist at the moment which for the decision of the dispute must be considered as critical.

Territorial sovereignty involves the exclusive right to display the activities of a state and has as a corollary certain international duties. It cannot limit itself to the negative side of excluding the activities of other states. International law cannot be presumed to reduce a right such as territorial sovereignty, with which almost all international relations are bound up, to the category of an abstract right, without concrete manifestations.

The claim of the United States to sovereignty over the Island of Palmas (or Miangas) is derived from Spain by way of cession under the Treaty of Paris of 1898. The treaty, though it comprises the island in dispute within the limits of cession, and in spite of the absence of any reserves or protest by the Netherlands as to these limits, has not created in favor of the United States any title of sovereignty such as was not already vested in Spain.

The United States base their claim on the titles of discovery, of recognition by treaty, and of contiguity. They have, however, not established the fact that the sovereignty so acquired was effectively displayed at any time. The title of discovery, if it had not been already disposed of by the treaties of Münster and Utrecht, would exist only as an inchoate title, as a claim to establish sovereignty by effective occupation. An inchoate title, however, can not prevail over a definite title founded on continuous and peaceful display of sovereignty. The title of contiguity as a basis of territorial sovereignty has no foundation in international law. The title of recognition by treaty does not apply.

The Netherlands found their claim to sovereignty essentially on a title of the peaceful and continuous display of state authority over the island (so-called prescription). The Netherlands have established by competent evidence that the island has formed a part of native states which were from 1677 onwards connected with the East India Company, and thereby with the Netherlands, by contracts of suzerainty which conferred upon the suzerain such powers as would justify his considering the vassal state as a part of his territory. Acts characteristic of state authority exercised either by the vassal state or by the Suzerain Power have been established as occurring at different epochs between 1700 and 1906.

The acts of Netherlands sovereignty displayed in the eighteenth and early nineteenth centuries are not numerous, but the manifestations of sovereignty over a small and distant island, inhabited only by natives, can not be expected to be frequent. Neither is it necessary that the display of sovereignty should be established as having been begun at a precise date in and continued from a far distant period. It suffices if such display existed openly and publicly in the critical period preceding the year 1898 and had existed as continuous and peaceful before that date long enough to give any other claimant Power a reasonable possibility, according to local conditions, to ascertain the existing state of things.

The evidence relating to the period after the middle of the nineteenth century makes it clear that the Netherlands Indian Government considered the island distinctly as a part of its possessions and that, in the years immediately preceding 1898 an intensification of display of sovereignty took place. There is, moreover, no evidence which would establish any act of display of sovereignty over the island by Spain or another Power to counterbalance or annihilate the manifestations of Netherlands sovereignty.

The evidence which tends to show the unchallenged acts of peaceful display of Netherlands sovereignty in the period from 1700 to 1906 may be regarded as sufficiently proving the existence of Netherlands sovereignty.

[Part I omitted]

II

The subject of the dispute is the sovereignty over the Island of Palmas (or Miangas) . . . a single, isolated island . . . about half way between Cape San Augustin (Mindanao, Philippine Islands) and the most northerly island of the Nanusa (Nanoesa) group (Netherlands East Indies).

The origin of the dispute is to be found in the visit paid to the Island of Palmas (or Miangas) on January 21, 1906, by General Leonard Wood, who was then Governor of the Province of Moro [Philippines]. . . . This visit led to the statement that the Island . . . undoubtedly included in the "archipelago known as the Philippine Islands," as delimited by Article III of the treaty of peace between the United States and Spain, dated December 10, 1898 (hereinafter also called Treaty of Paris) and ceded in virtue of the said article to the United States, was considered by the Netherlands as forming part of the territory of their possessions in the West Indies. There followed a diplomatic correspondence, beginning on March 31, 1906, and leading up to the special agreement of January 23, 1925 [providing for this arbitration].

. . . sovereignty in relation to a portion of the surface of the globe is the legal condition necessary for the inclusion of such portion in the territory of any particular State. . . .

Sovereignty in the relation between States signifies independence. Independence in regard to a portion of the globe is the right to exercise therein to the exclusion of any other State, the functions of a State. The development of the national organization of States during the last few centuries and, as a corollary, the development of international law, have established this principle of the exclusive competence of the State in regard to its own territory in such a way as to make it the point of departure in settling most questions that concern international relations. . . .

Territorial sovereignty is, in general, a situation recognized and delimited in space, either by so-called natural frontiers as recognized by international law or by outward signs of delimitation that are undisputed, or else by legal engagements entered into between interested neighbors, such as frontier conventions, or by acts of recognition of States within fixed boundaries. If a dispute arises as to the sovereignty over a portion of territory, it is customary to examine which of the states claiming sovereignty possesses a title—cession, conquest, occupation, etc.—superior to that which the other state might possibly bring forward against it. However, if the contestation is based on the act that the other party has actually displayed sovereignty, it cannot be sufficient to establish the title by which territorial sovereignty was validly acquired at a certain moment; it must also be shown that the territorial sovereignty has continued to exist and did exist at the moment which for the decision of the dispute must be considered as critical. The demonstration consists in the actual display of state activities, such as belongs only to the territorial sovereign.

Titles of acquisition of territorial sovereignty in present-day international law are either based on an act of effective apprehension, such as occupation or conquest, or, like cession, presuppose that the ceding and the cessionary Powers or at least one of them, have the faculty of effectively disposing of the ceded territory. In the same way natural accretion can only be conceived of as an accretion to a portion of territory where there exists an actual sovereignty capable of extending to a spot which falls within its sphere of activity. It seems therefore natural that an element which is essential for the constitution of sovereignty should not be lacking in its continuation. So true is this, that practice, as well as doctrine, recognizes—though under different legal formulae and with certain differences as to the conditions required—that the continuous and peaceful display of territorial sovereignty (peaceful in relation to other States) is as good as a title. The growing insistence with which international law, ever since the middle of the eighteenth century, has demanded that the occupation shall be effective would be inconceivable, if effectiveness were required only for the act of acquisition and not equally for the maintenance of the right. If the effectiveness has above all been insisted on in regard to occupation, this is because the question rarely arises in connection with territories in which there is already an established order of things. Just as before the rise of international law, boundaries of lands were necessarily determined by the fact that the power of a State was exercised within them, so too, under the reign of international law, the fact of peaceful and continuous display is still one of the most important considerations in establishing boundaries between states.

Territorial sovereignty, as has already been said, involves the exclusive right to display the activities of a state. This right has as corollary a duty: the obligation to protect within the territory the rights of other states, in particular their right to integrity and inviolability in peace and in war, together with the rights which each state may claim for its nationals in foreign territory. Without manifesting its territorial sovereignty in a manner corresponding to circumstances, the state cannot fulfil this duty. Territorial sovereignty cannot limit itself to its negative side, i.e., to excluding the activities of other states; for it serves to divide between nations the space upon which human activities are employed, in order to assure them at all points the minimum of protection of which international law is the guardian.

Although municipal law, thanks to its complete judicial system, is able to recognize abstract rights of property as existing apart from any material display of them, it has none the less limited their effect by the principles of prescription and the protection of possession. International law, the structure of which is not based on any super-State organisation, cannot be presumed to reduce a right such as territorial sovereignty, with which almost all international relations are bound up, to the category of an abstract right, without concrete manifestations.

The principle that continuous and peaceful display of the functions of State within a given region is a constituent element of territorial sovereignty is not only based on the conditions of the formation of independent States and their boundaries (as shown by the experience of political history) as well as on an international jurisprudence and doctrine widely accepted; this principle has further been recognized in more than one federal State, where a jurisdiction is established in order to apply, as need arises, rules of international law to the interstate relations of the States members. This is the more significant, in that it might well be conceived that in a federal State possessing a complete judicial system for interstate matters far more than in the domain of international relations properly so-called—there should be applied to territorial questions the principle that, failing any specific provision of law to the contrary, a *jus in re* once lawfully acquired shall prevail over *de facto* possession however well established.

It may suffice to quote among several non-dissimilar decisions of the Supreme Court of the United States of America that in the case of the State of Indiana *v.* State of Kentucky, (1890) 136 U.S. 479, where the precedent of the case of Rhode Island *v.* Massachusetts, 4 How. 591, 639, is supported by quotations from Vattel and Wheaton, who both admit prescription founded on length of time as a valid and incontestable title.

Manifestations of territorial sovereignty assume, it is true, different forms, according to conditions of time and place. Although continuous in principle, sovereignty cannot be exercised in fact at every moment on every point of a territory. The intermittence and discontinuity compatible with the maintenance of the right necessarily differ according as inhabited or uninhabited regions are involved, or regions enclosed within territories in which sovereignty is uncontestably displayed or again regions accessible from, for instance, the high seas. It is true that neighbouring States may by convention fix limits to their own sovereignty, even in regions such as the interior of scarcely explored continents where such sovereignty is scarcely manifested, and in this way each may prevent the other from any penetration of its territory. The delimitation of hinterland may also be mentioned in this connection.

If, however, no conventional line of sufficient topographical precision exists or if there are gaps in the frontiers otherwise established, or if a conventional line leaves room for doubt, or if, as *e.g.* in the case of an island situated in the high seas, the question arises whether a title is valid *erga omnes,* the actual continuous and peaceful display of State functions is in case of dispute the sound and natural criterium of territorial sovereignty.

. . . .

III

The title alleged by the United States of America as constituting the immediate foundation of its claim is that of cession, brought about by the Treaty of Paris, which cession transferred all rights of sovereignty which Spain may have possessed in the region indicated in Article III of the said Treaty and therefore also those concerning the Island of Palmas (or Miangas).

It is evident that Spain could not transfer more rights than she herself possessed. This principle of law is expressly recognized in a letter dated April 7, 1900, from the Secretary of State of the United States to the Spanish Minister at Washington concerning a divergence of opinion which arose about the question whether two islands claimed by Spain as Spanish territory and lying just outside the limits traced by the Treaty of Paris were to be considered as included in, or excluded from the cession. This letter, reproduced in the explanations of the United States Government, contains the following passage: "The metes and bounds defined in the treaty were not understood by either party to limit or extend Spain's right of cession. Were any island within those described bounds ascertained to belong in fact to Japan, China, Great-Britain or Holland, the United States could derive no valid title from its ostensible inclusion in the Spanish cession. The compact upon which the United States negotiators insisted was that all Spanish title to the archipelago known as the Philippine Islands should pass to the United States—no less or more than Spain's actual holdings therein, but all. This Government must consequently hold that the only competent and equitable test of fact by which the title to a disputed cession in that quarter may be determined is simply this: 'Was it Spain's to give? If valid title belonged to Spain, it passed; if Spain had no valid title, she could convey none.'"

Whilst there existed a divergence of views as to the extension of the cession to certain Spanish islands outside the treaty limits, it would seem that the cessionary power never envisaged that the cession, in spite of the sweeping terms of Article III, should comprise territories on which Spain had not a valid title, though falling within the limits traced by the treaty. It is evident that whatever may be the right construction of a treaty, it cannot be interpreted as disposing of the rights of independent third Powers.

. . . .

It is recognized that the United States communicated, on February 3, 1899, the Treaty of Paris to the Netherlands, and that no reservations were made by the latter in respect to the delimitation of the Philippines in Article III. The question whether the silence of a third Power, in regard to a treaty notified to it, can exercise any influence on the rights of this Power, or on those of the Powers signatories of the treaty, is a question the answer to which may depend on the nature of such rights. Whilst it is conceivable that a conventional delimitation duly notified to third Powers and left without contestation on their part may have some bearing on an inchoate title not supported by any actual display of sovereignty, it would be entirely contrary to the principles laid down above as to territorial sovereignty to suppose that such sovereignty could be affected by the mere silence of the territorial sovereign as regards a treaty which has been notified to him and which seems to dispose of a part of his territory.

The essential point is therefore whether the Island of Palmas (or Miangas) at the moment of the conclusion and coming into force of the Treaty of Paris formed a part of the Spanish or Netherlands territory. The United States declares that Palmas (or Miangas) was Spanish territory and denies the existence of Dutch sovereignty; the Netherlands maintain the existence of their sovereignty and deny that of Spain. Only if the examination of the arguments of both Parties should lead to the conclusion that the Island of Palmas (or Miangas) was at the critical moment neither Spanish nor Netherlands territory, would the question arise whether—and, if so, how—the conclusion of the Treaty of Paris and its notification to the Netherlands might have interfered with the rights which the Netherlands or the United States of America may claim over the island in dispute.

. . . [T]he United States bases its claim, as successor of Spain, in the first place on discovery. . . . It is admitted by both sides that international law underwent profound modifications between the end of the Middle-Ages and the end of the 19th century, as regards the rights of discovery and acquisition of uninhabited regions or regions inhabited by savages or semi-civilised peoples. Both parties are also agreed that a juridical fact must be appreciated in the light of the law contemporary with it, and not of the law in force at the time when a dispute in regard to it arises or falls to be settled. The effect of discovery by Spain is therefore to be determined by the rules of international law in force in the first half of the sixteenth century—or (to take the earliest date) in the first quarter of it, *i.e.* at the time when the Portuguese or Spaniards made their appearance in the Sea of Celebes.

If the view most favourable to the American arguments is adopted—with every reservation as to the soundness of such view—that is to say, if we consider as positive law at the period in question the rule that discovery as such, *i.e.* the mere fact of seeing land, without any act, even symbolical, of taking possession, involved *ipso jure* territorial sovereignty and not merely an "inchoate title," a *jus ad rem*, to be completed eventually by an actual and durable taking of possession within a reasonable time, the question arises whether sovereignty yet existed at the critical date, *i.e.* the moment of conclusion and coming into force of the Treaty of Paris.

As regards the question which of different legal systems prevailing at successive periods is to be applied in a particular case (the so-called intertemporal law), a distinction must be made between the creation of rights and the existence of rights. The same principle which subjects the act creative of a right to the law in force at the time the right arises, demands that the existence of the right, in other words its continued manifestation, shall follow the conditions required by the evolution of law. International law in the 19th century, having regard to the fact that most parts of the globe were under the sovereignty of States members of the commmunity of nations, and that territories without a master had become relatively few, took account of a tendency already existing and especially developed since the middle of the 18th century, and laid down the principle that occupation, to constitute a claim to territorial sovereignty, must be effective, that is, offer certain guarantees to other States and their nationals. It seems therefore incompatible with this rule of positive law that there should be regions which are neither under the effective sovereignty of a State, nor without a master, but which are reserved for the exclusive influence of one State, in virtue solely of a title of acquisition which is no longer recognized by existing law, even if such a title ever conferred territorial sovereignty. For these reasons, discovery alone, without any subsequent act, cannot at the present time suffice to prove sovereignty over the Island of Palmas (or Miangas); and in so far as there is no sovereignty, the question of an abandonment properly speaking of sovereignty by one State in order that the sovereignty of another may take its place does not arise.

If on the other hand the view is adopted that discovery does not create a definitive title of sovereignty, but only an "inchoate" title, such a title exists, it is true, without external manifestation. However, according to the view that has prevailed at any rate since the nineteenth century, an inchoate title of discovery must be completed within a reasonable period by the effective occupation of the region claimed to be discovered. This principle must be applied in the present case, for the reasons given above in regard to the rules determining which of successive legal systems is to be applied. . . . Now, no act of occupation nor, except as to a recent period, any exercise of sovereignty at Palmas by Spain has been alleged. But even admitting that the Spanish title still existed as inchoate in 1898 and must be considered as included in the cession under Article III of the Treaty of Paris, an inchoate title could not prevail over the continuous and peaceful display of authority by another State; for such display may prevail even over a prior, definitive title put forward by another State. This point will be considered, when the Netherlands argument has been examined and the allegations of either Party as to the display of their authority can be compared.

. . . .

In the last place there remains to be considered title arising out of contiguity. Although States have in certain circumstances maintained that islands relatively close to their shores belonged to them in virtue of their geographical situation, it is impossible to show the existence of a rule of positive international law to the effect that islands situated outside territorial waters should belong to a State from the mere fact that its territory forms the *terra firma* (nearest continent or island of considerable size). Not only would it seem that there are no precedents sufficiently frequent and sufficiently precise in their bearing to establish such a rule of international law, but the alleged principle itself is by its very nature so uncertain and contested that even governments of the same State have on different occasions maintained contradictory opinions as to its soundness. The principle of contiguity, in regard to islands, may not be out of place when it is a question of allotting them to one State rather than another, either by agreement between the parties, or by a decision not necessarily based on law; but as a rule establishing *ipso jure* the presumption of sovereignty in favour of a particular State, this principle would be in conflict with what has been said as to territorial sovereignty and as to the necessary relation between the right to exclude other States from a region and the duty to display therein the activities of a State. Nor is this principle of contiguity admissible as a legal method of deciding questions of territorial sovereignty; for it is wholly lacking in precision and would in its application lead to arbitrary results.

. . . .

[IV]

The questions to be solved in the present case are the following:

Was the Island of Palmas (or Miangas) in 1898 a part of territory under Netherlands sovereignty?

Did this sovereignty actually exist in 1898 in regard to Palmas (or Miangas) and are the facts proved which were alleged on this subject?

If the claim to sovereignty is based on the continuous and peaceful display of state authority, the fact of such display must be shown precisely in relation to the disputed territory. It is not necessary that there should be a special administration established in this territory; but it cannot suffice for the territory to be attached to another by a legal relation which is not recognized in international law as valid against a state contesting this claim to sovereignty; what is essential in such a case is the continuous and peaceful display of actual power in the contested region.

. . . .

However much the opinions of the parties may differ as to the existence of proof of the display of Dutch sovereignty over the Island of Palmas (or Miangas), the reports, furnished by both sides, of the visit of General Wood, in January 1906, show that at that time there were at least traces of continuous relations between the island in dispute and neighboring Dutch possessions, and even traces of Dutch sovereignty. General Wood noted his surprise that the Dutch flag was flying on the beach and on the boat which came to meet the American ship. According to information gathered by him, the flag had been there for 15 years and perhaps even longer. Since the contract of 1885 with Taruna and that of 1899 with Kandahar-Taruna comprise Palmas (or Miangas) within the territories of a native state under the suzerainty of the Netherlands and since it has been established that in 1906 on the said island a state of things existed showing at least certain traces of display of Netherlands sovereignty, it is now necessary to examine what is the nature of the facts invoked as proving such sovereignty, and to what periods such facts relate. This examination will show whether or not the Netherlands have displayed sovereignty over the Island of Palmas (or Miangas) in an effective continuous and peaceful manner at a period at which such exercise may have excluded the acquisition of sovereignty, or a title to such acquisition, by the United States of America.

Before beginning to consider the facts alleged by the Netherlands in support of their arguments, there are two preliminary points, in regard to which the parties also put forward different views, which require elucidation. These relate to questions raised by the United States: firstly the power of the East India Company to act validly under international law, on behalf of the Netherlands, in particular by concluding so-called political contracts with native rulers; secondly the identity or non-identity of the island in dispute with the island to which the allegations of the Netherlands as to display of sovereignty would seem to relate.

The acts of the East India Company *Generale Geoctroyeerde Nederlandsch Oost-Indische Compagnie*), in view of occupying or colonizing the regions at issue in the present affair must, in international law, be entirely assimilated to acts of the Netherlands state itself. From the end of the sixteenth till the nineteenth century, companies formed by individuals and engaged in economic pursuits (chartered companies), were invested by the states to whom they were subject with public powers for the acquisition and administration of colonies. The Dutch East India Company is one of the best known. Article V of the Treaty of Münster and consequently also the Treaty of Utrecht clearly show that the East and West India Companies were entitled to create situations recognized by international law; for the peace between Spain and the Netherlands extends to *"tous Potentats, nations et peuples"* with whom the said companies, in the name of the States of the Netherlands, *"entre les limites de leurdits Octroys sont en Amitié et Alliance."* The conclusion of conventions, even of a political nature, was, by Article XXXV of the charter of 1602, within the powers of the company. It is a question for decision in each individual case whether a contract concluded by the company falls within the range of simple economic transactions or is of a political and public administrative nature.

As regards contracts between a state or a company such as the Dutch East India Company and native princes or chiefs of peoples not recognized as members of the community of nations, they are not, in the international law sense, treaties or conventions capable of creating rights and obligations such as may, in international law, arise out of treaties. But, on the other hand, contracts of this nature are not wholly void of indirect effects on situations governed by international law; if they do not constitute titles in international law, they are nonetheless facts of which that law must in certain circumstances take account. From the time of the discoveries until recent times, colonial territory has very often been acquired, especially in the East Indies, by means of contracts with the native authorities, which contracts leave the existing organization more or less intact as regards the native population, whilst granting to the colonizing Power, besides economic advantages such as monopolies or navigation and commercial privileges, also the exclusive direction of relations with other Powers, and the right to exercise public authority in regard to their own nationals and to foreigners. The form of the legal relations created by such contracts is most generally that of suzerain and vassal, or of the so-called colonial protectorate.

In substance, it is not an agreement between equals; it is rather a form of internal organization of a colonial territory, on the basis of autonomy for the natives. In order to regularize the situation as regards other states, this organization requires to be completed by the establishment of powers to ensure the fulfilment of the obligations imposed by international law on every state in regard to its own territory. And thus suzerainty over the native state becomes the basis of territorial sovereignty as towards other members of the community of nations. It is the sum-total of functions thus allotted either to the native authorities or to those of the colonial Power which decides the question whether at any certain period the conditions required for the existence of sovereignty are fulfilled. It is a question to be decided in each case whether such a régime is to be considered as effective or whether it is essentially fictitious, either for the whole or a part of the territory. There always remains reserved the question whether the establishment of such a system is not forbidden by the pre-existing rights of other states.

The point of view here adopted by the arbitrator is—at least in principle—in conformity with the attitude taken up by the United States in the note already quoted above, from the Secretary of State to the Spanish Minister, dated January 7, 1900 and relating to two small islands lying just outside the line drawn by the Treaty of Paris, but claimed by the United States under the said treaty. The note states that the two islands "have not hitherto been directly administered by Spain, but have been successfully claimed by Spain as a part of the dominions of her subject, the Sultan of Sulu. As such they have been administered by Sulu agencies, under some vague form of resident supervision by Spanish agencies, which latter have been withdrawn as a result of the recent war."

This system of contracts between colonial Powers and native princes and chiefs is even expressly approved by Article V of the Treaty of Münster quoted above; for, among the "Potentates, Nations and Peoples," with whom the Dutch state or companies may have concluded treaties of alliance and friendship in the East and West Indies, are necessarily the native princes and chiefs.

The arbitrator can therefore not exclude the contracts invoked by the Netherlands from being taken into consideration in the present case.

. . . .

V

The conclusions to be derived from the above examination of the arguments of the Parties are the following:

The claim of the United States to sovereignty over the Island of Palmas (or Miangas) is derived from Spain by way of cession under the Treaty of Paris. The latter Treaty, though it comprises the island in dispute within the limits of cession, and in spite of the absence of any reserves or protest by the Netherlands as to these limits, has not created in favour of the United

States any title of sovereignty such as was not already vested in Spain. The essential point is therefore to decide whether Spain had sovereignty over Palmas (or Miangas) at the time of the coming into force of the Treaty of Paris.

The United States base their claim on the titles of discovery, of recognition by treaty and of contiguity, *i.e.* titles relating to acts or circumstances leading to the acquisition of sovereignty; they have however not established the fact that sovereignty so acquired was effectively displayed at any time.

The Netherlands on the contrary found their claim to sovereignty essentially on the title of peaceful and continuous display of State authority over the island. Since this title would in international law prevail over a title of acquisition of sovereignty not followed by actual display of State authority, it is necessary to ascertain in the first place, whether the contention of the Netherlands is sufficiently established by evidence, and, if so, for what period of time.

In the opinion of the Arbitrator the Netherlands have succeeded in establishing the following facts:

a. The Island of Palmas (or Miangas) is identical with an island designated by this or a similar name, which has formed, at least since 1700, successively a part of two of the native States of the Island of Sangi (Talautse Isles).

b. These native States were from 1677 onwards connected with the East India Company, and thereby with the Netherlands, by contracts of suzerainty, which conferred upon the suzerain such powers as would justify his considering the vassal State as a part of his territory.

c. Acts characteristic of State authority exercised either by the vassal State or by the suzerain Power in regard precisely to the Island of Palmas (or Miangas) have been established as occurring at different epochs between 1700 and 1898, as well as in the period between 1898 and 1906.

The acts of indirect or direct display of Netherlands sovereignty at Palmas (or Miangas), especially in the 18th and early 19th centuries are not numerous, and there are considerable gaps in the evidence of continuous display. But apart from the consideration that the manifestations of sovereignty over a small and distant island, inhabited only by natives, cannot be expected to be frequent, it is not necessary that the display of sovereignty should go back to a very far distant period. It may suffice that such display existed in 1898, and had already existed as continuous and peaceful before that date long enough to enable any Power who might have considered herself as possessing sovereignty over the island, or having a claim to sovereignty, to have, according to local conditions, a reasonable possibility for ascertaining the existence of a state of things contrary to her real or alleged rights.

It is not necessary that the display of sovereignty should be established as having begun at a precise epoch; it suffices that it had existed at the critical period preceding the year 1898. It is quite natural that the establishment of sovereignty may be the outcome of a slow evolution, of a progressive intensification of state control. This is particularly the case, if sovereignty is acquired by the establishment of the suzerainty of a colonial Power over a native state, and in regard to outlying possessions of such a vassal state.

Now the evidence relating to the period after the middle of the 19th century makes it clear that the Netherlands Indian Government considered the island distinctly as a part of its possessions and that, in the years immediately preceding 1898, an intensification of display of sovereignty took place.

Since the moment when the Spaniards, in withdrawing from the Moluccas in 1666, made express reservations as to the maintenance of their sovereign rights up to the contestation made by the United States in 1906, no contestation or other action whatever or protest against the exercise of territorial rights by the Netherlands over the Talautse (Sangi) Isles and their dependencies (Miangas included) has been recorded. The peaceful character of the display of Netherlands sovereignty for the entire period to which the evidence concerning acts of display relates (1700–1906) must be admitted.

There is moreover no evidence which would establish any act of display of sovereignty over the island by Spain or another Power, such as might counterbalance or annihilate the manifestations of Netherlands sovereignty. As to third Powers, the evidence submitted to the Tribunal does not disclose any trace of such action, at least from the middle of the 17th century onwards. These circumstances, together with the absence of any evidence of a conflict between Spanish and Netherlands authorities during more than two centuries as regards Palmas (or Miangas), are an indirect proof of the exclusive display of Netherlands sovereignty.

This being so, it remains to be considered first whether the display of State authority might not be legally defective and therefore unable to create a valid title of sovereignty, and secondly whether the United States may not put forward a better title to that of the Netherlands.

As to the conditions of acquisition of sovereignty by way of continuous and peaceful display of State authority (so-called prescription), some of which have been discussed in the United States counter memorandum, the following must be said:

The display has been open and public, that is to say that it was in conformity with usages as to exercise of sovereignty over colonial States. A clandestine exercise of State authority over an inhabited territory during a considerable length of time would seem to be impossible. An obligation for the Netherlands to notify to other Powers the establishment of suzerainty over the Sangi States or of the display of sovereignty in these territories did not exist.

Such notification, like any other formal act, can only be the condition of legality as a consequence of an explicit rule of law. A rule of this kind adopted by the Powers in 1885 for the African continent does not apply *de plano* to other regions, and thus the contract with Taruna of 1885, or with Kandahar-Taruna of 1889, even if they were to be considered as the first assertions of sovereignty over Palmas (or Miangas) would not be subject to the rule of notification.

There can further be no doubt that the Netherlands exercised the State authority over the Sangi States as sovereign in their own right, not under a derived or precarious title.

. . . .

The conditions of acquisition of sovereignty by the Netherlands are therefore to be considered as fulfilled. It remains now to be seen whether the United States as successors of Spain are in a position to bring forward an equivalent or stronger title. This is to be answered in the negative.

The title of discovery, if it had not been already disposed of by the Treaties of Münster and Utrecht would, under the most favourable and most extensive interpretation, exist only as an inchoate title, as a claim to establish sovereignty by effective occupation. An inchoate title however cannot prevail over a definite title founded on continuous and peaceful display of sovereignty.

The title of contiguity, understood as a basis of territorial sovereignty, has no foundation in international law.

. . . .

The Netherlands title of sovereignty, acquired by continuous and peaceful display of State authority during a long period of time going probably back beyond the year 1700, therefore holds good.

. . . .

Supposing that, at the time of the coming into force of the Treaty of Paris, the Island of Palmas (or Miangas) did not form part of the territory of any State, Spain would have been able to cede only the rights which she might possibly derive from discovery or contiguity. On the other hand, the inchoate title of the Netherlands could not have been modified by a treaty concluded between third Powers; and such a treaty could not have impressed the character of illegality on any act undertaken by the Netherlands with a view to completing their inchoate title—at least as long as no dispute on the matter had arisen, *i.e.* until 1906.

Now it appears from the report on the visit of General Wood to Palmas (or Miangas), on January 21, 1906, that the establishment of Netherlands authority, attested also by external signs of sovereignty, had already reached such a degree of development, that the importance of maintaining this state of things ought to be considered as prevailing over a claim possibly based either on discovery in very distant times and unsupported by occupation, or on mere geographical position.

This is the conclusion reached on the ground of the relative strength of the titles invoked by each Party, and founded exclusively on a limited part of the evidence concerning the epoch immediately preceding the rise of the dispute.

This same conclusion must impose itself with still greater force if there be taken into consideration—as the Arbitrator considers should be done—all the evidence which tends to show that there were unchallenged acts of peaceful display of Netherlands sovereignty in the period from 1700 to 1906, and which—as has been stated above—may be regarded as sufficiently proving the existence of Netherlands sovereignty.

For these reasons the Arbitrator, in conformity with Article I of the Special Agreement of January 23, 1925 decides that: The Island of Palmas (or Miangas) forms in its entirety a part of Netherlands territory.

CLIPPERTON ISLAND ARBITRATION

France–Mexico, 1931

As Translated in 26 *A.J.I.L.* (1932), 390

Victor Emmanuel III, Arbitrator

. . . .

Considering the agreement signed at Mexico March 2, 1909, by which the Government of the French Republic and that of the Republic of Mexico have referred to our arbitration the solution of the difference which has arisen between the high contracting parties on the subject of the sovereignty over Clipperton Island; . . . we find, in the first place, that on November 17, 1858, Lieutenant Victor Le Coat de Kerwéguen, of the French Navy, commissioner of the French Government, while cruising about one-half mile off Clipperton, drew up, on board the commercial vessel *L'Amiral,* an act by which, conformably to the orders which had been given to him by the Minister of Marine, he proclaimed and declared that the sovereignty of the said island beginning from that date belonged in perpetuity to His Majesty the Emperor Napoleon III and to his heirs and successors. During the cruise, careful and minute geographical notes were made; a boat succeeded, after numerous difficulties, in landing some members of the crew; and on the evening of November 20, after a second unsuccessful attempt to reach the shore, the vessel put off without leaving in the island any sign of sovereignty. Lieut. de Kerwéguen officially notified the accomplishment of his mission to the Consulate of France at Honolulu, which made a like communication to the Government of Hawaii. Moreover, the same consulate had published in English in the journal *The Polynesian,* of Honolulu, on December 8, the declaration by which French sovereignty over Clipperton had already been proclaimed.

Thereafter, until the end of 1887 no positive and apparent act of sovereignty can be recalled either on the part of France or on the part of any other Powers. The island remained without population, at least stable, and no administration was organized there. A concession for the exploitation of guano beds existing there, which had been approved by the Emperor on April 8, 1858, in favor of a certain Mr. Lockart, and which had given rise to the expedition of Lieut. de Kerwéguen, had not been followed up, nor had its exploitation been undertaken on the part of any other French subjects.

Towards the end of 1897, precisely the 24th of November of that year,

France stated, through the Chief of the Naval Division of the Pacific Ocean, which was charged with the examination of the matter, that three persons were found in the island collecting guano for the account of the Oceanic Phosphate Co., of San Francisco, and that they had, on the appearance of the French vessel, raised the American flag. Explanations were demanded on this subject from the United States, which responded that it had not granted any concession to the said company and did not intend to claim any right of sovereignty over Clipperton (January 28, 1898).

About a month after this act of surveillance had been accomplished by the French Navy, and while the diplomatic action with the United States was in progress, Mexico, ignoring the occupation claimed by France and considering that Clipperton was territory belonging to her for a long time, sent to the place a gun-boat, *La Democrata*, which action was caused by the report, afterwards acknowledged to be inaccurate, that England had designs upon the island. A detachment of officers and marines landed from the said ship December 13, 1897, and again found the three persons who resided on the island at the time of the preceding arrival of the French ship. It made them lower the American flag and hoist the Mexican flag in its place. Of the three individuals above mentioned, two consented to leave the island, and the third declared his wish to remain there, and in fact remained there until an unknown date. After that the *Democrata* left on December 15.

On January 8, France, having learned of the Mexican expedition, reminded that Power of its rights over Clipperton. From then a very long diplomatic discussion took place which lasted until the date when, by the agreement of March 2, 1909, the two governments decided to refer to our arbitration the solution of the difference relative to sovereignty over the island.

. . . Mexico [maintains] that Clipperton Island already belonged to her before France had proclaimed her sovereignty over the said island. If this claim should be recognized as founded, it would be necessary to conclude that the occupation of the said island by France was unlawful.

According to Mexico, Clipperton Island, which had been given the name of the famous English adventurer who, at the beginning of the 18th century, used it as a place of refuge, was none other than Passion Island, called also Medano or Medanos Island, that this island had been discovered by the Spanish Navy and, by virtue of the law then in force, fixed by the Bull of Alexander VII, had belonged to Spain, and afterwards, from 1836, to Mexico as the successor state of the Spanish State.

But according to the actual state of our knowledge, it has not been proven that this island, by whatever name one may call it, had been actually discovered by the Spanish navigators. . . . However, even admitting that the discovery had been made by Spanish subjects, it would be necessary, to establish the contention of Mexico, to prove that Spain not only had the right, as a state, to incorporate the island in her possessions, but also had effectively exercised the right. But that has not been demonstrated at all. . . .

Moreover, the proof of an historic right of Mexico's is not supported by any manifestation of her sovereignty over the island, a sovereignty never exercised until the expedition of 1897; and the mere conviction that this was territory belonging to Mexico, although general and of long standing, cannot be retained.

Consequently, there is ground to admit that, when in November, 1858, France proclaimed her sovereignty over Clipperton, that island was in the legal situation of *territorium nullius,* and, therefore, susceptible of occupation.

The question remains whether France proceeded to an effective occupation, satisfying the conditions required by international law for the validity of this kind of territorial acquisition. In effect, Mexico maintains, secondarily to her principal contention which has just been examined, that the French occupation was not valid, and consequently her own right to occupy the island which must still be considered as *nullius* in 1897.

In whatever concerns this question, there is, first of all, ground to hold as incontestable, the regularity of the act by which France in 1858 made known in a clear and precise manner, her intention to consider the island as her territory.

On the other hand, it is disputed that France took effective possession of the island, and it is maintained that without such a taking of possession of an effective character, the occupation must be considered as null and void.

It is beyond doubt that by immemorial usage having the force of law, besides the *animus occupandi,* the actual, and not the nominal, taking of possession is a necessary condition of occupation. This taking of possession consists in the act, or series of acts, by which the occupying State reduces to its possession the territory in question and takes steps to exercise exclusive authority there. Strictly speaking, and in ordinary cases, that only takes place when the State establishes in the territory itself an organization capable of making its laws respected. But this step is, properly speaking, but a means of procedure to the taking of possession, and, therefore, is not identical with the latter. There may also be cases where it is unnecessary to have recourse to this method. Thus, if a territory, by virtue of the fact that it was completely uninhabited, is, from the first moment when the occupying State makes its appearance there, at the absolute and undisputed disposition of that State, from that moment the taking of possession must be considered as accomplished, and the occupation is thereby completed. . . .

The regularity of the French occupation has also been questioned because the other Powers were not notified of it. But . . . the notoriety given to the act, by whatever means, sufficed at the time, and that France provoked that notoriety by publishing the said act in the manner above indicated.

It follows from these premises that Clipperton Island was legitimately acquired by France on November 17, 1858. There is no reason to suppose that France has subsequently lost her right by *derelictio,* since she never had the *animus* of abandoning the island, and the fact that she has not exercised her authority there in a positive manner does not imply the forfeiture of an acquisition already definitively perfected.

FOR THESE REASONS, we decide, as arbiter, that the sovereignty over Clipperton Island belongs to France, dating from November 17, 1858.

No matter how a state acquires control over its territory, it may exercise full jurisdiction over it—prescribing property rights, regulating trade and the practice of professions, defining civil rights for nationals and aliens, and establishing judicial processes among other things—so long as it does not, in exercising its jurisdiction, interfere with the authority of other states.[17] A state must protect the rights of other states within its own territory and may not lawfully use its own territory as a base of operations designed to injure neighboring states.

A state may, for instance, lawfully expropriate property if, at the same time, it protects the property rights of foreign nationals and foreign governments (see Chapter V). A state may raise troops for its own defense, but it may not lawfully use those troops to harass its neighbors. Thus the Security Council and General Assembly of the United Nations acted fully in accordance with existing law when they sought to protect the territorial integrity of Lebanon in 1958. The words of the resolutions follow:

The Security Council
Having heard the charges of the representative of Lebanon concerning interference by the United Arab Republic in the internal affairs of Lebanon and the reply of the representative of the United Arab Republic,
Decides to dispatch urgently an observation group to proceed to Lebanon so as to ensure that there is no illegal infiltration of personnel or supply of arms or other *matériel* across the Lebanese borders. . . .[18]

The General Assembly. . . .
Noting that the Arab States have agreed, in the Pact of the League of Arab States, to strengthen the close relations and numerous ties which link the Arab States, and to support and stabilize these ties upon a basis of respect for the independence and sovereignty of these States, and to direct their efforts toward the common good of all the Arab countries, the improvement of their status, the security of their future and the realization of their aspirations and hopes,
Desiring to relieve international tension,

I

1. *Welcomes* the renewed assurances given by the Arab States to observe the provision of article 8 of the Pact of the League of Arab States that each member State shall respect the systems of government established in the other member States and regard them as exclusive concerns of these

[17] See *The Lotus*, p. 4, and the Trail Smelter Arbitration, p. 180–181.
[18] S/4023 (11 June 1958).

States, and that each shall pledge to abstain from any action calculated to change established systems of government;

2. *Calls upon* all States Members of the United Nations to act strictly in accordance with the principles of mutual respect for each other's territorial integrity and sovereignty, of non-aggression of strict non-interference in each other's internal affairs, and of equal and mutual benefit, and to ensure that their conduct by word and deed conforms to these principles. . . .[19]

In December 1965, the United Nations General Assembly attempted to put the seal on the integrity of states by adopting a declaration (G.A. Res. 2131 [XX], adopted by a vote of 109-0-1, the U.K. abstaining) on the inadmissibility of intervention in the domestic affairs of other states and the protection of their independence and sovereignty. Although heavily laden with political overtones and originally intended when introduced by the Soviet Union as a weapon against United States policies in Vietnam, the declaration, as amended, may be read to condemn those policies which both the Soviet Union and the United States object to in each other:

The General Assembly

Deeply concerned at the gravity of the international situation and the increasing threat soaring over universal peace due to armed intervention and other direct or indirect forms of interference threatening the sovereign personality and the political independence of States,

Considering that the United Nations, according to their aim to eliminate war, threats to the peace and acts of aggression, created an Organization, based on the sovereign equality of States, whose friendly relations would be based on respect for the principle of equal rights and self-determination of peoples and on the obligation to its Members to refrain from the threat or use of force against the territorial integrity or political independence of any State,

Recognizing that, in fulfilment of the principle of self-determination, the General Assembly, by the Declaration on the Granting of Independence to Colonial Countries and Peoples contained in resolution 1514 (XV), stated its conviction that all peoples have an inalienable right to complete freedom, the exercise of their sovereignty and the integrity of their national territory and that, by virtue of that right, they freely determine their political status and freely pursue their economic, social and cultural development,

Recalling that in the Universal Declaration of Human Rights the Assembly proclaimed that recognition of the inherent dignity and of the equal and inalienable rights of all members of the human family is the foundation of freedom, justice and peace in the world, without distinction of any kind,

Reaffirming the principle of non-intervention, proclaimed in the charters of the Organization of American States, the League of Arab States and of

[19] G. A. Res. 1237 (ES-III), 21 August 1958.

the Organization of African Unity and affirmed in the Conferences of Montevideo, Buenos Aires, Chapultepec and Bogotá, as well as in the decisions of the Afro-Asian Conference in Bandung, the Conference of Non-aligned Countries in Belgrade, in the "Programme for Peace and International Co-operation," adopted at the end of the Cairo Conference of Non-Aligned Countries, and in the declaration on subversion adopted in Accra by the Heads of State or Government of the African States,

Recognizing that full observance of the principle of the non-intervention of States in the internal and external affairs of other States is essential to the fulfilment of the purposes and principles of the United Nations,

Considering that armed intervention is synonymous with aggression, and as such is contrary to the basic principles on which peaceful international co-operation between States should be built,

Considering further that direct intervention, subversion, as well as all forms of indirect intervention are contrary to these principles and, consequently, a violation of the Charter of the United Nations,

Mindful that violation of the principle of non-intervention poses a threat to the independence and freedom and normal political, economic, social and cultural development of countries, particularly those which have freed themselves from colonialism, and can pose a serious threat to the maintenance of peace,

Fully aware of the imperative need to create appropriate conditions which would enable all States, and in particular the developing countries, to choose without duress or coercion their own political, economic and social institutions,

In the light of the foregoing considerations, the General Assembly of the United Nations solemnly declares:

1. No State has the right to intervene, directly or indirectly, for any reason whatever, in the internal or external affairs of any other State. Consequently, armed intervention as well as all other forms of interference or attempted threats against the personality of the State or against its political, economic and cultural elements, are condemned;

2. No State may use or encourage the use of economic, political or any other type of measures to coerce another State in order to obtain from it the subordination of the exercise of its sovereign rights or to secure from it advantages of any kind. Also, no State shall organize, assist, foment, finance, incite or tolerate subversive, terrorist or armed activities directed to the violent overthrow of the régime of another State, or interfere in civil strife in another State;

3. The use of force to deprive peoples of their national identity constitutes a violation of their inalienable rights and of the principle of non-intervention;

4. The strict observance of these obligations is an essential condition to ensure that the nations live together in peace with one another, since the practice of any form of intervention not only violates the spirit and letter of the Charter but also leads to the creation of situations which threaten international peace and security;

5. Every State has an inalienable right to choose its political, economic, social and cultural systems, without interference in any form by another State;

6. All States shall respect the right of self-determination and independence of peoples and nations, to be freely exercised without any foreign pressure, and with absolute respect to human rights and fundamental freedoms. Consequently, all States shall contribute to the complete elimination of racial discrimination and colonialism in all its forms and manifestations;

7. For the purpose of this Declaration, the term "State" covers both individual States and groups of States;

8. Nothing in this Declaration shall be construed as affecting in any manner the relevant provisions of the Charter of the United Nations relating to the maintenance of international peace and security, in particular those contained in Chapters VI, VII, and VIII.

New problems of protecting state territory have arisen from so-called "pirate" broadcasting stations, and the states concerned have attempted, by treaty, to deal with the matter.

EUROPEAN AGREEMENT FOR THE PREVENTION OF "PIRATE" BROADCASTS[20]

[Open for signature, January 20, 1965]

C (64) 32
PL:DM:ajk
17. 12. 64.

PIRATE RADIO STATIONS

The Committee of Ministers of the Council of Europe has decided to open for signature the European Agreement for the prevention of broadcasts transmitted from stations outside national territories from 20 January 1965 onwards.

This Agreement is designed to prevent the operation of "pirate" radio stations, that is stations established outside national territories on board ships, aircraft or any other floating or airborne objects.

Contracting States will undertake to take appropriate steps, in accordance with their domestic law, against the activities of these broadcasting stations. They will punish as offences not only the establishment and the operation of "pirate" radio stations, but also any assistance to them.

Assistance, referred to in the Agreement as "acts of collaboration" will include the provision, maintenance or repairing of equipment, the provision of transport or supplies, the order or production of material for broadcasting, and the provision of services concerning advertising for the benefit of the stations.

Three ratifications or acceptances are required for the Agreement to enter into force.

[20] Council of Europe press release, December 17, 1964.

When these have been obtained, the Committee of Ministers may agree to the joining of States not members of the Council of Europe but belonging to the international Telecommunications Union.

EUROPEAN AGREEMENT FOR THE PREVENTION OF BROADCASTS TRANSMITTED FROM STATIONS OUTSIDE NATIONAL TERRITORIES

The member States of the Council of Europe signatory hereto,

Considering that the aim of the Council of Europe is to achieve a greater unity between its members;

Considering that the Radio Regulations annexed to the International Tele-communication Convention prohibit the establishment and use of broadcasting stations on board ships, aircraft or any other floating or airborne objects outside national territories;

Considering also the desirability of providing for the possibility of preventing the establishment and use of broadcasting stations on objects affixed to or supported by the bed of the sea outside national territories;

Considering the desirability of European collaboration in this matter;

Have agreed as follows:

ARTICLE 1

This Agreement is concerned with broadcasting stations which are installed or maintained on board ships, aircraft, or any other floating or airborne objects and which, outside national territories, transmit broadcasts intended for reception or capable of being received, wholly or in part, within the territory of any Contracting Party, or which cause harmful interference to any radio-communication service operating under the authority of a Contracting Party in accordance with the Radio Regulations.

ARTICLE 2

1. Each Contracting Party undertakes to take appropriate steps to make punishable as offences, in accordance with its domestic law, the establishment or operation of broadcasting stations referred to in Article 1, as well as acts of collaboration knowingly performed.

2. The following shall, in relation to broadcasting stations referred to in Article 1, be acts of collaboration:

(a) the provision, maintenance or repairing of equipment;

(b) the provision of supplies;

(c) the provision of transport for, or the transporting of, persons, equipment or supplies;

(d) the ordering or production of material of any kind; including advertisements, to be broadcast;

(e) the provision of services concerning advertising for the benefit of the stations.

ARTICLE 3

Each Contracting Party shall, in accordance with its domestic law, apply the provisions of this Agreement in regard to:

(a) its nationals who have committed any act referred to in Article 2 on its territory, ships, or aircraft, or outside national territories on any ships, aircraft or any other floating or airborne object;

(b) non-nationals who, on its territory, ships or aircraft, or on board any floating or airborne object under its jurisdiction have committed any act referred to in Article 2.

ARTICLE 4

Nothing in this Agreement shall be deemed to prevent a Contracting Party:

(a) from also treating as punishable offences acts other than those referred to in Article 2 and also applying the provisions concerned to persons other than those referred to in Article 3;

(b) from also applying the provisions of this Agreement to broadcasting stations installed or maintained on objects affixed to or supported by the bed of the sea.

ARTICLE 5

The Contracting Parties may elect not to apply the provisions of this Agreement in respect of the services of performers which have been provided elsewhere than on the stations referred to in Article 1.

ARTICLE 6

The provisions of Article 2 shall not apply to any acts performed for the purpose of giving assistance to a ship or aircraft or any other floating or airborne object in distress or of protecting human life.

ARTICLE 7

No reservation may be made to the provisions of this Agreement.

. . . .

Air and Outer Space

Jurisdiction over air and outer space is quite clearly a problem of international concern. Airplanes can move freely from one state to another only by agreement, and the rights of aircraft flow essentially from international treaties on civil aviation, such as the Chicago Convention of 1944, ratified by 115 states, which provides that every nation "has complete and exclusive sovereignty over the air space above its territory." States, for the most part, can control these air spaces either from the ground or from the air. They thus apply above the earth the essential principles that they have in modern times applied over land and water: jurisdiction rests on the ability to control the space.

For instance, American reconnaissance planes apparently surveyed the territory of the Soviet Union at an altitude of twelve miles without incident for several years in the late 1950's. The first Soviet protest came only on May 1, 1960, when the Soviet Union shot down the U-2 plane of Captain Francis Powers. The United States, while not admitting that its flights were illegal—"a distasteful but vital necessity" was what President Eisenhower called them—did not challenge the legality of the Soviet action in shooting down the plane.[21]

Control of states over the air above their territory has long been conceded. It is embraced by the Chicago convention and was conceded in 1956 in an exchange of notes between the United States and the Soviet Union regarding the flights of meteorological balloons.

SOVIET NOTE OF FEBRUARY 4 [1956][22]

[UNOFFICIAL TRANSLATION]

The Soviet Government considers it necessary to state the following to the Government of the USA:

During January of this year there have been seized in the air space of the Soviet Union a large number of aerial balloons up to fifteen meters in diameter with apparatus of various types, devices and other cargoes suspended therefrom. The above-mentioned balloons are balloons of polyethylene with capacity of up to 1600 cubic meters. The total weight of the cargo suspended from one such balloon reaches 650 kilos.

According to information at the disposal of the Soviet Government the release of these aerial balloons is carried out by American military organizations from the territory of Western Germany, and also from American air bases located on the territory of certain states bordering on the Soviet Union. The apparatus suspended from these aerial balloons includes automatically operated photo cameras for aerial survey, radio transmitters, radio receivers and other things. An examination of the captured balloons shows that both the balloons themselves and the apparatus suspended therefrom are manufactured in the United States of America. This is shown in part by such labels on various parts of the apparatus as "Made in USA" and the names of the American firms producing these parts. . . .

In addition to the above-mentioned balloons American organizations con-

---

[21] See *D.S.B.*, XLII (1960), 851–854, 900 for statements by U.S. and Soviet spokesmen. See also Quincy Wright, "Legal Aspects of the U-2 Incident." *A.J.I.L.*, LIV (1960), 836–854.

[22] *D.S.B.*, XXXIV (February 20, 1956), 293–295. See also pp. 426–428.

tinue to release into the air spaces of the Soviet Union balloons with cargo consisting of leaflets hostile to the USSR and propaganda literature.

As is known, already on September 28, 1955 the Soviet Government approached the Government of the United States on the question of the adoption of necessary measures in order that American organizations should cease the release from the territory of Western Germany of aerial balloons with cargo suspended therefrom. The Soviet Government pointed out that the flights of such balloons create a danger for airplanes flying on the internal lines of the Soviet Union and also on international lines going over the territories of the Soviet Union and of a series of European states.

. . . .

The release into the air space of the Soviet Union of balloons with the cargoes mentioned above which are carried out by American military organizations represents a crude violation of the air space of the Soviet Union and a violation of the generally accepted principle of international law in accordance with which each state has full and exclusive sovereignty in regard to the air space over its territory.

In accordance with this principle of the sovereignty of states over their air space the flight of any form of flying apparatus into the air space of any state can take place only with the permission of the state in question. In view of the foregoing the above-mentioned activities of the American military organizations represent violation of the territorial integrity of the USSR, are contrary to the obligations assumed by the United States Government under the Charter of the United Nations and are incompatible with normal relations between states.

The Soviet Government makes a decisive protest and demands from the United States Government the taking of measures for the immediate cessation of the above-mentioned impermissible activities of the American military organizations.

CORRESPONDENCE WITH U.S.S.R.
CONCERNING WEATHER BALLOONS

U.S. NOTE OF FEBRUARY 8 [1956]

PRESS RELEASE 72 DATED FEBRUARY 8 [1956]

Following is the text of the U.S. reply to the Soviet note of February 4, 1956, regarding meteorological balloons which was delivered on February 8 by the American Embassy at Moscow to the Soviet Ministry of Foreign Affairs.

The Ambassador of the United States of America presents his compliments to the Soviet Minister for Foreign Affairs and, under instructions from his Government, has the honor to reply as follows to the Soviet Government's note of February 4, 1956.

In the Soviet Government note there is an apparent confusion between a publicized meteorological operation and previous Soviet allegations concerning the launching of propaganda balloons directed toward the Soviet Union. In this latter connection, the U.S. Government recalls certain oral observations were made by the Soviet Foreign Ministry on September 28 to the American Chargé d'Affaires in Moscow who denied any U.S. Government responsibility for activities of which the Soviet Government complained. The U.S. Government wishes to reaffirm that it is not directly or indirectly participating in any project to despatch propaganda balloons over the Soviet Union.

Insofar as the Soviet Government's note pertains to meteorological balloons, the U.S. Government is happy to supply information complementary to what is already public knowledge. Under United States auspices, a meteorological survey is being carried out by the launching of balloons which are in effect miniature "satellites" and which remain aloft for several days at a very considerable height placing them out of the range of commercial aircraft. A number of balloons have been launched in several parts of the world and many have been passing over the United States. For example, a balloon sent up on January 8 in California, transited the U.S., the Atlantic Ocean, and the Eurasian Continent and was identified on January 20 transmitting homing signals from the Western Pacific.

The project was explained in a press release issued in Washington on January 8 which included pictures and details of the balloons. The Soviet Government is presumably aware of this announcement, but for convenient reference a copy is attached. While most of the balloon flights have taken place in the U.S., the announced opening of additional research stations in Europe, Alaska and Hawaii raised no objection by any government.

The balloons are equipped with instruments to measure and record meteorological phenomena such as air jet streams, and with photographic apparatus to provide pictures of cloud formations which bear on air movements at various velocities. Much valuable scientific information is being accumulated. It is hoped that this method of meteorological research will contribute substantially to the forthcoming International Geophysical Year programs.

The declared purpose of the project is made clear by the fact that the equipment itself contains instructions in several languages, including Russian, for its recovery and delivery to the authorities charged with the evaluation of the data obtained. In the interest of scientific research, it would be much appreciated if the Soviet Government would return the instruments which have come into its possession.

Similar surveys have been conducted for some time through the launching of some thousands of meteorological balloons over the United States. These have been equipped with safety devices and have constituted no hazard even to dense civilian air traffic. As explained in the announcement, the balloons observed by the Soviet Government are equipped with the same safety devices.

The United States Government would be happy to explain further to the Soviet Government the safety measures incorporated in the project. Provisionally, however, in order to avoid misunderstandings, and in view of the Soviet Government's objection, the United States Government will seek to avoid the launching of additional balloons which, on the basis of known data, might transit the USSR.

When planes are not over the territory of particular states, problems have arisen over jurisdiction, and it was to remove these difficulties in part that the members of the International Civil Aviation Organization drafted the "Convention on Offenses and Certain Other Acts Committed on Board Aircraft," opened for signature at Tokyo in September 1963.[23]

CONVENTION ON OFFENCES AND CERTAIN OTHER ACTS COMMITTED ON BOARD AIRCRAFT

THE STATES Parties to this Convention
HAVE AGREED as follows:

Chapter I—Scope of the Convention

ARTICLE 1

1. This Convention shall apply in respect of:
   (a) offences against penal law;
   (b) acts which, whether or not they are offences may or do jeopardize the the safety of the aircraft or of persons or property therein or which jeopardize good order and discipline on board.
2. Except as provided in Chapter III, this Convention shall apply in respect of offences committed or acts done by a person on board any aircraft registered in a Contracting State, while that aircraft is in flight or on the surface of the high seas or of any other area outside the territory of any State.
3. For the purposes of this Convention, an aircraft is considered to be in flight from the moment when power is applied for the purpose of take-off until the moment when the landing run ends.
4. This Convention shall not apply to aircraft used in military, customs or police services.

ARTICLE 2

Without prejudice to the provisions of Article 4 and except when the safety of the aircraft or of persons or property on board so requires, no provision

[23] The original signatories were Congo (Brazzaville), Federal Republic of Germany, Guatemala, Holy See, Indonesia, Italy, Japan, Liberia, Panama, Philippines, Republic of China, Republic of Upper Volta, Sweden, United Kingdom of Great Britain and Northern Ireland, United States of America, and Yugoslavia. The Convention remains open for signature at the Headquarters of the International Civil Aviation Organization in Montreal. It will enter into force when twelve signatory states have deposited instruments of ratification. For text. see *I.L.M.*, II (1963), 1042.

of this Convention shall be interpreted as authorizing or requiring any action in respect of offences against penal laws of a political nature or those based on racial or religious discrimination.

Chapter II—Jurisdiction

ARTICLE 3

1. The State of registration of the aircraft is competent to exercise jurisdiction over offences and acts committed on board.
2. Each Contracting State shall take such measures as may be necessary to establish its jurisdiction as the State of registration over offences committed on board aircraft registered in such State.
3. This Convention does not exclude any criminal jurisdiction exercised in accordance with national law.

ARTICLE 4

A Contracting State which is not the State of registration may not interfere with an aircraft in flight in order to exercise its criminal jurisdiction over an offence committed on board except in the following cases:
  (a) the offence has effect on the territory of such State;
  (b) the offence has been committed by or against a national or permanent resident of such State;
  (c) the offence is against the security of such State;
  (d) the offence consists of a breach of any rules or regulations relating to the flight or manoeuvre of aircraft in force in such State;
  (e) the exercise of jurisdiction is necessary to ensure the observance of any obligation of such State under a multilateral international agreement.

Chapter III—Powers of the aircraft commander

ARTICLE 5

1. The provisions of this Chapter shall not apply to offences and acts committed or about to be committed by a person on board an aircraft in flight in the airspace of the State of registration or over the high seas or any other area outside the territory of any State unless the last point of take-off or the next point of intended landing is situated in a State other than that of registration, or the aircraft subsequently flies in the airspace of a State other than that of registration with such person still on board.
2. Notwithstanding the provisions of Article 1, paragraph 3, an aircraft shall for the purposes of this Chapter, be considered to be in flight at any time from the moment when all its external doors are closed following embarkation until the moment when any such door is opened for disembarkation. In the case of a forced landing, the provisions of this Chapter shall continue to apply with respect to offences and acts committed on board until competent

authorities of a State take over the responsibility for the aircraft and for the persons and property on board.

<h2 style="text-align:center">ARTICLE 6</h2>

1. The aircraft commander may, when he has reasonable grounds to believe that a person has committed, or is about to commit, on board the aircraft, an offence or act contemplated in Article 1, paragraph 1, impose upon such person reasonable measures including restraint which are necessary:
    (a) to protect the safety of the aircraft, or of persons or property therein; or
    (b) to maintain good order and discipline on board; or
    (c) to enable him to deliver such person to competent authorities or to disembark him in accordance with the provisions of this Chapter.
2. The aircraft commander may require or authorize the assistance of other crew members and may request or authorize, but not require, the assistance of passengers to restrain any person whom he is entitled to restrain. Any crew member or passenger may also take reasonable preventive measures without such authorization when he has reasonable grounds to believe that such action is immediately necessary to protect the safety of the aircraft, or of persons or property therein.

<h2 style="text-align:center">ARTICLE 7</h2>

1. Measures of restraint imposed upon a person in accordance with Article 6 shall not be continued beyond any point at which the aircraft lands unless:
    (a) such point is in the territory of a non-Contracting State and its authorities refuse to permit disembarkation of that person or those measures have been imposed in accordance with Article 6, paragraph 1 (c) in order to enable his delivery to competent authorities;
    (b) the aircraft makes a forced landing and the aircraft commander is unable to deliver that person to competent authorities; or
    (c) that person agrees to onward carriage under restraint.
2. The aircraft commander shall as soon as practicable, and if possible before landing in the territory of a State with a person on board who has been placed under restraint in accordance with the provisions of Article 6, notify the authorities of such State of the fact that a person on board is under restraint and of the reasons for such restraint.

<h2 style="text-align:center">ARTICLE 8</h2>

1. The aircraft commander may, in so far as it is necessary for the purpose of subparagraph (a) or (b) or paragraph 1 of Article 6, disembark in the territory of any State in which the aircraft lands any person who he has reasonable ground to believe has committed, or is about to commit, on board the aircraft an act contemplated in Article 1, paragraph 1 (b).
2. The aircraft commander shall report to the authorities of the State in which he disembarks any person pursuant to this Article, the fact of, and the reasons for, such disembarkation.

ARTICLE 9

1. The aircraft commander may deliver to the competent authorities of any Contracting State in the territory of which the aircraft lands any person who he has reasonable grounds to believe has committed on board the aircraft an act which, in his opinion, is a serious offence according to the penal law of the State of registration of the aircraft.

2. The aircraft commander shall as soon as practicable and if possible before landing in the territory of a Contracting State with a person on board whom the aircraft commander intends to deliver in accordance with the preceding paragraph, notify the authorities of such State of his intention to deliver such person and the reasons therefor.

3. The aircraft commander shall furnish the authorities to whom any suspected offender is delivered in accordance with the provisions of this Article with evidence and information which, under the law of the State of registration of the aircraft, are lawfully in his possession.

ARTICLE 10

For actions taken in accordance with this Convention, neither the aircraft commander, any other member of the crew, any passenger, the owner or operator of the aircraft, nor the person on whose behalf the flight was performed shall be held responsible in any proceeding on account of the treatment undergone by the person against whom the actions were taken.

Chapter IV—Unlawful Seizure of Aircraft

ARTICLE 11

1. When a person on board has unlawfully committed by force or threat thereof an act of interference, seizure, or other wrongful exercise of control of an aircraft in flight or when such an act is about to be committed, Contracting States shall take all appropriate measures to restore control of the aircraft to its lawful commander or to preserve his control of the aircraft.

2. In the cases contemplated in the preceding paragraph, the Contracting State in which the aircraft lands shall permit its passengers and crew to continue their journey as soon as practicable, and shall return the aircraft and its cargo to the persons lawfully entitled to possession.

Chapter V—Powers and Duties of States

ARTICLE 12

Any Contracting State shall allow the commander of an aircraft registered in another Contracting State to disembark any person pursuant to Article 8, paragraph 1.

ARTICLE 13

1. Any Contracting State shall take delivery of any person whom the aircraft commander delivers pursuant to Article 9, paragraph 1.

2. Upon being satisfied that the circumstances so warrant, any Contracting State shall take custody or other measures to ensure the presence of any person suspected of an act contemplated in Article 11, paragraph 1 and of any person of whom it has taken delivery. The custody and other measures shall be as provided in the law of that State but may only be continued for such time as is reasonably necessary to enable any criminal or extradition proceedings to be instituted.

3. Any person in custody pursuant to the previous paragraph shall be assisted in communicating immediately with the nearest appropriate representative of the State of which he is a national.

4. Any Contracting State, to which a person is delivered pursuant to Article 9, paragraph 1, or in whose territory an aircraft lands following the commission of an act contemplated in Article 11, paragraph 1, shall immediately make a preliminary enquiry into the facts.

5. When a State, pursuant to this Article, has taken a person into custody, it shall immediately notify the State of registration of the aircraft and the State of nationality of the detained person and, if it considers it advisable, any other interested State of the fact that such person is in custody and of the circumstances which warrant his detention. The State which makes the preliminary enquiry contemplated in paragraph 4 of this Article shall promptly report its findings to the said States and shall indicate whether it intends to exercise jurisdiction.

ARTICLE 14

1. When any person has been disembarked in accordance with Article 8, paragraph 1, or delivered in accordance with Article 9, paragraph 1, or has disembarked after committing an act contemplated in Article 11, paragraph 1, and when such person cannot or does not desire to continue his journey and the State of landing refuses to admit him, that State may, if the person in question is not a national or permanent resident of that State, return him to the territory of the State of which he is a national or permanent resident or to the territory of the State in which he began his journey by air.

2. Neither disembarkation, nor delivery, nor the taking of custody or other measures contemplated in Article 13, paragraph 2, nor return of the person concerned, shall be considered as admission to the territory of the Contracting State concerned for the purpose of its law relating to entry or admission of persons and nothing in this Convention shall affect the law of a Contracting State relating to the expulsion of persons from its territory.

ARTICLE 15

1. Without prejudice to Article 14, any person who has been disembarked in accordance with Article 8, paragraph 1, or delivered in accordance with Article 9, paragraph 1, or has disembarked after committing an act contemplated in Article 11, paragraph 1, and who desires to continue his journey shall be at liberty as soon as practicable to proceed to any destination of

his choice unless his presence is required by the law of the State of landing for the purpose of extradition or criminal proceedings.

2. Without predudice to its law as to entry and admission to, and extradition and expulsion from its territory, a Contracting State in whose territory a person has been disembarked in accordance with Article 8, paragraph 1, or delivered in accordance with Article 9, paragraph 1 or has disembarked and is suspected of having committed an act contemplated in Article 11, paragraph 1, shall accord to such person treatment which is no less favourable for his protection and security than that accorded to nationals of such Contracting State in like circumstances.

Chapter VI—Other Provisions

ARTICLE 16

1. Offences committed on aircraft registered in a Contracting State shall be treated, for the purpose of extradition, as if they had been committed not only in the place in which they have occurred but also in the territory of the State of registration of the aircraft.

2. Without prejudice to the provisions of the preceding paragraph, nothing in this Convention shall be deemed to create an obligation to grant extradition.

ARTICLE 17

In taking any measures for investigation or arrest or otherwise exercising jurisdiction in connection with any offence committed on board an aircraft the Contracting States shall pay due regard to the safety and other interests of air navigation and shall so act as to avoid unnecessary delay to the aircraft, passengers, crew or cargo.

ARTICLE 18

If Contracting States establish joint air transport operating organizations or international operating agencies, which operate aircraft not registered in any one State those States shall, according to the circumstances of the case, designate the State among them which, for the purposes of this Convention, shall be considered as the State of registration and shall give notice thereof to the International Civil Aviation Organization which shall communicate the notice to all States Parties to this Convention.

[Chapter VII omitted.]

The problems of regulating aircraft are as nothing, however, when compared with the difficulties posed by satellites. These devices raise questions that are far less conventional for international law because they may pass over states, other than those which launch them, after they are beyond the control of any state. The neutral state must ponder the dilemma posed by satellites with military objectives passing over its territory; problems of ownership may arise if satellites or parts of them fall on the territory of states other than those that launch them; and the use of the upper atmosphere for thermonuclear tests raises questions of the right of states to pollute the atmosphere above other states.

Actually, neither the United States nor the Soviet Union protested flights of satellites launched by either over the other's territory until the Soviet Union in July 1961 objected to the flights of United States satellites carrying instruments that would transmit to the United States information about conditions over the Soviet Union.

The devices that evoked the protest were carried by the Midas III, a thirty-foot cylinder weighing 3500 pounds, which the United States had sent into polar orbit at an altitude of 1850 miles. Equipped with "sensors" to detect infrared radiation generated by the heat of missile exhausts, it passed over the Soviet Union once every three days. Tiros III, a 285-pound satellite launched the same month, carried television cameras and transmitters for photographing the earth's weather from 450 miles up and for relaying the pictures to receiving stations in the United States.[24] The Soviet Union argued that both launchings were acts of espionage and aggression and compared the two satellites to the U-2 flights. "A spy is a spy no matter at what height it flies," the official army newspaper, *Red Star,* commented. The United States has taken no position on the legality of the satellites.

These events suggest that an adequate law for outer space must divide *air* space (the area in which states can and may exercise complete national control) from *outer* space (the area subject to international control). The law must also define what activities states may undertake in outer space, where no state can exercise complete jurisdiction. Some preliminary efforts along these lines have already been undertaken.

Law for outer space has been considered by scientists and lawyers in committees of the American Rocket Society, the International Institute of Space Law of the International Astronautical Federation (composed of learned societies from thirty-six nations, including most of the states of Eastern Europe), and the American Bar Association. Colloquia on the law of outer space have been held at The Hague, London, and Stockholm (1960), and the United Nations has established an *ad hoc* Committee on the Peaceful Uses of Outer Space.

From these deliberations the shape of a rational law is already visible. Irrational theories have gone into the discard.

Russian lawyers like A. Kislov and S. B. Krylov originally contended that Russia might claim sovereignty of its air space, reaching into the infinity of space in wedges like the spokes of a wheel, a restatement of an ancient Roman law theory, *cuius est solum eius est usque ad*

[24] *New York Times,* July 16, 1961, p. E-2 and July 24, 1961, pp. 1–2.

coelum et al inferos (he who owns the ground owns everything to the heavens and to the depths). When the U.S.S.R. first penetrated outer space on October 4, 1957, the Soviet Union changed its views and supported the theory of G. P. Zadorozhnyi and the principles of the freedom of outer space, since supported by Soviet publicists Galina, Kovalev, Cheprov, and E. A. Korovin. Authority at present favors the "primary jurisdiction line," suggested by Dr. Theodore von Karman. The Karman line falls at approximately 275,000 feet (eight-three kilometers), where an object traveling at 25,000 feet (seven kilometers) a second loses its aerodynamic lift and centrifugal force takes over. This line may be changed, as physicists and lawyers attempt to define exactly where an aeronautical vehicle can no longer perform and where molecular oxygen dissociates and airspace no longer exists. But the final boundary is not likely to differ materially from the Karman line.

Officials of the Soviet Union and the United States at Barcelona, during October 1960, agreed that a line not materially different (100 kilometers) from the Karman line would divide airspace and outer space in keeping the records of the International Sporting Committee of the Federation Aeronautique Internationale, and that may well be a precedent, minor though it is, which will ultimately support a final determination of the legal divide between air and outer space.[25]

As for the uses of outer space, it may be possible to distinguish between aggressive and defensive satellites. Aggressive satellites (which presumably would be illegal) would be those capable of causing damage to other states, whereas reconnaissance or warning satellites, like Midas III, would be classified as defensive. The most desirable way of establishing such distinctions in law would be by a treaty creating a warning system under international control, but no such agreement exists as yet.

Earthbound analogies do suggest ways of creating a legal order for outer space. The Antarctic agreement is one such precedent. Another precedent for barring the use of outer space to nuclear explosions, exists in the decision of an arbitral tribunal that:

. . . under the principles of international law, as well as the law of the United States, no State has the right to use or permit the use of its territory in such a manner as to cause injury by fumes in or to the territory of another or the properties or persons therein, when the case is of serious consequence and the injury is established by clear and conflicting evidence.[26]

[25] Andrew G. Haley, "Rule of Law in Outer Space," *New York Times*, February 18, 1961, p. 18. See C. Wilfred Jenks, *Space Law* (New York: Frederick A. Praeger, 1965) and Howard J. Taubenfeld, ed., *Space and Society* (Dobbs Ferry, N.Y.: Oceana Publications, 1964).

[26] Trail Smelter Arbitration, March 11, 1941, U.S. Department of State Arbitration Series 8, pp. 36–37.

The Tribunal held Canada responsible for the damage caused in the United States by fumes blown into the United States from a Canadian smelter.

Although the optimistic expectations aroused by the Antarctic treaty have not been fulfilled, the United States and the Soviet Union observed a voluntary test ban from 1958 to 1961, and on August 5, 1963, signed a treaty which banned nuclear tests in the atmosphere, under water, and in outer space. Moreover, on December 13, 1963, the United Nations General Assembly unanimously adopted a Declaration of Legal Principles Governing Activities of States in the Exploration and Use of Outer Space (Resolution 1962 [XVIII]); in 1966 it unanimously endorsed a treaty on the subject, which was opened for signature in 1967; and in 1967, exactly a year later, it approved an agreement on rescuing and returning astronauts and returning objects launched into outer space, which 44 states signed in April 1968.[27]

TREATY OF PRINCIPLES GOVERNING THE ACTIVITIES OF STATES IN THE EXPLORATION AND USE OF OUTER SPACE, INCLUDING THE MOON AND OTHER CELESTIAL BODIES

The States Parties to this Treaty,

Inspired by the great prospects opening up before mankind as a result of man's entry into outer space,

Recognizing the common interest of all mankind in the progress of the exploration and use of outer space for peaceful purposes,

Believing that the exploration and use of outer space should be carried on for the benefit of all peoples irrespective of the degree of their economic or scientific development,

Desiring to contribute to broad international co-operation in the scientific as well as the legal aspects of the exploration and use of outer space for peaceful purposes,

Believing that such co-operation will contribute to the development of mutual understanding and to the strengthening of friendly relations between States and peoples,

Recalling resolution 1962 (XVIII) entitled "Declaration of Legal Principles Governing the Activities of States in the Exploration and Use of Outer Space," which was adopted unanimously by the United Nations General Assembly on 13 December 1963,

Recalling resolution 1884 (XVIII), calling upon States to refrain from placing in orbit around the earth any objects carrying nuclear weapons or any other kinds of weapons of mass destruction or from installing such weapons on celestial bodies, which was adopted unanimously by the United Nations General Assembly on 17 October 1963,

[27] GA Res. 2222 (XXI), 19 December 1966, and 2345 (XXII), 19 December 1967.

Taking account of United Nations General Assembly resolution 110 (II) of 3 November 1947, which condemned propaganda designed or likely to provoke or encourage any threat to the peace, breach of the peace or act of aggression, and considering that the aforementioned resolution is applicable to outer space,

Convinced that a Treaty on Principles Governing the Activities of States in the Exploration and Use of Outer Space, including the Moon and Other Celestial Bodies, will further the purposes and principles of the Charter of the United Nations,

Have agreed on the following:

ARTICLE I

The exploration and use of outer space, including the moon and other celestial bodies, shall be carried out for the benefit and in the interests of all countries, irrespective of their degree of economic or scientific development, and shall be the province of all mankind.

Outer space, including the moon and other celestial bodies, shall be free for exploration and use by all States without discrimination of any kind, on a basis of equality and in accordance with international law, and there shall be free access to all areas of celestial bodies.

There shall be freedom of scientific investigation in outer space, including the moon and other celestial bodies, and States shall facilitate and encourage international co-operation in such investigation.

ARTICLE II

Outer space, including the moon and other celestial bodies, is not subject to national appropriation by claim of sovereignty, by means of use or occupation, or by any other means.

ARTICLE III

States Parties to the Treaty shall carry on activities in the exploration and use of outer space, including the moon and other celestial bodies, in accordance with international law, including the Charter of the United Nations, in the interest of maintaining international peace and security and promoting international co-operation and understanding.

ARTICLE IV

States Parties to the Treaty undertake not to place in orbit around the earth any objects carrying nuclear weapons or any other kinds of weapons of mass destruction, install such weapons on celestial bodies, or station such weapons in outer space in any other manner.

The moon and other celestial bodies shall be used by all States Parties to the Treaty exclusively for peaceful purposes. The establishment of military bases, installations and fortifications, the testing of any type of weapons and the conduct of military manoeuvres on celestial bodies shall be forbidden. The use of military personnel for scientific research or for any other peaceful purposes shall not be prohibited. The use of any equipment or facility necessary for peaceful exploration of the moon and other celestial bodies shall also not be prohibited.

ARTICLE V

States Parties to the Treaty shall regard astronauts as envoys of mankind in outer space and shall render to them all possible assistance in the event of accident, distress, or emergency landing on the territory of another State Party or on the high seas. When astronauts make such a landing, they shall be safely and promptly returned to the State of registry of their space vehicle.

In carrying on activities in outer space and on celestial bodies, the astronauts of one State Party shall render all possible assistance to the astronauts of other States Parties.

States Parties to the Treaty shall immediately inform the other States Parties to the Treaty or the Secretary-General of the United Nations of any phenomena they discover in outer space, including the moon and other celestial bodies, which could constitute a danger to the life or health of astronauts.

ARTICLE VI

States Parties to the Treaty shall bear international responsibility for national activities in outer space, including the moon and other celestial bodies, whether such activities are carried on by governmental agencies or by nongovernmental entities, and for assuring that national activities are carried out in conformity with the provisions set forth in the present Treaty. The activities of non-governmental entities in outer space, including the moon and other celestial bodies, shall require authorization and continuing supervision by the State concerned. When activities are carried on in outer space, including the moon and other celestial bodies, by an international organization, responsibility for compliance with this Treaty shall be borne both by the international organization and by the States Parties to the Treaty participating in such organization.

ARTICLE VII

Each State Party to the Treaty that launches or procures the launching of an object into outer space, including the moon and other celestial bodies, and each State Party from whose territory or facility an object is launched, is internationally liable for damage to another State Party to the Treaty or to its natural or juridical persons by such object or its component parts on the earth, in air space or in outer space, including the moon and other celestial bodies.

ARTICLE VIII

A State Party to the Treaty on whose registry an object launched into outer space is carried shall retain jurisdiction and control over such object, and over any personnel thereof, while in outer space or on a celestial body. Ownership of objects launched into outer space, including objects landed or constructed on a celestial body, and of their component parts, is not affected by their presence in outer space or on a celestial body or by their return to the earth. Such objects or component parts found beyond the limits of the State Party to the Treaty on whose registry they are carried shall be returned to that State, which shall upon request, furnish identifying data prior to their return.

ARTICLE IX

In the exploration and use of outer space, including the moon and other celestial bodies, States Parties to the Treaty shall be guided by the principle of co-operation and mutual assistance and shall conduct all their activities in outer space, including the moon and other celestial bodies, with due regard to the corresponding interests of all other States Parties to the Treaty. States Parties to the Treaty shall pursue studies of outer space, including the moon and other celestial bodies, and conduct exploration of them so as to avoid their harmful contamination and also adverse changes in the environment of the earth resulting from the introduction of extraterrestrial matter and, where necessary, shall adopt appropriate measures for this purpose. If a State Party to the Treaty has reason to believe that an activity or experiment planned by it or its nationals in outer space, including the moon and other celestial bodies, would cause potentially harmful interference with activities of other States Parties in the peaceful exploration and use of outer space, including the moon and other celestial bodies, it shall undertake appropriate international consultations before proceeding with any such activity or experiment. A State Party to the Treaty which has reason to believe that an activity or experiment planned by another State Party in outer space, including the moon and other celestial bodies, would cause potentially harmful interference with activities in the peaceful exploration and use of outer space, including the moon and other celestial bodies, may request consultation concerning the activity or experiment.

ARTICLE X

In order to promote international co-operation in the exploration and use of outer space, including the moon and other celestial bodies, in conformity with the purposes of this Treaty, the States Parties to the Treaty shall consider on a basis of equality any requests by other States Parties to the Treaty to be afforded an opportunity to observe the flight of space objects launched by those States.

The nature of such an opportunity for observation and the conditions under which it could be afforded shall be determined by agreement between the States concerned.

ARTICLE XI

In order to promote international co-operation in the peaceful exploration and use of outer space, States Parties to the Treaty conducting activities in outer space, including the moon and other celestial bodies, agree to inform the Secretary-General of the United Nations as well as the public and the international scientific community, to the greatest extent feasible and practicable, of the nature, conduct, locations and results of such activities. On receiving the said information, the Secretary-General of the United Nations should be prepared to disseminate it immediately and effectively.

ARTICLE XII

All stations, installations, equipment and space vehicles on the moon and other celestial bodies shall be open to representatives of other States Parties to the Treaty on a basis of reciprocity. Such representatives shall give reasonable advance notice of a projected visit in order that appropriate consultations may be held and that maximum precautions may be taken to assure safety and to avoid interference with normal operations in the facility to be visited.

ARTICLE XIII

The provisions of this Treaty shall apply to the activities of States Parties to the Treaty in the exploration and use of outer space, including the moon and other celestial bodies, whether such activities are carried on by a single State Party to the Treaty or jointly with other States, including cases where they are carried on within the framework of international intergovernmental organizations.

Any practical questions arising in connexion with activities carried on by international inter-governmental organizations in the exploration and use of outer space, including the moon and other celestial bodies, shall be resolved by the States Parties to the Treaty either with the appropriate international organization or with one or more States members of that international organization, which are Parties to this Treaty.

ARTICLE XIV

1. This Treaty shall be open to all States for signature. Any State which does not sign this Treaty before its entry into force in accordance with paragraph 3 of this article may accede to it at any time.

2. This Treaty shall be subject to ratification by signatory States. Instruments of ratification and instruments of accession shall be deposited with the Governments of the Union of Soviet Socialist Republics, the United Kingdom of Great Britain and Northern Ireland and the United States of America, which are hereby designated the Depositary Governments.

3. This Treaty shall enter into force upon the deposit of instruments of ratification by five Governments including the Governments designated as Depositary Governments under this Treaty.

4. For States whose instruments of ratification or accession are deposited subsequent to the entry into force of this Treaty, it shall enter into force on the date of the deposit of their instruments of ratification or accession.

5. The Depositary Governments shall promptly inform all signatory and

acceding States of the date of each signature, the date of deposit of each instrument of ratification of and accession to this Treaty, the date of its entry into force and other notices.

6. This Treaty shall be registered by the Depositary Governments pursuant to Article 102 of the Charter of the United Nations.

ARTICLE XV

Any State Party to the Treaty may propose amendments to this Treaty. Amendments shall enter into force for each State Party to the Treaty accepting the amendments upon their acceptance by a majority of the States Parties to the Treaty and thereafter for each remaining State Party to the Treaty on the date of acceptance by it.

ARTICLE XVI

Any State Party to the Treaty may give notice of its withdrawal from the Treaty one year after its entry into force by written notification to the Depositary Governments. Such withdrawal shall take effect one year from the date of receipt of this notification.

ARTICLE XVII

This Treaty, of which the Chinese, English, French, Russian and Spanish texts are equally authentic, shall be deposited in the archives of the Depositary Governments. Duly certified copies of this Treaty shall be transmitted by the Depositary Governments to the Governments of the signatory and acceding States.

IN WITNESS WHEREOF the undersigned, duly authorized, have signed this Treaty.

Rivers

In the Middle Ages, peoples looked upon rivers as neutral barriers separating them from alien groups rather than as areas subject to the control of a riparian people. With the rise of commerce and navigation on both sides of rivers, however, the need to define legal rights over rivers increased. Early views, espoused by Grotius and Vattel, that international boundaries passed through the middle of streams proved incompatible with the needs of navigators, for the main channels were often not in the geometrical center, and channels, as the Chamizal Case shows, sometimes change.

At the beginning of the nineteenth century, therefore, States bordering rivers began to conclude treaties which agreed upon the *thalweg,* or "downway," as the proper dividing line between states separated by rivers. A treaty between the United States and Canada, respecting the St. Croix River, signed April 11, 1908, is the first American treaty to use the word *thalweg*, but European treaties employed the term nearly one hundred years earlier.[28]

LOUISIANA v. MISSISSIPPI

UNITED STATES, SUPREME COURT, 1906

202 U.S. 1

If the doctrine of the thalweg is applicable, the correct boundary line separating Louisiana from Mississippi in these waters is the deep water channel.

The term "thalweg" is commonly used by writers on international law in definition of water boundaries between States, meaning the middle or deepest or most navigable channel. And while often styled "fairway" or "midway" or "main channel," the word itself has been taken over into various languages. Thus in the treaty of Luneville, February 9, 1801, we find "le Thalweg de l'Adige," "le Thalweg du Rhin," and it is similarly used in English treaties and decisions, and the books of publicists in every tongue.

In *Iowa* v. *Illinois*, 147 U.S. 1, the rule of the thalweg was stated and applied. The controversy between the States of Iowa and Illinois on the Mississippi river, which flowed between them, was as to the line which separated "the jurisdiction of the two States for the purposes of taxation and other purposes of government." Iowa contended that the boundary line was the middle of the main body of the river, without regard to the "steamboat channel" or deepest part of the stream. Illinois claimed that its jurisdiction extended to the channel upon which commerce on the river by steamboats or other vessels was usually conducted. This court held that the true line in a navigable river between States is the middle of the main channel of the river.

Mr. Justice Field, delivering the opinion of the court, said:

"When a navigable river constitutes the boundary between two independent States, the line defining the point at which the jurisdiction of the two separates is well established to be the middle of the main channel of the stream. The interest of each State in the navigation of the river admits of no other line. The preservation by each of its equal right in the navigation of the stream is the subject of paramount interest. It is, therefore, laid down in all the recognized treatises on international law of modern times that the middle of the channel of the stream marks the true boundary between the adjoining States up to which each State will on its side exercise jurisdiction. In international law, therefore, and by the usage of European nations, the

---

[28] See Hyde, I, 443–445.

term 'middle of the stream,' as applied to a navigable river, is the same as the middle of the channel of such stream, and in that sense the terms are used in the treaty of peace between Great Britain, France, and Spain, concluded at Paris in 1763. By the language, 'a line drawn along the middle of the river Mississippi from its source to the river Iberville,' as there used, is meant along the middle of the channel of the river Mississippi."

This judgment related to navigable rivers. But we are of opinion that, on occasion, the principle of the thalweg is applicable, in respect of water boundaries, to sounds, bays, straits, gulfs, estuaries and other arms of the sea.

As to boundary lakes and landlocked seas, where there is no necessary track of navigation, the line of demarcation is drawn in the middle, and this is true of narrow straits separating the lands of two different States; but whenever there is a deep water sailing channel therein, it is thought by the publicists that the rule of the thalweg applies. 1 Martens (F. de), 2d ed. 134; Hall § 38; Bluntschli, 5th ed. §§ 298, 299; 1 Oppenheim, 254, 255.

Thus Martens writes: "What we have said in regard to rivers and lakes is equally applicable to the straits or gulfs of the sea, especially those which do not exceed the ordinary width of rivers or double the distance that a cannon can carry."

So Pradier Fodéré says (Vol. II, p. 202), that as to lakes, "in communication with or connected with the sea, they ought to be considered under the same rules as international rivers."

The same view is confirmed by decisions of this court and of many arbitral tribunals.

Before 1815, states disagreed constantly about the right to navigate rivers separating or crossing two or more states. Every state generally tried to monopolize the right of navigating streams flowing through its own territory and even to deny states farther upstream the right to send ships through to the sea. By the end of the Napoleonic wars, statesmen came to realize that these restrictions prevented commerce from developing and also engendered hostility, and they provided in the Final Act of the Congress of Vienna (1815) that states separated or traversed by the same navigable river should appoint commissioners to set the rules for navigation by mutual agreement according to certain basic principles. The first basic principle was that the right to navigate rivers from the point where each became navigable to its mouth should be open to all. The powers also agreed that navigation dues should be uniform, a special service should collect the dues, national customs houses should not interfere with navigation on the rivers, states should maintain navigable channels and towing paths, and rules should apply equally to all in the interest of international commerce.

Despite this general agreement, disputes have arisen with regard to the rights of states on internationalized rivers, as in the Faber Case between Venezuela and Germany in 1903.

STATUTE ON THE REGIME OF NAVIGABLE WATERWAYS OF INTERNATIONAL CONCERN

ANNEXED TO THE CONVENTION SIGNED AT BARCELONA, APRIL 20, 1921

7 *L.N.T.S.*, 51

Article 1. In the application of the Statute, the following are declared to be navigable waterways of international concern:

1. All parts which are naturally navigable to and from the sea of a waterway which in its course, naturally navigable to and from the sea, separates or traverses different States, and also any part of any other waterway naturally navigable to and from the sea, which connects with the sea a waterway naturally navigable which separates or traverses different States.

It is understood that:

(a) Trans-shipment from one vessel to another is not excluded by the words "navigable to and from the sea";

(b) Any natural waterway or part of a natural waterway is termed "naturally navigable" if now used for ordinary commercial navigation, or capable by reason of its natural conditions of being so used; by "ordinary commercial navigation" is to be understood navigation which, in view of the economic condition of the riparian countries, is commercial and normally practicable;

(c) Tributaries are to be considered as separate waterways;

(d) Lateral canals constructed in order to remedy the defects of a waterway included in the above definition are assimilated thereto.

(e) The different States separated or traversed by a navigable waterway of international concern, including its tributaries of international concern, are deemed to be "riparian States."

2. Waterways, or parts of waterways, whether natural or artificial, expressly declared to be placed under the régime of the General Convention regarding navigable waterways of international concern either in unilateral Acts of the States under whose sovereignty or authority these waterways or parts of waterways are situated, or in agreements made with the consent, in particular, of such States. . . .

Article 3. Subject to the provisions contained in Articles 5 and 17, each of the Contracting States shall accord free exercise of navigation to the vessels flying the flag of any one of the other Contracting States on those parts of navigable waterways specified above which may be situated under its sovereignty or authority.

Article 4. In the excerise of navigation referred to above, the nationals, property and flags of all Contracting States shall be treated in all respects on a footing of perfect equality. No distinction shall be made between the nationals, the property and the flags of the different riparian States, including the riparian States exercising sovereignty or authority over the portion of the navigable waterway in question: similarly, no distinction shall be made between the nationals, the property and the flags of riparian and non-riparian States. It is understood, in consequence, that no exclusive right of navigation shall be accorded on such navigable waterways to companies or to private persons.

No distinction shall be made in the said exercise, by reason of the point of departure or of destination, or of the direction of the traffic.

. . . .

Article 13. Treaties, conventions or agreements in force relating to navigable waterways, concluded by the contracting States before the coming into force of this Statute, are not, as a consequence of its coming into force, abrogated so far as concerns the States signatories to those treaties.

Nevertheless the Contracting States undertake not to apply among themselves any provisions of such treaties, conventions or agreements which may conflict with the rules of the present Statute.

[This Convention and Statute came into force on 31 October 1922. By 1939, it had been ratified by Albania, Bulgaria, Chile, Czechoslovakia, Denmark, Finland, France, Great Britain, Greece, Hungary, India, Italy, Luxembourg, New Zealand, Norway, Romania, Sweden, Thailand, and Turkey. See League of Nations Doc. A. 6. 1939, Annex I.V.2, p. 16. India denounced it on 26 March 1956, but other states still regard it as being in force, Norway, Sweden, and the United Kingdom having affirmed it as recently as 1965. See UN Doc. A/5759, "General Multilateral Treaties . . . Under the League of Nations, Report of the Secretary-General," 25 Feb. 1965, pp. 27–28.]

THE FABER CASE

GERMANY—VENEZUELA, COMMISSION UNDER THE AGREEMENT
OF FEBRUARY 13, 1903

RALSTON'S REPORT, P. 600

[Opinions of Goetsch and Zuloaga, Commissioners, omitted.]

DUFFIELD, Umpire. This is one of several claims which grow out of the suspension of river traffic on the river Zulia by Executive decrees of Venezuela in 1900, 1901, and 1902. The claimant Faber is a German subject who resides and has his place of business in Cúcuta, in Colombia. . . .

As to the main objection of the Commissioner for Venezuela that her acts in closing the ports in question were fully within the attributes of her sovereignty, the Commissioner for Germany insists to the contrary. In the course of a very able discussion of the question, to which he has brought great research, he maintains:

"To begin, it can not be denied that a sovereign state possesses absolute authority over its rivers and water courses as far as the boundary lines of other states. This principle is nevertheless limited in two ways in international law. When a river is the only route of communication and indispensable to the existence of another state or part of it, its use can not be entirely prohibited." (Citing Heffter, Int. Law of Europe, Berlin, 1857, 147.)

He also cites Heffter, Puffendorf, Groot, and Vattel, that a state can not deny to another nation without committing an act of hostility, and no state can prevent another from getting its commerce to the market of a third without giving offence and inflicting injury, and he claims "these international maxims whose object is to draw nations together have been at different times embraced in treaties," a number of which he cites, and concludes:

"It must be considered as an international doctrine that the navigation of rivers passing through the territory of several states, together with all their affluents, must be free from the point where they begin to be navigable to the point where they empty into the sea. . . . ."

We are met on the threshold of the discussion with the fact that no direct oceanic navigation was interrupted. Physical limitations deprive Colombia of the enjoyment of direct oceanic traffic through Venezuelan territory. No sea-going vessels can thus pass into Colombian territory. All must stop at Maracaibo, where all ocean freight must be reshipped. The case, therefore, is not one in which a foreigner is deprived by the act of Venezuela of the use of waters to which nature has given him direct access. The right Venezuela has not attempted to restrict. She permits him to carry his goods in the vessel in which they entered her territory as far as nature permits him. But the claimant insists that because of the nature of his business he suffers damage because goods are not permitted to be twice reshipped in the territory of Venezuela and thus transported into Colombia. Obviously this is a very different matter. First, it of necessity involves the use of land of Venezuela not incidental to navigation merely, but for the transshipment, carriage, and handling of freight on her shores. Second, it extends the claim of free navigation of rivers to a new case, for which I have found no precedent.

It is one thing for a foreigner to claim, "I have a right to navigation for my vessels wherever natural conditions permit, and Venezuela can not restrict it." But it is quite another thing to claim, "I have a right to send my goods over the inland waters of Venezuela, reshipping them into smaller and smaller vessels as often as the lessening depth of water may require." The question seems to be one of regulating commerce, rather than restricting internal navigation. It also appears that the laws of Venezuela with reference to internal navigation over its rivers and lakes require a nationalization of the vessels engaged therein. They also define interior maritime commerce of coast or river trade to be that which is established between ports and points on the banks of the rivers or shores of Venezuela in national boats with foreign merchandise which has paid duty, or fruits or other productions of the country. Another provision of law requires captains of vessels engaged in this trade to be Venezuelan citizens.

That these provisions were within the proper exercise of Venezuela's sovereignty can not be doubted. It results, therefore, that in the lawful exercise of such sovereignty she has excluded from her internal commerce boats of other nationalities and required even the boats of Venezuelan nationality to be commanded by Venezuelans.

For a considerable period before the decree of September 11, 1900, was issued there were internal political disturbances in the territory tributary to the Catatumbo and Zulia rivers. The relations between Venezuela and Colombia were at the same time seriously strained, and the former complained that revolutionist plans and movements found moral and material support on Colombian territory, which afforded a secure base of operation for them.

In this state of affairs the various decrees complained of were promulgated. It is evident that their purpose was to control the passage of vessels, especially steamers, to and fro between Colombia and Venezuela. The language of some of the decrees intimate fears of hostile forces entering Venezuela in that way. In July, 1901, Gen. Rángel Garbiras had begun his insurrection, which at one time seemed threatening, from Colombia. A part of his forces came into Venezuela by way of the Zulia and Catatumbo rivers. It may be reasonably presumed that this was the cause of the decree of July 29, 1901, revoking the permission given in that of March 4, 1901.

The concrete question, therefore, in the case is whether, under these physical and political conditions, Venezuela had the right to suspend the traffic on these rivers by the closing of these ports. She was in full possession of them and they were actually under her sovereignty. This distinguishes the case from that of the Orinoco Asphalt Company. . . . [Ralston's *Report*, p. 586.]

As has been shown above, there is no substantial contradiction of authorities as to the rights of a state to regulate, and, if necessary to the peace, safety, and convenience of her own citizens, to prohibit temporarily navigation on rivers which flow to the sea. What is necessary to peace, safety, and convenience of her own citizens she must judge, and it seems to the umpire quite clear that in any case calling for an exercise of that judgment her decision is final. That a case for the exercise of this discretion did exist at the dates of the various decrees complained of is obvious, and in the opinion of the umpire the decision of Venezuela in the premises can not be reviewed by this Commission or any other tribunal. Being of the opinion that the closing of the ports of the Catatumbo and Zulia rivers under the circumstances which existed at the time was a lawful exercise of sovereignty by the Republic of Venezuela, the claim is disallowed.

A complete examination of the question leads back to the differing theories of the true source of natural law. It would extend this opinion to too great a length to discuss them, but a brief statement of them is pertinent.

Some philosophers, while admitting that human ideas of right spring solely from revelation, do not agree that natural law is but the consequence of revelation of divine or moral law. (Statel. Rechts philosophie, V. I.)

Others derive their idea of natural law from the most abstract theories of reason, without taking into account the continual changes of social relations, which, being the practical basis of that law, necessarily exert an influence of the idea itself. (Grotius-Kant.)

While others, still, putting aside both the abstract and objective idea of a Supreme Being, discuss the source of natural law in the supreme and absolute faculty of the abstraction they call *esprit du monde*. (Hegel.) They construct the moral and material world by the dialectic process of an abstract idea, and define the state as the realization of God in the world. The consequence is the complete absorption of the citizen in the state and the individual in the "pantheistic chaos of universal reason," which, on the other hand, has no conscience of its own. Still another school recognizes natural law as the science which exhibits the first principles of right founded in the nature of man and conceived by reason. (Ahrens.)

But when the crucial question comes, from what authority natural law is derived, each publicist seeks to solve it in his own way.

The theory of Grotius was that on the establishment of separate property, which he conceived grew by agreement out of an original community of goods, there were reserved for the public benefit certain of the preexisting natural rights, and that one of these was the passage over territory, whether by land or by water, and whether in the form of navigation of rivers for commercial purposes, or of an army over neutral ground, which he held to be an innocent use, the concession of which it was not competent to a nation to refuse.

It is on this doctrine that some writers on international law uphold the principle of the freedom of river navigation.

Gronovius and Barbeyrac, in their notes to Grotius, consider the right of levying dues for permission to navigate rivers. This would seem to imply the right to prohibit navigation. It has been decided by the Supreme Court of the United States in the lottery cases that the right to regulate commerce includes the right to prohibit.

Bluntschli (par. 314) broadly states that water courses which flow into the sea, and navigable rivers which are in communication with an independent sea, are open to the commerce of all nations, but he restricts the right to the time of peace.

Calvo holds that where a river traverses more than one territory the right of navigation and of commerce on it is common to all who inhabit its banks, but when it is wholly within the territory of a single state it is considered as within the exclusive sovereignty of that state. He limits the exercise of that sovereignty to fiscal regulations, but seems to subordinate the right of property to that of navigation.

Fiore (758–768) agrees in the main with Calvo, that in the case of a river flowing through one state only, that state may close the river if it chooses.

It is difficult to sustain the distinction of a navigable river running into the sea.

Heffter, paragraph 77, says that each of the proprietors of a river flowing through several states, the same as the sole proprietor of a river, can, *stricti jure*, regulate the proper use of the waters, and restrict it to the inhabitants of the country and exclude others. But, on the other hand, he agrees with Grotius, Puffendorf, and Vattel, at least in principle, that the privilege of innocent use should not be refused absolutely to any nation and its subjects in the interest of universal commerce.

Wheaton (Elements of International Law, pt. 2, ch. 4, par. 11, Lawrence's ed.) declares that the right of navigation, for commercial purposes, of a river which flows through the territories of different states, is common to all the nations inhabiting *the different parts of its banks*. But this right of innocent passage being what the text writers call an *imperfect right*, its exercise is necessarily modified by the *safety and convenience* of the state affected by it, and can only be effectively secured by mutual convention regulating the mode of its exercise, citing Grotius, Vattel, and Puffendorf.

Halleck says (vol. 1, p. 147, chap. 6 sec. 23) that the right of navigation for commercial purposes is common to *all the nations inhabiting the banks* of a navigable river, subject to such provisions as are necessary to secure the *safety and convenience* of the several states affected.

De Martens, Précis, paragraph 84, recognizes, as a general rule, that the exclusive right of each nation to its territory authorizes a country to close its entry to strangers, but that it is wrong to refuse them innocent passage. It is for the state to judge what passage is innocent. But he seems to think that the geographical position of another state may give it a right *to* demand, and in case of need to *force a passage* for its commerce.

Woolsey, paragraph 62, says:

"When a river rises within the bounds of one state and empties into the sea in another, international law allows to the inhabitants of the upper waters only a moral claim or imperfect right to its navigation."

Phillimore, in speaking of the refusal of England to open the St. Lawrence unconditionally to the United States, says (pt. 1, Par. CLXX):

"It seems difficult to deny that Great Britain may have grounded her refusal on strict law; but it is at least equally difficult to deny that by so doing she put in force an extreme and hard law," not consistent with her conduct with respect to the Mississippi.

Klüber, paragraph 76, considers that the independence of the states is to be particularly noted in the free and exclusive usage of the right over water courses—at least in the territory of the state in which the water course flows into the sea, navigable rivers, channels, and lakes are situate. . . .

And that "a state can not be accused of injustice *if it forbids all passage of foreign vessels on its water courses*," flowing to the sea, rivers, channels, or lakes in its territory.

Twiss (Volume I, section 145, page 233, second edition) declares that "a nation having physical possession of both banks of a river is held to be in juridical possession of the stream of water contained within its banks, and may rightfully exclude at its pleasure every other nation from the use of the stream whilst it is passing through its territory."

It is to be observed that distinctions are drawn by some of the above text writers, some declaring that the right of innocent use is confined to time of peace; others that only the inhabitants of those countries through which the river passes have the right of innocent use, while still others sustain the right without any limitation, save the right of the state to make necessary and proper regulations in respect to the use of the stream within its boundaries.

The theory of Grotius, mentioned above, has been said to be the "root of such legal authority as is now possessed by the principle of the freedom of river navigation." (Hall's Treatise on International Law, p. 137). It does not appear to have been adopted by the best annotators on international law. Hall says: "It can no longer be accepted as an argumentative starting point." (Hall . . . , p. 139.)

Phillimore speaks of it as a "fiction which this great man believed," and says:

"But as the basis of this opinion clearly was, and is now universally acknowledged to be a fiction, this reason, built upon the supposition of its being a truth, can be of no avail." (Phillimore's Com. on International Law, p. 190, sec. CLVII.)

The other theory, also of Grotius, was because the use of rivers belonged to the class of things "*utilitatis innoxiae*," the value of streams being in no way whatever diminished to the proprietors by this innocent use of them by others, inasmuch as the use of them is inexhaustible. (Vattel, Bk. I, chap. 23.)

This right of mere passage by one nation over the domain of another, whether it be an arm of the sea, or lake or river, or even the land, is considered by him as one of strict law, and not of comity. It is said on the other hand that it is not founded on any sound or satisfactory reason, and is at variance with that of almost all other jurists. (Phillimore, *ubi sup.*)

"The same view was taken by Grotius, but the great weight of authority since Vattel is that the state through which a river flows is to be the sole judge of the right of foreigners to the use of such river." (Wheaton's International Law, Vol. I, p. 229, cited from Wharton, Vol. I, sec. 30, p. 97.)

Still another ground is asserted as a basis for this free use of rivers, viz. that conceding the proprietary rights of the state over that portion of the river within its boundaries, nevertheless these should be subordinated to the general interests of mankind as the proprietary rights of individuals in organized communities are governed by the requirements of the general good. It is pertinently remarked by an eminent jurist that this "involved the broad assertion that the opening of all waterways to the general commerce of nations is an end which the human race has declared to be as important to it as those ends to which the rights of the individual are sacrificed by civil communities, are to the latter." (Hall, p. 139.)

Most of the advocates of the innocent use of rivers base their claim upon the grounds that the inhabitants of lands traversed by another portion of the stream have a special right of use of the other portions because such use is highly advantageous to them. If the proprietary right of the state to the portion of the river within its boundaries be conceded, as it must be generally, there can be no logical defense of this position. It certainly is a novel proposition that because one may be so situated that the use of the property of another will be of special advantage to him he may on that ground demand such use *as a right*. The rights of an individual are not created or determined by his wants or even his necessities. The starving man who takes the bread of another without right is none the less, a thief, legally, although the immorality of the act is so slight as to justify it. Wants or necessities of individuals can not create legal rights for them, or infringe the existing right of others. (Hall, p. 149.)

It seems difficult upon principle to support the right to the free use of rivers as a right stricti juris. While this is not expressly admitted, it is tacitly conceded by nearly all the advocates. They define this right of use as an "imperfect right." The term is an anomaly. The fallacy is thus aptly stated by a learned authority on international law:

"A right, it is alleged, exists; but it is an imperfect one, and therefore its enjoyment may always be subjected to such conditions as are required in the judgment of the state whose property is affected, and for sufficient cause it may be denied altogether." (Hall, p. 140.)

Woolsey terms it "only a moral or imperfect right to navigation."

However, it is no longer to be doubted that the reason of the thing and the opinion of other jurists, spoken generally, seem to agree in holding that the *right* can only be what is called (however improperly) by Vattel and other writers imperfect, and that the state through whose domain the passage is to be made *"must be the sole judge* as to whether it is innocent or injurious in its character." (Phillimore, CLVII, citing Puffendorf, Wheaton's Elements of International Law, Hesty's Law of Nations, Wolff's Institutes, Vattel.)

From this review of the authorities it seems that even in respect of rivers capable of navigation by sea-going vessels carrying oceanic commerce the weight of authority sustains the right of Venezuela to make the decrees complained of. But in the opinion of the umpire there are other considerations which control the decision in this case.

If the case before the umpire turned upon this general question of international law, the umpire is inclined to the opinion that he would be compelled to sustain the right of Venezuela to the complete control of navigation of the Catatumbo and Zulia rivers. In his opinion it is not necessary to decide the case on this ground. As has been shown above, there is no contradiction of authority as to the right of Venezuela to regulate, and, if necessary to the peace, safety, or convenience of her own citizens, to prohibit altogether navigation on these rivers. It is also equally without doubt that her judgment in the premises can not be reviewed by this Commission or any other tribunal. That a case for the exercise of discretion did exist is obvious.

. . . .

In 1927, the Permanent Court of International Justice had to decide a claim by Rumania that the European Commission of the Danube (established in 1921) did not control harbor zones along the Danube River. The court argued that Rumania's territorial sovereignty over the Danube was complete "in all respects not incompatible with the powers possessed by the European Commission."[29] Thus, the state and the international institution shared control over vessels moored in river ports and using port services and installations: the state enjoyed the power of regulating them and had jurisdiction over the ships, but the Commission had the right to supervise them, with a view to insuring freedom of navigation to all.

After World War II, the United States very much wanted the wartime United Nations to maintain the Danube as an internationalized river. By 1948, however, the Soviet Union dominated all the riparian states except Germany and Austria, and a conference in July of that year among the seven Danubian states, France, the United Kingdom, and the United States met in Belgrade to draft a new treaty defining the rights of shipping on the Danube. Czechoslovakia, functioning along Communist lines since the previous February, argued for "free navigation . . . under the control of the riparians," and this view prevailed. The United States denies that the Convention of 1948 is valid, contending that it contravenes the rights of Belgium, Greece, and Italy; ignores the nonriparian states; violates the concept of international waterways recognized in Europe for more than 130 years; runs counter to the peace treaties with Bulgaria, Hungary, and Rumania; and fails to carry out the decision of the Council of Foreign Ministers in December 1946.[30]

Disputes over rivers continue to be extremely important today, especially in the nations which, as they industrialize, wish to develop their natural resources. In general, when a river separates two states, "neither of them possesses the right to change, by means of artificial works or otherwise, the natural course of the thalweg, and so alter the line of demarcation or affect the navigability of the stream."[31]

The ideal solution to navigation and power problems involving the use of rivers which interest several states is to agree on a regime for the river by treaty; in other words, to internationalize international rivers. Such international regimes exist in regard to great international rivers like the Rhine and the St. Lawrence. Other examples are agreements between India and Pakistan affecting the Indus River and between the United States and Mexico affecting the Colorado. India and Pakistan negotiated for eight years under the auspices of the International Bank

[29] *P. C. I. J.*, Ser. B, No. 14 (1927), p. 64, Jurisdiction of the European Commission of the Danube Case.
[30] See Department of State, *Documents and State Papers*, I (1948), 487–513 and *D.S.B.*, XXI (1949), 832.
[31] Hyde, I, 448.

for Reconstruction and Development, finally agreeing in 1960 to prepare a one-billion dollar program to develop the hydroelectric power and agriculture of the Indus River Basin.[32] The American agreement, which follows, deals with salinity.

MEXICO–U.S. AGREEMENT ON COLORADO RIVER SALINITY PROBLEM[33]

ANNOUNCEMENT OF AGREEMENT

DEPARTMENT OF STATE PRESS RELEASE 54 DATED MARCH 22 [1965]

JOINT STATE-INTERIOR PRESS RELEASE

The Presidents of the United States and Mexico on March 22 announced approval of an agreement on the lower Colorado River salinity problem. The agreement takes the form of a "Minute" of the International Boundary and Water Commission, United States and Mexico. Attached are a copy of the Minute (i.e., record of a Commission decision) and an explanatory map of the directly affected areas.[34]

Under the arrangements agreed upon for a 5-year period, the United States through the Interior Department's Bureau of Reclamation will, subject to the availability of appropriations, undertake to construct by October of this year an extension of the drainage channel of the Wellton-Mohawk Irrigation and Drainage District in Arizona. The extension will permit discharge of Wellton-Mohawk drainage into the Colorado River either above or below Mexico's Morelos Dam, as Mexico may request. The discharges above Morelos Dam would be diverted for irrigation of Mexican lands, while discharges below the dam would flow to the Gulf of California.

All Wellton-Mohawk drainage will be acounted for as a part of the water delivered to Mexico under the treaty of 1944.[35] The United States will control the flows in the river reaching Morelos Dam during the winter months so that, excluding this drainage, those flows will meet Mexico's minimum scheduled deliveries under the treaty. The discharge of Wellton-Mohawk drainage above Morelos Dam is to be coordinated, insofar as practicable, with Mexico's scheduled deliveries in order to minimize the salinity of its irrigation water.

The International Commission will keep the operation continually under review. Both Governments reserve all legal rights.

Essentially, the proposed works would be operated so as to discharge the most highly saline drainage water from the Wellton-Mohawk District below

[32] See the *New York Times,* September 20, 1960, p. 6, for summary of the Indus River treaty.
[33] *D.S.B.,* LII (1965), 555–557.
[34] Not printed here.
[35] 59 Stat. 1219.

Mexico's principal diversion point during the winter months when irrigation requirements in the Mexicali Valley are at their lowest. During this period, this would be accomplished by pumping the most saline drainage water into the extension channel for discharge below Morelos Dam.

At other times, when Mexico schedules increased deliveries of irrigation water, drainage water woud be pumped from the less saline wells in the Wellton-Mohawk District so that most or all of it may be discharged from the extension channel into the Colorado above Morelos Dam. There it would mingle with other Colorado River flows and be diverted by Mexico for irrigation.

CHAPTER V

Jurisdiction: The Sea

The extent to which nations control the seas has concerned statesmen and legal authorities since men first took to the sea in ships. In the sixteenth and seventeenth centuries, the claim to dominion over large areas of the sea was one of the principal subjects of legal debate in Europe. Fishing, navigation, trade, and defense—all raised problems for maritime states, and much was written on these subjects, largely to bolster the claims of particular sovereigns. Under Elizabeth I, for instance, England argued for a *mare liberum* and, as her interests changed under Elizabeth's Stuart successors, for a *mare clausam;* England under Elizabeth and Spain under Philip II argued over their rights to navigate, trade, and colonize in the Indies; Britain and Denmark disagreed over the rights to fish in the Baltic and the North Seas; and Hugo Grotius in *Mare Liberum* (1609) defended the Dutch interest in navigating around the Cape of Good Hope and trading with the Indies.[1]

Although international concern over the law of the sea has a long history, the pressures of twentieth century life arising from new and faster ships, more international travel and trade, exhaustion of fisheries, increasing population, and a growing awareness of the riches of the sea have all increased the need for states to agree on rules. Three times in recent decades, states have attempted to agree on a comprehensive law of the sea: at the Hague Codification Conference in 1930 and at two United Nations Conferences on the Law of the Sea in 1958 and 1960. The results of the 1930 and 1960 meetings can perhaps best be seen in terms of the meeting in 1958, which adopted four important conventions, based largely upon draft rules which the United Nations International Law Commission devised in 1956. The conventions dealt with the High Seas, Fishing and Conservation of Living Resources of

[1] For an entertaining and instructive account of these developments, see Percy E. Corbett, *Law in Diplomacy* (Princeton: Princeton University Press, 1959), pp. 11–13, 110–135.

the High Seas, the Continental Shelf, and the Territorial Sea and Contiguous Zone. They confirmed many long-established rules of international law and included some innovations. All are now in force.

The High Seas

Those waters "not included in the territorial sea or in the internal waters of a state,"[2] *i.e.,* waters outside the exclusive control of any state or group of states and which therefore belong to none of them, are traditionally known as the "high seas." Ships of all states are entitled to ply these waters freely.[3] As one jurist has put it, "The high seas are free and *res nullius,* and, apart from certain exceptions or restrictions imposed in the interest of the common safety of States, they are subject to no territorial authority."[4] And in the words of another authority, "in conformity with the principle of the equality of independent States, all nations have an equal right to the uninterrupted use of the unappropriated parts of the ocean for their navigation, and no State is authorized to interfere with the navigation of other States on the high seas in the time of peace except in the case of piracy by law of nations or in extraordinary cases of self defense."[5] Freedom of the high seas was formally confirmed in Article 2 of the 1958 Convention on the High Seas:

The high seas being open to all nations, no State may validly purport to subject any part of them to its sovereignty. Freedom of the high seas . . . comprises . . .

(1) Freedom of navigation;
(2) Freedom of fishing;
(3) Freedom to lay submarine cables and pipelines;
(4) Freedom to fly over the high seas.[6]

These rights exist for both coastal and noncoastal states, all of whom are supposed to exercise them "with reasonable regard" to the interests of one another and subject to the rules of international law.[7] Coastal

[2] Convention on the High Seas (1958), Article 1.
[3] Hyde, I, 751–753.
[4] Judge Weiss, *The Lotus* (dissenting opinion), *Publications, Permanent Court of International Justice,* Series A, No. 10, pp. 40, 45.
[5] Judge Moore, *ibid.,* pp. 65, 69.
[6] Convention on the High Seas, U.N. Doc. A/Conf. 13/L.53, United Nations Conference on the Law of the Sea, *OR,* II 135–139.
[7] This restriction, originally proposed by the United Kingdom (Doc. A/Conf. 13/C.2/L.68), was adopted at the behest of many states, not least Japan, who were eager to protect seafarers and fishermen on the high seas against the risks produced by military tests and exercises of all kinds, but particularly nuclear tests. The Conference also adopted a resolution "recognizing that there is a serious and genuine apprehension on the part of many States that nuclear explosions constitute

states which ratify the Convention obligate themselves to allow states without seacoasts free transit through their territory to the sea (Article 3).

States generally regard ships registered in their merchant marine as assimilated to their territory and possessing their nationality. Through this nationality tie, states ordinarily exercise complete jurisdiction over their own ships on the high seas. "The merchant ship, while on the high seas, is, as the ship of war everywhere, a part of the territory of the nation to which she belongs."[8] Under the 1958 Convention on the High Seas, this rule is also confirmed.

REGINA v. ANDERSON

GREAT BRITAIN, COURT OF CRIMINAL APPEAL, 1868

11 COX'S CRIMINAL CASES, P. 198

Case reserved by Byles, J., at the October Sessions of the Central Criminal Court, 1868, for the opinion of this court.

James Anderson, an American citizen, was indicted for murder on board a vessel, belonging to the port of Yarmouth in Nova Scotia. She was registered in London, and was sailing under the British flag.

At the time of the offence committed the vessel was in the river Garonne, within the boundaries of the French empire, on her way up to Bordeaux, which city is by the course of the river about ninety miles from the open sea. The vessel had proceeded about half-way up the river, and was at the time of the offence about three hundred yards from the nearest shore, the river at that place being about a half mile wide.

The tide flows up to the place and beyond it.

No evidence was given whether the place was or was not within the limits of the port of Bordeaux.

It was objected for the prisoner that the offence having been committed within the empire of France, the vessel being a colonial vessel, and the prisoner an American citizen, the court had no jurisdiction to try him.

I expressed an opinion unfavourable to the objection, but agreed to grant a case for the opinion of this Court [i.e., the Court of Criminal Appeal].

The prisoner was convicted of manslaughter.

J. Barnard Byles.

. . . .

---

an infringement of the freedom of the seas," and referred the matter to the General Assembly. Conference *OR*, II, 95, and 143. See also Max Sørensen, "Law of the Sea," *International Conciliation* No. 520 (November 1958), pp. 195–256.

[8] Moore, *Digest*, I, 933.

BOVILL, C. J.—There is no doubt that the place where the offence was committed was within the territory of France, and that the prisoner was therefore subject to the laws of France, which the local authorities of that realm might have enforced if so minded; but at the same time, in point of law, the offence was also committed within British territory, for the prisoner was a seaman on board a merchant vessel, which, as to her crew and master, must be taken to have been at the time under the protection of the British flag, and, therefore, also amenable to the provision of the British law. It is true that the prisoner was an American citizen, but he had with his own consent embarked on board a British vessel as one of the crew. Although the prisoner was subject to the American jurisprudence as an American citizen, and to the law of France as having committed an offence within the territory of France, yet he must also be considered as subject to the jurisdiction of British law, which extends to the protection of British vessels, though in ports belonging to another country. From the passage in the treaties of Ortolan, already quoted, it appears that, with regard to offences committed on board of foreign vessels within the French territory, the French nation will not assert their police law unless invoked by the master of the vessel, or unless the offence leads to a disturbance of the peace of the port; and several instances where that course was adopted are mentioned. Among these are two cases where offences were committed on board American vessels—one at the port of Antwerp, and the other at Marseilles and where, on the local authorities interfering, the American court claimed exclusive jurisdiction. As far as America herself is concerned, it is clear that she, by the statutes of the 23d of March, 1825, has made regulations for persons on board her vessels in foreign parts, and we have adopted the same course of legislation. Our vessels must be subject to the laws of the nation at any of whose ports they may be, and also to the laws of our country, to which they belong. As to our vessels when going to foreign parts we have the right, if we are not bound, to make regulations. America has set us a strong example that we have the right to do so. In the present case, if it were necessary to decide to question on the 17 & 18 Vict. c. 104, I should have no hesitation in saying that we now not only legislate for British subjects on board of British vessels, but also for all those who form the crews thereof, and that there is no difficulty in so construing the statute; but it is not necessary to decide that point now. Independently of that statute, the general law is sufficient to determine this case. Here the offence was committed on board a British vessel by one of the crew, and it makes no difference whether the vessel was within a foreign port or not. If the offence had been committed on the high seas it is clear that it would have been within the jurisdiction of the Admiralty, and the Central Criminal Court has now the same extent of jurisdiction. Does it make any difference because the vessel was in the river Garonne half-way between the sea and the head of the river? The place where the offence was committed was in a navigable part of the river below bridge, and where the tide ebbs and flows, and great ships do lie and hover. An offence committed at such a place, according to the authorities, is within the Admiralty jurisdiction, and it is the same as if the offence had been committed on the high seas. On the whole I come to the conclusion that the prisoner was amenable to the British law, and that the conviction was right.

. . . .

BYLES, J.—I am of the same opinion. I adhere to the opinion that I expressed at the trial. A British ship is, for the purposes of this question, like a floating island; and, when a crime is committed on board a British ship, it is within the jurisdiction of the Admiralty Court, and therefore of the Central Criminal Court, and the offender is as amenable to British law as if he had stood on the Isle of Wight and committed the crime. Two English and two American cases decide that a crime committed on board a British vessel in a river like the one in question, where there is the flux and reflux of the tide, and wherein great ships do hover, is within the jurisdiction of the Admiralty Court; and that is also the opinion expressed in Kent's Commentaries. The only effect of the ship being within the ambit of French territory is that there might have been concurrent jurisdiction had the French claimed it. . . . .

Conviction affirmed.

STAMPFER v. ATTORNEY-GENERAL[9]

ISRAEL, SUPREME COURT (SITTING AS THE COURT OF CRIMINAL APPEALS)

(CHESHIN, DEPUTY PRESIDENT; GOITEIN AND VITKON JJ.)

JANUARY 4, 1956

The appellant was prosecuted in the District Court of Haifa and convicted on several counts of manslaughter under s. 212 of the Palestine Criminal Code Ordinance, 1936. The act on which the charge was based occurred on the s.s. *Massada*, which sank on the high seas, or in one of her boats immediately before the sinking, when the appellant, an Israel national, was one of her crew. It is not in dispute that the vessel, after acquisition by its owners, an Israeli corporation, had been provisionally registered at the Israel Consulate in Copenhagen and was flying the Israel flag. The question of public international law which thus arose was whether the Israel courts have criminal jurisdiction over offences committed by Israel nationals in Israel ships on the high seas. . . .

It is an important rule of public international law that merchant vessels on the high seas are under the jurisdiction of the State whose flag they lawfully fly and that the law of the flag State prescribes the rights and

[9] Adapted from *International Law Reports*, (1956), p. 284.

obligations of every person on board. The essential purpose of this rule is to protect the public from the law of the jungle (or here perhaps more exactly, the law of the sea). It is imperative for law and order to be established on ships sailing the high seas, lest they become places of lawlessness, where everybody does as he pleases and brute force prevails. The establishment of law and order in the remote and undefined spaces of the sea may be effected in one of two ways: (1) the State concerned in the matter may assume jurisdiction over persons and property situated in such a place; (2) every State may exercise unlimited jurisdiction in such a place, regardless of the rights and claims of other States. The first of these two ways has been adopted in international law, and the accepted principle is that persons under the protection of the flag of a particular State, when in places not under the sovereignty of any other State, are amenable to the laws and jurisdiction of that State as if they were within its territory. Therefore, by general consent, a merchant vessel on the high seas is deemed to be the State, or part of the State, whose flag she flies.

[The judge then quoted and cited several cases, including Regina v. Anderson and the Lotus Case, above.]. . . . The position is the same with regard to the law of non-Anglo-Saxon countries. . . .

In short: this jurisdiction, in both criminal and civil matters, is claimed by all countries which send their fleets—merchantmen and warships—to the high seas. The principle is a universal one, and as far as I have been able to ascertain it is not in dispute. The debate among lawyers is merely concerned with its source and *raison d'être*. Some explain its development by the "floating island" theory, according to which every ship on the high seas is deemed to be a floating part of the flag State (Oppenheim's *International Law*, 7th ed. (1948), vol. I, p. 458). Others connect it with the ownership of the State and its right of control over its property and assets when these are in a place where no other State claims local jurisdiction (Hall, *International Law*, 5th ed. (1904), p. 253). Mention has been made in these proceedings of the English case of *R*. v. *Gordon-Finlayson*, [1941] 1 K.B. 171,[10] and it has been suggested that that decision marks a new departure in the question under discussion. But in my opinion that case has brought no revolution, great or small, into the concepts current in the legal field concerned. The Judges who sat in that case dissociated themselves from the "floating island" theory, *i.e.*, the notion that a ship on the high seas is a limb torn from the parent territory and floating on the high seas whilst retaining the properties of the living body which has stayed in its place; but it never occurred to them to deny the age-old principle that the jurisdiction of the courts of a particular State extends over merchant ships at sea flying the flag of that State. On the contrary, they repeatedly emphasized that the said rule prevailed in English law unchallenged. [The Judge here quoted passages from the judgments of Justice Humphreys, Justice Tucker and Justice Oliver in that case, and went on:] They repudiated, for the purpose of the question before

[10] See *Annual Digest*, 1941–1942, Case No. 67.

them, the "floating island" theory, but in no way disputed the close connection between the flag of the ship and the law of the flag State, as regards the powers of the courts of that State.

It may not be superfluous to quote here a short passage representing one of the latest utterances on the subject. Hans Kelsen, in *Principles of International Law* (1952), discusses the rule of international law that on the high seas, outside the territorial waters of any State, every State may exercise jurisdiction over ships lawfully flying its flag. Here is what he says (at p. 223):

"The usual way to describe the legal situation of a vessel on the open sea is to say that it has to be considered as a floating part of its home state. That means that a vessel on the open sea is under the exclusive jurisdiction of the state under the flag of which it legitimately sails. Exclusive jurisdiction means that no other state but the flag state is entitled to exercise coercive power on board the ship which legitimately sails under its flag. That the ship is considered to be a floating part of its home state means further that the law of the flag state may provide that anything which happens on the ship shall be considered as if it happened on the territory of the flag state, such as the birth of a child, a commercial transaction, a crime, and the like."

Summing up, Kelsen remarks more pointedly (at p. 225):

". . . each state is authorized by general international law . . . to exercise its own law and especially to perform coercive acts on the open sea . . . on board its own ships. . . ."

It is interesting to note that although the *Finlayson* case disapproves the "floating island" theory, Kelsen quotes Justice Humphreys' words in that case in support of his remarks on the principle of a State's jurisdiction over ships flying its flag and on the origin and *raison d'être* of that principle in international law (*ibid.*, p. 223, n. 14). That principle has, in my opinion, become a part of the law of this country in three ways: first, by Article 46 of the [Palestine] Order-in-Council of 1922; second, by section 1 of the Admirality Offences (Colonial) Act, 1849, which was incorporated in the laws of this country by Article 35 of the Order-in-Council of 1922; third, by virtue of the sovereignty of the State of Israel.

We have already seen that this principle has its place in the English common law (see Justice Bovill's remarks in the above-cited *Anderson* case, pp. 166–167). It does not conflict with conditions in the State of Israel or the situation of its population, nor, as we have seen, does it conflict with any local law. . . .

To recapitulate: when the State prosecuted the appellant for the offence it imputed to him, it did so not only in virtue of its written laws, but also in virtue of its sovereignty and in virtue of the jurisdiction of its courts over ships on the high seas flying its flag. No national or international principle has thereby been infringed by it, and thus it cannot be impugned on that account. For this reason I would dismiss the preliminary plea of Counsel for the appellant concerning the jurisdiction of the District Court of Haifa.

WILDENHUS' CASE

UNITED STATES, SUPREME COURT, 1887

120 U.S. 1

Appeal from the Circuit Court of the United States for the District of New Jersey. [28 F. 924.]

. . . .

This appeal brought up an application made to the Circuit Court of the United States for the District of New Jersey, by Charles Mali, the "Consul of His Majesty the King of the Belgians, for the States of New York and New Jersey, in the United States," for himself, as such consul, "and in behalf of one Joseph Wildenhus, one Gionvienne Gobnbosich, and John J. Ostenmeyer," for the release, upon a writ of *habeas corpus,* of Wildenhus, Gobnbosich, and Ostenmeyer from the custody of the keeper of the common jail of Hudson county, New Jersey, and their delivery to the consul, "to be dealt with according to the law of Belgium." The facts on which the application rests are thus stated in the petition for the writ:

Second. That on or about the sixth day of October, 1886, on board the Belgian steamship *Noordland,* there occurred an affray between the said Joseph Wildenhus and one Fijens, wherein and whereby it is charged that the said Wildenhus stabbed with a knife and inflicted upon the said Fijens a mortal wound, of which he afterwards died.

Third. That the said Wildenhus is a subject of the kingdom of Belgium, and has his domicile therein, and is one of the crew of the said steamship *Noordland,* and was such when the said affray occurred.

Fourth. That the said Fijens was also a subject of Belgium, and had his domicile and residence therein, and at the time of the said affray, as well as at the time of his subsequent death, was one of the crew of the said steamship.

Fifth. That, at the time said affray occurred, the said steamship *Noordland* was lying moored at the dock of the port of Jersey City, in said state of New Jersey.

Sixth. That the said affray occurred and ended wholly below the deck of the said steamship, and that the tranquillity of the said port of Jersey City was in nowise disturbed or endangered thereby.

Seventh. That said affray occurred in the presence of several witnesses, all of whom were and still are of the crew of the said vessel, and that no other person or persons except those of the crew of said vessel were present or near by.

Eighth. Your petitioner therefore respectfully shows unto this honorable court that the said affray occurred outside of the jurisdiction of the said state of New Jersey.

Ninth. But, notwithstanding the foregoing facts, your petitioner respectfully further shows that the police authorities of Jersey City, in said state of New Jersey, have arrested the said Joseph Wildenhus, and also the said Gionviennie Gobnbosich and John J. Ostenmeyer, of the crew of the said vessel (one of whom is a quartermaster thereof), and that said Joseph Wildenhus has been committed by a police magistrate, acting under the authority of the said state, to the common jail of the county of Hudson, on a charge of an indictable offense under the laws of the said state of New Jersey, and is now held in confinement by the keeper of the said jail, and that the others of the said crew, arrested as aforesaid, are also detained in custody and confinement as witnesses to testify in such proceedings as may hereafter be had against the said Wildenhus.

Articles 8, 9, and 10 of the royal decree of the king of the Belgians, made on the eleventh of March, 1857, relating to consuls and consular jurisdiction, are as follows:

Art. 8. Our consuls have the right of discipline on Belgian merchant vessels in all the ports and harbors of their district. In matters of offenses or crimes they are to make the examination conformably to the instructions of the disciplinary and penal code of the merchant service. They are to claim, according to the terms of the conventions and laws in force, the assistance of the local authorities for the arrest and taking on board of deserting seamen.

Art. 9. Except in the case where the peace of the port shall have been compromised by the occurrence, the consul shall protest against every attempt that the local authority may make to take cognizance of crimes or offenses committed on board of a Belgian vessel by one of the ship's company towards one, either of the same company, or of the company of another Belgian vessel. He shall take the proper steps to have the cognizance of the case turned over to him, in order that it be ultimately tried according to Belgian laws.

Art. 10. When men belonging to the company of a Belgian vessel shall be guilty of offenses or crimes out of the ship, or even on board the ship, but against persons not of the company, the consul shall, if the local authority arrests or prosecutes them, take the necessary steps to have the Belgians so arrested treated with humanity, defended, and tried impartially.

The application in this case was made under the authority of these articles.

Article 11 of a convention between the United States and Belgium "concerning the rights, privileges, and immunities of consular officers," concluded March 9, 1880, and proclaimed by the president of the United States, March 1, 1881 (21 Stat. 776, 781), is as follows:

The respective consuls general, consuls, vice-consuls, and consular agents shall have exclusive charge of the internal order of the merchant vessels of their nation, and shall alone take cognizance of all differences which may arise, either at sea or in port, between the captains, officers, and crews, without exception, particularly with reference to the adjustment of wages and the execution of contracts. The local authorities shall not interfere, except when the disorder that has arisen is of such a nature as to disturb tranquillity and public order on shore or in the port, or when a person of the country, or not belonging to the crew, shall be concerned therein. In all other cases, the aforesaid authorities shall confine themselves to lending aid to the consuls and vice-consuls or consular agents, if they are requested by them to do so, in causing the arrest and imprisonment of any person whose name is inscribed on the crew list, whenever, for any cause, the said officers shall think proper.

The claim of the consul is that, by the law of nations and the provisions of this treaty, the offense with which Wildenhus has been charged is "solely cognizable by the authority of the laws of the kingdom of Belgium," and that the state of New Jersey is without jurisdiction in the premises. The circuit court refused to deliver the prisoners to the consul, and remanded them to the custody of the jailer. 28 F. 924. To reverse that decision this appeal was taken. . . .

Mr. Chief Justice Waite . . . delivered the opinion of the court.

By 751 and 753 of the Revised Statutes the courts of the United States have power to issue writs of *habeas corpus* which shall extend to prisoners in jail when they are in "custody in violation of the constitution or a law or treaty of the United States," and the question we have to consider is whether these prisoners are held in violation of the provisions of the existing treaty between the United States and Belgium.

It is part of the law of civilized nations that, when a merchant vessel of one country enters the ports of another for the purposes of trade, it subjects itself to the law of the place to which it goes, unless, by treaty or otherwise, the two countries have come to some different understanding or agreement; for, as was said by Chief Justice Marshall in *The Exchange*, 7 Cranch, 116, 144: "It would be obviously inconvenient and dangerous to society, and would subject the laws to continual infraction, and the government to degradation, if such . . . merchants did not owe temporary and local allegiance, and were not amenable to the jurisdiction of the country." . . . As the owner has voluntarily taken his vessel for his own private purposes to a place within the dominion of a government other than his own, and from which he seeks protection during his stay, he owes that government such allegiance for the time being as is due for the protection to which he is entitled.

From experience, however, it was found long ago that it would be beneficial to commerce if the local government would abstain from interfering with the internal discipline of the ship, and the general regulation of the rights and duties of the officers and crew towards the vessel, or among themselves. And so by comity it came to be generally understood among civilized nations that all matters of discipline, and all things done on board, which affected only the vessel, or those belonging to her, and did not involve the peace or dignity of the country, or the tranquillity of the port, should be left by the local government to be dealt with by the authorities of the nation to which the vessel belonged as the laws of that nation, or the interests of its commerce should require. But, if crimes are committed on board of a character to disturb the peace and tranquillity of the country to which the vessel has been brought, the offenders have never, by comity or usage, been entitled to any exemption from the operation of the local laws for their punishment, if the local tribunals see fit to assert their authority. Such being the general public law on this subject, treaties and conventions have been entered into by nations having commercial intercourse, the purpose of which was to settle and define the rights and duties of the contracting parties with respect to each other in these particulars, and thus prevent the inconvenience that might arise from attempts to exercise conflicting jurisdictions.

. . . .

The form of the provision found in the present convention with Belgium first appeared in a convention with Austria concluded in 1870, Art XI, 17 Stat. 827, and it is found now in substantially the same language in all the treaties and conventions which have since been entered into by the United States on the same subject. . . .

It thus appears that at first provision was made only for giving consuls police authority over the interior of the ship, and jurisdiction in civil matters arising out of disputes or differences on board; that is to say, between those belonging to the vessel. Under this police authority the duties of the consuls were evidently confined to the maintenance of order and discipline on board. This gave them no power to punish for crimes against the peace of the country. In fact, they were expressly prohibited from interfering with the local police in matters of that kind. . . .

In the next conventions consuls were simply made judges and arbitrators to settle and adjust differences between those on board. This clearly related to such differences between those belonging to the vessel as are capable of adjustment and settlement by judicial decision or by arbitration, for it simply made the consuls judges or arbitrators in such matters. That would of itself exclude all idea of punishment for crimes against the state which affected the peace and tranquillity of the port; but, to prevent all doubt on this subject, it was expressly provided that it should not apply to differences of that character.

Next came a form of convention which in terms gave the consuls authority to cause proper order to be maintained on board, and to decide disputes between the officers and crew, but allowed the local authorities to interfere if the disorders taking place on board were of such a nature as to disturb the public tranquillity, and that is substantially all there is in the convention with Belgium which we have now to consider. This treaty is the law which now governs the conduct of the United States and Belgium towards each other in this particular. Each nation has granted to the other such local jurisdiction within its own dominion as may be necessary to maintain order on board a merchant vessel, but has reserved to itself the right to interfere if the disorder on board is of a nature to disturb the public tranquillity.

The treaty is part of the supreme law of the United States, and has the same force and effect in New Jersey that it is entitled to elsewhere. If it gives the consul of Belgium exclusive jurisdiction over the offense which it is alleged has been committed within the territory of New Jersey, we see no reason why he may not enforce his rights under the treaty by writ of *habeas corpus* in any proper court of the United States. This being the case, the only important question left for our determination is whether the thing which has been done—the disorder that has arisen—on board this vessel is of a nature to disturb the public peace, or, as some writers term it, the "public repose," of the people who look to the state of New Jersey for their protection. If the thing done—"the disorder," as it is called in the treaty—is of a character to affect those on shore or in the port when it becomes known, the fact that only those on the ship saw it when it was done, is a matter of no moment. Those who are not on the vessel pay no special attention to the mere disputes or quarrels of the seamen while on board, whether they occur under deck or above. Neither do they, as a rule, care for anything done on board which relates only to the discipline of the ship, or to the preservation of order and authority. Not so, however, with crimes which from their gravity awaken a public interest as soon as they become known, and especially those of a character which every civilized nation considers itself bound to provide a severe punishment for when committed within its own jurisdiction. In such cases inquiry is certain to be instituted at once to ascertain how or why the thing was done, and the popular excitement rises or falls as the news spreads, and the facts become known. It is not alone the publicity of the act, or the noise and clamor which attends it, that fixes the nature of the crime, but the act itself. If that is of a character to awaken public interest when it becomes known, it is a "disorder," the nature of which is to affect the community at large, and consequently to invoke the power of the local government whose people have been disturbed by what was done. The very nature of such an act is to disturb the quiet of a peaceful community, and to create, in the language of the treaty, a "disorder" which will "disturb tranquillity and public order on shore or in the port." The principle which governs the whole matter is this: Disorders which disturb only the peace of the ship or those on board are to be dealt with exclusively by the sovereignty of the home of the ship, but those which disturb the public peace may be suppressed, and, if need be, the offenders punished, by the proper authorities of the local jurisdiction. It may not be easy at all times to determine to which of the two jurisdictions a particular act of disorder belongs. Much will undoubtedly depend on the attending circumstances of the particular case, but all must concede that felonious homicide is a subject for the local jurisdiction; and that, if the proper authorities are proceeding with the case in a regular way, the consul has no right to interfere to prevent it. That, according to the petition for the *habeas corpus,* is this case.

This is fully in accord with the practice in France, where the government has been quite as liberal towards foreign nations in this particular as any other, and where, as we have seen in the cases of *The Sally* and *The Newton,* by a decree of the Council of State, representing the political department of the government, the French courts were prevented from exercising jurisdiction. But afterwards, in 1859, in the Case of Jally, the mate of an American merchantman, who had killed one of the crew and severely wounded another on board the ship in the port of Havre, the Court of Cassation, the highest judicial tribunal of France, upon full consideration, held, while the convention of 1853 was in force, that the French courts had rightful jurisdiction, for reasons which sufficiently appear in the following extract from its judgment: "Considering that it is a principle of the law of nations that every state has jurisdiction throughout its territory; considering that, by the terms of article 3 of the Code Napoleon, the laws of police and safety bind all those who inhabit French territory, and that consequently foreigners, even *transeuntes,* find themselves subject to those laws; considering that merchant vessels entering the port of a nation other than that to which they belong cannot be withdrawn from the territorial jurisdiction, in any case in which the interest of the state of which that port forms part finds itself concerned, without danger to the good order and to the dignity of the government; considering that every state is interested in the repression of crimes and offenses that may be committed in the ports of its territory, not only by the men of the ship's company of a foreign merchant vessel towards men not forming part of that company, but even by men of the ship's company among themselves, whenever the act is of a nature to compromise the tranquillity of the port, or the intervention of the local authority is invoked, or the act constitutes a crime by common law [*droit commun,* the law common to all civilized nations,] the gravity of which does not permit any nation to leave it unpunished, without impugning its rights of jurisdictional and territorial sovereignty, because that crime is in itself the most manifest as well as the most flagrant violation of the laws which it is the duty of every nation to cause to be respected in all parts of its territory." 1 Ortolan, *Diplomatie de la Mer* (4th ed.), 455, 456; Sirey (N.S.) 1859, p. 189.

The judgment of the Circuit Court is affirmed.

Although a ship's nationality does not derive from the nationality of its owners or builders, states may decide to grant documents only to ships built or owned by its nationals. In general, every state is free to fix the conditions under which it grants its nationality to ships, registers them, and permits them to fly its flag,[11] except that "there must be a genuine link between the State and the ship; in particular, the State must effectively exercise its jurisdiction and control in administrative, technical, and social matters over ships flying its flag." This proviso was aimed at states like Liberia, Panama and, to a certain extent, Honduras and Costa Rica, which have registered ships even when owned and operated by foreigners and, in effect, permitted them to escape higher taxes, operating costs, insurance rates, and wages; and allowed them to avoid labor, safety, and social security legislation in effect in the traditional maritime states. Because the Convention does not define "genuine link," it does not eliminate the economic competition implicit in the "flags of convenience," nor did the conferees go so far as the International Law Commission suggested by making recognition of a ship's nationality depend on their being such a genuine link.[12]

The Convention also contains provisions obliging each state: to make sure that its ships conform to generally accepted international standards of lighting (Article 10); to require ship's masters to assist persons and

[11] Convention on the High Seas (1958), Article 5.
[12] For a discussion of this and other problems related to the 1958 Conference, see Sørensen, who discusses "flags of convenience" on pp. 201–206.

vessels in distress at sea (Article 12); to punish the slave trade (Article 14); to prevent pollution of the seas with oil or radioactive wastes (Articles 24 and 25); and to repress and punish piracy (Article 14).

Piracy

The 1958 Convention also defines piracy (Article 15) as follows.

Piracy consists of any of the following acts:

1. Any illegal acts of violence, detention or any act of depredation, committed for private ends by the crew or the passengers of a private ship or a private aircraft, and directed:

(a) On the high seas, against another ship or aircraft, or against persons or property on board such ship or aircraft;

(b) Against a ship, aircraft, persons or property in a place outside the jurisdiction of any State;

2. Any act of voluntary participation in the operation of a ship or of an aircraft with knowledge of facts making it a pirate ship or aircraft;

3. Any act of inciting or of intentionally facilitating an act described in sub-paragraph 1 or sub-paragraph 2 of this article.

The Convention goes on (Article 16) to make clear that this definition applies to such acts whether committed on a private or government ship or aircraft and then confirms the universal jurisdiction of states over pirate ships:

ARTICLE 19

On the high seas, or in any other place outside the jurisdiction of any State, every State may seize a pirate ship or aircraft, or a ship taken by piracy and under the control of pirates, and arrest the persons and seize the property on board. The courts of the State which carried out the seizure may decide upon the penalties to be imposed, and may also determine the action to be taken with regard to the ships, aircraft or property, subject to the rights of third parties acting in good faith.

States must, however, proceed with caution in seizing ships, because they are responsible for any seizure without cause (Article 20). In any case, the seizures may be carried out only by warships or military aircraft or other ships specifically authorized to make the seizure (Article 21).

Some of the diplomatic and legal risks involved became manifest in 1961, when Henrique Galvao seized a ship of Portuguese registry in the Caribbean, alleging that he was signalling the start of a revolt against the Salazar regime. Compare, for instance, these statements by the U.S. Department of State, issued on successive days:

[At the request of the Portuguese government] destroyers and airplanes have been dispatched to intercept the vessel under the well-defined terms of international law governing piracy and insurrection aboard ship.[13]

[The] facts . . . are not entirely clear . . . and not sufficiently detailed to form a . . . firm opinion as to whether the crime of piracy under international law has been committed.[14]

Ultimately, Captain Galvao surrendered to Brazilian authorities who promised him asylum and returned the ship to Portugal, thus making it unnecessary for other governments to decide for themselves whether or not Galvao and his supporters had committed piracy. There was no doubt that they had seized the ship; their intentions, however, seemed to be wholly political.

Hot Pursuit

The 1958 Convention has one article dealing with "hot pursuit":

ARTICLE 23

1. The hot pursuit of a foreign ship may be undertaken when the competent authorities of the coastal State have good reason to believe that the ship has violated the laws and regulations of that State. Such pursuit must be commenced when the foreign ship or one of its boats is within the internal waters or the territorial sea or the contiguous zone of the pursuing State, and may only be continued outside the territorial sea or the contiguous zone if the pursuit has not been interrupted. It is not necessary that, at the time when the foreign ship within the territorial sea or the contiguous zone receives the order to stop, the ship giving the order should likewise be within the territorial sea or the contiguous zone. If the foreign ship is within a contiguous zone, as defined in article 24 of the Convention on the Territorial Sea and the Contiguous Zone, the pursuit may only be undertaken if there has been a violation of the rights for the protection of which the zone was established.

2. The right of hot pursuit ceases as soon as the ship pursued enters the territorial sea of its own country or of a third State.

3. Hot pursuit is not deemed to have begun unless the pursuing ship has satisfied itself by such practicable means as may be available that the ship pursued or one of its boats or other craft working as a team and using the ship pursued as a mother ship are within the limits of the territorial sea, or as the case may be within the contiguous zone. The pursuit may only be commenced after a visual or auditory signal to stop has been given at a distance which enables it to be seen or heard by the foreign ship.

4. The right of hot pursuit may be exercised only by warships or military aircraft, or other ships or aircraft on government service specially authorized to that effect.

5. Where hot pursuit is effected by an aircraft:

[13] *New York Times*, January 25, 1961, p. 32.
[14] *Ibid.*, January 26, 1961, p. 1.

(a) The provisions of paragraphs 1 to 3 of this article shall apply *mutatis mutandis;*

(b) The aircraft giving the order to stop must itself actively pursue the ship until a ship or aircraft of the coastal State, summoned by the aircraft, arrives to take over the pursuit, unless the aircraft is itself able to arrest the ship. It does not suffice to justify an arrest on the high seas that the ship was merely sighted by the aircraft as an offender or suspected offender, if it was not both ordered to stop and pursued by the aircraft itself or other aircraft or ships which continue the pursuit without interruption.

6. The release of a ship arrested within the jurisdiction of a State and escorted to a port of that State for the purposes of an inquiry before the competent authorities may not be claimed solely on the ground that the ship, in the course of its voyage, was escorted across a portion of the high seas, if the circumstances rendered this necessary.

7. Where a ship has been stopped or arrested on the high seas in circumstances which do not justify the exercise of the rights of hot pursuit, it shall be compensated for any loss or damage that may have been thereby sustained.

THE *I'M ALONE*

U.S. ARBITRATION SERIES, No. 2 (1-7) 1931-1935

[The U.S. Coast Guard cutter, *Wolcott,* operating off the Louisiana coast, hailed a Canadian schooner, the *I'm Alone,* suspected of smuggling liquor, on March 20, 1929. Although the *I'm Alone* was outside the three-mile limit, it was within one hour's sailing distance of the shore when first sighted. The *I'm Alone* refused to stop, and the captain of the *Wolcott* ordered three blank shells to be fired in the direction of the *I'm Alone.* He then received permission to board, but was denied permission to search. He returned to his own ship, whereupon the *I'm Alone* headed for the open sea. The *Wolcott* pursued the *I'm Alone,* fired another three blank shots across its bow and, then commenced firing upon the ship in earnest, until its gun jammed. Still in hot pursuit, the master of the *Wolcott* called for help, and on March 22, the pursuit continuing, the *Wolcott* was joined by another cutter, the *Dexter,* which sank the *I'm Alone* two hundred miles from the coast. The crew of the *I'm Alone* jumped overboard and were rescued, except for the boatswain, Leon Mainguy, who was drowned. The master and the crew of the *I'm Alone* were placed in irons and conveyed to New Orleans, where they were kept in custody for 48 hours.

[Arbitration between the United States and Canada went forward under Article IV of a Convention of January 28, 1924, between the United States and Great Britain, which dealt with means of suppressing liquor smuggling into the United States. Canada argued that "hot pursuit" was not a wholly acceptable doctrine in international law, and that where it was accepted, it always assumed that the pursuit would begin within the territorial waters of the offended state. The United States noted that its own courts had upheld the right of pursuing ships that had offended against U.S. laws so long as they were not more than one hour's sailing distance from the coast of the United States when pursuit began.

[Canada also objected to the role of the *Dexter,* maintaining that it had substituted for the *Wolcott* and thereby interrupted the hot pursuit, which had to be continuous. Finally the Canadian authorities said that sinking the *I'm Alone* was not justified in any case. The United States maintained that since the *Wolcott* had been present throughout the case, the pursuit was hot and continuous, and that the sinking would not have taken place if the master of the *I'm Alone* had ordered his ship to stop when requested. The sinking was therefore owing to "the unlawful act of her master in refusing to heave to." Furthermore, the United States pointed out, the *Dexter* had injured no one by its gun fire; and the death by drowning would not have occurred if the *I'm Alone* had had life-preservers on board. Finally, the U.S. Government maintained that the beneficial ownership of the *I'm Alone* was American, even though it was registered in Canada, which gave the United States a jurisdictional claim to the *I'm Alone* no matter where it was.]

In an Interim Report the Commissioner stated: . . . The question is whether, in the circumstances, the Government of the United States was legally justified in sinking the *I'm Alone.*

The answer given to this question is as follows:

On the assumptions stated in the question, the United States might, consistently with the Convention, use necessary and reasonable force for the purpose of effecting the objects of boarding, searching, seizing and bringing into port the suspected vessel; and if sinking should occur incidentally, as a result of the exercise of necessary and reasonable force for such purpose, the pursuing vessel might be entirely blameless. But the Commissioners think that, in the circumstances stated . . . , the admittedly intentional sinking of the suspected vessel was not justified. . . .

In their Final Report the Commissioners stated:

It will be recalled that the *I'm Alone* was sunk on the 22nd day of March, 1929, on the high seas, in the Gulf of Mexico, by the United States revenue cutter *Dexter.* By their interim report the Commissioners found that the sinking of the vessel was not justified by anything in the Convention. The Commissioners now add that it could not be justified by any principle of international law.

The vessel was a British ship of Canadian registry; after her construction she was employed for several years in rum running, the cargo being destined for illegal introduction into, and sale in, the United States. In December, 1928, and during the early months of 1929, down to the sinking of the vessel on the 22nd of March, of that year, she was engaged in carrying liquor from Belize, in British Honduras, to an agreed point or points in the Gulf of Mexico, in convenient proximity to the coast of Louisiana, where the liquor was taken from her in smaller craft, smuggled into the United States, and sold there.

We find as a fact that, from September, 1928, down to the date when she was sunk, the *I'm Alone*, although a British ship of Canadian registry, was *de facto* owned, controlled, and at the critical times, managed, and her movements directed and her cargo dealt with and disposed of, by a group of persons acting in concert who were entirely, or nearly so, citizens of the United States, and who employed her for the purposes mentioned. The possibility that one of the group may not have been of United States nationality we regard as of no importance in the circumstances of this case.

The Commissioners consider that, in view of the facts, no compensation ought to be paid in respect of the loss of the ship or the cargo.

The act of sinking the ship, however, by officers of the United States Coast Guard, was, as we have already indicated, an unlawful act; and the Commissioners consider that the United States ought formally to acknowledge its illegality, and to apologize to His Majesty's Canadian Government therefor; and, further, that as a material amend in respect of the wrong the United States should pay the sum of $25,000 to His Majesty's Canadian Government; and they recommend accordingly.

The Commissioners have had under consideration the compensation which ought to be paid by the United States to His Majesty's Canadian Government for the benefit of the captain and members of the crew, none of whom was a party to the illegal conspiracy to smuggle liquor into the United States and sell the same there. [The Commissioners recommended that the U.S. pay $25,666.50 for the benefit of the captain and crew.]

Fishing and Conservation

As Article 2 of the Convention on the High Seas (*supra* page 201) makes clear, states today generally include in freedom of the sea the right to fish outside the territorial waters of coastal states. Some states argued at the 1958 meetings that this right was not one of the freedoms of the sea,[15] but legal formulas going back to the seventeenth century and before prevailed. Fishing has been carried on so extensively, however, that there is in some parts of the world real danger of reducing the stocks of fish to a very dangerous degree.[16] States have attempted individually to introduce conservation measures, in some cases by creating conservation zones, but where they have failed to conclude agreements with other states concerned, their conservation measures have in effect defined exclusive fishing zones. One of the largest was proclaimed by Chile, Ecuador, and Peru in 1952 under the Santiago Declaration wherein, to preserve the natural resources of the sea, they claimed

[15] U.N. Conference on the Law of the Sea, *OR*, III, 6–7, Statement of Mr. Ulloa Sótomayer (Peru), 5 March 1958.
[16] A/Conf. 13/16, "The Economic Importance of the Sea Fisheries in Different Countries," 1958 Conference on the Law of the Sea, *OR*, Vol. I: Preparatory Documents, pp. 245–287.

sovereignty and jurisdiction over 200 miles of ocean off their coasts.[17] Under this Declaration, the three states fired upon and seized ships in 1954 which were operating without a permit.[18]

In 1958, the very year of the first U.N. Conference, British frigates clashed with Icelandic coastal vessels attempting to enforce Iceland's decision to extend her territorial waters from four to twelve miles and thus close traditional fishing grounds to British fishermen.

A "little war" between the two powers ensued, involving many clashes at sea in which ships exchanged gunfire, and the fighting continued fitfully for about thirty months. But in March 1961, after a "truce" arranged in 1960, Britain agreed to object no more to the twelve-mile fishing zone around Iceland. Up to 1964, Iceland would permit British ships to fish in parts of the six-to-twelve-mile zone at certain times of the year. The base lines used in delineating the six- and twelve-mile limits were redrawn in Iceland's favor, however, for instead of measuring the distances from the indentations of the coast, the authorities agreed to measure them from straight lines drawn between headlands.[19]

Some states have concluded treaties under which they cooperate in conserving fish by coordinating research programs through an international body.[20] Other states have established commissions to recommend conservation measures or to adopt regulations subject to governmental approval.[21] One Convention binds the parties to adopt certain conservation measures, but creates a commission which can propose changes in the Convention; the changes come automatically into effect if unanimously adopted.[22] States have given even wider powers to other bodies, for example, the International Whaling Commission, which has the power to close the whaling season when quotas that it establishes are reached, and which may modify conservation measures established by the Convention for the Regulation of Whaling (1946) by determining the length

---

[17] Text in *Laws and Regulations on the Regime of the Territorial Sea* (New York: United Nations Sale No. 1957.V.2), p. 723. For comments on the material in this and the succeeding paragraph, see Sørensen, pp. 213–215.

[18] See the *New York Times,* November 6, 17, 23, 27, 1954.

[19] For accounts of the controversy, see the *New York Times* for the years involved. 1958: May 1, June 3, July 3, 6, 23; 1959: Feb. 3, March 26, April 16, May 6, 23, 24, June 6, 8, 28, July 7, Sept. 3, Nov. 11; 1960: Aug. 12, Sept. 22, Oct. 12; 1961: Feb. 28, March 10. For episodes after the treaty was signed, see *ibid.,* 1963; April 28, Oct. 28. See also p. 271 below for account of the European Fisheries Convention. For the treaty itself, see the *New York Times,* Feb. 28, 1961, p. 10 and n. 46 below.

[20] The Indo-Pacific Fisheries (est. 1949) and the General Fisheries Council for the Mediterranean (1952) are examples.

[21] Examples are the Northwest Atlantic Fisheries Convention (1949), the North Pacific High Seas Fisheries Convention (1952), the Northern Pacific Halibut Fisheries Convention (1953).

[22] See, for example, the 1946 Convention for the Regulation of Meshes of Fishing Nets and the Size Limits of Fish, which applies in the northeastern Atlantic.

of the closed season and the maximum number of whales to be caught. The International Whaling Commission's rules are enforced by a board that sits in Sandefjord, Norway. They regulate the number of blue-whale "units" or their equivalent (two fin whales, two and one-half humpback whales, or six sei whales) that may be taken from the Southern Ocean in one season by the fifteen or twenty expeditions of various nationalities that sail there. The regulations are enforced by two whaling inspectors who sail with every expedition. British inspectors sail with British expeditions, Norwegian inspectors with Norwegian expeditions, and so on.

The whaling inspectors, like many officials of international organizations today, have a double loyalty—a first loyalty to the government that employs and pays them, and a second (but no less demanding) one to the organization they serve. Their job is mainly to curb overzealous whalemen, in order to preserve the various species of whale and to see to it that despite the slaughter they even get a chance to breed and increase. The inspectors must keep in mind a hundred or more regulations and restrictions. They must make sure that no whale shorter than the lengths internationally agreed upon for the several species is taken; they must preserve the rarer species, such as the right whale and the gray whale, inviolate; they must limit whaling to the times and seas prescribed by the Commission; and they must keep the expeditions they accompany from trespassing on great whale sanctuaries that have been set aside in the oceans of the world. They must be seamen, zoologists, mathematicians, and men of absolute integrity, who will refuse the bribes that are presented daily in sundry attractive forms. They must be detectives with the acumen of Holmes, and they must also be lawyers and arbitrators. At the same time, they must have the ability to keep on terms of good will with the whale-fleet owners and the whalemen, all of whom, they must assume, are trying to hoodwink them. For doing this job and possessing these qualities, the British government pays its senior inspectors sixty pounds ($168) a month and its junior inspectors fifty pounds ($140). . . . The inspector's job is to enforce the law of his nation and the rules of the International Commission, but he is given no power to do so. He cannot *order* the expedition's manager or the gunners—or, indeed, any man at all—to do anything. He can only "advise," and, long afterward, when he has returned home, report any delinquencies of which he has absolute proof. Most breaches of the whaling laws carry a penalty of three months' imprisonment or a fine of fifty pounds, but I have heard of no case of a man's doing time or paying for a whaling offense.[23]

The Whaling Inspector's job, to enforce the law without any real authority, in a way symbolizes the present status of international law enforcement. On the face of it, it seems to provide no real enforcement at all; and yet, without truly strong enforcement agencies, the record of

[23] R. B. Robertson, "And There Was Whale, Part III: A Matter of Proportion," *The New Yorker* XXIX (January 23, 1954), 47–48. See also R. B. Robertson, *Of Whales and Men* (New York: Alfred A. Knopf, 1954), pp. 195–196.

enforcing the law is remarkable. Certainly without this much law, the chances of any whales surviving (and therefore the chance of preserving the whale industry) would be nil.[24]

Not all the fishing agreements work equally well: some governments do not participate; some areas of the world are not covered; and some species of fish are not protected. Moreover, even participating governments sometimes find it impossible to approve conservation regulations because of local pressure groups concerned with immediate profits rather than with long-term conservation measures.

Recognizing that existing treaties do not form a coherent and complete system, international legal experts have favored either additional regional arrangements or some universal system. It was to provide such a universal system that the International Law Commission, the General Assembly, and the delegates to the 1958 Conference were working. The 1958 Convention on Fishing and Conservation of the Living Resources of the High Seas takes a middle path by including in a universal treaty provisions for using *ad hoc* seven-member commissions to arbitrate interstate disagreements over conservation measures.

The Convention, like all efforts to regulate fishing beforehand, has had to deal with one overriding problem—the right of a coastal state to impose conservation measures upon foreigners fishing in areas of the high seas adjacent to its territorial sea.[25] Clearly conservation measures observed internationally are an alternative to exclusive control of fishing within large areas of the sea. The problem is complicated because the interests of coastal and high-sea fishermen differ, and states' positions are determined in large part by the dominant fishing interest within their own economies:

> The interests of coastal fisheries and high seas fisheries clash most conspicuously in areas such as the northern Atlantic, where sea-going fishing vessels must approach foreign coasts to exploit rich fishing grounds. High sea fishing fleets, with trawlers, factory ships, and other efficiently operating vessels, may deplete the stocks on which local fisheries depend. The understandable reaction of the costal state is to claim an extension either of the territorial sea or the sea in which it can exercise exclusive rights.[26]

[24] As a supplemental measure, the governments of Japan, the Netherlands, Norway, the U.S.S.R., and the U.K., all parties to the 1946 International Convention for the Regulation of Whaling, agreed in London in 1963 to establish an international observer scheme for factory ships engaged in pelagic whaling in the Antarctic. By this arrangement, factory ships are to carry as an observer someone not a national of the country sending out the ship. The observers were empowered to receive all the information they need to report independently to the International Whaling Commission.
[25] See F. V. Garcia Amador, *The Exploitation and Conservation of the Resources of the Sea* (2d ed., Leyden: A. W. Sythoff, 1959), Part III.
[26] Sørensen, p. 219. For more recent, far-reaching recommendations for international conservation measures, see Commission to Study the Organization of Peace, *New*

The basic principles of the Convention on Fishing and Conservation appear in the first article.[27]

ARTICLE 1

1. All States have the right for their nationals to engage in fishing on the high seas, subject (a) to their treaty obligations, (b) to the interest and rights of coastal States as provided for in this Convention, and (c) to the provisions contained in the following articles. . . .

2. All States have the duty to adopt, or to co-operate with other States in adopting, such measures for their respective nationals as may be necessary for the conservation of the living resources of the high seas.

States are supposed to adopt conservation measures to govern their own nationals' fishing any stocks of fish where the nationals of other states are not involved (Article 3) and to negotiate agreements with other states in cases where the nationals of two or more states are involved in fishing the same stocks of fish (Article 4).[28] The special rights of coastal states referred to in Article 1 (b) are spelled out in the treaty:

ARTICLE 7

1. . . . any coastal State may, with a view to the maintenance of the productivity of the living resources of the sea, adopt unilateral measures of conservation appropriate to any stock of fish or other marine resources in any area of the high seas adjacent to its territorial sea, provided that negotiations to that effect with the other States concerned have not led to an agreement within six months.

2. The measures which the coastal State adopts under the previous paragraph shall be valid as to other States only if the following requirements are fulfilled:

(a) That there is a need for urgent application of conservation measures in the light of existing knowledge of the fishery;

(b) That the measures adopted are based on appropriate scientific findings;

(c) That such measures do not discriminate in form or in fact against foreign fishermen.

3. These measures shall remain in force pending the settlement, in accordance with the relevant provisions of this Convention, of any disagreement as to their validity.

4. If the measures are not accepted by the other States concerned, any of the parties may initiate the procedure contemplated by article 9. Subject to paragraph 2 of article 10, the measures adopted shall remain obligatory pending the decision of the special commission.

Dimensions for the United Nations (New York: The Commission, 1966), Introduction, Part IV, Chapter IV.

[27] A/Conf. 13/L.54, "Conference on the Law of the Sea," *OR*, II, 139–141.

[28] Note that the Convention does not cover the situation where nationals of different states are fishing different stocks of fish in the same area. See Sørensen, p. 221.

The quotation below Article 7 is from Sørensen, p. 223.

5. The principles of geographical demarcation as defined in article 12 of the Convention of the Territorial Sea and the Contiguous Zone shall be adopted when coasts of different states are involved.

This provision marks "a radical departure from the established principle of the freedom of the seas" by authorizing states to adopt measures binding upon the nationals of other states. It also leaves open a number of troublesome questions: how far from the coast such measures can apply and who is to enforce the measures, for instance. As a safeguard against abuses of these rights by the coastal-fishing states, the high seas fishing nations looked to the arbitral scheme set out in the treaty:

ARTICLE 9

1. Any dispute which may arise between States under articles 4, 5, 6, 7, and 8 shall, at the request of any of the parties, be submitted for settlement to a special commission of five members, unless the parties agree to seek a solution by another method of peaceful settlement, as provided for in Article 33 of the Charter of the United Nations.

2. The members of the commission, one of whom shall be designated as chairman, shall be named by agreement between the States in dispute within three months of the request for settlement in accordance with the provisions of this article. Failing agreement they shall, upon the request of any State party, be named by the Secretary-General of the United Nations, within a further three-month period, in consultation with the States in dispute and with the President of the International Court of Justice and the Director-General of the Food and Agriculture Organization of the United Nations, from amongst well-qualified persons being nationals of States not involved in the dispute and specializing in legal, administrative or scientific questions relating to fisheries, depending upon the nature of the dispute to be settled. Any vacancy arising after the original appointment shall be filled in the same manner as provided for the initial selection.

3. Any State party to proceedings under these articles shall have the right to name one of its nationals to the special commission, with the right to participate fully in the proceedings on the same footing as a member of the commission, but without the right to vote or to take part in the writing of the commission's decision.

4. The commission shall determine its own procedure, assuring each party to the proceedings a full opportunity to be heard and to present its case. It shall also determine how the costs and expenses shall be divided between the parties to the dispute, failing agreement by the parties on this matter.

5. The special commission shall render its decision within a period of five months from the time it is appointed unless it decides, in case of necessity, to extend the time limit for a period not exceeding three months.

6. The special commission shall, in reaching its decisions, adhere to these articles and to any special agreements between the disputing parties regarding settlement of the dispute.

7. Decisions of the commission shall be by majority vote.

Seizures, detentions, and other harassments of tuna vessels

THE FOLLOWING INFORMATION IS BASED UPON OFFICIAL BUSINESS RECORDS OF THE AMERICAN TUNABOAT ASSOCIATION, UPON AFFIDAVITS OF MASTERS OF TUNA CLIPPERS, AND UPON VERBAL REPORTS RECEIVED BY THE ASSOCIATION FROM OTHER MASTERS AND MANAGING OWNERS OF TUNA CLIPPERS

Name of motor vessel	Date	Location	Remarks
Marico	Sept. 15, 1951	Puerto Bolivar, Ecuador	Seized by Ecuadoran frigate *Guayas*. Vessel was entering port because of repairs. Vessel was fined $5,500.
Tesoro del Mar	November 1951		Seized by Ecuadorans, vessel was of Panamanian registry, no information available.
Notre Dame	Nov. 4, 1951	51 miles west-northwest of Isla de la Plata, Ecuador.	Vessel seized while en route to fishing banks in high seas off Peru. Vessel fined $8,000, released after fine paid under protest.
Sun Pacific	July 30, 1952	1°52′ south latitude 81°4′′ west longitude (18 miles off coast of Ecuador).	Vessel released Aug. 18, 1952, upon deposit of cash bond of $11,600.
Equator	July 31, 1952	0°52′ south latitude 81°3′′ west longitude (12 to 13 miles off coast of Ecuador).	Vessel in possession of Ecualoran fishing license issued in Panama. Vessel paid $1,000. Released after being in custody 3 weeks.
Venus	April 1952	Off coast of Colombia	Vessels seized and taken into port of Buenaventura. Reference: El Tiempo, newspaper in Bogotá, Colombia, dated July 25, 1952.
Cesare Augustus	do	do	
Jackie Sue	do	Off coast of Colombia beyond 3 miles	
Lima B	do	El Salvador	Seizure of vessel, no other facts available.
American Beauty	Aug. 9, 1952	Ecuador, 00° north latitude, 80°42′′ west longitude.	Ecuadoran merchant vessel *Rio Guayas* attempted to stop and board vessel, but *Martin B.* did not stop or permit boarding.
Martin B	Oct. 21, 1952		Fine imposed and paid $3,000 for vessel and bail for crew in the amount of $2,000.
Starcrest	May 20, 1953	Panama	
Conte Bianco	Mar. 1, 1954	Galapagos Islands, Ecuador.	Vessel boarded by naval officers. Vessel had purchased Ecuadoran fishing license. Vessel charged with failure to clear vessel and vessel assessed penalty $8,848.50.
Santa Rosa	do	do	Assessed penalty $9,040.50. Same as above.
Helen Ann	do	do	$9,040.50. Same as above.
Bernadette	do	do	Vessel boarded and documents inspected by naval officers of Ecuadoran patrol vessel *Bae Manabi*. Fined $10,240.50.
Conte di Savoia	do	do	Abandonment of Ecuadoran waters without presenting for inspection of the captain of the port, the fishing license as well as other pertinent documents. $9,068.50.
Sun Beam	Apr. 14, 1954	In waters between port of Salinas and Santa Clara Island, Ecuador.	Seized by Ecuadoran patrol vessel *El Oro*; fine imposed (amount unknown). Vessel in distress at time of seizure.
Janus	June 1954	3°15′ south latitude, 80°54′ west longitude (12 miles west of Santa Clara Island, Ecuador).	No further information.
Sun Streak	Sept. 4, 1954	San Cristobal, Galapagos Islands, Ecuador.	Seized by patrol vessel *Bae Manabi*. Fine imposed, $12,000.
Belle of Portugal	Sept. 25, 1954	31 miles, 304° true from Foca Island, Peru.	Charged that in July this vessel was sighted 12 miles off Manta, Ecuador, during July. Vessel released after boarding by naval officers. Peruvian cutter D-3 *Rodriquez* advised master to "come aboard immediately or we will sink you." Master refused, vessel continued to operate 3 miles off the coast.
Portuguesa	Nov. 19, 1954	23 miles southwest of Foca Islands, Peru.	Boarded by Peruvian naval vessel, and request for fishing license. Released and told to get license from Peruvian consul in Los Angeles.
Invader	Nov. 14, 1954	4° 47′′ south latitude, 81° 28′′ west longitude, about 15 miles off coast of Peru.	Boarded by Peruvian naval vessel D2 *Aguirre*. Advised to proceed 200 miles off coast.
Renown	do	4° 81′ south latitude, 81° 37′ west longitude.	Same as above.
Seafarer	Feb. 18, 1955	Off the coast of Peru beyond 3 miles	Seized and fined $2,000. Taken into port of Talara.
Stanford	do	do	Do.
E. S. Lucido	do	do	Do.
Miss Universe	do	do	Do.
Martha Ann	do	do	Do.
Alaska Reefer	do	do	Do.
Sea King	do	do	Do.

223

Vessel	Date	Location	Remarks
Tony B.	Jan. 18, 1955	Entered Port of Callao, Peru	*Tony B.* had engine trouble.
Western Clipper	do.	do.	Sick crewmember aboard the *Western Clipper*.
Arctic Maid	Mar. 27, 1955	35 miles off coast of Ecuador	Vessel stopped, shot at, Chief Engineer William Peck severely wounded. Vessel impounded. $43,481.20 fine imposed.
Santa Anna	do.	do.	Vessel seized. $5,881.10 fine imposed.
Magellan	Mar. 26, 1955	25 miles off the coast of Ecuador	Vessel boarded and inspected then released.
Western Pride	do.	do.	Do.
Katie Lou	Nov. 25, 1955	do.	Do.
Historic	Jan. 20, 1956	3°4' south latitude, 80°43' west longitude (18 miles from Santa Clara Island, Gulf of Guayaquil, Ecuador).	Seized and taken into port of Guayaquil. Released Nov. 28, 1955. Other vessels were boarded, but their names are unknown. Ambassador of Peru notified by letter from ATA dated Nov. 23, 1954.
Santa Anita	do.	2°48' south latitude, 80°40' west longitude (about 18 miles from the coast of Ecuador).	Vessel stopped by Ecuadoran naval vessel *Atahualpa* ordered to proceed to nearest port. Ship's documents taken and then vessel released.
do.	do.	2°48' south latitude, 80°40' west longitude (about 18 miles from the coast of Ecuador).	Vessel stopped by Ecuadoran naval vessel *Atahualpa*, ship's documents taken and then vessel released.
Commodore	Jan. 29, 1956	32 miles, 280° true from Cape Pasado, Ecuador.	Vessel stopped by Ecuador patrol vessel, *President Velasco*, detained 1 hour, boarded by armed personnel. Released after search indicated no bait. ATA sent letter dated Feb. 8, 1956, to the Secretary of State, outlining the above events.
Normandie	Dec. 13, 1957	19°45' south latitude, 70°37' west longitude (20 to 25 miles off the coast of Chile).	Chilean airplane shot across the bow of vessel, ordered vessel to go into port of Iqueque. Other vessels in vicinity, *Chicken of the Sea*, *Starcrest*, *Southern Pacific*, and *Excalibur*. Total fine imposed, $5,000.
Shamrock	Feb. 7, 1961	Off coast of Ecuador beyond 3 miles.	Ecuadoran gunboat stops vessel, master of *Shamrock* leaves his vessel and shows documents to patrol boat.
Do.	Mar. 21, 1961	11.9 miles of island in Gulf of Panama.	Vessel seized, crew and master imprisoned by Panama. Paid $2,500 fine plus costs. At time of seizure vessel having mechanical problems and under repair.
Normandie	May 1961	11 miles of Manta, Ecuador.	Vessel stopped, fishing activities interrupted, and master left and boarded Ecuadoran patrol vessel. License and other ship's documents inspected. Vessel permitted to continue fishing. 4 other vessels in vicinity.
Do.	Nov. 29, 1961	15 miles west of Cape Pasado.	Vessel stopped by Ecuadoran patrol boat while it was working on school of fish. Papers inspected and then vessel released.
Nautilus	Dec. 15, 1961	Salinas, Ecuador.	Master required to pay port captain in Salinas, Ecuador, $300 to avoid trouble with authorities and fish off the coast. This vessel has paid $200 for annual registration fee and $4,884 for fishing license for trip commencing on Nov. 22, 1961.
Equator	Jan. 27, 1962	Sank approximately 40 miles off Gorgona Island, Colombia.	Crew used vessel's powerboat to escape to Gorgona Island. Crew denied opportunity to purchase fuel, and required to leave the small vessel at the island. After clearance from U.S. Embassy in Bogota and Colombian authorities, MV *Cabrillo* went to Gorgona Island to pick up powerboat. At island, master of *Cabrillo* was told that powerboat would not be released. Commandant on island told him that unless the *Cabrillo* leaves, the vessel would be seized and fined. Powerboat was eventually removed from island after U.S. Embassy took further action.
San Joaquin	Feb. 12, 1962	Seized about 8 or 9 miles off the coast of Colombia.	Colombian patrol vessel *Arc Gorgona* seized the vessel, placed armed guards aboard. Vessel fined $2,318.20; vessel released.
Jo Linda	Feb. 23, 1962	4°10' north latitude, 78°10' west longitude (25 miles off the Colombian coast).	Colombian gunboat No. 71 came on the vessel during early morning hours, fired 12 rounds. *Jo Linda* escaped into the darkness after a 30-minute chase.
Saratoga	do.	4°10' north latitude, 78°10' west longitude.	Same Colombian gunboat that shot at *Jo Linda* chased *Saratoga*, darkness prevented capture.

[This table was prepared by the United States Department of the Interior, and covers the period September 15, 1951, to June 28, 1963. Reproduced from 109 Congressional Record 20181–20182 (November 6, 1963).]

Name of motor vessel	Date	Location	Remarks
Western Ace	Mar. 28, 1962	Off coast of Ecuador beyond 3 miles	Vessel seized, held in port of Salinas for 3 days. No fine imposed.
Normandie	Apr. 3, 1962	00° 08' south latitude, 80° 59' west longitude (28 miles west of Cape Pasado, Ecuador)	Stopped by Ecuadoran patrol vessel. Master of Normandie left vessel, and showed logbook and other documents.
Constitution	Apr. 16, 1962	1°05' north latitude, 80°21' west longitude (20 miles northwest of Punta Galera, Ecuador).	Ecuadoran patrol vessel President Velasco stopped vessel and requested master to leave vessel. Vessel boarded by armed personnel, who checked papers and then released the vessel for fishing.
Normandie	Apr. 17, 1962	2°10' south latitude, 81°08' west longitude (8 miles west of Cape San Elena, Ecuador).	Vessel was setting net; armed men from Ecuadoran patrol vessel boarded and inspected the ship's log. Master of the vessel ordered in to port of Salinas. Master paid captain of port $60 and left to continue fishing.
Lou Jean	Apr. 28, 1962	About 15 miles off coast of El Salvador	Vessel shot at, boarded, and seized while it was en route to San Diego with load of fish caught 80 miles off Costa Rica. No fine.
Mauritania	June 1962	Peruvian coast	Vessels chased off fishing banks 25 miles off Peruvian coast by Peruvian patrol vessels.
Seapreme			
White Star	Aug. 3, 1962	Beyond 3 miles off coast of Ecuador between Manta and Isla La Plata.	Vessel seized and taken into port and held for about 5 weeks. No fine imposed.
Cabrillo	Aug. 6, 1962	5 miles off Isla La Plata, Ecuador	Vessel boarded by armed soldiers and commandant of the island. Threatened to seize the vessel. Master gave whisky and tuna, then vessel permitted to continue fishing.
Larry Roe	Aug. 24, 1962	Galapagos Island, Ecuador	Vessel taken under custody on ground ship's papers irregular. Vessel released for fishing after a few days delay. No fine imposed.
Evelyn R.	Sept. 10, 1962	do	Vessel held under custody on ground that it abandoned islands without proper clearance, and that it unloaded fish in Panama. Released Sept. 13, 1962. No fine on vessel but master fined.
Chicken of the Sea	Oct. 28, 1962	12 miles off Peru	Fined $5,000 for fishing without license.
Western Ace	do	Peru	Fined $10,000 for fishing without license.
Mayflower	Nov. 5, 1962	Peru	Seized and fined $4,000 for alleged fishing without license in Peruvian waters some 6 months earlier.
Nautilus	Nov. 14, 1962	do	Forced into port but released within 24 hours without any fines.
Royal Pacific	do	do	Do.
Elsinore	Nov. 18, 1962	Galapagos, Ecuador	Taken into custody but released without fines.
Larry Roe	do	do	Taken into custody and fined $150.
Cabrillo	November 1962	15 miles off Ecuador	Harassment by patrol boat but evaded seizure under cover of darkness.
Ecuador	do	do	Do.
Jeanne Lynn	do	do	Do.
White Star	May 25, 1963	5.5 miles off Ecuador	Fined $11,184 and charged license fee of $3,002.
Ranger	do	5.5 miles off Ecuador	Fined $9,504 and charged license fee of $2,582. The White Star and Ranger were joined by 19 other vessels as a protest. The 19 vessels were not charged or held.
Espiritu Santo	June 12, 1963	Ecuador	Held temporarily pending issuance of a matricula.
United States	June 19, 1963	do	Boarded but released.
Ranger	June 28, 1962 *	Isla de la Plata, Ecuador	Do.

Continental Shelf[29]

Only in recent years has international law taken account of the continental shelf, the underwater land that declines moderately from the coasts of most continents to a depth of a few hundred meters before dropping steeply into deep ocean, because only within the last few decades has it become accessible to human beings and legal claims. Techniques for drilling on the seabed and from floating derricks were necessary before states could claim rights over the seabed not only below the territorial sea, but also beyond its limits.

Proclamations asserting exclusive rights to exploit the subsoil outside their coasts have been issued by various states, and some of them, in particular Latin American states, claimed not only the subsoil and seabed, but also sovereignty over the superjacent waters. Most states objected, however, to claims to the superjacent waters, which are clearly unfounded in law. Claims to the subsoil and seabed have been generally accepted, at least tacitly, and rules that have gained considerable acceptance found their way into the Convention on the Continental Shelf:

ARTICLE 1

. . . "continental shelf" is used as referring (a) to the seabed and subsoil of the submarine areas adjacent to the coast but outside the area of the territorial sea, to the depth of 200 metres or, beyond that limit, to where the depth of the superjacent waters admits of the exploitation of the natural resources of the said areas; (b) to the seabed and subsoil of similar submarine areas adjacent to the coasts of islands.

ARTICLE 2

1. The coastal State exercises over the continental shelf sovereign rights for the purpose of exploring it and exploiting its natural resources.

2. The rights referred to in paragraph 1 of this article are exclusive in the sense that if the coastal State does not explore the continental shelf or exploit its natural resources, no one may undertake these activities, or make a claim to the continental shelf, without the express consent of the coastal State.

3. The rights of the coastal State over the continental shelf do not depend on occupation, effective or national, or on any express proclamation.

ARTICLE 3

The rights of the coastal State over the continental shelf do not affect the legal status of the superjacent waters as high seas, or that of the air space above those waters.

[29] The following discussion is drawn from Sørensen, pp. 226–231 and the 1958 Conference proceedings.

By these provisions, the Convention rejects the right of states to establish exclusive fishing rights over the continental shelf: states remain free to navigate, fish, lay cables, conduct scientific research, and enjoy all the other freedoms of the seas in the waters over the continental shelf, and the coastal state may not interfere with these freedoms when it constructs installations to exploit the resources of the shelf (Article 5).

These provisions, adopted in 1958, conform with earlier practice by states very much involved with the continental shelf as, for instance, the United States, which has always carefully distinguished its right to control the resources in and under the sea from control of the sea itself, as indicated in the following case.

MATSON NAVIGATION CO. AND UNION OIL CO. OF CALIFORNIA v. U. S.

UNITED STATES, COURT OF CLAIMS, JUNE 5, 1956

135 CT. CL. 526, 141 F. SUPP. 929 (1956)

(Brief adapted from International Law Reports 1956)

The Facts. The Union Oil Co. claimed indemnity from the United States for the sinking of its tanker, the *Montebello,* by a Japanese submarine on December 23, 1941, at a point three to five and a half miles off the shore of the United States, but over the continental shelf. The plaintiff claimed that the loss of the vessel was covered by the free insurance against war damage provided by the Reconstruction Finance Corporation Act, 5 (g), as added by the Act of March 27, 1942, 2 (56 Stat. 175), as regards "property situated in the United States . . . and in such other places as may be determined by the President to be under the dominion and control of the United States." The President had proclaimed on September 28, 1945, that the United States regards the natural resources of the subsoil and sea bed of the continental shelf beneath the high seas but contiguous to the coasts of the United States as appertaining to the United States, subject to its jurisdiction and control [Presidential Proclamation No. 2667 (59 Stat. 884)]. The plaintiff contended that the Proclamation demonstrated that the seas over the continental shelf were under the "dominion and control of the United States."

[After discussing a related claim and matters of the municipal law of the United States, the Court said:] The remaining legal question is whether the *Montebello* was, for purposes of determining whether its cargo was covered by the free insurance, "situated in the United States" or in a place "determined by the President to be under the dominion and control of the United States" when sunk. The jury found that the *Montebello* was sunk beyond the 3-mile limit and Union's suit was dismissed by the District Court. It is conceded that the *Montebello* was over the continental shelf when sunk. . . .

Union's contention [that the ship was either in the United States or under the dominion and control of the United States] is not well founded. Vessels on the high seas are not within the United States and while on the high seas are not under the dominion and control of the United States. The Presidential Proclamation specifically stated: "The character as high seas of the waters above the continental shelf and the right to their free and unimpeded navigation are in no way thus affected." Further the Presidential Proclamation was [made] after the *Montebello* was sunk, and the terms of the Proclamation indicate it was prospective only. . . .

Territorial Sea

Freedom of the sea has never extended to that part of the sea nearest the coast of states; states have always assumed the right to control the territorial sea, although they have differed from time to time (and differ today) about the nature of that control and the distance from the shore over which they can exercise it. The two problems are closely related, since the wider and more complete the control that coastal states exercise over the sea, the narrower the freedom of the seas becomes.

Whatever the width of the territorial sea (a question to which we must return), the Convention on the Territorial Sea and the Contiguous Zone[30] restated the traditional view that "The sovereignty of a State extends, beyond its land territory and its internal waters, to a belt of sea adjacent to its coast, described as the territorial sea" (Article 1). The rights of coastal states over this sea are the same as the rights that states exercise over other parts of their territory,[31] which means that states have full authority over persons and ships of all nationalities within the territorial sea unless the persons or ships enjoy immunity for some other reason recognized by international law. States may, if they wish, exclude foreign ships and nationals from the territorial sea as, for instance, Cuba did in 1961, while it was exchanging old currency for new.[32] State's rights in the territorial sea are subject to other rules of international law, primarily the right of "innocent passage" by foreign ships.

Ten articles of the 1958 Convention on the Territorial Sea (numbers 14 to 23) deal with the right of innocent passage in an attempt to strike a balance between the interests of states in securing the rights for their ships to pass through the territorial waters of other states and their interest in security in their own territorial waters. Under the 1958 Convention, passage through the territorial sea "is innocent so long as it is not prejudicial to the peace, good order or security of the coastal State" (Article 14 [4]), but the treaty implies that a state may, if it

[30] A/Conf. 13/L.52, 1958 Conference of the Law of the Sea, *OR*, II, 132–135.
[31] See the commentary by the International Law Commission, GA *OR* XI (1956), Suppl. No. 9, Article 1, commentary, par. 1.
[32] *New York Times*, August 6, 1961, p. 1ff.

believes its security is endangered, interfere with ships carrying certain cargoes to certain destinations. In passing through territorial waters, foreign ships must "comply with the laws and regulations enacted by the coastal State" (Article 17), a provision which authorizes coastal states to enforce their rules on foreign ships in territorial waters, even if they may not prevent such ships from passing through. These rules apply both to privately owned merchant ships and government-owned ships operated for commercial purposes (Article 21), a statement which refutes the Soviet claim of immunity for all government-owned vessels. Passage is not innocent, however, for fishing vessels which do not observe laws and regulations prohibiting fishing in the territorial sea, nor for submarines (which must navigate on the surface and show their flag in territorial waters). Presumably a state might prohibit such vessels from passing through its waters and penalize them for violating its rules (Article 14, [5, 6]).

Warships are required (Article 23) to "comply with the regulations of the coastal state concerning passage through the territorial sea," and if a warship "disregards any request for compliance . . . , the coastal State may require the warship to leave the territorial sea." Presumably under this article a state might surround the innocent passage of a warship with certain restrictions, while not being able to prohibit it altogether because Article 14 grants innocent passage to all ships. Despite this provision, many states at the 1958 conference believed that a warship needed specific permission from a coastal state before making an innocent passage or that it needed at least to notify the coastal state of its intention to navigate in territorial waters. These restrictions failed to find their way into the final document because of a complicated parliamentary situation at the 1958 conference. In fact, therefore, no consensus exists on this particular point.[33]

Public Law 88-308
88th Congress, S. 1988
May 20, 1964

An Act

To prohibit fishing in the territorial waters of the United States and in certain other areas by vessels other than vessels of the United States and by persons in charge of such vessels.

Be it enacted by the Senate and House of Representatives of the United States of America in Congress assembled, That it is unlawful for any vessel, except a vessel of the United States, or for any master or other person in charge of such a vessel, to engage in the fisheries within the territorial waters of the United States, its territories and possessions and the Commonwealth of Puerto Rico, or within any waters in which the United States has the same rights in respect to fisheries as it has in its territorial waters or to engage in the taking of

Fishing in territorial waters of U. S. Prohibition.

---

[33] "This is a typical illustration of the shortcomings inherent in the drafting of rules of international law through a process based upon the formalistic rules of procedure and voting of the United Nations." Sørensen, p. 235.

any Continental Shelf fishery resource which appertains to the United States except as provided in this Act or as expressly provided by an international agreement to which the United States is a party. However, sixty days after written notice to the President of the Senate and the Speaker of the House of Representatives of intent to do so, the Secretary of the Treasury may authorize a vessel other than a vessel of the United States to engage in fishing for designated species within the territorial waters of the United States or within any waters in which the United States has the same rights in respect to fisheries as it has in its territorial waters or for resources of the Continental Shelf which appertain to the United States upon certification by the Secretaries of State and of the Interior that such permission would be in the national interest and upon concurrence of any State, Commonwealth, territory, or possession directly affected. The authorization in this section may be granted only after a finding by the Secretary of the Interior that the country of registry, documentation, or licensing extends substantially the same fishing privileges for a fishery to vessels of the United States. Notwithstanding any other provision of law, the Secretary of State, with the concurrence of the Secretaries of the Treasury and of the Interior, may permit a vessel, other than a vessel of the United States, owned or operated by an international organization of which the United States is a member, to engage in fishery research within the territorial waters of the United States or within any waters in which the United States has the same rights in respect to fisheries as it has in its territorial waters, or for resources of the Continental Shelf which appertain to the United States and to land its catch in a port of the United States in accordance with such conditions as the Secretary may prescribe whenever they determine such action is in the national interest.

78 STAT. 194.
78 STAT. 195.

SEC. 2. (a) Any person violating the provisions of this Act shall be fined not more than $10,000, or imprisoned not more than one year, or both.

(b) Every vessel employed in any manner in connection with a violation of this Act including its tackle, apparel, furniture, appurtenances, cargo, and stores shall be subject to forfeiture and all fish taken or retained in violation of this Act or the monetary value thereof shall be forfeited.

(c) All provisions of law relating to the seizure, summary and judicial forfeiture, and condemnation of a vessel, including its tackle, apparel, furniture, appurtenances, cargo, and stores for violation of the customs laws, the disposition of such vessel, including its tackle, apparel, furniture, appurtenances, cargo, and stores or the proceeds from the sale thereof, and the remission or mitigation of such forfeitures shall apply to seizures and forfeitures incurred, or alleged to have been incurred, under the provisions of this Act, insofar as such provisions of law are applicable and not inconsistent with the provisions of this Act.

SEC. 3. (a) Enforcement of the provisions of this Act is the joint responsibility of the Secretary of the Interior, the Secretary of the Treasury, and the Secretary of the Department in which the Coast Guard is operating. In addition, the Secretary of the Interior may designate officers and employees of the States of the United States, of the Commonwealth of Puerto Rico, and of any territory or possession of the United States to carry out enforcement activities hereunder. When so designated, such officers and employees are authorized to function as Federal law enforcement agents for these purposes, but they shall not be held and considered as employees of the United States for the purposes of any laws administered by the Civil Service Commission.

(b) The judges of the United States district courts, the judges of the highest courts of the territories and possessions of the United States, and United States commissioners may, within their respective jurisdictions, upon proper oath or affirmation showing probable cause, issue such warrants or other process, including warrants or other process issued in admiralty proceedings in Federal District Courts, as may be required for enforcement of this Act and any regulations issued thereunder.

(c) Any person authorized to carry out enforcement activities hereunder shall have the power to execute any warrant or process issued by any officer or court of competent jurisdiction for the enforcement of this Act.

Enforcement powers.

(d) Such person so authorized shall have the power—

(1) with or without a warrant or other process, to arrest any person committing in his presence or view a violation of this Act or the regulations issued thereunder;

(2) with or without a warrant or other process, to search any vessel and, if as a result of such search he has reasonable cause to believe that such vessel or any person on board is in violation of any provision of this Act or the regulations issued thereunder, then to arrest such person.

78 STAT. 195.
78 STAT. 196.

(e) Such person so authorized may seize any vessel, together with its tackle, apparel, furniture, appurtenances, cargo and stores, used or employed contrary to the provisions of this Act or the regulations issued hereunder or which it reasonably appears has been used or employed contrary to the provisions of this Act or the regulations issued hereunder.

(f) Such person so authorized may seize, whenever and wherever lawfully found, all fish taken or retained in violation of this Act or the regulations issued thereunder. Any fish so seized may be disposed of pursuant to the order of a court of competent jurisdiction pursuant to the provisions of subsection (g) of this section, or if perishable, in a manner prescribed by regulations of the Secretary of the Treasury.

Seizure and disposal of fish.

(g) Notwithstanding the provisions of section 2464 of title 28 when a warrant of arrest or other process in rem is issued in any cause under this section, the United States marshal or other officer shall discharge any fish seized if the process has been levied, on receiving from the claimant of the fish a bond or stipulation for the value of the fish with sufficient surety to be approved by a judge of the district court having jurisdiction of the offense, conditioned to deliver the fish seized, if condemned, without impairment in value or, in the discretion of the court, to pay its equivalent value in money or otherwise to answer the decree of the court in such cause. Such bond or stipulation shall be returned to the court and judgment thereon against both the principal and sureties may be recovered in event of any breach of the conditions thereof as determined by the court. In the discretion of the accused, and subject to the direction of the court, the fish may be sold for not less than its reasonable market value and the proceeds of such sale placed in the registry of the court pending judgment in the case.

62 Stat. 974.

SEC. 4. The Secretaries of the Treasury and Interior are authorized jointly or severally to issue such regulations as they determine are necessary to carry out the provisions of this Act.

Regulations.

SEC. 5. (a) As used in this Act, the term "Continental Shelf fishery resource" includes the living organisms belonging to sedentary species; that is to say, organisms which, at the harvestable stage, either are immobile on or under the seabed or are unable to move except in constant physical contact with the seabed or the subsoil of the Continental Shelf.

"Continental Shelf fishery resource".

(b) The Secretary of the Interior in consultation with the Secretary of State is authorized to publish in the Federal Register a list of the species of living organisms covered by the provisions of subsection (a) of this section.

Publication in F. R.

(c) As used in this Act, the term "fisheries" means the taking, planting, or cultivation of fish, mollusks, crustaceans, or other forms of marine animal or plant life by any vessel or vessels; and the term "fish" includes mollusks, crustaceans, and all other forms of marine animal or plant life.

Definitions.

(d) As used in this Act, the term "Continental Shelf" refers (a) to the seabed and subsoil of the submarine areas adjacent to the coast but outside the area of the territorial sea, to a depth of 200 meters or, beyond that limit, to where the depth of the superjacent waters admits

of the exploitation of the natural resources of the said areas; (b) to
the seabed and subsoil of similar submarine areas adjacent to the coasts
of islands.

Approved May 20, 1964.

LEGISLATIVE HISTORY:

HOUSE REPORT No. 1356 (Comm. on Merchant Marine & Fisheries).
SENATE REPORT No. 500 (Comm. on Commerce).
CONGRESSIONAL RECORD:
    Vol. 109 (1963): Oct. 1, considered and passed Senate.
    Vol. 110 (1964): May 4, considered and passed House, amended.
                  May 6, Senate concurred in House amendments.

STATEMENT BY PRESIDENT JOHNSON

White House press release dated May 20

I have today [May 20] signed into law S. 1988, a bill which prohibits fishing by foreign vessels in the territorial waters of the United States. This law fills a longstanding need for legislation to prevent foreign fishing vessels, which in recent years have appeared off our coast in increasing numbers, from fishing in our territorial waters.

The new law will not establish any new rights to the continental shelf. But it will make possible the enforcement of whatever rights now exist or may be established. Since the waters over the continental shelf are high seas, efforts will be made to work out in advance with foreign countries procedures for enforcement there. In this connection, the United States has assured Japan that in such consultations with Japan full consideration will be given to Japan's long-established king crab fishery.

DEPARTMENT STATEMENT

The Governments of Japan and the United States have held a series of discussions in Washington on the effect of the U.S. legislation S. 1988, which was signed by President Johnson today.

The United States Government has explained to the Japanese Government that this legislation would not, of itself, constitute the assertion of any right to jurisdiction over resources that does not already exist and that it is concerned primarily with providing meaningful protection to such rights as now exist or which might be acquired at some time in the future.

The position of the Government of Japan is that it is not bound by the convention on the continental shelf, to which Japan is not a party, and that therefore the rights of the Government of Japan will not be affected by the provisions of S. 1988 relating to fishery resources of the continental shelf. The Government of the United States has taken note of this position.

The United States Government has assured the Japanese Government that prior to implementing this legislation with respect to fishery resources of the continental shelf, the United States Government will consult with the Japanese Government and that in such consultations full consideration will be given to the views of the Japanese Government and to Japan's long-established king crab fishery.

936

[Reproduced from 50 <u>Department of State Bulletin</u> 936 (1964).]

EXCHANGE OF REMARKS

Press release 503 dated November 25

Remarks by Secretary Rusk

For a month, representatives of Japan and the United States discussed important issues affecting the fishermen of both countries arising from the presence of a Japanese king crab fishery on the continental shelf of the United States in the Bering Sea.[1] When President Johnson signed the Bartlett Act, which makes possible the enforcement of rights which now exist or may be established in the resources of the continental shelf, he assured the Government of Japan that we would give full consideration to Japan's long-established king crab fishery in the east Bering Sea.[2]

I am deeply gratified that our two Governments have agreed on an interim 2-year *modus operandi* for accommodating our separate interests. Our representatives have faced the question of conservation of the resource, how to take account of Japan's historical fishery, our different legal concepts on the continental shelf convention, and the interest of the United States crab fishing industry in the area previously fished predominantly by Japan. The king crab in the east Bering Sea is not the only issue upon which we have, and can be expected to have in the future, differing interests and perspectives. I consider it encouraging for the future that by mutual understanding and rational balancing of our respective national interests we have reached an agreement which is equitable and to our common benefit.

---

[1] For text of a joint announcement made when the notes were initialed on Nov. 14, see BULLETIN of Dec. 7, 1964, p. 829.

[2] *Ibid.*, June 15, 1964, p. 936.

In the light of the difficult nature of their tasks, I think both Governments can take pride in the achievement of agreement.

Remarks by Ambassador Takeuchi

It is a great honor and privilege for me to represent Japan on this occasion of the exchanging of notes on the king crab fishery in the eastern Bering Sea.

The core of the problem lies in the fact that the two Governments hold fundamentally different legal positions with respect to the king crab resource in this area. However, as a result of the long and patient consultation aimed at a realistic solution of the problem between two friendly nations, we have reached agreement in spite of difficulties.

As the relationship between our two countries becomes ever closer, we are bound to encounter many complicated problems. But I believe that the present agreement very clearly demonstrates that, however difficult these problems may be, they can be solved if we engage in frank and constructive discussions with determination and mutual understanding in the broader interest of our firm friendship.

I should like to congratulate the representatives of both Governments for their untiring efforts and zeal, which contributed so much to bringing about the present agreement.

TEXT OF U.S. NOTE

DEPARTMENT OF STATE,
Washington, November 25, 1964.

EXCELLENCY: I have the honor to refer to Your Excellency's note of November 25, 1964, which reads with Appendix as follows:

[Reproduced from 51 Department of State _Bulletin_ 892-93 (December 21, 1964).]

I have the honor to refer to the consultation between the representatives of the Government of Japan and the Government of the United States of America in regard to the king crab fishery in the eastern Bering Sea, held in Washington from October 15 to November 14, 1964, and to confirm, on behalf of the Government of Japan, the following understandings reached as the result of this consultation:

1. The Government of Japan holds the view that king crabs are a high seas fishery resource, and that nationals and vessels of Japan are entitled to continue fishing for king crabs in the eastern Bering Sea.

2. The Government of the United States of America is of the view that the king crab is a natural resource of the continental shelf over which the coastal state (in this case the United States of America) has exclusive jurisdiction, control and rights of exploitation.

3. However, the two Governments, having regard to the historical fact that nationals and vessels of Japan have over a long period of years exploited the king crab resource in the eastern Bering Sea, have agreed, without prejudice to their respective positions as described above, as follows:

1) The king crab fishery by nationals and vessels of Japan in the eastern Bering Sea will continue in and near the waters which have been fished historically by Japan, that is, those waters in which migrate the king crab stocks exploited historically by Japan, provided that, in order to avoid possible overfishing of the king crab resource in the eastern Bering Sea, the Government of Japan ensures that the annual commercial catch of king crabs by nationals and vessels of Japan for the years 1965 and 1966 shall be equivalent to 185,000 cases respectively (one case being equivalent to 48 half-pound cans).

2) The two Governments shall apply such interim measures as described in the Appendix to this note to their respective nationals and vessels fishing for king crabs in the eastern Bering Sea.

3) The International Commission under the North Pacific Fishery Convention will be asked by the two Governments to continue and intensify the study of the king crab resource in the eastern Bering Sea and to transmit to the two Governments annually by November 30 the findings of such study, including also, to the extent possible, an estimate of the maximum sustainable yield of the resource.

4) For the purpose of carrying out faithfully measures under the provisions of the proviso of sub-paragraph (1) and the provisions of sub-paragraph (2) of this paragraph, the two Governments shall take appropriate and effective measures respectively, and either Government shall, if requested by the other Government, provide opportunity for observation of the conduct of enforcement.

5) The two Governments shall meet before December 31, 1966 to review the operation of these arrangements and the conditions of the king crab fishery of the eastern Bering Sea, and decide on future arrangements in the light of paragraphs 1 and 2, and the introductory part of this paragraph, and the United States President's assurance of May 20, 1964 that full consideration would be given to Japan's long established fishery.

I have further the honor to propose that this note and your Excellency's reply confirming the above understandings on behalf of your Government shall be regarded as constituting an agreement between the two Governments.

APPENDIX

a) Female king crabs, small king crabs less than 14.5 cms. in maximum carapace width and soft-shelled king crabs shall not be retained and used. Any such crabs taken incidentally shall be returned immediately to the sea with a minimum of injury.

b) King crabs shall not be taken by means of fishing gear other than pot and tangle net. The stretched diagonal measure of tangle net mesh shall be no less than 50 cms.

c) Unless otherwise agreed by the two Governments, only pots may be used to capture king crabs for commercial purposes in that area lying seaward of the United States territorial sea and within the following described boundaries: a line running due west through Sea Lion Rock light and along 55°28' N. latitude to 165°34' W. longitude, thence southwesterly to an intersection of a line passing between Cape Navarin and Cape Sarichef at 55°16' N. latitude and 166°10' W. longitude, thence southeasterly along the Cape Navarin-Sarichef line to Cape Sarichef.

I have the honor to inform Your Excellency that the above understandings reached by representatives of our two Governments are acceptable to the Government of the United States of America and that Your Excellency's note and this reply are considered as an agreement between our two Governments.

Accept, Excellency, the renewed assurances of my highest consideration.

DEAN RUSK

His Excellency
RYUJI TAKEUCHI,
Ambassador of Japan.

234

International Straits

The Convention permits a state "without discrimination amongst foreign ships," to "suspend temporarily in specified areas of its territorial sea the innocent passage of foreign ships if such suspension is essential for the protection of its security" (Article 16 [3]), but "There shall be no suspension of the innocent passage of foreign ships through straits which are used for international navigation between one part of the high seas and another part of the high seas or the territorial sea of a foreign State." (Article 16 [4].) As worded, this article would prohibit such acts as Egypt's (1955, 1967) barring the Strait of Tiran entrance to the Gulf of Aqaba, which gives access from the Red Sea to Israel's port of Eilath.[34]

THE CORFU CHANNEL CASE (MERITS)

UNITED KINGDOM—ALBANIA, INTERNATIONAL
COURT OF JUSTICE, APRIL 9, 1949

I.C.J. REPORTS 1949

By the first part of the Special Agreement, the following question is submitted to the Court:

(1) Is Albania responsible under international law for the explosions which occurred on the 22nd October 1946 in Albanian waters and for the damage and loss of human life which resulted from them and is there any duty to pay compensation?

On October 22nd, 1946, a squadron of British warships, the cruisers *Mauritius* and *Leander* and the destroyers *Saumarez* and *Volage,* left the port of Corfu and proceeded northward through a channel previously swept for mines in the North Corfu Strait. The cruiser *Mauritius* was leading, followed by the destroyer *Saumarez;* at a certain distance thereafter came the cruiser *Leander* followed by the destroyer *Volage.* Outside the Bay of Saranda, *Saumarez* struck a mine and was heavily damaged. *Volage* was ordered to give her assistance and to take her in tow. Whilst towing the damage ship, *Volage* struck a mine and was much damaged. Nevertheless, she succeeded in towing the other ship back to Corfu.

Three weeks later, on November 13th, the North Corfu Channel was swept by British minesweepers and twenty-two moored mines were cut. Two mines were taken to Malta for expert examination.

[34] Egyptian shore batteries fired on a British ship in the Straits on April 10, 1955. The U.K. government, in notes dated July 6 and September 12 maintained that the waters were international, whereas Egyptian regulations issued on September 11 regarded them as "Egyptian territorial waters."

. . . .

The Court consequently finds that the following facts are established. The two ships were mined in Albanian territorial waters in a previously swept and check-swept channel just at the place where a newly laid minefield consisting of moored contact German GY mines was discovered three weeks later. The damage sustained by the ships was inconsistent with damage which could have been caused by floating mines, magnetic ground mines, magnetic moored mines, or German GR mines, but its nature and extent were such as would be caused by mines of the type found in the minefield. In such circumstances the Court arrives at the conclusion that the explosions were due to mines belonging to that minefield.

* * *

Such are the facts upon which the Court must, in order to reply to the first question of the Special Agreement, give judgment as to Albania's responsibility for the explosions on October 22nd, 1946, and for the damage and loss of human life which resulted, and for the compensation, if any, due in respect of such damage and loss.

To begin with, the foundation for Albania's responsibility, as alleged by the United Kingdom, must be considered. On this subject, the main position of the United Kingdom is to be found in its submission No. 2: that the minefield which caused the explosions was laid between May 15th, 1946, and October 22nd, 1946, by or with the connivance or knowledge of the Albanian Government.

The Court considered first the various grounds for responsibility alleged in this submission.

. . . .

It is clear that knowledge of the minelaying cannot be imputed to the Albanian Government by reason merely of the fact that a minefield discovered in Albanian territorial waters caused the explosions of which the British warships were the victims. It is true, as international practice shows, that a State on whose territory or in whose waters an act contrary to international law has occurred, may be called upon to give an explanation. It is also true that that State cannot evade such a request by limiting itself to a reply that it is ignorant of the circumstances of the act and of its authors. The State may, up to a certain point, be bound to supply particulars of the use made by it of the means of information and inquiry at its disposal. But it cannot be concluded from the mere fact of the control exercised by a State over its territory and waters that that State necessarily knew, or ought to have known, of any unlawful act perpetrated therein, nor yet that it necessarily knew, or should have known, the authors. This fact, by itself and apart from other circumstances, neither involves *prima facie* responsibility nor shifts the burden of proof.

On the other hand, the fact of this exclusive territorial control exercised by a State within its frontiers has a bearing upon the methods of proof available to establish the knowledge of that State as to such events. By reason of this exclusive control, the other State, the victim of a breach of international law, is often unable to furnish direct proof of facts giving rise to responsibility. Such a State should be allowed a more liberal recourse to inferences of fact and circumstantial evidence. This indirect evidence is admitted in all systems of law, and its use is recognized by international decisions. It must be regarded as of special weight when it is based on a series of facts linked together and leading logically to a single conclusion.

The Court must examine therefore whether it has been established by means of indirect evidence that Albania has knowledge of minelaying in her territorial waters independently of any connivance on her part in this operation. The proof may be drawn from inferences of fact, provided that they leave *no room* for reasonable doubt. The elements of fact on which these inferences can be based may differ from those which are relevant to the question of connivance.

From all the facts and observations mentioned above, the Court draws the conclusion that the laying of the minefield which caused the explosions on October 22nd, 1946, could not have been accomplished without the knowledge of the Albanian Government.

The obligations resulting for Albania from this knowledge are not disputed between the Parties. Counsel for the Albanian Government expressly recognized that [*translation*] "if Albania had been informed of the operation before the incidents of October 22nd, and in time to warn the British vessels and shipping in general of the existence of mines in the Corfu Channel, her responsibility would be involved. . . ."

The obligations incumbent upon the Albanian authorities consisted in notifying, for the benefit of shipping in general, the existence of a minefield in Albanian territorial waters and in warning the approaching British warships of the imminent danger to which the minefield exposed them. Such obligations are based, not on the Hague Convention of 1907, No. VIII, which is applicable in time of war, but on certain general and well-recognized principles, namely: elementary considerations of humanity, even more exacting in peace than in war; the principle of the freedom of maritime communication; and every State's obligation not to allow knowingly its territory to be used for acts contrary to the rights of other States.

In fact, Albania neither notified the existence of the minefield, nor warned the British warships of the danger they were approaching.

But Albania's obligation to notify shipping of the existence of mines in her waters depends on her having obtained knowledge of that fact in sufficient time before October 22nd; and the duty of the Albanian coastal authorities to warn the British ships depends on the time that elapsed between the moment that these ships were reported and the moment of the first explosion.

On this subject, the Court makes the following observations. As has already been stated. The Parties agree that the mines were recently laid. It must be concluded that the minelaying, whatever may have been its exact date, was done at a time when there was a close Albanian surveillance over the

Strait. If it be supposed that it took place at the last possible moment, *i.e.*, in the night of October 21st–22nd, the only conclusion to be drawn would be that a general notification to the shipping of all States before the time of the explosions would have been difficult, perhaps even impossible. But this would certainly not have prevented the Albanian authorities from taking, as they should have done, all necessary steps immediately to warn ships near the danger zone, more especially those that were approaching that zone. When on October 22nd about 13.00 hours the British warships were reported by the look-out post at St. George's Monastery to the Commander of the Coastal Defences as approaching Cape Long, it was perfectly possible for the Albanian authorities to use the interval of almost two hours that elapsed before the explosion affecting *Saumarez* (14.53 hours or 14.55 hours) to warn the vessels of the danger into which they were running.

In fact, nothing was attempted by the Albanian authorities to prevent the disaster. These grave omissions involve the international responsibility of Albania.

The Court therefore reaches the conclusion that Albania is responsible under international law for the explosions which occurred on October 22nd, 1946, in Albanian waters, and for the damage and loss of human life which resulted from them, and that there is a duty upon Albania to pay compensation to the United Kingdom.

In the second part of the Special Agreement [of March 25, 1948], the following question is submitted to the Court:

(2) Has the United Kingdom under international law violated the sovereignty of the Albanian People's Republic by reason of the acts of the Royal Navy in Albanian waters on the 22nd October and on the 12th and 13th November 1946 and is there any duty to give satisfaction?

The Court will first consider whether the sovereignty of Albania was violated by reason of the acts of the British Navy in Albanian waters on October 22nd, 1946.

On May 15th, 1946, the British cruisers *Orion* and *Superb*, while passing southward through the North Corfu Channel, were fired at by an Albanian battery in the vicinity of Saranda. It appears from the report of the commanding naval officer dated May 29th, 1946, that the firing started when the ships had already passed the battery and were moving away from it; that from 12 to 20 rounds were fired; that the firing lasted 12 minutes and ceased only when the ships were out of range; but that the ships were not hit although there were a number of "shorts" and of "overs." An Albanian note of May 21st states that the Coastal Commander ordered a few shots to be fired in the direction of the ships "in accordance with a General Order founded on international law."

The United Kingdom Government at once protested to the Albanian Government, stating that innocent passage through straits is a right recognized by international law. There ensued a diplomatic correspondence in which the Albanian Government asserted that foreign warships and merchant vessels

had no right to pass through Albanian territorial waters without prior notification to, and the permission of, the Albanian authorities. This view was put
into effect by the communication of the Albanian Chief of Staff, dated May
17th, 1946, which purported to subject the passage of foreign warships and
merchant vessels in Albanian territorial waters to previous notification to and
authorization by the Albanian Government. The diplomatic correspondence
continued, and culminated in a United Kingdom note of August 2nd, 1946,
in which the United Kingdom Government maintained its view with regard
to the right of innocent passage through straits forming routes for international
maritime traffic between two parts of the high seas. The note ended with
the warning that if Albanian coastal batteries in the future opened fire on
any British warship passing through the Corfu Channel, the fire would be
returned.

The contents of this note were, on August 1st, communicated by the British
Admiralty to the Commander-in-Chief, Mediterranean, with the instruction
that he should refrain from using the Channel until the note had been presented to the Albanian Government. On August 10th, he received from the
Admiralty the following telegram: "The Albanians have now received the note.
North Corfu Strait may now be used by ships of your fleet, but only when
essential and with armament in fore and aft position. If coastal guns fire
at ships passing through the Strait, ships should fire back." On September
21st, the following telegram was sent by the Admiralty to the Commander-in-
Chief, Mediterranean: "Establishment of diplomatic relations with Albania
is again under consideration by His Majesty's Government who wish to know
whether the Albanian Government have learnt to behave themselves. Information is requested whether any ships under your command have passed through
the North Corfu Strait since August and, if not, whether you intend them
to do so shortly." The Commander-in-Chief answered the next day that his
ships had not done so yet, but that it was his intention that *Mauritius* and
Leander and two destroyers should do so when they departed from Corfu
on October 22nd.

It was in such circumstances that these two cruisers together with the
destroyers *Saumarez* and *Volage* were sent through the North Corfu Strait
on that date.

The Court will now consider the Albanian contention that the United Kingdom Government violated Albanian sovereignty by sending the warships
through this Strait without the previous authorization of the Albanian
Government.

It is, in the opinion of the Courts, generally recognized and in accordance
with international custom that States in time of peace have a right to send
their warships through straits used for international navigation between two
parts of the high seas without the previous authorization of a coastal State,
provided that the passage is *innocent*. Unless otherwise prescribed in an
international convention, there is no right for a coastal State to prohibit such
passage through straits in time of peace.

The Albanian Government does not dispute that the North Corfu Channel is a strait in the geographical sense; but it denies that this Channel belongs to the class of international highways through which a right of passage exists, on the grounds that it is only of secondary importance and not even a necessary route between two parts of the high seas, and that it is used almost exclusively for local traffic to and from the ports of Corfu and Saranda.

It may be asked whether the test is to be found in the volume of traffic passing through the Strait or in its greater or lesser importance for international navigation. But in the opinion of the Court the decisive criterion is rather its geographical situation as connecting two parts of the high seas and the fact of its being used for international navigation. Nor can it be decisive that this Strait is not a necessary route between two parts of the high seas, but only an alternative passage between the Aegean and the Adriatic Seas. It has nevertheless been a useful route for international maritime traffic. In this respect, the Agent of the United Kingdom Government gave the Court the following information relating to the period from April 1st, 1936, to December 31st, 1937: "The following is the total number of ships putting in at the Port of Corfu after passing through or just before passing through the Channel. During the period of one year nine months, the total number of ships was 2,884. The flags of the ships are Greek, Italian, Roumanian, Yugoslav, French, Albanian and British. Clearly, very small vessels are included, as the entries for Albanian vessels are high and of course one vessel may make several journeys, but 2,884 ships for a period of one year nine months is quite a large figure. These figures relate to vessels visited by the Customs at Corfu and so do not include the large number of vessels which went through the Strait without calling at Corfu at all." There were also regular sailings through the Strait by Greek vessels three times weekly, by a British ship fortnightly, and by two Yugoslav vessels weekly and by two others fortnightly. The Court is further informed that the British Navy has regularly used this Channel for eighty years or more, and that it has also been used by the navies of other States.

One fact of particular importance is that the North Corfu Channel constitutes a frontier between Albania and Greece, that a part of it is wholly within the territorial waters of these States, and that the Strait is of special importance to Greece by reason of the traffic to and from the port of Corfu.

Having regard to these various considerations, the Court has arrived at the conclusion that the North Corfu Channel should be considered as belonging to the class of international highways through which passage cannot be prohibited by a coastal State in time of peace.

On the other hand, it is a fact that the two coastal States did not maintain normal relations, that Greece had made territorial claims precisely with regard to a part of Albanian territory bordering on the Channel, that Greece had declared that she considered herself technically in a state of war with Albania, and that Albania, invoking the danger of Greek incursions, had considered it necessary to take certain measures of vigilance in this region. The Court is of opinion that Albania, in view of these exceptional circumstances, would have been justified in issuing regulations in respect of the passage of warships through the Strait, but not in prohibiting such passage or in subjecting it to the requirement of special authorization.

For these reasons the Court is unable to accept the Albanian contention that the Government of the United Kingdom has violated Albanian sovereignty by sending the warships through the Strait without having obtained the previous authorization of the Albanian Government.

In these circumstances, it is unnecessary to consider the more general question, much debated by the Parties, whether States under international law have a right to send warships in time of peace through territorial waters not included in a strait.

The Albanian Government has further contended that the sovereignty of Albania was violated because the passage of the British warships on October 22nd, 1946, was not an *innocent passage*. The reasons advanced in support of this contention may be summed up as follows: The passage was not an ordinary passage, but a political mission; the ships were manoeuvring and sailing in diamond combat formation with soldiers on board; the position of the guns was not consistent with innocent passage; the vessels passed with crews at action stations; the number of the ships and their armament surpassed what was necessary in order to attain their object and showed an intention to intimidate and not merely to pass; the ships had received orders to observe and report upon the coastal defences and this order was carried out.

It is shown by the Admiralty telegram of September 21st, cited above, and admitted by the United Kingdom Agent, that the object of sending the warships through the Strait was not only to carry out a passage for purposes of navigation, but also to test Albania's attitude. As mentioned above, the Albanian Government, on May 15th, 1946, tried to impose by means of gunfire its view with regard to the passage. As the exchange of diplomatic notes did not lead to any clarification, the Government of the United Kingdom wanted to ascertain by other means whether the Albanian Government would maintain its illegal attitude and again impose its view by firing at passing ships. The legality of this measure taken by the Government of the United Kingdom cannot be disputed, provided that it was carried out in a manner consistent with the requirements of international law. The "mission" was designed to affirm a right which had been unjustly denied. The Government of the United Kingdom was not bound to abstain from exercising its right of passage, which the Albanian Government had illegally denied.

It remains, therefore, to consider whether the *manner* in which the passage was carried out was consistent with the principle of innocent passage and to examine the various contentions of the Albanian Government in so far as they appear to be relevant.

When the Albanian coastguards at St. George's Monastery reported that the British warships were sailing in combat formation and were manoeuvring, they must have been under a misapprehension. It is shown by the evidence that the ships were not proceeding in combat formation, but in line, one after the other, and that they were not manoeuvring until after the first explosion. Their movements thereafter were due to the explosions and were made necessary in order to save human life and the mined ships. It is shown by the evidence of witnesses that the contention that soldiers were on board must be due to a misunderstanding probably arising from the fact that the two cruisers carried their usual detachment of marines.

It is known from the above-mentioned order issued by the British Admiralty on August 10th, 1946, that ships, when using the North Corfu Strait, must pass with armament in fore and aft position. That this order was carried out during the passage on October 22nd is stated by the Commander-in-Chief, Mediterranean, in a telegram of October 26th to the Admiralty. The guns were, he reported, "trained fore and aft, which is their normal position at sea in peace time, and were not loaded." It is confirmed by the commanders of *Saumarez* and *Volage* that the guns were in this position before the explosions. The navigating officer on board *Mauritius* explained that all guns on that cruiser were in their normal stowage position. The main guns were in the line of the ship, and the anti-aircraft guns were pointing outwards and up into the air, which is the normal position of these guns on a cruiser both in harbour and at sea. In the light of this evidence, the Court cannot accept the Albanian contention that the position of the guns was inconsistent with the rules of innocent passage.

In the above-mentioned telegram of October 26th, the Commander-in-Chief reported that the passage "was made with ships at action stations in order that they might be able to retaliate quickly if fired upon again." In view of the firing from the Albanian battery on May 15th, this measure of precaution cannot, in itself, be regarded as unreasonable. But four warships—two cruisers and two destroyers—passed in this manner, with crews at action stations, ready to retaliate quickly if fired upon. They passed one after another through this narrow channel, close to the Albanian coast, at a time of political tension in this region. The intention must have been, not only to test Albania's attitude, but at the same time to demonstrate such force that she would abstain from firing again on passing ships. Having regard, however, to all the circumstances of the case, as described above, the Court is unable to characterize these measures taken by the United Kingdom authorities as a violation of Albania's sovereignty. . . . Lastly, as the Court has to judge of the innocent nature of the passage, it cannot remain indifferent to the fact that, though two warships struck mines, there was no reaction, either on their part or on that of the cruisers that accompanied them. . . .

Having thus examined the various contentions of the Albanian Government in so far as they appear to be relevant, the Court has arrived at the conclusion that the United Kingdom did not violate the sovereignty of Albania by reason of the acts of the British Navy in Albanian waters on October 22nd, 1946.

In addition to the passage of the United Kingdom warships on October 22nd, 1946, the second question in the Special Agreement relates to the acts of the Royal Navy in Albanian waters on November 12th and 13th, 1946. This is the minesweeping operation called "Operation Retail" by the Parties during the proceedings. This name will be used in the present Judgment.

After the explosions of October 22nd, the United Kingdom Government sent a note to the Albanian Government, in which it announced its intention to sweep the Corfu Channel shortly. The Albanian reply, which was received in London on October 31st, stated that the Albanian Government would not give its consent to this unless the operation in question took place outside Albanian territorial waters. Meanwhile, at the United Kingdom Government's request, the International Central Mine Clearance Board decided, in a resolution of November 1st, 1946, that there should be a further sweep of the Channel, subject to Albania's consent. The United Kingdom Government having informed the Albanian Government, in a communication of November 10th, that the proposed sweep would take place on November 12th, the Albanian Government replied on the 11th, protesting against this "unilateral decision of His Majesty's Government." It said it did not consider it inconvenient that the British fleet should undertake the sweeping of the channel of navigation, but added that, before sweeping was carried out, it considered it indispensable to decide what area of the sea should be deemed to constitute this channel, and proposed the establishment of a Mixed Commission for the purpose. It ended by saying that any sweeping undertaken without the consent of the Albanian Government outside the channel thus constituted, *i.e.*, inside Albanian territorial waters where foreign warships have no reason to sail, could only be considered as a deliberate violation of Albanian territory and sovereignty.

After this exchange of notes, "Operation Retail" took place on November 12th and 13th. Commander Mestre, of the French Navy, was asked to attend as observer, and was present at the sweep on November 13th. The operation was carried out under the protection of an important covering force composed of an aircraft carrier, cruisers and other war vessels. This covering force remained throughout the operation at a certain distance to the west of the Channel, except for the frigate *St. Bride's Bay*, which was stationed in the Channel southeast of Cape Kiephali. The sweep began in the morning of November 13th, at about 9 o'clock, and ended in the afternoon near nightfall. The area swept was in Albanian territorial waters, and within the limits of the channel previously swept.

The United Kingdom Government does not dispute that "Operation Retail" was carried out against the clearly expressed wish of the Albanian Government. It recognized that the operation had not the consent of the international mine clearance organizations, that it could not be justified as the exercise of a right of innocent passage, and lastly that, in principle, international law does not allow a State to assemble a large number of warships in the territorial waters of another State and to carry out mine-sweeping in those waters. The United Kingdom Government states that the operation was one of extreme urgency, and that it considered itself entitled to carry it out without anybody's consent.

The United Kingdom Government put forward two reasons in justification. First, the Agreement of November 22nd, 1945, signed by the Governments of the United Kingdom, France, the Soviet Union and the United States of America, authorizing regional mine clearance organizations, such as the

Mediterranean Zone Board, to divide the sectors in their respective zones amongst the States concerned for sweeping. Relying on the circumstance that the Corfu Channel was in the sector allotted to Greece by the Mediterranean Zone Board on November 5th, *i.e.*, before the signing of the above-mentioned Agreement, the United Kingdom Government put forward a permission given by the Hellenic Government to resweep the navigable channel.

The Court does not consider this argument convincing.

It must be noted that, as the United Kingdom Government admits, the need for resweeping the Channel was not under consideration in November 1945; for previous sweeps in 1944 and 1945 were considered as having effected complete safety. As a consequence, the allocation of the sector in question to Greece, and, therefore, the permission of the Hellenic Government which is relied on, were both of them merely nominal. It is also to be remarked that Albania was not consulted regarding the allocation to Greece of the sector in question, despite the fact that the Channel passed through Albanian territorial waters.

But, in fact, the explosions of October 22nd, 1946, in a channel declared safe for navigation, and one which the United Kingdom Government, more than any other government, had reason to consider safe, raised quite a different problem from that of a routine sweep carried out under the orders of the mine-clearance organizations. These explosions were suspicious; they raised a question of responsibility.

Accordingly, this was the ground on which the United Kingdom Government chose to establish its main line of defence. According to that Government, the *corpora delicti* must be secured as quickly as possible, for fear they should be taken away, without leaving traces, by the authors of the minelaying or by the Albanian authorities. This justification took two distinct forms in the United Kingdom Government's arguments. It was presented first as a new and special application of the theory of intervention, by means of which the State intervening would secure possession of evidence in the territory of another State, in order to submit it to an international tribunal and thus facilitate its task.

The Court cannot accept such a line of defence. The Court can only regard the alleged right of intervention as the manifestation of a policy of force, such as has, in the past, given rise to most serious abuse and such as cannot, whatever be the present defects in international organization, find a place in international law. Intervention is perhaps still less admissible in the particular form it would take here; for, from the nature of things, it would be reserved for the most powerful States, and might easily lead to perverting the administration of international justice itself.

The United Kingdom Agent, in his speech in reply, has further classified "Operation Retail" among methods of self-protection or self-help. The Court cannot accept this defence either. Between independent States, respect for territorial sovereignty is an essential foundation of international relations. The Court recognizes that the Albanian Government's complete failure to carry out its duties after the explosions, and the dilatory nature of its diplomatic notes, are extenuating circumstances for the action of the United Kingdom Government. But to ensure respect for international law, of which it is the organ, the Court must declare that the action of the British Navy constituted a violation of Albanian sovereignty.

This declaration is in accordance with the request made by Albania through her Counsel, and is in itself appropriate satisfaction.

The method of carrying out "Operation Retail" has also been criticized by the Albanian Government, the main ground of complaint being that the United Kingdom, on that occasion, made use of an unnecessarily large display of force, out of proportion to the requirements of the sweep. The Court thinks that this criticism is not justified. It does not consider that the action of the British Navy was a demonstration of force for the purpose of exercising political pressure on Albania. The responsible naval commander, who kept his ships at a distance from the coast, cannot be reproached for having employed an important covering force in a region where twice within a few months his ships had been the object of serious outrages.

For These Reasons, The Court on the first question put by the Special Agreement . . . by eleven votes to five,

Gives judgment that the People's Republic of Albania is responsible under international law for the explosions which occurred on October 22nd, 1946, in Albanian waters, and for the damage and loss of human life that resulted therefrom; and

by ten votes to six,

Reserves for further consideration the assessment of the amount of compensation and regulates the procedure on this subject by an Order dated this day; [and]

on the second question put by the Special Agreement . . . by fourteen votes to two,

Gives judgment that the United Kingdom did not violate the sovereignty of the People's Republic of Albania by reason of the acts of the British Navy in Albanian waters on October 22nd, 1946; and

unanimously,

Gives judgment that by reason of the acts of the British Navy in Albanian waters in the course of the Operation of November 12th and 13th, 1946, the United Kingdom violated the sovereignty of the People's Republic of Albania, and that this declaration by the Court constitutes in itself appropriate satisfaction.

Delimiting the Territorial Sea

In determining the width of the territorial sea, it is important to decide the point from which to measure. The conventional line is the low-water mark along the coast, but special problems arise in connection with bays, with coastlines at points where rivers flow into the sea, and where the coast is too jagged and irregular to permit navigators to measure territorial waters conveniently.

Fishing rights have been particularly troublesome in bays. The Hague Codification Conference of 1930 revealed three major problems that prevented states from agreeing about jurisdiction over bays. First, some states claim control of some bays, regardless of their size or shape. Second, states differ about width of the entrance to a territorial bay. Third, states do not agree on the methods they should use in measuring bays, although some very elaborate techniques have been developed for so doing.[35]

In general, the Conference tended to favor a ten-mile entrance width of territorial bays. States are inclined to claim bays as part of their territories whenever the national interest dictates the need for the claim and regardless of the distance between the headlands which mark the entrance to the bay. Many bays, such as Chesapeake Bay, are often described as "historic bays," in acknowledging that the waters are territorial. But no rule of law as yet lays down exact tests for defining a bay.

CONVENTION ON THE TERRITORIAL SEA AND THE CONTIGUOUS ZONE

U.N. Document A/Conf.13/L.52

SECTION II. LIMITS OF THE TERRITORIAL SEA

ARTICLE 3

Except where otherwise provided in these articles, the normal baseline for measuring the breadth of the territorial sea is the low-water line along the coast as marked on large-scale charts officially recognized by the coastal State.

ARTICLE 4

1. In localities where the coastline is deeply indented and cut into, or if there is a fringe of islands along the coast in its immediate vicinity, the method of

[35] Hyde, I, 479–481.

straight baselines joining appropriate points may be employed in drawing the baseline from which the breadth of the territorial sea is measured.

2. The drawing of such baselines must not depart to any appreciable extent from the general direction of the coast, and the sea areas lying within the lines must be sufficiently closely linked to the land domain to be subject to the régime of internal waters.

3. Baselines shall not be drawn to and from low-tide elevations, unless lighthouses or similar installations which are permanently above sea level have been built on them.

4. Where the method of straight baselines is applicable under the provisions of paragraph 1, account may be taken, in determining particular baselines, of economic interests peculiar to the region concerned, the reality and the importance of which are clearly evidenced by a long usage.

5. The system of straight baselines may not be applied by a State in such a manner as to cut off from the high seas the territorial sea of another State.

6. The coastal State must clearly indicate straight baselines on charts, to which due publicity must be given.

ARTICLE 5

1. Waters on the landward side of the baseline of the territorial sea form part of the internal waters of the State.

2. Where the establishment of a straight baseline in accordance with article 4 has the effect of enclosing as internal waters areas which previously had been considered as part of the territorial sea or of the high seas, a right of innocent passage, as provided in articles 14 to 23, shall exist in those waters.

ARTICLE 6

The outer limit of the territorial sea is the line every point of which is at a distance from the nearest point of the baseline equal to the breadth of the territorial sea.

ARTICLE 7

1. This article relates only to bays the coasts of which belong to a single State.

2. For the purposes of these articles, a bay is a well-marked indentation whose penetration is in such proportion to the width of its mouth as to contain landlocked waters and constitute more than a mere curvature of the coast. An indentation shall not, however, be regarded as a bay unless its area is as large as, or larger than, that of the semi-circle whose diameter is a line drawn across the mouth of that indentation.

3. For the purpose of measurement, the area of an indentation is that lying between the low-water mark around the shore of the indentation and a line joining the low-water mark of its natural entrance points. Where, because of the presence of islands, an indentation has more than one mouth, the semi-circle shall be drawn on a line as long as the sum total of the lengths of

the lines across the different mouths. Islands within an indentation shall be included as if they were part of the water area of the indentation.

4. If the distance between the low-water marks of the natural entrance points of a bay does not exceed twenty-four miles, a closing line may be drawn between these two low-water marks, and the waters enclosed thereby shall be considered as internal waters.

5. Where the distance between the low-water marks of the natural entrance points of a bay exceeds twenty-four miles, a straight baseline of twenty-four miles shall be drawn within the bay in such a manner as to enclose the maximum area of water that is possible with a line of that length.

6. The foregoing provisions shall not apply to so-called "historic" bays, or in any case where the straight baseline system provided for in article 4 is applied.

ARTICLE 8

For the purpose of delimiting the territorial sea, the outermost permanent harbour works which form an integral part of the harbour system shall be regarded as forming part of the coast.

ARTICLE 9

Roadsteads which are normally used for the loading, unloading and anchoring of ships, and which would otherwise be situated wholly or partly outside the outer limit of the territorial sea, are included in the territorial sea. The coastal State must clearly demarcate such roadsteads and indicate them on charts together with their boundaries, to which due publicity must be given.

ARTICLE 10

1. An island is a naturally formed area of land, surrounded by water, which is above water at high tide.

2. The territorial sea of an island is measured in accordance with the provisions of these articles.

ARTICLE 11

1. A low-tide elevation is a naturally formed area of land which is surrounded by and above water at low-tide but submerged at high tide. Where a low-tide elevation is situated wholly or partly at a distance not exceeding the breadth of the territorial sea from the mainland or an island, the low-water line on that elevation may be used as the baseline for measuring the breadth of the territorial sea.

2. Where a low-tide elevation is wholly situated at a distance exceeding the breadth of the territorial sea from the mainland or an island, it has no territorial sea of its own.

ARTICLE 12

1. Where the coasts of two States are opposite or adjacent to each other, neither of the two States is entitled, failing agreement between them to the contrary, to extend its territorial sea beyond the median line every point of which is equidistant from the nearest points on the baselines from which the breadth of the territorial seas of each of the two States is measured. The provisions of this paragraph shall not apply, however, where it is necessary by reason of historic title or other special circumstances to delimit the territorial seas of the two States in a way which is at variance with this provision.

2. The line of delimitation between the territorial seas of two States lying opposite to each other or adjacent to each other shall be marked on large-scale charts officially recognized by the coastal States.

ARTICLE 13

If a river flows directly into the sea, the baseline shall be a straight line across the mouth of the river between points on the low-tide line of its banks.

These articles establish rules of the sea for many circumstances, but still leave unresolved: (a) the maximum permissible length of baselines (many states feel that the maximum of 44 miles approved in the Anglo-Norwegian Fisheries Case was too long and would prefer a rule of fifteen miles); and (b) whether the method of straight baselines applies to "mid-ocean" groups of islands or archipelagos, like Indonesia and the Philippines.[36]

NORTH ATLANTIC COAST FISHERIES (1910)

PERMANENT COURT OF ARBITRATION, AWARD OF THE TRIBUNAL
(UNITED STATES—GREAT BRITAIN)

PROCEEDINGS IN THE NORTH ATLANTIC COAST FISHERIES ARBITRATION—
SEN. DOC. 870, I, 64, 61ST CONG., 3D SESS.

[Great Britain and the United States agreed on a Treaty signed in London on October 20, 1818, that both Americans and British subjects might fish off the coasts of Newfoundland, but the United States renounced "forever, any liberty . . . to take, dry, or cure fish on, or within three marine miles

---

[36] Indonesia in December 1957 proclaimed that all its islands were grouped together within one single system of baselines enclosing vast areas of the sea between the islands. The Philippines also considers the sea areas between its islands as belonging to its territory. Proposals approving this conception were presented to the 1958 Conference, but were withdrawn before being voted upon.

For the Anglo-Norwegian Fisheries Case, see pp. 255, 264.

of any . . . coasts, bays, creeks, or harbours" outside certain specified limits. Among the questions that arose in connection with this treaty was where the three marine miles were to be measured from.]

In regard to this question, Great Britain claims that the renunciation applies to all bays generally, and

The United States contend that it applies to bays of a certain class or condition.

Now, considering that the treaty used the general term "bays" without qualification, the tribunal is of opinion that these words of the treaty must be interpreted in a general sense as applying to every bay on the coast in question that might be reasonably supposed to have been considered as a bay by the negotiators of the treaty under the general conditions then prevailing, unless the United States can adduce satisfactory proof that any restrictions or qualifications of the general use of the term were or should have been present to their minds. . . .

4. It has been further contended by the United States that the renunciation applies only to bays six miles or less in width *inter fauces terrae,* those bays only being territorial bays, because the three-mile rule is, as shown by this treaty, a principle of international law applicable to coasts and should be strictly and systematically applied to bays.

But the tribunal is unable to agree with this contention:

(a) Because admittedly the geographical character of a bay contains conditions which concern the interests of the territorial sovereign to a more intimate and important extent than do those connected with the open coast. Thus conditions of national and territorial integrity, of defense, of commerce and of industry are all vitally concerned with the control of the bays penetrating the national coast line. This interest varies, speaking generally, in proportion to the penetration inland of the bay; but as no principle of international law recognizes any specified relation between the concavity of the bay and the requirements for control by the territorial sovereignty, this tribunal is unable to qualify by the application of any new principle its interpretation of the treaty of 1818 as excluding bays in general from the strict and systematic application of the three-mile rule; nor can this tribunal take cognizance in this connection of other principles concerning the territorial sovereignty over bays such as ten-mile or twelve-mile limits of exclusion based on international acts subsequent to the treaty of 1818 and relating to coasts of a different configuration and conditions of a different character;

(b) Because the opinion of jurists and publicists quoted in the proceedings conduce to the opinion that speaking generally the three-mile rule should not be strictly and systematically applied to bays; . . .

(f) Because from the information before this tribunal it is evident that the three-mile rule is not applied to bays strictly or systematically either by the United States or by any other power;

(g) It has ben recognized by the United States that bays stand apart, and that in respect of them territorial jurisdiction may be exercised farther than the marginal belt in the case of Delaware Bay by the report of the

United States Attorney General of May 19, 1793; and the letter of Mr. Jefferson to Mr. Genet of November 8, 1793, declares the bays of the United States generally to be, "as being landlocked, within the body of the United States."

5. In this latter regard it is further contended by the United States, that such exceptions only should be made from the application of the three-mile rule to bays as are sanctioned by conventions and established usage; that all exceptions for which the United States of America were responsible are so sanctioned; and that His Majesty's government are unable to provide evidence to show that the bays concerned by the treaty of 1818 could be claimed as exceptions on these grounds either generally, or except possibly in one or two cases, specifically.

But the tribunal, while recognizing that conventions and established usage might be considered as the basis for claiming as territorial those bays which on this ground might be called historic bays, and that such claims should be held valid in the absence of any principle of international law on the subject; nevertheless is unable to apply this, *a contrario*, so as to subject the bays in question to the three-mile rule, as desired by the United States:

(a) Because Great Britain has during this controversy asserted a claim to these bays generally, and has enforced such claim specifically in statutes or otherwise, in regard to the more important bays such as Chaleurs, Conception and Miramichi; . . .

6. It has been contended by the United States that the words "coasts, bays, creeks or harbors" are here used only to express different parts of the coast and are intended to express and be equivalent to the word "coast," whereby the three marine miles would be measured from the sinuosities of the coast and the renunciation would apply only to the waters of bays within three miles.

But the tribunal is unable to agree with this contention: . . .

(f) Because the tribunal is unable to understand the term "bays" in the renunciatory clause in other than its geographical sense, by which a bay is to be considered as an indentation of the coast, bearing a configuration of a particular character easy to determine specifically, but difficult to describe generally.

The negotiators of the treaty of 1818 did probably not trouble themselves with subtle theories concerning the notion of "bays"; they most probably thought that everybody would know what was a bay. In this popular sense the term must be interpreted in the treaty. The interpretation must take into account all the individual circumstances which for any one of the different bays are to be appreciated, the relation of its width to the length of penetration inland, the possibility and the necessity of its being defended by the state in whose territory it is indented; the special value which it has for the industry of the inhabitants of its shores; the distance which it is secluded from the highways of nations on the open sea and other circumstances not possible to enumerate in general.

For these reasons the tribunal decides and awards:

In case of bays, the three marine miles are to be measured from a straight line drawn across the body of water at the place where it ceases to have the configuration and characteristics of a bay. At all other places the three marine miles are to be measured following the sinuosities of the coast.

But considering the tribunal cannot overlook that this answer to Question 5, although correct in principle and the only one possible in view of the want of a sufficient basis for a more concrete answer, is not entirely satisfactory as to its practical applicability, and that it leaves room for doubts and differences in practice. Therefore the tribunal considers it its duty to render the decision more practicable and to remove the danger of future differences by adjoining to it, a recommendation. . . .

Considering, moreover, that in treaties with France, with the North German Confederation and the German Empire and likewise in the North Sea convention, Great Britain has adopted for similar cases the rule that only bays of ten miles width should be considered as those wherein the fishing is reserved to nationals. And that in the course of the negotiations between Great Britain and the United States a similar rule has been on various occasions proposed and adopted by Great Britain in instructions to the naval officers stationed on these coasts. And that though these circumstances are not sufficient to constitute this a principle of international law, it seems reasonable to propose this rule with certain exceptions, all the more that this rule with such exceptions has already formed the basis of an agreement between the two Powers.

Now therefore this tribunal . . . hereby recommends for the consideration and acceptance of the high contracting Parties the following rules and method of procedure for determining the limits of the bays hereinbefore enumerated:

1. In every bay not hereinafter specifically provided for, the limits of exclusion shall be drawn three miles seaward from a straight line across the bay in the part nearest the entrance at the first point where the width does not exceed ten miles. . . .

It is understood that nothing in these rules refers either to the Bay of Fundy considered as a whole apart from its bays and creeks or as to the innocent passage through the Gut of Canso, which were excluded by the agreement made by exchange of notes between Mr. Bacon and Mr. Bryce dated February 21, 1909, and March 4, 1909; or to Conception Bay, which was provided for by the decision of the Privy Council in the case of the *Direct United States Cable Company* v. *The Anglo-American Telegraph Company,* in which decision the United States have acquiesced.

THE SECRETARY OF STATE
Washington

January 15, 1963

Dear Mr. Attorney General:

   Your letter of January 8, 1963 called my attention to a
case now on appeal in the Supreme Court of Alaska, the <u>Arctic
Maid Fisheries, Inc</u>. v. <u>State of Alaska</u>, which involves the
territorial extent of the State's jurisdiction, for taxing
purposes, in Bristol Bay. In a decision rendered in this case
on September 4, 1962, the Alaska Superior Court held that
"the territorial waters of the State of Alaska in Bristol Bay
are those waters landward or northerly and easterly of a line
drawn from Cape Newenham to Cape Menshikof." The defendant
fishing companies appealed. All of the fishing activities
involved in the case took place landward of the line from
Cape Newenham to Cape Menshikof.

   Your letter states that it is your understanding that
the Department of State takes a more limited view of the extent of territorial waters in Bristol Bay and in these circumstances you inquire whether we think it would be desirable
for you to file an <u>amicus</u> <u>curiae</u> brief in the Supreme Court of
Alaska stating our position. It is your thought that a letter
from me setting forth our position would be submitted to the
Court as an authoritative determination of a policy question
within the province of this Department. You add that the
specific issue in this case is Alaska's jurisdiction in the
years 1951 through 1954 so that my letter should deal with
the national maritime boundary in Bristol Bay as of that time,
but that it would also be useful to have a statement as to
the present boundary for the future guidance of the Court and
of the State.

The Honorable
     Robert F. Kennedy,
          Department of Justice.

Article 7 of the Convention on the Territorial Sea and
the Contiguous Zone, which was adopted at the First Law of the
Sea Conference at Geneva in 1958, and which was ratified by the
President on March 24, 1961, deals with the status of bays,
the coasts of which belong to a single State. Paragraph 2
of that article defines a bay and prescribes the semi-
circular test. Paragraph 3 describes the method of measurement of the area of the bay, and paragraph 4 provides that
the closing line of the bay shall not exceed twenty-four miles.
Paragraph 5 states that where the distance between the low
water marks of the natural entrance points of the bay exceeds
twenty-four miles, a straight base line of twenty-four miles
shall be drawn within the bay in such a manner as to enclose
the maximum area of water that is possible with a line of that
length. Although the Convention is not yet in force according
to its terms because twenty-two States have not yet ratified
or acceded to it, nevertheless, it must be regarded in view
of its adoption by a large majority of the States of the
world as the best evidence of international law on the subject at the present time. This is particularly so in view
of the rejection by the International Court of Justice in
the Anglo-Norwegian Fisheries case of the so-called ten-mile
rule previously considered as international law by the United
States and other countries. Furthermore, in view of the
ratification of the Convention by the President with the
advice and consent of the Senate, it must be regarded as
having the approval of this Government and as expressive of
its present policy. Since the line drawn from Cape Newenham
to Cape Menshikof is some 162 miles long, it will be apparent
at once that the waters landward of that line cannot be regarded as internal waters of the United States under the law
as set forth in Article 7 of the Convention. Consequently,
the Department considers that there is no basis in international law as presently understood and approved by the
United States for Alaska's claim to the waters in question
as within its domain unless these waters can be considered
an "historic bay."

An extensive search of the records of the Department and
of the historical records of the Government at the National
Archives has revealed no evidence that the United States has
claimed the waters of Bristol Bay within the line referred to
as internal waters of the United States. It is noted from
your letter and from the decision of the Superior Court of
Alaska in this case that the Court's conclusion that Alaska's

claim to these waters is valid was based on a finding that "The Government of the United States has asserted a claim to all Bristol Bay waters landward of a line drawn between Cape Newenham and Cape Menshikof as inland waters through inter-related administrative and legislative action." It is also noted that it is your view that the statutes and regulations referred to, relating to fishing in Alaskan waters, do not justify the Court's conclusion. These statutes and regulations and the administrative practice thereunder have not been examined by the Department in the limited time available since they are regarded as matters more properly within the competence of other Departments of the Government and in view of what has been said it is not conceived that they would be decisive.

From the foregoing, it is evident that the Department is not aware of any basis in international law or on historic grounds for now considering all of the waters of Bristol Bay in question as internal waters of the United States. However, your letter requested the Department to indicate the maritime boundary of the United States in Bristol Bay during the years 1951 to 1954 when the tax claims of the State of Alaska involved in the present case accrued. Prior to the decision of the International Court of Justice in the Anglo-Norwegian Fisheries case rendered on December 10, 1951 the United States, as indicated above, followed the so-called ten-mile rule for bays, i.e., that under international law the closing line of bays could not exceed that limit. In a note verbale to the United Nations dated March 12, 1956, the United States took exception to a twenty-five mile proposal in the International Law Commission's 1955 draft code on the law of the sea and advocated instead maintaining the ten-mile rule for bays. Thus, during the 1951-1954 period, the United States either supported the ten-mile rule as international law or after the rejection of that rule by the International Court of Justice advocated its adoption by the United Nations. If the line between Cape Newenham and Cape Menshikof cannot be justified now under the twenty-four mile rule a fortiori, it was not valid under the ten-mile rule.

It is believed that future difficulties in our relations with other countries may be avoided if the Supreme Court of Alaska is advised of the position of the Government on the matters referred to. I therefore concur in your suggestion that an amicus curiae brief setting forth our position be filed. In that connection you may make such use of this letter as you consider advisable.

Sincerely yours,

s/ Dean Rusk

Dean Rusk

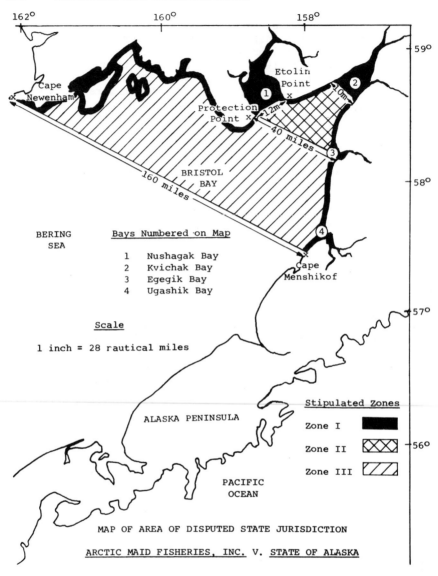

162°   160°   158°

59°

Cape
Newenham

Etolin
Point
x

1   10m

2

12m

Protection
Point x

40 miles

3

160 miles

BRISTOL
BAY

58°

BERING
SEA

Bays Numbered on Map

1   Nushagak Bay
2   Kvichak Bay
3   Egegik Bay
4   Ugashik Bay

4

Cape
Menshikof

57°

Scale

1 inch = 28 nautical miles

Stipulated Zones

Zone I

ALASKA PENINSULA

Zone II

56°

Zone III

PACIFIC
OCEAN

MAP OF AREA OF DISPUTED STATE JURISDICTION

ARCTIC MAID FISHERIES, INC. V. STATE OF ALASKA

[Chart prepared by Richard W. Edwards, Jr.]

Contiguous Zone

The traditional concept that the sea includes a zone contiguous to the territorial sea where a state may exercise certain functions was embraced in the 1958 Convention.

ARTICLE 24

1. In a zone of the high seas contiguous to its territorial sea, the coastal State may exercise the control necessary to:

(*a*) Prevent infringement of its customs, fiscal, immigration or sanitary regulations within its territory or territorial sea;

(*b*) Punish infringement of the above regulations committed within its territory or territorial sea.

2. The contiguous zone may not extend beyond twelve miles from the baselines from which the breadth of the territorial sea is measured.

. . . .

Among the purposes for which states may exercise authority in the contiguous zone, Article 24 does not include fishing. The Convention also treats the contiguous zone in a separate part of the document, thus emphasizing its legal status as an entity separate from the territorial sea. In fact, the contiguous zone is traditionally part of the high seas; states may exercise certain functions in the zone, but do not exercise sovereignty over it.

States, like the United States and the United Kingdom, not wishing to encourage wider claims to territorial waters, have been content to exercise their authority outside the territorial sea without claiming exclusive jurisdiction. For example, the United States asserted the right during Prohibition (1919–1933) to seize ships in the contiguous zone which wished unlawfully to introduce intoxicating liquor into American territory. And both the United States and Britain during wartime asserted the right under "hovering laws" to interfere with foreign ships outside their territorial waters. Neither state asserted, however, that the waters in which they carried on these activities were part of the territorial sea. In fact, without asserting territorial claims, states for hundreds of years have acted within the contiguous zone to prevent the use of the seas for certain purposes injurious to their territorial interests. As one authority has put it:

The significant fact is that the law of nations does not in a variety of situations forbid a State to exercise a protective and preventive jurisdiction for special purposes within waters beyond the marginal sea, and that it does not infer from that exercise an attempt to extend the limits of that sea.[37]

CHURCH v. HUBBART

UNITED STATES, SUPREME COURT, 1804

6 U.S. (2 CRANCH) 187

[John Barker Church, Jr., insured the cargo of the brigantine *Aurora* for a voyage from New York to one or two Portuguese ports in Brazil. The insurance policies stated that "The insurers are not liable for seizure by the Portuguese for illicit trade," and "The insurers do not take the risk of illicit trade with the Portuguese." In Rio de Janeiro, having received permission

[37] Hyde, I, 460–461.

to remain there for fifteen days, the *Aurora* sold $700-worth of goods with the apparent consent of customs officers. The ship then sailed to the Brazilian port of Para, where Portuguese authorities seized it at anchor "about four or five leagues from land" and arrested Church, who alleged that the *Aurora* had put in only for wood and water and to refit. The insurers maintained that the *Aurora* had been engaging in precisely the trade excluded by the clauses quoted above and that they were, therefore, not liable to pay. They introduced copies of Portuguese laws, certified by the U.S. Consul at Lisbon, as well as copies of sequestration proceedings against the vessel, and their position was upheld by the circuit court.]

MARSHALL, C. J. . . . [N]o error is perceived in the opinion given on the construction of the policies. If the proof is sufficient to show that the loss of the vessel and cargo was occasioned by attempting an illicit trade with the Portuguese; that an offence was actually committed against the laws of that nation, and that they were condemned by the government on that account, the case comes fairly within the exception of the policies, and the risk was one not intended to be insured against.

. . . .

For the plaintiff it is contended, that the terms used require an actual traffic between the vessel and inhabitants, and a seizure in consequence of that traffic, or at least that the vessel should have been brought into port, in order to constitute a case which comes within the exception of the policy. But such does not seem to be the necessary import of the words. The more enlarged and liberal construction given to them by the defendants, is certainly warranted by common usage; and wherever words admit of a more extensive or more restricted signification, they must be taken in that sense which is required by the subject matter, and which will best effectuate what it is reasonable to suppose was the real intention of the parties.

In this case, the unlawfulness of the voyage was perfectly understood by both parties. That the crown of Portugal excluded, with the most jealous watchfulness, the commercial intercourse of foreigners with their colonies, was, probably, a fact of as much notoriety as that foreigners had devised means to elude this watchfulness, and to carry on a gainful but very hazardous trade with those colonies. If the attempt should succeed it would be very profitable, but the risk attending it was necessarily great. It was this risk which the underwriters, on a fair construction of their words, did not mean to take upon themselves. "They are not liable," they say, "for seizure by the Portuguese for illicit trade." "They do not take the risk of illicit trade with the Portuguese." Now this illicit trade was the sole and avowed object of the voyage, and the vessel was engaged in it from the time of her leaving the port of New York. The risk of this illicit trade is separated from the various other perils to which vessels are exposed at sea, and excluded from the policy. Whenever the risk commences, the exception commences also for it is apparent that the underwriters meant to take upon themselves no portion of that hazard which was occasioned by the unlawfulness of the voyage.

If it could have been presumed by the parties to this contract, that the laws of Portugal, prohibiting commercial intercourse between their colonies and foreign merchants, permitted vessels to enter their ports, or to hover off their coasts for the purposes of trade, with impunity, and only subjected them to seizure and condemnation after the very act had been committed, or if such are really their laws, then indeed the exception might reasonably be supposed to have been intended to be as limited in its construction as is contended for by the plaintiff. If the danger did not commence till the vessel was in port, or till the act of bargain and sale, without a permit from the governor, has been committed, then it would be reasonable to consider the exception as only contemplating that event. But this presumption is too extravagant to have been made. If, indeed, the fact itself should be so, then there is an end of presumption, and the contract will be expounded by the law. But as a general principle, the nation which prohibits commercial intercourse with its colonies must be supposed to adopt measures to make that prohibition effectual. They must, therefore, be supposed to seize vessels coming into their harbours, or hovering on their coasts in a condition to trade, and to be afterwards governed in their proceedings with respect to those vessels by the circumstances which shall appear in evidence. That the officers of that nation are induced occasionally to dispense with their laws, does not alter them, or legalize the trade they prohibit. As they may be executed at the will of the governor, there is always danger that they will be executed, and that danger the insurers have not chosen to take upon themselves.

That the law of nations prohibits the exercise of any act of authority over a vessel in the situation of the *Aurora*, and that this seizure is, on that account, a mere marine trespass, not within the exception, cannot be admitted. To reason from the extent of protection a nation will afford to foreigners to the extent of the means it may use for its own security does not seem to be perfectly correct. It is opposed by principles which are universally acknowledged. The authority of a nation within its own territory is absolute and exclusive. The seizure of a vessel within a range of its cannon by a foreign force is an invasion of that territory, and is a hostile act which it is its duty to repel. But its power to secure itself from injury may certainly be exercised beyond the limits of its territory. Upon this principle the right of a belligerent to search a neutral vessel on the high seas for contraband of war is universally admitted, because the belligerent has a right to prevent the injury done to himself by the assistance intended for his enemy: so too a nation has a right to prohibit any commerce with its colonies. Any attempt to violate the laws made to protect this right, is an injury to itself which it may prevent, and it has a right to use the means necessary for its prevention. These means do not appear to be limited within any certain marked boundaries, which remain the same at all times and in all situations. If they are such as unnecessarily to vex and harass foreign lawful commerce, foreign nations will resist their exercise. If they are such as are reasonable and necessary to secure their laws from violation, they will be submitted to.

In different seas, and on different coasts, a wider or more contracted range, in which to exercise the vigilance of the government, will be assented to. Thus in the Channel, where a very great part of the commerce to and from all the north of Europe, passes through a very narrow sea, the seizure of vessels on suspicion of attempting an illicit trade, must necessarily be restricted to very narrow limits; but on the coast of South America, seldom frequented by vessels but for the purpose of illicit trade, the vigilance of the government may be extended somewhat further; and foreign nations submit to such regulations as are reasonable in themselves, and are really necessary to secure that monopoly of colonial commerce, which is claimed by all nations holding distant possessions.

If this right be extended too far, the exercise of it will be resisted. It has occasioned long and frequent contests, which have sometimes ended in open war. The English, it will be well recollected, complained of the right claimed by Spain to search their vessels on the high seas, which was carried so far that the *guarda costas* of that nation seized vessels not in the neighborhood of their coasts. This practice was the subject of long and fruitless negotiations, and at length of open war. The right of the Spaniards was supposed to be exercised unreasonably and vexatiously, but it never was contended that it could only be exercised within the range of the cannon from their batteries. Indeed, the right given to our own revenue cutters, to visit vessels four leagues from our coast, is a declaration that in the opinion of the American government, no such principle as that contended for has a real existence.

Nothing, then, is to be drawn from the laws or usages of nations, which gives to this part of the contract before the court the very limited construction which the plaintiff insists on, or which proves that the seizure of the *Aurora*, by the Portuguese governor, was an act of lawless violence.

The argument that such act would be within the policy, and not within the exception, is admitted to be well founded. That the exclusion from the insurance of the "risk of illicit trade with the Portuguese," is an exclusion only of that risk, to which such trade is by law exposed, will be readily conceded.

It is unquestionably limited and restrained by the terms "illicit trade." No seizure, not justifiable under the laws and regulations established by the crown of Portugal, for the restriction of foreign commerce with its dependencies, can come within this part of the contract, and every seizure which is justifiable by those laws and regulations must be deemed within it. . . .

[The court reversed the lower court's judgment and remanded the case to be tried again because, in its view, the copies of the Portuguese edicts were not properly authenticated. The Supreme Court held that no provision in the consular treaty with Portugal gave U.S. consuls the authority to authenticate copies of foreign laws.]

THE GRACE AND RUBY

UNITED STATES, DISTRICT COURT, DISTRICT OF MASSACHUSETTS, 1922

283 F. 475

MORTON, District Judge. These are libels for the forfeiture of the schooner *Grace and Ruby* for smuggling liquor in violation of of Rev. St. §§ 2872, 2874, and the National Prohibition Act (41 Stat. 305). They were heard upon exceptions to the libels, raising solely the question of jurisdiction. The facts are settled by stipulation of the parties. Those essential to a decision may be briefly stated as follows:

The *Grace and Ruby* was a British vessel owned and registered in Yarmouth, Nova Scotia, and commanded by one Ross, a British subject. He sailed from the Bahama Islands, British West Indies, with a St. John, N.B., clearance, on February 10, 1922, having a cargo of liquor, part of which was owned by one Sullivan, of Salem, Mass., who was on board. From the Bahamas she proceeded directly to a point about six miles off Gloucester, Mass., where Sullivan was set on shore and the schooner stood off and on, keeping always more than three miles from land. Two days later Sullivan came out to her in motorboat *Wilkin II*, owned in Gloucester and manned by two men, to bring provisions to the schooner and to take on shore part of her cargo. At that time the schooner was about ten miles from the nearest land. About 8,000 bottles of whisky and some other liquors were there transferred from the *Grace and Ruby* into the motorboat and taken to shore at night. Three members of the crew of the schooner, as well as Sullivan, went in the *Wilkin II*, and a dory belonging to the schooner was towed along, presumably for use in landing the liquor, or to enable the men to return to the schooner after the liquor was landed. The attempt to land the liquor was discovered by revenue officers, and *Wilkin II* and her cargo were seized.

The next day the revenue cutter *Tampa* was ordered to find the *Grace and Ruby* and bring her into port. Two days later, on February 23d, she discovered the schooner, and after some show of resistance on her part, which was overcome by a display of force by the cutter, the schooner was seized and brought into the port of Boston by the *Tampa*. At the time of the seizure the *Grace and Ruby* was about four miles from the nearest land. She had on board the balance of her cargo of liquor. Her master in no way assented to the seizure. After the schooner was brought into Boston the present libels were filed, a warrant for her arrest issued, and she was taken into custody by the United States marshal.

From the agreed facts it is clearly inferable that the master of the *Grace and Ruby* knew that she was engaged in an enterprise forbidden by the laws of the United States; that he knew her cargo was contraband; that she was lying off the coast beyond the three-mile limit, but within the four-league limit, for the purpose of having her cargo taken ashore in other boats; and that before her seizure part of her cargo had been transferred to *Wilkin II* for the purpose, as her master knew, of being smuggled into this country, with the assistance of the schooner's crew and boat. There is nothing to suggest any intent on his part, if that be material, that the *Grace and Ruby* herself should go within the territorial jurisdiction of this country, and so far as appears she never did. She was hovering on the coast for the purpose of landing contraband goods, and had actually sent, at night, a part of her cargo ashore, with her boat and three of her men to assist in landing it.

While the question is not free from doubt, and no decision upon the point has come to my notice, it seems to me that this action on her part constituted an unlawful unlading by the *Grace and Ruby* at night within the territorial limits of the United States, in violation of Rev. St. §§ 2872, 2874. See 1 Wheaton, *Criminal Law* (11th ed.) §§ 324, 330, 341, for a discussion of the principles involved and a collection of cases. The act of unlading, although beginning beyond the three-mile limit, continued until the liquor was landed, and the schooner was actively assisting in it by means of her small boat and three of her crew, who were on the motorboat for that purpose. It was none the less an unlawful unlading, within the section referred to, because by the transfer to the motorboat an offense was committed under section 2867, which rendered the motorboat and liquor liable to seizure for forfeiture, and the persons who aided and assisted liable to a penalty for so doing. . . .

The case, then, is that the *Grace and Ruby,* having violated our law and laid herself liable to forfeiture under it if she could be reached, was forcibly taken four miles off the coast by an executive department of the government and brought within our jurisdiction. The present question is whether on such facts this court has jurisdiction of a libel brought by the government for the forfeiture of the vessel. It is to be noticed that the schooner is held in these proceedings on the arrest made by the marshal under the warrant that was issued on the filing of the libels, and not under the seizure made by the cutter, when the schooner was taken and brought into Boston. Whether she could have been seized beyond the three-mile limit for an offense committed wholly beyond that limit is not the present question.

The high seas are the territory of no nation; no nation can extend its laws over them; they are free to the vessels of all countries. But this has been thought not to mean that a nation is powerless against vessels offending against its laws which remain just outside the three-mile limit. . . .

Church v. *Hubbart* has never been overruled, and I am bound by it until the law is clearly settled otherwise. Moreover, the principle there stated seems to me such a sensible and practical rule for dealing with cases like the present that it ought to be followed until it is authoritatively repudiated. This is not to assert a right generally of search and seizure on the high seas, but only a limited power, exercised in the waters adjacent to our coasts, over vessels which have broken our laws.

The mere fact, therefore, that the *Grace and Ruby* was beyond the three-mile limit, does not of itself make the seizure unlawful and establish a lack of jurisdiction.

As to the seizure: The line between territorial waters and the high seas is not like the boundary between us and a foreign power. There must be, it seems to me, a certain width of debatable waters adjacent to our coasts. How far our authority shall be extended into them for the seizure of foreign vessels which have broken our laws is a matter for the political departments of the government rather than for the courts to determine.

It is a question between governments; reciprocal rights and other matters may be involved. *In re* Cooper, 143 U.S. 472, 503; *The Kodiak* (D.C.) 53 F. 126, 130. In the case of *The Cagliari,* Dr. Twiss advised the Sardinian government that: "In ordinary cases, where a merchant ship has been seized on the high seas, the sovereign whose flag has been violated waives his privilege, considering the offending ship to have acted with *mala fides* toward the other state with which he is in amity, and to have consequently forfeited any just claim to his protection."

He considered the revenue regulations of many states authorizing visit and seizure beyond their waters to be enforceable at the peril of such states, and to rest on the express or tacit permission of the states whose vessels may be seized, 1 Moore's *Digest*, 729, 730.

It seems to me that this was such a case. The *Grace and Ruby* had committed an offense against our law, if my view as to the unlading is right, and was lying just outside the three-mile limit for purposes relating to her unlawful act. In directing that she be seized there and brought into the country to answer for her offense, I am not prepared to say that the Treasury Department exceeded its power.

An order may be entered, overruling the exceptions to each libel alleging lack of jurisdiction.

Breadth of the Territorial Sea

There remains to consider the breadth of the territorial sea, which is the fundamental consideration upon which many of the other rules above depend. It is one of the most controversial questions in contemporary international law, involving political and economic interests that differ from state to state. The much-publicized three-mile limit to the territorial sea originated in a prescription by a Dutch jurist, Cornelius Bynkershoek, who in 1703 declared that a state might control as much of the sea as it might command from the land. The test of that power, Bynkershoek held, was the range of a cannon, a range that came to be regarded in his time as three marine miles. That limit continued to be respected long after its theoretical base had disappeared and short-based guns acquired ranges far beyond their original capabilities.[38]

The United States and Britain have quite consistently adhered to the three-mile limit. Other states have not been so conservative. Norway, with the other Scandinavian states, for instance, because of her need to fish in wider waters, has traditionally regarded her territorial waters as extending four miles from her coast.

The Norwegian Government [an official made clear in 1957] would consider it futile to seek general agreement on rules governing the extent of the territorial sea which would deprive any country of stretches of its territorial sea over which today it enjoys uncontested jurisdiction. Thus the Norwegian Government would find it impossible to accept a breadth of less than four miles for its own coasts.[39]

[38] Hyde, I, 453.
[39] Letter from the Permanent Mission of Norway to the United Nations, 12 August 1957, U.N. Conference on the Law of the Sea, *OR*, I, 93. See also Hyde, I, 463–464 and Sørensen, pp. 242–252.

Mediterranean states have held to a limit of six miles, and Czarist Russia in some instances, to twelve. The great maritime states have not been eager to change the three-mile rule, fearing that extensions might eventually swallow up the high seas, disrupt fishing and navigation, seriously hamper air traffic, and interfere with defense. Their unwillingness to change the rule prevented the Hague Conference of 1930 from reaching any solution, and they could agree only that there was such a thing as a territorial sea.[40] Ever since then, however, states have in practice shown a tendency to extend the limits of the territorial sea, and in 1958, hardly more than twenty of 73 coastal states adhered to the three-mile rule. The International Court of Justice has pronounced against states unilaterally extending their territorial waters in an arbitrary manner,[41] but the Court has not attempted to decide how broad territorial waters are. Nor could the International Law Commission draft an acceptable rule on the subject. It contented itself instead with expressing the view that international law did not permit states to extend the territorial sea beyond twelve miles.

The problem was resolved neither by the 1958 or 1960 United Nations Conferences on the Law of the Sea. The several proposals before the Conferences, together with the vote for each, appear below.

FIRST U.N. CONFERENCE ON THE LAW OF THE SEA[42]

Alternate Texts of Article 3 of The Convention on the Territorial Sea

United Nations Document A/Conf.13/L.29

United States of America: Proposal (1958)

1. The maximum breadth of the territorial sea of any State shall be six miles.

2. The coastal State shall in a zone having a maximum breadth of twelve miles, measured from the applicable baseline, determined as provided in these rules, have the same rights in respect of fishing and the exploitation of the living resources of the sea as it has in its territorial sea; provided that such rights shall be subject to the right of the vessels of any State whose vessels have fished regularly in that portion of the zone having a continuous baseline and located in the same major body of water for the period of five years immediately preceding the signature of this convention, to fish in the outer six miles of that portion of the zone under obligation to observe therein such conservation regulations as are consistent with the rules on fisheries adopted by this conference and other rules of international law.

[40] Article I, Final Act of the Hague Codification Conference, League Doc. 1930, V.7, p. 15. The preparatory documents show that all states agreed beforehand that territorial waters included a three-mile belt, but only as a minimum. League of Nations, Conference for the Codification of International Law, Bases of Discussion, Vol. II—Territorial Waters, 1929, V.2, p. 17.

[41] *Fisheries case (United Kingdom v. Norway)*, [1951] *I.C.J.*, p. 132.

[42] For the texts of the Documents see, U.N. Conference on the Law of the Sea, *OR*, II, 116, 125, 126, 128. For account of the voting, see pp. 39–40.

Vote: 45, yes; 33 no; 7 abstentions. (Not adopted because two-thirds of those present and voting were needed, *i.e.* 52 in this case.)

United Nations Document A/Conf.13/L.30

U.S.S.R. Proposal

Each State shall determine the breadth of its territorial waters in accordance with established practice within the limits, as a rule, of three to twelve miles, having regard to historical and geographical conditions, economic interests of the security of the coastal State and the interests of international navigation.
Vote: 21 in favor; 45 opposed; 17 abstentions.

United Nations Document A/Conf.13/L.34

Burma, Colombia, Indonesia, Mexico, Morocco, Saudi Arabia
United Arab Republic and Venezuela, Proposal

1. Every State is entitled to fix the breadth of its territorial sea up to a limit of twelve nautical miles measured from the baseline which may be applicable in conformity with articles 4 and 5.
2. Where the breadth of its territorial sea is less than twelve nautical miles measured as above, a State has a fishing zone contiguous to its territorial sea extending to a limit twelve nautical miles from the baseline from which the breadth of its territorial sea is measured in which it has the same rights in respect of fishing and the exploitation of the living resources of the sea as it has in its territorial sea.
Vote: 39 in favor; 38 opposed; 8 abstentions.

United Nations Document A/Conf.13/L.28/Rev.1

Report of the First Committee

ARTICLE 3

A State has a fishing zone contiguous to its territorial sea, extending to a limit twelve nautical miles from the baseline from which the breadth of its territorial sea is measured, in which it has the same rights in respect of fishing and the exploitation of the living resources of the sea as it has in its territorial sea.
Vote: 35 in favor; 30 against; 20 abstentions.

SECOND U.N. CONFERENCE ON THE LAW OF THE SEA[43]

United Nations Document A/Conf.19/C.1/L.2/Rev.1

Ethiopia, Ghana, Guinea, Indonesia, Iran, Iraq, Jordan, Lebanon, Libya, Mexico, Morocco, Philippines, Saudi Arabia, Sudan, Tunisia, United Arab Republic, Venezuela, and Yemen, a Proposal (1960)

ARTICLE 1

A State has the right to fix the breadth of its territorial sea up to a maximum of twelve miles measured from the applicable baseline.

ARTICLE 2

A State, if the breadth of its territorial sea is less than twelve miles, has the right to establish a fishing zone contiguous to its territorial sea extending to a maximum of twelve miles measured from the applicable baseline.

ARTICLE 3

A State has in this fishing zone the same rights of fishing and of exploitation of the living resources of the sea as it has in its territorial sea.

ARTICLE 4

A State, if it has fixed the breadth of its territorial or contiguous fishing zone at less than twelve miles, has the right, vis-à-vis any other State with a different delimination thereof, to exercise the same sovereignty or exclusive fishing rights beyond its fixed limits up to the limits fixed by that other State.

ARTICLE 5

The foregoing provisions shall not apply to historic waters.

Vote: 36 in favor; 36 against; 13 abstentions.

United Nations Document A/Conf.19/C.1/L.10

Canada and United States of America: proposal (1960)

1. A State is entitled to fix the breadth of its territorial sea up to a maximum of six nautical miles measured from the applicable baseline.

2. A State is entitled to establish a fishing zone contiguous to its territorial sea extending to a maximum limit of twelve nautical miles from the baselines from which the breadth of its territorial sea is measured, in which it shall have the same rights in respect of fishing and the exploitation of the living resources of the sea as it has in its territorial sea.

3. Any State whose vessels have made a practice of fishing in the outer six miles of the fishing zone established by the coastal State, in accordance with paragraph 2 above, for the period of five years immediately preceding 1 January 1958, may continue to do so for a period of ten years from 31 October 1960.

Vote in Committee of the Whole: 43 in favor; 33 opposed; 12 abstentions.

Vote in Plenary Sessions: 54 in favor, 28 against, 5 abstentions. (Not adopted, having failed to obtain a two-thirds majority.)

At the 1960 conference, the vote on the Canadian-United States proposal failed by but one vote to achieve the required two-thirds majority.

[43] For documents, see Second United Nations Conference on the Law of the Sea, *OR*, pp. 158ff.; for voting, see *ibid.*, p. 170.

The statement thus represents something of a consensus, but in effect weakens the three-mile rule without substituting anything positive for it. All one can say at present about the existing rules of the breadth of the territorial sea is that some states object to extending the limits beyond three miles; most states agree that twelve miles is a maximum limit; and that it is likely that fishing rights will be recognized in a contiguous zone beyond the territorial sea when the law is finally formulated.

Defining the areas of the sea reserved for the fishing industry of one state and the areas of the sea open to all states is bound to raise continuing difficulties. In the absence of any clear legal rule on the subject, the Second United Nations Conference on the Law of the Sea attempted to deal with the situation by adopting a resolution (68 in favor; none opposed; 20 abstentions) which looked to mitigating quarrels over fisheries through technical assistance.

Annex II

The Second United Nations Conference on the Law of the Sea,
Having considered the question of fishery limits,

Recognizing that the development of international law affecting fishing may lead to changes in the practices and requirements of many States,

Recognizing further that economic development and the standard of living in many coastal States require increased international assistance to improve and expand their fisheries and fishing industries, which in many cases are handicapped by a lack of modern equipment, technical knowledge, and capital,

1. *Expresses* the view that technical and other assistance should be available to help States in making adjustments to their coastal and distant-waters fishing in the light of new developments in international law and practices;

2. *Draws the attention of* Governments participating in the facilities for assistance already available through the United Nations and specialized agencies;

3. *Urges* the appropriate organs of the United Nations and the specialized agencies and in particular the Food and Agriculture Organization of the United Nations, the Technical Assistance Board, and the United Nations Special Fund to give sympathetic and urgent consideration to any requests for assistance made by member Governments based on the new developments, and also urges them to consider, jointly or separately, further comprehensive studies and programmes of technical and material assistance;

4. *Invites* the Economic and Social Council to inform the General Assembly through its annual reports of the action taken in response to this resolution;

5. *Requests* the Secretary-General of the United Nations to bring this reso-

lution to the attention of the appropriate organs of the United Nations and the specialized agencies for suitable action at the earliest practicable time.[44]

Summary Record of a Statement by the Honorable Arthur H. Dean,
Chairman, Delegation of the United States of America
to the Second United Nations Conference on the Law of the Sea

[The] offer to agree on a six-mile breadth of territorial sea, provided that agreement could be reached on such a breadth on certain conditions, had been no more than an offer; its nonacceptance therefore left the pre-existing situation unchanged. His country was satisfied with the three-mile rule and would continue to regard it as established international law. Three miles was the sole breadth of territorial sea on which there had ever been anything like common agreement, and was a time-tested principle which offered the greatest opportunity to all nations without exception. Unilateral acts by States claiming a greater breadth of territorial sea were not sanctioned by international law, and conflicted with the universally accepted principles of freedom of the seas. In his Government's view there was no obligation on the part of States adhering to the three-mile rule to recognize claims of other States to a greater national agreement on the breadth of the territorial sea and on fishing rights, so that a regime of law might be established and the often conflicting national interests of States be prevented from jeopardizing the peace of the international community. His Government believed that such agreement was possible and would continue to lend its efforts to that end.

CANADIAN ANNOUNCEMENT OF ESTABLISHMENT OF 12-MILE FISHING ZONE[45]

Right Honorable L. B. Pearson (Prime Minister):

Mr. Speaker, I should like to make a statement to the House on the law of the sea, a subject of considerable importance in international affairs and of particular significance for Canada, the seventh largest fishing nation in the world and the fourth largest trading nation, possessing the world's longest coastlines.

Traditionally the breadth of the territorial sea has been three nautical miles, but the Canadian view has long been that breadth of three miles is not adequate for all purposes. It was on December 7, 1956, that a Canadian representative put forward at a meeting of the Sixth Committee of the United Nations the proposal, which later came to be known at Geneva as the Canadian proposal, of a contiguous fishing zone beyond the three mile territorial sea which would extend to a limit of 12 miles.

In the light of the failure of efforts to bring about an agreement on the breadth of the territorial sea and the contiguous fishing zone, the Government

---

[44] *Ibid.*, p. 176. The statement by Arthur H. Dean, that follows, may be found in *ibid.*, p. 34.
[45] 108 House of Commons Debates 621 (June 4, 1963).

has decided, after careful deliberation, that the time has come to take firm action to protect Canada's fishing industry. It is well known that foreign fishing operations off Canada's east coast, which have increased enormously over the past five years, are not only depleting our off-shore fisheries resources but are posing other problems. There are indications also that Canada's west coast fisheries may soon be threatened. In similar circumstances an increasing number of countries have felt themselves compelled to abandon the three mile fishing limit. All told, more than 40 countries have already extended their territorial limits, and more than 50 countries their fisheries limits beyond three miles.

With these considerations in mind the Canadian Government has decided to establish a 12 mile exclusive fisheries zone along the whole of Canada's coastline as of mid-May, 1964, and to implement the straight base line system at the same time as the basis from which Canada's territorial sea and exclusive fisheries zone shall be measured.

The Government recognizes that such action will necessarily have implications for other countries, particularly the United States of America and France, both of which have treaty fishing rights in some of the areas affected and claims to "historic" fishing rights in other areas in question. In the case of Canada and the U.S.A. in particular, there is a long tradition of friendly and fruitful co-operation of fisheries problems, and any action by Canada on these matters will, as in the past, take full account of United States interests, as well as those other countries affected.

It may be recalled that in my discussions with President Kennedy at Hyannis Port, I informed him that the Canadian Government would shortly be taking decisions to establish a 12 mile fishing zone. The President reserved the longstanding American position in support of the three mile limit. He also called attention to the "historic" and treaty fishing rights of the U.S.A. and I assured him that these rights would be taken into account. Discussions will be held with the United States with a view to determining the nature and extent of the U.S.A. rights and interests which may be affected by the action which Canada is taking. Discussions will also be opened as soon as possible with other countries affected, and it is our hope and belief that we will be able to reach agreement with such countries on mutually satisfactory arrangements.

POSITIONS OF OTHER STATES

DEPARTMENT OF STATE,
Washington, D.C., June 17, 1963.
Hon. ERNEST GRUENING,
U.S. Senate.

DEAR SENATOR GRUENING: A representative of your office recently requested a list of countries which claim more than 3 miles of territorial sea or exclusive fishing rights. A comprehensive survey of such claims was made in connection with the two United Nations Law of the Sea Conferences held at Geneva 1958 and 1960, and a synoptical table was prepared by these conferences showing the breadth of the territorial sea and adjacent zones claimed by the various states. A reproduction of the table is enclosed for your information. **

Since that time several countries have made claims to an extended territorial sea or exclusive fishing zone. A summary of such claims since the 1960 Law of the Sea Conference, based on information reaching the Department, is also enclosed. In addition to the countries which have asserted claims, a number have indicated that they intend to do so. Legislation has been introduced (1) in Colombia to extend the territorial sea from 6 to 12 miles; (2) in Ghana to establish a 12-mile territorial sea, with an undefined protective area seaward of this, and up to 100 miles of fishing conservation zone; (3) in South Africa, Costa Rica, and Turkey to extend the territorial sea to 6 miles with a 6-mile contiguous fishing zone; and (4) in the Ivory Coast to extend the territorial sea to 12 miles. Moreover, Canada recently announced a decision to establish a 12-mile fishing zone, and the United Kingdom has renounced certain fisheries treaties apparently as a first move toward abandoning the 3-mile limit for fisheries.

I hope this informaton will be helpful to you.

Sincerely yours,
FREDERICK G. DUTTON,
Assistant Secretary.

SUMMARY OF UNILATERAL CLAIMS TO EXTENDED TERRITORIAL SEAS OR EXCLUSIVE FISHING ZONES, SINCE THE 1960 UNITED NATIONS CONFERENCE ON LAW OF THE SEA

Albania: March 1, 1960, restricted innocent passage in a 10-mile territorial sea. Fishing jurisdiction claimed to 12 miles.

Cameroon: June 23, 1962, claimed a 6-mile territorial sea.

China: While the Republic of China recognizes the 3-nautical-mile territorial sea, Communist China claims a 12-mile territorial sea.

Denmark: June 1, 1963, extended the fisheries limits for Greenland to 12 miles. A similar limit for the Faroes Islands will take effect March 12, 1964. Certain countries are exempted from the Greenland limits until May 31, 1973.

Malagasy Republic: February 27, 1963, claimed a 12-mile territorial sea.

Morocco: Extended fishing jurisdiction to 12 miles, except for the Strait of Gibraltar, for which such jurisdiction was extended to 6 miles.

Norway: Extended fisheries jurisdiction to 6 miles on April 1, 1961, and to 12 miles on September 1, 1961.

Senegal: June 21, 1961, claimed a 6-mile territorial sea, plus a 6-mile contiguous zone.

Sudan: August 2, 1960, extended the territorial sea to 12 miles.

Tunisia: July 26, 1962, extended the territorial sea to 6 miles with an additional 6 miles of fisheries jurisdiction for a portion of its coast from the Algerian border to Ras Kapoudia, and extended the territorial sea from there to the Libyan border to the 50-meter isobath line.

Uruguay: February 21, 1963, claimed a 6-mile territorial sea plus a 6-mile contiguous zone for fishing and other purposes.

[Letter of Frederick G. Dutton, Assistant Secretary of State, to Ernest Gruening, Senator from Alaska. Reproduced from 109 Congressional Record 11279-11280 (June 28, 1963).]

**[This synoptical table is not reproduced here. It appears as United Nations Document A/Conf. 19/4 (February 8, 1960), and has been reprinted as an annex to the Summary Records of Plenary Meetings and of Meetings of the Committee of the Whole, Second United Nations Conference on the Law of the Sea, United Nations Document A/Conf. 19/8, Sales No. 60.V.6.]

DEPARTMENT OF STATE,
Washington, May 18, 1966.

Hon. WARREN G. MAGNUSON,
Chairman, Committee on Commerce,
U.S. Senate.

DEAR MR. CHAIRMAN: Your letter of June 30, 1965, enclosed copies of S. 2218, introduced by Senator Bartlett, and S. 2225, introduced by Senator Magnuson, on which the Department of State's comments were requested.

The purpose of the proposed legislation is to establish for the United States a 12-mile exclusive fisheries zone measured from the baseline from which the breadth of the territorial sea is measured but subject to the continuation of such traditional fishing by foreign states and their nationals as may be recognized by the U.S. Government.

Although the Geneva Conference of 1958 adopted four conventions on the law of the sea, it was recognized that the conventions left unresolved the twin questions of the width of the territorial sea and the extent to which a coastal state could claim exclusive fishing rights in the high seas off its coast. The Conference adopted a resolution suggesting that the United Nations call a second conference to deal with these unresolved problems, which the United Nations did. At the second conference, which was held in 1960, the United States and Canada put forward a compromise proposal for a 6-mile territorial sea, plus a 6-mile exclusive fisheries zone (12 miles of exclusive fisheries jurisdiction in all) subject to the continuation for 10 years of traditional fishing by other states in the outer 6 miles. This compromise proposal failed by one vote to obtain the two-thirds vote necessary for adoption.

Since the 1960 Law of the Sea Conference there has been a trend toward the establishment of a 12-mile fisheries rule in international practice. Many states acting individually or in concert with other states have extended or are in the process of extending their fisheries limits to 12 miles. Such actions have no doubt been accelerated by the support for the proposals made at the Geneva Law of the Sea Conferences in 1958 and 1960, of a fisheries zone totaling 12 miles as part of a package designed to achieve international agreement on the territorial sea.

In view of the recent developments in international practice, action by the United States at this time to establish in exclusive fisheries zone extending 9 miles beyond the territorial sea would not be contrary to international law. It should be emphasized that such action would not extend the territorial sea beyond our traditional 3-mile limit and would not affect such traditional freedoms of the sea as freedom of navigation or of overflight. With one or two possible exceptions, it is not likely that such action would be unfavorably received by other governments in view of the provision for recognition of traditional fishing, which the Department regards as a desirable provision.

In the above circumstances, the Department has no objection from the standpoint of U.S. foreign relations to establishing a 12-mile exclusive fisheries zone subject to the continuation of such traditional fishing by foreign states as may be recognized by the U.S. Government.

Whether the establishment at this time of a 12-mile exclusive fisheries zone would serve the longer term economic interests of the United States and the U.S. fishing industry is, of course, a separate question which is discussed in a report prepared by the Department of the Interior. Inasmuch as U.S. establishment of a 12-mile exclusive fisheries zone would tend to support the trend already referred to, the passage of the proposed legislation would make it more difficult, from the standpoint of international law, to extend the zone beyond 12 miles in the future.

Time has not permitted the Department to obtain the advice of the Bureau of the Budget with respect to this report.

Sincerely yours,

DOUGLAS MACARTHUR II,
Assistant Secretary for Congressional Relations
(For the Secretary of State).

[Reproduced from Senate Report No. 1280, 89th Congress, 2d Session (June 15, 1966), pp. 12-13.]

271

Breadth of fishery jurisdiction claimed by coastal nations

3 miles	3 to 12 miles	12 miles	Beyond 12 miles
*Australia	Cameroon (6)	Albania	Argentina (CS)
China	*Finland (4)	Algeria	*Cambodia (CS)
Cuba	Greece (6)	Belgium	Ceylon (100)
Ivory Coast	*Haiti (6)	Brazil	Chile (200)
Japan	Honduras (6)	Bulgaria	Costa Rica (200)
*Jamaica	Israel (6)	Burma	*Dominican Republic (15)
Jordan	Lebanon (6)	Canada	Ecuador (200)
Kenya	Maldive Island (6)	*Colombia	El Salvador (200)
Liberia	Mexico (9)	Cyprus	Ghana (100)
Malaysia	Yugoslavia (10)	Dahomey	Guinea (130)
Malta		Denmark	India (100)
Poland		Ethiopia	Korea (200)
The Gambia		France	Nicaragua (200)
Trinidad		Germany	Pakistan (100)
*United States		Guatemala	Panama (CS)
		Iceland	Peru (200)
		Indonesia	Tunisia (65)
		Iran	
		Iraq	
		Ireland	
		Italy	
		Libya	
		*Malagasy Republic	
		Mauritania	
		Morocco	
		*Netherlands	
		New Zealand	
		Norway	
		*Portugal	
		Romania	
		Saudi Arabia	
		*Senegal	
		*Sierra Leone	
		*South Africa	
		Spain	
		Sudan	
		Sweden	
		Syria	
		Tanzania	
		Thailand	
		Togo	
		Turkey	
		Ukrainian S.S.R.	
		U.S.S.R.	
		United Arab Republic	
		*United Kingdom	
		Uruguay	
		*Venezuela	
		Vietnam	

NOTES

1. 23 nations that are members of United Nations have no coast.
2. As of June 1, 1966, Department of State had incomplete information on fishery jurisdiction claims of 8 coastal nations—Congo (Brazzaville), Congo (Léopoldville), Gabon, Kuwait. *Nigeria (3-mile territorial sea, fishery jurisdiction uncertain), Philippines (expansive use of straight base lines, fishery jurisdiction uncertain), Somali Republic, and Yemen.
3. Numbers in parentheses indicate approximate number of miles claimed; "CS" means continental shelf.
4. The nature of the claims of several nations beyond 12 miles is uncertain.
5. "*" indicates nations that have ratified the 1958 Convention on Fishing and Conservation of the Living Resources of the Sea.

[Reproduced from Senate Report No. 1280, 89th Congress, 2d Session (June 15, 1966), p. 5. The information in the table, up-to-date as of June 1, 1966, was provided to the U.S. Senate Committee on Commerce by the Department of State.]

Efforts to define jurisdiction over the sea continued after the two United Nations conferences and resulted in March 1964 in a European Fisheries Convention signed by twelve of sixteen states represented at the International Conference on North European Waters which convened in London in December 1963. The Convention replaces the three-mile rule for fishing with a twelve-mile rule and thus reserves wider stretches of the marginal sea for domestic fishermen. Aliens who have customarily fished six to twelve miles out may, however, continue to do so forever, but with certain restrictions. They may not, for instance, in the interest of conservation, remove very small fish from the sea.

Agreement was not complete at the London meetings: Austria, Switzerland, Iceland, and Norway did not accept the treaty, while Denmark accepted it for its own coastline, but not on behalf of the Faroe islands or Greenland. These exceptions leave ample room for continuing controversy, because it is in these very waters that most difficulties have arisen among competing fishermen. Faroe islanders and Iceland refused to make any exceptions for "historic" rights, which was bound to irk British trawlermen who have traditionally fished off these islands.[46]

Offshore Mineral and Oil Rights

Improved techniques for drilling for oil, which make it possible to conduct such operations farther offshore than in the past and in deeper waters, have increased pressure upon governments to extend their claims farther and farther into the sea. The conflicts of interest among states are real, and the complexity of the questions enormous, as indicated below in *U.S. v. California* (382 U.S. 448).

In 1947, the U.S. Supreme Court decided that the United States had "paramount rights in, and full dominion and power over, the lands, minerals and other things underlying the Pacific Ocean lying seaward of the ordinary low-water mark on the coast of California, and outside of the inland waters, extending seaward three nautical miles. . . .The State of California has no title thereto or property interest therein."[47] The Court appointed a Special Master to define these lands in detail, and the Special Master completed his report in 1952.[48] Before the Court could act on this report, Congress passed the Submerged Lands Act,[49] which reversed the Supreme Court's 1947 decision and granted the States "title to and ownership of the lands beneath navigable waters within the boundaries of the respective States" (Sec. 3a). The Act limited boundaries to lines extending from the coastline no more than three geographical miles into the Atlantic or Pacific Oceans and no more than three marine leagues into the Gulf of Mexico (Sec. 2b). The Court defined *coastline* as the composite "line of ordinary low water along that portion of the coast which is in direct contact with the open sea and the line marking the seaward limit of inland waters" (Sec. 2c), but it did not define *inland waters*. California claimed that *inland waters* meant those waters which the State considered to be inland when it entered the Union and that the lines drawn in the Special Master's report (based on those which the United States would have claimed as such for purposes of international relations) should be redrawn. The Court, asserting first that Congress meant the Court to define the term, then addressed itself to that task, as the excerpt below indicates.

---

[46] See *Final Act of the European Fisheries Conference*, Misc. No. 11 (1964), Cmnd. 2335 (London: HMSO, 1965).
[47] *U.S. v. California, Order and Decree*, 332 U.S. 804, 805.
[48] 344 U.S. 872.
[49] 67 Stat. 29, 43 U.S.C. Secs. 1301–15 (1958 ed.).

UNITED STATES V. CALIFORNIA

UNITED STATES, SUPREME COURT, 1965

382 U.S. 448

III

THE MEANING OF INLAND WATERS IN THE SUBMERGED LANDS ACT
SHOULD CONFORM TO THE CONVENTION ON THE TERRITORIAL SEA
AND THE CONTIGUOUS ZONE

We turn, then, to determining the judicial definition of "inland waters." It immediately appears that the bulk of cases cited by congressmen during debates on the Submerged Lands Act for the proposition that inland waters "have been defined time and again by the courts" deal with interior waters such as lakes and rivers, and provide no assistance in classifying bodies of water which join the open sea.[50] In this latter context no prior case in this Court has ever precisely defined the term. The 1947 *California* opinion clearly indicated that "inland waters" was to have an international content since the outer limits of inland waters would determine the Country's international coastline, but the Court did not particularize the definition.[51] It was that task which subsequently led to the appointment of the Special Master.

[50] See, *e.g.*, 99 Cong. Rec. 3110–3112 (remarks of Senator Hill).
[51] The 1947 case raised the purely legal question—who owned the lands and mineral rights beneath the marginal sea belt? In deciding that they belonged to the United States the Court relied heavily on the international responsibilities of the Federal Government.
"But whatever any nation does in the open sea, which detracts from its common usefulness to nations, or which another nation may charge detracts from it, is a question for consideration among nations as such, and not their separate governmental units. What this Government does, or even what the states do, anywhere in the ocean, is a subject upon which the nation may enter into and assume treaty or similar international obligations." 322 U.S., at 35 (footnote omitted).
The opinion also established that landlocked waters not a part of the open sea are not part of the marginal belt, and belong to the States. The only problem remaining in the way of actually fixing the location of the marginal belt, and hence the dividing line of ownership between the State and the United States, was that of determining where the open sea ends and landlocked waters begin. The Court specifically left that question unresolved. It is precisely that problem of defining what constitutes open sea and what constitutes inland waters which we must decide in the present case.
Resolution of that question will (1) determine for the present the location of the marginal belt which we claim against other nations, and (2) define the areas within which ships of foreign nations have no right of innocent passage. Unquestionably, the definitions of what constitutes open sea and inland waters is, to borrow the words of the 1947 opinion, "a subject upon which the nation may enter and assume treaty or similar international obligations." Negotiations at the Hague beginning in 1930 were directed to just that end, and the Convention of the Territorial Sea and the Contiguous Zone, to which we became a party in 1961, now establishes rules for separating the open sea from inland waters. . . .

The Special Master found that there was no internationally accepted definition for inland waters, and decided, in those circumstances, that it was the position which the United States took on the question in the conduct of its foreign affairs which should be controlling. He considered the relevant date on which to determine our foreign policy position to be the date of the *California* decree, October 27, 1947. He therefore rejected the assertion that letters from the State Department written in 1951 and 1952[52] declaring the then present policy of the United States were conclusive on the question before him. At the same time that decision required the Special Master to consider a great deal of foreign policy materials dating back to 1793 in an attempt to discern a consistent threat of United States policy on the definition of inland waters. He ultimately decided that as of 1947 the United States had taken the position that a bay was inland water only if a closing line could be drawn across its mouth less than 10-miles long enclosing a sufficient water area to satisfy the Boggs formula.[53]

Since the filing of the Special Master's Report the policy of the United States has changed significantly. Indeed it may now be said that there is a settled international rule defining inland waters. On March 24, 1961, the United States ratified the Convention on the Territorial Sea and the Contiguous Zone (T.I.A.S. No. 5639) and on September 10, 1964, when the requisite number of nations had ratified it, the Convention went into force. For nations which do not use a straight-baseline method[54] to define inland waters (see *United Kingdom* v. *Norway*, [1951] I.C.J. Rep. 116), the Convention permits a 24-mile maximum closing line for bays and a "semicircle" test for testing the sufficiency of the water area enclosed. The semicircle test requires that a bay must comprise at least as much water area within its closing line as would be contained in a semicircle with a diameter equal to the length of the closing line. Unquestionably the 24-mile closing line together with the semicircle test now represents the position of the United states.[55]

The United States contends that we must ignore the Convention of the

---

[52] Letter from Acting Secretary of State Webb to Attorney General McGrath, November 13, 1951. Senate Hearings 460; letter from Secretary of State Acheson to Attorney General McGrath, February 12, 1952. Senate Hearings 462.

[53] . . . Neither the Special Master nor the United States treated the Boggs formula as having been the "definitive" United States position. The Special Master recommended it as an "appropriate technical method" for measuring the sufficiency of the depth of bays. Report of Special Master 26. [The Boggs formula draws a closing line across the mouth of an indentation; draws a belt around the shore of the indentation having a width equal to one-fourth the length of the closing line; compares the remaining area inside the closing line with the area of a semicircle having a diameter equal to one-half the length of the closing line. If the enclosed area is larger than the semicircle, the indentation is inland water; if the enclosed area is smaller than the semicircle, the indentation is high seas. See Boggs, "Delimination of the Territorial Sea," *A.J.I.L.*, XXIV (1930), 541, 548.]

[54] See n. 60, *infra*.

[55] Letter from Dean Rusk, Secretary of State, to Robert Kennedy, Attorney General, January 15, 1963, 2 International Legal Materials 527.

Territorial Sea and the Contiguous Zone in performing our duty of giving content to "inland waters" as used in the Submerged Lands Act, and must restrict ourselves to determining what our decision would have been had the question been presented to us for decision on May 22, 1953, the passage date of the Act. At that time there was no international accord on any definition of inland waters, and the best evidence (although strenuously contested by California) of the position of the United States was the letters of the State Department which the Special Master refused to treat as conclusive.

We do not think that the Submerged Lands Act has so restricted us. Congress, in passing the Act, left the responsibility for defining inland waters to this Court.[56] We think that it did not tie our hands at the same time. Had Congress wished us simply to rubber stamp the statements of the State Department as to its policy in 1953, it could readily have done so itself.[57] It is our opinion that we best fill our responsibility of giving content to the words which Congress employed by adopting the best and most workable definitions available. The Convention of the Territorial Sea and the Contiguous Zone, approved by the Senate and ratified by the President,[58] provides such definitions. We adopt them for purposes of the Submerged Lands Act. This establishes a single coastline for both the administration of the Submerged Lands Act and the conduct of our future international relations (barring an unexpected change in the rules established by the Convention). Furthermore the comprehensiveness of the Convention provides answers to many of the lesser problems related to coastlines which, absent the Convention, would be most troublesome.[59]

[56] See discussion and legislative history, Part II, *supra* [not reproduced here].
[57] See 99 Cong. Rec. 2633 (remarks of Senators Long and Cordon).
[58] The Convention was approved by the Senate May 26, 1960, 106 Cong. Rec. 11196, and was ratified by the President March 24, 1961, 44 State Dept. Bull. 609. See Treaties in Force—January 1, 1965, 263.
[59] In support of the position that we should ignore the developments in the law and practice of nations respecting the concept of inland waters which have transpired subsequent to the passage of the Submerged Lands Act—a position which the Solicitor General frankly recognized in his oral presentation was not an easy one for the Government to maintain—the United States cites a statement made by Senator Cordon during the hearings.
"Those who prepared the bill over the years took the view—and that is the way the bill is before us—that 'coastline' means the line of ordinary low water along that portion of the coast which is in direct contact with the open sea and the line marking the seaward limit of inland waters. That is in the present tense. It is the coastline as of now. We have confirmed here 3 miles from the coastline as of now. . . .
"If we attempt now to discuss a coastline of 1783, or whenever the Revolutionary War was concluded and the treaty was signed—and I do not just now recall the date—if we attempt now to determine a coastline as of then, it would seem to me that we increase our difficulties beyond what, as I understand the bill, we envisioned in the first place, but which we left where they were." Senate Hearings 1354–1355.
That statement was made in reply to a suggestion that a State should have the choice of extending its boundaries three miles from its present coastline or three miles from its coastline as of the time it entered the Union. Senator Cordon's reply

California argues, alternatively to its claim that "inland waters" embrace all ocean areas lying within a State's historic seaward boundaries, that if Congress intended "inland waters" to be judicially defined in accordance with international usage, such definition should possess an ambulatory quality so as to encompass future changes in international law or practice. Thus, if 10 years from now the definitions of the Convention were amended, California would say that the extent of the Submerged Lands Act grant would automatically shift, at least if the effect of such amendment were to enlarge the extent of submerged lands available to the States. We reject this open-ended view of the Act for several reasons. Before today's decision no one could say with assurance where lay the line of inland waters as contemplated by the Act; hence there could have been no tenable reliance on any particular line. After today that situation will have changed. Expectations will be established and reliance placed on the line we define. Allowing future shifts of international understanding respecting inland waters to alter the extent of the Submerged Lands Act grant would substantially undercut the definiteness of expectation which should attend it. Moreover, such a view might unduly inhibit the United States in the conduct of its foreign relations by making its ownership of submerged lands *vis-à-vis* the States continually dependent upon the position it takes with foreign nations. "Freezing" the meaning of "inland waters" in terms of the Convention definition largely avoids this, as well as serving to fulfill the requirements of definiteness and stability which should attend any congressional grant of property rights belonging to the United States.

IV

SUBSIDIARY ISSUES

Once it is decided that the definitions of the Convention on the Contiguous Zone apply, many of the subsidiary issues before us fall into place.

1. *Straight Base Lines.* California argues that because the Convention permits a nation to use the straight base line method for determining its seaward boundaries if its "coast line is deeply indented and cut into, or if there is a fringe of islands along the coast in its immediate vicinity," California is therefore free to use such boundary lines across the openings of its bay and around its islands.[60] We agree with the United States that the Convention

---

expresses his opposition to that idea on the ground that the exact location of the ancient shoreline would be extremely difficult to determine. It reveals no intent to restrict the courts in framing the definitions to be used to determine the present coastline.

[60] Article 4 of the Convention provides:

"1. In localities where the coast line is deeply indented and cut into, or if there is a fringe of islands along the coast in its immediate vicinity, the method of straight baselines joining appropriate points may be employed in drawing the baseline from which the breadth of the territorial sea is measured.

"2. The drawing of such baselines must not depart to any appreciable extent from the general direction of the coast, and the sea areas lying within the lines

recognizes the validity of straight base lines used by other countries, Norway for instance, and would *permit* the United States to use such base lines if it chose, but that California may not use such base lines to extend our international boundaries beyond their traditional international limits against the expressed opposition of the United States. The national responsibility for conducting our international relations obviously must be accommodated with the legitimate interests of the States in the territory over which they are sovereign. Thus a contraction of a State's recognized territory imposed by the Federal Government in the name of foreign policy would be highly questionable. But an extension of state sovereignty to an international area by claiming it as inland water would necessarily also extend national sovereignty, and unless the Federal Government's responsibility for questions of external sovereignty is hollow, it must have the power to prevent States from so enlarging themselves. We conclude that the choice under the Convention to use the straight-baseline method for determining inland waters claimed against other nations is one that rests with the Federal Government, and not with the individual States.

California relies upon *Manchester v. Massachusetts*, 139 U.S. 240, for the proposition that a State may draw its boundaries as it pleases with limits recognized by the law of nations regardless of the position taken by the United States. Although some dicta in the case may be read to support that view, we do not so interpret the opinion. The case involved neither an expansion of our traditional international boundary nor opposition by the United States to the position taken by the State.

2. *Twenty-four Mile Closing Rule.* The Convention recognizes, and it is the present United States position,[61] that a 24-mile closing rule together with the semicircle test should be used for classifying bays in the United States.[62]

---

must be sufficiently closely linked to the land domain to be subject to the régime of internal waters.

"3. Baselines shall not be drawn to and from low-tide elevations, unless lighthouses or similar installations which are permanently above sea level have been built on them.

"4. Where the method of straight baselines is applicable under the provisions of paragraph 1, account may be taken, in determining particular baselines, of economic interests peculiar to the region concerned, the reality and the importance of which are clearly evidenced by a long usage.

"5. The system of straight baselines may not be applied by a State in such a manner as to cut off from the high seas the territorial sea of another State.

"6. The coastal State must clearly indicate straight baselines on charts, to which due publicity must be given."

[61] Letter from Dean Rusk, Secretary of State, to Robert Kennedy, Attorney General January 5, 1963, 2 International Legal Materials 527; Brief for the United States in Answer to California's Exceptions 148.

[62] The full text of Article 7 is as follows:

"1. This article relates only to bays the coasts of which belong to a single State.

"2. For the purposes of these articles, a bay is a well-marked indentation whose penetration is in such proportion to the width of its mouth as to contain landlocked

Applying these tests to the segments of California's coast here in dispute, it appears that Monterey Bay is inland water and that none of the other coastal segments in dispute[63] fulfill these aspects of the Convention test. We so hold.

California asserts that the Santa Barbara Channel may be considered a "fictitious bay" because the openings at both ends of the channel and between the islands are each less than 24 miles.[64] The United States argues that the

---

waters and constitute more than a mere curvature of the coast. An indentation shall not however, be regarded as a bay unless its area is as large as, or larger than, that of the semi-circle whose diameter is a line drawn across the mouth of that indentation.

"3. For the purpose of measurement, the area of an indentation is that lying between the low-water mark around the shore of the indentation and a line joining the low-water marks of its natural entrance points. Where, because of the presence of islands, an indentation has more than one mouth, the semi-circle shall be drawn on a line as long as the sum total of the lengths of the lines across the different mouths. Islands within an indentation shall be included as if they were part of the water area of the indentation.

"4. If the distance between the low-water marks of the natural entrance points of a bay does not exceed twenty-four miles, a closing line may be drawn between these two low-water marks, and the waters enclosed thereby shall be considered as internal waters.

"5. Where the distance between the low-water marks of the natural entrance points of a bay exceeds twenty-four miles, a straight baseline of twenty-four miles shall be drawn within the bay in such a manner as to enclose the maximum area of water that is possible with a line of that length.

"6. The foregoing provisions shall not apply to so-called 'historic' bays, or in any case where the straight baseline system provided for in article 4 applied."
[63] The parties stated that Crescent City Bay is no longer an area in dispute.
[64] The United States asserts that "international law recognizes no principle of 'fictitious bays.'" We find it unnecessary to decide that question. The Government states:

"The expression seems to have originated in a proposal by the Committee of Experts, made to the Fifth Session of the International Law Commission, suggesting a 10-mile rule for bays, a general 10-mile limit for straight baselines, providing that baselines should not be drawn to islands more than 5 miles from shore, and limiting baselines to 5 miles in groups of islands or between such groups and the mainland, except that in such a group one opening could be 10 miles. The latter situation was called a 'fictitious bay.' The Special Rapporteur adopted this proposal in an Addendum to the Second Report of the Regime of the Territorial Sea, International Law Commission, Fifth Session, 18 May 1953. English text, U. N. Doc. A/CN·4/61/Add.1, p. 7, and Annex, p. 4. The subject of groups of islands was postponed by the Commission in 1954 (Article 11, *Report of the International Law Commission Covering the Work of Its Sixth Session* (U. N. Doc. A/CN.4/88, p. 42), and there is no special provision of the subject in the Convention on the Territorial Sea and the Contiguous Zone as finally adopted. The Report of the International Law Commission on the Work of Its Eighth Session, p. 45, fn. 1 (U. N. Doc. A/C.6/L.378) makes clear that the original proposal on the subject was an attempt to formulate a rule and not an expression of a rule already in existence." Brief for the United States in answer to California's Exceptions, p. 149, n. 112.

The openings at the ends of the Santa Barbara Channel are 11 miles and 21 miles.

channel is no bay at all; that it is a strait which serves as a useful route of communication between two areas of open sea and as such may not be classified as inland waters.[65]

By way of analogy California directs our attention to the Breton and Chandleur Sounds off Louisiana which the United States claims as inland waters, *United States v. Louisiana*, 363 U.S. 1, 66–67, n. 108. Each of these analogies only serves to point up the validity of the United States' argument that the Santa Barbara Channel should not be treated as a bay. The Breton Sound is a *cul de sac*. The Chandleur Sound, if considered separately from the Breton Sound which it joins, leads only to the Breton Sound. Neither is used as a route of passage between two areas of open sea. In fact both are so shallow as to not be readily navigable.[66] California also points to the Strait of Juan de Fuca. That strait is not claimed by the United States as a "fictitious bay" and it does not connect two areas of open sea.

Evidence submitted to the Master on the extent of international use made of the Santa Barbara Channel was sparse. What evidence there was indicated the usefulness of the route, but did not specify whether the ships so using it were domestic or international.[67] California now regards the point as important, for under international law as expressed in the *Corfu Channel Case*, I.C.J. Reports, 1949, p. 4, the International Court of Justice held that a country could not claim a straight as inland water if, in its natural state, it served as a useful route for *international* passage. We do not consider the point of controlling importance. The United States has not in the past claimed the Santa Barbara Channel as inland water and opposes any such claim now. The channel has not been regarded as a bay either historically or geographically. In these circumstances, as with the drawing of straight baselines, we hold that if the United States does not choose to employ the concept of a "fictitious bay" in order to extend our international boundaries around the islands framing Santa Barbara Channel, it cannot be forced to do so by California. It is, therefore, unnecessary to reinstitute proceedings before a master to determine the factual question of whether the passageway is internationally useful.

---

[65] See letter from Acting Secretary of State Webb to Attorney General McGrath, November 13, 1951, Senate Hearings 460. See also Senate Hearings 1084–1085 (remarks of Jack B. Tate).

[66] The depth in general ranges between 6 and 12 feet according to Coast and Geodetic Survey Chart No. 1270, but there is no passage as much as 12 feet deep connecting the ends of the sounds. The sounds are "navigable waters" in the legal sense even in the parts too shallow for navigation. See *United States v. Turner*, 175 F. 2d 644, 647, cert. denied, 338 U.S. 851.

[67] Testimony before the Special Master indicated that the channel provided a substantial amount of protection from the rough seas of the Pacific and was used as an alternate route of passage for ships "coming down from the Pacific Northwest." (Tr. 595. See also Tr. 608.) In its appendix, p. 57, California points to a statement in Davidson, Coast Pilot of California, Oregon and Washington (4th ed. 1889), p. 53, "The islands break the force of the large westerly swell of the Pacific along the coastline, and in winter afford good lee from the full force of the southeast gales."

3. *Historic Inland Waters.* By the terms of the Convention the 24-mile closing rule does not apply to so-called "historic" bays.[68] Essentially these are bays over which a coastal nation has traditionally asserted and maintained dominion with the acquiescence of foreign nations.[69] California claims that virtually all the waters here in dispute are historic inland waters as the term is internationally understood. It relies primarily on an interpretation of its State Constitution to the effect that the State boundaries run three miles outside the islands and bays,[70] plus several court decisions which so interpret it as applied to Monterey, Santa Monica, and San Pedro Bays.[71] The United States counters that, as with straight base lines, California can maintain no claim to historic inland waters unless the claim is endorsed by the United States. The Special Master found it unnecessary to decide that question because, on the evidence before him, he concluded that California had not traditionally exercised dominion over any of the claimed waters.

Since the 24-mile rule includes Monterey Bay, we do not consider it here. As to Santa Monica Bay, San Pedro Bay, and the other water areas in dispute, we agree with the Special Master that they are not historic inland waters of the United States.

California contends that two studies of the criteria for determining historic waters have been made since the Special Master filed his report[72] which show that he applied the wrong standards, thus vitiating his conclusions. In particular it is said that the Special Master erroneously thought the concept of historic waters to be an exception to the general rule of inland waters requiring a rigorous standard of proof. We find no substantial indication of this in his report.

On the evidence, California's claim that its constitution set a boundary beyond the bays and islands is arguable, but many of the state statutes drawing county boundaries which supposedly run to the limit of the state boundaries cut the other way by indicating a line only three miles from shore.[73]

---

[68] See Art. 7, § 6, *supra*, n. 62.
[69] See generally, Juridical Regime of Historic Waters, Including Historic Bays, U. N. Doc. A/CN.4/143 (1962).
[70] Article XII of the California Constitution of 1849 described the sea boundary of the State of California as follows:
". . . thence running west and along said boundary line to the Pacific Ocean, and extending therein three English miles; thence running in a northwesterly direction and following the direction of the Pacific Coast to the 42d degree of north latitude, thence on the line of said 42d degree of north latitude to the place of beginning. Also all the islands, harbors, and bays, along and adjacent to the Pacific Coast."
[71] *Ocean Industries, Inc.* v. *Superior Court,* 200 Cal. 235, 252 P. 722 (1927); *Ocean Industries, Inc.* v. *Greene,* 15 F. 2d 862 (D.C.N.D. Cal. 1926) (Monterey Bay). *People v. Stralla,* 14 Cal. 2d 617, 96 P. 2d 941 (1939) (Santa Monica Bay). *United States* v. *Carrillo,* 13 F. Supp. 121 (1935) (San Pedro Bay).
[72] Historic Bays, U. N. Doc. A/CN.13/1 (1957), and Juridical Regime of Historic Waters, including Historic Bays, U. N. Doc. A/N.4/143 (1962).
[73] *E.g.,* for San Diego County, see Cal. Stat. 1850, c. 15, § 2, p. 58; Cal. Stat. 1851, c. 14, § 2, p. 172; Cal. Political Code 1872, §§ 3907, 3944; Cal. Political Code § 3945; Cal. Stat. 1919, c. 470, § 38, p. 895; Cal. Stat. 1923, c. 160, § 38, p. 361; Cal.

Furthermore, a legislative declaration of jurisdiction without evidence of further active and continuous assertion of dominion over the waters is not sufficient to establish the claim.[74] There is a federal district court opinion, *United States* v. *Carillo,* 13 F. Supp. 121 (1935), which dismissed federal criminal charges for an offense which took place more than three miles from the shore of San Pedro Bay on the ground that the bay was within California, not federal, jurisdiction; but it is difficult to see this dismissal as an assertion of dominion. In Santa Monica Bay, California did successfully prosecute a criminal offense which took place more than three miles from the shore, *People* v. *Stralla,* 14 Cal. 2d 617, 96 P. 2d 941 (1939). However, the decision stands as the only assertion of criminal jurisdiction of which we have been made aware.[75]

The United States disclaims that any of the disputed areas are historic inland waters. We are reluctant to hold that such a disclaimer would be decisive in all circumstances, for a case might arise in which the historic evidence was clear beyond doubt. But in the case before us, with its questionable evidence of continuous and exclusive assertions of dominion over the disputed waters, we think the disclaimer decisive.

4. *Harbors and Roadsteads.* The parties disagree as to whether inland waters should encompass anchorages beyond the outer harborworks of harbors. The Convention on the Contiguous Zone and the Territorial Sea (Art. 8) states without qualification that "the outermost permanent harbour works which form an integral part of the harbour system shall be regarded as forming part of the coast." We take that to be the line incorporated in the Submerged Lands Act.

As to open roadsteads used for loading, unloading and anchoring ships, the Convention (Art. 9) provides that such areas should be included in the territorial sea, and, by implication, that they are not to be considered inland waters. We adopt that interpretation.

5. *The Line of Ordinary Low Water.* Along the California coast there are two low tides each day, one of which is generally lower than the other. The assertion of the United States, with which the Special Master agreed, is that the line of ordinary low water is obtained by taking the average of all low tides. California would average only the lower low tides.

Govt. Code 1947, § 23137, Cal. Stat. 1957, c. 424, p. 1069. For Los Angeles County, see Cal. Stat. 1850, c. 15, § 3, p. 59; Cal. Stat. 1851, c. 14, § 3, p. 172; Cal. Stat. 1856, c. 46, § 1, p. 53; Cal. Political Code 1872, § 3945; Cal. Stat. 1919, c. 470, p. 877; Cal. Political Code 1923, § 3927; Cal. Stat. 1923, c. 160, § 20, p. 343; Cal. Govt. Code § 23119; Cal. Stat. 1947, c. 424, p. 1055.
[74] See generally, Juridical Regime of Historic Waters, Including Historic Bays, U. N. Doc. A/CN.4/143, §§ 80–105 (1962).
[75] The United States Attorney for the Southern District of California participated as an *amicus curiae* in the *Stralla* case and supported the position of California. We do not consider this action so significant as to foreclose the United States in the controversy before us. Compare the discussion of actions taken by the Secretary of the Interior in *United States* v. *California,* 332 U.S. 19, 39–40.

We hold that California's position represents the better view of the matter. The Submerged Lands Act defines coastline in terms of the "line of ordinary low water." The Convention (Art. 3) uses "the low water line along the coast as marked on large-scale charts officially recognized by the coastal State" (*i.e.*, the United States). We interpret the two lines thus indicated to conform, and on the official United States coastal charts of the Pacific coast prepared by the United States Coast and Geodetic Survey, it is the lower low water line which is marked.

6. *Artificial Accretions.* When this case was before the Special Master, the United States contended that it owned all mineral rights to lands outside inland waters which were submerged at the date California entered the Union, even though since enclosed or reclaimed by means of artificial structures. The Special Master ruled that lands so enclosed or filled belonged to California because such artificial changes were clearly recognized by international law to change the coastline. Furthermore, the Special Master recognized that the United States, through its control over navigable waters, had power to protect its interests from encroachment by unwarranted artificial structures, and that the effect of any future changes could thus be the subject of agreement between the parties.

The United States now contends that whereas the Submerged Lands Act recognized and confirmed state title within all artificial as well as natural modifications to the shoreline prior to the passage of the Act, Congress meant to recognize only natural modifications after the date of the Act. The Act, however, makes no specific reference to artificial accretions, and nowhere in the legislative history did anyone focus on the question.[76] The United States points by analogy to the rule of property law that artificial fill belongs to the owner of the submerged land onto which it is deposited. *Marine R. & Coal Co.* v. *United States*, 257 U.S. 47, 65. We think the situation different when a State extends its land domain by pushing back the sea; in that case its sovereignty should extend to the new land, as was generally thought to be the case prior to the 1947 *California* opinion.[77] The considerations which led us to reject the possibility of wholesale changes in the location of the line of inland waters caused by future changes in international law, *supra*, pp. 25–26, do not apply with force to the relatively slight and sporadic changes which can be brought about artificially. Arguments based on the inequity to the United States of allowing California to effect changes in the

---

[76] See, *e.g.*, 99 Cong. Rec. 2697 (remarks of Senator Cordon); Senate Hearings 1344–1345; 1353–1385, 1374.

[77] See, *e.g.*, Statement of Robert Moses and the discussion following it. Senate Hearings 137.

The United States points by analogy to judicial interpretations of the Swamp Lands Act of 1850, 9 Stat. 519, to the effect that it granted only those lands which were swamp at the date of its passage. However, the terms of that Act were specific; ". . . those swamp and overflowed lands . . . which shall remain unsold at the passage of this act, shall be, and the same are hereby granted . . ."; and it granted lands sovereignty over which had never been thought to change because the nature of the land changed.

boundary between federal and state submerged lands by making future artificial changes in the coastline are met, as the Special Master pointed out, by the ability of the United States to protect itself through its power over navigable waters.

With the modifications set out in this opinion we approve the recommendations of the Special Master. The Parties, or either of them, may, before September 1, 1965, submit a proposed decree to carry this opinion into effect, failing which the Court will prepare and enter an appropriate decree at the next Term of Court.

It is so ordered.

THE CHIEF JUSTICE and MR. JUSTICE CLARK took no part in the consideration or decision of this case.

Governments have in recent years become increasingly concerned about the potential uses of the sea-bed, the ocean floor, and its subsoil, beyond the limits of national jurisdiction. The United Nations General Assembly adopted a resolution (2340 [XXII]) on December 28, 1967, calling for a study of practical ways of promoting international cooperation aimed at reserving the sea-bed exclusively for peaceful purposes "in accordance with the principles and purposes of the Charter, in the interest of maintaining international peace and security, and for the benefit of mankind." Some private groups have suggested that one way of guaranteeing the peaceful uses of the sea-bed and ocean floor would be to give the U.N. authority to license their use.

Postscript. Inasmuch as the United Nations Conferences on the Law of the Sea have been so important in recent years in codifying the law, a final postscript, describing the conferences as law-making forums, may be interesting.

Loftus Becker, "Some Political Problems of the Legal Advisor"[78]

CONFERENCE ON LAW OF THE SEA

Now I should like to discuss with you some personal observations as to the conditions under which international law is being formulated today.

On February 24, 1958, there was convened in Geneva, Switzerland, an International Conference on the Law of the Sea. Eighty-six states are participating in this conference, which is now drawing to a close—more than double the number that attended the Hague conference of 1930. We regard this conference as one of the most important of those convened since the end of World War II.

[78] *D.S.B.*, XXXVIII (1958), 834–836.

Perhaps the most important single issue that came before this conference was the breadth of the territorial sea in which a state may exercise sovereign rights. That is the sole issue to which I shall advert this evening.

As all of you know, the United States adopted a 3-mile limit for its territorial sea in 1793 and our Government has not since departed from that position. The United States Government believes that the 3-mile limit, which affords a maximum freedom of the seas, is in the best interests of all states—large and small, old and new.

By the latter part of the 19th century or the early part of the 20th century, the 3-mile limit was firmly established as customary international law. It has been the consistent position of the Department of State that no greater breadth of territorial sea can be justified in international law, and numerous protests have been filed on this basis when broader claims have been asserted.

There have, of course, been various states which have asserted from time to time a right to a broader territorial sea—to 6, to 12, and even to 200 miles. In some instances such broader claims have been based upon security grounds, as, for example, in the case of the U.S.S.R., which claims 12 miles. In other instances these broader claims were based upon the alleged economic requirements of the coastal states, which maintained that they were entitled to appropriate to their own use all fishing grounds lying between 3 and 12 miles off their coasts or even farther, even though such offshore fishing grounds had theretofore been regarded as the common property of all nations. Insofar as the United States is concerned, such unilateral appropriations of vast areas of the high seas are contrary to the common good, contrary to our own security interests, and contrary to the valuable economic interests of our overseas fishing industry.

Unfortunately, at Geneva, from which I have just now returned, there was a minimum of debate and even less inclination to vote upon the merits, as principles of international law, of the various specific proposals submitted for conference approval. The reasons for this are even more important than the proposals made and the various votes cast for or against them, which I shall not attempt to detail.

The principle of the freedom of the seas, with its corollary, the 3-mile limit, was established before many of the states represented at the Geneva conference had gained their independence. In large measure at the conference such states made no serious effort to weigh the advantages they might retain by maintaining the freedom of the seas as against the disadvantages of an extension of territorial seas, such as the obligation of patrolling such an expanded territorial sea. They opposed the 3-mile limit upon the ground that it had been adopted by the major maritime powers before they had come into existence. For that reason alone, the preexisting rule had to be changed. That was regarded as progress.

Such states, moreover, took the position that they must be free to fix the breadth of their territorial sea up to 12 miles or to exercise exclusive fishing control for the same distance from their coasts because that was the only rule that would be consistent with their dignity and sovereignty as new nations.

These same new states regarded the freedom of the high seas—rather than as a common heritage—as a legal fiction invented by the major maritime nations, or their lawyers, in order to rob the populations of newly created nations of the living resources of the seas located off their coasts. Those other states which desired to fish up to 3 miles off the coasts of these newly created nations, or to overfly the high seas between 3 and 12 miles off their coasts without express permisssion, were regarded as motivated wholly by selfish motives. The use of large mother or cannery ships off coastal waters was frequently denounced as a means of taking the bread out of the mouths of local coastal fishermen operating out of port on small boats on a 1-day basis.

They were wholly unmoved by the fact that a nation such as Portugal had fished for centuries on the high seas off the coasts of other nations and relied upon such fishing for the protein in the diet of its population, particularly the poorer elements thereof.

Those who opposed a coastal state's legal right to annex neighboring areas of the high seas in order to improve its economic position—additional land being unavailable—were denounced as reactionary or predatory.

These same new nations viewed as progressive and desirable—because it constituted a change from the existing order—the Mexican proposal, supported without deviation by the entire Soviet bloc, that the territorial sea could be fixed by the coastal state anywhere between 3 and 12 miles off its coast.

BLOC VOTING

With these views there was combined the practice of bloc voting. The entire Soviet bloc came to the conference instructed to support a 12-mile limit and never deviated from this position from beginning to end of the conference. The Arab bloc in its entirety was also pledged to the 12-mile limit, and the members of that bloc had no hesitance in declaring that their position was principally motivated by their desire to close off the Gulf of Aqaba. Argument or persuasion, even with the most friendly members of that bloc, was wholly wasted. A vote against this principle by any member of the bloc for any reason whatever was regarded as disloyalty to the bloc.

In caucuses of the Afro-Asian and the Latin American blocs every effort was made to exert pressure to insure that members of the bloc would vote as a unit. Even countries to which the United States had extended extensive aid and which have a long record of friendship with the United States deemed themselves bound to vote solidly with the other bloc members. Nations which indicated an intention to vote in favor of the United States, contrary to the bloc, were threatened with economic reprisals.

In one instance, in Committee I, when it appeared that the chairman was about to announce a tie vote on the optional 3- to 12-mile proposal advanced by Mexico, one delegate favoring this proposal ran to the seat of a South American delegate and sought to coerce him into changing his vote from abstention to an affirmative vote in favor of the Mexican proposal not only by shouting at him but also by lifting his arm in order to attract the attention of the chair. I am glad to note that, even though the other delegate was coerced into making this attempt, the chairman ruled that the vote, once having been made and recorded, could not thereafter be changed, and his ruling was sustained on appeal by a vote of 48 to 17 with 17 abstentions. The tactics used in that instance clearly shocked the conscience of the conference.

These, I regret to say, are the practicalities of the development of one branch of international law today. Principle, reason, and persuasion, as well as common security interests of the utmost importance, are subordinated to "ward politics" of the most ruthless character. Whether we like it or not, this is a political reality of which we must take account.

We are fortunate, indeed, that, notwithstanding the attitudes and practices that I have just described, the compromise proposal made by the United States at Geneva gained the largest majority of any of those voted upon in plenary session (45-33-7), although none received the two-thirds required for conference approval. This, I should like to make plain, we owe to the outstanding performance of the United States delegation under the leadership of Mr. Arthur Dean of New York, who is well known to most of those here present. This result could not have been accomplished, moreover, had not a number of our good friends firmly resisted bloc pressure to vote against us.

The United States Government has made it plain that unless the conference approved its compromise proposal—involving a 6-mile territorial sea with a contiguous fishing zone of an additional 6 miles, in which historical fishing rights would have to be respected by the coastal state—this Government would continue to conform, and to expect others to conform, to the 3-mile limit now firmly established as customary international law. It is interesting to note that, as among the 3-, 6-, and 12-mile limits, the 3-mile limit was the only one that was not expressly rejected by the Geneva conference.

The attitudes and activities of the newly formed nations and the members of blocs at the Geneva conference pose a serious and continuing problem for which I have no immediate answer. Such attitudes and activities in the political sphere are regrettable, but they are even more reprehensible when they appear at a conference dedicated to the statement, the codification, or the formulation of sound international law.

I do not wish to end upon too gloomy a note. The 86 nations represented at Geneva did get together constructively in order to agree upon many important facets of the law of the sea. These included agreement upon important rules relating to fisheries, to the high seas generally, and to the continental shelf, the last mentioned being the first time agreement has been reached upon this principle.

As far as this Government is concerned, the United States comes out of the Geneva conference with a greatly enhanced international reputation. I was deeply impressed by the fact that speaker after speaker, even those who were opposing the United States proposal, paid tribute to the honesty and sincerity of the United States and its clearly demonstrated willingness to compromise and, in so doing, to sacrifice valuable interests of its own. The attitude of our Government and its delegation compared most favorably with the monolithic immobility of the U.S.S.R. and its bloc.

CHAPTER VI

Individuals in International Law

Conventionally, states are the traditional *subjects* of international law (see Chapter II), and individuals are the traditional *objects;* the law theoretically affects states directly, individuals indirectly. To many students of the law, the theoretical barriers that prevent international law from operating directly on individuals are major hurdles in the way of making international law effective.[1] Some of these problems arise acutely as states attempt to protect their nationals abroad, as this chapter shows, but present practice also raises significant questions about the usefulness of current theory. For instance, is *nationality,* which states still look upon as the bond between man and the state, necessary to protect individual human rights? Also might not states create new institutions to protect human rights?

Notwithstanding future developments, however, states still insist that they, and not international law directly, exercise jurisdiction over individuals. They claim jurisdiction on five grounds:

1. the *territorial principle,* which gives them jurisdiction over everyone within their domain;

2. the *nationality principle,* whereby they have jurisdiction over those persons wherever they are, who possess a special tie to the state;

3. the *protective principle,* whereby they may take jurisdiction over persons who pose a threat to the national interest;

4. the *universality principle,* whereby they may take jurisdiction over a person, wherever he is, because he has committed an offense which the entire world recognizes as a crime; and

---

[1] See, for instance, Brierly, "Le Fondement du caractère obligatoire du droit international" (1928), 23 *Recueil de cours,* 467, 531; Phillip C. Jessup, *A Modern Law of Nations* (New York: The Macmillan Company, 1948), chaps. IV and V; H. Lauterpacht, *International Law and Human Rights* (New York: Frederick A. Praeger, 1950).

5. the *passive personality principle,* whereby they may take jurisdiction over a person who has injured one of their own nationals. Of these five, the territorial principle is the most fundamental; the nationality principle is universally accepted, although states draw widely differing conclusions from it; the protective principle is usually looked upon as an auxiliary basis for competence; universality is largely limited to piracy; and the last is admittedly auxiliary and not often relied upon.[2]

Nationality

All states look upon individuals owing allegiance to them as their *nationals* and as possessing their *nationality.* States offer nationals protection in exchange for their allegiance. Although "in a broad sense international law limits the right of a State to impress its national character upon an individual, or to prevent that character from being lost or transferred,"[3] every state may specify for itself how individuals may acquire and lose nationality. As a result, state rules on nationality sometimes conflict, and some persons possess dual nationality while others have no nationality and are stateless. Both groups, but especially stateless persons, find themselves in difficulties in a world in which the state plays so important a part. Eliminating statelessness and dual nationality, which in theory is a simple thing to do, has proved difficult because of the varying interests of states. Thus, at the Hague Conference on Nationality in 1930, the representatives of 37 states affirmed "that it is in the general interest of the international community to secure that all its members should recognize that every person should have a nationality and should have one nationality only"; and then went on to restate the very rules that make it impossible to carry out the principle:

Article 1. It is for each State to determine under its own law who are its nationals. . . .

Article 2. Any question as to whether a person possesses the nationality of a particular State shall be determined in accordance with the law of that State.[4]

The basic problem is that some states are eager to encourage immigration; others are unwilling to encourage immigration; some are willing to allow individuals to choose their national allegiance; others not. Na-

[2] *Harvard Research,* Draft Convention on Jurisdiction with Respect to Crime, p. 445.
[3] Hyde, II, 1066.
[4] Convention on Certain Questions Relating to the Conflict of Nationality Laws, April 12, 1930. Up to 1968, only 14 states had ratified, the most recent being Malta (1966). See *Multilateral Treaties in Respect of which the Secretary-General Performs Depositary Functions* (U.N. Sales No.: E.68.V.3), pp. 347–348.

tionality laws thus reflect the varying ways that states look upon the bond between individuals—particularly naturalized persons and nationals born abroad—and the state. Some states assert the right to deprive persons of their nationality if they reside abroad and fail to declare that they intend to retain their nationality. Other states set up certain standards of behavior as criteria for acquiring nationality and will deprive persons of their nationality if they violate these criteria. In fact, states that freely bestow their nationality are quicker than others to assert the right to withdraw it, while states which set up stringent requirements for acquiring nationality often deny themselves the right to deprive individuals of their nationality. Unfortunately, in most cases, states grant and withdraw nationality without determining whether the person affected has another nationality, a practice that in itself adds to the numbers of stateless persons.

To eliminate statelessness completely in the future, national laws would have to provide that everyone would acquire the nationality of the country with which he is at the time most closely connected, according to uniform criteria; no one could lose a nationality acquired at birth unless he first obtained another; and anyone who lost a connection with one country and acquired a connection with another would have to receive the second country's nationality. So far, the diverse interests of states have precluded their adopting a treaty based on these simple, uniform principles. The international community has, as a consequence, chosen not to adopt an ideal set of rules that only few states could accept, but rather to draft a less perfect international arrangement that might find favor with more states.

The United Nations, like the League before it, has addressed itself to the problem of eliminating or, at least, reducing statelessness. The numbers of refugees and stateless persons[5] had risen in the aftermath of World War II, a circumstance that led the General Assembly to proclaim in the Universal Declaration on Human Rights that everyone has the right to a nationality (Article 15) and that no one should be denied the right to change his nationality (Article 14, paragraph 2). This Declaration was not, however, a legally binding commitment on the part of the signatory states. The United Nations next adopted a Convention on Refugees, which came into force in April 1954, at a Geneva Conference of Plenipotentiaries in July 1951. The conferees believed that states should consider the question of statelessness further,

---

[5] A *stateless* person obviously is one who, regardless of where he lives, has no nationality; a *refugee* may be stateless, have one or several nationalities, but be unable, usually for reasons of persecution, to return to the country where he habitually resides. For full definitions, see the relevant treaties.

and they referred a draft Protocol on the Status of Stateless Persons, which they had considered, back to the appropriate U.N. organs for further study.

States evidently wished to consider separately the treaties on refugees and stateless persons, partly because they were unwilling to extend to the stateless all the privileges of refugees—for example, preferential treatment in assistance and social security; partly because some persons might have become stateless because they had evaded certain normal duties of citizenship, such as military service; partly because they regarded the matter as essentially within their domestic jurisdiction; or because, as in the United States, except for certain matters, such as the right to vote and to practice certain occupations, the state treated the stateless no less favorably than other aliens.[6]

As a result, another Conference met in New York at U.N. Headquarters in the fall of 1954 and adopted a 42-article "Convention Relating to the Status of Stateless Persons," which came into force in June 1960. The drafters included in it many of the articles of the Refugee Convention, but the separate instrument made it possible for states to consider ratifying the Refugee Convention or the Convention on Stateless Persons without accepting both. The Convention put stateless persons on an equal footing with nationals of the contracting states with regard to such matters as freedom of religion, protection of artistic rights and industrial property, access to courts of law, elementary education, public relief, labor legislation, and social security. In other matters, such as wage-earning employment, public housing, higher education, and freedom of movement, stateless persons received the same privileges as those generally granted to aliens. The Convention also provided for states to issue special travel documents to stateless persons.

Further conferences on reducing statelessness were held in 1959 (in Geneva) and 1961 (in New York). At the second conference, the delegates adopted a Convention on the Reduction of Statelessness (signed at the United Nations on August 30, 1961).[7] Under the Convention

---

[6] "Whoever, under color of any law, statute, ordinance, regulation, or custom, willfully subjects any inhabitant of any State, Territory, or District to the deprivation of any rights, privileges, or immunities secured or protected by the Constitution or laws of the United States or to different punishments, pains, or penalties, on account of such inhabitant being an alien, or by reason of his color, or race, than are prescribed for the publishment of citizens, shall be fined not more than $1000 or imprisoned not more than one year, or both." U.S.C., 1958 ed., Title 18, Sec. 242.

[7] For text, see U.N. Doc. A/Conf.9/15. In 1968, the treaty was not yet in force. It had been signed by the Dominican Republic, France, Israel, Netherlands, and the United Kingdom, which ratified it on 29 March 1966. For the Convention relating to the status of Refugees, see 189 *U.N.T.S.*, 137; for Convention relating to the status of Stateless Persons, see 360 *U.N.T.S.*, 117.

the possibilities of persons becoming stateless do not disappear, but they would diminish if sufficient states ratified the agreement.

The Convention deals with ways of acquiring nationality (Articles 1 to 4), the automatic loss of nationality (Articles 5 to 7), and states' rights to deprive persons of nationality (Articles 8 and 9).

As regards means of acquiring nationality, the Convention incorporates *ius soli* (law of the soil) by providing that a person acquires the nationality of the state in which he is born; the Convention also incorporates *ius sanguinis* (law of the blood) by providing that a person born outside the territory of a contracting state acquires the nationality of a parent who may be a national of a contracting state. States may impose additional requirements, but they are strictly circumscribed.

The Convention takes account of the principal means by which persons have become stateless in the past and binds the ratifying states to make the loss of nationality for these reasons conditional upon the affected person's acquiring a new nationality. In the states ratifying the Convention, national laws would presumably have to provide that no person could lose his nationality by marriage, termination of marriage, legitimation, recognition, or adoption (Article 5), or because a spouse or parent (Article 6) had changed nationality, unless at the same time he possessed or acquired another nationality (Article 5). Where states that are parties to the Convention transfer territory to one another, the treaty embodying the transfer must guard against statelessness by providing that no person shall become stateless as a result of the transfer. If the treaty has no such provisions, a state acquiring territory obligates itself to confer its nationality on persons who would otherwise become stateless because the territory had changed hands (Article 10). Foundlings, in the absence of proof, are assumed to have been born of parents possessing the nationality of the state in which they are found (Article 2); a child born in wedlock in the territory of contracting states, whose mother has the nationality of that state, acquires his mother's nationality if it otherwise would be stateless (Article 1, paragraph 3).

In naturalizing individuals born on their own territory who would otherwise be stateless,[8] states may impose certain conditions (Article 1). For instance, they need not allow persons to apply for naturalization except between the ages of eighteen and twenty-one just so long as they allow a person at least one year when he may legally apply for naturalization without the permission of parents or guardians. States may require an applicant to have lived on their territory up to five years

[8] For example, the children of stateless persons, or an illegitimate child born in Germany of an English mother would not acquire either German or English nationality under existing law.

immediately before applying (but no more than ten years in all); they need not permit a person to apply who has "been convicted of an offense against national security" or "sentenced to imprisonment for a term of five years or more on a criminal charge"; and they need not accept applications from persons who have previously had another nationality.

States may impose similar conditions on persons not born in the territory of a contracting state who would otherwise be stateless, if one of his parents had the nationality of the contracting state (Article 4). Even after the normal time limits for applying for nationality expire in the state where one was born, a person may under certain conditions obtain nationality from a contracting state if one of his parents had its nationality at the time of his birth (Article 1, paragraphs 4 and 5). The treaty permits states to make comparable arrangements even for persons not born in the territory of a contracting state (Article 4). And a child born out of wedlock, who has lost his nationality because a parent possessing a different nationality has acknowledged the child as his own, may recover his earlier nationality by applying to the original state under comparable provisions (Article 5).

The Convention also attempts to reduce the numbers of stateless persons created when persons renounce their nationality or are deprived of it. Thus if a state permits persons to renounce their nationality, it would have to provide that the actual renunciation did not take effect until the person had acquired a new nationality. The only exception is that this restriction may not apply where it would contravene Articles 13 and 14 of the Universal Declaration of Human Rights, *i.e.*, it must not operate to prevent a person from leaving his country or from seeking asylum in another country (Article 7, paragraph 1). Similarly, a person who seeks naturalization in a foreign country retains his original nationality until he acquires a new one or is sure that he will obtain it (paragraph 2). Nor can a person ordinarily lose his nationality, and thereby become stateless, just because he has left his own country, lived abroad, or failed to register with designated officials. But a naturalized person may lose his nationality if he lives abroad more than seven years and fails to indicate to his consulate or embassy that he plans to retain his nationality. And a state may also require a national born outside its territory, to reside in its territory or register with a consul or embassy official at the end of the first year after he attains his majority. No other grounds are recognized for a contracting state's rendering a person stateless even if the Convention does not expressly forbid it (paragraphs 3–6).

Contracting states thus enjoin themselves not to deprive persons of their nationality if, by so doing, they will render them stateless. The only exceptions, other than those mentioned above, arise in cases where a person has obtained his nationality by misrepresenting the facts or by fraud. Contracting states also allow themselves the possibility of stating, in reservations to the treaty, other reasons for depriving persons of their nationality. But such exceptions have to exist in the national law at the time the treaty is ratified and must rest on one of several specified grounds—namely,

(a) that, inconsistently with his duty of loyalty to the Contracting State, the person

(i) has, in disregard of an express prohibition by the Contracting State rendered or continued to render services to, or received or continued to receive emoluments from, another State, or

(ii) has conducted himself in a manner seriously prejudicial to the vital interests of the State;

(b) that the person has taken an oath, or made a formal declaration, of allegiance to another State, or given definite evidence of his determination to repudiate his allegiance to the Contracting State (Article 8, paragraph 3).

The national laws which permit states to deprive persons of their nationality under these provisions must, under the treaty, allow the person involved a fair hearing by a court or other independent body (Article 8, paragraph 4). States are also specifically enjoined from depriving any person or group of persons of nationality for racial, ethnic, religious, or political reasons (Article 9).

Finally, the Convention takes a modest step in the direction of allowing for some international check on the way the states themselves are carrying out the treaty by providing that states will establish within the framework of the United Nations, as soon as possible after the sixth state deposits with the United Nations an instrument of ratification or accession, some international body to which a person claiming a benefit under the treaty may apply to have his claim examined and from which he could obtain help in presenting his claim to an appropriate authority (Article 11).

The Convention does not eliminate all possibilities of future statelessness among contracting states. As long as states, before granting nationality, can require persons to do more than be born on their territory or to descend from a national, the problem will exist. Also, if states will permit persons to lose a nationality before they acquire a new one, persons can continue to be rendered stateless. And as long as states can require persons to live up to certain standards as the price of retaining their nationality, the possibility will exist that some persons will suffer the loss of nationality as a penalty. The Convention tries to limit these instances, but new cases of statelessness could arise even if all states adhered to the treaty. It does, however, reduce the possibilities of statelessness to a practicable minimum. More far-reaching suggestions—for example, that states create an international body to settle disputes among themselves that penalize individuals—have so far come to nought.[9]

Citizenship is a term often used in common parlance as synonomous with nationality. In fact, the two may be distinguished. Citizenship "refers to rights which a state sees fit to confer upon certain individuals who are also its nationals,"[10] and although all citizens are nationals, not all nationals are citizens. Thus legal entities, like corporations, may have nationality; so do ships and airplanes; and some persons—for instance, those in outlying possessions of the United States (American Samoa and Swains Island)—are nationals but not citizens. Under the terms of the Immigration and Nationality Act of 1952 as amended,

> The term "national of the United States" means (A) a citizen of the United States, or (B) a person, who, though not a citizen of the United States, owes permanent allegiance to the United States.[11]

Each of us acquires nationality either at birth or by naturalization. Nationality at birth may result in two ways: by being born in the territory of a state (*jus soli*); or by being born outside the territory of the state to parents who are nationals of the state (*jus sanguinis*).[12] One may acquire nationality by naturalization in several ways: (a) in one's own right under a state's general naturalization laws; (b) in a derivative way (*e.g.*, a minor child may be naturalized if one or both parents become naturalized; a wife, if her husband is naturalized; an alien, if he or she marries a national. In the United States, since 1922, only a minor child may be nationalized in a derivative manner; all other persons must apply for naturalization themselves); (c) by adoption

---

[9] For surveys of the nationality problem, see U.N. Docs. A/Cn.4/81, "Nationality, Including Statelessness," *International Law Commission Yearbook*, 6th Session (1954), II, 26–111, U.N. Sales No. 59.V.7, Vol. II and Roberto Cordova, "Report [and Second Report] on . . . Statelessness," *ibid.*, (1953), II, 167–199.

The U.N. High Commissioner for Refugees has cited the case of a State A maintaining that an individual was a national of State B, while State B denied it. Such a person would not get nationality A and would therefore be stateless. See U.N. Doc. A/Conf.9/11, pp. 1–4.

[10] Hyde, II, 1066.

[11] 8 U.S.C. 1964 ed., Sec. 1101 (a) (22); see *infra*, p. 300.

[12] Hackworth, III, 2.

(possible in only a few countries); (d) collectively (when a state acquires territory by cession); or (e) by special legislation.

Similarly, a person may lose his nationality in different ways. In the United States, for instance, the Nationality Act of 1940 originally provided that a national might lose his status by taking an oath of allegiance to a foreign state, by being naturalized by a foreign state, by entering another state's armed forces, by working for a foreign government in a position for which only nationals are eligible, by voting in a foreign political election, by formally renouncing his nationality before an American diplomatic or consular officer, by deserting the armed forces in time of war or remaining outside the country in time of emergency to avoid the military draft, by being convicted of treason against the United States or by attempting to overthrow the U.S. government or, in the case of naturalized citizens, subject to certain exceptions, by residing out of the United States for specificed periods of time.[13]

Since 1940, however, the United States Supreme Court has narrowed these grounds considerably by striking down expatriation of draft dodgers, military deserters, women who marry foreign nationals, persons who vote in foreign elections, and naturalized citizens who stay abroad indefinitely.[14] There are no obstacles in international law, however, to making these provisions grounds for withdrawing citizenship, and many states still have such restrictions.

SCHNEIDER v. RUSK

United States, Supreme Court, 1964

377 U.S. 163

Mr. Justice Douglas delivered the opinion of the Court.

The Immigration and Nationality Act of 1952, 66 Stat. 163, 269, U.S.C. §§ 1101, 1484, provides by § 352:

(a) A person who has become a national by naturalization shall lose his nationality by

(1) *having a continuous residence for three years* in the territory of a foreign state of which he was formerly a national or in which the place of his birth is situated. . . ." (Italics added.)

Appellant, a German national by birth, came to this country with her parents when a small child, acquired derivative American citizenship at the age of 16 through her mother, and, after graduating from Smith College,

---

[13] Nationality and Immigration Act of 1940, as amended in 1952 and 1961, 8 U.S.C., 1964 ed., Secs. 1481 and 1484.
[14] See, esp. Trop v. Dulles, 356 U.S. 86 (1958), Nishikawa v. Dulles, 356 U.S. 129 (1958), Kennedy v. Mendoza-Martineez, 372 U.S. 144 (1963), Schneider v. Rusk, 377 U.S. 163 (1964).

went abroad for postgraduate work. In 1956 while in France she became engaged to a German national, returned here briefly, and departed for Germany, where she married and where she has resided ever since. Since her marriage she has returned to this country on two occasions for visits. Her husband is a lawyer in Cologne where appellant has been living. Two of her four sons, born in Germany, are dual nationals, having acquired American citizenship under § 301 (a) (7) of the 1952 Act. The American citizenship of the other two turns on this case. In 1959 the United States denied her a passport, the State Department certifying that she had lost her American citizenship under § 352 (a) (1), quoted above. Apellant sued for a declaratory judgment that she still is an American citizen. The District Court held against her, 218 F. Supp. 302, and the case is here on appeal.[15] 375 U.S. 893.

The Solicitor General makes his case along the following lines.

Over a period of many years this Government has been seriously concerned by special problems engendered when naturalized citizens return for a long period to the country of their former nationalities. It is upon this premise that the argument derives that Congress, through its power over foreign relations, has the power to deprive such citizen of his or her citizenship.

Other nations, it is said, frequently attempt to treat such persons as their own citizens, thus embroiling the United States in conflicts when it attempts to afford them protection. It is argued that expatriation is an alternative to withdrawal of diplomatic protection. It is also argued that Congress reasonably can protect against the tendency of three years' residency in a naturalized citizen's former homeland to weaken his or her allegiance to this country. The argument continues that it is not invidious discrimination for Congress to treat such naturalized citizens differently from the manner in which it treats native-born citizens and that Congress has the right to legislate with respect to the general class without regard to each factual violation. It is finally argued that Congress here, unlike the situation in *Kennedy v. Mendoza-Martinez*, 372 U.S. 164, was aiming only to regulate and not to punish, and that what Congress did had been deemed appropriate not only by this country but by many others,[16] and is in keeping with traditional American concepts of citizenship.

. . . .

[15] For other aspects of the case see 372 U.S. 224.

[16] In arguing the reasonableness of the requirement Congress established limiting residence abroad, Justice Clark, in his dissent, stated:

"Nor is the United States alone in making residence abroad cause for expatriation. Although the number of years of foreign residence varies from two to 10 years, 29 countries, including the United Kingdom and seven commonwealth countries, expatriate naturalized citizens residing abroad. Only four—Czechoslovakia, Poland, Afghanistan, and Yugoslavia—apply expatriation to both native-born and naturalized citizens. Even the United Nations sanctions different treatment for naturalized and native-born citizens; Article 7 of the United Nations Convention on the Reduction of Statelessness provides that naturalized citizens who reside abroad for seven years may be expatriated unless they declare their intent to retain citizenship."

We are faced with the issue presented and decided in *Perez v. Brownell* [356 U.S. 44], *i.e.,*

> Is the means, withdrawal of citizenship, reasonably calculated to effect the end that is within the power of Congress to achieve, the avoidance of embarrassment in the conduct of our foreign relations . . . ? 356 U.S., at 60.

In that case, where an American citizen voted in a foreign election, the answer was in the affirmative. In the present case the question is whether the same answer should be given merely because the naturalized citizen lived in her former homeland for three years. We think not.

. . . .

> . . . such legislation, touching as it does on the "most precious right" of citizenship (*Kennedy* v. *Mendoza-Martinez,* 372 U.S., at 159), would have to be justified under the foreign relations power "by some more urgent public necessity than substituting administrative convenience for the individual right of which the citizen is deprived." 218 F. Supp. 302, 320.

In *Kennedy* v. *Mendoza-Martinez, supra,* a divided Court held that it was beyond the power of Congress to deprive an American of his citizenship automatically and without any prior judicial or administrative proceedings because he left the United States in time of war to evade or avoid training or service in the Armed Forces. The Court held that it was an unconstitutional use of congressional power because it took away citizenship as punishment for the offense of remaining outside the country to avoid military service, without, at the same time, affording him the procedural safeguards granted by the Fifth and Sixth Amendments. Yet even the dissenters, who felt that flight or absence to evade the duty of helping to defend the country in time of war amounted to manifest nonallegiance, made a reservation. JUSTICE STEWART stated:

> Previous decisions have suggested that congressional exercise of the power to expatriate may be subject to a further constitutional restriction—a limitation upon the kind of activity which may be made the basis of denationalization. Withdrawal of citizenship is a drastic measure. Moreover, the power to expatriate endows government with authority to define and to limit the society which it represents and to which it is responsible.
> This Court has never held that Congress' power to expatriate may be used unsparingly in every area in which it has general power to act. Our previous decisions upholding involuntary denationalization all involved conduct inconsistent with undiluted allegiance to this country. 372 U.S., at 214.

This statute proceeds on the impermissible assumption that naturalized citizens as a class are less reliable and bear less allegiance to this country than do the native born. This is an assumption that is impossible for us to make. Moreover, while the Fifth Amendment contains no equal protection clause, it does forbid discrimination that is "so unjustifiable as to be violative of due process." *Bolling* v. *Sharpe,* 347 U.S. 497, 499. A native-born citizen is free to reside abroad indefinitely without suffering loss of citizenship. The discrimination aimed at naturalized citizens drastically limits their rights to live and work abroad in a way that other citizens may. It creates indeed a second-class citizenship. Living abroad, whether the citizen be naturalized or native born, is no badge of lack of allegiance and in no way evidences a voluntary renunciation of nationality and allegiance. It may indeed be compelled by family, business, or other legitimate reasons.

Reversed.

Mr. Justice Brennan took no part in the decision of this case.

UNITED STATES CODE
TITLE 8.—ALIENS AND NATIONALITY
CHAPTER 12. IMMIGRATION AND NATIONALITY

SUBCHAPTER I. GENERAL PROVISIONS

§ 1101. Definitions.

(a) As used in this chapter—

. . . .

(3) The term "alien" means any person not a citizen or national of the United States.

. . . .

(14) The term "foreign state" includes outlying possessions of a foreign state, but self-governing dominions or territories under mandate or trusteeship shall be regarded as a separate foreign state.

. . . .

(22) The term "national of the United States" means (A) a citizen of the United States, or (B) a person who, though not a citizen of the United States, owes permanent allegiance to the United States.

(23) The term "naturalization" means the conferring of nationality of a state upon a person after birth, by any means whatsoever.

. . . .

(27) The term "special immigrant" means—

(A) an immigrant who was born in any independent foreign country of the Western Hemisphere or in the Canal Zone and the spouse and children of any such immigrant, if accompanying, or following to join him: *Provided,* That no immigrant visa shall be issued pursuant to this clause until the consular officer is in receipt of a determination made by the Secretary of Labor pursuant to the provisions of section 1182(a) (14) of this title;

(B) an immigrant, lawfully admitted for permanent residence, who is returning from a temporary visit abroad;

(C) an immigrant who was a citizen of the United States and may, under section 1435(a) or 1438 of this title, apply for reacquisition of citizenship;

(D) (i) an immigrant who continuously for at least two years immediately preceding the time of his application for admission to the United States has been, and who seeks to enter the United States solely for the purpose of carrying on the vocation of minister of a religious denomination, and whose services are needed by such religious denomination having a bona fide organization in the United States; and (ii) the spouse or the child of any such immigrant, if accompanying or following to join him; or

(E) an immigrant who is an employee, or an honorably retired former employee, of the United States Government abroad, and who has performed faithful service for a total of fifteen years, or more, and his accompanying spouse and children: *Provided,* That the principal officer of a Foreign Service establishment, in his discretion, shall have recommended the granting of special immigrant status to such alien in exceptional circumstances and the Secretary of State approves such recommendation and finds that it is in the national interest to grant such status.

. . . .

(29) The term "outlying possession of the United States" means American Samoa and Swains Island.

. . . .

(38) The term "United States," except as otherwise specifically provided, when used in a geographical sense, means the continental United States, Alaska, Hawaii, Puerto Rico, Guam, and the Virgin Islands of the United States. . . .

SUBCHAPTER III. NATIONALITY AND NATURALIZATION

PART I. NATIONALITY AT BIRTH AND COLLECTIVE NATURALIZATION

§ 1401. Nationals and citizens of United States at birth.

(a) The following shall be nationals and citizens of the United States at birth:

(1) a person born in the United States, and subject to the jurisdiction thereof;

(2) a person born in the United States to a member of an Indian, Eskimo, Aleutian, or other aboriginal tribe. *Provided,* That the granting of citizenship

under this subsection shall not in any manner impair or otherwise affect the right of such person to tribal or other property;

(3) a person born outside of the United States and its outlying possessions of parents both of whom are citizens of the United States and one of whom has had a residence in the United States or one of its outlying possessions, prior to the birth of such person;

(4) a person born outside of the United States and its outlying possessions of parents one of whom is a citizen of the United States who has been physically present in the United States or one of its outlying possessions for a continuous period of one year prior to the birth of such person, and the other of whom is a national, but not a citizen of the United States;

(5) a person born in an outlying possession of the United States of parents one of whom is a citizen of the United States who has been physically present in the United States or one of its outlying possessions for a continuous period of one year at any time prior to the birth of such person;

(6) a person of unknown parentage found in the United States while under the age of five years, until shown, prior to his attaining the age of twenty-one years, not to have been born in the United States;

(7) a person born outside the geographical limits of the United States and its outlying possessions of parents one of whom is an alien, and the other a citizen of the United States who, prior to the birth of such person, was physically present in the United States or its outlying possessions for a period or periods totaling not less than ten years, at least five of which were after attaining the age of fourteen years: *Provided,* That any periods of honorable service in the Armed Forces of the United States, or periods of employment with the United States Government or with an international organization as that term is defined in section 288 of Title 22 by such citizen parent, or any periods during which such citizen parent is physically present abroad as the dependent unmarried son or daughter and a member of the household of a person (A) honorably serving with the Armed Forces of the United States, or (B) employed by the United States Government or an international organization as defined in section 288 of Title 22, may be included in order to satisfy the physical-presence requirement of this paragraph. This proviso shall be applicable to persons born on or after December 24, 1952, to the same extent as if it had become effective in its present form on that date.[17]

. . . .

[17] 1966—Subsec. (a)(7). Pub. L. 89–770 authorized periods of employment with the United States Government or with an international organization by the citizen parent, or any periods during which the citizen parent is physically present abroad as the dependent unmarried son or daughter and a member of the household of a person (A) honorably serving with the Armed Forces of the United States, or (B) employed by the United States Government or an international organization, to be included in order to satisfy the physical presence requirement, and permitted the proviso to be applicable to persons born on or after December 24, 1952.

Part II. Nationality Through Naturalization

. . . .

§ 1422. Eligibility for naturalization.

The right of a person to become a naturalized citizen of the United States shall not be denied or abridged because of race or sex or because such person is married. Notwithstanding section 405 (b) of this Act, this section shall apply to any person whose petition for naturalization shall hereafter be filed, or shall have been pending on the effective date of this chapter. (June 27, 1952, ch. 477, title III, ch. 2, § 311, 66 Stat. 239.)

. . . .

§ 1423. Requirements as to understanding the English language, history, principles and form of government of the United States.

No person except as otherwise provided in this subchapter shall hereafter be naturalized as a citizen of the United States upon his own petition who cannot demonstrate—

(1) an understanding of the English language, including an ability to read, write, and speak words in ordinary usage in the English language: *Provided,* That this requirement shall not apply to any person physically unable to comply therewith, if otherwise qualified to be naturalized, or to any person who, on the effective date of this chapter, is over fifty years of age and has been living in the United States for periods totaling at least twenty years: *Provided further,* That the requirements of this section relating to ability to read and write shall be met if the applicant can read or write simple words and phrases to the end that a reasonable test of his literacy shall be made and that no extraordinary or unreasonable condition shall be imposed upon the applicant; and

(2) a knowledge and understanding of the fundamentals of the history, and of the principles and form of government, of the United States. (June 27, 1952, ch. 477, title III, ch. 2, § 312, 66 Stat. 239.)

. . . .

§ 1424. Prohibition upon the naturalization of persons opposed to government or law, or who favor totalitarian forms of government.

(a) Notwithstanding the provisions of section 405 (b) of this act, no person shall hereafter be naturalized as a citizen of the United States—

(1) who advocates or teaches, or who is a member of or affiliated with any organization that advocates or teaches, opposition to all organized government; or

(2) who is a member of or affiliated with (A) the Communist Party of the United States; (B) any other totalitarian party of the United States; (C) the Communist Political Association; (D) the Communist or other totalitarian party of any State of the United States, of any foreign state, or of

any political or geographical subdivision of any foreign state; (E) any section, subsidiary, branch, affiliate, or subdivision of any such association or party; (F) the direct predecessors or successors of any such association or party, regardless of what name such group or organization may have used, may now bear, or may hereafter adopt; (G) who, regardless of whether he is within any of the other provisions of this section, is a member of or affiliated with any Communist-action organization during the time it is registered or required to be registered under the provisions of section 786 of Title 50; or (H) who, regardless of whether he is within any of the other provisions of this section, is a member of or affiliated with any Communist-front organization during the time it is registered or required to be registered under section 786 of Title 50, unless such alien establishes that he did not have knowledge or reason to believe at the time he became a member of or affiliated with such an organization (and did not thereafter and prior to the date upon which such organization was so registered or so required to be registered have such knowledge or reason to believe) that such organization was a Communist-front organization; or

(3) who, although not within any of the other provisions of this section, advocates the economic, international, and governmental doctrines of world communism or the establishment in the United States of a totalitarian dictatorship, or who is a member of or affiliated with any organization that advocates the economic, international, and governmental doctrines of world communism or the establishment in the United States of a totalitarian dictatorship, either through its own utterances or through any written or printed publications issued or published by or with the permission or consent of or under authority of such organization or paid for by the funds of such organization; or

(4) who advocates or teaches or who is a member of or affiliated with any organization that advocates or teaches (A) the overthrow by force or violence or other unconstitutional means of the Government of the United States or of all forms of law; or (B) the duty, necessity, or propriety of the unlawful assaulting or killing of any officer or officers (either of specific individuals or of officers generally) of the Government of the United States or of any other organized government because of his or their official character; or (C) the unlawful damage, injury, or destruction of property; or (D) sabotage; or

(5) who writes or publishes or causes to be written or published, or who knowingly circulates, distributes, prints, or displays, or knowingly causes to be circulated, distributed, printed, published, or displayed, or who knowingly has in his possession for the purpose of circulation, publication, distribution, or display, any written or printed matter, advocating or teaching opposition to all organized government, or advocating (A) the overthrow by force, violence or other unconstitutional means of the Government of the United States or of all forms of law; or (B) the duty, necessity, or propriety of the unlawful assaulting or killing of any officer or officers (either of specific individuals or of officers generally) of the Government of the United States or of any other organized government, because of his or their official character; or

(C) the unlawful damage, injury, or destruction of property; or (D) sabotage; or (E) the economic, international, and governmental doctrines of world communism or the establishment in the United States of a totalitarian dictatorship; or

(6) who is a member of or affiliated with any organization that writes, circulates, distributes, prints, publishes, or displays, or causes to be written, circulated, distributed, printed, published, or displayed, or that has in its possession for the purpose of circulation, distribution, publication, issue, or display, any written or printed matter of the character described in subparagraph (5) of this subsection.

(b) The provisions of this section or of any other section of this title shall not be construed as declaring that any of the organizations referred to in this section or in any other section of this title do not advocate the overthrow of the Government of the United States by force, violence, or other unconstitutional means.

(c) The provisions of this section shall be applicable to any applicant for naturalization who at any time within a period of ten years immediately preceding the filing of the petition for naturalization or after such filing and before taking the final oath of citizenship is, or has been found to be within any of the classes enumerated within this section, notwithstanding that at the time the petition is filed he may not be included within such classes.

(d) Any person who is within any of the classes described in subsection (a) of this section solely because of past membership in, or past affiliation with, a party or organization may be naturalized without regard to the provisions of subsection (c) of this section if such person establishes that such membership or affiliation is or was involuntary, or occurred and terminated prior to the attainment by such alien of the age of sixteen years, or that such membership or affiliation is or was by operation of law, or was for purposes of obtaining employment, food rations, or other essentials of living and where necessary for such purposes. (June 27, 1952, ch. 477, title III, ch. 2. § 313, 66 Stat. 240.)

§ 1425. Ineligibility to naturalization of deserters from the armed forces.

A person who, at any time during which the United States has been or shall be at war, deserted or shall desert the military, air, or naval forces of the United States, or who, having been duly enrolled, departed, or shall depart from the jurisdiction of the district in which enrolled, or who, whether or not having been duly enrolled, went or shall go beyond the limits of the United States, with intent to avoid any draft into the military, air, or naval service, lawfully ordered, shall, upon conviction thereof by a court martial or a court of competent jurisdiction, be permanently ineligible to become a citizen of the United States; and such deserters and evaders shall be forever incapable of holding any office of trust or of profit under the United States, or of exercising any rights of citizens thereof. (June 27, 1952, ch. 477, title III, ch. 2, § 314, 66 Stat. 241.)

§ 1426. Citizenship denied alien relieved of service in armed forces because of alienage: conclusiveness of records.

(a) Notwithstanding the provisions of section 405 (b) of this Act, any alien who applies or has applied for exemption or discharge from training or service in the Armed Forces or in the National Security Training Corps of the United States on the ground that he is an alien, and is or was relieved or discharged from such training or service on such ground, shall be permanently ineligible to become a citizen of the United States.

(b) The records of the Selective Service System or of the National Military Establishment shall be conclusive as to whether an alien was relieved or discharged from such liability for training or service because he was an alien. (June 27, 1952, ch. 477, title III, ch. 2, § 315, 66 Stat. 242.)

§ 1427. Requirements of naturalization.

(a) Residence

No person, except as otherwise provided in this subchapter, shall be naturalized unless such petitioner, (1) immediately preceding the date of filing his petition for naturalization has resided continuously, after being lawfully admitted for permanent residence, within the United States for at least five years and during the five years immediately preceding the date of filing his petition has been physically present therein for periods totaling at least half of that time, and who has resided within the State in which the petitioner filed the petition for at least six months, (2) has resided continuously within the United States from the date of the petition up to the time of admission to citizenship, and (3) during all the period referred to in this subsection has been and still is a person of good moral character, attached to the principles of the Constitution of the United States, and well disposed to the good order and happiness of the United States.

(b) Absences

Absence from the United States of more than six months but less than one year during the period for which continuous residence is required for admission to citizenship, immediately preceding the date of filing the petition for naturalization, or during the period between the date of filing the petition and the date of final hearing, shall break the continuity of such residence, unless the petitioner shall establish to the satisfaction of the court that he did not in fact abandon his residence in the United States during such period.

Absence from the United States for a continuous period of one year or more during the period for which continuous residence is required for admission to citizenship (whether preceding or subsequent to the filing of the petition for naturalization) shall break the continuity of such residence, except that in the case of a person who has been physically present and residing in the United States, after being lawfully admitted for permanent residence, for an uninterrupted period of at least one year, and who thereafter is employed by or under contract with the Government of the United States or an American institution of research recognized as such by the Attorney General, or is employed by an American firm or corporation engaged in whole or in part in the development of foreign trade and commerce of the United States, or a subsidiary thereof more than 50 per centum of whose stock is owned by an American firm or corporation, or is employed by a public international organization of which the United States is a member by treaty or statute and by which the alien was not employed until after being lawfully admitted for permanent residence, no period of absence from the United States shall break the continuity of residence if—

(1) prior to the beginning of such period of employment (whether such period begins before or after his departure from the United States), but prior to the expiration of one year of continuous absence from the United States, the person has established to the satisfaction of the Attorney General that his absence from the United States for such a period is to be on behalf of such Government, or for the purpose of carrying on scientific research on behalf of such institution, or to be engaged in the development of such foreign trade and commerce or whose residence abroad is necessary to the protection of the property rights in such countries in such firm or corporation, or to be employed by a public international organization of which the United States is a member by treaty or statute and by which the alien was not employed until after being lawfully admitted for permanent residence; and

(2) such person proves to the satisfaction of the court that his absence from the United States for such period has been for such purpose.

(c) Physical presence

The granting of the benefits of subsection (b) of this section shall not relieve the petitioner from the requirement of physical presence within the United States for the period specified in subsection (a) of this section, except in the case of those persons who are employed by, or under contract with, the Government of the United States. In the case of a person employed by or under contract with Central Intelligence Agency, the requirement in subsection (b) of this section of an uninterrupted period of at least one year of physical presence in the United States may be complied with by such person at any time prior to filing a petition for naturalization.

(d) Moral character

No finding by the Attorney General that the petitioner is not deportable shall be accepted as conclusive evidence of good moral character.

(e) Same; determination

In determining whether the petitioner has sustained the burden of establishing good moral character and the other qualifications for citizenship specified in subsection (a) of this section, the court shall not be limited to the petitioner's conduct during the five years preceding the filing of the petition, but may take into consideration as a basis for such determination the petitioner's conduct and acts at any time prior to that period.

(f) Restrictions

Naturalization shall not be granted to a petitioner by a naturalization court while registration proceedings or proceedings to require registration against an organization of which the petitioner is a member or affiliate are pending under section 792 or 793 of Title 50. (June 27, 1952, ch. 477, title III, ch. 2, § 316, 66 Stat. 242.)

§ 1451. Revocation of naturalization.

(a) Concealment of material evidence; refusal to testify

It shall be the duty of the United States attorneys for the respective districts, upon affidavit showing good cause therefor, to institute proceedings in any court specified in subsection (a) of section 1421 of this title in the judicial district in which the naturalized citizen may reside at the time of bringing suit, for the purpose of revoking and setting aside the order admitting such person to citizenship and canceling the certificate of naturalization on the ground that such order and certificate of naturalization were procured by concealment of a material fact or by willful misrepresentation, and such revocation and setting aside of the order admitting such person to citizenship and such canceling of certificate of naturalization shall be effective as of the original date of the order and certificate, respectively: *Provided,* That refusal on the part of a naturalized citizen within a period of ten years following his naturalization to testify as a witness in any proceeding before a congressional committee concerning his subversive activities, in a case where such person has been convicted of contempt for such refusal, shall be held to constitute a ground for revocation of such person's naturalization under this subsection as having been procured by concealment of a material fact or by willful misrepresentation. If the naturalized citizen does not reside in any judicial district in the United States at the time of bringing such suit, the proceedings may be instituted in the United States District Court for the District of Columbia or in the United States district court in the judicial district in which such person last had his residence.

(b) Notice to party

The party to whom was granted the naturalization alleged to have been procured by concealment of a material fact or by willful misrepresentation shall, in any such proceedings under subsection (a) of this section, have sixty days' personal notice, unless waived by such party, in which to make answers to the petition of the United States; and if such naturalized person be absent from the United States or from the judicial district in which such person last had his residence, such notice shall be given either by personal service upon him or by publication in the manner provided for the service of summons by publication or upon absentees by the laws of the State or the place where such suit is brought.

(c) Membership in certain organizations; prima facie evidence

If a person who shall have been naturalized after the effective date of this chapter shall within five years next following such naturalization become a member of or affiliated with any organization, membership in or affiliation with which at the time of naturalization would have precluded such person from naturalization under the provisions of section 1424 of this title, it shall be considered prima facie evidence that such person was not attached to the principles of the Constitution of the United States and was not well disposed to the good order and happiness of the United States at the time of naturalization, and, in the absence of countervailing evidence, it shall be sufficient in the proper proceeding to authorize the revocation and setting aside of the order admitting such person to citizenship and the cancellation of the certificate of naturalization as having been obtained by concealment of a material fact or by willful misrepresentation, and such revocation and setting aside of the order admitting such person to citizenship and such canceling of certificate of naturalization shall be effective as of the original date of the order and certificate, respectively.

(d) Foreign residence

If a person who shall have been naturalized shall, within five years after such naturalization, return to the country of his nativity, or go to any other foreign country, and take permanent residence therein, it shall be considered prima facie evidence of a lack of intention on the part of such person to reside permanently in the United States at the time of filing his petition for naturalization, and, in the absence of countervailing evidence, it shall be sufficient in the proper proceeding to authorize the revocation and setting aside of the order admitting such person to citizenship and the cancellation of the certificate of naturalization as having been obtained by concealment of a material fact or by willful misrepresentation, and such revocation and setting aside of the order admitting such person to citizenship and such canceling of certificate of naturalization shall be effective as of the original date of the order and certificate, respectively. The diplomatic and consular officers of the United States in foreign countries shall from time to time, through the Department of State, furnish the Department of Justice with statements of the names of those persons within their respective jurisdictions who have been so naturalized and who have taken permanent residence in the country of their nativity, or in any other foreign country, and such statements, duly certified, shall be admissable in evidence in all courts in proceedings to revoke and set aside the order admitting to citizenship and to cancel the certificate of naturalization.

PART III. LOSS OF NATIONALITY

§ 1481. Loss of nationality by native-born or naturalized citizens; voluntary action.

(a) From and after the effective date of this chapter a person who is a national of the United States whether by birth or naturalization, shall lose his nationality by—

(1) obtaining naturalization in a foreign state upon his own application, upon an application filed in his behalf by a parent, guardian, or duly autho-

rized agent, or through the naturalization of a parent having legal custody of such person: *Provided,* That nationality shall not be lost by any person under this section as the result of the naturalization of a parent or parents while such person is under the age of twenty-one years, or as the result of a naturalization obtained on behalf of a person under twenty-one years of age by a parent, guardian, or duly authorized agent, unless such person shall fail to enter the United States to establish a permanent residence prior to his twenty-fifth birthday: *And provided further,* That a person who shall have lost nationality prior to January 1, 1948, through the naturalization in a foreign state of a parent or parents, may, within one year from the effective date of this chapter, apply for a visa and for admission to the United States as nonquota immigrant under the provisions of section 1101 (a) (27) (E) of this title; or

(2) taking an oath or making an affirmation or other formal declaration of allegiance to a foreign state or a political subdivision thereof; or

(3) entering, or serving in, the armed forces of a foreign state unless, prior to such entry or service, such entry or service is specifically authorized in writing by the Secretary of State and the Secretary of Defense: *Provided,* That the entry into such service by a person prior to the attainment of his eighteenth birthday shall serve to expatriate such person only if there exists an option to secure a release from such service and such person fails to exercise such option at the attainment of his eighteenth birthday; or

(4) (A) accepting, serving in, or performing the duties of any office, post, or employment under the government of a foreign state or a political subdivision thereof, if he has or acquires the nationality of such foreign state; or (B) accepting, serving in, or performing the duties of any office, post, or employment under the government of a foreign state or a political subdivision thereof, for which office, post, or employment an oath, affirmation, or declaration of allegiance is required; or

(5) voting in a political election in a foreign state or participating in an election or plebiscite to determine the sovereignty over foreign territory or

(6) making a formal renunciation of nationality before a diplomatic or consular officer of the United States in a foreign state, in such form as may be prescribed by the Secretary of State; or

(7) making in the United States a formal written renunciation of nationality in such form as may be prescribed by, and before such officer as may be designated by, the Attorney General, whenever the United States shall be in a state of war and the Attorney General shall approve such renunciation as not contrary to the interests of national defense; or

(8) deserting the military, air, or naval forces of the United States in time of war, if and when he is convicted thereof by court martial and as the result of such conviction is dismissed or dishonorably discharged from the service of such military, air, or naval forces: *Provided,* That, notwithstanding loss of nationality or citizenship under the terms of this chapter or previous laws by reason of desertion committed in time of war, restoration to active duty with such military, air, or naval forces in time of war or the reenlistment

or induction of such a person in time of war with permission of competent military, air, or naval authority shall be deemed to have the immediate effect of restoring such nationality or citizenship heretofore or hereafter so lost; or

(9) committing any act of treason against, or attempting by force to overthrow, or bearing arms against, the United States, violating or conspiring to violate any of the provisions of section 2383 of Title 18 or willfully performing any act in violation of section 2385 of Title 18, or violating section 2384 of Title 18 by engaging in a conspiracy to overthrow, put down, or to destroy by force the Government of the United States, or to levy war against them, if and when he is convicted thereof by a court martial or by a court of competent jurisdiction; or

(10) departing from or remaining outside of the jursidiction of the United States in time of war or during a period declared by the President to be a period of national emergency for the purpose of evading or avoiding training and service in the military, air, or naval forces of the United States. For the purposes of this paragraph failure to comply with any provision of any compulsory service laws of the United States shall raise the presumption that the departure from or absence from the United States was for the purpose of evading or avoiding training and service in the military, air, or naval forces of the United States.

(b) Any person who commits or performs any act specified in subsection (a) of this section shall be conclusively presumed to have done so voluntarily and without having been subjected to duress of any kind, if such person at the time of the act was a national of the state in which the act was performed and had been physically present in such state for a period or periods totaling ten years or more immediately prior to such act. (June 27, 1952, ch. 477, title III, ch. 3, § 349, 66 Stat. 267; Sept. 3, 1954, ch. 1256, § 2, 68 Stat. 1146.)

(c) Whenever the loss of United States nationality is put in issue in any action or proceeding commenced on or after September 26, 1961 under, or by virtue of, the provisions of this chapter or any other Act, the burden shall be upon the person or party claiming that such loss occurred, to establish such claim by a preponderance of the evidence. Except as otherwise provided in subsection (b) of this section, any person who commits or performs, or who has committed or performed, any act of expatriation under the provisions of this chapter or any other Act shall be presumed to have done so voluntarily, but such presumption may be rebutted upon a showing, by a preponderance of the evidence, that the act or acts committed or performed were not done voluntarily. (June 27, 1952, ch. 477, title III, ch. 3, § 349, 66 Stat. 267; Sept. 3, 1954 ch. 1256, § 2, 68 Stat. 1146; Sept. 26, 1961, Pub. 87–301, § 19, 75 Stat. 656.)

. . . .

RIGHT OF EXPATRIATION

R.S. § 1999 provided that: "Whereas the right of expatriation is a natural and inherent right of all people, indispensable to the enjoyment of the rights of life, liberty, and the pursuit of happiness; and whereas in the recognition of this principle this Government has freely received emigrants from all nations, and invested them with the rights of citizenship; and whereas it is claimed that such American citizens, with their descendants, are subjects of foreign states, owing allegiance to the governments thereof; and whereas it is necessary to the maintenance of public peace that this claim of foreign allegiance should be promptly and finally disavowed: Therefore any declaration, instruction, opinion, order, or decision of any officer of the United States which denies, restricts, impairs, or questions the right of expatriation, is declared inconsistent with the fundamental principles of the Republic."

§ 1482. Dual nationals; divestiture of nationality.

A person who acquired at birth the nationality of the United States and of a foreign state and who has voluntarily sought or claimed benefits of the nationality of any foreign state shall lose his United States nationality by hereafter having a continuous residence for three years in the foreign state of which he is a national by birth at any time after attaining the age of twenty-two years unless he shall—

(1) prior to the expiration of such three-year period, take an oath of allegiance to the United States before a United States displomatic,[18] or consular officer in a manner prescribed by the Secretary of State; and

(2) have his residence outside of the United States solely for one of the reasons set forth in paragraphs (1), (2)–(7), or (8) of section 1485 of this title, or paragraph (1) or (2) of section 1486 of this title: *Provided, however,* That nothing contained in this section shall deprive any person of his United States nationality if his foreign residence shall begin after he shall have attained the age of sixty years and shall have had his residence in the United States for twenty-five years afer having attained the age of eighteen years.

(June 27, 1952, ch. 477, title III, ch. 3, § 350, 66 Stat. 269.)

. . . .

AFROYIM v. RUSK, SECRETARY OF STATE

UNITED STATES, SUPREME COURT, 1967

387 U.S. 253

MR. JUSTICE BLACK delivered the opinion of the Court.

Petitioner, born in Poland in 1893, emigrated to this country in 1912 and became a naturalized American citizen in 1926. He went to Israel in 1950, and in 1951 he voluntarily voted in an election for the Israeli Knesset, the legislative body of Israel. In 1960, when he applied for renewal of his United States passport, the Department of State refused to grant it on the sole ground that he had lost his American citizenship by virtue of § 401 (e) of the

---

[18] So in original. Probably read "diplomatic."

Nationality Act of 1940 which provides that a United States citizen shall "lose" his citizenship if he votes "in a political election in a foreign state."[19] Petitioner then brought this declaratory judgment action in federal district court alleging that § 401 (e) violates both the Due Process Clause of the Fifth Amendment and § 1, cl. 1, of the Fourteenth Amendment[20] which grants American citizenship to persons like petitioner. Because neither the Fourteenth Amendment nor any other provision of the Constitution expressly grants Congress the power to take away that citizenship once it has been acquired, petitioner contended that the only way he could lose his citizenship was by his own voluntary renunciation of it. Since the Government took the position that § 401 (e) empowers it to terminate citizenship without the citizen's voluntary renunciation, petitioner argued that this section is prohibited by the Constitution. The District Court and the Court of Appeals, rejecting this argument, held that Congress has constitutional authority forcibly to take away citizenship for voting in a foreign country based on its implied power to regulate foreign affairs. Consequently, petitioner was held to have lost his American citizenship regardless of his intention not to give it up. This is precisely what this Court held in *Perez* v. *Brownell*, 356 U.S. 44.

Petitioner, relying on the same contentions about voluntary renunciation of citizenship which this Court rejected in upholding § 401 (e) in *Perez*, urges us to reconsider that case, adopt the view of the minority there, and overrule it. That case, decided by a 5–4 vote 10 years ago, has been a source of controversy and confusion ever since, as was emphatically recognized in the opinion of all the judges who participated in this case below.[21] Moreover, in the other cases decided with[22] and since[23] *Perez*, this Court has consistently invalidated on a case-by-case basis various other statutory sections providing for involuntary expatriation. It has done so on various grounds and has refused to hold that citizens can be expatriated without their voluntary renunciation of citizenship. These cases, as well as many commentators,[24] have cast great

[19] 54 Stat. 1137, as amended, 58 Stat. 746, 8 U.S.C. § 801:
"A person who is a national of the United States, whether by birth or naturalization, shall lose his nationality by:

. . . .

"(e) Voting in a political election in a foreign state or participating in an election or plebiscite to determine the sovereignty over foreign territory."
This provision was re-enacted as § 349 (a)(5) of the Immigration and Nationality Act of 1952, 66 Stat. 267, 8 U.S.C. § 1481 (a)(5).
[20] "All persons born or naturalized in the United States and subject to the jurisdiction thereof. are citizens of the United States. . . ."
[21] 250 F. Supp. 686; 361 F. 2d 102, 105.
[22] *Trop* v. *Dulles*, 356 U.S. 86; *Nishikawa* v. *Dulles*, 356 U.S. 129.
[23] *Kennedy* v. *Mendoza-Martinez*, 372 U.S. 144; *Schneider* v. *Rusk*, 377 U.S. 163; In his concurring opinion in *Mendoza-Martinez*, MR. JUSTICE BRENNAN expressed "felt doubts of the correctness of *Perez* . . . ." 372 U.S., at 187.
[24] See, *e.g.*, Agata, Involuntary Expatriation and Schneider v. Rusk, 27 U. Pitt. L. Rev. 1 (1965); Hurst, Can Congress Take Away Citizenship?, 29 Rocky Mt. L. Rev. 62 (1956); Kurland, Foreword: "Equal in Origin and Equal in Title

doubt upon the soundness of *Perez*. Under these circumstances, we granted certiorari to reconsider it, 385 U.S. 917. In view of the many recent opinions and dissents comprehensively discussing all the issues involved,[25] we deem it unnecessary to treat this subject at great length.

The fundamental issue before this Court here, as it was in *Perez*, is whether Congress can consistently with the Fourteenth Amendment enact a law stripping an American of his citizenship which he has never voluntarily renounced or given up. The majority in *Perez* held that Congress could do this because withdrawal of citizenship is "reasonably calculated to effect the end that is within the power of Congress to achieve." 356 U.S., at 60. That conclusion was reached by this chain of reasoning: Congress has an implied power to deal with foreign affairs as an indispensable attribute of sovereignty; this implied power, plus the Necessary and Proper Clause, empowers Congress to regulate voting by American citizens in foreign elections; involuntary expatriation is within the "ample scope" of "appropriate modes" Congress can adopt to effectuate its general regulatory power. *Id.*, at 57–60. Then upon summarily concluding that "there is nothing . . . in the Fourteenth Amendment to warrant drawing from it a restriction upon the power otherwise possessed by Congress to withdraw citizenship," *id.*, at 58, n. 3, the majority specifically rejected the "notion that the power of Congress to terminate citizenship depends upon the citizen's assent," *id.*, at 61.

First we reject the idea expressed in *Perez* that, aside from the Fourteenth Amendment, Congress has any general power, express or implied, to take away an American citizen's citzenship without his assent. This power cannot as *Perez* indicated, be sustained as an implied attribute of sovereignty possessed by all nations. Other nations are governed by their own constitutions, if any, and we can draw no support from theirs. In our country the people are sovereign and the Government cannot sever its relationship to the people by taking away their citizenship. Our Constitution governs us and we must never forget that our Constitution limits the Government to those powers specifically granted or those that are necessary and proper to carry out the specifically granted ones. The Constitution, of course, grants Congress no express power to strip people of their citizenship, whether in the exercise of the implied power to regulate foreign affairs or in the exercise of any specifically granted power. And even before the adoption of the Fourteenth Amendment, views were expressed in Congress and by this Court that under the Constitution the Government was granted no power, even under its express

to the Legislative and Executive Branches of the Government," 78 Harv. L. Rev. 143, 169–175; Comment, 56 Mich. L. Rev. 1142 (1958); Note, Forfeiture of Citizenship Through Congressional Enactment, 21 U. Cin. L. Rev. 59 (1952); 40 Cornell L. Q. 365 (1955); 25 U. So. Cal. L. Rev. 196 (1952). But see, *e.g.*, Comment, The Expatriation Act of 1954, 64 Yale L. J. 1164 (1955).

[25] See *Perez* v. *Brownell, supra*, at 62 (dissenting opinion of THE CHIEF JUSTICE), 79 (dissenting opinion of MR. JUSTICE DOUGLAS); *Trop* v. *Dulles, supra*, at 91–93 (part I of opinion of Court); *Nishikawa* v. *Dulles, supra*, at 138 (concurring opinion of MR. JUSTICE BLACK).

power to pass a uniform rule of naturalization, to determine what conduct should and should not result in the loss of citizenship. On three occasions, in 1795, 1797, and 1818, Congress considered and rejected proposals to enact laws which would describe certain conduct as resulting in expatriation.[26] On each occasion Congress was considering bills that were concerned with recognizing the right of voluntary expatriation and with providing some means of exercising that right. In 1795 and 1797, many members of Congress still adhered to the English doctrine of perpetual allegiance and doubted whether a citizen could even voluntarily renounce his citizenship.[27] By 1818, however, almost no one doubted the existence of the right of voluntary expatriation, but several judicial decisions had indicated that the right could not be exercised by the citizens without the consent of the Federal Government in the form of enabling legislation.[28] Therefore, a bill was introduced to provide that a person could voluntarily relinquish his citizenship by declaring such relinquishment in writing before a district court and then departing from the country.[29] The opponents of the bill argued that Congress had no constitutional authority, either express or implied, either under the Naturalization Clause or the Necessary and Proper Clause, to provide that a certain act would constitute expatriation.[30] They pointed to a proposed Thirteenth Amendment, subsequently not ratified, which would have provided that a person would lose his citizenship by accepting an office or emolument from a foreign government.[31] Congressman Anderson of Kentucky argued:

The introduction of this article declares the opinion . . . that Congress could not declare the acts which should amount to a renunciation of citizenship; otherwise there would have been no necessity for this last resort. When it was settled that Congress could not declare that the acceptance of a pension or office from a foreign Emperor amounted to a disfranchisement of the citizen, it must surely be conceded that they could not declare that any other act did. The cases to which their powers before this amendment confessedly did not extend, are very strong, and induce a belief that Congress could not in any case declare the acts

[26] For a history of the early American view of the right of expatriation, including these congressional proposals, see generally Roche, The Early Development of United States Citizenship (1949); Tsiang, Expatriation in America Prior to 1907 (1942); Dutcher, The Right of Expatriation, 11 Am. L. Rev. 447 (1877); Roche, The Loss of American Nationality—The Development of Statutory Expatriation, 99 U. Pa. L. Rev. 25 (1950); Slaymaker, The Right of the American Citizen to Expatriate, 37 Am. L. Rev. 191 (1903).
[27] Annals of Cong. 1005, 1027–1030 (1793–1795); 7 Annals of Cong. 349 *et seq.* (1797–1798).
[28] See, *e.g., Talbot* v. *Jansen,* 3 Dall. 133.
[29] 31 Annals of Cong. 495 (1817–1818).
[30] *Id.,* at 1036–1037, 1058. Although some of the opponents, believing that citizenship was derived from the States, argued that any power to prescribe the mode for its relinquishment rested in the States, they were careful to point out that "the absence of all power from the State Legislatures would not vest it in us." *Id.,* at 1039.
[31] The amendment had been proposed by the 11th Cong., 2d Sess. See The Constitution of the United States of America, S. Doc. No. 39, 88th Cong., 1st Sess., 77–78 (1964).

which should cause 'a person to cease to be a citizen.' The want of power in a case like this, where the individual has given the strongest evidence of attachment to a foreign potentate and an entire renunciation of the feelings and principles of an American citizen, certainly establishes the absence of all power to pass a bill like the present one. Although the intention with which it was introduced, and the title of the bill declare that it is to insure and foster the right of the citizens, the direct and inevitable effect of the bill, is an assumption of power by Congress to declare that certain acts when committed shall amount to a renunciation of citizenship. [31 Annals of Congress 1038–1039 (1817–1818).]

Congressman Pindall of Virginia rejected the notion, later accepted by the majority in *Perez*, that the nature of sovereignty gives Congress a right to expatriate citizens:

[A]llegiance imports an obligation on the citizen or subject, the correlative right to which resides in the sovereign power; allegiance in this country is not due to Congress, but to the people, with whom the sovereign power is found; it is, therefore, by the people only that any alteration can be made of the existing institutions with respect to allegiance. (*Id.,* at 1045.)

Although he recognized that the bill merely sought to provide a means of voluntary expatriation, Congressman Lowndes of South Carolina argued:

But, if the Constitution had intended to give to Congress so delicate a power, it would have been expressly granted. That it was a delicate power and ought not to be loosely inferred, . . appeared in a strong light, when it was said, and could not be denied, that to determine the manner in which a citizen may relinquish his right of citizenship, is equivalent to determining how he shall be divested of that right. The effect of assuming the exercise of these powers will be, that by acts of Congress a man may not only be released from all the liabilities, but from all the privileges of a citizen. If you pass this bill, . . . you have only one step further to go, and say that such and such acts shall be considered as presumption of the intention of the citizen to expatriate, and thus take from him the privileges of a citizen. . . . [Q]uestions affecting the right of the citizen were questions to be regulated, not by the laws of the General or State Governments, but by Constitutional provisions. If there was anything essential to our notion of a Constitution, . . . it was this: that while the employment of the physical force of the country is in the hands of the Legislature, those rules which determine what constitutes the rights of the citizen, shall be a matter of Constitutional provision. (*Id.,* at 1050–1051.)

The bill was finally defeated.[32] It is in this setting that six years later, in *Osborn* v. *Bank of the United States,* 9 Wheat, 738, 87, this Court, speaking through Chief Justice Marshall, declared in what appears to be a mature and well-considered dictum that Congress, once a person becomes a citizen, cannot deprive him of that status:

---

[32] *Id.,* at 1071. It is interesting to note that the proponents of the bill, such as Congressman Cobb of Georgia, considered it to be "the simple declaration of the manner in which a voluntary act, in the exercise of a natural right, may be performed" and denied that it created or could lead to the creation of "a presumption of relinquishment of the right of citizenship." *Id.,* at 1068.

[The naturalized citizen] becomes a member of the society, possessing all the rights of a native citizen, and standing, in the view of the constitution, on the footing of a native. The constitution does not authorize Congress to enlarge or abridge those rights. The simple power of the national Legislature, is to prescribe a uniform rule of naturalization, and the exercise of this power exhausts it, so far as respects the individual.

Although these legislative and judicial statements may be regarded as inconclusive and must be considered in the historical context in which they were made,[33] any doubt as to whether prior to the passage of the Fourteenth Amendment Congress had the power to deprive a person against his will of citizenship once obtained should have beem removed by the unequivocal terms of the Amendment itself. It provides its own constitutional rule in language calculated completely to control the status of citizenship: "All persons born or naturalized in the United States . . . are citizens of the United States. . . ." There is no indication in these words of a fleeting citizenship, good at the moment it is acquired but subject to destruction by the Government at any time. Rather the Amendment can most reasonably be read as defining a citizenship which a citizen keeps unless he voluntarily relinquishes it. Once acquired, this Fourteenth Amendment citizenship was not to be shifted, canceled, or diluted at the will of the Federal Government, the States, or any other governmental unit.

It is true that the chief interest of the people in giving permanence and security to citizenship in the Fourteenth Amendment was the desire to protect Negroes. The *Dred Scott* decision, 19 How. 393, had shortly before greatly disturbed many people about the status of Negro citizenship. But the Civil Rights Act of 1866, 14 Stat. 27, had already attempted to confer citizenship on all persons born or naturalized in the United States. Nevertheless, when the Fourteenth Amendment passed the House without containing any definition of citizenship, the sponsors of the Amendment in the Senate insisted on inserting a constitutional definition and grant of citizenship. They expressed fears that the citizenship so recently conferred on Negroes by the Civil Rights Act could be just as easily taken away from them by subsequent Congresses, and it was to provide an insuperable obstacle against every governmental effort to strip Negroes of their newly acquired citizenship that the first clause was added to the Fourteenth Amendment.[34] Senator Howard, who sponsored the Amendment in the Senate, thus explained the purpose of the clause:

It settles the great question of citizenship and removes all doubt as to what persons are or are not citizens of the United States. . . . We desired to put this question of citizenship and the rights of citizens . . . under the civil rights bill

[33] The dissenting opinion here points to the fact that a Civil War Congress passed two Acts designed to deprive military deserters to the Southern side of the rights of citizenship. Measures of this kind passed in those days of emotional stress and hostility are by no means the most reliable criteria for determining what the Constitution means.

[34] Cong. Globe, 39th Cong., 1st Sess., 2768, 2769, 2869, 2890 *et seq.* (1866). See generally, Flack, Adoption of the Fourteenth Amendment 88–94 (1908).

beyond the legislative power. . . . [Cong. Globe, 39th Cong., 1st Sess., 2890, 2896 (1866).]

This undeniable purpose of the Fourteenth Amendment to make citizenship of Negroes permanent and secure would be frustrated by holding that the Government can rob a citizen of his citizenship without his consent by simply proceeding to act under an implied general power to regulate foreign affairs or some other power generally granted. Though the framers of the Amendment were not particularly concerned with the problem of expatriation, it seems undeniable from the language they used that they wanted to put citizenship beyond the power of any governmental unit to destroy. In 1868, two years after the Fourteenth Amendment had been adopted, Congress specifically considered the subject of expatriation. Several bills were introduced to impose involuntary expatriation on citizens who committed certain acts.[35] With little discussion, these proposals were defeated. Other bills, like the one proposed but defeated in 1818, provided merely a means by which the citizen could himself voluntarily renounce his citizenship.[36] Representative Van Trump of Ohio, who proposed such a bill, vehemently denied in supporting it that his measure would make the Government "a party to the act dissolving the tie between the citizen and his country . . . where the statute simply prescribes the manner in which the citizen shall proceed to perpetuate the evidence of his intention, or election, to renounce his citizenship by expatriation." Cong. Globe, 40th Cong., 2d Sess., 1804 (1868). He insisted that "inasmuch as the act of expatriation depends almost entirely upon a question of intention on the part of the citizen," *id.,* at 1801, "the true question is, that not only the right of expatriation, but the whole power of its exercise, rests solely and exclusively in the will of the individual," *id.,* at 1804.[37] In strongest of terms, not contradicted by any during the debates, he concluded:

[35] Representative Jenckes of Rhode Island introduced an amendment that would expatriate those citizens who became naturalized by a foreign government, performed public duties for a foreign government, or took up domicile in a foreign country without intent to return. Cong. Globe, 40th Cong., 2d Sess., 968, 1129, 2311 (1868). Although he characterized his proposal as covering "cases where citizens may voluntarily renounce their allegiance to this country," *id.,* at 1159, it was opposed by Representative Chanler of New York who said, "So long as a citizen does not expressly dissolve his allegiance and does not swear allegiance to another country, his citizenship remains in *statu quo,* unaltered and unimpaired." *Id.,* at 1016.
[36] Proposals of Representatives Pruyn of New York (*id.,* at 1130) and Van Trump of Ohio (*id.,* at 1801, 2311).
[37] While Van Trump disagreed with the 1818 opponents as to whether Congress had power to prescribe a means of voluntary renunciation of citizenship, he wholeheartedly agreed with their premise that the right of expatriation belongs to the citizen, not to the Government, and that the Constitution forbids the Government from being party to the act of expatriation. Van Trump simply thought that the opponents of the 1818 proposal failed to recognize that their mutual premise would not be violated by an Act which merely prescribed "how . . . [the rights of citizenship] might be relinquished at the option of the person in whom they were vested." Cong. Globe, 40th Cong., 2d Sess., 1804 (1868).

To enforce expatriation or exile against a citizen without his consent is not a power anywhere belonging to this Government. No conservative-minded statesman, no intelligent legislator, no sound lawyer has ever maintained any such power in any branch of the Government. The lawless precedents created in the delirium of war, . . . of sending men by force into exile, as a punishment for political opinion, were violations of this great law . . . of the Constitution. . . . . The men who debated the question in 1818 failed to see the true distinction. . . . They failed to comprehend that it is not the Government, but that it is the individual, who has the right and the only power of expatriation. . . . [I]t belongs and appertains to the citizen and not to the Government; and it is the evidence of his election to exercise his right, and not the power to control either the election or the right itself, which is the legitimate subject matter of legislation. There has been, and there can be, no legislation under our Constitution to control in any manner the right itself. (*Ibid.*)

But even Van Trump's proposal, which went no further than to provide a means of evidencing a citizen's intent to renounce his citizenship, was defeated.[38] The Act, as finally passed, merely recognized the "right of expatriation" as an inherent right of all people.[39]

The entire legislative history of the 1868 Act makes it abundantly clear that there was a strong feeling in the Congress that the only way the citizenship it conferred could be lost was by the voluntary renunciation or abandonment by the citizen himself. And this was the unequivocal statement of the Court in the case of *United States* v. *Wong Kim Ark*, 169 U.S. 649. The issues in that case were whether a person born in the United States to Chinese aliens was a citizen of the United States and whether, nevertheless, he could be excluded under the Chinese Exclusion Act. The Court first held that within the terms of the Fourteenth Amendment, Wong Kim Ark was a citizen of the United States, and then pointed out that though he might "renounce this citizenship, and become a citizen of . . . any other country," he had never done so. *Id.*, at 704–705. The Court then held[40] that Congress could not do anything to abridge or affect his citizenship conferred by the Fourteenth Amendment. Quoting Chief Justice Marshall's well-considered and oft-repeated dictum in *Osborn* to the effect that Congress under the power of naturalization

---

[38] *Id.*, at 2317. Representative Banks of Massachusetts, the Chairman of the House Committee on Foreign Affairs which drafted the bill eventually enacted into law, explained why Congress refrained from providing a means of expatriation:

"It is a subject which, in our opinion, ought not to be legislated upon. . . . [T]his comes within the scope of natural rights which no Government has the right to control and which no Government can confer. And wherever this subject is alluded to in the Constitution— . . . it is in the declaration that Congress shall have no power whatever to legislate upon these matters." *Id.*, at 2316.

[39] 15 Stat. 223, R. S. § 1999.

[40] Some have referred to this part of the decision as a holding, see, *e.g.*, Hurst, *supra*, 29 Rocky Mt. L. Rev., at 78–79); Comment, 56 Mich. L. Rev., at 1153–1154; while others have referred to it as *obiter dictum*, see, *e.g.*, Roche, *supra*, 99 U. Pa. L. Rev., at 26–27. Whichever it was, the statement was evidently the result of serious consideration and is entitled to great weight.

has "a power to confer citizenship, not a power to take it away," the Court said:

Congress having no power to abridge the rights conferred by the Constitution upon those who have become naturalized citizens by virtue of acts of Congress, *a fortiori* no act . . . of Congress . . . can affect citizenship acquired as a birthright, by virtue of the Constitution itself. . . . The Fourteenth Amendment, while it leaves the power, where it was before, in Congress, to regulate naturalization, has conferred no authority upon Congress to restrict the effect of birth, declared by the Constitution to constitute a sufficient and complete right to citizenship. (*Id.*, at 703.)

To uphold Congress' power to take away a man's citizenship because he voted in a foreign election in violation of § 401 (e) would be equivalent to holding that Congress has the power to "abridge," "affect," "restrict the effect of," and "take . . . away" citizenship. Because the Fourteenth Amendment prevents Congress from doing any of these things, we agree with the Chief Justice's dissent in the *Perez* case that the Government is without power to rob a citizen of his citizenship under § 401 (e).[41]

Because the legislative history of the Fourteenth Amendment and the expatriation proposals which preceded and followed it, like most other legislative history, contains many statements from which conflicting inferences can be drawn, our holding might be unwarranted if it rested entirely or principally upon that legislative history. But it does not. Our holding we think is the only one that can stand in view of the language and the purpose of the Fourteenth Amendment, and our construction of that Amendment, we believe, comports more nearly than *Perez* with the principles of liberty and equal justice to all that the entire Fourteenth Amendment was adopted to guarantee. Citizenship is no light trifle to be jeopardized any moment Congress decides to do so under the name of one of its general or implied grants of power. In some instances, loss of citizenship can mean that a man is left without the protection of citizenship in any country in the world—as a man without a country. Citizenship in this Nation is a part of a cooperative affair. Its citizenry is the country and the country is its citizenry. The very nature of our free government makes it completely incongruous to have a rule of law under which a group of citizens temporarily in office can deprive another group of citizens of their citizenship. We hold that the Fourteenth Amendment was designed to, and does, protect every citizen of this Nation against a congressional forcible destruction of his citizenship, whatever his creed, color, or race. Our holding does no more than to give to this citizen that which is his own, a constitutional right to remain a citizen in a free country unless he voluntarily relinquishes that citizenship.

Perez v. *Brownell* is overruled. The judgment is

Reversed.

[41] Of course, as THE CHIEF JUSTICE said in his dissent, 356 U.S., at 66, naturalization unlawfully procured can be set aside. See, *e.g.*, *Knauer* v. *United States*, 328 U.S. 654; *Baumgartner* v. *United States*, 322 U.S. 665; *Schneiderman* v. *United States*, 320 U.S. 118.

Except in cases of annexation, states object to having other states impose nationality upon individuals against their will. Thus, for instance, the United States objected in 1886 when Mexico passed a law providing that foreigners who acquired real estate or had children born to them in Mexico would become Mexican citizens unless they officially declared that they intended to retain their original nationality. The Mexican law was in fact discarded later.[42] Even in cases of annexation, a conquering state can impose citizenship only on those persons who actually lived within the conquered state at the time of conquest, unless persons abroad at the time accepted their new citizenship. Acting on this principle, American courts refused to allow the United States to intern an immigrant from Austria under the Alien Enemy Act in 1941 just because Austria had been conquered by Germany and Germany was then at war with the United States.[43]

The jurisdiction of states over their own territory does not prevent states from prosecuting and punishing their nationals for acts committed in the territory of other states. States may prosecute their nationals abroad and execute judgments against either their property within the state, or upon them personally when they return.[44]

HARRY M. BLACKMER v. UNITED STATES OF AMERICA

United States, Supreme Court, 1932

284 U.S. 421

Mr. Chief Justice Hughes delivered the opinion of the Court.

The petitioner, Harry M. Blackmer, a citizen of the United States resident in Paris, France, was adjudged guilty of contempt of the Supreme Court of the District of Columbia for failure to respond to subpoenas served upon him in France and requiring him to appear as a witness on behalf of the United States at a criminal trial in that court. Two subpoenas were issued, for appearances at different times, and there was a separate proceeding with respect to each. The two cases were heard together, and a fine of $30,000 with costs was imposed in each case, to be satisfied out of the property of the petitioner which had been seized by order of the court. The decrees were affirmed by the Court of Appeals of the District, 49 F (2d) 523, and this Court granted writs of *certiorari*.

[42] U.S. For. Rel., 1866: 723; 1887: 672, 678, 681, 717, 731–733; Moore, *Digest*, III, 305–307; and Maximilian Koessler, "The Reformed Mexican Nationality Law," 5 Louisiana L.R. (1942–44), 420, 424, 425.

[43] U.S. ex rel. Schwarzkopf v. Uhl, U.S.C.A., 2d Circ., 1943, 137 F. 2d 898.

[44] Harvard Research Draft Convention on Jurisdiction with Respect to Crime (Edwin D. Dickinson, Reporter) *A.J.I.L.*, XXIX (1935), Supp., pp. 439–442.

The subpoenas were issued and served, and the proceedings to punish for contempt were taken, under the provisions of the Act of July 3, 1926, c. 762, 44 Stat. 835, *U.S.C.*, Tit. 28, §§ 711–718. The statute provides that whenever the attendance at the trial of a criminal action of a witness abroad, who is "a citizen of the United States or domiciled therein," is desired by the Attorney General, or any assistant or district attorney acting under him, the judge of the court in which the action is pending may order a subpoena to issue, to be addressed to a consul of the United States and to be served by him personally, upon the witness with a tender of traveling expenses. §§ 2, 3. Upon proof of such service and of the failure of the witness to appear, the court may make an order requiring the witness to show cause why he should not be punished for contempt, and upon the issue of such an order the court may direct that property belonging to the witness and within the United States may be seized and held to satisfy any judgment which may be rendered against him in the proceeding. §§ 4, 5. Provision is made for personal service of the order upon the witness and also for its publication in a newspaper of general circulation in the district where the court is sitting. § 6. If, upon the hearing, the charge is sustained, the court may adjudge the witness guilty of contempt and impose upon him a fine not exceeding $100,000, to be satisfied by a sale of the property seized. § 7. This statute and the proceedings against the petitioner are assailed as being repugnant to the Constitution of the United States.

First. The principal objections to the statute are that it violates the due process clause of the Fifth Amendment. These contentions are (1) that the "Congress has no power to authorize United States consuls to serve process except as permitted by treaty"; (2) that the Act does not provide "a valid method of acquiring judicial jurisdiction to render personal judgment against defendant and judgment against his property"; (3) that the Act "does not require actual or any other notice to defendant of the offense or of the Government's claim against his property"; (4) that the provisions "for hearing and judgment in the entire absence of the accused and without his consent" are invalid; and (5) that the Act is "arbitrary, capricious and unreasonable."

While it appears that the petitioner moved his residence to France in the year 1924, it is undisputed that he was, and continued to be, a citizen of the United States. He continued to owe allegiance to the United States. By virtue of the obligations of citizenship, the United States retained its authority over him, and he was bound by its laws made applicable to him in a foreign country. Thus, although resident abroad, the petitioner remained subject to the taxing power of the United States. *Cook* v. *Tait,* 265 U.S. 47, 54, 56. For disobedience to its laws through conduct abroad he was subject to punishment in the courts of the United States. *United States* v. *Bowman,* 260 U.S. 94, 102. With respect to such an exercise of authority, there is no question of international law, but solely of the purport of the municipal law which establishes the duties of the citizen in relation to his own government. While the legislation of the Congress, unless the contrary intent appears, is construed to apply only within the territorial jurisdiction of the United States, the question of its application, so far as citizens of the United States in foreign countries are concerned, is one of construction, not of legislative power. *American Banana Co.* v. *United Fruit Co.*, 213 U.S. 347, 357; *United States* v. *Bowman*, 260 U.S. 94, *supra; Robertson* v. *Railroad Labor Board*, 268 U.S. 619, 622. Nor can it be doubted that the United States possesses the power inherent in sovereignty to require the return to this country of a citizen, resident elsewhere, whenever the public interest requires it, and to penalize him in case of refusal. Compare *Bartue & Duchess of Suffolk's Case*, 2 Dyer, 176b, 73 Eng. Rep. 388; *Knowles* v. *Luce*, Moore, 109, 72 Eng. Rep. 473. . . . It is also beyond controversy that one of the duties which the citizen owes to his government is to support the administration of justice by attending its courts and giving his testimony whenever he is properly summoned. *Blair* v. *United States*, 250 U.S. 273, 281. And the Congress may provide for the performance of his duty and prescribe penalties for disobedience.

In this present instance, the question concerns only the method of enforcing the obligation. The jurisdiction of the United States over its absent citizen, so far as the binding effect of its legislation is concerned, is a jurisdiction *in personam*, as he is personally bound to take notice of the laws that are applicable to him and to obey them. *United States* v. *Bowman*, 260 U.S. 94, *supra*. But for the exercise of judicial jurisdiction *in personam*, there must be due process, which requires appropriate notice of the judicial action and an opportunity to be heard. For this notice and opportunity the statute provides. The authority to require the absent citizen to return and testify necessarily implies the authority to give him notice of the requirement. As his attendance is needed in court, it is appropriate that the Congress should authorize the court to direct the notice to be given and that it should be in the customary form of a subpoena. Obviously, the requirement would be nugatory, if provision could not be made for its communication to the witness in the foreign country. The efficacy of an attempt to provide constructive service in this country would rest upon the presumption that the notice would be given in a manner calculated to reach the witness abroad. *McDonald* v. *Mabee*, 243 U.S. 90, 92. The question of the validity of the provision for actual service of the subpoena in a foreign country is one that arises solely between the Government of the United States and the citizen. The mere giving of such a notice to the citizen in the foreign country of the requirement of his government that he shall return is in no sense an invasion of any right of the foreign government and the citizen has no standing to invoke any such supposed right. While consular privileges in foreign countries are the appropriate subjects of treaties, it does not follow that every act of a consul, as, *e.g.*, in communicating with citizens of his own country, must be predicated upon a specific provision of a treaty. The intercourse of friendly nations, permitting travel and residence of the citizens of each in the territory of the other, presupposes and facilitates such communications. In selecting the consul for the service of the subpoena, the Congress merely prescribed a method deemed to assure the desired result but in no sense essential. The consul was not directed to perform any function involving consular privileges or depending upon any treaty relating to them, but simply to act as any designated person might act for the Government in conveying to the citizen the actual notice of the requirement of his attendance. The point raised by the petitioner with respect to the provision for the service of the subpoena abroad is without merit.

As the Congress could define the obligation, it could prescribe a penalty to enforce it. . . . Decrees affirmed.

Treatment of Nationals. Traditionally, states have been free under international law to treat their nationals as they wished. After World War II, believing that the German persecution of Jewish and other German nationals was intimately related to German plans to wage war, the victorious United Nations powers (France, the U.S.S.R., the United Kingdom, and the United States) decided to give the Nuremberg Tribunal jurisdiction over "*Crimes Against Humanity:* namely, murder, extermination, enslavement, deportation, and other inhumane acts committed against any civilian population, before or during the war; or persecutions on political, racial or religious grounds in execution of or in connection with any crime within the jurisdiction of the Tribunal, whether or not in violation of domestic law of the country where perpetrated."[45] The charge was unprecedented and looked at askance, as was the entire Nuremberg proceeding, by more conservative members of the legal community. Taking account of the objections, Robert H. Jackson, Chief of Counsel for the United States, replied to them in the terms already quoted in Chapter 1.[46]

Although the Tribunal proceeded to find many defendants guilty of crimes against humanity, as well as other crimes, it had by the Berlin Protocol of October 6, 1945, limited itself to judging only such crimes against humanity as were ancillary or subsidiary to other criminal acts within its jurisdiction. Moreover, the Tribunal's judgment ignored the body's jurisdiction over crimes against humanity "before or during the war" and declined to judge acts committed before the start of hostilities. But the Tribunal did conclude that crimes against humanity were crimes "regardless of whether they were committed in accordance with and in obedience to the national law of the accused. Such acts were deemed to violate the sanctity of human personality to such a degree as to make irrelevant reliance upon the law of the State which ordered them."[47] In effect the Tribunal's judgment amounts to international rec-

[45] Article 6, Charter of the International Military Tribunal, Department of State Publication 2461, Executive Agreements Series 472.
[46] See pp. 46–47.
[47] H. Lauterpacht, *International Law and Human Rights* (New York: Frederick A. Praeger, Inc., 1950), pp. 35–36. For comment on the Tribunal's jurisdiction

ognition of fundamental principles of human rights. The principles received further recognition in Article 5 of the Charter of the International Military Tribunal for the Far East; in the Paris Peace Treaties of 1947 with Italy, Roumania, Hungary, Bulgaria, and Finland, which called for the states to surrender persons accused of such crimes; in the laws enacted by the Four Powers occupying Germany, which provided for the prosecution of crimes against humanity committed in Germany before and during the war; and in General Assembly resolutions.[48]

In order to make these principles legally binding, the United Nations General Assembly approved in 1948 a Convention on the Prevention and Punishment of the Crime of Genocide. The Treaty, which came into force on January 12, 1951, with 27 ratifications and which by 1968 had 71 ratifications, confirms that genocide, "whether committed in time of peace or in time of war is a crime under international law," which the parties agree to punish in their own courts under their own laws. In Article II, the treaty defines genocide as "any of the following acts committed with intent to destroy, in whole or in part, a national, ethnical, racial or religious group, as such:

(a) Killing members of the group;

(b) Causing serious bodily or mental harm to members of the group;

(c) Deliberately inflicting on the group conditions of life calculated to bring about its physical destruction in whole or in part;

(d) Imposing measures intended to prevent births within the group;

(e) Forcibly transferring children of the group to another group.

The Parties undertake to enact legislation to give effect to the Convention and if the parties wish, they can also agree separately to establish an "international penal tribunal" with jurisdiction over cases of genocide.

Enforcement of the treaty thus rests by and large with the states signing it. Nonetheless it has provoked vigorous opposition in the United States, which has not ratified it, on the grounds that it does not define genocide to include the acts directed against political and economic groups (to which the proponents reply that because the Convention sets

---

over crimes against humanity, see *The Trial of the Major War Criminals Before the International Military Tribunal* (Nuremberg, 1948), XXII, 495–498; E. Schwelb, "Crimes Against Humanity," *British Yearbook of International Law*, 1946, pp. 178–226; A. L. Goodhart, "Questions and Answers Concerning the Nuremberg Trial," *Juridical Review*, LVIII (April 1946), 1–19; Quincy Wright, "The Law of the Nuremberg Trial," *A.J.I.L.*, XXXXI (1947), 38–72; and Robert K. Woetzel, *The Nuremberg Trials in International Law* (London: Stevens & Sons Limited, 1960).

[48] Lauterpacht, *International Law and Human Rights, supra,* pp. 37–38; see also: Department of State Publication 2613, Far Eastern Series 12, pp. 39–44; Control Council Law No. 10 of December 20, 1945; General Assembly Resolution 95 (I), 1946, 177 (II) 1947, 260B (III) 1948, 489 (V) 1950; Report of the International Law Commission, 2d Session (1950).

only minimum standards is no reason to oppose it); that the Convention would create new categories of crime that are vague, ill-defined, and inappropriate subjects for international agreement (the proponents believe that the definitions are quite adequate); that the Convention would automatically incorporate its provisions into American law without regard for the distinction in the Tenth Amendment to the Constitution between federal and state powers (the proponents point out that the Convention specifies in Article V the need for implementing acts by national governments); and that the Convention would enlarge the jurisdiction of the International Court of Justice by providing that disputes about interpreting, applying, or fulfilling the Convention are to go to the Court (which the proponents say is an exaggerated fear).[49]

Aliens

Admission. A state may, under international law, exclude aliens altogether, exclude certain categories of aliens, or admit some or all aliens on conditions of various kinds. A state may, for instance, require aliens to register themselves; it may restrict their right to hold certain jobs or acquire certain property, limit the time they may stay in the country, or regulate them in other ways.

THE CHINESE EXCLUSION CASE: CHAE CHAN PING v. U.S.

UNITED STATES, SUPREME COURT, 1888

130 U.S. 581

MR. JUSTICE FIELD delivered the opinion of the court.

The appeal involves a consideration of the validity of the act of Congress of October 1, 1888, prohibiting Chinese laborers from entering the United States who had departed before its passage, having a certificate issued under the act of 1882 as amended by the act of 1884, granting them permission to return. The validity of the act is assailed as being in effect an expulsion from the country of Chinese laborers, in violation of existing treaties between the United States and the government of China, and of rights vested in them under the laws of Congress.

. . . .

It must be conceded that the act of 1888 is in contravention of express stipulations of the treaty of 1868 and of the supplemental treaty of 1880,

[49] Association of the Bar of the City of New York, Committee on International Law, "Report on the United Nations Convention on . . . Genocide [1949]." For text of the Convention itself, see *U.N.T.S.,* LXXVIII, 277.

but it is not on that account invalid or to be restricted in its enforcement. The treaties were of no greater legal obligation than the act of Congress. By the Constitution, laws made in pursuance thereof and treaties made under the authority of the United States are both declared to be the supreme law of the land, and no paramount authority is given to one over the other. A treaty, it is true, is in its nature a contract between nations and is often merely promissory in its character, requiring legislation to carry its stipulations into effect. Such legislation will be open to future repeal or amendment. If the treaty operates by its own force, and relates to a subject within the power of Congress, it can be deemed in that particular only the equivalent of a legislative act, to be repealed or modified at the pleasure of Congress. In either case the last expression of the sovereign will must control.

The effect of legislation upon conflicting treaty stipulations was elaborately considered in *The Head Money Cases*, and it was there adjudged "that so far as a treaty made by the United States with any foreign nation can become the subject of judicial cognizance in the courts of this country, it is subject to such acts as Congress may pass for its enforcement, modification, or repeal." 112 U.S. 580, 599. This doctrine was affirmed and followed in *Whitney* v. *Robertson*, 124 U.S. 190, 195. . . .

To preserve its independence, and give security against foreign aggression and encroachment, is the highest duty of every nation, and to attain these ends nearly all other considerations are to be subordinated. It matters not in what form such aggression and encroachment come, whether from the foreign nation acting in its national character or from vast hordes of its people crowding in upon us. The government, possessing the powers which are to be exercised for protection and security, is clothed with authority to determine the occasion on which the powers shall be called forth; and its determination, so far as the subjects affected are concerned, are necessarily conclusive upon all its departments and officers. If, therefore, the government of the United States, through its legislative department, considers the presence of foreigners of a different race in this country, who will not assimilate with us, to be dangerous to its peace and security, their exclusion is not to be stayed because at the time there are no actual hostilities with the nation of which the foreigners are subjects. The existence of war would render the necessity of the proceeding only more obvious and pressing. The same necessity, in a less pressing degree, may arise when war does not exist, and the same authority which adjudges the necessity in one case must also determine it in the other. In both cases its determination is conclusive upon the judiciary. If the government of the country of which the foreigners excluded are subjects is dissatisfied with this action it can make complaint to the executive head of our government, or resort to any other measure which, in its judgment, its interests or dignity may demand; and there lies its only remedy.

The power of the government to exclude foreigners from the country whenever, in its judgment, the public interests require such exclusion, has been asserted in repeated instances, and never denied by the executive or legislative departments. In a communication made in December, 1852, to Mr. A. Dudley

Mann, at one time a special agent of the Department of State in Europe, Mr. Everett, then Secretary of State under President Fillmore, writes: "This government could never give up the right of excluding foreigners whose presence it might deem a source of danger to the United States." "Nor will this government consider such exclusion of American citizens from Russia necessarily a matter of diplomatic complaint to that country." In a dispatch to Mr. Fay, our minister to Switzerland, in March, 1856, Mr. Marcy, Secretary of State under President Pierce, writes: "Every society possesses the undoubted right to determine who shall compose its members, and it is exercised by all nations, both in peace and war." "It may always be questionable whether a resort to this power is warranted by the circumstances, or what department of the government is empowered to exert it; but there can be no doubt that it is possessed by all nations, and that each may decide for itself when the occasion arises demanding its exercise." In a communication in September, 1869, to Mr. Washburne, our minister to France, Mr. Fish, Secretary of State under President Grant, uses this language: "The control of the people within its limits, and the right to expel from its territory persons who are dangerous to the peace of the State, are too clearly within the essential attributes of sovereignty to be seriously contested. Strangers visiting or sojourning in a foreign country voluntarily submit themselves to its laws and customs, and the municipal laws of France, authorizing the expulsion of strangers, are not of such recent date, nor has the exercise of the power by the government of France been so infrequent, that sojourners within her territory can claim surprise when the power is put in force." . . .

The power of exclusion of foreigners being an incident of sovereignty belonging to the government of the United States, as a part of those sovereign powers delegated by the Constitution, the right to its exercise at any time when, in the judgment of the government, the interests of the country require it, cannot be granted away or restrained on behalf of any one. The powers of government are delegated in trust to the United States, and are incapable of transfer to any other parties. They cannot be abandoned or surrendered. Nor can their exercise be hampered, when needed for the public good, by any considerations of private interest. The exercise of these public trusts is not the subject of barter or contract. Whatever license, therefore, Chinese laborers may have obtained, previous to the act of October 1, 1888, to return to the United States after their departure, is held at the will of the government, revocable at any time, at its pleasure. Whether a proper consideration by our government of its previous laws, or a proper respect for the nation whose subjects are affected by its action, ought to have qualified its inhibition and made it applicable only to persons departing from the country after the passage of the act, are not questions for judicial determination. If there be any just ground of complaint on the part of China, it must be made to the political department of our government, which is alone competent to act upon the subject. The rights and interests created by a treaty, which have become so vested that its expiration or abrogation will not destroy or impair them, are such as are connected with and lie in property, capable of sale and transfer or other disposition, not such as are personal and untransferable in their character. . . .

Mr. Justice Washington in *Society for the Propagation of the Gospel* v. *New Haven*, 8 Wheat. 464, . . . observes that "if real estate be purchased or secured under a treaty, it would be most mischievous to admit that the extinguishment of the treaty extinguished the right to such estate. In truth, it no more affects such rights than the repeal of a municipal law affects rights acquired under it." Of this doctrine there can be no question in this court; but far different is this case, where a continued suspension of the exercise of a governmental power is insisted upon as a right, because, by the favor and consent of the government, it has not heretofore been exerted with respect to the appellant or to the class to which he belongs. Between property rights not affected by the termination or abrogation of a treaty, and expectations of benefits from the continuance of existing legislation, there is as wide a difference as between realization and hopes.

. . . .

Order affirmed.

FONG YUE TING [AND OTHERS] v. UNITED STATES

UNITED STATES, SUPREME COURT, 1893

149 U.S. 698

Appeals from the Circuit Court of the United States for the Southern District of New York.

These were three writs of *habeas corpus,* granted by the Circuit Court of the United States for the Southern District of New York, upon petitions of Chinese laborers, arrested and held by the marshal of the district for not having certificates of residence, under section 6 of the act of May 5, 1892, c. 60. . . .

The first petition alleged that the petitioner was a person of the Chinese race, born in China, and not a naturalized citizen of the United States; that in or before 1879 he came to the United States, with the intention of remaining and taking up his residence therein, and with no definite intention of returning to China, and had ever since been a permanent resident of the United States, and for more than a year last past had resided in the city, county and State of New York, and within the second district for the collection of internal revenue in that State; that he had not, since the passage of the act of 1892, applied to the collector of internal revenue of that district for a certificate of residence, as required by section 6, and was and always had been without such certificate of residence; and that he was arrested by the marshal, claiming authority to do so under that section, without any writ or warrant. The return of the marshal stated that the petitioner was found by him within the jurisdiction of the United States, and in the Southern District of New York, without the certificate of residence required by that section; that he had therefore arrested him with the purpose and intention of taking him before a United States judge within that district; and that the petitioner admitted to the marshal, in reply to questions put through an interpreter, that he was a Chinese laborer, and was without the required certificate of residence.

. . . .

In each case, the Circuit Court, after a hearing upon the writ of *habeas corpus* and the return of the marshal, dismissed the writ of *habeas corpus,* and allowed an appeal of the petitioner to this court, and admitted him to bail pending the appeal. . . .

GRAY, J. The general principles of public law which lie at the foundation of these cases are clearly established by previous judgments of this court, and by the authorities therein referred to.

In the recent case of *Nishimura Ekiu* v. *United States,* 142 U.S. 651, 659, the court, in sustaining the action of the executive department, putting in force an act of Congress for the exclusion of aliens, said: "It is an accepted maxim of international law, that every sovereign nation has the power, as inherent in sovereignty, and essential to self-preservation, to forbid the entrance of foreigners within its dominions, or to admit them in such cases and upon such conditions as it may see fit to prescribe. In the United States, this power is vested in the national government, to which the Constitution has committed the entire control of international relations, in peace as well as in war. It belongs to the political department of the government, and may be exercised either through treaties made by the President and Senate, or through statutes enacted by Congress."

The same views were more fully expounded in the earlier case of *Chae Chan Ping* v. *United States,* 130 U.S. 581, in which the validity of a former act of Congress, excluding Chinese laborers from the United States, under the circumstances therein stated, was affirmed.

In the elaborate opinion delivered by Mr. Justice Field, in behalf of the court, it was said: "Those laborers are not citizens of the United States; they are aliens. That the government of the United States, through the action of the legislative department, can exclude aliens from its territory is a proposition which we do not think open to controversy. Jurisdiction over its own territory to that extent is an incident of every independent nation. It is a part of its independence. If it could not exclude aliens, it would be to that extent subject to the control of another power." "The United States, in their relation to foreign countries and their subjects or citizens, are one nation, invested with powers which belong to independent nations, the exercise of which can be invoked for the maintenance of its absolute independence and security throughout its entire territory. . . .

. . . "To preserve its independence, and give security against foreign aggression and encroachment, is the highest duty of every nation, and to attain these ends nearly all other considerations are to be subordinated. It matters not in what form such aggression and encroachment come, whether from the foreign nation acting in its national character, or from vast hordes of its people crowding in upon us. The government, possessing the powers which are to be exercised for protection and security, is clothed with authority to determine the occasion on which the powers shall be called forth; and its determinations, so far as the subjects affected are concerned, are necessarily conclusive upon all its departments and officers. If, therefore, the government of the United States, through its legislative department, considers the presence of foreigners of a different race in this country, who will not assimilate with us, to be dangerous to its peace and security, their exclusion is not to be stayed because at the time there are no actual hostilities with the nation of which the foreigners are subjects. The existence of war would render the necessity of the proceeding only more obvious and pressing. The same necessity, in a less pressing degree, may arise when war does not exist, and the same authority which adjudges the necessity in one case must also determine it in the other. In both cases its determination is conclusive upon the judiciary. If the government of the country of which the foreigners excluded are subjects is dissatisfied with this action, it can make complaint to the executive head of our government, or resort to any other measure which, in its judgment, its interest or dignity may demand; and there lies its only remedy.

"The power of the government to exclude foreigners from the country whenever, in its judgment, the public interests require such exclusion, has been asserted in repeated instances, and never denied by the executive or legislative departments." 130 U.S. [603, 604] 606, 607. This statement was supported by many citations from the diplomatic correspondence of successive Secretaries of State, collected in Wharton's *International Law Digest*, § 206.

The right of a nation to expel or deport foreigners, who have not been naturalized or taken any steps towards becoming citizens of the country, rests upon the same grounds, and is as absolute and unqualified as the right to prohibit and prevent their entrance into the country.

This is clearly affirmed in dispatches referred to by the court in Chae Chan Ping's case. In 1856, Mr. Marcy wrote: "Every society possesses the undoubted right to determine who shall compose its members, and it is exercised by all nations, both in peace and war. . . ."

The statements of leading commentators on the law of nations are to the same effect.

Vattel says: "Every nation has the right to refuse to admit a foreigner . . . and in virtue of its natural liberty, it belongs to the nation to judge whether its circumstances will or will not justify the admission of a foreigner." "Thus also it has the right to send them elsewhere. . . ." Vattel's Law of Nations, lib. 1, c. 19, §§ 230, 231.

. . . .

The right to exclude or to expel all aliens, or any class of aliens, absolutely or upon certain conditions, in war or in peace, being an inherent and inalienable right of every sovereign and independent nation, essential to its safety, its independence and its welfare, the question now before the court is whether the manner in which Congress has exercised this right in sections 6 and 7 of the act of 1892 is consistent with the Constitution.

The United States are a sovereign and independent nation, and are vested by the Constitution with the entire control of international relations, and with all the powers of government necessary to maintain that control and to make it effective. The only government of this country, which other nations recognize or treat with, is the government of the Union; and the only American flag known throughout the world is the flag of the United States.

The Constitution of the United States speaks with no uncertain sound upon this subject. . . .

The power to exclude or to expel aliens, being a power affecting international relations, is vested in the political departments of the government, and is to be regulated by treaty or by act of Congress, and to be executed by the executive authority according to the regulations so established, except so far as the judicial department has been authorized by treaty or by statute, or is required by the paramount law of the Constitution, to intervene.

. . . .

The power to exclude aliens and the power to expel them rest upon one foundation, are derived from one source, are supported by the same reasons, and are in truth but parts of one and the same power.

The power of Congress, therefore, to expel, like the power to exclude aliens, or any specified class of aliens, from the country, may be exercised through executive officers; or Congress may call in the aid of the judiciary to ascertain any contested facts on which the alien's right to be in the country has been made by Congress to depend.

Congress, having the right, as it may see fit, to expel aliens of a particular class, or to permit them to remain, has undoubtedly the right to provide a system of registration and identification of the members of that class within the country, and to take all proper means to carry out the system which it provides.

. . . .

[In the case of Chae Chan Ping, 130 U.S. 600,] it was directly adjudged, upon full argument and consideration, that a Chinese laborer, who had been admitted into the United States while the treaty of 1868 was in force, by which the United States and China "cordially recognized the inherent and inalienable right of man to change his home and allegiance, and also the mutual advantage of the free migration and emigration of their citizens and subjects, respectively, from one country to the other," not only for the purpose of curiosity or of trade, but "as permanent residents;" and who had continued to reside here for twelve years, and who had then gone back to China, after receiving a certificate, in the form provided by act of Congress, entitling him to return to the United States; might be refused re-admission into the United States, without judicial trial or hearing, and simply by reason of another act of Congress, passed during his absence, and declaring all such certificates to be void, and prohibiting all Chinese laborers who had at any time been residents in the United States, and had departed therefrom and not returned before the passage of this act, from coming into the United States.

In view of that decision, which, as before observed, was a unanimous judgment of the court, and which had the concurrence of all the justices who had delivered opinions in the cases arising under the acts of 1882 and 1884, it appears to be impossible to hold that a Chinese laborer acquired, under any of the treaties or acts of Congress, any right, as denizen or otherwise, to be and remain in this country, except by the license, permission and sufferance of Congress, to be withdrawn whenever, in its opinion, the public welfare might require it.

By the law of nations, doubtless, aliens residing in a country, with the intention of making it a permanent place of abode, acquire, in one sense, a domicil there; and, while they are permitted by the nation to retain such a residence and domicil, are subject to its laws, and may invoke its protection against other nations. This is recognized by those publicists who, as has been seen, maintain in the strongest terms the right of the nation to expel any or all aliens at its pleasure. . . .

Chinese laborers, therefore, like all other aliens residing in the United States for a shorter or longer time, are entitled, so long as they are permitted by the government of the United States to remain in the country, to the safeguards of the Constitution, and to the protection of the laws, in regard to their rights of person and of property, and to their civil and criminal responsibility. But they continue to be aliens, having taken no steps towards becoming citizens, and incapable of becoming such under the naturalization laws; and therefore remain subject to the power of Congress to expel them, or to order them to be removed and deported from the country, whenever in its judgment their removal is necessary or expedient for the public interest. . . .

The act of May 5, 1892, c. 60, is entitled "An act to prohibit the coming of Chinese persons into the United States"; and . . . [the] manifest objects of these sections [6 and 7] is to provide a system of registration and identification of such Chinese laborers, to require them to obtain certificates of residence and, if they do not do so within a year, to have them deported from the United States. . . . The order of deportation is not a punishment for crime. It is not a banishment . . . of a citizen. . . . It is but a method of enforcing the return to his own country of an alien who has not complied with a condition upon the performance of which the government of the nation . . . has determined that continuing to reside here shall depend. He has not, therefore, been deprived of life, liberty, or property without due process of law. . . .

The question whether, and upon what condition, these aliens shall be permitted to remain within the United States being one to be determined by the political departments of the government, the judicial department cannot properly express an opinion upon the wisdom, the policy or the justice of the measures enacted by Congress in the exercise of the powers confided to it by the Constitution over this subject.

Upon careful consideration of the subject, the only conclusion which appears to us to be consistent with the principles of international law, with the Constitution and laws of the United States, and with the previous decisions of this court, is that in each of these cases the judgment of the Circuit Court, dismissing the writ of *habeas corpus,* is right and must be affirmed.

UNITED STATES CODE
TITLE 8.—ALIENS AND NATIONALITY
SUBCHAPTER II. IMMIGRATION

Part I. Selection System

§ 1151. Numerical limitations on total lawful admissions.

(a) Quarterly and yearly limitations.

Exclusive of special immigrants defined in section 1101(a) (27) of this title, and of the immediate relatives of United States citizens specified in subsection (b) of this section, the number of aliens who may be issued immigrant visas or who may otherwise acquire the status of an alien lawfully admitted to the United States for permanent residence, or who may, pursuant to section 1153(a) (7) of this title enter conditionally, (i) shall not in any of the first three quarters of any fiscal year exceed a total of 45,000 and (ii) shall not in any fiscal year exceed a total of 170,000.

(b) Immediate relatives defined.

The "immediate relatives" referred to in subsection (a) of this section shall mean the children, spouses, and parents of a citizen of the United States: *Provided,* That in the case of parents, such citizen must be at least twenty-one years of age. The immediate relatives specified in this subsection who are otherwise qualified for admission as immigrants shall be admitted as such, without regard to the numerical limitations in this chapter.

(c) Determination of unused quota numbers.

During the period from July 1, 1965, through June 30, 1968, the annual quota of any quota area shall be the same as that which existed for that area on June 30, 1965. The Secretary of State shall, not later than on the sixtieth day immediately following October 3, 1965, and again on or before September 1, 1966, and September 1, 1967, determine and proclaim the amount of quota numbers which remain unused at the end of the fiscal year ending on June 30, 1965, June 30, 1966, and June 30, 1967, respectively, and are available for distribution pursuant to subsection (d) of this section.

(d) Immigration pool; limitation on total numbers; allocations.

Quota numbers not issued or otherwise used during the previous fiscal year, as determined in accordance with subsection (c) hereof, shall be transferred to an immigration pool. Allocation of numbers from the pool and from national quotas shall not together exceed in any fiscal year the numerical limitations in subsection (a) of this section. The immigration pool shall be made available to immigrants otherwise admissible under the provisions of this chapter who are unable to obtain prompt issuance of a preference visa due to oversubscription of their quotas, or subquotas as determined by the Secretary of State. Visas and conditional entries shall be allocated from the immigration pool within the percentage limitations and in the order of priority specified in section 1153 of this title without regard to the quota to which the alien is chargeable.

(e) Termination of immigration pool; carryover of admissible immigrants.

The immigration pool and the quotas of quota areas shall terminate June 30, 1968. Thereafter immigrants admissable under the provisions of this chapter who are subject to the numerical limitations of subsection (a) of this section shall be admitted in accordance with the percentage limitations and in the order of priority specified in section 1153 of this title. (As amended Oct. 3, 1965, Pub. L. 89–236, § 1, 79 Stat. 911.)

AMENDMENTS

1965—Subsec. (a). Pub. L. 89–236 substituted provisions setting up a 170,000 maximum on total annual immigration and 45,000 maximum on total quarterly immigration without regard to national origins, for provisions setting an annual quota for quota areas which allowed admission of one-sixth of one per centum of the portion of the national population of the continental United States in 1920 attributable by national origin of that quota area and setting a minimum quota of 100 for each quota area.

Subsec. (b) Pub. L. 89–236 substituted provisions defining "immediate relatives," for provisions calling for a determination of the annual quota for each quota area by the Secretaries of State and Commerce and the Attorney General, and the proclamation of the quotas by the President.

Subsec. (c). Pub. L. 89–236 substituted provisions allowing the carryover through June 30, 1968, of the quotas for quota areas in effect on June 30, 1965, and the redistribution of unused quota numbers, for provisions which limited the issuance of immigrant visas.

Subsec. (d). Pub. L. 89–236 substituted provisions creating an immigration pool and allowing its numbers without reference to the quotas to which an alien is chargeable, for provisions allowing the issuance of an immigrant visa to an immigrant as a quota immigrant even though he might be a non-quota immigrant.

Subsec. (e). Pub. L. 89–236 substituted provisions terminating the immigration pool on June 30, 1968, for provisions permitting the reduction of annual quotas based on national origins pursuant to Act of Congress prior to the effective date of proclaimed quotas.

. . . .

SELECT COMMISSION ON WESTERN HEMISPHERE IMMIGRATION

Section 21 of Pub. L. 89–236 provided that:

"(a) There is hereby established a Select Commission on Western Hemisphere Immigration (hereinafter referred to as the 'Commission') to be composed of fifteen members. The President shall appoint the Chairman of the Commission and four other members thereof. The President of the Senate, with the approval of the majority and minority leaders of the Senate, shall appoint five members from the membership of the Senate. The Speaker of the House of Representatives, with the approval of the majority and minority leaders of the House, shall appoint five members from the membership of the House. Not more than three members appointed by the President of the Senate and the Speaker of the House of Representatives, respectively, shall be members of the same political party. A vacancy in the membership of the Commission shall be filled in the same manner as the original designation and appointment.

"(b) The Commission shall study the following matters:

"(1) Prevailing and projected demographic, technological, and economic trends, particularly as they pertain to Western Hemisphere nations;

"(2) Present and projected unemployment in the United States, by occupations, industries, geographic areas and other factors, in relation to immigration from the Western Hemisphere;

"(3) The interrelationships between immigration, present and future, and existing and contemplated national and international programs and projects of Western Hemisphere nations, including programs and projects for economic and social development;

"(4) The operation of the immigration laws of the United States as they pertain to Western Hemisphere nations, including the adjustment of status for Cuban refugees, with emphasis on the adequacy of such laws from the standpoint of fairness and from the standpoint of the impact of such laws on employment and working conditions within the United States;

"(5) The implications of the foregoing with respect to the security and international relations of Western Hemisphere nations; and

"(6) Any other matters which the Commission believes to be germane to the purposes for which it was established.

"(c) On or before July 1, 1967, the Commission shall make a first report to the President and the Congress, and on or before January 15, 1968, the Commission shall make a final report to the President and the Congress. Such reports shall include the recommendations of the Commission as to what changes, if any, are needed in the immigration laws in the light of its study.

The Commission's recommendations shall include, but shall not be limited to, recommendations as to whether, and if so how, numerical limitations should be imposed upon immigration to the United States from the nations of the Western Hemisphere. In formulating its recommendations on the latter subject, the Commission shall give particular attention to the impact of such immigration on employment and working conditions within the United States and to the necessity of preserving the special relationship of the United States with its sister Republics of the Western Hemisphere.

"(d) The life of the Commission shall expire upon the filing of its final report, except that the Commission may continue to function for up to sixty days thereafter for the purpose of winding up its affairs.

"(e) Unless legislation inconsistent herewith is enacted on or before June 30, 1968, in response to recommendations of the Commission or otherwise, the number of special immigrants within the meaning of section 101(a) (27) (A) of the Immigration and Nationality Act, as amended [section 1101 (a) (24) (A) of this title], exclusive of special immigrants who are immediate relatives of United States citizens as described in section 201(b) of that Act [subsec. (b) of this section], shall not, in the fiscal year beginning July 1, 1968, or in any fiscal year thereafter, exceed a total of 120,000.

"(f) All Federal agencies shall cooperate fully with the Commission to the end that it may effectively carry out its duties.

"(g) Each member of the Commission who is not otherwise in the service of the Government of the United States shall receive the sum of $100 for each day spent in the work of the Commission, shall be paid actual travel expenses, and per diem in lieu of subsistence expenses, when away from his usual place of residence, in accordance with section 5 of the Administrative Expenses Act of 1946, as amended [section 73b–2 of Title 5]. Each member of the Commission who is otherwise in the service of the Government of the United States shall serve without compensation in addition to that received for such other service, but while engaged in the work of the Commission shall be paid actual travel expenses, when away from his usual place of residence, in accordance with the Administrative Expenses Act of 1946, as amended.

"(h) There is authorized to be appropriated, out of any money in the Treasury not otherwise appropriated, so much as may be necessary to carry out the provisions of this section."

. . . .

§ 1152. Numerical limitations on individual foreign states.

(a) Prohibition against preference or priority because of race, sex, nationality, place of birth, or place of residence.

No person shall receive any preference or priority or be discriminated against in the issuance of an immigrant visa because of his race, sex, nationality, place of birth, or place of residence, except as specifically provided in sections 1101 (a) (27), 1151 (b), and 1153 of this title: *Provided,* That the total number of immigrant visas and the number of conditional entries made available to natives of any single foreign state under paragraphs (1) through (8) of section 1153(a) of this title shall not exceed 20,000 in any fiscal year: *Provided further,* That the foregoing proviso shall not operate to reduce the number of immigrants who may be admitted under the quota of any quota area before June 30, 1968.

(b) Determination of individual foreign states by Secretary of State; charging immigrant to proper foreign state.

Each independent country, self-governing dominion, mandated territory, and territory under the international trusteeship system of the United Nations, other than the United States and its outlying possessions shall be treated as a separate foreign state for the purposes of the numerical limitation set forth in the proviso to subsection (a) of this section when approved by the Secretary of State. All other inhabited lands shall be attributed to a foreign state specified by the Secretary of State. For the purposes of this chapter the foreign state to which an immigrant is chargeable shall be determined by birth within such foreign state except that (1) an alien child, when accompanied by his alien parent or parents, may be charged to the same foreign state as the accompanying parent or of either accompanying parent if such parent has received or would be qualified for an immigrant visa, if necessary to prevent the separation of the child from the accompanying parent or parents, and if the foreign state to which such parent has been or would be chargeable has not exceeded the numerical limitation set forth in the proviso to subsection (a) of this section for that fiscal year; (2) if an alien is chargeable to a different foreign state from that of his accompanying spouse, the foreign state to which such alien is chargeable may, if necessary to prevent the separation of husband and wife, be determined by the foreign state of the accompanying spouse, if such spouse has received or would be qualified for an immigrant visa and if the foreign state to which such spouse has been or would be chargeable has not exceeded the numerical limitation set forth in the proviso to subsection (a) of this section for that fiscal year; (3) an alien born in the United States shall be considered as having been born in the country of which he is a citizen or subject, or if he is not a citizen or subject of any country then in the last foreign country in which he had his residence as determined by the consular officer; (4) an alien born within any foreign state in which neither of his parents was born and in which neither of his parents had a residence at the time of such alien's birth may be charged to the foreign state of either parent.

(c) Immigrants born in colonies of foreign states.

Any immigrant born in a colony or other component or dependent area of a foreign state unless a special immigrant as provided in section 1101(a) (27) of this title or an immediate relative of a United States citizen as specified in section 1151 (b) of this title, shall be chargeable, for the purpose of limitation set forth in subsection (a) of this section, to the foreign state, except that the number of persons born in any such colony or other component or dependent area overseas from the foreign state chargeable to the foreign state in any one fiscal year shall not exceed 1 per centum of the maximum number of immigrant visas available to such foreign state.

(d) Changes in territorial limits of foreign states.

In the case of any change in the territorial limits of foreign states, the Secretary of State shall, upon recognition of such change issue appropriate instructions to all diplomatic and consular offices. (As amended Oct. 3, 1965, Pub. L. 89–236, § 2, 79 Stat. 911.)

AMENDMENTS

1965—Subsec. (a). Pub. L. 89–236 substituted provisions prohibiting preferences or priorities or discrimination in the issuance of an immigrant visa because of race, sex, nationality, place of birth, or place of residence, setting a limit of 20,000 per year on the total number of entries available to natives of any single foreign state, and prohibiting the 20,000 limitation from reducing the number of immigrants under the quota of any quota area before June 30, 1968, for provisions calling for the charging of immigrants, with certain exceptions, to the annual quota of the quota area of his birth.

Subsec. (b). Pub. L. 89–236 substituted provisions calling for treatment of each independent country, self-governing dominion, mandated territory, and trusteeship territory as a separate foreign state for purposes of determining the numerical limitation imposed on each foreign state, and chargeability of immigrants to the country of their birth except where such chargeability would cause the family unit to be divided, for provisions setting up the Asia-Pacific triangle and providing for the special treatment of quota chargeability thereunder on the basis of racial ancestry.

Subsec. (c). Pub. L. 89–236 substituted provisions making immigrants born in colonies or other component or dependent areas of a foreign state chargeable to the foreign state and placing a limitation on the number of such immigrants of 1 per centum of the maximum number of visas available to the foreign state, for provisions making immigrants born in colonies for which no specific quota are set chargeable to the governing country and placing a limit of 100 on such immigrants from each governing country each year, with special application to the Asia-Pacific triangle.

Subsec. (d). Pub. L. 89–236 substituted provisions requiring the Secretary of State, upon a change in the territorial limits of foreign states, to issue appropriate instructions to all diplomatic and consular offices, for provisions that the terms of an immigration quota for a quota area do not constitute recognition of the transfer of territory or of a government not recognized by the United States.

Subsec. (e). Pub. L. 89–236 repealed subsec. (e) which allowed revision of quotas.

. . . .

PART VII—REGISTRATION OF ALIENS

§ 1301. Alien seeking entry; contents.

No visa shall be issued to any alien seeking to enter the United States until such alien has been registered and fingerprinted in accordance with section 1201 (b) of this title, unless such alien has been exempted from being fingerprinted as provided in that section (June 27, 1952, ch. 477, title II, ch. 7, § 261, 66 Stat. 223.)

. . . .

§ 1302. Registration of aliens.

(a) It shall be the duty of every alien now or hereafter in the United States, who (1) is fourteen years of age or older, (2) has not been registered and fingerprinted under section 1201 (b) of this title or section 30 or 31 of the Alien Registration Act, 1940, and (3) remains in the United States for thirty days or longer, to apply for registration and to be fingerprinted before the expiration of such thirty days.

(b) It shall be the duty of every parent or legal guardian of any alien now or hereafter in the United States, who (1) is less than fourteen years of age, (2) has not been registered under section 1201 (b) of this title or section 30 or 31 of the Alien Registration Act, 1940, and (3) remains in the United States for thirty days or longer, to apply for the registration of such alien before the expiration of such thirty days. Whenever any alien attains his fourteenth birthday in the United States he shall, within thirty days thereafter, apply in person for registration and to be fingerprinted. (June 27, 1952, ch. 477, title II, ch. 7, § 262, 66 Stat. 224.)

§ 1304. Forms for registration and fingerprinting.

(a) Preparation; contents.

The Attorney General and the Secretary of State jointly are authorized and directed to prepare forms for the registration and fingerprinting of aliens under section 1301 of this title, and the Attorney General is authorized and directed to prepare forms for the registration and fingerprinting of aliens under section 1302 of this title. Such forms shall contain inquiries with respect to (1) the date and place of entry of the alien into the United States; (2) activities in which he has been and intends to be engaged; (3) the length of time he expects to remain in the United States; (4) the police and criminal record, if any, of such alien; and (5) such additional matters as may be prescribed.

Treatment of Aliens. Because under international law the sovereign territorial state has the right to exercise full authority in its domain, one might logically conclude that it has the right to treat aliens as it wishes. International law, however, imposes on states the duty to do justice within their domain even to aliens. The rights which aliens enjoy are established in national laws, practice, and in treaties. In addition, however, international law recognizes certain minimum standards of treatment determined by diplomatic practice and the decisions of international tribunals. "The rule of obligation is perfectly distinct and settled," said Elihu Root, sometime United States Secretary of State and President of the American Society of International Law. He continued:

> Each country is bound to give to the national of another country in its territories the benefit of the same laws, the same administration, the same protection, and the same redress for injury which it gives to its own citizens, and neither more nor less: provided the protection which the country gives to its own citizens conforms to the established standard of civilization.
>
> There is a standard of justice very simple, very fundamental, and of such general acceptance by all civilized countries as to form a part of the international law of the world. The condition upon which any country is entitled to measure the justice due from it to an alien by the justice which it accords to its own citizens is that its system of law and administration shall conform to this general standard. If any country's system of law and administration does not conform to that standard, although the people of the country may be content and compelled to live under it, no other country can be compelled to accept it as furnishing a satisfactory measure of treatment to its citizens.[50]

In general, the international standard requires that states allow an alien certain basic rights: to make contracts; to acquire personal property; to marry and raise a family; to have access to the courts either as a complainant in civil action or as instigator of criminal proceedings to be undertaken by the state. It requires that, in going before the local court, an alien should not be discriminated against because of his nationality (except, perhaps, by being asked to furnish security for costs in a civil action); he should be able to invoke the aid of a court without regard for the political importance of his adversaries; he should be able to obtain help from the courts and other local authorities to prevent wrongful or criminal acts; and he should be able to obtain restitution from guilty defendants. If the alien is the object of criminal prosecution, he must be able to summon witnesses in his own behalf and to interrogate them; he must be informed of the nature of the charges preferred against him; and he must receive the right to counsel.[51]

States accord rights to aliens because they want their nationals treated similarly, because they normally treat nationals and aliens alike in certain matters, or because they grant to the nationals of all states the same privileges they grant to the nationals of any state. As a statement of international aspirations, the Universal Declaration of Human Rights,

[50] *Proceedings,* American Society of International Law, IV (1910), 16, 20–21.
[51] Hyde, II, 879–881.

adopted by the United Nations in 1948, expresses rights which the General Assembly believed should be granted to all persons, aliens or nationals.

Although the text of the Universal Declaration of Human Rights is not legally binding, the practice of states indicates that the following actions have been regarded as falling below the minimum international standard: (a) executing an alien without trial; (b) wanton killing of aliens by local officials; and (c) unlawful arrest, imprisonment, or detention, and unduly harsh, oppressive, or unjust treatment.

These standards are sufficiently accepted for the Secretary-General of the United Nations to have invoked them in an attempt to protect persons rebelling against a government whose authority the United Nations itself was attempting to establish, as evidenced by the following letters written on December 3 and 5, 1960, from Mr. Dag Hammarskjöld to Joseph Kasavubu, President of the Republic of the Congo (Leopoldville).[52]

I

I have learnt about the arrest of Mr. Lumumba and note that according to newspaper reports Mr. Lumumba has now been brought to Leopoldville "for trial."

A great number of delegations have approached me expressing their grave concern that a situation might develop in which action against Mr. Lumumba would be taken contrary to recognized rules of law and order and outside the framework of due process of law. It is felt that such a development—which it is widely trusted would be entirely against your intentions and views—would put seriously in jeopardy the international prestige of the Republic of the Congo and mean a most serious blow to principles to be upheld by the United Nations and by its Members. . . .

. . . I feel sure that you share my view as to the imperative need for the young republic firmly to uphold those general principles by which it wishes to live and to which it has put its signature when it became a Member of the United Nations. . . .

II

I am sure you will already have given your closest examination to the effect upon world opinion of any departure from the observance of the principles of the United Nations Charter concerning "respect for human rights and for fundamental freedom for all." This respect is reflected in the provisions of the Fundamental Law on the structures of the Congo and on public liberties in the Congo, as well as in the Universal Declaration of Human Rights.

. . . Inasmuch as the principle of parliamentary immunity exists throughout

[52] For the full texts, see *SCORs. Supp.* (October, November, and December 1960), pp. 71–73.

the world as a means of protecting not the private interests of the individual but rather the structure of parliamentary democracy, world public opinion will be certain to give to this point great attention, without regard to the political positions of the various personages detained.

. . . .

In my previous letter . . . I made a strong appeal for application of due process of law, as generally understood . . . which . . . applies to every stage of police action or legal action, including arrest and detention. Of special importance in this context is the concept of due process of law as developed in general recognized law and the fundamental law of public liberties. I refer in particular to the questions of the necessity for and legality of the warrant of arrest, the requirements that the detainee be informed, with twenty-four hours at the latest, of the reasons for his arrest and of the formal charges in detail entered against him; that he shall not be prosecuted except in the cases provided for by legislation and in accordance with the procedures in force at the time when the offense was perpetrated, that he may have counsel of his own choice, and further, that he shall be entitled in full equality to a fair and public hearing by an independent and impartial tribunal in the determination of any criminal charge against him.[53]

Denial of Justice. When states fail to adhere to the international standard, a *denial of justice* may occur. Legal experts differ, however, about the exact meaning of this term. Some restrict it to illegal conduct of judicial authorities only; others believe the term can apply to illegal conduct by any official; there are also those who would use the term only to refer to a state's failure to provide redress in its courts to an individual who has already been injured by the state's conduct, *i.e.*, no denial of justice occurs until an individual has exhausted local remedies and the remedies themselves have been found wanting. But, as one student of the subject has pointed out, the outcome of particular controversies "has almost never depended upon the meaning attached to this term. . . In almost all cases the real question has always been whether or not a State was responsible internationally for a particular act or omission, and not whether such an act or omission can be called denial of justice."[54] Authorities seem to agree that a state that violates international law and in the process injures another state or the nationals of another state incurs a responsibility to repair that injury from the

---

[53] On February 10, 1961, the Minister for the Interior of the Katanga provincial government announced that Patrice Lumumba and two colleagues had escaped from detention the night before. On February 13, the same official announced that the three men had been killed the previous day by certain villagers.

[54] Oliver J. Lissitzyn, "The Meaning of the Term Denial of Justice in International Law," *A.J.I.L.*, XXX (1960), 645. See also Hyde, II, § 281.

moment it commits the injury. If it makes reparation through its own domestic processes, the matter may go no farther; if it fails to make reparation, its failure may lead the injured state to interpose diplomatically to obtain a remedy to which international law entitles it.

International law does not hold sovereigns responsible for guaranteeing the safety of foreign life or property within their borders; the state has merely a contingent liability when injuries are caused not by state officials, but by private individuals. When, for instance, aliens are injured by a mob, the state is responsible only if it fails to take police actions which are reasonable and proper under the circumstances. Claims by states or their nationals against other states exist then either when a state has violated international law by acting or failing to act under certain circumstances, or when a state fails to adopt a course of action that promises an effective way of doing justice. If a state remedies the injustice locally, the settlement does not assume an international aspect; on the other hand, if a state does not provide a local remedy, either because it fails to recognize its international obligations, differs with another state about them, or is defective when it comes to maintaining procedures by which injured parties can claim justice, the question is likely to become an international claim.[55]

Claims

"A claim in international law may be defined as a demand for redress made by one State upon another by reason of the alleged wrongful conduct of that other."[56] When one state makes a claim against another, it implies that the foreign power has, through some agency of its own (usually by an act or omission of an official) violated international law and that it has failed to provide adequate means of obtaining redress through any domestic institution. The injury may be to the state directly or indirectly through one of its nationals. The demand for redress may be made through diplomatic channels; demands have also been made by force (see Chapter VIII). The redress sought may be payment of an indemnity or a request that the offender relinquish control over territory or perform some ceremonial act as, for instance, arranging for a salute to the flag of the offended state. In 1950, for instance, the United States formally protested to Guatemala because a Guatemalan band played "La Borinquena," a popular dance tune, instead of the United States national anthem when a Puerto Rican color guard at the Central American "Olympic" games that year paraded the Stars and Stripes. By way of making amends, the Guatemalan officials arranged for two

[55] Hyde, II, 882–885.
[56] Hyde, II, 886.

United States flags to be flown from masts in the "Stadium of the Revolution" and for the band to play the "Star Spangled Banner."[57]

Claims fall into two classes: those made upon private complaints of individuals whose government represents them in espousing the cause; and those that concern the state as a whole. A demand upon a state to pay a reparation to an individual is commonly known as *interposition*. Essentially the issues that arise in claims have to do with four questions: (1) the relation of the aggrieved individual, in private claims, to the State asked to espouse his cause; (2) the relation of the person whose conduct has given rise to the complaint to the state against which the claim is to be made; (3) the responsibility of the state for the act committed; and (4) the procedure to follow in order to obtain redress. The United States, for instance, will not interpose on behalf of persons not nationals from the date a claim arises to the date it is settled; or when acts complained of have not been committed by public officials in a foreign state; or when the official acts have not been illegal; or when the claimant has failed to exhaust the local remedies. All claims by individuals must proceed through diplomatic channels, which means, of course, that states may for diplomatic, rather than legal reasons, choose to prosecute or choose not to prosecute a claim. "It is," as one justice has put it, "an elementary principle that, when a government officially intervenes on behalf of its citizen, it makes his claim its own, and may settle [it] . . . on such terms as it may conceive to be proper."[58]

States look upon claims in international law as public matters, even when they involve injuries to individuals. They may, of course, decline to prosecute claims when the claimant, even though he may have suffered a wrong, is himself without clean hands, *i.e.*, if he has suffered the injury while pursuing an illegal or immoral object or acted in some way that his own government does not condone.[59] The public nature of international claims may also be seen in the adamant position of states in denying to individuals the possibility of waiving the right to institute such claims: most states have taken the position that the right, as a state right, may not be waived by any individual. Established states, moreover, have resisted attempts by new states to bar diplomatic interposition, as proposed by the Argentine jurist, Carlos Calvo.[60]

[57] *New York Times*, February 26, 1950, pp. 1, 11; February 28, 1950, p. 19.
[58] Judge Moore, dissenting opinion in The Mavromattis Palestine Concessions Case, Publications, P.C.I.J., Series A, No. 2, 54, 63.
[59] See Hyde, II, 885–892.
[60] See his *Le Droit International Théorique et Pratique* (5th ed., 6 vols. Paris, 1896), I, iii, secs. 110, 185–296; III, xv, secs. 1278, 1280.

Some states attempted to endorse the *Calvo Doctrine* by inserting in bilateral treaties provisions that their nationals shall not be entitled in each other's territory to diplomatic intervention, or by securing from an alien a contractual agreement that he would waive his rights to call upon his government for diplomatic protection. Some states, while willing to concede that they are responsible for wrongful acts not involving breaches of contracts, *i.e.*, *torts*, have been reluctant to admit that they are obliged by international law to perform contracts made with aliens. Contracts are generally conceded to be matters of private, not international law. The law assumes that an alien making a contract with or buying the bonds of a foreign government has assessed his risk beforehand.[61] On the other hand, many states have willingly adjudicated contractual claims and have specifically provided for such adjudication in claims conventions—bilateral treaties obligating them to settle their differences with other parties by arbitration.[62]

THE UNITED STATES OF AMERICA ON BEHALF OF NORTH AMERICAN DREDGING COMPANY OF TEXAS, CLAIMANT, v. UNITED MEXICAN STATES

CLAIMS COMMISSION, UNITED STATES AND MEXICO, 1926

OPINIONS OF COMMISSIONERS (1927), 21

This case is before this Commission on a motion of the Mexican Agent to dismiss. It is put forward by the United States of America on behalf of North American Dredging Company of Texas, an American corporation, for the recovery of the sum of $233,523.30 with interest thereon, the amount of losses and damages alleged to have been suffered by claimant for breaches of a contract for dredging at the port of Salina Cruz, which contract was entered into between the claimant and the Government of Mexico, November 23, 1912. The contract was signed at Mexico City. The Government of Mexico was a party to it. It had for its subject matter services to be rendered by the claimant in Mexico. Payment therefor was to be made in Mexico. Article 18, incorporated by Mexico as an indispensable provision, not separable from the other provisions of the contract, was subscribed to by the claimant for the purpose of securing the award of the contract. Its translation by the Mexican Agent reads as follows:

[61] Edwin M. Borchard, *The Diplomatic Protection of Citizens Abroad* (New York, 1916), pp. 284 ff.
[62] See, for example, United-States-Mexico, General Claims Convention (1924), T.S., No. 678, and United States (Illinois Central R.R. Co., Claim) v. United Mexican States (United States-Mexico, General Claims Commission, 1926, *Opinions of Commissioners*, 1927), p. 15.

The contractor and all persons, who, as employees or in any other capacity may be engaged in the execution of the work under this contract either directly or indirectly, shall be considered as Mexicans in all matters, within the Republic of Mexico, concerning the execution of such work and the fulfillment of this contract. They shall not claim, nor shall they have, with regard to the interests and the business connected with this contract, any other rights or means to enforce the same than those granted by the laws of the Republic to Mexicans, nor shall they enjoy any other rights than those established in favor of Mexicans. They are consequently deprived of any rights as aliens, and under no conditions shall the intervention of foreign diplomatic agents be permitted, in any matter related to this contract.

1. The jurisdiction of the Commission is challenged in this case on the grounds (first) that claims based on an alleged nonperformance of contract obligations are outside the jurisdiction of this Commission and (second) that a contract containing the so-called Calvo clause deprives the party subscribing said clause of the right to submit any claims connected with his contract to an international commission.

2. The Commission, in its decision this day rendered on the Mexican motion to dismiss the *Illinois Central Railroad Company Case,* Docket No. 432, has stated the reasons why it deems contractual claims to fall within its jurisdiction. It is superfluous to repeat them. The first ground of the motion is therefore rejected.

The Calvo Clause

3. The Commission is fully sensible of the importance of any judicial decision either sustaining in whole or in part, or rejecting in whole or in part, or construing the so-called "Calvo clause" in contracts between nations and aliens. It appreciates the legitimate desire on the part of nations to deal with persons and property within their respective jurisdictions according to their own laws and to apply remedies provided by their own authorities and tribunals, which laws and remedies in no wise restrict or limit their international obligations, or restrict or limit or in any wise impinge upon the correlative rights of other nations protected under rules of international law. The problem presented in this case is whether such legitimate desire may be accomplished through appropriate and carefully phrased contracts; what form such a contract may take; what is its scope and its limitations; and does clause 18 of the contract involved in this case fall within the field where the parties are free to contract without violating any rule of international law?

4. The Commission does not feel impressed by arguments either in favor of or in opposition to the Calvo clause, in so far as these arguments go to extremes. The Calvo clause is neither upheld by all outstanding international authorities and by the soundest among international awards nor is it universally rejected. The Calvo clause in a specific contract is neither a clause which must be sustained to its full length because of its contractual nature nor can it be discretionarily separated from the rest of the contract as if

it were just an accidental postscript. The problem is not solved by saying yes or no; the affirmative answer exposing the rights of foreigners to undeniable dangers, the negative answer leaving to the nations involved no alternative except that of exclusion of foreigners from business. The present stage of international law imposes upon every international tribunal the solemn duty of seeking for a proper and adequate balance between the sovereign right of national jurisdiction, on the one hand, and the sovereign right of national protection of citizens on the other. No international tribunal should or may evade the task of finding such limitations of both rights as will render them compatible within the general rules and principles of international law. By merely ignoring worldwide abuses either of the right of national protection or of the right of national jurisdiction no solution compatible with the requirements of modern international law can be reached.

5. At the very outset the Commission rejects as unsound a presentation of the problem according to which if article 18 of the present contract were upheld Mexico or any other nation might lawfully bind all foreigners by contract to relinquish all rights of protection by their governments. It is quite possible to recognize as valid some forms of waiving the right of foreign protection without thereby recognizing as valid and lawful every form of doing so.

6. The Commission also denies that the rules of international public law apply only to nations and that individuals cannot under any circumstances have a personal standing under it. As illustrating the antiquated character of this thesis it may suffice to point out that in article 4 of the unratified International Prize Court Convention adopted at The Hague in 1907 and signed by both the United States and Mexico and by 29 other nations this conception, so far as ever held, was repudiated.

7. It is well known how largely the increase of civilization, intercourse, and interdependence as between nations has influenced and moderated the exaggerated conception of national sovereignty. As civilization has progressed individualism has increased; and so has the right of the individual citizen to decide upon the ties between himself and his native country. There was a time when governments and not individuals decided if a man was allowed to change his nationality or his residence, and when even if he had changed either of them his government sought to lay burdens on him for having done so. To acknowledge that under the existing laws of progressive, enlightened civilization a person may voluntarily expatriate himself but that short of expatriation he may not by contract, in what he conceives to be his own interest, to any extent loosen the ties which bind him to his country is neither consistent with the facts of modern international intercourse nor with corresponding developments in the field of international law and does not tend to promote good will among nations.

Lawfulness of the Calvo Clause

8. The contested provision, in this case, is part of a contract and must be upheld unless it be repugnant to a recognized rule of international law.

What must be established is not that the Calvo clause is universally accepted or universally recognized, but that there exists a generally accepted rule of international law condemning the Calvo clause and denying to an individual the right to relinquish to any extent, large or small, and under any circumstances or conditions, the protection of the government to which he owes allegiance. Only in case a provision of this or any similar tendency were established could a parallel be drawn between the illegality of the Calvo clause in the present contract and the illegality of a similar clause in the Arkansas contract declared void in 1922 by the Supreme Court of the United States [*Terral v. Burke Construction Co.*] (257 U.S. 529) because of its repugnance to American statute provisions. It is as little doubtful nowadays as it was in the day of the Geneva Arbitration that international law is paramount to decrees of nations and to municipal law; but the task before this Commission precisely is to ascertain whether international law really contains a rule prohibiting contract provisions attempting to accomplish the purpose of the Calvo clause.

9. The Commission does not hesitate to declare that there exists no international rule prohibiting the sovereign right of a nation to protect its citizens abroad from being subject to any limitation whatsoever under any circumstances. The right of protection has been limited by treaties between nations in provisions related to the Calvo clause. While it is true that Latin-American countries—which are important members of the family of nations and which have played for many years an important and honorable part in the development of international law—are parties to most of these treaties, still such countries as France, Germany, Great Britain, Sweden, Norway, and Belgium, and in one case at least even the United States of America (Treaty between the United States and Peru, dated September 6, 1870, Volume 2, Malloy's United States Treaties, at page 1426; article 37) have been parties to treaties containing such provisions.

10. What Mexico has asked of the North American Dredging Company of Texas as a condition for awarding it the contract which it sought is, "If all of the means of enforcing your rights under this contract afforded by Mexican law, even against the Mexican Government itself, are wide open to you, as they are wide open to our own citizens, will you promise not to ignore them and not to call directly upon your own Government to intervene in your behalf in connection with any controversy, small or large, but seek redress under the laws of Mexico through the authorities and tribunals furnished by Mexico for your protection?" and the claimant, by subscribing to this contract and seeking the benefits which were to accrue to him thereunder, has answered, "I promise."

11. Under the rules of international law may an alien lawfully make such a promise? The Commission holds that he may, but at the same time holds that he cannot deprive the government of his nation of its undoubted right of applying international remedies to violations of international law committed to his damage. Such government frequently has a larger interest in maintaining the principles of international law than in recovering damage for one of

its citizens in a particular case, and manifestly such citizen can not by contract tie in this respect the hands of his government. But while any attempt to so bind his government is void, the Commission has not found any generally recognized rule of positive international law which would give to his government the right to intervene to strike down a lawful contract, in the terms set forth in the preceding paragraph 10, entered into by its citizen. The obvious purpose of such a contract is to prevent abuses of the right to protection, not to destroy the right itself—abuses which are intolerable to any self-respecting nation and are prolific breeders of international friction. The purpose of such a contract is to draw a reasonable and practical line between Mexico's sovereign right of jurisdiction within its own territory, on the one hand, and the sovereign right of protection of the government of an alien whose person or property is within such territory, on the other hand. Unless such line is drawn and if these two coexisting rights are permitted constantly to overlap, continual friction is inevitable.

12. It being impossible to prove the illegality of the said provision, under the limitations indicated, by adducing generally recognized rules of positive international law, it apparently can only be contested by invoking its incongruity to the law of nature (natural rights) and its inconsistency with inalienable, indestructible, unprescriptible, uncurtailable rights of nations. The law of nature may have been helpful, some three centuries ago, to build up a new law of nations, and the conception of inalienable rights of men and nations may have exercised a salutary influence, some one hundred and fifty years ago, on the development of modern democracy on both sides of the ocean; but they have failed as a durable foundation of either municipal or international law and can not be used in the present day as substitutes for positive municipal law, on the one hand, and for positive international law, as recognized by nations and governments through their acts and statements, on the other hand. Inalienable rights have been the cornerstones of policies like those of the Holy Alliance and of Lord Palmerston; instead of bringing to the world the benefit of mutual understanding, they are to weak or less fortunate nations an unrestrained menace.

Interpretation of the Calvo Clause in the Present Contract

13. What is the true meaning of article 18 of the present contract? It is essential to state that the closing words of the article should be combined so as to read: "being deprived, in consequence, of any rights as aliens in *any matter connected with this contract,* and without the intervention of foreign diplomatic agents being in any case permissible *in any matter connected with this contract.*" Both the commas and the phrasing show that the words "in any matter connected with this contract" are a limitation on either of the two statements contained in the closing words of the article.

14. Reading this article as a whole, it is evident that its purpose was to bind the claimant to be governed by the laws of Mexico and to use the remedies existing under such laws. The closing words "in any matter connected with this contract" must be read in connection with the preceding phrase "in everything connected with the execution of such work and the

fulfillment of this contract" and also in connection with the phrase "regarding the interests or business connected with this contract." In other words, in executing the contract, in fulfilling the contract, or in putting forth any claim "regarding the interests or business connected with this contract," the claimant should be governed by those laws and remedies which Mexico had provided for the protection of its own citizens. But this provision did not, and could not, deprive the claimant of his American citizenship and all that that implies. It did not take from him his undoubted right to apply to his own Government for protection if his resort to the Mexican tribunals or other authorities available to him resulted in a denial or delay of justice as that term is used in international law. In such a case the claimant's complaint would be not that his contract was violated but that he had been denied justice. The basis of his appeal would be not a construction of his contract, save perchance in an incidental way, but rather an internationally illegal act.

15. What, therefore, are the rights which claimant waived and those which he did not waive in subscribing to article 18 of the contract? (a) He waived his right to conduct himself as if no competent authorities existed in Mexico; as if he were engaged in fulfilling a contract in an inferior country subject to a system of capitulations; and if the only real remedies available to him in the fulfillment, construction, and enforcement of this contract were international remedies. All these he waived and had a right to waive. (b) He did not waive any right which he possessed as an American citizen as to any matter not connected with the fulfillment, execution, or enforcement of this contract as such. (c) He did not waive his undoubted right as an American citizen to apply to his Government for protection against the violation of international law (internationally illegal acts) whether growing out of this contract or out of other situations. (d) He did not and could not affect the right of his Government to extend to him its protection in general or to extend to him its protection against breaches of international law. But he did frankly and unreservedly agree that in consideration of the Government of Mexico awarding him this contract, he did not need and would not invoke or accept the assistance of his Government with respect to the fulfillment and interpretation of his contract and the execution of his work thereunder. The conception that a citizen in doing so impinges upon a sovereign, inalienable, unlimited right of his government belongs to those ages and countries which prohibited the giving up of his citizenship by a citizen or allowed him to relinquish it only with the special permission of his government.

16. It is quite true that this construction of article 18 of the contract does not effect complete equality between the foreigner subscribing the contract on the one hand and Mexicans on the other hand. Apart from the fact that equality of legal status between citizens and foreigners is by no means a requisite of international law—in some respects the citizen has greater rights and larger duties, in other respects the foreigner has—article 18 only purposes equality between the foreigner and Mexicans with respect to the execution, fulfillment, and interpretation of this contract and such limited equality is properly obtained.

17. The Commission ventures to suggest that it would strengthen and stimulate friendly relations between nations if in the future such important clauses in contracts as article 18 in the contract in question were couched in such clear, simple, and straightforward language, frankly expressing its purpose with all necessary limitations and restraints as would preclude the possibility of misinterpretation and render it insusceptible of such extreme construction as sought to be put upon article 18 in this instance, which if adopted would result in striking it down as illegal.

The Calvo Clause and the Claimant

18. If it were necessary to demonstrate how legitimate are the fears of certain nations with respect to abuses of the right of protection and how seriously the sovereignty of those nations within their own boundaries would be impaired if some extreme conceptions of this right were recognized and enforced, the present case would furnish an illuminating example. The claimant, after having solemnly promised in writing that it would not ignore the local laws, remedies, and authorities, behaved from the very beginning as if article 18 of its contract had no existence in fact. It used the article to procure the contract, but this was the extent of its use. It has never sought any redress by application to the local authorities and remedies which article 18 liberally granted it and which, according to Mexican law, are available to it, even against the Government, without restrictions, both in matter of civil and of public law. It has gone so far as to declare itself freed from its contract obligations by its *ipse dixit* instead of having resort to the local tribunals to construe its contract and its rights thereunder. And it has gone so far as to declare that it was not bound by article 7 of the contract and to forcibly remove a dredge to which, under that article, the Government of Mexico considered itself entitled as security for the proper fulfillment of its contract with claimant. While its behavior during the spring and summer of 1914, the latter part of the Huerta administration, may be in part explained by the unhappy conditions of friction then existing between the two countries in connection with the military occupation of Veracruz by the United States, this explanation can not be extended from the year 1917 to the date of the filing of its claim before this Commission, during all of which time it has ignored the open doors of Mexican tribunals. The record before this Commission strongly suggests that the claimant used article 18 to procure the contract with no intention of ever observing its provisions.

The Calvo Clause and the Claims Convention

19. Claims accruing prior to the signing of the Treaty must, in order to fall within the jurisdiction of this Commission under Article I of the Treaty, either have been "presented" before September 8, 1923, by a citizen of one of the nations parties to the agreement "to [his] Government for its interposition with the other," or, after September 8, 1923, "such claims"—i.e., claims presented for interposition—may be filed by either Government with this Commission. Two things are therefore essential, (1) the presentation by the citizen of a claim to his Government and (2) the espousal of such claim

by that Government. But it is urged that when a Government espouses and presents a claim here, the private interest in the claim is merged in the Nation in the sense that the private interest is entirely eliminated and the claim is a national claim, and that therefore this Commission can not look behind the act of the Government espousing it to discover the private interest therein or to ascertain whether or not the private claimant has presented or may rightfully present the claim to his Government for interposition. This view is rejected by the Commission for the reasons set forth in the second paragraph of the opinion in the Parker claim [*Opinions of the Commissioners* (1927), 35] . . . and need not be repeated here.

20. Under article 18 of the contract declared upon the present claimant is precluded from presenting to its Government any claim relative to the interpretation or fulfillment of this contract. If it had a claim for denial of justice, for delay of justice or gross injustice, or for any other violation of international law committed by Mexico to its damage, it might have presented such a claim to its Government, which in turn could have espoused it and presented it here. Although the claim as presented falls within the first clause of Article I of the Treaty, describing claims coming within this Commission's jurisdiction, it is not a claim that may be rightfully presented by the claimant to its Government for espousal and hence is not cognizable here, pursuant to the latter part of paragraph 1 of the same Article I.

21. It is urged that the claim may be presented by claimant to its Government for espousal in view of the provision of Article V of the Treaty, to the effect "that no claim shall be disallowed or rejected by the Commission by the application of the general principle of international law that the legal remedies must be exhausted as a condition precedent to the validity or allowance of any claim." This provision is limited to the application of a general principle of international law to claims that may be presented to the Commission falling within the terms of Article I of the Treaty, and if under the terms of Article I the private claimant can not rightfully present its claim to its Government and the claim therefore can not become cognizable here, Article V does not apply to it, nor can it render the claim cognizable, nor does it entitle either Government to set aside an express valid contract between one of its citizens and the other Government.

Extent of the Present Interpretation of the Calvo Clause

22. Manifestly it is impossible for this Commission to announce an all-embracing formula to determine the validity or invalidity of all clauses partaking of the nature of the Calvo clause, which may be found in contracts, decrees, statutes, or constitutions, and under widely varying conditions. Whenever such a provision is so phrased as to seek to preclude a Government from intervening, diplomatically or otherwise, to protect its citizen whose rights of any nature have been invaded by another Government in violation of the rules and principles of international law, the Commission will have no hesitation in pronouncing the provision void. Nor does this decision in any way apply to claims not based on express contract provisions in writing and signed by the claimant or by one through whom the claimant has deraigned

title to the particular claim. Nor will any provision in any constitution, statute, law, or decree, whatever its form, to which the claimant has not in some form expressly subscribed in writing, howsoever it may operate or affect his claim, preclude him from presenting his claim to his Government or the Government from espousing it and presenting it to this Commission for decision under the terms of the Treaty.

23. Even so, each case involving application of a valid clause partaking of the nature of the Calvo clause will be considered and decided on its merits. Where a claim is based on an alleged violation of any rule or principle of international law, the Commission will take jurisdiction notwithstanding the existence of such a clause in a contract subscribed by such claimant. But where a claimant has expressly agreed in writing, attested by his signature, that in all matters pertaining to the execution, fulfillment, and interpretation of the contract he will have resort to local tribunals, remedies, and authorities, and then wilfully ignores them by applying in such matters to his Government, he will be held bound by his contract and the Commission will not take jurisdiction of such claim.

Summary of the Considerations on the Calvo Clause

24. (a) The Treaty between the two Governments under which this Commission is constituted requires that a claim accruing before September 8, 1923, to fall within its jurisdiction must be that of a citizen of one Government against the other Government and must not only be espoused by the first Government and put forward by it before this Commission but, as a condition precedent to such espousal, must have been presented to it for its interposition by the private claimant.

(b) The question then arises, Has the private claimant in this case put itself in a position where it has the right to present its claim to the Government of the United States for its interposition? The answer to this question depends upon the construction to be given to article 18 of the contract on which the claim rests.

(c) In article 18 of the contract the claimant expressly agreed that in all matters connected with the execution of the work covered by the contract and the fulfillment of its contract obligations and the enforcement of its contract rights it would be bound and governed by the laws of Mexico administered by the authorities and courts of Mexico and would not invoke or accept the assistance of his Government. Further than this it did not bind itself. Under the rules of international law the claimant (as well as the Government of Mexico) was without power to agree, and did not in fact agree, that the claimant would not request the Government of the United States, of which it was a citizen, to intervene in its behalf in the event of internationally illegal acts done to the claimant by the Mexican authorities.

(d) The contract declared upon, which was sought by claimant, would not have been awarded it without incorporating the substance of article 18 therein. The claimant does not pretend that it has made any attempt to comply with the terms of that article, which as here construed is binding on it. Therefore the claimant has not put itself in a position where it may rightfully present this claim to the Government of the United States for its interposition.

(e) While it is true that under Article V of the Treaty the two Governments have agreed "that no claim shall be disallowed or rejected by the Commission by the application of the general principle of international law that the legal remedies must be exhausted as a condition precedent to the validity or allowance of any claim," this provision is limited to claims falling under Article I and therefore rightfully presented by the claimant.

(f) If it were necessary to so construe article 18 of the contract as to bind the claimant not to apply to its Government to intervene diplomatically or otherwise in the event of a denial of justice to the claimant growing out of the contract declared upon or out of any other situation, then this Commission would have no hesitation in holding such a clause void *ab initio* and not binding on the claimant.

(g) The foregoing pertains to the power of the claimant to bind itself by contract. It is clear that the claimant could not under any circumstances bind its Government with respect to remedies for violations of international law.

(h) As the claimant voluntarily entered into a legal contract binding itself not to call as to this contract upon its Government to intervene in its behalf, and as all of its claim relates to this contract, and as therefore it can not present its claim to its Government for interposition or espousal before this Commission, the second ground of the motion to dismiss is sustained.

Decision

25. The Commission decides that the case as presented is not within its jurisdiction and the motion of the Mexican Agent to dismiss it is sustained and the case is hereby dismissed without prejudice to the claimant to pursue his remedies elsewhere or to seek remedies before this Commission for claims arising after the signing of the Treaty of September 8, 1923.

Done at Washington this 31st day of March, 1926.

C. von Vollenhoven, *Presiding Commissioner*
G. Fernández MacGregor, *Commissioner*

THE UNITED STATES OF AMERICA, ON BEHALF OF HARRY ROBERTS, CLAIMANT v. THE UNITED MEXICAN STATES

Claims Commission, United States and Mexico

Opinions of Commissioners (1927), 100

1. This claim is presented by the United States of America in behalf of Harry Roberts, an American citizen who, it is alleged in the Memorial, was

arbitrarily and illegally arrested by Mexican authorities, who held him prisoner for a long time in contravention of Mexican law and subjected him to cruel and inhumane treatment throughout the entire period of confinement.

2. From the Memorial filed by the Government of the United States and accompanying documents, the allegations upon which the claim is based are briefly stated as follows: Harry Roberts, together with a number of other persons, was arrested by Mexican Federal troops on May 12, 1922, in the vicinity of Ocampo, Tamaulipas, Mexico, charged with having taken part in an assault on the house of E. F. Watts, near Ebano, San Luis Potosí, Mexico, on the night of May 5, 1922. The claimant was taken prisoner and brought to Tampico, whence he was taken to Cuidad Valles, San Luis Potosí, where he was held under detention until he was placed at liberty on December 16, 1923, a period of nearly nineteen months. It is alleged that there were undue delays in the prosecution of the trial of the accused which was not instituted within one year from the time of his arrest, as required by the Constitution of Mexico. These delays were brought to the notice of the Government of Mexico, but no corrective measures were taken. During the entire period of imprisonment he was subjected to rude and cruel treatment from which he suffered great physical pain and mental anguish.

3. The United States asks that an idemnity be paid by the Government of Mexico in the sum of $10,000.00 for the wrongful treatment of the accused. It is stated in the Memorial that Roberts earned prior to the time of his arrest $350.00 a month; that he would have earned $6,650.00 during the nineteen months that he was under arrest; and that he spent $1,000.00 in fees paid to a lawyer resident in the United States to assist in obtaining his release. A total indemnity is asked in the sum of $17,650.00 together with a proper allowance of interest.

. . . .

6. The Commission is not called upon to reach a conclusion whether Roberts committed the crime with which he was charged. The determination of that question rested with the Mexican judiciary, and it is distinct from the question whether the Mexican authorities had just cause to arrest Roberts and to bring him to trial. Aliens of course are obliged to submit to proceedings properly instituted against them in conformity with local laws. In the light of the evidence presented in the case the Commission is of the opinion that the Mexican authorities had ample grounds to suspect that Harry Roberts had committed a crime and to proceed against him as they did. The Commission therefore holds that the claim is not substantiated with respect to the charge of illegal arrest.

7. In order to pass upon the complaint with reference to an excessive period of imprisonment, it is necessary to consider whether the proceedings instituted against Roberts while he was incarcerated exceeded reasonable limits within which an alien charged with crime may be held in custody pending the investigation of the charge against him. Clearly there is no definite stand-

ard prescribed by international law by which such limits may be fixed. Doubtless an examination of local laws fixing a maximum length of time within which a person charged with crime may be held without being brought to trial may be useful in determining whether detention has been unreasonable in a given case. The Mexican Constitution of 1917, provides by its Article 20, section 8, that a person accused of crime "must be judged within four months if he is accused of a crime the maximum penalty for which may not exceed two years' imprisonment, and within one year if the maximum penalty is greater." From the judicial records presented by the Mexican Agent it clearly appears that there was a failure of compliance with this constitutional provision, since the proceedings were instituted on May 17, 1922, and that Roberts had not been brought to trial on December 16, 1923, the date when he was released. It was contended by the Mexican Agency that the delay was due to the fact that the accused repeatedly refused to name counsel to defend him, and that as a result of such refusal on his part proceedings were to his advantage suspended in order that he might obtain satisfactory counsel to defend him. We do not consider that this contention is sound. There is evidence in the record that Roberts constantly requested the American Consul at Tampico to take steps to expedite the trial. Several communications were addressed by American diplomatic and consular officers in Mexico to Mexican authorities with a view to hastening the trial. It was the duty of the Mexican Judge under Article 20, section 9, of the Mexican Constitution to appoint counsel to act for Roberts from the time of the institution of the proceedings against him. The Commission is of the opinion that preliminary proceedings could have been completed before the lapse of a year after the arrest of Roberts. Even though it may have been necessary to make use of rogatory letters to obtain the testimony of witnesses in different localities, it would seem that that could have been accomplished at least within six or seven months from the time of the arrest. In any event, it is evident in the light of provisions of Mexican law that Roberts was unlawfully held a prisoner without trial for at least seven months. With respect to this point of unreasonably long detention without trial, the Mexican Agency contended that Roberts was undoubtedly guilty of the crime for which he was arrested; that therefore had he been tried he would have been sentenced to serve a term of imprisonment of more than nineteen months; and that, since, under Mexican law, the period of nineteen months would have been taken into account in fixing his sentence of imprisonment, it can not properly be considered that he was illegally detained for an unreasonable period of time. The Commission must reject this contention, since the Commission is not called upon to pass upon the guilt or innocence of Roberts but to determine whether the detention of the accused was of such an unreasonable duration as to warrant an award of indemnity under the principles of international law. Having in mind particularly that Roberts was held for several months without trial in contravention of Mexican law, the Commission holds that an indemnity is due on the ground of unreasonably long detention.

8. With respect to the charge of ill-treatment of Roberts, it appears from evidence submitted by the American Agency that the jail in which he was kept was a room thirty-five feet long and twenty feet wide with stone walls, earthen floor, straw roof, a single window, a single door and no sanitary accommodations, all the prisoners depositing their excrement in a barrel kept in a corner of the room; that thirty or forty men were at times thrown together in this single room; that the prisoners were given no facilities to clean themselves; that the room contained no furniture except that which the prisoners were able to obtain by their own means; that they were afforded no opportunity to take physical exercise; and that the food given them was scarce, unclean, and of the coarsest kind. The Mexican Agency did not present evidence disproving that such conditions existed in the jail. It was stated by the Agency that Roberts was accorded the same treatment as that given to all other persons, and with respect to the food Roberts received, it was observed in the Answer that he was given "the food that was believed necessary, and within the means of the municipality." All of the details given by Roberts in testimony which accompanies the Memorial with respect to the conditions of the jail are corroborated by a statement of the American Consul at Tampico who visited the jail. Facts with respect to equality of treatment of aliens and nationals may be important in determining the merits of a complaint of mistreatment of an alien. But such equality is not the ultimate test of the propriety of the acts of authorities in the light of international law. That test is, broadly speaking, whether aliens are treated in accordance with ordinary standards of civilization. We do not hesitate to say that the treatment of Roberts was such as to warrant an indemnity on the ground of cruel and inhumane imprisonment.

9. The respondent Government has not denied that, under the Convention of September 8, 1923, acts of authorities of San Luis Potosí may give rise to claims against the Government of Mexico. The Commission is of the opinion that claims can be predicated on such acts.

10. As has been stated, the Commission holds that damages may be assessed on two of the grounds asserted in the American Memorial, namely, (1) excessively long imprisonment—with which the Mexican Government is clearly chargeable for a period of seven months, and (2) cruel and inhumane treatment suffered by Roberts in jail during nineteen months. After careful consideration of the facts of the case and of similar cases decided by international tribunals, the Commission is of the opinion that a total sum of $8,000.00 is a proper indemnity to be paid in satisfaction of this claim.

11. For the reasons stated above the Commission decides that the Government of the United Mexican States must pay to the Government of the United States of America on behalf of Harry Roberts $8,000.00 . . . without interest.

Done at Washington, D.C., this 2nd day of November, 1926.

C. von Vollenhoven, *Presiding Commissioner*
Fred K. Nielsen, *Commissioner*
G. Fernández MacGregor, *Commissioner*

THE UNITED STATES OF AMERICA ON BEHALF OF LAURA M. B. JANES et al., CLAIMANTS v. THE UNITED MEXICAN STATES

CLAIMS COMMISSION, UNITED STATES AND MEXICO

OPINIONS OF COMMISSIONERS (1927), 108

1. Claim is made by the United States of America in this case for losses and damages amounting to $25,000.00, which it is alleged in the Memorial were "suffered on account of the murder, on or about July 10, 1918, at a mine near El Tigre, Sonora, Mexico, of Byron Everett Janes," an American citizen. The claim is presented, as stated in the Memorial, "on behalf of Laura May Buffington Janes, individually and as guardian of her two minor children, Byron Everett Janes, Jr., and Addison M. Janes; and Elizabeth Janes and Catherine Janes."

2. Briefly summarized, the allegations in the Memorial upon which the claim is based are as follows:

3. Byron Everett Janes, for some time prior to and until the time of his death on July 10, 1918, was Superintendent of Mines for the El Tigre Mining Company at El Tigre. On or about July 10, 1918, he was deliberately shot and killed at this place by Pedro Carbajal, a former employee of the Mining Company who had been discharged. The killing took place in the view of many persons resident in the vicinity of the company's office. The local police Comisario was informed of Janes' death within five minutes of the commission of the crime and arrived soon thereafter at the place where the shooting occurred. He delayed for half an hour in assembling his policemen and insisted that they should be mounted. The El Tigre Mining Company furnished the necessary animals and the posse, after the lapse of more than an hour from the time of the shooting, started in pursuit of Carbajal who had departed on foot. The posse failed to apprehend the fugitive. Carbajal remained at a ranch six miles south of El Tigre for a week following the shooting, and it was rumored at El Tigre that he came to that place on two occasions during his stay at the ranch. Subsequently information was received that Carbajal was at a mescal plant near Carrizal, about seventy-five miles south of El Tigre. This information was communicated to Mexican civil and military authorities, who failed to take any steps to apprehend Carbajal, until the El Tigre Mining Company offered a reward, whereupon a local military commander was induced to send a small detachment to Carrizal, which, upon its return, reported that Carbajal had been in this locality, but had left before the arrival of the detachment, and that it was therefore impossible to apprehend him.

4. It is alleged in the Memorial that the Mexican authorities took no proper steps to apprehend and punish Carbajal; that such efforts as were made were lax and inadequate; that if prompt and immediate action had been taken on one occasion there is reason to believe that the authorities would

have been successful; that it was only after a money reward for the capture of Carbajal had been offered that some dilatory steps were taken to apprehend him in a nearby town where he was staying.

5. The Memorial contains allegations with respect to the earning capacity of Janes, the loss suffered by his wife and children because of his death, and their want of means of support.

6. To substantiate the allegations of fact in the Memorial of the United States and the charge that Mexican authorities failed to take effective steps to apprehend the man who shot Janes, there were filed with the Memorial certain affidavits, statements and copies of reports of the American Consul at Tampico to the Department of State from which it appears that the consul addressed the Governor of Sonora, pointing out that the killing of other Americans in mining camps in Sonora in the past had gone unpunished and urging that the Mexican authorities take steps to apprehend Carbajal.

7. In the Answer filed by the Mexican Government it is denied that the Mexican authorities failed to take appropriate steps to arrest and punish Carbajal. Accompanying the Answer is a certified copy of judicial proceedings showing the action taken to investigate the killing of Janes and the orders given with respect to his apprehension. Attention is also called to the use of an armed force to capture the fugitive concerning which information is given in evidence accompanying the Memorial of the United States.

. . . .

9. An affidavit . . . was furnished by L. R. Budrow, the General Manager of the Lucky Tiger Combination Gold Mining Company, an American corporation, owners of the stock of the Tigre Mining Company. In this affidavit Mr. Budrow states that on a visit he made to El Tigre shortly after Janes' death, he obtained the impression that very limited efforts had been made by the authorities at the time to capture Carbajal and that there was a general rumor in El Tigre that Carbajal was seen at that place a few nights after the murder. The affiant attached to his affidavit a report made by R. T. Mishler, Manager of the El Tigre Mining Company on April 11, 1925, with respect to the killing of Janes. The following extract from that report doubtless states in a substantially accurate way the facts with respect to the killing of Janes and the steps taken shortly thereafter by Mexican authorities to apprehend Carbajal:

Mr. Janes had been Mine Superintendent of the Tigre Mine for six months preceding the tragedy.

He had had trouble with a trammer named Pedro Carbajal and had given orders for his discharge.

Mr. Janes and his Assistant, Mr. W. H. Williams, were accustomed to hire new men at the mine office, near the entrance to No. 4 Level which is situated about a hundred yards from the American quarters in the town of El Tigre. Carbajal had requested that he be re-instated in his work on two or three evenings before the tragedy and had been refused.

On the evening of July 10 (1918) at about 3:30 P.M. he again requested work and was again refused.

After Mr. Janes and Mr. Williams had left the office and were about half way up the path leading to their quarters, Carbajal started running after them brandishing a revolver. The Americans heard him when he had almost reached them. Mr. Janes dodged by him and started to run back toward the office. Mr. Williams stood still and said "don't shoot." Carbajal snapped his pistol, point blank at Mr. Williams, but it failed to go off. He then turned and fired at Mr. Janes as he was running down the path. The bullet entered the back near the spin causing Mr. Janes to fall. Carbejal ran up, placed his pistol at Mr. Janes' head and fired a second shot through the brain.

Carbajal then went down the path, threatening with his pistol, a half dozen Mexicans gathered around the office, and disappeared up the cañon.

The Comisario was advised within five minutes after the murder and was on the spot five minutes later. He lost a half hour in getting his policemen together and insisted that they should be mounted. The Company furnished the animals and the posse left Camp about 4:30 P.M. They returned about 7:00 P.M. and reported that they had not seen Carbajal. They were also out the following day, but without results.

It is current talk that Carbajal stayed at a ranch 6 miles south of Tigre, for a week following the murder, and that he came into Tigre on two nights during the week, but it is most difficult to prove this story.

Later word was received that Carbajal was at a mescal (native liquor) plant near Carrizal, 75 miles south of Tigre. Both the civil and military authorities were advised of this report. Finally the Major in charge of the District was persuaded to send a small detachment to Carrizal to investigate, with the promise by the Company of a substantial reward should Carbajal be captured. On their return the detachment reported that the man had left before they arrived.

10. Doubtless the evidence accompanying the Memorial of the United States furnishes accurate information with regard to the killing of Janes, and with regard to the preliminary steps taken looking to the apprehension of Carbajal. The evidence on this first-mentioned point is substantially the same as that given by witnesses whose statements are recorded in the record of judicial proceedings accompanying the Answer. With respect to these preliminary steps, we feel justified in reaching the conclusion that they were inefficient and dilatory. From an examination of the evidence on this point accompanying the Memorial, and more particularly from an examination of the records produced by the Mexican Government, we are constrained to reach the conclusion that there was clearly such a failure on the part of the Mexican authorities to take prompt and efficient action to apprehend the slayer as to warrant an award of indemnity. The grounds for such a conclusion can be shown by a brief statement of what those records reveal as to the action taken by the authorities.

11. It is shown that in the afternoon of July 10, 1918, the killing of Janes was brought to the notice of the local Judge, at El Tigre, and he appointed two men as experts to examine the body of the deceased. On the following day the Judge took the testimony of two persons employed by the El Tigre Mining Company. These men, who were not eyewitnesses of the murder, identified the corpse but gave no testimony concerning the facts of the killing. On July 12, the Judge took the statement of Guillermo A. Williams, an eye-

witness of the killing. On July 13, the Judge took the statement of another eyewitness. On July 14, the statement of another eyewitness was taken.

12. On July 15, five days after the killing of Janes, when statements had been obtained from five men, the Judge, reciting that there had resulted from the proceedings up to that time sufficient merit for the prosecution of the person who killed Janes, issued an order to the Comisario to proceed to the capture of Carbajal.

13. On July 16, the Judge took the statement of another eyewitness to the murder. The Comisario, in reply to the order directing him to proceed to capture Carbajal, stated that, following immediate steps looking to the capture of Carbajal, which were unsuccessful, orders were given by means of warrants to different authorities where it was thought the accused might take refuge. On July 17, all papers in the case were forwarded by the local Judge to the Judge of First Instance of the District. The papers were received by the latter on July 22.

14. On July 30, the Judge of First Instance directed the arrest of Carbajal, and on August 5, a communication in the nature of a circular was sent to the Judges of First Instance in the State of Sonora with the apparent purpose of enlisting their co-operation in the apprehension of the fugitive. This communication recited the facts with regard to the killing of Janes and the preliminary investigations which had been conducted, and requested that the communication be returned to the Judge who transmitted it.

15. The circular was received by the Judge of First Instance at Arizpe on August 13, and by him brought to the notice of the Municipal President on August 14. On August 16, the Municipal President felt himself to be in a position to report that Carbajal was not found "in this section." The circular was evidently not received by the next Judge of First Instance on the route of transmission (the Judge at Sahuaripa) until October 14, about two months after it had reached the Judge of First Instance to whom it was originally transmitted. On October 15, it was sent to the Municipal President. On November 15, the communication was received by the Judge at Cananea and transmitted to the Municipal President on November 16. On December 3, the communication was forwarded to the Judge of First Instance at Nogales, Sonora. It thus is shown that from August 5, the date when the circular was first dispatched, until December 3, a period of about four months, the circular had reached but three judges.

16. In this manner, as shown by the record, the circular proceeded to Judges at Magdalena, Alter, Hermosillo, Ures, Guaymas, and Alamos, being received on February 12, 1919, seven months after the killing of Janes, by the Judge of First Instance at this last mentioned place. Thereupon it was returned to the Judge of First Instance at Moctezuma who had initiated its dispatch.

17. Carbajal, the person who killed Janes, was well known in the community where the killing took place. Numerous persons witnessed the deed. The slayer, after killing his victim, left on foot. There is evidence that a Mexican police magistrate was informed of the shooting within five minutes

after it took place. The official records with regard to the action taken to apprehend and punish the slayer speak for themselves. Eight years have elapsed since the murder, and it does not appear from the records that Carbajal has been apprehended at this time. Our conclusions to the effect that the Mexican authorities did not take proper steps to apprehend and punish the slayer of Janes is based on the record before us consisting of evidence produced by both Governments.

18. The respondent Government has not denied that, under the Convention of September 8, 1923, acts of authorities of Sonora may give rise to claims against the Government of Mexico. The Commission is of the opinion that claims may be predicated on such acts.

Measure of Damages for Failure of Apprehension and Punishment

19. The liability of the Mexican Government being stated there remains to be determined for what they are liable and to what amount. At times international awards have held that, if a State shows serious lack of diligence in apprehending and/or punishing culprits, its liability is a derivative liability, assuming the character of some kind of complicity with the perpetrator himself in rendering the State responsible for the very consequences of the individual's misdemeanor. . . . The reasons upon which such finding of complicity is usually based in cases in which a Government could not possibly have prevented the crime, is that the nonpunishment must be deemed to disclose some kind of approval of what has occurred, especially so if the Government has permitted the guilty parties to escape or has remitted the punishment by granting either pardon or amnesty.

20. A reasoning based on presumed complicity may have some sound foundation in cases of nonprevention where a Government knows of an *intended* injurious crime, might have averted it, but for some reason constituting its liability did not do so. The present case is different; it is one of nonrepression. Nobody contends either that the Mexican Government might have prevented the murder of Janes, or that it acted in any other form of connivance with the murderer. The international delinquency in this case is one of its own specific type, separate from the private delinquency of the culprit. The culprit is liable for having killed or murdered an American national; the Government is liable for not having measured up to its duty of diligently prosecuting and properly punishing the offender. The culprit has transgressed the penal code of his country; the State, so far from having transgressed its own penal code (which perhaps not even is applicable to it), has transgressed a provision of international law as to State duties. The culprit can not be sentenced in criminal or civil procedure unless his guilt or intention in causing the victim's death is proven; the Government can be sentenced once the nonperformance of its judicial duty is proven to amount to an international delinquency, the theories on guilt or intention in criminal and civil law not being applicable here. The damage caused by the culprit is the damage caused to Janes' relatives by Janes' death; the damage caused by the Government's negligence is the damage resulting from the nonpunishment of the murderer.

If the murderer had not committed his delinquency—if he had not slain Janes—Janes (but for other occurrences) would still be alive and earning the livelihood for his family; if the Government had not committed its delinquency—if it had apprehended and punished Carbajal—Janes' family would have been spared indignant neglect and would have had an opportunity of subjecting the murderer to a civil suit. Even if the nonpunishment were conceived as some kind of approval—which in the Commission's view is doubtful—still approving of a crime has never been deemed identical with being an accomplice to that crime; and even if nonpunishment of a murderer really amounted to complicity in the murder, still it is not permissible to treat this derivative and remote liability not as an attenuate form of responsibility, but as just as serious as if the Government had perpetrated the killing with its own hands. The results of the old conception are unsatisfactory in two directions. If the murdered man had been poor, or if, in a material sense, his death had meant little to his relatives, the satisfaction given these relatives should be confined to a small sum, though the grief and the indignity suffered may have been great. On the other hand; if the old theory is sustained and adhered to, it would, in cases like the present one, be to the pecuniary benefit of a widow and her children if a Government did *not* measure up to its international duty of providing justice, because in such a case the Government would repair the pecuniary damage caused by the killing, whereas she practically never would have obtained such reparation if the State had succeeded in apprehending and punishing the culprit.

21. It can not surprise, therefore, that both international tribunals and Governments more than once took a different view, or at least abstained from sustaining the first view. The Commission is not aware of an international award in which the distinction has been set forth with clearness. But the Commission is aware of more than one award and governmental interposition which, in allowing or claiming damages in connection with nonpunishment of a wrongdoer, abstained from linking up the amount of these damages with the loss caused by the act of the individual. In the Glenn Case (Moore, 3138; under the Convention of July 4, 1868) the amount of damages was not connected with any assumption of complicity. In the Lenz Case the Government of the United States, on account of nonpunishment of the culprits, only claimed "a reasonable indemnity" (March 25, 1899; Moore, Digest VI, 794). In the Renton case the same Government for the same reason at the same date pleaded "gross negligence, if not complicity"—therefore leaving the assumption of complicity doubtful—and claimed a lump sum "for the murder of Renton and the failure promptly to apprehend and adequately punish the offenders," a position indicating that the Government did not consider the nonpunishment to be identical with the murder . . . Mr. Hyde, interpreting the policy in this respect of the Government of the United States, says: "The amount of the indemnity requested and obtained appears, at times, to have been out of proportion to the pecuniary loss sustained by the victims or their dependents *in consequence of the laches of the territorial sovereign.*" (Hyde I, 515). And how dangerous inferences from awards which are silent

on presumed complicity are is shown by the fact that, whereas the American Agency quoted the correspondence in the case of the Mexican shepherds as testimony in favor of the older doctrine, a German author quotes it as a striking example of the new one. . . .

22. The answer to the question, which of the two views should be accepted as consistent with international law in its present status, would seem to be suggested by the fact that here we have before us a case of denial of justice, which, but for some convincingly logical reason, should be judged in the same manner as any other case of the same category. Denial of justice, in its broader sense, may cover even acts of the executive and the legislative; in cases of improper governmental action of this type, a nation is never held to be liable for anything else than the damage caused by what the executive or the legislative committed or omitted itself. In cases of denial of justice in its narrower sense, Governments again are held responsible exclusively for what they commit or omit themselves. Only in the event of one type of denial of justice, the present one, a State would be liable not for what it committed or omitted itself, but for what an individual did. Such an exception to the general rule is not admissible but for convincing reasons. These reasons, as far as the Commission knows, never were given. One reason, doubtless lies in the well-known tendency of Governments (Hyde, I, 515; Ralston, 1926, 267) to claim exaggerated reparations for nonpunishment of wrongdoers, a tendency which found its most promising help in a theory advocating that the negligent State had to make good all of the damage caused by the crime itself. But since international delinquencies have been recognized next to individual delinquencies, since damages for denial of justice have been assessed by international tribunals in many other forms, and since exaggerated claims from the Government as against another have been repeatedly softened down as a consequence of arbitral methods, it would seem time to throw off the doctrine dating from the end of the eighteenth century, and return to reality.

23. Once this old theory, however, is thrown off, we should take care not to go to the opposite extreme. It would seem a fallacy to sustain that, if in case of nonpunishment by the Government it is not liable for the crime itself, then it can only be responsible, in a punitive way, to a sister Government, not to a claimant. There again, the solution in other cases of improper governmental action shows the way out. It shows that, apart from reparation or compensation for material losses, claimants always have been given substantial satisfaction for serious dereliction of duty on the part of a Government; and this world-wide international practice was before the Governments of the United States and Mexico when they framed the Convention concluded September 8, 1923. In the Davy case—a case, not of unpunished crime, but of inhuman treatment of a foreigner under the color of administration of justice—the award rightly stated (Ralston, Venzuelan Arbitrations of 1903, p. 412) that "there is left to the respondent Government only one way to signify . . . its desire to remove the stain which rests upon its department of criminal jurisprudence." In the Maal case—a case of attack on a foreigner's

personal dignity by officials—the award rightly stated (Ralston . . . , p. 916):
"The only way in which there can be an expression of regret on the part
of the Government and a discharge of its duty toward the subject of a sovereign and a friendly State is by making an indemnity therefore in the way
of money compensation." The indignity done the relatives of Janes by nonpunishment in the present case is, as that in other cases of improper governmental action, a damage directly caused to an individual by a Government.
If this damage is different from the damage caused by the killing, it is quite
as different from the wounding of the national honor and national feeling
of the State of which the victim was a national.

24. The Commission holds that the wording of Article I of the Convention,
concluded September 8, 1923, mentioning claims for losses or damages
suffered *by persons or* by their properties, is sufficiently broad to cover not
only reparation (compensation) for material losses in the narrow sense, but
also satisfaction for damages of the stamp of indignity, grief, and other similar
wrongs. The Davy and Maal cases quoted are just two among numerous
international cases in which arbitrators held this view. The Commission does
not think lightly of the additional suffering caused by the fact that a Government apparently neglects its duty in cases of so outstanding an importance
for the near relatives of a victim.

25. As to the measure of such a damage caused by the delinquency of
a Government, the nonpunishment, it may be readily granted that its computation is more difficult and uncertain than that of the damage caused by the
killing itself. The two delinquencies being different in their origin, character,
and effect, the measure of damages for which the Government should be
liable can not be computed by merely stating the damages caused by the
private delinquency of Carbajal. But a computation of this character is not
more difficult than computations in other cases of denial of justice such as
illegal encroachment on one's liberty, harsh treatment in jail, insults and
menaces of prisoners, or even nonpunishment of the perpetrator of a crime
which is not an attack on one's property or one's earning capacity, for instance
a dangerous assault or an attack on one's reputation and honor. Not only
the individual grief of the claimants should be taken into account, but a
reasonable and substantial redress should be made for the mistrust and lack
of safety, resulting from the Government's attitude. If the nonprosecution
and nonpunishment of crimes (or of specific crimes) in a certain period
and place occurs with regularity, such nonrepression may even assume the
character of a nonprevention and be treated as such. One among the advantages of severing the Government's dereliction of duty from the individual's
crime is in that it grants an opportunity to take into account several shades
of denial of justice, more serious ones and lighter ones (no prosecution at
all; prosecution and release; prosecution and light punishment; prosecution,
punishment, and pardon), whereas the old system operates automatically
and allows for the numerous forms of such a denial one amount only, that
of full and total reparation.

26. Giving careful consideration to all elements involved, the Commission

holds that an amount of $12,000, without interest, is not excessive as satisfaction for the personal damage caused by the claimants by the nonapprehension and nonpunishment of the murderer of Janes.

Decision

27. On the above grounds, the Commission decides that the Government of the United Mexican States is obligated to pay to the Government of the United States of America $12,000.00 . . . , without interest, on behalf of Laura May Buffington Janes, widow of Byron Everett Janes, and Elizabeth Janes, Catherine Janes, Byron E. Janes, Jr., and Addison M. Janes, their children.

Done at Washington, D.C., this 16th day of November, 1926.

C. van Vollenhoven, *Presiding Commissioner*
G. Fernández MacGregor, *Commissioner*

THE UNITED STATES OF AMERICA ON BEHALF OF THOMAS H. YOUMANS, CLAIMANT v. THE UNITED MEXICAN STATES

Claims Commission, United States and Mexico

Opinions of Commissioners (1927), 150

1. Claim for damages in the amount of $50,000.00 is made in this case by the United States of America against the United Mexican States in behalf of Thomas H. Youmans, the son of Henry Youmans, an American citizen, who, together with two other Americans, John A. Connelly and George Arnold, was killed at the hands of a mob on March 14, 1880, at Angangueo, State of Michoacán, Mexico. The occurrences giving rise to the claim as stated in the Memorial are substantially as follows:

2. At the time when the killing took place Connelly and Youmans were employed by Justin Arnold and Clinton Stephens, American citizens, who were engaged under a contract with a British corporation in driving a tunnel, known as the San Hilario Tunnel, in the town of Angangueo, a place having a population of approximately 7,000 people. The work was being done by Mexican laborers resident in the town under the supervision of the Americans. On the day when these men were killed Connelly, who was Managing Engineer in the construction of the tunnel at Angangueo, had a controversy with a laborer, Cayentano Medina by name, over a trifling sum of about twelve cents which the laborer insisted was due to him as wages. Connelly, considering the conduct of the laborer to be offensive, ejected the latter from the house in which Connelly lived and to which Medina had come to discuss the matter. Subsequently Medina, who was joined by several companions, began to throw stones at Connelly while the latter was sitting in front of

his house and approached the American with a drawn machete. Connelly, with a view to frightening his assailant, fired shots into the air from a revolver. The American having withdrawn into the house, Medina attempted to enter, and his companions followed. Connelly thereupon fired at Medina with a shotgun and wounded him in the legs. Soon the house was surrounded by a threatening mob, which increased until it numbered about a thousand people. Connelly, Youmans, and Arnold, realizing the seriousness of their situation, prepared to defend themselves against the mob. Connelly's employer, Clinton Stephens, on hearing shots, went to the house and learned from Connelly what had happened. Upon Stephens's advice Connelly undertook to surrender himself to the local authorities, but was driven back into the house by the mob. The attack against Connelly when he endeavored to surrender to police authorities was led by Pedro Mondragón, a person styled the *Jefe de Manzana*, with whom Connelly had been on friendly terms. Stephens, followed by a part of the mob, proceeded to the *Casa Municipal* and requested the Mayor, Don Justo Lopez, to endeavor to protect the Americans in the house. The Mayor promptly went to the house, but was unable to quiet the mob. He then returned to his office and ordered José Maria Mora, *Jefe de la Tropa de la Seguridad Publica*, who held the rank of Lieutenant in the forces of the State of Michoacán, to proceed with troops to quell the riot and put an end to the attack upon the Americans. The troops, on arriving at the scene of the riot, instead of dispersing the mob, opened fire on the house, as a consequence of which Arnold was killed. The mob renewed the attack, and while the Americans defended themselves as best they could, several members of the mob approached the house from the rear, where there were no windows, and set fire to the roof. Connelly and Youmans were forced to leave, and as they did so they were killed by the troops and members of the mob. Their bodies were dragged through the streets and left under a pile of stones by the side of the road so mutilated as scarcely to be recognizable. At night they were buried by employees of the Mining Company in its cemetery at Trojes.

3. On the morning following the murder of the Americans, Federal Troops arrived and established order. On March 17, the Government of the State was directed by the President of Mexico to take all possible measures to discover those who were responsible for the murders. Of the thousand or more who made up the mob, court action was instituted against about twenty-nine. Only eighteen of this number were arrested, but the record discloses that several were released on nominal bail, and were not apprehended after their release. Five were condemned to capital punishment, but their sentences were modified. This action of the court was to no avail; when it was taken one had died, and the remaining four left town before they could be arrested. Seven were acquitted. The cases of six others were discontinued, and the charges against the remaining eleven were left open in the year 1887 for prosecution when they might be apprehended.

4. There appears to be no reason to doubt the substantial accuracy of

the allegations in the Memorial upon which the claim is predicated. Some contention is made in the brief filed by the respondent Government to the effect that it is not proved by evidence in the record that the Mexican authorities were chargeable with negligence in the matter of protecting the men who were killed; or that soldiers participated in the assault on the men; or that proper efforts were not made to apprehend and punish the persons participating in the attack. We do not agree with that contention. In reaching conclusions respecting material facts we are confronted by no serious difficulties resulting from absence of or uncertainties in evidence. The riot took place in the day time. About one thousand persons participated. The incidents of the riot were therefore, of course, well known throughout the town. Pertinent facts are fully revealed by information collected and gathered immediately after the riot, by reports from American diplomatic and consular officers in Mexico, and by communications exchanged between the American Legation at Mexico City and the Mexican Foreign Office. Copies of official Mexican judicial records and other records accompany the Mexican Answer and throw considerable light on the character of the various steps taken to bring to justice the guilty persons. It is pertinent to note that counsel for Mexico in oral argument did not challenge the substantial accuracy of the evidence upon which the allegations in the Memorial with respect to the occurrences out of which the claim arises are based. However, mention may be made of some of the principal parts of that evidence.

5. Accompanying a despatch of April 2, 1880, from the American Legation at Mexico City to the Secretary of State at Washington . . . , is a lengthy communication sent to the Legation by Arthur B. Kitchener, Director of the Trojes Mining Company. That communication furnishes detailed information with respect to the incidents of the riot as they are described in the Memorial, and it contains the statement that the writer and Mr. Stephens had "several witnesses who saw the soldiers later on fire on the Americans." With a despatch of May 18, 1880, from the American Minister at Mexico City to the Department of State . . . , was enclosed another lengthy communication addressed by Mr. Kitchener to the Minister in reply to a request made by the latter for information regarding the steps taken by Mexican authorities to bring to justice the persons implicated in the murder. Mr. Kitchener furnishes details with regard to the arrest of a number of persons and the release on what he calls "nominal bail" of some of those who had been taken into custody. He mentioned two cases in which the bondsmen of men so released were common workmen of no property or position; another case in which the bondsman was a shopkeeper. He expresses great dissatisfaction with the manner in which the investigation of the crime was conducted. Evidence which undoubtedly is of much value in furnishing reliable information concerning the facts relative to the riot is found in a report . . . transmitted to the Secretary of State at Washington under date of May 16, 1881, by Mr. David H. Strother, American Consul General at Mexico City, who visited Angangueo for the purpose of making an investigation of the murder.

Although his investigation was made a year after the riot, it seems reasonable to believe that the facts in relation to the tragedy were so vividly in the minds of persons with whom the Consul General came into contact that he was able to obtain accurate and comprehensive information. From the Consul General's report it appears to be clear that he performed his work faithfully and with the sole purpose of ascertaining the truth. The manner in which he proceeded and the sources of his information may be shown to some extent by the following extract from his report:

> In conducting any investigation of the subject in hand I thought it advisable to conceal my official character and the motive of my visit, believing that I could thus obtain a more full and impartial statement of the facts. In this way I gathered evidence from Mexicans, English and Americans, all agreeing in the main facts and confirming generally the statements we have had heretofore. Some of the persons with whom I conversed were well acquainted with all the principal parties concerned and eye witnesses of some of the facts which they narrated. All told their stories clearly and dispassionately and seemed fairly to express the settled convictions of thinking men on events, which occurring more than a year before had been carefully sifted and conclusively established.

6. With respect to the participation of the soldiers in the attack on the Americans the Consul General said:

> It is believed by those who seem well acquainted with all the circumstances, that the appearance of the troops on the ground in behalf of public order, would of itself alone have been sufficient to have quelled the riot and put an end to all further turbulent and unlawful proceedings, but to the astonishment of all, they at once took position and opened fire on the Americans in the house. This act encouraged the mob to reopen their attack with redoubled fury. The soldiers continued their fire until they had expended their ammunition killing George Arnold by a shot through the head.

7. In submitting certain conclusions at the end of the report Mr. Strother stated:

> That there would in all probability have been no fatal results from the riot had it not been for the unaccountable and scandalous conduct of the State troops.

8. The American Minister at Mexico City in his despatch of April 2, 1880, reported to his Government that upon receiving telegraphic information regarding the murder of the Americans at Angangueo, he brought the matter to the attention of the Mexican Foreign Office in a communication of March 16, 1880, in which he expressed the feeling of assurance that such prompt and energetic measures would be taken by the Mexican Government as the circumstances of the case might require. In an instruction of April 20, 1880 . . . , Secretary of State Evarts directed the Minister to express to the Mexican Government, without any reference to the question of private

indemnity in advance of more complete information, the confident expectations on the part of the Government of the United States that nothing would be omitted in the matter of bringing the offenders to the strictest justice according to law. Following the receipt of Consul General Strother's despatch of May 16, 1881, the Department of State, in an instruction dated November 4, 1881 . . . , directed the American Minister at Mexico City to bring to the attention of the Mexican Government claims which had been presented to the Department by relatives of the three murdered men. The Department in this communication emphasized the participation of the troops in the riot and with respect to this point said:

These troops, at a moment when they had the mob under control, and when the complete quelling of the riot seemed an immediate possibility, in utter disregard of the obligations of their office as preservers of the peace and with wanton and deliberate violation of law, opened fire on the three Americans, instantly killing one and joining with the infuriated mob in the inhuman slaughter of the other two who were fleeing for their lives from their burning cabin, which had been deliberately set fire to over their heads.

It seems almost needless to remark that such conduct on the part of soldiers or police, under orders to preserve the peace and protect the lives and property of peaceable inhabitants, on the plainest principles of international law and independent of the treaty stipulations between the two nations, which are contravened by such proceedings, renders the Government in whose service they are employed, justly liable to the Government of the men, whose lives were thus wantonly and needlessly sacrificed.

9. Under date of May 15, 1882, the Mexican Foreign Office addressed a communication to the American Legation denying all liability with respect to these claims . . . . The Minister for Foreign Affairs, Senor Mariscal, challenged the right of the United States to intervene in the cases on the ground that the murdered men had not been matriculated under Mexican law. He asserted that there had been no negligence in the matter of giving protection to the men and denied that evidence had been furnished to prove that soldiers participated in the attack on the Americans. A reply to the Mexican Government's note was made at considerable length by the American Minister in a note of May 27, 1882. . . . In this communication the Minister referred to the participation in the riot by the Mexican officer and the men under his command as follows:

The above-mentioned officer and soldiers under his charge confessed to having done this, alleging in excuse that they feared the vengeance of the mob had they acted otherwise. A number of the towns-people were eye-witnesses of this fact. Amongst others, I may mention the following: Don Guillermo Zercero 2; Diputado de Mineria, an owner of mines and smelting works in the town; Don Justo Lopez, president of the Ayuntamiento of Angangueo; Don Ruperto Menchaca, butcher, well known to the Company and Antonio Alamio, storekeeper, besides many miners and work people of the District. For above a week after the disturbance the above-mentioned Mora and soldiers were still at liberty, but were then taken into custody on evidence against them by Don Justo Lopez.

10. In an instruction of September 4, 1882, the American Minister was informed that the Government of the United States did not deem it to be advisable to press the cases further at that time.

11. The claim made by the United States is predicated on the failure of the Mexican Government to exercise due diligence to protect the father of the claimant from the fury of the mob at whose hands he was killed, and the failure to take proper steps looking to the apprehension and punishment of the persons implicated in the crime. In connection with the contention with respect to the failure of the authorities to protect Youmans from the acts of the mob, particular emphasis is laid on the participation of soldiers which is asserted to be in itself a ground of liability. In behalf of the respondent Government it is contended that the Mexican Government and the Government of the State of Michoacán acted with due diligence in arresting and bringing to justice all persons against whom a reasonable suspicion of guilt existed; that the charge that some State troops participated in the riot is not proved by the evidence; and that, even if it were assumed that the soldiers were guilty of such participation, the Mexican Government should not be held responsible for the wrongful acts of ten soldiers and one officer of the State of Michoacán, who, after having been ordered by the highest official in the locality to protect American citizens, instead of carrying out orders given them acted in violation of them in consequence of which the Americans were killed.

12. We are of the opinion that the contentions advanced by the United States as to liability on the part of the Mexican Government are sustained by the evidence in the record. Without discussing the evidence at length, it may be stated that the Commission is of the opinion that the record shows a lack of diligence in the punishment of the persons implicated in the crime. Annex 3 accompanying the Mexican Answer reveals some interesting information with respect to the prosecution of persons who were arrested. There is not sufficient information before the Commission to warrant us in undertaking to draw any definite conclusions with respect to certain cases in which prisoners were released and other cases in which severe sentences imposed by the court of first instance were mitigated by a higher court. It may be mentioned, however, that this judicial record shows that seventeen prisoners escaped, some of them while they were at liberty on bail. Citations have been made to evidence with respect to participation of soldiers in the killing of the three Americans. We consider that evidence to be ample proof of such conduct on the part of the soldiers, and touching this point it is pertinent to note that evidence has not been adduced to disprove their guilt. It is also pertinent to note touching this point that some soldiers were arrested but were not sentenced. Evidence before the Commission does not disclose whose weapons killed the Americans, but the participation of the soldiers with mem-

bers of the mob is established. It can not properly be said that adequate protection is afforded to foreigners in a case in which the proper agencies of the law to afford protection participate in murder. The claim of *Alfred Jeannotat,* under the Convention of July 4, 1868, between the United States and Mexico, was a case very similar to the present one. Speaking of the participation of soldiers in riotous acts, Umpire Thornton said:

> It has been alleged that in the above-mentioned instance the sacking was done by the released prisoners, and by a mob belonging to the population of the town; but, if it were so, it was the military force commanded by officers who put it in the power of the convicts and incited the mob to assist them in their acts of violence and plunder. It does not appear that without the arrival of the military force, which ought to have protected the peaceable inhabitants of the town, there would have been any inclination to commit such acts of violence. The umpire is therefore of opinion that compensation is due to the claimant from the Mexican Government. (Moore, *International Arbitrations,* Vol. IV, 3673, 3674.)

13. With respect to the question of responsibility for the acts of soldiers there are citations in the Mexican Government's brief of extracts from a discussion of a subcommittee of the League of Nations Committee of Experts for the Progressive Codification of International Law. The passage quoted, which deals with the responsibility of a State for illegal acts of officials resulting in damages to foreigners, begins with a statement relative to the acts of an official accomplished "outside the scope of his competency, that is to say, if he has exceeded his powers." An illegal act of this kind, it is stated in the quotation, is one that can not be imputed to the State. Apart from the question whether the acts of officials referred to in this discussion have any relation to the rule of international law with regard to responsibility for acts of soldiers, it seems clear that the passage to which particular attention is called in the Mexican Government's brief is concerned solely with the question of the authority of an officer as defined by domestic law to act for his Government with reference to some particular subject. Clearly it is not intended by the rule asserted to say that no wrongful act of an official acting in the discharge of duties entrusted to him can impose responsibility on a Government under international law because any such wrongful act must be considered to be "outside the scope of his competency." If this were the meaning intended by the rule it would follow that no wrongful acts committed by an official could be considered as acts for which his Government could be held liable. We do not consider that any of these passages from the discussion of the subcommittee quoted in the Mexican brief are at variance with the view which we take that the action of the troops in participating in the murder at Angangueo imposed a direct responsibility on the Government of Mexico.

14. Citation is also made in the Mexican brief to an opinion rendered by Umpire Lieber in which effect is evidently given to the well-recognized

rule of international law that a government is not responsible for malicious acts of soldiers committed in their private capacity. Awards have repeatedly been rendered for wrongful acts of soldiers acting under the command of an officer. (See for example the claim of *Frederick A. Newton* v. *Mexico,* for the theft of property by Republican troops under Colonel Rijos, and the claim of *A. F. Lanfranco* v. *Mexico,* for the looting of a store at Tehuantepec by armed men under the command of the *Jefe Politico* of that place— Moore, *International Arbitrations,* Vol. III, p. 2997; also the . . . case of the German sentry who at the frontier near Vexaincourt shot from the German side and killed a person on French territory, mentioned by Oppenheim, *International Law,* 3d edit., Vol. I, pp. 218–219; and the opinion of the Commission in the *Falcon claim,* Docket No. 278 [*Opin'ons of Commissioners* (1927), p. 140].) Certain cases coming before the international tribunals may have revealed some uncertainty whether the acts of soldiers should properly be regarded as private acts for which there was no liability on the State, or acts for which the State should be held responsible. But we do not consider that the participation of the soldiers in the murder at Angangueo can be regarded as acts of soldiers committed in their private capacity when it is clear that at the time of the commission of these acts the men were on duty under the immediate supervision and in the presence of a commanding officer. Soldiers inflicting personal injuries or committing wanton destruction or looting always act in disobedience of some rules laid down by superior authority. There could be no liability whatever for such misdeeds if the view were taken that any acts committed by soldiers in contravention of instructions must always be considered as personal acts.

15. The respondent Government has not denied that, under the Convention of September 8, 1923, acts of authorities of Michoacán may give rise to claims against the Government of Mexico. The Commission is of the opinion that claims may be predicated on such acts.

16. Claim is made in this case for damages in the amount of $50,000.00. The Commission is of the opinion that an award may properly be made in the sum of $20,000.00.

Decision

17. The Commission therefore decides that the Government of the United Mexican States must pay to the Government of the United States of America the sum of $20,000.00 . . . without interest on behalf of Thomas H. Youmans.

Done at Washington, D.C., this 23rd day of November, 1926.

C. van Vollenhoven, *Presiding Commissioner.*
Fred K. Nielsen, *Commissioner*
G. Fernández MacGregor, *Commissioner*

U.S. FOREIGN CLAIMS SETTLEMENT COMMISSION DECISION IN
KOERBER CASE (Nationality of Claimants)
[Decision of August 18, 1965]

FOREIGN CLAIMS SETTLEMENT COMMISSION
OF THE UNITED STATES
WASHINGTON, D.C. 20579

IN THE MATTER OF THE CLAIM OF

WALTER LUDWIG KOERBER

Claim No. W- 3917

Decision No. W- 1322

Under Title II of the War Claims Act of 1948, as
amended by Public Law 87-846

Counsel for claimant: Ishmael Sklarew, Esq.

Appeal and objections from a Proposed Decision entered March 3, 1965;
oral hearing requested.

Hearing held May 11, 1965; appearance and argument by Ishmael Sklarew, Esq.;
testimony of WALTER LUDWIG KOERBER.

FINAL DECISION

This claim, for $50,000.00, under Section 202(a), Title II of the
War Claims Act of 1948, as amended, is based upon the asserted destruction
of an apartment building in Berlin, Germany during 1945. Claimant, who
became a citizen of the United States by naturalization on June 7, 1945,
contends that he was a national of the United States within the meaning
of the Act prior to the date of damage by the fact of filing his
declaration of intention to become a citizen on September 22, 1937, by
the naturalization hearing on October 18, 1943, and/or by the taking of
oaths at different times between 1937 and 1943 in connection with the
naturalization procedures.

The term "National of the United States" is defined in Section 201(c),
Title II, of the War Claims Act of 1948, as amended, which reads as
follows:

> ". . . (1) a natural person who is a citizen
> of the United States, (2) a natural person who,
> though not a citizen of the United States, owes
> permanent allegiance to the United States. . . ."
> (76 Stat. 1107 (1962); 50 U.S.C. App. 2017c (1962).)

In its Proposed Decision of March 3, 1965, the Commission found that the destruction of the property occurred during World War II, and that the claimant was not a national of the United States at that time. Accordingly, the Claim was denied under Section 204 of the Act on the ground that the property upon which the claim was based was not owned by a national of the United States at the time of its destruction.

The counsel for claimant contended in his briefs and oral argument that by virtue of the claimant filing a declaration of intention, by having a naturalization hearing, and/or by taking various oaths in connection with the claimant's naturalization proceedings, he became either (1) a de facto citizen of the United States or (2) a person who, though not a citizen of the United States, owes permanent allegiance to the United States.

After full consideration of the briefs filed by counsel for claimant on March 22, April 28, May 6, and May 17, 1965, of the oral argument, of the testimony of the claimant, and on re-examination of the pertinent statutes and authorities, the Commission is constrained to adhere to its position that the claimant was not a "National of the United States" within the meaning of Sections 201(c) and 204 of the Act at the time that his property was destroyed during World War II.

The claimant's contention that he became a de facto citizen is without basis under the law of the United States. The effect of filing a declaration of intention, the naturalization hearing, and the taking of oaths between 1937 and 1943 is determined by the Naturalization Act of 1906 (34 Stat. 596 (1906)), as amended, and the Nationality Act of 1940 (54 Stat. 1137 (1940)).

The declaration of intention was provided in the Naturalization Act of 1906, as amended, to be merely one of the preliminary steps to becoming admitted as a citizen of the United States (34 Stat. 596 (1906); 8 U.S.C. §408). A person was thereafter required to file a petition of naturalization (34 Stat. 597 (1906); 8 U.S.C. §379), take an oath of allegiance (34 Stat. 597-598 (1906); 8 U.S.C. §379), establish his residency, good character, and attachment to the Constitution (45 Stat 1513-1514 (1929); 8 U.S.C. §382), and have a final hearing in a court of competent jurisdiction

376

(34 Stat. 599 (1906); 8 U.S.C. §398). Although the claimant had filed
a declaration of intention and taken an oath that "it is my intention in
good faith to become a citizen of the United States of America" on
September 22, 1937, he had not fulfilled the other statutory requirements
necessary to becoming a citizen of the United States. The courts have
not recognised that substantial compliance with the requirements of the
Act would confer a special status of "de facto citizenship." Until all
the statutory requirements are fulfilled, and an order conferring
citizenship is issued by a court having jurisdiction, the petitioner
remains an alien. (Johnson v. Nickoloff, 52 F. 2d 1074 (9th Cir. (1931);
United States v. Uhl, 211 F. 628 (2d Cir. 1914).)

   To determine the significance of the declaration of intention,
the taking of oaths, and the naturalization hearing subsequent to
October 14, 1940, it is necessary to consider the provisions of the
Nationality Act of 1940, as amended. This Act has substantially the
same statutory requirements for the preliminary steps to becoming a
citizen of the United States as the prior legislation. The mere
filing of a declaration of intention and taking the required oath would
not have conferred citizenship on the person (See 54 Stat. 1153-1158
(1940); 8 U.S.C. §731-736). The hearing on the petition for naturalization (held on October 18, 1943) and the taking of the requisite oath,
were also merely further necessary requirements of the Act which had
to be completed prior to the claimant becoming a United States citizen
(54 Stat. 1556-1557 (1940); 8 U.S.C. §734). Although the claimant filed
a declaration of intention and a petition of naturalization, and took
certain oaths, he did not become a citizen of the United States until
such time as a court of competent jurisdiction entered its order of
naturalization. Until such act occurred, the claimant did not acquire
the status of citizenship, de facto or otherwise, but rather remained
an alien under both the Naturalization Act of 1906 and the Nationality
Act of 1940. (Petition of Moser, 182 F. 2d 734 (2d Cir. 1950), rev'd on
other grounds, 340 U.S. 41 (1951); Johnson v. Nickoloff, supra; United
States v. Uhl, supra).

The second contention of the claimant is that he was a person owing "permanent allegiance" to the United States at the time of the property destruction, within the meaning of Section 201(c)(2) of the Act. The phrase "a natural person who . . . owes permanent allegiance to the United States" is a term of art which has acquired a special meaning whenever used in the legislation of the United States, and refers to only those persons residing in the outlying possessions of the United States. Language substantially identical to that used in Public Law 87-846 was employed in the International Claims Settlement Act of 1949, in the Nationality Act of 1940, and in the Immigration and Nationality Act (66 Stat. 163 (1952).) It was even specifically stated in the legislative history of the International Claims Settlement Act of 1949 that the definition of "nationals" was that employed in the Nationality Act of 1940 (H.R. Rep. No. 770, 81st Cong., 1st Sess. 6 (1949); S.Rep. No. 899, 81st Cong., 1st Sess. 7 (1949)). Due to the continued use of the term "permanent allegiance", and particularly since it was employed in the related claims legislation of the International Claims Settlement Act of 1949, it is concluded that this phrase was intended to have the same meaning in Public Law 87-846 as it had in the prior legislation.

The specialized meaning of the phrase "owes permanent allegiance to the United States" is clearly explained in a comment on the Immigration and Nationality Act, which also applies in this situation to the Nationality Act of 1940:

> "The term 'national of the United States' is used
> in the new law, as it was used in the Nationality
> Act of 1940 [Act Oct. 14, 1940, c. 876, 56 Stat. 1137],
> to designate both a citizen of the United States
> and a person . . . who, though not a citizen of the
> United States, owes permanent allegiance to the
> United States. The only remaining non-citizen
> nationals under the present law are the inhabitants
> of American Samoa and Swains Island, both outlying
> possessions of the United States . . . ." (Besterman,
> Commentary on the Immigration and Nationality Act,
> 8 U.S.C.A., p. 75 (1953).)

The Nationality Act of 1940 specifically provided for a method by which those individuals who owed permanent allegiance to the United States could become citizens, rather than merely remaining as nationals (54 Stat. 1148 (1940); 8 U.S.C. §721). The historical background relative to this section was spelled out by the District Court as follows:

> "The history of Section 30 [now Section 321] is, broadly speaking, as follows: As a result of the Spanish-American War, the United States acquired certain territory, the inhabitants of which were held to be neither aliens nor citizens of the United States. There was then no way in which such persons, whatever their race, could be admitted to citizenship here, because they were not 'aliens'; and [R.S.] section 2169 extended the benefit of our naturalization laws only to aliens. This left a large class of persons, of various races, who owed allegiance to the United States, but who were incapable of obtaining citizenship here, and were more unfavorably treated by our laws than aliens from foreign countries. To meet this situation section 30, supra, was passed."
> (In re Mallari, 239 F. 416, 417 (D. Mass. 1916).)

The status of those persons in the outlying possessions who owe "permanent allegiance" to the United States may be illustrated by the situation in the Philippine Islands. Under the Treaty of Peace between the United States and Spain (30 Stat. 1754; T.S. No. 343), whereby Spain ceded the Philippine Islands to the United States, Congress was authorized to determine the civil rights and political status of the native inhabitants of the Philippine Islands. By Act of Congress of July 1, 1902 (32 Stat. 692 (1902)), it was declared that all inhabitants who were Spanish subjects on April 11, 1899, and then resided in the Islands, and their children born subsequent thereto, "shall be deemed and held to be citizens of the Philippine Islands and as such entitled to the protection of the United States, except such as shall have elected to preserve their allegiance to the Crown of Spain" according to the treaty. The citizens of the Philippine Islands were not aliens. They owed no allegiance to any foreign government, but did owe allegiance to the United States. (Hidemitsu Toyota v. United States, 268 U.S. 402, 410-12 (1925).) Inasmuch as citizens of the Philippines owed no allegiance to the former sovereign, the allegiance to the United States upon the cession of the Philippines to the United States under the terms of the treaty could have been nothing less than permanent. Subsequent enactment of laws dealing with nationality where reference is made to permanent allegiance can be interpreted only as having its origin in the outlying possessions and territories of the United States.

In determining the meaning of this phrase, the Commission has
stated with regard to the Nationality Act of 1940 "that the reference
to non-citizens owing permanent allegiance to the United States involved
persons in certain outlying possessions of the United States, who were
neither aliens nor United States citizens. The history of subsequent
legislation makes clear that . . . a declaration of intention to become
a United States citizen . . . [does] not bring a person within the
ambit of the phrase 'owe permanent allegiance to the United States'."
(See the Claim of Fajbus Zakrzewski, Claim No. PO-1695, 14 FCSC Semiann.
Rep. 198, 199 (Jan.-June 1961).) The same interpretation has been
employed in many other claims arising under the International Claims
Settlement Act of 1949, as amended (See, e.g., Claim of Edward Krukowski,
Claim No. PO-9532; Claim of Szobolcs Szunyogh, Claim No. HUNG-22,185,
10 FCSC Semiann. Rep. 34 (Jan.-June 1959)).

The Supreme Court of the United States has long recognized the
distinction between "temporary" allegiance, which is owed by an alien
living in a friendly country, and "permanent" allegiance, which is owed
by a national of a country. This distinction was defined by Mr. Justice
Field as follows:

> "By allegiance is meant the obligation of fidelity
> and obedience which the individual owes to the
> government under which he lives, or to his sovereign
> in return for the protection he receives. It may
> be an absolute and permanent obligation, or it may
> be a qualified and temporary one. The citizen or
> subject owes an absolute and permanent allegiance
> to his government or sovereign, or at least until,
> by some open and distinct act, he renounces it and
> becomes a citizen or subject of another government
> or another sovereign. The alien, whilst domiciled
> in the country, owes a local and temporary allegiance,
> which continues during the period of his residence."
> (Carlisle v. United States, 83 U.S. 147, 154 (1872).)

On the basis of this distinction, the claimant, an alien, owed temporary,
rather than permanent, allegiance to the United States on taking the
oaths, and on the filing of his declaration of intention and petition for
naturalization.

It is clear from the continued use of the phrase "owe permanent
allegiance to the United States" that this is a term of art applying only

380

to persons in certain outlying possessions of the United States. No
action by claimant could confer upon him this special status. It is
concluded, therefore, that the claimant did not become a "National of
the United States" within the meaning of Sections 201(c) and 204 of the
Act until the order of naturalization was issued by the court on June 7,
1945, which was a time subsequent to the destruction of the property
that is the subject matter of this claim.

In view of the foregoing, the Proposed Decision of March 3, 1965,
is hereby affirmed, and the claim is denied.

Dated at Washington, D. C.,
and entered as the Final
Decision of the Commission.

AUG 18 1965

Edward D. Re, Chairman

Theodore Jaffe, Commissioner

LaVern R. Dilweg, Commissioner

Nature and Measure of Damages. As noted above, the theories behind
claims in international law hold that states are responsible for injuries
caused to aliens by their own acts and the acts of their officials, and
that the injury is to the state and only incidentally to the individuals
involved. Every claims commission must therefore face the problem of
how to assess damages and, to be consistent, it should measure the
damage according to the extent of the injury done by one state to another
state. The question that claims commissions should logically answer is:
how much is the state injured because of the denial of justice? Specifically, in terms of the cases above, what was the extent of the damage
done to the United States by Mexico's failure either to protect the victims
or to prosecute the criminals?

The theory clearly breaks down, however, when commissions come
to making awards. The tribunals invariably tend to assess the losses
to the survivors rather than the damage to the offended state, even
though they often rest their official opinions on the fiction rather than
the fact. The disparity is clearest in the Janes Case in which Mexico

was not at all responsible for the original crime, and the tribunal assessed the grief allegedly caused by the Mexican failure to prosecute the murderer. In fact, Mrs. Janes' grief must really have stemmed from the murder (for which Mexico was not responsible), not the failure to prosecute. In a later case, the Mexican government actually argued that it had no responsibility because the one survivor, who was in a mental institution, could feel no distress, mistrust, or lack of safety when Mexico failed to prosecute. In that case, however,[63] a Mexican police official had been implicated in the original crime, and the Commission awarded money to the United States on those grounds. Neither case, therefore, answers the question of whether an award would be forthcoming if an official had not been implicated and there had been no survivor able to feel pain.[64] Awards thus rest on the theory that a state, being delinquent, in effect has condoned the crime and should therefore pay a penalty. But the awards in fact rest in part on the need to compensate the individual victim (not the state) and sometimes in part to punish the offender.

One way of removing many of the conflicting theoretical and practical difficulties inherent in the law of claims would be to permit individuals to come before a special international tribunal to present claims against states. No states are at present willing to advocate such an approach to settling claims, although prominent international lawyers have advanced such proposals.[65] A preferred means of reducing the conflicts and ambiguities is to remove all the claims questions from the mixed international commissions and to give them to national claims commissions, which apply international law standards. These municipal bodies "stamped with the features of internationality,"[66] award money to claimants out of lump sums negotiated between their government and the government against whom they have the claim. The national claims commissions save the individual claimants considerable difficulty, and remove the individual claim from the realm of diplomacy. In putting an end to the fiction that an injury to one of its nationals indirectly injures the state and, in assuming instead that it is desirable to eliminate conflicts among states expeditiously, the national commissions put the claims theory on a sounder basis. They will still, however, have to determine the extent to which states were responsible for the injury and the amounts owed to the aggrieved individuals. And as states come

---

[63] William T. Way Case, U.S. v. Mexico, Opinion of Commissioners, II, 94.

[64] See Frederick Sherwood Dunn, *Protection of Nationals* (Baltimore: Johns Hopkins Press, 1932).

[65] See, for instance, Louis B. Sohn, "Proposals for the Establishment of a System of International Tribunals," Martin Domke, ed., *International Trade Arbitration* (New York: American Arbitration Association, 1958), pp. 65–73.

[66] *Special Report of William E. Fuller* (Washington: U.S. Government Printing Office, 1907) p. 112.

to use them more and more, they will build up a case law of their own, drawing, however, upon the earlier international claims cases.[67]

THE LUSITANIA CASES

UNITED STATES—GERMANY, MIXED CLAIMS COMMISSION, 1923

CONSOLIDATED EDITION OF DECISIONS (1925), 17

PARKER, Umpire. These cases grew out of the sinking of the British ocean liner *Lusitania*, which was torpedoed by a German submarine off the coast of Ireland May 7, 1915, during the period of American neutrality. Of the 197 American citizens aboard the *Lusitania* at that time, 69 were saved and 128 lost. . . . liability for losses sustained by American nationals was assumed by the Government of Germany through its note of February 4, 1916. . . .

. . . Germany is financially obligated to pay to the United States all losses suffered by American nationals, stated in terms of dollars, where the claims therefor have continued in American ownership, which losses have resulted from death or from personal injury or from loss of, or damage to, property, sustained in the sinking of the *Lusitania*.

This finding disposes of this group of claims, save that there remain to be considered (1) issues involving the nationality of each claimant affecting the Commissioner's jurisdiction and (2) the measure of damages to be applied to the facts of each case.

. . . .

It is a general rule of both the civil and the common law that every invasion of private right imports an injury and that for every such injury the law gives a remedy. Speaking generally, that remedy must be commensurate with the injury received. It is variously expressed as "compensation," "reparation," "indemnity," "recompense," and is measured by pecuniary standards, because, says Grotius, "money is the common measure of valuable things."

In death cases the right of action is for the loss sustained by the *claimants*, not by the estate. The basis of damages is, not the physical or mental suffering of deceased or his loss or the loss to his estate, but the losses resulting to claimants from his death. The enquiry then is: What amount will compensate claimants for such losses?

Bearing in mind that we are not concerned with any problems involving the punishment of a wrongdoer but only with the naked question of fixing the amount which will compensate for the wrong done, our formula expressed in general terms for reaching that end is: Estimate the amounts (a) which the decedent, had he not been killed, would probably have contributed to the claimant, add thereto (b) the pecuniary value to such claimant of the deceased's personal services in claimant's care, education, or supervision, and also add (c) reasonable compensation for such mental suffering or shock, if any, caused by the violent severing of family ties, as claimant may actually have sustained by reason of such death. The sum of these estimates, reduced

---

[67] For a discussion of the national claims commissions, see Richard B. Lillich, *International Claims: Their Adjudication by National Claims Commissions* (Syracuse: Syracuse University Press, 1962).

to its present cash value, will generally represent the loss sustained by claimant.

In making such estimates there will be considered, among other factors, the following:

(a) The age, sex, health, condition and station in life, occupation, habits of industry and sobriety, mental and physical capacity, frugality, earning capacity and customary earnings of the deceased and the uses made of such earnings by him;

(b) The probable duration of the life of deceased but for the fatal injury, in arriving at which standard life-expectancy tables and all other pertinent evidence offered will be considered;

(c) The reasonable probability that the earning capacity of deceased, had he lived, would either have increased or decreased;

(d) The age, sex, health, condition and station in life, and probable life expectancy of each of the claimants;

(e) The extent to which the deceased, had he lived, would have applied his income from his earnings or otherwise to his personal expenditures from which claimants would have derived no benefits;

(f) In reducing to their present cash value contributions which would probably have been made from time to time to claimants by deceased, a 5 % interest rate and standard present-value tables will be used;

(g) Neither the physical pain nor the mental anguish which the deceased may have suffered will be considered as elements of damage;

(h) The amount of insurance on the life of the deceased collected by his estate or by the claimants will not be taken into account in computing the damages which claimants may be entitled to recover;

(i) No exemplary, punitive, or vindictive damages can be assessed.

The foregoing statement of the rules for measuring damages in death cases will be applied by the American Agent and the German Agent and their respective counsel in the preparation and submission of all such cases. The enumeration of factors to be taken into account in assessing damages will not be considered as exclusive of all others. When either party conceives that other factors should be considered, having a tendency either to increase or decrease the *quantum* of damages, such factors will be called to the attention of the Commission in the presentation of the particular case.

Most of the elements entering into the rules here expressed for measuring damages, and the factors to be taken into account in applying them, are so obviously sound and firmly established by both the civil and common law authorities as to make further elaboration wholly unnecessary. As counsel for Germany, however, very earnestly contends that the mental suffering of a claimant does not constitute a recoverable element of damage in death cases, and also contends that life insurance paid claimants on the happening of the death of deceased should be deducted in estimating the claimant's loss, we will state the reasons why we are unable to adopt either of these contentions. The American counsel, with equal earnestness, contends that exemplary, punitive, and vindictive damages should be assessed against Germany for the use and benefit of each private claimant. For the reasons hereinafter set forth at length this contention is rejected.

Mental Suffering.—The legal concept of damages is judicially ascertained compensation for wrong. The compensation must be adequate and balance as near as may be the injury suffered. In many tort cases, including those for personal injury and for death, it is manifestly impossible to compute mathematically or with any degree of accuracy or by the use of any precise formula the damages sustained, involving such inquiries as how long the deceased would probably have lived but for the fatal injury; the amount he would have earned, and of such earnings the amount he would have contributed to each member of his family; the pecuniary value of his supervision over the education and training of his children; the amount which will reasonably compensate an injured man for suffering excruciating and prolonged physical pain; and many other inquiries concerning elements universally recognized as constituting recoverable damages. This, however, furnishes no reason why the wrongdoer should escape repairing his wrong or why he who has suffered should not receive reparation therefor measured by rules as nearly approximating accuracy as human ingenuity can devise. To deny such reparation would be to deny the fundamental principle that there exists a remedy for the direct invasion of every right.

Mental suffering is a fact just as real as physical suffering, and susceptible of measurement by the same standards. The interdependency of the mind and the body, now universally recognized, may result in a mental shock producing physical disorders. But quite apart from any such result, there can be no doubt of the reality of mental suffering, of sickness of mind as well as sickness of body, and of its detrimental and injurious effect on the individual and on his capacity to produce. Why, then, should he be remediless for this injury? The courts of France under the provisions of the Code Napoleon have always held that mental suffering or *préjudice morale* is a proper element to be considered in actions brought for injuries resulting in death. A like rule obtains in several American States, including Louisiana, South Carolina, and Florida. The difficulty of measuring mental suffering or loss of mental capacity is conceded, but the law does not refuse to take notice of such injury on account of the difficulty of ascertaining its degree.

On careful analysis it will be found that decisions announcing a contrary rule by some of the American courts are measurably influenced by the restrictions imposed by the language of the statutes creating the right of action for injuries resulting in death. As hereinafter pointed out, these very restrictions have in some instances driven the courts to permit the juries to award as exemplary damages what were in truth compensatory damages for mental suffering, rather than leave the plaintiff without a remedy for a real injury sustained.

Mental suffering to form a basis of recovery must be real and actual, rather than purely sentimental and vague.

Insurance.—Counsel for Germany insist that in arriving at claimants' net loss there should be deducted from the present value of the contributions which the deceased would probably have made to claimants had he lived all payments made to claimants under policies of insurance on the life of deceased. The contention is opposed to all American decisions and the more recent decisions of the English courts. The various reasons given for these decisions are, however, for the most part inconclusive and unsatisfactory.

But it is believed that the contention here made by the counsel for Germany is based upon a misconception of the essential nature of life insurance and the relations of the beneficiaries thereto.

Unlike marine and fire insurance, a life insurance contract is not one of indemnity, but a contract absolute in its terms for the payment of an amount certain on the happening of an event certain—death—at a time uncertain. The consideration for the claimants' contract rights is the premiums paid. Those premiums are based upon the risk taken and are proportioned to the amount of the policy. The contract is in the nature of an investment made either by, or in behalf of, the beneficiaries. The claimants' rights under the insurance contracts existed prior to the commission of the act complained of, and prior to the death of deceased. Under the terms of the contract these rights were to be exercised by claimants upon the happening of a certain event. The mere fact that the act complained of hastened that event can not inure to Germany's benefit, as there was no uncertainty as to the happening of the event, but only as to the *time* of its happening. Sooner or later payment must be made under the insurance contract. Such payment of insurance, far from springing from Germany's act, is entirely foreign to it. If it be said that the acceleration of death secures to the claimants now what might otherwise have been paid to others had deceased survived claimants, and that therefore claimants may *possibly* have benefited through Germany's act, the answer is that the law will not for the benefit of the wrongdoer enter the domain of speculation and consider the probability of probabilities in order to offset an absolute and certain contract right against the uncertain damages flowing from a wrong.

Use of Life-Expectancy and Present-Value Tables.—Ordinarily the facts to which must be applied the rules of law in measuring damages in death cases lie largely in the future. It results that, absolute knowledge being impossible, the law of probabilities and of averages must be resorted to in estimating damages, and these preclude the possibility of making any precise computations or mathematical calculations. As an aid—but solely as an aid—in estimating damages in this class of cases, the Commission will consider the standard life-expectancy and present-value tables. These will be used not as absolute guides but in connection with other evidence, such as the condition of the health of deceased, the risks incident to his vocation, and any other circumstances tending to throw light on the probable length of his life but for the act of Germany complained of. To the extent that happenings subsequent to the death of deceased make certain what was before uncertain, to such extent the rules of probabilities will be discarded.

Neither will we lose sight of the fact that life tables are based on statistics of the length of life of individuals, not upon the duration of their physical or mental capacity or of their earning powers. In using such tables it will be borne in mind that the present value of the probable earnings of deceased depends on many more unknowable contingencies than does the present value of a life annuity or dower. Included among these contingencies are possible and probable periods of illness, periods of unemployment even when well, and various degrees of disability arising from gradually increasing age. The weight to be given to such tables will, therefore, be determined by the Commission in the light of the facts developed in each particular case.

Exemplary Damages.—American counsel with great earnestness insists that exemplary, or, as they are frequently designated, punitive and vindictive, damages should be assessed by this Commission against Germany in behalf of private claimants. Because of the importance of the question presented the nature of exemplary damages will be examined and the Commission's reasons for declining to assess such damages will be fully stated.

. . . .

In our opinion the words exemplary, vindictive, or punitive as applied to *damages* are misnomers. The fundamental concept of "damages" is satisfaction, reparation for a *loss* suffered; a judicially ascertained *compensation* for wrong. The remedy should be commensurate with the loss, so that the injured party may be made whole. The superimposing of a penalty in addition to full compensation and naming it damages, with the qualifying word exemplary, vindictive, or punitive, is a hopeless confusion of terms, inevitably leading to confusion of thought. Many of the American authorities lay down the rule that where no actual damage has been suffered no exemplary damages can be allowed, giving as a reason that the latter are awarded, not because the *plaintiff* has any right to recover them, but because the *defendant* deserves punishment for his wrongful acts; and that, as the plaintiff cannot maintain an action merely to inflict punishment upon a supposed wrongdoer, if he has no cause of action independent of a supposed right to recover exemplary damages, he has no cause of action at all. It is apparent that the theory of the rule is not based upon any right of the plaintiff to receive the award assessed against the defendant, but that the defendant should be punished. The more enlightened principles of government and of law clothe the state with the sole power to punish but insure to the individual full, adequate, and complete compensation for a wrong inflicted to his detriment.

. . . .

But it is not necessary for this Commission to go to the length of holding that exemplary damages cannot be awarded in *any* case by *any* international arbitral tribunal. A sufficient reason why such damages cannot be awarded by *this* Commission is that it is without the power to make such awards under the terms of its charter—the Treaty of Berlin. It will be borne in mind that this is a "Treaty between the United States and Germany Restoring Friendly Relations"—a Treaty of Peace. Its terms negative the concept of the imposition of a penalty by the United States against Germany, save that the undertaking by Germany to make reparation to the United States and its nationals as stipulated in the Treaty may partake of the nature of a penalty.

Part VII of the Treaty of Versailles (Articles 227 to 230, inclusive) deals with "Penalties." It is significant that these provisions were not incorporated in the Treaty of Berlin.

In negotiating the Treaty of Peace, the United States and Germany were of course dealing directly with each other. Had there been any intention on the part of the United States to exact a penalty either as a punishment or as an example and a deterrent, such intention would have been clearly expressed in the Treaty itself; and, had it taken the form of a money payment, would have been claimed by the Government of the United States on its own behalf and not on behalf of its nationals. As to such nationals, care was taken to provide for full and adequate "indemnities," "reparations," and "satisfaction" of their claims for losses, damages, or injuries suffered by them. While under that portion of the Treaty of Versailles which has by reference been incorporated in the Treaty of Berlin, Germany "accepts" responsibility for all loss and damage to which the United States and its nationals have been subjected as a consequence of the war, nevertheless the United States frankly recognizes the fact "that the resources of Germany are not adequate . . . to make complete reparation for all such loss and damage," but requires that Germany make "compensation" for specified damages suffered by American nationals. For the enormous cost to the Government of the United States in prosecuting the war no claim is made against Germany. No claims against Germany are being asserted by the Government of the United States on account of pensions paid, and compensation in the nature of pensions paid, to naval and military victims of the war and to their families and dependents. In view of this frank recognition by the Government of the United States of Germany's inability to make to it full and complete reparation for all of the consequences of the war, how can it be contended that there should be read into the Treaty an obligation on the part of Germany to pay penalties to the Government of the United States for the use and benefit of a small group of American nationals for whose full and complete compensation for losses sustained adequate provision has been made?

. . . .

The treaty is one between two sovereign nations—a Treaty of Peace. There is no place in it for any vindictive or punitive provisions. Germany must make compensation and reparation for all losses falling within its terms sustained by American nationals. That compensation must be full, adequate, and complete. To this extent Germany will be held accountable. But this Commission is without power to impose penalties for the use and benefit of private claimants when the Government of the United States has exacted none.

This decision in so far as applicable shall be determinative of all cases growing out of the sinking of the Steamship *Lusitania*. All awards in such cases shall be made as of this date and shall bear interest from this date at the rate of five per cent (5%) per annum.

Extradition

Because states have a mutual interest in prosecuting crime, extradition (the surrender of an alleged criminal by one state to another) is a common practice among them. During the nineteenth century, states signed many bilateral agreements providing for extradition, for as travel and communication became easier, so too it became easier to flee across a frontier to escape the law. Without some treaty, there is no basis in law for extradition, and some alleged criminals have taken advantage of that fact to escape the jurisdiction of a prosecuting state.

The early extradition treaties listed the crimes for which the contracting states agreed to grant extradition. This *list system* proved unsatisfactory, however, since there were inevitably crimes for which contracting states were willing to extradite, but which they had neglected to list. To overcome errors of omission, states began to employ the more inclusive *general system,* whereby the treaties provided for extradition in cases of the more serious crimes—for example, crimes carrying a prison penalty of over two years.

Extradition treaties customarily provide for extradition only if the alleged criminal has committed his crime on the territory of one of the contracting states; that is to say, they acknowledge jurisdiction only on the territorial principle. Moreover, states agree that they will try persons only for the crimes for which they are extradited (the *specialty* principle) and only if the crime is recognized as a crime in both countries (the *double criminality* rule) and if the person has not already been tried for the crime (the *non bis idem* rule).

Some states do not extradite their own nationals (among them, France, Germany, and Italy). The United States has extradited its own nationals on some occasions and, on other occasions, it has refused to do so.

In determining whether to allow a state to extradite an alleged criminal under an extradition treaty, the courts of a contracting state have to determine whether grounds for extradition exist. They are not supposed to try the case, but merely to determine whether, on the face of it, there is sufficient evidence to justify a trial. The line between assessing the weight of evidence and judging the alleged crime is not always easy to determine. In the Case of Samuel Insull in 1933, for instance, a Greek Court refused to extradite Insull, who was wanted in the United States for violating the income tax laws, because "there is not sufficient evidence to justify the commitment for trial of the accused."[68] The United States protested that the Greek Government had actually attempted to try the case and had thereby exceeded its authority, especially since Greece admitted that Insull had committed the acts with which he was charged and that the acts were crimes under the laws of both Greece and the United States. The United States was so incensed by the behavior of the Greek court that it moved to terminate the extra-

[68] See the translation in the *American Journal of International Law,* XXVIII (1934), 362–372. See also James Hyde, "The Extradition Case of Samuel Insull," *ibid.,* 307–312.

dition treaty between the two countries, relenting only in 1937, when the two governments signed a protocol stating explicitly that Article 1 of the Treaty of Extradition of May 6, 1931, did not signify "that the court or magistrate is authorized to determine the question of the guilt or innocence of the person charged."[69]

JIMENEZ v. U.S. DISTRICT COURT FOR THE SOUTHERN DISTRICT OF FLORIDA

84 S.Ct. 14 (1963)

Background. Marcos Perez Jimenez, former Head of State of the Republic of Venezuela, applied to former Supreme Court Justice Arthur Goldberg for a stay of extradition pending review of a jurisdictional question and his argument that he should be released persuant to 18 U.S.C. Sec. 3188:

> Whenever any person who is committed for rendition to a foreign government to remain until delivered up in pursuance of a requisition, is not so delivered up and conveyed out of the United States within two calendar months after such commitment, over and above the time actually required to convey the prisoner from the jail to which he was committed, by the readiest way, out of the United States, any judge of the United States, or of any State, upon application made to him by or on behalf of the person so committed, and upon proof made to him that reasonable notice of the intention to make such application has been given to the Secretary of State, may order the person so committed to be discharged out of custody, unless sufficient cause is shown to such judge why such discharge ought not to be ordered. [9 Stat. 302, as amended 62 Stat. 824.]

Venezuela first moved to extradite Jimenez in August 1959, so that he could stand trial on charges of murder, embezzlement, and related financial crimes. A U.S. District Judge in Florida, in a hearing held to determine whether the evidence justified extradition, found that the evidence failed "to show the necessary direct connection between the defendant and the commission of such murders" [see Petition for writ of certiorari. No. 958, Oct. Term, 1962, for text of report] but he found it sufficient to justify trial for embezzlement and related financial crimes. He also noted that these crimes were encompassed in the extradition treaty and were not political in character.

On June 16, 1961, Jimenez was committed to the custody of a U.S. Marshal to await action by the Secretary of State, who, after a long series of legal moves by Jimenez had concluded, issued a warrant of surrender on August 12, 1963, accompanied by the following letter:

Excellency:

I have the honor to refer to note No. 320, dated August 5, 1961, in which the Government of Venezuela formally requested the extradition of Marcos Perez

[69] Ex. Ag. Series No. 114 (see Hackworth, V, 315).

Jimenez for the crimes of embezzlement or criminal malversation, receiving money or valuable securities knowing the same to have been unlawfully obtained, and fraud or breach of trust, as specified in paragraphs 14, 18 and 20 of Article II of the Extradition Treaty of 1922, between our two countries.

As you are aware, an extradition hearing was held pursuant to the provisions of Section 3184, Title 18, United States Code, at the conclusion of which the Honorable George W. Whitehurst, United States Distict Judge for the Southern District of Florida, sitting as extradition magistrate, found that the evidence presented by your Government showed probable cause to believe Marcos Perez Jimenez guilty of the above-mentioned crimes, but that insufficient evidence had been presented to warrant his extradition on the charges of complicity in murder with which he was also charged in Venezuela. Habeas Corpus proceedings brought to challenge the decision of the extradition magistrate resulted in his decision being upheld by the United States District Court for the Southern District of Florida and by the United States Court of Appeals for the Fifth Circuit. On June 17, 1963, the United States Supreme Court denied the petition of Marcos Perez Jimenez for a rehearing on that Court's denial of his petition for certiorari to review the decision of the Court of Appeals.

I have taken note of your Government's assurances, contained in your note No. 1396, dated July 22, 1963, that careful security arrangements have been made by your Government to eliminate any risk of physical harm to Marcos Perez Jimenez should he be extradited, that he would be tried only for those offenses for which his extradition is granted, that he would be given all the rights accorded an accused under the laws of your country, including the right to full and effective defense, and that he would have the right to adequate legal counsel of his own choice.

Accordingly, there is enclosed my warrant directing the United States Marshal for the Southern District of Florida or any other public officer or person having charge or custody of Marcos Perez Jimenez to surrender and deliver him up to such person or persons as may be duly authorized by your Government to receive him in order that he may be returned to Venezuela for trial for the crimes of embezzlement or criminal malversation, receiving money or valuable securities knowing the same to have been unlawfully obtained, and fraud or breach of trust. The specific offenses which are considered, in this case, to be encompassed by the crimes and those for which extradition is granted are those charges set forth in paragraphs 15.B, 15.C and 15.D (3) of the Second Amended Complaint for Extradition filed March 8, 1960, in the District Court of the United States for the Southern District of Florida, Miami Division, by Manuel Aristeguieta in case No. 9425-M-Civil entitled *Manuel Aristeguieta, Consul General of the Republic of Venezuela, Plaintiff,* v. *Marcos Perez Jimenez, Defendant.*

Inasmuch as the extradition magistrate found sufficient evidence of criminality of Marcos Perez Jimenez only with respect to these crimes, his extradition is granted on the condition, specified in Article XIV of the Extradition Treaty of 1922, that he shall be tried only for those crimes.

Accept, Excellency, the renewed assurances of my highest consideration.

/s/ Dean Rusk

His Excellency
    Dr. Enrique Tejera-Paris,
        Ambassador of Venezuela.
Enclosure:
    Warrant of surrender.

[Justice Goldberg handed down this opinion, in which he said that he was:] mindful that this is the first time in our history a former head of state has been extradited for offenses allegedly committed during his incumbency. I am equally aware and respectful of the long tradition, reflected in our treaties and statutes, against extradition for political offenses. The extraditing magistrate determined, however, that the crimes for which petitioner is being extradited were not of "a political character" and that a solemn treaty between the United States and Venezuela requires extradition for "Embezzlement . . . by public officers."[70] A petition for a writ of habeas corpus challenging this determination was dismissed by a district judge. A Court of Appeals painstakingly reviewed this issue and concluded that the crimes in question were not political. This Court denied certiorari and rehearing, thereby leaving the judgment of the Court of Appeals undisturbed. The alleged political nature of the crimes does not form the basis for the present application; the contention here is that 18 U.S.C. § 3188 requires petitioner's release because he was not delivered to the extraditing government within two months of his commitment.

Petitioner construes the two-month period in § 3188 to run from the time of the original commitment order of the extraditing magistrate, not from the time his legal rights were finally determined by this Court's denial of certiorari and rehearing. From this construction, one of two results must follow: If the Government were prevented from removing him during the pendency of review proceedings, then the accused could readily frustrate this country's treaty obligations simply by invoking such proceedings for two months; if, on the other hand, the Government were permitted to remove him while proceedings were pending, then the statute would effectively foreclose review of extradition orders. A construction which compels a choice between such alternatives is untenable.

Section 3188, originally enacted in 1848[71] as part of a general scheme governing extradition from this country, was intended to implement our treaty obligations "without delay and the danger of a denial of justice" to the accused.[72] Its purpose was to ensure prompt action by the extraditing government as well as by this government so that the accused would not suffer incarceration in this country or uncertainty as to his status for long periods of time through no fault of his own.

The procedural history of this litigation leaves no doubt that the Government of Venezuela has acted with diligence to effect petitioner's extradition. The United States Government has acted with equal diligence, consistent with its duty to protect the rights of all within its jurisdiction by affording them recourse to its courts. Petitioner having sought review of the extradition order, the Secretary of State properly deferred execution of the surrender warrant until petitioner's claims were fully adjudicated. This case is unlike *In re Dawson*, 101 F. 253 (C.C. N.Y.). There, "petitioner had interposed

[70] [43 stat. 1698 (1922).]
[71] 9 Stat. 302.
[72] Cong. Globe, 30 Cong., 1st Sess. 868 (1948).

no captious objection to the proceeding"; the two-month delay was caused solely by "the leisurely movements" of the extraditing government which had acted without "any measure of diligence" upon being informed of this country's readiness to deliver up the accused. Here, the delays resulted from petitioner's pursuit of legal remedies, not from the dilatory actions of either party to the extradition treaty.

The common-sense reading of § 3188 is that where as here, the accused has instituted and pursued review of his extradition order, the two-month period runs from the time his claims are finally adjudicated, not from the time of the original commitment order he has been challenging. In any event, since the delays were attributable to the proceedings prosecuted by petitioner, there certainly was "sufficient cause" for the delay, within the intended meaning of § 3188. Thus petitioner's contention regarding the two-month limitation is without merit. [Justice Goldberg then discussed the jurisdictional question raised by Jimenez and found it, too, to be without merit. He denied Jimenez's application for a stay of extradition, and Jimenez was taken from the United States to stand trial in Venezuela—both on August 16, 1963.]

United Nations and European Developments

Attempts to use international law to protect the rights of individuals have proceeded under the aegis of the United Nations and the Council of Europe.

In the United Nations, the third General Assembly adopted the Universal Declaration of Human Rights, which is not a statement of law, but a standard toward which all nations may aspire. As such, it has exhortatory, but no legal force. Beyond that, states labored from 1948 to 1966 to draft two Covenants of Human Rights.[73] Lawyers have attempted to cite these United Nations efforts in defending the rights of their clients. United States courts have been careful not to attribute to the United Nations Charter, the Declaration, and the draft Covenants the force of law. They have thus avoided the technical issue on which so much opposition to these documents rests—namely, that the Covenants (like the Genocide Convention) could become devices for circumventing the Constitution of the United States.[74]

[73] Originally, the U.N. Commission on Human Rights attempted to draft a single Covenant, but in 1951, the General Assembly asked the Commission to separate the legal and political rights from the economic and social. By separating the two draft documents, the delegates hoped to attract the maximum support from governments that might be free to sign one but not the other. In 1953, the United States indicated that it would not sign either document and proposed that the United Nations abandon its attempt to draft the Covenants and concentrate instead on educational and legal research into common problems of human rights. The United Nations adopted the United States program in addition, but not instead of, its own program. See *D.S.B.*, XXVIII (1953), 579–582, 842–848.
[74] See Chap. VII for the discussion of the status of treaties under the United States Constitution. For texts of Convenants, see G.A. Res. 2200 (XXI), 1966.

In actual fact, the United States can safeguard its legitimate interests and still ratify the Covenants. The Covenants themselves contain ample safeguards for the United States. Thus the obligations under the Covenant on Economic, Social and Cultural Rights are, in Article 2, limited to progressive implementation and will cause no difficulties. Moreover, each Covenant, in paragraph 2 of Article 5, provides that in no case can these pacts in any way restrict the rights of a citizen of a state under its Constitution or laws. The Covenants can provide only additional guarantees; they cannot diminish existing rights. These provisions should, according to supporters of the Covenants, make ratification possible and reservations unnecessary. Reservations might be necessary, however, because of the federal-state relationship in the United States, since both Covenants provide that they will apply throughout Federal states. In the United States, since all powers not specifically delegated to the federal government are, under the tenth amendment to the Constitution, reserved to the states, some reservation to protect this constitutional balance might be necessary.

To assist in implementing the Covenant on Civil and Political Rights, the pact envisages a Human Rights Committee of 18 persons with special competence in human rights, elected as individuals by representatives of the parties. The parties would then report on measures they have taken to implement the Covenant and on difficulties encountered in implementing it. After studying these reports, the Committee is supposed to transmit "general comments" on them to the parties and, if it wishes, to the Economic and Social Council.

In addition, by making a separate declaration, a state party may recognize the competence of the Committee to consider communications from one party claiming that another party is not fulfilling its obligations under the Covenant. Ten states would have to file such declarations to bring the provisions into force, and the communications would be received only from and about parties who had filed the declarations, and only after domestic remedies had been exhausted. The Committee would deal with such matters only at closed meetings and offer its good offices to try to solve the matter in a friendly fashion. If the matter is not settled through the Committee's good offices, it would state the facts and record the respective submissions of the parties. Then, if the parties agree, the Committee may appoint an *ad hoc* Conciliation Commission which, if the parties have not resolved their differences within a year, may report its findings on all relevant questions of fact as well as its views on the possibilities of settling the matter amicably.

There is also a separate optional protocol, by which parties may empower the Human Rights Committee to consider communications from individuals, subject to its jurisdiction, claiming that their rights under the Covenant have been violated by that state. Again, once domestic remedies have been exhausted, the Committee would be able to consider the communication and a state's explanation at a closed meeting and forward its views to both parties. The communications would receive only the publicity arising out of the Committee's annual report to the General Assembly.

Some more far-reaching steps have been taken by members of the Council of Europe under the European Convention on Human Rights. This Convention, signed in Rome on November 4, 1950, guarantees certain rights and freedoms to all persons (and not just nationals) within the jurisdiction of the contracting parties.[75] It also establishes a Commission (with one member from each of the contracting parties) and a Court (with one member from each of the 20 states in the Council of Europe). These bodies help make the guarantees under the Convention effective. The Convention provides options, whereby, under Article 25, states parties may agree to allow individuals to bring their own cases before the Commission, thus marking an important step in the development of international law, and whereby, under Article 46, states may recognize the Court's jurisdiction as compulsory.

In general, the Convention guarantees the right to life, liberty, and security of the person; and the individual's freedom of thought, conscience, expression, assembly, association, education, and religion. It also guarantees respect for his private and family life, his home and correspondence, and his right to marry, to found a family, and to enjoy his possessions peacefully. It prohibits torture, inhuman or degrading treatment or punishment, slavery, servitude, and forced labor. It guarantees to individuals fair administration of justice and free elections, and requires states to define offenses and penalties by law.

States which have signed and ratified the Convention have in effect agreed to restrict the free exercise of their rights under international law to the extent of the obligations they have accepted under the Convention, and many cases now exist where national courts have applied

[75] The parties are the following 15 states, an asterisk (*) indicating that the party has also accepted the two optional arrangements under Articles 25 and 46: Austria*, Belgium*, Cyprus, Denmark*, the Federal Republic of Germany*, Greece, Iceland*, Ireland*, Italy, Luxembourg*, Netherlands*, Norway*, Sweden*, Turkey, and the United Kingdom*. The Convention entered into force on September 3, 1953.

For basic information about the Convention, see Council of Europe, *European Convention on Human Rights: Collected Texts* (5th ed., Strasbourg: The Council of Europe, 1966) and Council of Europe, *European Convention on Human Rights: Manual* (Strasbourg: Council of Europe, 1963).

the Convention.[76] In addition, changes in domestic law and administration have come about, directly or indirectly, because of the Convention. For instance, since ratifying the Convention, the Norwegian government has withdrawn a prohibition against the work of Jesuits in Norway;[77] Belgium in 1961 adjusted penalties for persons convicted of collaborating with the enemy, so as not to interfere with the collaborators' freedom of expression;[78] Britain abolished whipping of youths under 18 years of age and eliminated collective fines from the penalties imposed in Cyprus when Greece protested that these penalities violated the Convention's prohibition against degrading treatment and punishment;[79] German courts refused to deport an alien to Belgium in order to preserve the unity of his family life;[80] and Austria in 1962 and 1963 revised its Code of Penal Procedures to permit accused persons to attend certain hearings relating to their cases before court.[81] These actions show in practice how states have attempted to meet Convention provisions requiring them to adjust their domestic laws and procedures, if need be, to guarantee the rights under the Covenant and to provide effective national remedies for violations of the guaranteed rights. The Convention also protects the state in certain ways, permitting signatories "in time of war or other public emergency" to take measures derogating from their obligations as may be required.

The Commission and Court provided for in the Convention are both elected. For Commission elections, the Consultative Assembly (144 parliamentarians from the member states of the Council of Europe) nominates candidates. The Committee of Ministers (in effect, the Foreign Ministers of the states in the Council of Europe) then elects the members of the Commission. Member governments of the Council nominate candidates for the Court, who are then elected by the Consultative Assembly.

The Commission receives applications from states or from individuals, provided that the signatory state has consented to allow its nationals to address grievances directly to the Commission. By the end of 1966, only three applications had been received from states,[82] but individual

---

[76] A convenient summary of these cases may be found in Council of Europe, "European Convention on Human Rights: Decisions of National Courts relating to the Convention," (2d ed., Strasbourg: Council of Europe, 1965), Doc. H (65) 7.
[77] *Yearbook of the European Convention on Human Rights* (The Hague: Nijhoff, annual), I, 41–42.
[78] *Yearbook*, II, 214; European Court of Human Rights, *De Becker Case*, Series B, 1962, pp. 11–153.
[79] Application of Greece v. United Kingdom No. 176/56.
[80] Lebeau Case, *Yearbook*, II, 355.
[81] Applications by Ofner, Hopfinger, Pataki, and Dunshirn, *Yearbook*, VI.
[82] Two came from Greece and were directed against the United Kingdom, relating to Cyprus. In these cases, the Committee of Ministers took no further action after

applications number more than 2500. The Commission has declared only about 30 of these admissible. Most of the others have been declared inadmissible because they did not conform with the requirements of the Convention. Some were not directed against signatory states which had recognized the right of individual application, or against states which were members of the Council of Europe or parties to the Convention.

Applications have also been ruled inadmissible because they did not deal with rights covered by the Convention, *e.g.*, the right to practice a profession, to enter into public service, to serve in the armed forces, to receive a pension, to have an adequate standard of living, to be given nationality or a passport, to receive a specific type of prison treatment or legal assistance of one's own choosing, or to obtain exclusive custody of children (in the case of one parent opposing another); to receive social security, proper housing, holidays with pay; and many others.

The Commission has also rejected cases, as the Convention requires it to do, where applicants have not exhausted all domestic remedies or have waited more than six months to appeal against a final national decision. The Commission does not entertain anonymous petitions, petitions dealing with matters it has already adjudicated, complaints that are manifestly ill-founded or that abuse the right of petition.

The Commission notifies states of complaints made against them by other states. When a complaint comes from an individual, however, three members of the Commission examine the application and report to the Commission on whether it is admissible. If they agree unanimously that it is, the Commission invites the state against which the claim is made to submit its views on the question of admissibility. Where the three disagree, the entire Commission either decides that the application is inadmissible, without informing the state involved, or else asks the state to comment on the application's admissibility.

Once the Commission declares an application admissible, it examines it and investigates the facts, placing itself all the while at the disposal of the parties concerned in the hope of securing a friendly settlement of the matter. If the Commission cannot arrange a friendly settlement, it submits a report to the Committee of Ministers, stating whether it

---

the British Government altered its procedures. See Resolutions (59) 12 and (59) 32 and *Yearbook*, II, 174–197. A third came from Austria and was directed against Italy and had to do with the trial of some German-speaking youths for the murder of a customs officer in the Upper Adige. The complaints had to do with the conduct of the trial, but the Commission and, later, the Committee of Ministers found no violation of the Convention. Resolution (63) DH 3.

believes that a state has violated its obligations under the Covenant. These reports are not published at first, to give the Ministers a chance to reconcile the parties. By 1968, four reports had been published: in one of them the Commission decided that the disputed legislation, a provision of the Belgian penal code, did not conform to the Convention; in the three others, the Commission found no violation of the Covenant.[83] As matters now stand, only the Committee of Ministers or the Court can terminate a case where there has been no friendly settlement, but a Protocol is pending which will, when ratified, give the Commission itself the power to terminate proceedings by a unanimous vote.

After submitting a report to the Committee of Ministers, the Commission considers whether to refer a case to the Court. It can do so only after determining that all efforts at a friendly settlement have failed. It then assists the Court in the matter. The Commission refers matters to the Court in order that the Court may decide whether the Convention has been violated. The Commission itself expresses an opinion on that point in its reports, but its opinions are not legal decisions; they are expert opinions that provide the basis for legally binding decisions, either by the Committee of Ministers or by the Court.[84] To date the Court has dealt with three cases: the Lawless case, the De Becker case, and the case "relating to certain aspects of the laws on the use of languages in education in Belgium."

There follow extracts from the Lawless case and examples of decisions by the Commission of Human Rights.

"LAWLESS" CASE

EUROPEAN COURT OF HUMAN RIGHTS

1st July 1961

In the "Lawless" Case,

The European Court of Human Rights, sitting, in accordance with the provisions of Article 43 of the Convention for the Protection of Human Rights and Fundamental Freedoms (hereinafter referred to as "the Convention") and of Rules 21 and 22 of the Rules of the Court, as a Chamber composed of:

[83] The De Becker Case concerned the Belgian penal code, since amended; the others were the Cases of Nielsen against Denmark, Ofner-Hopfinger against Austria, and the Lawless Case.
[84] Sir Humphrey Waldock, 3 Oct. 1960, in the Lawless Case, Verbatim Report, pp. 32–33, quoted in Council of Europe, European Convention on Human Rights, *Manual*, p. 129.

Mr. R. CASSIN, *President*
and MM. G. MARIDAKIS
      E. RODENBOURG
      R. McGONIGAL, *ex officio* member
      G. BALLADORE PALLIERI
      E. ARNALDS
      K. F. ARIK, *Judges*
      P. MODINOS, *Registrar,*

delivers the following judgment:
[A section on procedure and Part I of the facts are omitted.]

II

5. Under the Treaty establishing the Irish Free State, signed on 6th December 1921 between the United Kingdom and the Irish Free State, six counties situated in the North of the Island of Ireland remained under British sovereignty.

6. On several occasions since the foundation of the Irish Free State, armed groups, calling themselves the "Irish Republican Army" (IRA), have been formed, for the avowed purpose of carrying out acts of violence to put an end to British sovereignty in Northern Ireland. At times the activities of these groups have been such that effective repression by the ordinary process of law was not possible. From time to time, the legislature has, therefore, conferred upon the Government special powers to deal with the situation created by these unlawful activities; and such powers have sometimes included the power of detention without trial.

. . . .

12. The powers of detention referred to in the Act are vested in Ministers of State. Section 4 of the Act provides as follows:

(1) Whenever a Minister of State is of opinion that any particular person is engaged in activities which, in his opinion, are prejudicial to the preservation of public peace and order or to the security of the State, such Minister may by warrant under his hand and sealed with his official seal order the arrest and detention of such person under this section.

(2) Any member of the *Gárda Síochána* may arrest without warrant any person in respect of whom a warrant has been issued by a Minister of State under the foregoing sub-section of this section.

(3) Every person arrested under the next preceding sub-section of this section shall be detained in a prison or other place prescribed in that behalf by regulations made under this Part of this Act until this Part of this Act ceases to be in force or until he is released under the subsequent provisions of this Part of this Act, whichever first happens.

(4) Whenever a person is detained under this section, there shall be furnished to such person, as soon as may be after he arrives at a prison or other place of detention prescribed in that behalf by regulations made under this Part of this Act, a copy of the warrant issued under this section in relation to such person and of the provisions of section 8 of this Act.

13. Under section 8 of the Offences against the State (Amendment) Act, 1940, the Government is required to set up, as soon as conveniently may be after the entry into force of the powers of detention without trial, a Commission (hereinafter referred to as "Detention Commission") to which any person arrested or detained under the Act may apply, through the Government, to have his case considered. The Commission is to consist of three persons, appointed by the Government, one to be a commissioned officer of the Defence Forces with not less than seven years' service and each of the others to be a barrister or solicitor of not less than seven years' standing or a judge or former judge of one of the ordinary courts. Lastly, section 8 of the Act provides that, if the Commission reports that no reasonable grounds exist for the continued detention of the person concerned, such person shall, with all convenient speed, be released.

IV

14. After several years during which there was very little IRA activity, there was a renewed outbreak in 1954 and again in the second half of 1956.

In the second half of December 1956 armed attacks were made on a number of Northern Ireland police barracks and at the end of the month a policeman was killed. In the same month a police patrol on border roads was fired on, trees were felled across roads and telephone wires cut, *etc.* In January 1957 there were more incidents of the same kind. At the beginning of the month there was an armed attack on Brookeborough Police Barracks during which two of the assailants were killed; both of them came from the 26-county area. Twelve others, of whom four were wounded, fled across the border and were arrested by the police of the Republic of Ireland. Thereupon, the Prime Minister of the Republic of Ireland, in a public broadcast address on 6th January 1957, made a pressing appeal to the public to put an end to these attacks.

Six days after this broadcast, namely, on 12th January 1957, the IRA carried out an armed raid on an explosives store in the territory of the Republic of Ireland, situated at Moortown, County Dublin, for the purpose of stealing explosives. On 6th May 1957, armed groups entered an explosives store at Swan Laois, held up the watchman and stole a quantity of explosives.

On 18th April 1957, the main railway line from Dublin to Belfast was closed by an explosion which caused extensive damage to the railway bridge at Ayallogue in County Armagh, about 5 miles on the northern side of the border.

During the night of 25th-26th April, three explosions between Lurgan and Portadown, in Northern Ireland, also damaged the same railway line.

On the night of 3rd/4th July a Northern Ireland police patrol on duty a short distance from the border was ambushed. One policeman was shot dead and another injured. At the scene of the ambush 87 sticks of gelignite were found to have been placed on the road and covered with stones, with wires leading to a detonator.

This incidence occurred only eight days before the annual Orange Processions which are widespread through Northern Ireland on 12th July. In the past, this date has always been particularly critical for the maintenance of peace and public order.

V

15. The special powers of arrest and detention conferred upon the Minister of State by the 1940 (Amendment) Act were brought into force on 8th July 1957 by a Proclamation of the Irish Government published in the Official Gazette on 5th July 1957.

On 16th July 1957, the Government set up the Detention Commission provided for in section 8 of that Act and appointed as members of that Commission an officer of the Defence Forces, a judge and a district Justice.

. . . .

17. By letter of 20th July 1957 the Irish Minister for External Affairs informed the Secretary-General of the Council of Europe that Part II of the Offences against the State Act, 1940 (No. 2) had come into force on 8th July 1957.

Paragraph 2 of that letter read as follows:

. . . Insofar as the bringing into operation of Part II of the Act, which confers special powers of arrest and detention, may involve any derogation from the obligations imposed by the Convention for the Protection of Human Rights and Fundamental Freedoms, I have the honour to request you to be good enough to regard this letter as informing you accordingly, in compliance with Article 15 (3) of the Convention.

The letter pointed out that the detention of persons under the Act was considered necessary "to prevent the commission of offences against public peace and order and to prevent the maintaining of military or armed forces other than those authorized by the Constitution."

. . . .

18. Soon after the publication of the Proclamation of 5th July 1957 bringing into force the powers of detention provided for under the 1940 Act, the Prime Minister of the Government of the Republic of Ireland announced that the Government would release any person held under that Act who undertook "to respect the Constitution and the laws of Ireland" and "to refrain from being a member of or assisting any organisation declared unlawful under the Offenses against the State Act, 1939."

VI

19. G. R. Lawless was first arrested with three other men on 21st September 1956 in a disused barn at Keshcarrigan, County Leitrim. The police discovered in the barn a Thompson machine-gun, six army rifles, six sporting guns, a revolver, an automatic pistol and 400 magazines. Lawless admitted that he was a member of the IRA and that he had taken part in an armed raid

when guns and revolvers had been stolen. He was subsequently charged on 18th October with unlawful possession of firearms under the Firearms Act, 1935 and under Section 21 of the Offenses against the State Act, 1939.

G. R. Lawless, together with the other accused, was sent forward for trial to the Dublin Circuit Criminal Court. On 23rd November 1956, they were acquitted of the charge of unlawful possession of arms. The trial judge had directed the jury that the requirements for proving the accused's guilt had not been satisfied in that it had not been conclusively shown that no competent authority had issued a firearm certificate authorizing him to be in possession of the arms concerned.

At the hearing before this Court on 26th October, the District Justice asked one of the accused, Sean Geraghty, whether he wished to put any questions to any of the policemen present. Sean Geraghty replied as follows:

As a soldier of the Irish Republican Army and as leader of these men, I do not wish to have any part in proceedings in this Court.

When asked by the Justice whether he pleaded guilty or not guilty to the charge, he again said:

On behalf of my comrades and myself I wish to state that any arms and ammunition found on us were to be used against the British Forces of occupation to bring about the re-unification of our country and no Irishman or woman of any political persuasion had anything to fear from us. We hold that it is legal to possess arms and also believe it is the duty of every Irishman to bear arms in defense of his country.

Subsequently, G. R. Lawless in reply to a question by the Justice said: "Sean Geraghty spoke for me."

Lawless was again arrested in Dublin on 14th May 1957 under section 30 of the 1939 Act, on suspicion of engaging in unlawful activities. A sketch map for an attack of certain frontier posts between the Irish Republic and Northern Ireland was found on him bearing the inscription "Infiltrate, annihilate and destroy."

On the same day his house was searched by the police who found a manuscript document on guerilla warfare containing, *inter alia*, the following statements:

The resistance movement is the armed vanguard of the Irish people fighting for the freedom of Ireland. The strength of the movement consists in the popular patriotic character of the movement. The basic mission of local resistance units are the destruction of enemy installations and establishments, that is TA halls, special huts, BA recruiting offices, border huts, depots, *etc.*

Attacks against enemy aerodromes and the destruction of aircraft hangars, depots of bombs and fuel, the killing of key flying personnel and mechanics, the killing or capture of high-ranking enemy officers and high officials of the enemy's colonial Government and traitors to our country in their pay, that is, British officers, police agents, touts, judges, high members of the Quisling party, *etc.*

After being arrested, G. R. Lawless was charged:

(*a*) with possession of incriminating documents contrary to section 12 of the 1939 Act;

(*b*) with membership of an unlawful organisation, the IRA, contrary to section 21 of the 1939 Act.

On 16th May 1957, G. R. Lawless was brought before the Dublin District Court together with three other men who were also charged with similar offenses under the 1939 Act. The Court convicted Lawless on the first charge and sentenced him to one month's imprisonment; it acquitted him on the second charge. The Court record showed that the second charge was dismissed "on the merits" of the case but no official report of the proceedings appears to be available. The reasons for this acquittal were not clearly established. G. R. Lawless was released on about 16th June 1957, after having served his sentence in Mountjoy Prison, Dublin.

20. G. R. Lawless was re-arrested on 11th July 1957 at Dune Laoghaire by Security Officer Connor when about to embark on a ship for England. He was detained for 24 hours at Bridewell Police Station in Dublin under section 30 of the 1939 Act, as being a suspected member of an unlawful organisation, namely the IRA.

Detective-Inspector McMahon told the Applicant on the same day that he would be released provided that he signed an undertaking in regard to his future conduct. No written form of the undertaking proposed was put to G. R. Lawless and its exact terms are in dispute.

On 12th July 1957, the Chief Superintendent of Police, acting under section 30, sub-section 3 of the 1939 Act, made an order that G. R. Lawless be detained for a further period of 24 hours expiring at 7:45 P.M. on 13th July 1957.

At 6 A.M. on 13th July 1957, however, before Lawless' detention under section 30 of the 1939 Act had expired, he was removed from the Bridewell Police Station and transferred to the military prison in the Curragh, Co. Kildare (known as the "Glass House"). He arrived there at 8 A.M. on the same day and was detained from that time under an order made on 12th July 1957 by the Minister for Justice under section 4 of the 1940 Act. Upon his arrival at the "Glass House," he was handed a copy of the above-mentioned detention order in which the Minister for Justice declared that G. R. Lawless was, in his opinion, engaged in activities prejudicial to the security of the State and he ordered his arrest and detention under section 40 of the 1940 Act.

From the "Glass House," G. R. Lawless was transferred on 17th July 1957 to a camp known as the "Curragh Internment Camp," which forms part of the Curragh Military Camp and Barracks in County Kildare, and together with some 120 other persons, was detained there without charge or trial until 11th December 1957 when he was released.

21. On 16th August 1957 G. R. Lawless was informed that he would be released provided he gave an undertaking in writing "to respect the Consti-

tution and laws of Ireland" and not to "be a member of or assist any organisation which is an unlawful organisation under the Offences against the State Act, 1939." G. R. Lawless declined to give this undertaking.

[The Court then relates how Lawless applied to appear before the Detention Commission; how he appeared at a session devoted largely to procedural matters; and how his counsel applied to the Irish High Court for a Conditional Order of *habeas corpus ad subjiciendum*, so that the Court itself would examine and decide upon the validity of Lawless' detention. The Detention Commission thereupon suspended its proceedings to await the outcome of the *habeas corpus* application, which the High Court ultimately dismissed on the grounds that the Commandant of the Detention Camp had "shown cause" for detaining Lawless. Lawless then appealed to the Supreme Court of Ireland, which also dismissed his appeal on the grounds that the 1940 Act was not unconstitutional and that the European Convention of Human Rights, on which Lawless had also based his appeal, was not part of the Irish internal law and did not therefore apply in proceedings before the Supreme Court.]

. . . .

26. Meanwhile, on 8th November 1957—that is two days after the announcement of the Supreme Court's rejection of his appeal—G. R. Lawless had introduced his Application before the European Commission of Human Rights, alleging that his arrest and detention under the 1940 Act, without charge or trial, violated the Convention and he claimed:

(*a*) immediate release from detention;

(*b*) payment of compensation and damages for his detention; and

(*c*) payment of all the costs and expenses of, and incidental to the proceedings instituted by him in the Irish courts and before the Commission to secure his release.

27. Shortly afterwards the Detention Commission resumed its consideration of the case of G. R. Lawless under section 8 of the 1940 Act and held hearings for that purpose on 6th and 10th December 1957. On the latter date, at the invitation of the Attorney-General, G. R. Lawless in person before the Detention Commission gave a verbal undertaking that he would not "engage in any illegal activities under the Offences against the State Acts, 1939 and 1940," and on the following day an order was made by the Minister for Justice, under section 6 of the 1940 Act, releasing the Applicant from detention.

28. The release of G. R. Lawless from detention was notified to the European Commission of Human Rights by his solicitor in a letter dated 16th December 1957. The letter at the same time stated that G. R. Lawless intended to continue the proceedings before the Commission with regard to (*a*) the claim for compensation and damages for his detention and (*b*) the claim for reimbursement of all costs and expenses in connection with the proceedings undertaken to obtain his release.

[The Court then turned to questions of law, considered and decided several questions submitted by the Commission of Human Rights and the Government of Eire. It dismissed the Irish Government's contention that Lawless was using the Convention, contrary to Article 17, to establish the right to destroy the rights the Convention was designed to protect; it then agreed with Lawless that his detention was not "effected for the purpose of bringing him before the competent legal authority" and that he was not in fact brought before a judge for trial "within a reasonable time." The Court held therefore that his detention under Section 4 of the Irish 1940 Act contravened provisions of Article 5, paragraphs 1 (c) and 3 of the Convention. It found that the Irish Government had not violated Article 7 of the Convention, however, because Lawless had been detained, not because he had been convicted of a crime, but because the Government believed him to be "engaged in activities prejudicial to the preservation of public peace and order. . . . [p. 54]." The Court then turned to the following question:]

As to whether, despite Articles 5[85] *and 6 of the Convention, the detention of G. R. Lawless was justified by the right of derogation allowed to the High Contracting Parties in certain exceptional circumstances under Article 15 of the Convention.*

[85] Article 5 of the Convention reads as follows:

"(1) Everyone has the right to liberty and security of person. No one shall be deprived of his liberty save in the following cases and in accordance with a procedure prescribed by law:

(a) the lawful detention of a person after conviction by a competent court;

(b) the lawful arrest or detention of a person for non-compliance with the lawful order of a court or in order to secure the fulfillment of any obligation prescribed by law;

(c) the lawful arrest or detention of a person effected for the purpose of bringing him before the competent legal authority on reasonable suspicion of having committed an offence or when it is reasonably considered necessary to prevent his committing an offence or fleeing after having done so;

(d) the detention of a minor by lawful order for the purpose of educational supervision of his lawful detention for the purpose of bringing him before the competent legal authority;

(e) the lawful detention of persons for the prevention of the spreading of infectious diseases, of persons of unsound mind, alcoholics or drug addicts or vagrants;

(f) the lawful arrest or detention of a person to prevent his effecting an unauthorised entry into the country or of a person against whom action is being taken with a view to deportation or extradition.

(2) Everyone who is arrested shall be informed promptly, in a language which he understands, of the reasons for his arrest and of any charge against him.

(3) Everyone arrested or detained in accordance with the provisions of paragraph 1 (c) of this Article shall be brought promptly before a judge or other officer authorised by law to exercise judicial power and shall be entitled to trial within a reasonable time or to release pending trial. Release may be conditioned by guarantees to appear for trial.

(4) Everyone who is deprived of his liberty by arrest or detention shall be entitled to take proceedings by which the lawfulness of his detention shall be decided speedily by a court and his release ordered if the detention is not lawful.

(5) Everyone who has been the victim of arrest or detention in contravention of the provisions of this Article shall have an enforceable right to compensation."

20. *Whereas* the Court is called upon to decide whether the detention of G. R. Lawless from 13th July to 11th December 1957 under the Offences against the state (Amendment) Act, 1940, was justified, despite Articles 5 and 6 of the Convention, by the right of derogation allowed to the High Contracting Parties in certain exceptional circumstances under Article 15 of the Convention;

21. *Whereas* Article 15 reads as follows:

(1) In time of war or other public emergency threatening the life of the nation any High Contracting Party may take measures derogating from its obligations under this Convention to the extent strictly required by the exigencies of the situation, provided that such measures are not inconsistent with its other obligations under international law.

(2) No derogation from Article 2, except in respect of deaths resulting from lawful acts of war, or from Articles 3, 4 (paragraph 1) and 7 shall be made under this provision.

(3) Any High Contracting Party availing itself of this right of derogation shall keep the Secretary-General of the Council of Europe fully informed of the measures which it has taken and the reasons therefor. It shall also inform the Secretary-General of the Council of Europe when such measures have ceased to operate and the provisions of the Convention are again being fully executed.

22. *Whereas* it follows from these provisions that, without being released from all its undertakings assumed in the Convention, the Government of any High Contracting Party has the right, in case of war or public emergency threatening the life of the nation, to take measures derogating from its obligations under the Convention other than those named in Article 15, paragraph 2, provided that such measures are strictly limited to what is required by the exigencies of the situation and also that they do not conflict with other obligations under international law; whereas it is for the Court to determine whether the conditions laid down in Article 15 for the exercise of the exceptional right of derogation have been fulfilled in the present case;

(a) *As to the existence of a public emergency threatening the life of the nation.*

23. *Whereas* the Irish Government, by a Proclamation dated 5th July 1957 and published in the Official Gazette on 8th July 1957, brought into force the extraordinary powers conferred upon it by Part II of the Offences against the State (Amendment) Act, 1940, "to secure the preservation of public peace and order";

24. *Whereas*, by letter dated 20th day July 1957 addressed to the Secretary-General of the Council of Europe, the Irish Government expressly stated that "the detention of persons under the Act is considered necessary to prevent the commission of offences against public peace and order and to prevent the maintaining of military or armed forces other than those authorized by the Constitution,"

25. *Whereas*, in reply to the Application introduced by G. R. Lawless before the Commission, the Irish Government adduced a series of facts from which they inferred the existence, during the period mentioned, of "a public emergency threatening the life of the nation" within the meaning of Article 15;

26. *Whereas,* before the Commission, G. R. Lawless submitted in support of his application that the aforesaid facts, even if proved to exist, would not have constituted a "public emergency threatening the life of the nation" within the meaning of Article 15; whereas, moreover, he disputed some of the facts adduced by the Irish Government;

27. *Whereas* the Commission, following the investigation carried out by it in accordance with Article 28 of the Convention expressed a majority opinion in its Report that in "July 1957 there existed in Ireland a public emergency threatening the life of the nation within the meaning of Article 15, paragraph 1, of the Convention";

28. *Whereas,* in the general context of Article 15 of the Convention, the natural and customary meaning of the words "other public emergency threatening the life of the nation" is sufficiently clear; whereas they refer to an exceptional situation of crisis or emergency which affects the whole population and constitutes a threat to the organised life of the community of which the State is composed; whereas, having thus established the natural and customary meaning of this conception, the Court must determine whether the facts and circumstances which led the Irish Government to make their Proclamation of 5th July 1957 come within this conception; whereas the Court, after an examination, find this to be the case; whereas the existence at the time of a "public emergency threatening the life of the nation," was reasonably deduced by the Irish Government from a combination of several factors, namely: in the first place, the existence in the territory of the Republic of Ireland of a secret army engaged in unconstitutional activities and using violence to attain its purposes; secondly, the fact that this army was also operating outside the territory of the State, thus seriously jeopardising the relations of the Republic of Ireland with its neighbour; thirdly the steady and alarming increase in terrorist activities from the autumn of 1956 and throughout the first half of 1957;

29. *Whereas,* despite the gravity of the situation, the Government had succeeded, by using means available under ordinary legislation, in keeping public institutions functioning more or less normally, but whereas the homicidal ambush on the night of 3rd to 4th July 1957 in the territory of Northern Ireland near the border had brought to light, just before 12th July—a date, which, for historical reasons is particularly critical for the preservation of public peace and order—the imminent danger to the nation caused by the continuance of unlawful activities in Northern Ireland by the IRA and various associated groups, operating from the territory of the Republic of Ireland;

30. *Whereas,* in conclusion, the Irish Government were justified in declaring that there was a public emergency in the Republic of Ireland threatening the life of the nation and were hence entitled, applying the provisions of Article 15, paragraph 1, of the Convention for the purposes for which those provisions were made, to take measures derogating from their obligations under the Convention;

(b) *As to whether the measures taken in derogation from obligations under the Convention were "strictly required by the exigencies of the situation."*

31. *Whereas* Article 15, paragraph 1, provides that a High Contracting Party may derogate from its obligations under the Convention only "to the extent strictly required by the exigencies of the situation"; whereas it is therefore necessary, in the present case, to examine whether the bringing into force of Part II of the 1940 Act was a measure strictly required by the emergency existing in 1957;

32. *Whereas* G. R. Lawless contended before the Commission that even if the situation in 1957 was such as to justify derogation from obligations under the Convention, the bringing into operation and the enforcement of Part II of the Offences against the State (Amendment) Act 1940 were disproportionate to the strict requirements of the situation;

33. *Whereas* the Irish Government, before both the Commission and the Court, contended that the measures taken under Part II of the 1940 Act were, in the circumstances, strictly required by the exigencies of the situation in accordance with Article 15, paragraph 1, of the Convention;

34. *Whereas* while the majority of the Commission concurred with the Irish Government's submissions on this point, some members of the Commission drew from the facts established different legal conclusions;

35. *Whereas* it was submitted that in view of the means available to the Irish Government in 1957 for controlling the activities of the IRA and its splinter groups the Irish Government could have taken measures which would have rendered superfluous so grave a measure as detention without trial; whereas, in this connection, mention was made of the application of the ordinary criminal law, the institution of special criminal courts of the type provided for by the Offences against the State Act, 1939, or of military courts; whereas it would have been possible to consider other measures such as the sealing of the border between the Republic of Ireland and Northern Ireland;

36. *Whereas,* however, considering, in the judgment of the Court, that in 1957 the application of the ordinary law had proved unable to check the growing danger which threatened the Republic of Ireland; whereas the ordinary criminal courts, or even the special criminal courts or military courts, could not suffice to restore peace and order; whereas, in particular, the amassing of the necessary evidence to convict persons involved in activities of the IRA and its splinter groups was meeting with great difficulties caused by the military, secret and terrorist character of those groups and the fear they created among the population; whereas the fact that these groups operated mainly in Northern Ireland, their activities in the Republic of Ireland being virtually limited to the preparation of armed raids across the border was an additional impediment to the gathering of sufficient evidence; whereas the sealing of the border would have had extremely serious repercussions on the population as a whole, beyond the extent required by the exigencies of the emergency.

Whereas it follows from the foregoing that none of the abovementioned means would have made it possible to deal with the situation existing in Ireland in 1957; whereas, therefore, the administrative detention—as instituted under the Act (Amendment) of 1940—of individuals suspected of intending to take part in terrorist activities, appeared, despite its gravity, to be a measure required by the circumstances;

37. *Whereas*, moreover, the Offences against the State (Amendment) Act of 1940, was subject to a number of safeguards designed to prevent abuses in the operation of the system of administrative detention; whereas the application of the Act was thus subject to constant supervision by Parliament, which not only received precise details of its enforcement at regular intervals but could also at any time, by a Resolution, annul the Goverment's Proclamation which had brought the Act into force; whereas the Offences against the State (Amendment) Act of 1940, provided for the establishment of a "Detention Commission" made up of three members, which the Government did in fact set up, the members being an officer of the Defence Forces and two judges; whereas any person detained under this Act could refer his case to that Commission whose opinion, if favourable to the release of the person concerned, was binding upon the Government; whereas, moreover, the ordinary courts could themselves compel the Detention Commission to carry out its functions;

Whereas, in conclusion, immediately after the Proclamation which brought the power of detention into force, the Government publicly announced that it would release any person detained who gave an undertaking to respect the Constitution and the Law and not to engage in any illegal activity, and that the wording of this undertaking was later altered to one which merely required that the person detained would undertake to observe the law and refrain from activities contrary to the 1940 Act; whereas the persons arrested were informed immediately after their arrest that they would be released following the undertaking in question; whereas in a democratic country such as Ireland the existence of this guarantee of release given publicly by the Government constituted a legal obligation on the Government to release all persons who gave the undertaking;

Whereas, therefore, it follows from the foregoing that the detention without trial provided for by the 1940 Act, subject to the above-mentioned safeguards, appears to be a measure strictly required by the exigencies of the situation within the meaning of Article 15 of the Convention;

38. *Whereas*, in the particular case of G. R. Lawless, there is nothing to show that the powers of detention conferred upon the Irish Government by the Offenses against the State (Amendment) Act 1940, were employed against him, either within the meaning of Article 18 of the Convention, for a purpose other than that for which they were granted, or within the meaning of Article 15 of the Convention, by virtue of a measure going beyond what was strictly required by the situation at that time; whereas on the contrary, the Commission, after finding in its Decision of 30th August 1958 on the admissibility of the Application that the Applicant had in fact submitted his Application to it after having exhausted the domestic remedies, observed in its Report that the general conduct of G. R. Lawless, "his association with persons known to be active members of the IRA, his conviction for carrying incriminating documents and other circumstances were such as to draw upon the Applicant the gravest suspicion that, whether or not he was any longer a member, he still was concerned with the activities of the IRA at the time of his arrest in July 1957"; whereas the file also shows that, at the beginning of G. R. Lawless's detention under Act No. 2 of 1940,

the Irish Government informed him that he would be released if he gave a written undertaking "to respect the Constitution of Ireland and the Laws" and not to "be a member of or assist any organisation that is an unlawful organisation under the Offences against the State Act, 1939"; whereas in December 1957 the Government renewed its offer in a different form, which was accepted by G. R. Lawless, who gave a verbal undertaking before the Detention Commission not to "take part in any activities that are illegal under the Offences against the State Acts 1939 and 1940" and was accordingly immediately released;

(c) *As to whether the measures derogating from obligations under the Convention were "inconsistent with . . . other obligations under international law."*

39. *Whereas* Article 15, paragraph 1, of the Convention authorises a High Contracting Party to take measures derogating from the Convention only provided that they "are not inconsistent with . . . other obligations under international law";

40. *Whereas,* although neither the Commission nor the Irish Government have referred to this provision in the proceedings, the function of the Court, which is to ensure the observance of the engagements undertaken by the Contracting Parties in the Convention (Article 19 of the Convention), requires it to determine *proprio motu* whether this condition has been fulfilled in the present case;

41. *Whereas* no facts have come to the knowledge of the Court which give it cause to hold that the measures taken by the Irish Government derogating from the Convention may have conflicted with the said Governments other obligations under international law;

. . . .

48. For these reasons,

THE COURT,

Unanimously,

. . . .

(ii) *States* that Articles 5 and 6 of the Convention provided no legal foundation for the detention without trial of G. R. Lawless from 13th July to 11th December 1957, by virtue of Article 4 of the Offences against the State (Amendment) Act, 1940;

(iii) *States* that there was no breach of Article 7 of the Convention;

(iv) *States* that the detention of G. R. Lawless from 13th July to 11th December 1957 was founded on the right of derogation duly exercised by the Irish Government in pursuance of Article 15 of the Convention in July 1957.

APPLICATION NO. 2518/65

X. Against Denmark

(Decision of 14th December, 1965)

I. *"Fair hearing"* (Article 6, paragraph (1), of the Convention) and *"presumption of innocence"* (Article 6, paragraph (2), of the Convention)—jury informed of previous convictions—practice in other countries.

II. *Detention in a special institution for an indefinite period* (Article 5 of the Convention)

THE FACTS

Whereas the facts of the case as presented by the Applicant may be summarised as follows:

The Applicant is a Danish citizen, born in 1931 and at present detained in prison in Copenhagen. He is represented before the Commission by Mr. C, a barrister practising in Copenhagen.

The Applicant was charged before the High Court of Eastern Denmark (Ostre Landsret) with rape committed on two occasions in 1963, and, according to the procedure applicable, a jury was set up to determine the question of his guilt.

During the proceedings before the Court on . . . 1964, the Applicant's counsel requested that an account of the Applicant's previous convictions should not be given to the Court until the jury had reached its decision as to his guilt in the present case. This request was rejected by the Court which, in its decision on this point, referred to Article 877 of the Code of Procedure (retsplejeloven) which expressly provides that records of previous convictions may be used as evidence during proceedings before the High Court.

Following this decision of the Court, the Public Prosecutor gave an account of the Applicant's numerous previous convictions; in particular, on one occasion in 1956, he had already been convicted of rape and sentenced to six years' imprisonment.

On . . . 1964, the jury found that the Applicant was guilty of the offences charged and on the same day the High Court, considering that the Applicant would not be susceptible to the effects of a penal sentence, decided to place him in a special detention centre (saerlig forvaringsanstalt) as provided for in Article 70 of the Penal Code.

The Applicant appealed against the decision of the High Court, requesting primarily that the case be returned to the High Court for a new examination and, alternatively, that he be sentenced to detention for a fixed period of time. He maintained in his appeal that information about his criminal record ought not to have been given before the jury had decided upon the question of his guilt and that, moreover, it could be assumed that he would not have been found guilty, if his previous convictions had not been known to the jury. He alleged that the procedure followed did not meet the requirements for a fair trial within the meaning of Article 6 of the Convention.

On . . . 1965, the Supreme Court (Hojesteret) rejected his appeal. In its decision, the Supreme Court stated that information about previous convictions had been given in accordance with Article 877 of the Code of Procedure and that, moreover, the detention of the Applicant in a special detention centre as provided for in Article 70 of the Penal Code was justified.

The Applicant now complains:

(1) that the Public Prosecutor was allowed to inform the jury of his previous convictions, not only in general terms but in considerable detail; and

(2) that he has been sentenced to detention for an indefinite period of time.

He alleges violations of Articles 3, 4 paragraph (1), 6, paragraphs (1) and (2), of the Convention and requests a new trial before an unbiased jury and the annulment of his sentence of detention for an unlimited period.

THE LAW

Whereas, as regards the complaint that the jury was informed of the Applicant's previous convictions before determining the issue of his guilt in respect of two charges of rape, the Commission considers that the Application gives rise to questions of the interpretation of Article 6, paragraphs (1) and (2), of the Convention; whereas, when interpreting such fundamental concepts as "fair hearing" within the meaning of Article 6, paragraph (1), and "presumption of innocence" within the meaning of Article 6, paragraph (2), the Commission finds it necessary to take into consideration the practice in different countries which are members of the Council of Europe; whereas it is clear that in a number of these countries information as to previous convictions is regularly given during the trial before the court has reached a decision as to the guilt of an accused; whereas the Commission is not prepared to consider such a procedure as violating any provision of Article 6 of the Convention, not even in cases where a jury is to decide on the guilt of an accused;

Whereas it follows that this part of the Application is manifestly ill-founded within the meaning of Article 27, paragraph (2), of the Convention;

Whereas, as regards the Applicant's complaint that he was sentenced to detention for an indefinite time, it is to be considered whether the Applicant's detention is contrary to Article 5, paragraph (1) (a), of the Convention which deals with "the lawful detention of a person after conviction by a competent court";

Whereas detention in a special detention centre, as provided for in Article 70 of the Penal Code, is a measure which, in the interests of public safety, is applied to persons with certain mental defects; whereas, at certain intervals, the detention may be re-examined by a court at the instance of the Public Prosecutor, the director of the institution concerned or the supervising guardian;

Whereas the Commission has previously been called upon to consider whether other similar measures involving detention for an indefinite period are contrary to Article 5, paragraph (1) (a); whereas, in these cases, the Commission has concluded that the measures concerned did not violate the said provision of the Convention (see for instance, in regard to the German "Sicherungsverwahrung," the Commission's decision regarding Application No. 99/55 X. against the Federal Republic of Germany, Annuaire I, p. 160);

Whereas, having regard to the nature of the measure complained of and to the Commission's previous jurisprudence in regard to similar measures, the Commission does not find any appearance of a violation of the rights and freedoms set forth in the Convention and, in particular, in Article 5, paragraph (1) (a); whereas it follows that this part of the Application is also manifestly ill-founded within the meaning of Article 27, paragraph (2) of the Convention.

Now therefore the Commission

DECLARES THIS APPLICATION INADMISSIBLE

Law Report, September 13

COMMITTEE OF MINISTERS OF THE COUNCIL OF EUROPE

GIVING EFFECT TO CONVENTION ON HUMAN RIGHTS

Before THE MINISTERS' DEPUTIES

The Committee of Ministers today adopted the text of a resolution in which they considered the question of a violation of the European Convention on Human Rights and Fundamental Freedoms as alleged in the application lodged by Pataki and Dunshirn against Austria.

The committee also took note of the report submitted by the European Commission of Human Rights and decided that it should be published. This report was completed by the commission as no friendly settlement of the matter had been achieved. It sets out the facts of the two applications, which had been joined by the commission, and also the written and oral submissions of the parties.

Both applicants had been represented by the same counsel, Dr. Hans Gurtler, of Vienna, in the proceedings before the commission.

The applicants were separately convicted in March, 1959, and February, 1960, respectively, of certain criminal offences, and sentenced to terms of imprisonment. The proceedings took place before the regional court of Vienna and, in each case, the public prosecutor appealed to the regional court of appeal against the sentence passed. Pataki's sentence was increased from three to six years and Dunshirn's sentence was increased from 14 months to 30 months.

In accordance with section 294, paragraph (3) of the Austrian Code of Criminal Procedure the proceedings before the court of appeal took place in a non-public session at which neither of the accused nor his lawyer was allowed to be present, while the public prosecutor was present and was heard by the court.

The applicants submitted that section 294, paragraph (3), of the Austrian Code of Criminal Procedure and the procedure before the court of appeal in their cases gave rise to an inequality of arms, in the representation of the parties and thereby violated certain provisions of Article 6 of the Convention on Human Rights, which guarantees to an accused person the right to a fair hearing and a proper administration of justice. In particular, it was pointed out that the public prosecutor remained present during the court's deliberations and voting on the case.

The principal submissions of the respondent Government were that:

1.—A convicted person had the right to submit within 14 days a written reply to the public prosecutor's notice of appeal.

2.—The public prosecutor's case is limited to the facts mentioned in the documents already filed and to the grounds expressed in the notice of appeal. He is also obliged to adopt an objective attitude in considering the circumstances which are in favour of or against the accused.

3.—In regard to Pataki, the increase of sentence had been proposed by the Judge Rapporteur of the appeal court. The chief public prosecutor had made a written submission, as had the applicant, but had expressed no opinion during the proceedings.

4.—In regard to Dunshirn, the increase of sentence was determined on the grounds mentioned in the notice of appeal and independently of any representation made by the chief public prosecutor.

The commission stated its opinion in the report that the proceedings conducted in these two cases on the basis of Article 294, paragraph (3) of the Code of Criminal Procedure were not in conformity with the convention.

The main grounds of this opinion were:—

(a) That this procedure was essentially different from appeal proceedings before the supreme court. In the cases of Ofner and Hopfinger against Austria, the commission had stated its opinion and the Committee of Ministers had decided that these proceedings were not inconsistent with the convention.

(b) That the principle of the equality of arms, that is the procedural equality of the accused with the public prosecutor, is an inherent element of a fair trial, within the meaning of Article 6, paragraph (1).

(c) That, even if the public prosecutor did not play an active role at that stage of the proceedings, the fact that he was present and thereby had an opportunity of influencing the Court, without the accused or his counsel having any similar opportunity or any possibility of contesting any statements made by the prosecutor, constitutes an inequality which is incompatible with the notion of a fair trial.

MODIFICATION TO CODE

The commission also included in its report a note on certain relevant new legislation which was enacted during the course of the present proceedings. On July 18, 1962, an Act was passed which, *inter alia*, amended section 294 paragraph (3) by providing for the representation of the defence at appeal proceedings other than proceedings where a rejection of the appeal was proposed on technical grounds.

On April 5, 1963, a further Act was promulgated, which gave the right to persons, whose applications had been declared admissible by the Commission of Human Rights, to claim a new hearing of their appeal before the Austrian courts. Certain conditions, including the fixing of a time-limit of six months, were also mentioned and the new proceedings will, of course, be subject to the amended procedure.

The explanatory grounds of this legislation, when in bill form, referred expressly to the series of applications pending before the commission. The commission considered that a new remedy had thus been given to the applicants and a new procedure had been instituted which would not give rise to the objections regarding the previous procedure. It accordingly proposed to the Committee of Ministers that no further action should be taken in these cases.

PROPOSALS ACCEPTED

The COMMITTEE in their resolution have followed the commission's proposals made under Article 31 of the convention. They agree with the reasoning of the commission. They take note of the commission's report. They take account of the law of March 27, 1963, and express satisfaction with the legislative measures put into force in Austria with a view to giving full effect to the Convention on Human Rights. They decided that no further action is required in the present case.

[(c) The Times Publishing Company Limited, 1963. All Rights Reserved. Reprinted from The Times of September 14, 1963, with the permission of The Times Publishing Company Limited and The New York Times Company.]

FORCED SERVICE FOR DENTIST: HELD, NOT SLAVERY

IVERSEN v. NORWAY

Before the PRESIDENT *and* MEMBERS OF THE COMMISSION

The COMMISSION issued the full text of its decision taken on December 17, 1963, by which it declared inadmissible the application lodged in June, 1962, by Dr. Iversen against Norway under article 25 of the European Convention on Human Rights and Fundamental Freedoms.

The COMMISSION also decided that, having regard to the important question of principle involved by the issue of "forced or compulsory labour", it would for the first time indicate the voting and the various opinions of its members.

Extensive written and oral pleadings had been submitted by both parties.

Dr. Iversen qualified as a dentist in 1958, having studied in Germany and Norway and then carried out his military service in Norway for one year as a dentist. In June, 1956, a provisional Act had been passed which provided for obligatory public service for dentists and, in November, 1959, the Minister for Social Affairs, in pursuance of that Act, directed Dr. Iversen to fill a dental post in Nordland in northern Norway for one year. Dr. Iversen took up the post but left six months later after notifying the Ministry.

Criminal proceedings were brought against him in November, 1960, and he was convicted by the court of first instance of a violation of the Act and sentenced to a fine of 2,000 kroner or, in default, to go to prison for 30 days. Dr. Iversen appealed to the Supreme Court on the grounds that the Act was contrary both to the Norwegian Constitution and to the Convention on Human Rights, further that the Act was not applicable to him as, unlike other students, he had given no undertaking to serve in the public dental service after completing his studies. In December, 1961, his appeal was rejected by a majority judgment of the Supreme Court, while the minority opinion was that the Act of 1956 did not apply to him, and Dr. Iversen duly paid the fine in question.

Dr. Iversen alleged before the commission that the Act of 1956 and the Minister's order made under it violated articles 4, 8, and 11 of the Convention.

Article 4 guarantees to an individual freedom from forced or compulsory labour which, however, does not include service, *inter alia*, in case of an emergency threatening the life or wellbeing of the community. Articles 8 and 11 refer respectively to the rights of family life and of freedom of association.

The Norwegian Government's principal submissions were that the application was abusive, in that it was designed to use the Commission as a forum for domestic politics and that, as regards article 4, it was manifestly ill-founded. In regard to the latter ground the Government referred to the deplorable lack of dentists in northern Norway and to the problems, in view also of the difficult communications, of maintaining an adequate health service. It also submitted that the Act of 1956, and the Act of 1949 which had established a public dental service, were humanitarian attempts to overcome these difficulties, particularly as other arrangements made with students for that purpose had failed. Article 8, in the Government's submission, was drafted in the light of Nazi excesses and Soviet ideology and the concept of "forced labour" was close to that of slavery. The article was applicable to concentration and labour camps but not to reasonable and democratic measures taken to solve urgent social needs.

The Government also referred to the International Labour Organization Conventions of 1930 and 1957 and to its subsequent jurisprudence which showed that "forced or compulsory labour" had been defined in the special content of forced labour in colonial or dependent territories.

To sum up, the Government submitted that the following elements should be considered: (*a*) The scope and object of the Act of 1956. (*b*) The Act of 1956, by reason of its provisional character, did not impose conditions equivalent to slavery. (*c*) The short duration of the service required. (*d*) The comparatively high remuneration paid. (*e*) The service required was in the profession of the person affected. (*f*) The lightness of the sanctions. (*g*) The voluntary or contractual aspect of the present case.

Dr. Iversen submitted in reply that the fundamental issue was whether or not the Act of 1956 was contrary to the Convention. In this respect, he contended that the Act of 1956 was unnecessary, as the students were ready to cooperate; further, that neither the period of service, nor the pay, nor the nature of the sanctions, was relevant but only the compulsory nature of the service required.

As to the interpretation of article 4 of the Convention, Dr. Iversen submitted that the preparatory work showed clearly that its scope was wider than the prevention of overt criminal acts. He agreed that the 1930 and 1957 I.L.O. Conventions were highly relevant and considered that the Act of 1956 would have been considered contrary to the 1957 Convention had it been submitted to the I.L.O. for examination.

In a further reply to the Government, Dr. Iversen submitted that the Act of 1956 had been prolonged until 1966 and thus to some extent lost its temporary character. Finally, he argued that the so-called "contractual" element was irrelevant to the fundamental issue and, indeed, had not been raised before the Norwegian court and that in any event he was compelled to accept the post in Nordland as the alternative was criminal prosecution.

The Government submitted that there was an "emergency" within the meaning of article 4 (3) (*c*), or that the service required was a "normal civic obligation" within the meaning of paragraph (3) (*b*).

DECISION OF THE COMMISSION

The Commission dealt mainly with the questions whether or not the application was an abuse of the right of petition or, as regards article 4, manifestly ill-founded.

In regard to the "abuse" issue, the Commission referred to its findings in the Lawless Case (Yearbook, vol. 2, p. 308) that the fact of the applicant being inspired by motives of publicity and political propaganda would not by itself necessarily cause the application to be abusive. The Commission took note of the political interest raised in Norway in the present case but did not find that it established that Dr. Iversen had unduly emphasized the political aspect in the foundation of his case. It also found that Dr. Iversen's allegations were sufficiently clear and substantiated and rejected the Government's objection to admissibility.

The Commission then decided, by a majority of six votes to four, to reject the allegations under article 4 as being manifestly ill-founded on the ground that Dr. Iversen's service in Nordland did not constitute forced or compulsory labour within the meaning of that article. Four members of the majority, in referring particularly to the I.L.O. conventions and resolutions on forced labour, considered that certain elements of forced labour were lacking both in the Act of 1956 and in its application to Dr. Iversen. The two other members held that, having regard to the serious situation of the dental service in 1956 and 1960, Dr. Iversen's service in Nordland was a service reasonably required of him in "an emergency . . . threatening the well-being of the community" within the meaning of article 4 (3).

The minority of four members considered that the conditions of Dr. Iversen's service in regard, for example, to salary, time-limit and professional facilities, did not exclude the application of article 4 (2), since the service imposed was subject to penal sanctions. The minority further considered that, having regard to the complexity of the legal problems raised and the varying opinions in the Commission, the application should be declared admissible as it was not manifestly ill-founded.

Two other objections to admissibility raised by the Government were rejected unanimously by the Commission which, on the other hand, found unanimously that Dr. Iversen's allegations of violations of articles 8 (right to family life) and 11 (right to freedom of association) were manifestly ill-founded.

[(c) The Times Publishing Company Limited, 1964. All rights reserved. Reproduced, with permission, from the Law Report of March 12 that appeared in The Times of March 13, 1964.]

Conclusion

After considering the law on the subject of individuals, one may well ponder the difficulties of asserting that men everywhere have rights in their own capacity and not merely because they are nationals of certain states. To make such an assertion would be to assert that rights do not depend on possessing a nationality, and would lead logically to a demand for international institutions to protect the individual. Such international institutions might in effect reduce the existing states to administrative entities in protecting the rights of individuals everywhere, and would revolutionize international practice. None of the practical problems that arise are impossible to solve;[86] the problem which has, however, resisted solution is how to bring enough men and governments to support international efforts to enhance human rights. Even aside from legal objections, many persons oppose such efforts on philosophical grounds because they do not admit the justice of allowing international efforts to override or modify national constitutions and laws. They find it unacceptable to have the international community set standards, no matter how worthy. The European Convention on Human Rights is a noteworthy exception.

[86] See the works by Brierly, Jessup, and Lauterpacht, cited above.

CHAPTER VII

Relations Among States

Although the modern state system dates only from 1648 and the signing of the Treaty of Westphalia, laws relating to diplomacy go back to the earliest recorded history when men in different groups first attempted to deal with one another. The oldest recorded treaty dates from 3000 B.C. between the kings of Lagash and Umma, and many of our diplomatic practices were well established in past centuries by the ancient Hebrews, Greeks, and Romans. Much of international law itself has developed from these contacts among peoples, so that the law of diplomatic practice and the law of treaties, both of which we examine in this chapter, have a fundamental place in international law.

Privileges and Immunities (Individual)

Privileges and immunities are accorded diplomats, consuls, and international civil servants, and it is logical to discuss them in that order because that is the order in which the several categories came into being.

Ambassadors have been considered inviolable ever since man has been recording his association with groups other than his own. Biblical Israel looked upon ambassadors as inviolable.[1] The ancient Greeks believed that heralds, ambassadors, and their retinues were sacrosanct in all matters having to do with public office and executing their duties. They could go anywhere by land or sea in all proceedings having to do with peace and justice. For instance, Thucydides tells of a truce between the Athenians and Lacedaemonians in 423 B.C., which provided in Article V for safe conduct by land and sea for heralds and envoys and as many attendants as the two parties agreed upon.[2] In the fifth century B.C., as now, of course, the guarantees of diplomatic immunity were

[1] I Chronicles xix.
[2] Thucydides, *History of the Peloponnesian War*, IV, 118.

416

not always respected, but it is significant that the violations were punished. Thus, Herodotus tells of the remorse and expiation of the Spartans for mistreating envoys of the Persian king, Darius. The emissaries had been dispatched to Athens and to Sparta to demand for Persia control over land and sea or, symbolically, to demand "earth and water." The Athenians threw the emissaries into a pit, and the Spartans threw them into a well, telling them to carry earth and water to their king from those two places. Subsequently, Herodotus speculates that the Athenians may have suffered for their offense by the destruction of their city. However, two Spartan nobles offered their lives to Persia to atone for the violence done to the Persian representatives. Darius' son, Xerxes, interestingly enough, "replied that he would not behave like the Spartans, who by murdering the ambassadors of a foreign power had broken the law which all the world holds sacred."[3] He thus refused to taint Persian diplomatic practice by violating the common laws of mankind. What is especially significant here is that even between peoples who did not consider themselves part of the same civilization, the idea of a common standard of conduct, superior to them both, had already come into being. In fact, ancient history records few instances of violence offered to the persons of ambassadors, even in cases where the envoys themselves committed offenses in states to which they were accredited. Violence done to an ambassador was seen as a crime against a higher law and as a cause of war.

In ancient Rome, officials demonstrated much the same attitude toward ambassadors. They looked upon the diplomats as personifying the sovereignty and majesty of the states they represented, as bearing with them "the personality of the senate, the authority of the republic."[4] Any offense against an envoy was therefore an offense against the state, against the sovereign power, a deliberate infraction of the *ius gentium*, the law assumed to be common to all peoples. And unless the offender made some reparation, his act was for the Romans, as for the Greeks before, a cause for war. These immunities which ambassadors enjoyed in Rome extended to their attachés, to their correspondence, and to all things the envoys needed to perform their duties, but they did not extend, as they do today, to the entire ambassadorial suite or to the ambassador's families.

In times of war, enemy envoys remained as inviolable as the representatives of friendly states. Like the Greeks, the Romans showed their high regard for diplomatic practice by refusing to engage in reprisals

---

[3] Herodotus, *The Histories*, trans. by Aubrey de Selincourt (London: Penguin, 1954), vii, 133–137.
[4] Cicero, *Philippics*, viii:8.

against foreign ambassadors even when their own were ill-treated. Scipio's envoys in the second Punic war were ill-treated by the Carthagenians, but Romans scorned to violate diplomatic immunity even when the opportunity presented itself. Rome in fact severely punished those who committed offenses against foreign ambassadors. The College of Fetials investigated all complaints, and those found guilty were offered to the injured state, both to satisfy the authorities and also to appease the gods. Alternatively, the culprits might be deported, and, if later permitted to return to Rome, they were sometimes deprived of their citizenship. Sometimes the miscreants were even sentenced to death. Ambassadors to Rome were not subject to local law: they were exempt from local civil and criminal jurisdiction even when, as happened on some occasions, they were guilty of plotting against the state to which they were accredited; their houses were not regarded as immune, however, and they could not furnish asylum to others attempting to escape the authorities.

This general survey suggests the ancient lineage of modern diplomatic privileges and immunities, which we may examine under seven basic headings:

1. inviolability of person;
2. exemption from local civil and criminal jurisdiction;
3. freedom of domicile;
4. other privileges and immunities, for example:
   (a) exemption from taxation and other civic burdens;
   (b) freedom to correspond;
   (c) freedom from religious restrictions; and
   (d) protection of reputation.

Inviolability of Person. The person of the ambassador has generally been regarded as inviolable so as to allow different groups to conduct their relations with one another in an orderly manner. Obviously, if ambassadors cannot carry out their missions safely, diplomatic relations would be impossible. This point was already well established when Grotius laid down the consensus "everywhere recognized as prescribed by the law of nations, first, that ambassadors are to be admitted; and then that they are not to have violence offered them."[5] Ambassadorial immunity has always been closely connected to the mystique of the sovereign, whether a personal ruler or the collectivity of a state, and the ambassador generally enjoys some of the privileges due a head of state. He is, in fact, the personal representative of the head of state,

[5] *De Jure Belli ac Paris,* II, Chap. XVIII.

even in republics like the United States, where ambassadorial appointments are confirmed by the Senate, but ambassadors hold office only at the pleasure of the President. In the words of Blackstone,

The rights, the powers, the duties and the privileges of ambassadors are determined by the law of nature and nations, and not by any municipal constitutions. For, as they represent the person of their respective masters, who owe no subjection to any laws but those of their own country, their actions are not subject to the control of the private law of that state wherein they are appointed to reside.[6]

Because of the ambassador's fundamental role in diplomacy, states regard any injury to them quite seriously, and prompt apologies and redress are readily forthcoming. A state's failure to make these amends could be serious, for as an American judge pointed out in dealing with an attack on a Spanish *chargé d'affaires* "A neglect or refusal to perform the duty [of giving redress for violating the law on this point] might lead to retaliation upon our own ministers and even to war."[7] The mutual interest here is a real one. In consequence, the laws of most countries severely punish those who offend public ministers. Even in time of war, modern states, like their precursors, take care to protect accredited diplomats and allow them to return home.

Exemption from Local Jurisdiction. This exemption, which states accord ambassadors, is not a license granted to a privileged group to violate laws wholesale. Ambassadors are expected to obey the local laws voluntarily or to run the risk of becoming *persona non grata.* Even if states do not assume the right to punish an ambassador, they may ask the sending state to recall him, which is, in most cases, quite a sufficient sanction for most diplomats. Some authorities have at times wanted to whittle down ambassadorial privileges in order to make envoys available for private suits, but states have generally resisted such incursions into ambassadorial status on the solid ground that suits of any kind would keep the ambassador from doing his job and thus negate the very reason why the privileges were accorded in the first place. The extent to which his immunities protect him from jurisdiction over his private acts has rarely been a cause of dispute among states. Ambassadors may, of course, appear as witnesses in trials if they wish to; and if they refuse to appear, they may so offend the receiving state as to bring about their recall. Just what their responsibilities are in such matters is sometimes unclear. The United States, for instance, asked

[6] Sir William Blackstone, *Commentaries on the Law of England* (London, 1803), 4 vols., 4th ed., I, 223.
[7] United States v. Ortega, 4 Wash. C.C. 531.

the Dutch government to recall one of its ministers, Dubois, in 1856, when he refused to appear in a homicide case. The immunity which an ambassador enjoys is clearly not a personal privilege: it appertains to his state, as is illustrated in the case of Dickinson v. Del Solar.

DICKINSON v. DEL SOLAR

GREAT BRITAIN, KING'S BENCH DIVISION, 1929

[1930] 1 K.B. 376

LORD HEWART, C. J. This was an action in which the plaintiff, Mr. Robert Edmund Dickinson, sought to recover damages against the defendant, Emilio Del Solar, for injuries to the plaintiff caused by the negligent driving of a motor car by the defendant or his servant. That action was tried before me with a special jury on July 9 last, and in the result the jury awarded £856 damages to the plaintiff. Judgment was entered accordingly with costs against the defendant, Emilio Del Solar. That defendant however had a policy of insurance with the third parties, the Mobile and General Insurance Company, Ltd., and he claims against those third parties a declaration that he is entitled to be indemnified against any amount that he might be adjudged and ordered to pay to the plaintiff by way of damages in the action. . . . The third party alleged further that if the plaintiff in the action was injured, nevertheless the defendant was under no legal liability to the plaintiff by reason of the fact that the defendant was at all material times First Secretary of the Peruvian Legation and immune from civil process; alternatively, the third party relied upon certain alleged breaches of conditions.

. . . .

There followed correspondence; the representative of the insurance company was seen again by the defendant and it was made quite clear that the Minister of the Peruvian Legation had intervened and had forbidden the defendant to rely upon diplomatic immunity, inasmuch as the collision had taken place when the car was being used not for official but for private purposes. In the meantime certain steps had been taken in the action; an appearance had been entered by the insurance company for the defendant, other steps had been taken, and finally, when it was made abundantly clear that diplomatic privilege was not to be pleaded, this letter of March 5, 1929, was written by Mr. Del Solar's solicitors to the solicitors to the insurance company:

We have seen His Excellency the Peruvian Minister personally on this matter, and he has definitely repeated the instructions he has already given to his first secretary, Mr. Del Solar, to the effect that diplomatic privilege is not to be pleaded in this action; in our submission, therefore, the effect is that, so far at any rate as this claim is concerned, Mr. Del Solar has not and never did have any diplomatic privilege at all, so that it is impossible for him to claim it even if he wished to do so.

. . . .

Diplomatic agents are not, in virtue of their privileges as such, immune from legal liability for any wrongful acts. The accurate statement is that they are not liable to be sued in the English Courts unless they submit to the jurisdiction. Diplomatic privilege does not import immunity from legal liability, but only exemption from local jurisdiction. The privilege is the privilege of the Sovereign by whom the diplomatic agent is accredited, and it may be waived with the sanction of the Sovereign or of the official superior of the agent: Taylor v. Best (1854) 14 C.B. 487; *In re* Suarez [1918] 1 Ch. 176, 193. In the present case the privilege was waived and jurisdiction was submitted to by the entry of appearance: *In re* Suarez; Duff Development Co. v. Government of Kelantan (1924) A.C. 797, 830, and as Mr. Del Solar had so submitted to the jurisdiction it was no longer open to him to set up privilege. If privilege had been pleaded as a defence, the defence could, in the circumstances, have been struck out. Mr. Del Solar was bound to obey the direction of his Minister in the matter. In these circumstances it does not appear to me that there has been, on the part of Mr. Del Solar, any breach of the conditions of the policy, and the judgment clearly creates a legal liability against which the insurance company have agreed to indemnify him. It has been argued that by reason of the privilege execution cannot issue against Mr. Del Solar on the judgment. That is perhaps an open question: Duff Development Co. v. Government of Kelantan. But in my opinion it is not necessary to decide it. Even if execution could not issue in this country while Mr. Del Solar remains a diplomatic agent, presumably it might issue if he ceased to be a privileged person, and the judgment might also be the foundation of proceedings against him in Peru at any time. I hold therefore that the third parties here are liable.

Freedom of Domicile. Originally, the freedom from taxes and legal process that the residences of ambassadors enjoy was bolstered by the fiction of extraterritoriality, that is, the law assumed that the land on which the residence stood was temporarily removed from the jurisdiction of the receiving state and part of the territory of the sending state. As one writer has put it,

. . . when the ambassadors or public ministers of one state go upon a diplomatic mission to another and establish a residence there [t]he fiction is that such a residence is a part of the state from which the envoys have come, with all of its domestic institutions, including its special forms of religous worship, in full force; and with perfect immunity from the jurisdiction, both civil and criminal of the country to which it has been temporarily transferred.[8]

[8] Hannis Taylor, *International Public Law* (Chicago, 1901), p. 207.

This fiction, dating from the sixteenth and seventeenth centuries, was in time seen to be unnecessary, since it was perfectly possible to agree on immunity for an ambassadorial residence on functional grounds without going as far as to say that the land it occupied was temporarily outside the territorial domain of the state in which it was located. The embassy buildings remained immune because the immunity was essential if the ambassador was to carry out his functions.

Whatever the justification, certain general principles grew up about the residence and the embassy. For instance, no one could enter the embassy without the permission of the ambassador unless some emergency prevented authorities from seeking permission. Acting in accordance with this principle, for instance, the United States in 1836 discharged a constable who entered the house of the Secretary of the British legation to remove a fugitive slave.[9] Freedom of domicile is not unlimited, however, for ambassadors are expected not to make the shelter of diplomatic immunity available to common criminals. In general, governments will not protect anyone from processes of justice. Thus, in the Ripperda case (1726), Spain used force to remove the Duke of Ripperda, first minister of Philip V of Spain, accused of high treason, from the British embassy in Madrid, "since otherwise a privilege designed to maintain a closer connection among sovereigns could turn to their ruin and cause their destruction."[10] States may, however, provide asylum for persons accused of political crimes or fleeing from persecution. The liberality of governments varies in these matters. For instance, the United States normally does not grant asylum except in cases of public disorder or to protect someone from imminent mob violence.

Other Privileges and Immunities. Once states concede immunity from judicial process to ambassadors, they must logically extend to them freedom from taxation and other civic burdens since, if the envoys were not exempt, the receiving state could not collect taxes from them in the courts. Freedom of correspondence (the diplomatic pouch) is an obvious essential for the practice of diplomacy. And freedom of religious worship hardly raises any questions today, although when it was established in the sixteenth century, it was far more important: the unwillingness of Roman Catholic Spain to grant the emissary of Elizabeth I—one Dr. Marr—the right to worship as a Protestant once led the English

[9] U.S. v. Jeffers, 4 Cranch C. C. 704. But see Lincoln, At. Gen., 1804, 1 Op. 141, where the seizing of a slave was not regarded as such an offence.
[10] Letter from the Marquis de la Paz, Secretary of State of the King of Spain, to the Marquis Pozzo Bueno, Ambassador of the King in London, 25 May 1726, quoted, in French, in Charles de Martens, *Causes Célèbres du Droit des Gens* (2 vols., Leipzig, 1827), I, 195.

to break diplomatic relations with the Spanish Government.[11] As for protecting reputations, states undertake to guard diplomatic personnel from libelous attacks in the mutual interest of promoting good relations. Thus in 1784, the American Attorney-General, undertook to institute proceedings against those who had vilified the British ambassador:

> To represent in the public prints, such an officer as a contemptible person, to style him an incendiary jack-in-office, to charge him with deceiving the nation which sends him, and with inspiring another foreign minister with fears of being killed by certain citizens of the United States, is, no doubt, a publication that may be made the subject of legal prosecution.[12]

RESPUBLICA v. DE LONGCHAMPS

COURT OF OYER AND TERMINER—PHILADELPHIA 1784

1 DALLAS 111

McKean, Chief Justice. Charles Julian de Longchamps: You have been indicted for unlawfully and violently threatening and menacing bodily harm and violence to the person of the Honorable Francis Barbe de Marbois, secretary to the legation from France, and consul-general of France to the United States of America, in the mansion-house of the minister plenipotentiary of France; and for an assault and battery committed upon the said secretary and consul, in a public street in the city of Philadelphia. . . .

These offenses having been thus legally ascertained and fixed upon you, his Excellency the President, and the Honorable the Supreme Executive Council, attentive to the honor and interest of this state, were pleased to inform the judges of this court, as they had frequently done before, that the minister of France had earnestly repeated a demand, that you, having appeared in his house in the uniform of a French regiment, and having called yourself an officer in the troops of his Majesty, should be delivered up to him for these outrages, as a Frenchman, to be sent to France; and wished us in this stage of your prosecution, to take into mature consideration, and in the most solemn manner to determine:

1. Whether you could be legally delivered up by council, according to the claim made by the late minister of France?

2. If you could not be thus legally delivered up, whether your offenses in violation of the law of nations, being now ascertained and verified according to the laws of this commonwealth, you ought not be imprisoned, until his most Christian Majesty shall declare, that the reparation is satisfactory?

[11] Butler and Jacoby, p. 89.
[12] Opinion of Bradford, At. Gen., Sept. 17, 1794, 1 Op. 52 (Moore, IV, 629).

3. If you can be imprisoned, whether any legal act can be done by council, for causing you to be so imprisoned?

To these questions we have given the following answers in writing:

. . . .

1. . . . . Charles Julian de Longchamps cannot be legally delivered up by council, according to the claim made by the minister of France. Though, we think, cases may occur, where council could, *pro bono publico,* and to prevent atrocious offenders evading punishment, deliver them up to the justice of the country to which they belong, or where the offences were committed.

2. Punishments must be inflicted in the same county where the criminals were tried and convicted, unless the record of the attainder be removed into the supreme court, which may award execution in the county where it sits; they must be such as the laws expressly prescribe; or where no stated or fixed judgment is directed, according to the legal direction of the court; but judgments must be certain and definite in all respects. Therefore, we conclude, that the defendant cannot be imprisoned, until his most Christian Majesty shall declare that the reparation is satisfactory.

3. The answer to the last question is rendered unnecessary, by the above answer to the second question.

The foregoing answers having been given, it only remains for the court to pronounce sentence upon you. This sentence must be governed by a due consideration of the enormity and dangerous tendency of the offences you have committed, of the wilfulness, deliberation and malice wherewith they were done, of the quality and degree of the offended and offender, the provocation given, and all the other circumstances which may any way aggravate or extenuate the guilt.

The first crime in the indictment is an infraction of the law of nations. This law, in its full extent, is a part of the law of this state, and is to be collected from the practice of different nations, and the authority of writers. The person of a public minister is sacred and inviolable. Whoever offers any violence to him, not only affronts the sovereign he represents, but also hurts the common safety and well-being of nations—he is guilty of a crime against the whole world.

All the reasons, which establish the independency and inviolability of the person of a minister, apply likewise to secure the immunities of his house. It is to be defended from all outrage; it is under a peculiar protection of the laws; to invade its freedom, is a crime against the state and all other nations.

The *comites* of a minister or those of his train, partake also of his inviolability. The independence of a minister extends to all his household; these are so connected with him, that they enjoy his privileges and follow his fate. The secretary to the embassy has his commission from the sovereign himself; his is the most distinguished character in the suit of a public minister, and is, in some instances, considered as a kind of public minister himself. Is it not, then, an extraordinary insult, to use threats of bodily harm to his person, in the domicile of the minister plenipotentiary? If this is tolerated, his freedom of conduct is taken away, the business of his sovereign cannot be transacted, and his dignity and grandeur will be tarnished.

You then have been guilty of an atrocious violation of the law of nations; you have grossly insulted gentlemen, the peculiar objects of this law (gentlemen of amiable characters, and highly esteemed by the government of this state), in a most wanted and unprovoked manner; and it is now the interest as well as the duty of the government to animadvert upon your conduct with a becoming severity—such a severity as may tend to reform yourself, to deter others from the commission of the like crime, preserve the honor of the state, and maintain peace with our great and good ally, and the whole world.

A wrong opinion has been entertained concerning the conduct of Lord Chief Justice Holt and the court of King's bench, in England in the noted case of the Russian ambassador. They detained the offenders, after conviction, in prison, from term to term, until the Czar Peter was satisfied, without ever proceeding to judgment; and from this, it has been inferred, that the court doubted, whether they could inflict any punishment for an infraction of the law of nations. But this was not the reason. The court never doubted, that the law of nations formed a part of the law of England, and that a violation of this general law could be punished by them; but no punishment less than death would have been thought by the Czar an adequate reparation for the arrest of his ambassador. This punishment they could not inflict, and such a sentence as they could have given, he might have thought a fresh insult. Another expedient was, therefore, fallen upon. However, the princes of the world, at this day, are more enlightened, and do not require impracticable nor unreasonable reparations for injuries of this kind.

The second offence charged in this indictment, namely, the assault and battery, needs no observations.

Upon the whole, THE COURT, after a most attentive consideration of every circumstance in this case, do award, and direct me to pronounce the following sentence:

That you pay a fine of one hundred French crowns to the commonwealth; that you be imprisoned until the 4th day of July 1786, which will make a little more than two years' imprisonment in the whole; that you then give good security to keep the peace, and be of good behavior to all public ministers, secretaries to embassies and consuls, as well as to all the liege people of Pennsylvania, for the space of seven years, by entering into a recognisance, yourself in a thousand pounds, and two securities in five hundred pounds each; that you pay the costs of this prosecution, and remain committed until this sentence be complied with.

Problems Relating to Diplomatic Immunity. Problems sometimes arise in the relations among states in determining exactly who on the ambassadorial staff is entitled to diplomatic immunity. In general, immunities extend to the ambassador's official staff, immediate family, and to his personal staff. To determine whether or not someone should enjoy diplomatic privileges, courts consult the Diplomatic List, an official publication of the receiving state. Sending states are expected not to abuse the privilege of including persons on the diplomatic list, as was reportedly done in some English cases by audacious foreign ministers.

Thus in one case an attempt was made to protect a debtor on the ground of his being ostler to a foreign minister, who it was proven never kept horses; in another, on the ground of the defendant's being coachman to a foreign minister who kept no coach; in a third, of his being cook to one who kept no kitchen nor culinary instruments; in a fourth, of his being gardener to one who had no garden; in a fifth, of his being a physician, although there was no proof that he had ever prescribed in his life; and in a sixth, on the ground of his being English chaplain to the ambassador from Morocco, who was a Mahometan.[13]

On the other hand, states refusing to grant sending states the right to maintain an adequate staff may create the immediate cause for breaking diplomatic relations, as in 1961, when the United States refused to accede to a Cuban demand to limit the American Embassy staff in Havana to eleven persons. The United States protest follows:

Note of United States Government to Cuba, 3 January 1961

This unwarranted action by the Government of Cuba places crippling limitations on the ability of the U.S. Mission to carry on its normal diplomatic and consular functions. It would consequently appear that it is designed to achieve an effective termination of diplomatic and consular relations between the Government of Cuba and the Government of the United States. Accordingly the Government of the United States hereby notifies the Government of Cuba of the termination of such relations.[14]

At other times, a state may retaliate in kind as, for instance, the United States did in restricting the movements of Rumanian diplomats and asking the Czechs to reduce the size of their mission—both in 1950. Other problems that have from time to time troubled the international community include defining the time limits on diplomatic privileges and immunities. Do the time limits extend, for instance, from the time the ambassador leaves his home country, and therefore guard him from the action of third states? Do they begin only after he has been received at his post, and do they last until he returns home or only up to the moment he is recalled?

Codifying Diplomatic Privileges and Immunities. The most recent attempt to answer some of the questions that have arisen over the years

---

[13] Moore, IV, 655.
[14] *D.S.B.*, XLIV (1961), 103–104 and *The Annual Register* (1950), pp. 261, 277.

in connection with ambassadorial privileges and immunities is contained in the Vienna Convention on Diplomatic Relations (1961).

The Vienna Convention on Diplomatic Relations contains 53 articles codifying existing practice and clarifying some matters previously unclear. Its preamble specifies that diplomatic privileges and immunities are not designed to benefit individual diplomats but to help diplomatic missions perform efficiently. It provides, among other things, as follows:

(a) A receiving state may require the size of a mission to be "reasonable and normal" in size (Article 11).

(b) Receiving states shall regard diplomatic premises as inviolable, that local authorities must receive the consent of heads of mission to enter the premises, and that receiving states must protect foreign missions against searches, requisitions, legal attachments, damage, and acts that injure their dignity (Article 22).

(c) Receiving states must exempt mission premises from taxes (Article 23), treat their archives and documents as inviolable (Article 24), and provide missions with full facilities to perform their functions (Article 25).

(d) Receiving states must leave the members of a mission free to move and travel within their territory "subject to . . . laws and regulations concerning zones, entry into which is prohibited or regulated for reasons of national security" (Article 26).

(e) A diplomatic agent who is a national or permanent resident of the receiving state will have immunity only for his official acts, unless the receiving state grants other immunities; and that other staff members and private servants, also nationals or permanent residents, also enjoy immunity only for their official acts, except that the receiving states undertake to exercise jurisdiction over them so as not to interfere "unduly" with the missions' work (Article 38).

(f) Diplomatic privileges and immunities start from the moment a diplomatic agent enters the territory of the receiving state en route to his post or, if already there, from the moment the receiving state receives notice of his appointment; and that once the diplomat's functions have come to an end, he keeps his privileges and immunities until he leaves the country or until a reasonable period for leaving the country has expired; and that, furthermore, should a diplomat die at his post, his family continues to enjoy its immunity for a reasonable period after his death, no taxes are levied against the diplomat's personal estate, and his family may remove their movable property, except for goods acquired locally whose export is prohibited (Article 39).

(g) "Third" states, having granted visas to diplomats going to or coming from posts elsewhere, also accord immunities and inviolability to the traveling diplomats, their families, and other members of the diplomatic staff and family, their correspondence, and couriers (Article 40).[15]

Consular Privileges

Consuls, who are primarily commercial officers of states, enjoy privileges and immunities commensurate with their lesser responsibilities, but there is no doubt here, that their privileges extend only to their official functions, not to their personal affairs: they have absolutely no immunity for their private acts in the receiving countries. At one point in history, they enjoyed no privileges at all, but as their duties have grown, so have the number of treaties defining their rights. In any case, the basis of such privileges as they do enjoy is clearly a matter of treaty rights and not ancient custom, as in the case of their ambassadorial superiors.

International Civil Servants

The newest categories of persons entitled to privileges and immunities are those civil servants who work for international organizations like the United Nations and the specialized agencies. Their rights, like those of consuls, rest upon treaties, specifically the League of Nations Covenant, the United Nations Charter, and agreements between the international organizations and the member states. In addition, international organizations make special arrangements with those countries in which they have their headquarters, in order to cover the wider range of problems that inevitably arise in defining the relations between a host state and international organizations. In general, the organizations ask only for privileges for their staffs that will permit them to carry out their functions. Ironically enough, those who in theory most need the privileges, the nationals of the host state working for an international organization, are the ones least likely to receive them. Thus, the United States has refused to ratify the General Convention on Privileges and Immunities, which would grant to its nationals (the largest group working for the international organizations) working for the United Nations the immunities from taxation and police interference which a truly international status would require.

Persons with Business before International Organizations

Such persons have the right of access to international organizations, under headquarters agreements with host countries, like the United States. In general, these agreements require the host country to admit

[15] By 1968, 65 states had ratified the Convention. For text, see 500 U.N.T.S. 95.

persons to their territory so as to give them access to the international organization doing business there, even if such persons might ordinarily not be admissible under immigration laws. The host state may impose restrictions on persons so admitted, and the United States has done so from time to time, either by limiting the geographical area of the United States such persons may visit or the length of their stay. The rights of access are limited quite strictly, in any case, as became apparent when Henrique Galvão, wanted by the government of Portugal for alleged acts of piracy, was to appear at the United Nations.[16]

Eighteenth session
FOURTH COMMITTEE
Agenda item 23

Distr.
GENERAL

A/C.4/621
15 November 1963

ORIGINAL: ENGLISH

TERRITORIES UNDER PORTUGUESE ADMINISTRATION

Opinion of the Legal Counsel on the question of the right of transit to the Headquarters district raised in the Fourth Committee at its 1475th meeting in connexion with a request for a hearing concerning Territories under Portuguese administration (A/C.4/600/Add. 4 and 5)

Note by the Secretariat: This Opinion, which was given in accordance with a decision taken by the Fourth Committee at its 1475th meeting and which was originally made available as a Conference Room Paper, is now circulated as a document in accordance with a decision taken by the Fourth Committee at its 1481st meeting.

1. At its 1475th meeting on 11 November 1963 the Fourth Committee requested an opinion as to the legal implications of the possible appearance before it of Mr. Galvão.

2. The Committee will wish to take into accournt the limited character of the legal status of an individual invited to the Headquarters for the purpose of appearing before a Committee of the General Assembly or other organ of the United Nations.

3. Section 11 of the Headquarters Agreement between the United Nations and the United States of America provides that the federal, state or local authorities of the United States shall not impose any impediments to transit

[16] By a vote of 49 to 4, with 41 abstentions, the Fourth Committee of the U.N. General Assembly on November 14, 1963, decided to grant the request for hearing of Henrique Galvão. On December 9 and 10, 1963, Mr. Galvão appeared before the Committee, and he left the United States on December 10, 1963.

to or from the Headquarters District of (among other classes of persons) persons invited to the Headquarters District by the United Nations on official business. While such a person is in transit to or from the Headquarters District, the appropriate American authorities are required to accord him any necessary protection.

4. Apart from police protection, therefore, the obligations imposed on the host Government by the Headquarters Agreement are limited to assuring the right of access to the Headquarters and an eventual right of departure. The Headquarters Agreement does not confer any diplomatic status upon an individual invitee because of his status as such. He therefore cannot be said to be immune from suit or legal process during his sojourn in the United States and outside of the Headquarters District.

5. Two other provisions of the Headquarters Agreement serve to reinforce the right of access to the Headquarters. Section 13(a) specifies that the laws and regulations in force in the United States regarding the *entry* of aliens shall not be applied in such manner as to interfere with the privilege of transit to the Headquarters District. This provision, however, clearly assures admission to the United States without conferring any other privilege or immunity during the sojourn. Similarly, Section 13(b) interposes certain limitations on the right of the host Government to require the departure of persons invited to the Headquarters District while they continue in their official capacity; but this plainly relates to restrictions on the power of deportation and not, conversely, on a duty to bring about departure. Moreover, Section 13(d) makes clear that, apart from the two foregoing restrictions, "the United States retains full control and authority over the entry of persons or property into the territory of the United States and the conditions under which persons may remain or reside there."

6. It is thus clear that the United Nations would be in no position to offer general assurances to Mr. Galvão concerning immunity from legal process during his sojourn in the United States. It might be that individual citizens of the United States might have civil causes of action against him and could subject him to service of process. While the Federal Government might have no intention, and might lack jurisdiction, to initiate any criminal proceedings against him, it is a known fact that there are legal limitations on the powers of the Executive Branch of the United States Government to ensure against any type of proceeding by another branch of the Government, including the Judicial Branch.

7. Moreover, apart from general restrictions in the Federal Regulations on the departure of an alien from the United States when he is needed in connexion with any proceeding to be conducted by any executive, legislative, or judicial agency in the United States, the attention of the Committee has already been invited to the possibility that extradition proceedings might be instituted against Mr. Galvão during his presence in this country. By an Extradition Convention of 1908 between Portugal and the United States

persons may be delivered up who are charged, among other crimes, with piracy or with mutiny or conspiracy by two or more members of the crew or other persons on board of a vessel on the high seas, for the purpose of rebelling against the authority of the captain of the vessel, or by fraud or violence taking possession of the vessel, or with assault on board ships upon the high seas with intent to do bodily harm, or with abduction or detention of persons for any unlawful end. The extradition is also to take place for the participation in any such crimes as an accessory before or after the fact. The Convention contains the usual exception for any crime or offence of a political character, or for acts connected with such crimes or offences. (II Mallory Treaties 1469, Articles II, III.)

8. Whenever there is an extradition convention between the United States and any foreign Government, any federal or state judge of the United States may issue a warrant for the apprehension of any person found within his jurisdiction who is properly charged with having committed within the jurisdiction of any such foreign Government any of the crimes provided for by the Convention. If, after hearing and considering the evidence of criminality, the judge deems it sufficient to sustain the charge under the convention, he must certify this conclusion to the Secretary of State of the United States in order that a warrant may issue upon the requisition of the proper authorities of the foreign Government for the surrender of the person according to the terms of the convention. (18 U.S. Code 3184.)

9. There is no precedent in the history of the Headquarters Agreement which would indicate whether an application of Federal Regulations restricting departure of an alien, by reason of proceedings against him not related to his presence at the United Nations, would constitute an impediment to transit "from the Headquarters District" within the meaning of Section 11 of the Agreement. There is likewise no precedent which would indicate whether compliance by the Federal Government with the terms of an extradition treaty would conflict with the right of transit of an invitee from the Headquarters District. In this connexion it is important to note that what the United States Government has undertaken not to do, by the terms of Section 11, is to "impose" an impediment to transit from the Headquarters. To the extent that the presence of Mr. Galvão in the United States might in one manner or another give rise to proceedings against him by operation of existing law in relation to pre-existing facts (such as previous activities on his part), it could be argued that this did not constitute an action taken by the Government to impose an impediment on his departure.

10. The Legal Counsel is of course not in a position to pass upon the internal operations of United States law, much less upon the relations between the Executive and Judicial Branches of the Government. Even if it should prove possible that the Executive Branch could, in the exercise of its authority over foreign affairs, certify and allow to the Judicial Branch that the freedom of Mr. Galvão to depart without impediment should override the authority of the courts to detain him, it is not clear on what basis an advance assurance

could be given him. Likewise, even if a dispute were to arise between the United Nations and the United States on such an issue, it might eventually require referral to a tribunal of arbitrators under the terms of Section 21 of the Headquarters Agreement.

11. In these circumstances, it must be recognized that a situation could arise by which the Fourth Committee was deprived of the advantage ot receiving oral testimony from Mr. Galvão. Should he not be prepared to attend because of the inability of the host Government to confer upon him a general immunity, it is clear that his abstention from appearing would be his own, and not the affirmative imposition of an impediment to his transit. For it might only be at the moment of his attempted departure from the United States that an arbitrable dispute could arise as to whether he was entitled to depart notwithstanding proceedings which might in the meantime have been instituted against him.

12. Two other points of law were raised in the 1475th meeting of the Committee. It was suggested that, in the event of a conflict between the obligations of the United States under its Extradition Treaty with Portugal and the Charter, the obligations under the Charter would prevail by virtue of its Article 103. The difficulty here is that such rights as enure Mr. Galvão stem directly from the Headquarters Agreement and not from any provision of the Charter, which does not cover invitees. The question was also raised as to whether the Treaty could be invoked before the General Assembly under Article 102 of the Charter. The sanction in the second paragraph of that Article, however, relates to treaties required to be registered with the Secretariat under that Article. The Extradition Treaty in question dates from the year 1908, whereas the duty to register relates only to treaties entered into by a Member after the coming into force of the Charter. It is also true that, in the hypothetical situation dealt with above, the risk is that the Extradition Treaty would be invoked in the United States courts rather than in the General Assembly.

*   *   *

UNITED STATES DELEGATION
TO THE GENERAL ASSEMBLY

FOR IMMEDIATE RELEASE   Press Release No. 4297
                                         November 11, 1963

Statement by Ambassador Sidney R. Yates, United States Representative, in Committee Four, on the request for a hearing by Mr. Galvão.

. . . .

Mr. Chairman:

I have asked for the floor briefly at this point to bring to the Committee's attention certain factors in connection with the request for a hearing we are now considering. Let me say first, we do not object to Mr. Galvão's appearance. We desire only to point out possible consequences of Mr. Galvão's appearance before this Committee. This Committee should be fully aware it could raise serious problems because of certain unique aspects of his situation. Granting the request for a hearing could set in motion a sequence of events which could pose most serious consequences for Mr. Galvão. Because it could be later asserted that responsibility for those consequences rested in part with the Committee, I believe the Committee in reaching its decision should give careful thought to certain factors.

I would point out, Mr. Chairman, that the United States has extradition agreements with some 78 countries. Under these agreements, a country has the right to undertake measures to extradite persons accused, in that country, of serious crimes.

First of all, let me make clear at the outset that there is no question that, if Mr. Galvão is invited to appear before this Committee at UN Headquarters, the United States will—as in the case of other petitioners—take the necessary steps to enable him to travel to the headquarters district, in accordance with Section 11 of the Headquarters Agreement. However, the members of this Committee will also be aware that Section 11, while entitling invited persons to travel to the headquarters district, and contemplating routine measures of protection while they are in transit, does not grant them immunity from legal process. Such immunity is granted by Section 15 of the Headquarters Agreement, whose benefits are limited by its own terms, to resident representatives of members of the Organization, and to certain members of their staffs. Accordingly, Mr. Galvão, while present in the United States, would not enjoy immunity from legal process.

May I note, in passing, that while the United States is not party to the General Convention on Privileges and Immunities of the United Nations, the situation would in no way be changed if we were party, since the General Convention does not confer any immunity on invitees.

As members of the Committee are aware, the Government of Portugal seeks custody over Mr. Galvão in connection with certain serious charges, alleging criminal acts. It may be that some of these charges, at least by name, might prove to come within terms of the Extradition Convention of May 7, 1908 between Portugal and the United States. Accordingly, it would appear very likely that the Government of Portugal will initiate proceedings in the courts of this country for Mr. Galvão's extradition.

The United States is prepared as I noted earlier to comply fully with its obligations under the Headquarters Agreement. At the same time, however, neither the Government nor the courts of this country have any choice but to comply with whatever legal obligations they may have under the Extradition Convention. In the light of these considerations, we think it incumbent upon the United States Delegation to set forth this situation unequivocally to the Committee in order that its decision regarding the issuance of an invitation or the granting of the request for a hearing to Mr. Galvão may proceed without any possible misunderstanding.

Mr. Chairman, in view of these considerations, we suggest that the Committee, rather than granting Mr. Galvão's request for a hearing, might wish to invite him to submit a statement in writing or make an audiotape recording which could be heard by the Committee. While we recognize that such a procedure is not as satisfactory as having a petitioner present in person, it would, nevertheless, permit Mr. Galvão to submit his views to the Committee and would at the same time eliminate the difficulties I have described.

Privileges and Immunities (States and International Organizations)

Cases presented earlier in Chapter II have indicated implicitly that states, as sovereigns, are immune from the jurisdiction of foreign courts. Questions of immunity have arisen in connection with recognition problems; they also arise when states engage in activities traditionally regarded as commercial or, to use the Latin phrase, as part of the *jus gestionis* (the law of management or transactions), as opposed to the *jus imperii* (law of command).

With the development of state trading, especially since the Soviet Revolution of 1918, more and more states, communist and noncommunist, have engaged in transactions that in earlier centuries might have been carried on as private undertakings. The difficulties these undertakings pose for courts appear clearly in the case of *N. V. Cabolent* v. *National Iranian Oil Company.*

N. V. CABOLENT v. NATIONAL IRANIAN OIL COMPANY

The Netherlands, District Court of the Hague, 2d Chamber
63/2217 and 63/2467, Decision of April 15, 1965

Note on Factual Background of Case[17]

This suit was brought by N. V. Cabolent, the Netherlands subsidiary of Cabol Enterprises, Ltd., of Toronto, Canada, to enforce an arbitration award against the National Iranian Oil Company (hereafter NIOC).

On June 16, 1958, Sapphire Petroleums, Ltd., a subsidiary of Cabol Enterprises, concluded an agreement with NIOC for exploration for and production of oil in southern Iran. When disagreements between Sapphire and NIOC arose and were not resolved, Sapphire instituted arbitration proceedings against NIOC in Switzerland pursuant to the agreement. NIOC did not appear in these proceedings; and the arbitrator, Judge Pierre Cavin of Lausanne, on March 15, 1963, rendered an award in favor of Sapphire. Sapphire later assigned its rights under the award to N. V. Cabolent. Cabolent initiated the present suit through service of process in the Netherlands upon NIOC and its Dutch subsidiaries.

In this case in the District Court of the Hague, NIOC claimed sovereign immunity as the Iranian governmental body for developing the nationalized

[17] Prepared by the editors of *International Legal Materials*, V, 477.

petroleum industry. The Court held NIOC was entitled to sovereign immunity and did not reach the question of the enforceability of Judge Cavin's award.

Judgment of the Court[18]

Considering with respect to the law:
in the joint cases:

Preceding to all other pleas the defendant—hereinafter to be called NIOC—argued, that on the strength of the rule of unwritten international law mentioned by it in its statements it can, with respect to the present claims, only be taken into the competent Iranian Court, so that this Court has no jurisdiction with respect to the claims.

It may be premised that it is generally recognized in international law, that in principle a sovereign state cannot be submitted to the jurisdiction of a foreign state against its will. However, a tendency can be shown in jurisprudence and case law to limit this immunity of the state, that is to the so-called "acta iure imperii."

If such an act of the foreign state "iure imperii" has to be deemed to exist in the present case, the Court then ought to refuse to entertain jurisdiction in pursuance of art. 13a of the "Wet houdende Algemene Bepalingen der Wetgeving van het Koninkrijk" (Statute containing General Provisions of the legislation of the Kingdom). Together with the learned authors and the case law, who reject unlimited immunity, the Court holds that the acceptance of unlimited immunity cannot be justified any longer at this present time, when a great number of states take it to their public responsibility to interfere actively and drastically with the regulation of the economic life in particular and thus participate in economic life in nearly the same way as a private person. This active responsibility and activity of the state in the economic field, specifically to be seen in countries like Iran where the exploitation of the natural resources is by far the most important source of revenue, is considered to be of equal importance for life and well being of country and people as compared with *e.g.* the care for the military defence, which of old is part of the responsibility of the state. This actual development of the function and the activity of the state had as a result that the state, for the sake of a well-balanced and efficient execution of same, started to use forms of organization other than the public law ones that were customary before. Whether the foreign state chooses to use one or the other form of organization to reach its goals is naturally to be left to its discretion. It it not incumbent upon the Dutch Courts to pass judgment on this choice.

This course of events with respect to the economic activity of the state entails, however, that, whenever a foreign defendant invokes the immunity to which it is allegedly entitled under international law, the Court will have to examine whether with respect to the issue brought before the Court this

---

[18] [Reprinted from a translation provided by M. P. Bloemsma, The Hague, attorney for N. V. Cabolent. The summary of the facts and the arguments of the parties have been omitted.]

defendant has acted "iure imperii" as an organ of the foreign state, which has to be identified with that state.

After Iran had nationalized, by Statute of March 15th and 20th, 1951, the entire oil industry, *i.e.* the exploration, winning and exploitation of oil on its territory, NIOC was established as "a commercial joint-stock company" by Iranian legislative decree of April 30th, 1951. The by-laws of NIOC were drawn up by a commission, composed of five members of the Iranian Senate and five members of the Iranian Parliament, and the Minister of Finance. They were subsequently approved by both Chambers of the Iranian Parliament. According to their unofficial English translation—of which, however, during the speeches of counsel both parties declared that they accepted this translation as correct—the by-laws stipulate i.a.:

(a) all NIOC-shares are property of Iran and are not transferable (sect. 3);

(b) at the general shareholders' meeting the shareholders—the state of Iran—are represented by three Ministers, to wit the Minister of Finance, who also acts as Chairman, the Minister of Industry and Mining and a third Minister appointed by the Cabinet Council (sect. 14);

(c) the "High Council"—its function as an organ of NIOC is described in section 24 of the by-laws—is composed of seven members chosen from and by the Iranian Parliament, the Minister of Finance who acts as Chairman at the meetings of the Council, the Minister of Industry and Mining and the Attorney-General with the Iranian Court of Cassation (sect. 21);

(d) the by-laws can be amended by the general shareholders' meeting; each amendment, however, has to be approved by the Iranian Parliament (sect. 19, sub a);

(e) NIOC is responsible for the preservation of the natural resources in the soil and the Iranian continental shelf; wherever this responsibility has been entrusted to others than NIOC by statute, NIOC has the supreme control (sect. 58).

According to sections 1 and 2 of the Petroleum Act of July 31st, 1957 all activities pertaining to exploration and winning of oil and oil products, wherever in Iran and in the Iranian continental shelf—with the exception of those territories, with respect to which a concession has been granted to an international consortium—and all activities pertaining to refining, transport and sale of oil and oil products belong to the sphere of actions of NIOC. NIOC also has the right to negotiate with third parties and to enter into agreements with respect to the above mentioned activities. These agreements have to be submitted to the Iranian Parliament for approval. The agreement will be effective from the day of approval by the Parliament only.

On the strength of the above mentioned provisions of statute and by-laws the Court holds, that NIOC is an organization of the company-type, wholly controlled and managed by the Iranian Government, subject to parliamentary control and promoting the primordial economic and social interests of the state of Iran in the oil industry on her territory, which promotion that state has made part of its public responsibility as appears from the nationalization in 1951. Whether the state of Iran gives effect to its self-imposed responsibility in the official departmental form or in the form of a "commercial joint stock company" which meets the demands of modern economic intercourse in a better way, and whether NIOC, when acting, is also now and then participating in this intercourse on the same footing as a private person, the Court does not deem to be decisive for the question whether immunity has been invoked rightly or not. The basis of this suit is the agreement—governed by Iranian law—of June 16th, 1958 concluded between NIOC and Sapphire Petroleum Limited, a Canadian Company, pertaining to the exploration for and possible exploitation of oil on part of the Iranian territory as specified in the Agreement. This agreement, granting a concession to the Canadian company, has been concluded in compliance with the provisions of the Petroleum Act of 1957. It has been approved by the Iranian Government and the Iranian Parliament and was promulgated by the Shah of Iran in compliance with section 27 of the Iranian constitution, by Imperial Decree of July 23rd, 1958.

On the strength of the preceding the Court holds, that NIOC, when entering into this agreement, was acting as an organ of the central government which has to be identified with that government, and that it acted thereby "iure imperii," so that NIOC like Iran itself, cannot be submitted against its will to the jurisdiction of the Dutch Courts.

Neither the fact that arbitration has been agreed to in that agreement, which has no connection with Dutch Sphere of jurisdiction, nor the fact that NIOC has argued the case on its merits can be construed as a waiver of the right to invoke immunity.

Thus it has to be decided as follows:

DOING JUSTICE
in the joint cases:

The Court declares itself without jurisdiction to take cognizance of the claims.

It gives judgement against the plaintiff for the costs of the proceedings in this suit and in the incident, estimated at the side of the defendant up till this verdict at Dfl.2.650,—(TWO THOUSAND SIX HUNDRED AND FIFTY GUILDERS).

This given by J. Schaafsma, Vice-President, B. Pronk and S. F. Kootte, Judges, and pronounced at the public session of this Court and Chamber of April 15th, 1965 by mouth of the Vice-President mentioned before in the presence of C. J. Konijnenburg, Substitute-Clerk of the Court.

signed: J. Schaafsma.
signed: C. J. Konijnenburg.

      ❅   ❅   ❅

By treaty or statute, or both, states have accorded to international organizations the rights and privileges which they, as entities and as distinguished from their employees, need to carry on their functions in the international community. One instance of an attempt to challenge and restrict these privileges occurred in the case of *Lutcher, S. A.* v. *Inter-American Development Bank.*

LUTCHER S. A. . . . v. INTER-AMERICAN DEVELOPMENT BANK

UNITED STATES DISTRICT COURT, DISTRICT OF COLUMBIA, 1966

253 F. SUPP. 568

GASCH, District Judge.

This cause came on for hearing on plaintiffs' motion for preliminary injunction and defendant's motion to dismiss. Plaintiffs seek to enjoin the Inter-American Development Bank from augmenting a loan to one of plaintiffs' competitors. The loan would facilitate the development of a pulp mill in Brazil. Plaintiffs are engaged in a similar business and contend that the market will not support two mills. Plaintiffs further contend that the Bank has ignored certain alleged market conditions and that if consummated, the additional loan to plaintiffs' competitor would not be a prudent act.

Defendant's motion to dismiss is predicated upon two points: (1) the Bank is immune from suit, such as the one filed in the instant case; and (2) the complaint does not state a claim upon which relief can be granted. For the reasons hereinafter set forth, the Court agrees with both of defendant's contentions.

The International Organizations Immunities Act provides, in part:

"International organizations, their property and their assets, wherever located, and by whomsoever held, shall enjoy the same immunity from suit in every form of judicial process as is enjoyed by foreign governments, except to the extent that such organizations may expressly waive their immunity for the purpose of any proceedings or by the terms of any contract."[19]

An Executive Order of President Eisenhower dated April 8, 1960, designated the Inter-American Development Bank as a public international organization which would be entitled to the immunities and exemptions flowing from the above-quoted statute.[20] A subsequent Executive Order promulgated by President Kennedy provided that the first Executive Order should not be construed as affecting a certain provision of the Bank's Charter, which provides:

Actions may be brought against the Bank only in a court of competent jurisdiction in the territories of a member in which the Bank has an office, has appointed an agent for the purpose of accepting service or notice of process, or has issued or guaranteed securities.

No action shall be brought against the Bank by members or persons acting

[19] 22 U.S.C. sec. 288a(b).
[20] Executive Order 10873, 3 C.F.R. 404 (1959–1963 Comp.).

for or deriving claims from members. However, member countries shall have recourse to such special procedures to settle controversies between the Bank and its members as may be prescribed in this Agreement, in the by-laws and regulations of the Bank or in contracts entered into with the Bank.

Property and assets of the Bank shall, wheresoever located and by whomsoever held, be immune from all forms of seizure, attachment or execution before the delivery of final judgment against the Bank.

These pronouncements of executive policy and the Bank's position on its amenability to suit should be considered as important factors relating to the existence of jurisdiction of this Court in the instant case.

The Supreme Court has recognized that sovereign immunity has become part of the fabric of our judicial system through the adjudications of the courts.[21] While there is nothing in the Constitution on the subject, it was early recognized that the dignity and standing of foreign sovereigns could be preserved and maintained by not subjecting them or their agents to the jurisdiction of the United States Courts.[22] When a suit filed in a court of law could conceivably involve delicate matters of international relations, the courts should recognize that under our Constitution such matters are confided to the judgment and discretion of the Executive Branch of the Government.[23] Plaintiff argues that the Bank has been sued in previous situations: where a customer fell on the floor,[24] where there was an alleged breach of a contractual relationship with a coffee shop,[25] and where workmen's compensation was involved.[26] However, situations comparable to the one in which the Court is confronted are clearly distinguishable for the reason that cases involving the discretion and judgment of the Bank's governing board in matters of economic policy closely associated with consideration of international politics are vastly different from cases involving simple torts and contracts. Where delicate, complex issues of international economic policy are involved, jurisdiction should be denied.

Assuming *arguendo* that this Court does have jurisdiction, it is highly questionable whether even a domestic bank could properly be sued by one of two competing customers who alleged that the Bank had imprudently loaned money to the second customer and thereby made more difficult the customer's obligation to respond. Here, it is clear that the situation with which the Court is confronted in this complaint is even more lacking in merit in the judicial sense. Plaintiffs' standing to raise the issues on which they rely is by no means established irrespective of the foreign policy consideration.[27] Counsel does not urge that there is any clause of the contract between plain-

---

[21] *National City Bank v. Republic of China*, 348 U.S. 356, 358 (1955).

[22] *The Schooner Exchange v. M'Fadden* 11 U.S. (7 Cranch) 116 (1812).

[23] *United States v. Curtiss-Wright Export Corp.*, 299 U.S. 304 (1936).

[24] *Schutz, Et Al. v. Ship Shape Maintenance Corp., Et Al.*, 2860–65.

[25] *808 Coffee Shop v. Inter-American Development Bank*, 3202–65.

[26] *Commerce Insurance Company of Newark, N.J. v. Red Coats, Inc.*, 2267–64.

[27] *Alabama Power Company v. Ickes*, 302 U.S. 464 (1938); *Kansas City Power & Light Company v. McKay*, 96 U.S. App. D.C. 273, 225 F. 2d 924 (D.C. D.C. 1955), *cert. denied* 350 U.S. 884 (1955).

tiffs and the Bank which specifically concerns the matter of limiting possible competition. He relies on implication. The contract provides for the ultimate sale of Twenty-five Percent (25%) of plaintiffs' stock. Plaintiffs contend that the Bank is required to act prudently in other matters so that the plaintiffs' stock will be marketable. Plaintiffs also complain about repayment features of the loan. In the opinion of the Court, none of these contentions are sufficient to establish an implied contract guaranteeing plaintiffs what amounts to a virtual monopoly in the borrowing of the Bank's funds to establish a pulp mill in Brazil. Furthermore, where the contract between the parties is detailed and specific, as in the instant case, the courts will not improvise an implied contract.[28]

Plaintiffs have failed to demonstrate irreparable injury or the probability of ultimate success.

Although counsel for the Bank has not raised the question of an indispensable party, nevertheless, the Court notes that the competing customer (the Klabin group) is not before the Court. This familiar doctrine alone would preclude the taking of such action as is sought by the plaintiffs in that it would be highly prejudicial to this missing indispensable party.[29]

For these reasons, plaintiffs' motion for preliminary injunction should be and is denied, and defendant's motion to dismiss is granted.

Agreements Among States

General

In the absence of an international legislative body to order matters of international concern among states, specific agreements between and among them (sometimes called "international legislation") have been the principal means of making peaceful changes in the international order.

International agreements take many forms, and out of the practice of states has arisen a considerable body of law regarding the means by which parties enter into, try to perform, and seek to terminate their understandings.[30] As relations of all kinds among states have increased, so has the number of treaties regulating those relations, defining states' mutual interests, and limiting the individual freedom of states. From December 14, 1946, to June 15, 1967, for instance, states that were members of the United Nations registered or filed and recorded 12,636 treaties with the Secretariat.[31] States have also bound themselves increasingly

[28] *Roebling v. Dillon*, 109 U.S. App. D.C. 42, 288 F. 2d 386 (1961), *cert. denied* 366 U.S. 918 (1961); *Fort Sill Gardens, Inc. v. United States*, 355 F. 2d 636 (Ct. Cl. 1966).
[29] *Lumbermen's Mutual Casualty Company v. Elbert*, 348 U.S. 48 (1954).
[30] Hyde, II, 1369–1373.
[31] U.N. GA OR XXII (1967), Supp. No. 1, p. 182.

by multilateral conventions as the complexity of international relations has grown.

Many examples of states violating treaties come to mind, but no instances of states violating treaties without attempting to justify their violation in legal or moral terms. This manifestation of concern for legal or moral niceties may be sheer hypocrisy or it may arise because of an ingrown acknowledgement of law among all men, even among those who break it. Whatever the reason, it has proved sufficiently strong to hold together a considerable structure of international relations. In quantitative terms, the number of treaties observed certainly outstrips the number violated, although the violations of major treaties undoubtedly produce repercussions all out of proportion to their number. The mere fact that thousands of treaties may be observed when only one is violated pales into insignificance when the one that is violated results in a major world war. There are those who maintain, however, that if there is one single fundamental rule at the base of international law, it is *pacta sunt servanda* (treaties must be observed), for without respect for treaties, states would be unable to stabilize their relations in any way, and all law and order would fail.

Duress

The consent of a state is theoretically necessary before it becomes party to a treaty. In fact, however, states, particularly when they are vanquished in combat, but also when considerable political pressure is brought against them, may sign agreements that they would not make if they had true freedom of choice. Ideally, treaty law would incorporate the provisions of private contract law, which invalidates any agreement entered into under duress. Treaties concluded as a result of force or undue pressure will be deemed void, however, only when a more nearly perfect system exists for righting wrongs in the international community.

The true anomaly in the present law is not that it should be legal to coerce a state into accepting obligations which it does not like, but that it should be legal for a state which has been victorious in a war to do the coercing; and the change to which we ought to look forward is not the elimination of the use of coercion from the transaction, but the establishment of international machinery to ensure that when coercion is used it shall be in a proper case and by due process of law, and not, as at present it may be, arbitrarily. The problem of treaties imposed by force is therefore in its essence not a problem of treaty law, but a particular aspect of that much wider problem which pervades the whole system, that of subordinating the use of force to law.[32]

[32] Brierly, *Law of Nations,* 6th ed. p. 319.

At the same time, it is worth noting that long-lived treaties are those which record a true mutual interest on the part of all signatories. Treaties, which statesmen are in effect forced to sign, for example, at the end of a war in which their state has been defeated, may seem to be so punitive as to create almost automatically a resentment that will lead those statesmen or their successors to devote considerable energy to overthrowing the order established by the agreements. This resentment was clearly visible with regard to the "settlements" after the first World War, which Germany and Italy eventually regarded as mere scraps of paper. Those states which impose onerous treaties upon other states must be prepared either to enforce those terms for all time or to change the treaty when the conditions begin to rankle. Thus the United States in 1961 revised the security treaty signed with defeated Japan in 1954.

The League of Nations formerly had and the United Nations now has the legal and political apparatus to adjust the international order.

League of Nations Covenant Article 19

The Assembly may from time to time advise the reconsideration by Members of the League of treaties which have become inapplicable and the consideration of international conditions whose continuance might endanger the peace of the world.

United Nations Charter Article 14

. . . the General Assembly may recommend measures for the peaceful adjustment of any situation, regardless of origin, which it deems likely to impair the general welfare or friendly relations among nations, including situations resulting from a violation of the provisions of the present Charter setting forth the Purposes and Principles of the United Nations.

Unfortunately, states desiring change do not always choose to wait for the slow processes of international political negotiation or legal adjudication. They sometimes prefer, often for reasons of national politics, to take action into their own hands, as Hitler and Mussolini did in the years between World Wars I and II.

Definition

A treaty is sometimes known by other names: agreement, convention, compact, covenant, protocol, Charter, and *modus vivendi*. Regardless of the name, an instrument recording an agreement between two states is a treaty in international law, including even those documents that the United States styles "Executive Agreements." The President often makes such agreements on his own authority (as in the destroyer-base agreement with Britain in 1940 discussed below) or under grants of congressional power (engagements concerning trade, commerce, and navigation; copyrights, trademarks, postal conventions, loans, and territory). Sometimes the United States has undertaken international commitments by presidential action after a joint congressional resolution (membership in many international organizations like the International Labour Organisation in 1934, and others). The courts traditionally regard all of these arrangements as having the same effect as the more formal treaties. As the Supreme Court stated in 1912:

> While it may be true that this commercial agreement [with France, 30 Stat. 1774 made under the authority of the Tariff Act of 1897] was not a treaty possessing the dignity of one requiring ratification by the Senate of the United States, it was made in the name and on behalf of the contracting countries and dealing with important commercial relations between the two countries, and was proclaimed by the President. If not technically a treaty requiring ratification, nevertheless it was a compact authorized by the Congress of the United States, negotiated and proclaimed under the authority of its President.[33]

The opinion of the Attorney General in 1940 on the power of President Franklin D. Roosevelt to arrange to transfer certain overage destroyers to the United Kingdom in exchange for leases to certain British possessions in the American hemisphere demonstrates the wide-ranging purposes to which executive agreements may be put.

OPINION OF ATTORNEY-GENERAL ROBERT H. JACKSON ON TREATIES (1940)[34]

There is, of course, no doubt concerning the authority of the President to negotiate with the British Government for the proposed exchange. The

---

[33] Altman v. United States, 224 U.S. 583, 601 (1912); and U.S. v. Belmont, 301 U.S. 324, 331 (1937): "A treaty signifies 'a compact made between two or more independent nations with a view of the public welfare.' *Altman & Co. . . . v. U.S.*, 224 U.S. 583, 600. But an international compact, as this was, is not always a treaty which requires the participation of the Senate There are many such compacts, of which a protocol, a modus vivendi, a postal convention, and agreements like that now under consideration are illustrations." [The particular arrangement here was between the U.S. and the U.S.S.R. in 1933, whereby the U.S.S.R. agreed not to enforce claims against American nationals. The claims were instead to be assigned to the U.S.] Hyde II, 1406.
[34] *D.S.B.*, III (1940), 202–203.

only questions that might be raised in connection therewith are (1) whether the arrangement must be put in the form of a treaty and await ratification by the Senate or (2) whether there must be additional legislation by the Congress. Ordinarily (and assuming the absence of enabling legislation) the question whether such an agreement can be concluded under Presidential authority or whether it must await ratification by a two-thirds vote of the United States Senate involves consideration of two powers which the Constitution vests in the President.

One of these is the power of the Commander-in-Chief of the Army and Navy of the United States, which is conferred upon the President by the Constitution but is not defined or limited. Happily, there has been little occasion in our history for the interpretation of the powers of the President as Commander-in-Chief of the Army and Navy. I do not find it necessary to rest upon that power alone to sustain the present proposal. But it will hardly be open to controversy that the vesting of such a function in the President also places upon him a responsibility to use all constitutional authority which he may possess to provide adequate bases and stations for the utilization of the naval and air weapons of the United States at their highest efficiency in our defense. It seems equally beyond doubt that present world conditions forbid him to risk any delay that is constitutionally avoidable.

The second power to be considered is that control of foreign relations which the Constitution vests in the Presidents as a part of the Executive function. The nature and extent of this power has recently been explicitly and authoritatively defined by Mr. Justice Sutherland, writing for the Supreme Court. In 1936, in *United States* v. *Curtiss-Wright Export Corp., et al*, 299 U.S. 304, he said:

It is important to bear in mind that we are here dealing not alone with an authority vested in the President by an exertion of legislative power, but with such an authority plus the very delicate, plenary and exclusive power of the President as the sole organ of the federal government in the field of international relations—a power which does not require as a basis for its exercise an act of Congress, but which, of course, like every other governmental power, must be exercised in subordination to the applicable provisions of the Constitution. It is quite apparent that if, in the maintenance of our international relations, embarrassment—perhaps serious embarrassment—is to be avoided and success for our aims achieved, congressional legislation which is to be made effective through negotiation and inquiry within the international field must often accord to the President a degree of discretion and freedom from statutory restriction which would not be admissible were domestic affairs alone involved. Moreover, he, not Congress, has the better opportunity of knowing the conditions which prevail in foreign countries, and especially is this true in time of war. He has his confidential sources of information. He has his agents in the form of diplomatic consular and other officials. Secrecy in respect of information gathered by them may be highly necessary, and the premature disclosure of it productive of harmful results.

The President's power over foreign relations while "delicate, plenary and exclusive" is not unlimited. Some negotiations involve commitments as to the future which would carry an obligation to exercise powers vested in the Congress. Such Presidential arrangements are customarily submitted for ratification by a two-thirds vote of the Senate before the future legislative power of the country is committed. However, the acquisitions which you are proposing to accept are without express or implied promises on the part of the United States to be performed in the future. The consideration, which we later discuss, is completed upon transfer of the specified items. The Executive Agreement obtains an opportunity to establish naval and air bases for the protection of our coastline but it imposes no obligation upon the Congress to appropriate money to improve the opportunity. It is not necessary for the Senate to ratify an opportunity that entails no obligation.

There are precedents which might be cited, but not all strictly pertinent. The proposition falls far short in magnitude of the acquisition by President Jefferson of the Louisiana Territory from a belligerent during a European war, the Congress later appropriating the consideration and the Senate later ratifying a treaty embodying the agreement.

I am also reminded that in 1850, Secretary of State Daniel Webster acquired Horse Shoe Reef, at the entrance of Buffalo Harbor, upon condition that the United States would engage to erect a lighthouse and maintain a light but would erect no fortification thereon. This was done without awaiting legislative authority. Subsequently the Congress made appropriations for the lighthouse, which was erected in 1856. *Malloy, Treaties and Conventions,* Vol. 1, p. 663.

It is not believed, however, that it is necessary here to rely exclusively upon your constitutional power. . . . There is also ample statutory authority to support the acquisition of these bases, and the precedents perhaps most nearly in point are the numerous acquisitions of rights in foreign countries for sites of diplomatic and consular establishments—perhaps also the trade agreements recently negotiated under statutory authority and the acquisition in 1903 of the coaling and naval stations and rights in Cuba under the act of March 2, 1901, c. 803, 31 Stat. 895, 898. In the last-mentioned case the agreement was subsequently embodied in a treaty but it was only one of a number of undertakings, some clearly of a nature to be dealt with ordinarily by treaty, and the statute had required "that by way of further assurance the government of Cuba will embody the foregoing provisions in a permanent treaty with the United States."

The transaction now proposed represents only an exchange with no statutory requirement for the embodiment thereof in any treaty and involving no promises or undertakings by the United States that might raise the question of the propriety of incorporation in a treaty. I therefore advise that acquisition by Executive Agreement of the rights proposed to be conveyed to the United States by Great Britain will not require ratification by the Senate.

MEMORANDUM OF UNDERSTANDING BETWEEN
THE UNITED STATES OF AMERICA AND
THE UNION OF SOVIET SOCIALIST REPUBLICS
REGARDING THE ESTABLISHMENT OF
A DIRECT COMMUNICATIONS LINK*
[Signed on June 20, 1963, at Geneva, Switzerland]

For use in time of emergency, the Government of the United States of America and the Government of the Union of Soviet Socialist Republics have agreed to establish as soon as technically feasible a direct communications link between the two governments.

Each government shall be responsible for the arrangements for the link on its own territory. Each government shall take the necessary steps to ensure continuous functioning of the link and prompt delivery to its head of government of any communications received by means of the link from the head of government of the other party.

Arrangements for establishing and operating the link are set forth in the Annex which is attached hereto and forms an integral part hereof.

Done in duplicate in the English and Russian languages at Geneva, Switzerland, this 20th day of June, 1963.

For the Government of the   For the Government of the
Union of Soviet Socialist   United States of America:
Republics:

/s/ Semyon Tsarapkin   /s/ Charles C. Stelle
Acting Representative of   Acting Representative of
the Union of Soviet Socialist   the United States of America
Republics to the Eighteen   to the Eighteen Nation
Nation Committee on   Committee on Disarmament
Disarmament

---

*[Reprinted from a text issued by the Department of State.]

446

ANNEX TO THE MEMORANDUM OF UNDERSTANDING BETWEEN
THE UNITED STATES OF AMERICA AND
THE UNION OF SOVIET SOCIALIST REPUBLICS
REGARDING THE ESTABLISHMENT OF
A DIRECT COMMUNICATIONS LINK

The direct communications link between Washington and Moscow established in accordance with the memorandum, and the operation of such link, shall be governed by the following provisions:

1. The direct communications link shall consist of:

A. Two terminal points with telegraph-teleprinter equipment between which communications shall be directly exchanged;

B. One full-time duplex wire telegraph circuit, routed Washington-London-Copenhagen-Stockholm-Helsinki-Moscow, which shall be used for the transmission of messages;

C. One full-time duplex radio telegraph circuit, routed Washington-Tangier-Moscow, which shall be used for service communications and for coordination of operations between the two terminal points.

If experience in operating the direct communications link should demonstrate that the establishment of an additional wire telegraph circuit is advisable, such circuit may be established by mutual agreement between authorized representatives of both governments.

2. In case of interruption of the wire circuit, transmission of messages shall be effected via the radio circuit, and for this purpose provision shall be made at the terminal points for the capability of prompt switching of all necessary equipment from one circuit to another.

3. The terminal points of the link shall be so equipped as to provide for the transmission and reception of messages from Moscow to Washington in the Russian language and from Washington to Moscow in the English language. In this connection, the USSR shall furnish the United States four sets of telegraph terminal equipment, including page printers, transmitters, and reperforators, with one year's supply of spare parts and all necessary special tools, test equipment, operating instructions and other technical literature, to provide for transmission and reception of messages in the Russian language. The United States shall furnish the Soviet Union

four sets of telegraph terminal equipment including page printers, transmitters, and reperforators, with one year's supply of spare parts and all necessary special tools, test equipment, operating instructions and other technical literature, to provide for transmission and reception of messages in the English language. The equipment described in this paragraph shall be exchanged directly between the parties without any payment being required therefor.

4. The terminal points of the direct communications link shall be provided with encoding equipment. For the terminal point in the USSR, four sets of such equipment (each capable of simplex operation), with one year's supply of spare parts, with all necessary special tools, test equipment, operating instructions and other technical literature, and with all necessary blank tape, shall be furnished by the United States to the USSR against payment of the cost thereof by the USSR.

The USSR shall provide for preparation and delivery of keying tapes to the terminal point of the link in the United States for reception of messages from the USSR. The United States shall provide for preparation and delivery of keying tapes to the terminal point of the link in the USSR for reception of messages from the United States. Delivery of prepared keying tapes to the terminal points of the link shall be effected through the Embassy of the USSR in Washington (for the terminal of the link in the USSR) and through the Embassy of the United States in Moscow (for the terminal of the link in the United States).

5. The United States and the USSR shall designate the agencies responsible for the arrangements regarding the direct communications link, for its technical maintenance, continuity and reliability, and for the timely transmission of messages.

Such agencies may, by mutual agreement, decide matters and develop instructions relating to the technical maintenance and operation of the direct communications link and effect arrangements to improve the operation of the link.

6. The technical parameters of the telegraph circuits of the link and of the terminal equipment, as well as the maintenance of such circuits and equipment, shall be in accordance with CCITT and CCIR recommendations.

Transmission and reception of messages over the direct communications link shall be effected in accordance with applicable recommendations of international telegraph and radio communications regulations, as well as with mutually agreed instructions.

7. The costs of the direct communications link shall be borne as follows:

>   A. The USSR shall pay the full cost of leasing the por-
>   tion of the telegraph circuit from Moscow to Helsinki and 50
>   percent of the cost of leasing the portion of the telegraph
>   circuit from Helsinki to London. The United States shall pay
>   the full cost of leasing the portion of the telegraph circuit
>   from Washington to London and 50 percent of the cost of leas-
>   ing the portion of the telegraph circuit from London to
>   Helsinki.

>   B. Payment of the cost of leasing the radio telegraph
>   circuit between Moscow and Washington shall be effected with-
>   out any transfer of payments between the parties. The USSR
>   shall bear the expenses relating to the transmission of mes-
>   sages from Moscow to Washington. The United States shall
>   bear the expenses relating to the transmission of messages
>   from Washington to Moscow.

Validity of Treaties

Treaties may be made on any subject, as long as the agreement does not call for the parties to perform acts that international law proscribes. In practice it is very difficult to challenge a treaty on the grounds that it has an illegal purpose: the parties are not willing to admit the possibility, and there is as yet no way for "third parties" to challenge a questionable agreement.[35] The United Nations Charter attempts to establish a widespread standard for treaties by asserting in Article 103 that:

In the event of a conflict between the obligations of the Members of the United Nations under the present Charter and their obligations under any other international agreement, their obligations under the present Charter shall prevail.

The difficulty in applying this standard, however, arose very clearly in the case of various regional agreements concluded by groups of states which were members of the United Nations. A case has been made, for instance, that the North Atlantic Treaty (1949) and the Warsaw Pact (1955) are both inconsistent with the United Nations Charter, even though each contains provisions disavowing any intention of conflicting with the United Nations Charter and even associates itself with Chapter VIII of the Charter (regional arrangements). There is no way, however, of reaching any definite conclusions on the subject or determining the matter legally, since none of the parties is inclined to ask the International Court of Justice to consider the legal questions. Despite the difficulty of determining whether or not a treaty is compatible with

[85] Consider, for instance, the problem of the Western Powers alleging in 1961 that it was illegal for the U.S.S.R. to sign a separate peace treaty with the [East] German Democratic Republic.

the Charter, the Charter assumes the character of basic law for the more than 120 states in the international community, and even nonmembers are expected to recognize this law (Article 1 [6]).

The United Nations is also involved in current treaty law by the provisions of Article 102:

1. Every treaty and every international agreement entered into by any Member of the United Nations after the present Charter comes into force shall as soon as possible be registered with the Secretariat and published by it.

2. No party to any such treaty or international agreement which has not been registered in accordance with the provisions of paragraph 1 of this Article may invoke that treaty or agreement before any organ of the United Nations.

Under these provisions, the Secretariat registers and publishes not only bilateral and multilateral treaties and international agreements, but even unilateral engagements of an international character, such as arise when a state accedes to an existing treaty. The provisions of paragraph 2 of Article 102 represent a more modest view of the responsibilities of an international organization than was taken in the League of Nations Covenant, whose Article 18 stated that no treaty was binding until it had been registered. Article 18 was never applied, however, which means that the change of wording does not represent any real loss for the international community, even though the Charter pretensions are more modest.[36]

Who May Make Treaties?

The capacity to conduct international relations is part of the definition of a state (see p. 58), so that it may be assumed generally that all states have the capacity to make treaties. Occasionally, states have restricted their own capacity to carry on international relations and to make treaties, but such arrangements are exceptional.[37] Such limitations are likely to become less frequent as states become increasingly jealous of their authority. Nonetheless, as recently as 1954, the Federal Republic of Germany undertook by treaty not to manufacture atomic, bacteriological, and chemical weapons, as well as other types of specified weapons.[38]

[36] For comments on these and other articles of the Charter, see Leland M. Goodrich and Edvard Hambro, *Charter of the United Nations: Commentary and Documents* (Boston: World Peace Foundation, 1949).

[37] Under the Platt Amendment, which Cuba included in a treaty with the United States in May 22, 1903, and by a constitutional declaration on June 12, 1901, Cuba relinquished throughout the life of that agreement the capacity to make a treaty which would impair or tend to impair Cuban independence, or which would permit a power to colonize or control in any other way, any portion of the island. See Malloy, I, 363; Articles I and II.

[38] For examples of such limitations in the 19th century, see Hyde, II, 1378, notes 4–7. In the German case, see *D.S.B.*, XXXI (Nov. 15, 1954), 519, 725–729 for text of Annex I to Protocol III on Control of Armaments of London and Paris Agreements.

Besides states, international organizations are now also more and more frequently parties to rule-making agreements. Their activities, including their part in making agreements, are an important element of what some authors have styled *transnational law*.[39]

Treaties—Duration

A treaty does not come into force automatically when it is negotiated, signed, and sealed by the representatives of states. States must formally confirm and approve of the written document by *ratifying* it. Individual states have their own ways of ratifying treaties: in the United States, under the terms of Article II of the Constitution, the President has the "power, by and with the advice and consent of the Senate to make treaties, provided two-thirds of the Senators present concur." The President may, of course, decline to exercise his power to ratify by withholding a treaty from the Senate, even though U.S. negotiators have signed it; he may refuse to ratify a treaty even if the Senate recommends otherwise; or he may withdraw a treaty from the Senate after he has submitted it. Conversely, the Senate itself may refuse to consent to the ratification—the most publicized instance of such a refusal to consent being in the matter of the Treaty of Versailles in 1919. Treaties normally do not go into effect, in any case, until (in the case of bilateral treaties) after the two parties have informed each other that the competent municipal authorities have ratified the document or (in the case of multilateral treaties) a specified number of states have deposited notices of ratification with designated authorities (usually the United Nations, but sometimes one or more of the seats of signatory governments). Well drafted treaties make the effective date quite clear in their own texts.

Well drafted treaties also specify the conditions under which and the means by which they shall come to an end. Either the treaty text provides that the treaty will be valid for a specified number of years, or it may run for an indefinite term, with the provision that either party may relieve himself of the obligation it has undertaken by giving proper notice. Treaties may also come to an end by the provisions of later treaties on the same subject.

Statesmen have often tried to relieve their governments of treaty obligations by appealing to the so-called doctrine of *rebus sic stantibus*—namely, that treaties endure only as long as the conditions which led to their coming into being remain the same. To define legally when conditions have changed is difficult, however, and open to much abuse as, for instance in 1914, when Germany violated the Belgian neutrality treaties of 1839 on these grounds.[40] To avoid such abuses under present

---

[39] See Philip C. Jessup, *Transnational Law* (New Haven: Yale University Press, 1956).

[40] See Ch. de Visscher, *Belgium's Case, A Juridical Enquiry* (London, 1916), pp. 89–110.

world conditions is also difficult, for states may preserve the sanctity of treaties only by making treaties which truly serve their mutual interests for the lifetime of a treaty or, alternatively, by restricting the meaning of "changed conditions" to those occasions when they can show that circumstances exist which the contracting parties never intended a treaty to cover.[41]

Treaties do not come to an end merely because the form of an existing government changes, although the Soviet Union argued after its own revolution in 1917 that its "complete" social revolution had invalidated the undertakings of its czarist predecessors. Most states which were parties to treaties with the U.S.S.R. have in practice had to acquiesce in Soviet refusals to carry out czarist treaty obligations, but they have not accepted the Soviet practice as establishing a new doctrine in international law. Treaties do come to an end, however, if a state is incorporated into or absorbed by another state, as when the United States absorbed the Republic of Texas, an act which extinguished treaties of the former independent Republic. Where states change their territorial boundaries, but remain in being, treaties do not necessarily come to an end, although the treaties will not operate with regard to territory that has been alienated in a territorial change.

When new states come into being after separating from another, as in the case of many African states which began their national life in the second half of the 20th century, they, as sovereign entities, may determine for themselves to what extent they will be bound by treaties signed by states formerly exercising sovereignty over their territory. Thus Article 6 of the Franco-Moroccan Diplomatic Accord, initialed May 20 and signed on May 28, 1956, reads:

> None of the present provisions can be interpreted as infringing upon the obligations which result either from the United Nations Charter, or from commitments, treaties or conventions in force between one of the High Contracting Parties and a third power.
>
> None of the present provisions must, furthermore, be interpreted as limiting the power of one of the High Contracting Parties to negotiate and conclude treaties, conventions or other international acts.

Article 11 thereof states:

> Morocco hereby assumes the obligations resulting from international treaties concluded by France in the name of Morocco, as well as those which result from the international acts concerning Morocco, on which it has made no observations.

[41] See the discussion in Hyde II, § 541.

The Moroccan Government stated in a note of May 20 to the French Government:

I have the honor of informing you that the Moroccan Government entirely reserves its position as regards the Franco-American agreement of December 22, 1950 [Base Agreement].

The French note of the same date, acknowledging receipt of the Moroccan note, stated:

The French Government has taken cognizance of your reservations on the Franco-American agreement of December 22, 1950. I hereby confirm to you, in this respect, the fact that this agreement does not come under the same head as the acts and treaties referred to in Article 11 of the Diplomatic Accord between France and Morocco dated today.[42]

By article VII of the Treaty of General Relations Between the United States and the Republic of the Philippines, signed on July 4, 1946, the Republic of the Philippines agreed "to assume all continuing obligations assumed by the United States of America under the Treaty of Peace between the United States of America and Spain concluded at Paris on the 10th day of December, 1898, by which the Philippine Islands were ceded to the United States of America, and under the Treaty between the United States of America and Spain concluded at Washington on the 7th day of November, 1900."[43]

If war breaks out between signatories to treaties, the treaties may well remain in force unless the treaty itself provides that it lapses in time of war or it is plain that the parties did not intend the treaty to operate in time of war. Regardless of treaty language, the true test as to whether or not a treaty survives an outbreak of war between the parties "is to be found in the intention of the parties at the time when they concluded the treaty."[44]

Interpreting Treaties

Contemporary treaties usually provide for some way of resolving disputes between the parties over the meaning of the documents. Sometimes the parties agree to refer any such disputes to the International Court of Justice, although they may also agree to settle disputes by using

[42] For the Franco-Moroccan Diplomatic Accord, May 28, 1956, and the Franco-Moroccan exchange of notes, May 20, 1956, see *A.J.I.L.*, LI (1957), 679, 682. See also *Annuaire français de droit international*, 1956, p. 133.
[43] U.S. TIAS 1568; 61 Stat. 1174, 1176. For 1898 Treaty, see 30 Stat. 1754. For 1900 Treaty, see 31 Stat. 1942. (The material on the Franco-Moroccan Diplomatic Accord and the U.S.-Philippine Treaty is quoted from Whiteman, II, 984–985.)
[44] Sir Cecil J. B. Hurst, "The Effect of War on Treaties," *British Yearbook of International Law, 1921–1922*, p. 47.

the services of arbitrators. In interpreting a treaty, the competent inter-
preters may study its historical background, the preparatory papers,
the circumstances of the parties at the time they made the treaty,
changes in those circumstances which the treaty itself was supposed
to bring about, and conditions prevailing at the time the treaty is being
interpreted.[45]

Reservations

In ratifying treaties, a state may attach to it certain reservations. In
general, a reservation is a formal statement made by a prospective party
to a treaty which is intended to modify the conditions that the treaty
would ordinarily create. In bilateral treaties, states may decline to exchange ratifications if they disapprove of reservations by the other party.
Reservations to bilateral treaties therefore cause few problems. If the
parties do exchange ratifications, they usually acquiesce in any reservations made.

Reservations to multilateral treaties cause more problems, however,
which have not yet been fairly resolved. Ideally every state would obtain
the consent of all other parties to any reservations it had; in practice,
such a procedure may be impractical because the pressure of business
is so great and the number of parties so high. The problem falls with
particular force upon the Secretary-General of the United Nations who
has to know whether he is justified in accepting a treaty ratification
with reservations: when does a reservation in effect vitiate a treaty and
when does it not? And what are his obligations if a state files reservations
in depositing its ratification?

In an attempt to answer these questions for the Secretary-General,
the U.N. General Assembly asked the International Court of Justice,
with regard to the Convention on the Prevention and Punishment of
the Crime of Genocide, "in the event of a State ratifying or acceding
to the Convention subject to a reservation made either on ratification
or on accession, or on signature followed by ratification":

I. Can the reserving State be regarded as being a party to the Convention
while still maintaining its reservation if the reservation is objected to by
one or more of the parties to the Convention but not by others?

II. If the answer to Question I is in the affirmative, what is the effect
of the reservation as between the reserving State and:
  (a) The parties which object to the reservation?
  (b) Those which accept it?

[45] See Article 19 (a), Harvard Draft Convention on the Law of Treaties, *A.J.I.L.*,
XXIX (1935), Supp., 66, 937–971.

III. What would be the legal effect as regards the answer to Question I if an objection to a reservation is made:

(a) By a signatory which has not yet ratified?

(b) By a State entitled to sign or accede but which has not yet done so?[46]

RESERVATIONS TO THE CONVENTION ON THE PREVENTION AND PUNISHMENT OF THE CRIME OF GENOCIDE

INTERNATIONAL COURT OF JUSTICE, 1951

ADVISORY OPINION, [1951] I.C.J. REP. 15

The Court observes that the three questions which have been referred to it for an Opinion have certain common characteristics.

All three questions are expressly limited by the terms of the Resolution of the General Assembly to the Convention on the Prevention and Punishment of the Crime of Genocide, and the same Resolution invites the International Law Commission to study the general question of reservations to multilateral conventions both from the point of view of codification and from that of the progressive development of international law. The questions thus having a clearly defined object, the replies which the Court is called upon to give to them are necessarily and strictly limited to that Convention. The Court will seek these replies in the rules of law relating to the effect to be given to the intention of the parties to multilateral conventions.

The three questions are purely abstract in character. They refer neither to the reservations which have, in fact, been made to the Convention by certain States, nor to the objections which have been made to such reservations by other States. They do not even refer to the reservations which may in future be made in respect of any particular article; nor do they refer to the objections to which these reservations might give rise.

. . . .

The Court observes that . . . question [I] refers, not to the possibility of making reservations to the Genocide Convention, but solely to the question whether a contracting State which has made a reservation can, while still maintaining it, be regarded as being a party to the Convention, when there is a divergence of views between the contracting parties concerning this reservation, some accepting the reservation, others refusing to accept it.

It is well established that in its treaty relations a State cannot be bound without its consent, and that consequently no reservation can be effective against any State without its agreement thereto. It is also a generally recognized principle that a multilateral convention is the result of an agreement freely concluded upon its clauses and that consequently none of the contract-

[46] I.C.J., Advisory Opinion, 1951; I.C.J. Rep. 15.

ing parties is entitled to frustrate or impair, by means of unilateral decisions or particular agreements, the purpose and *raison d'être* of the convention. To this principle was linked the notion of the integrity of the convention as adopted, a notion which in its traditional concept involved the proposition that no reservation was valid unless it was accepted by all the contracting parties without exception, as would have been the case if it had been stated during the negotiations.

This concept, which is directly inspired by the notion of contract, is of undisputed value as a principle. However, as regards the Genocide Convention, it is proper to refer to a variety of circumstances which would lead to a more flexible application of this principle. Among these circumstances may be noted the clearly universal character of the United Nations under whose auspices the Convention was concluded, and the very wide degree of participation envisaged by Article XI of the Convention. Extensive participation in conventions of this type has already given rise to greater flexibility in the international practice concerning multilateral conventions. More general resort to reservations, very great allowance made for tacit assent to reservations, the existence of practices which go so far as to admit that the author of reservations which have been rejected by certain contracting parties is nevertheless to be regarded as a party to the convention in relation to those contracting parties that have accepted the reservations—all these factors are manifestations of a new need for flexibility in the operation of multilateral conventions.

It must also be pointed out that although the Genocide Convention was finally approved unanimously, it is nevertheless the result of a series of majority votes. The majority principle, while facilitating the conclusion of multilateral conventions, may also make it necessary for certain States to make reservations. This observation is confirmed by the great number of reservations which have been made of recent years to multilateral conventions.

In this state of international practice, it could certainly not be inferred from the absence of an article providing for reservations in a multilateral convention that the contracting States are prohibited from making certain reservations. Account should also be taken of the fact that the absence of such an article or even the decision not to insert such an article can be explained by the desire not to invite a multiplicity of reservations. The character of a multilateral convention, its purpose, provisions, mode of preparation and adoption, are factors which must be considered in determining, in the absence of any express provision on the subject, the possibility of making reservations, as well as their validity and effect.

Although it was decided during the preparatory work not to insert a special article on reservations, it is none the less true that the faculty for States to make reservations was contemplated at successive stages of the drafting of the Convention. In this connection, the following passage may be quoted from the comments on the draft Convention prepared by the Secretary-General: ". . . (1) It would seem that reservations of a general scope have no place in a convention of this kind which does not deal with the private interests of a State, but with the preservation of an element of international order . . . ; (2) perhaps in the course of discussion in the General Assembly it will be possible to allow certain limited reservations."

Even more decisive in this connection is the debate on reservations in the Sixth Committee at the meetings (December 1st and 2nd, 1948) which immediately preceded the adoption of the Genocide Convention by the General Assembly. Certain delegates clearly announced that their governments could only sign or ratify the Convention subject to certain reservations.

Furthermore, the faculty to make reservations to the Convention appears to be implicitly admitted by the very terms of Question I.

The Court recognizes that an understanding was reached within the General Assembly on the faculty to make reservations to the Genocide Convention and that it is permitted to conclude therefrom that States becoming parties to the Convention gave their assent thereto. It must now determine what kind of reservation may be made and what kind of objections may be taken to them.

The solution of these problems must be found in the special characteristics of the Genocide Convention. The origins and character of that Convention, the objects pursued by the General Assembly and the contracting parties, the relations which exist between the provisions of the Convention, *inter se,* and between those provisions and these objects, furnish elements of interpretation of the will of the General Assembly and the parties. The origins of the Convention show that it was the intention of the United Nations to condemn and punish genocide as "a crime under international law" involving a denial of the right of existence of entire human groups, a denial which shocks the conscience of mankind and results in great losses to humanity, and which is contrary to moral law and to the spirit and aims of the United Nations (Resolution 96 (I) of the General Assembly, December 11th, 1946). The first consequence arising from this conception is that the principles underlying the Convention are principles which are recognized by civilized nations as binding on States, even without any conventional obligation. A second consequence is the universal character both of the condemnation of genocide and of the co-operation required "in order to liberate mankind from such an odious scourge" (Preamble to the Convention). The Genocide Convention was therefore intended by the General Assembly and by the contracting parties to be definitely universal in scope. It was in fact approved on December 9th, 1948, by a resolution which was unanimously adopted by fifty-six States.

The objects of such a convention must also be considered. The Convention was manifestly adopted for a purely humanitarian and civilizing purpose. It is indeed difficult to imagine a convention that might have this dual character to a greater degree, since its object on the one hand is to safeguard the very existence of certain human groups and on the other to confirm and endorse the most elementary principles of morality. In such a convention the contracting States do not have any interests of their own; they merely have, one and all, a common interest, namely, the accomplishment of those high purposes which are the *raison d'être* of the convention. Consequently, in a convention of this type one cannot speak of individual advantages or disadvantages to States or of the maintenance of a perfect contractual balance between rights and duties. The high ideals which inspired the Convention provide, by virtue of the common will of the parties, the foundation and measure of all its provisions.

The foregoing considerations, when applied to the question of reservations, and more particularly to the effects of objections to reservations, lead to the following conclusions.

The object and purpose of the Genocide Convention imply that it was the intention of the General Assembly and of the States which adopted it that as many States as possible should participate. The complete exclusion from the Convention of one or more States would not only restrict the scope of its application, but would detract from the authority of the moral and humanitarian principles which are its basis. It is inconceivable that the contracting parties readily contemplated that an objection to a minor reservation should produce such a result. But even less could the contracting parties have intended to sacrifice the very object of the Convention in favour of a vain desire to secure as many participants as possible. The object and purpose of the Convention thus limit both the freedom of making reservations and that of objecting to them. It follows that it is the compatibility of a reservation with the object and purpose of the Convention that must furnish the criterion for the attitude of a State in making the reservation on accession as well as for the appraisal by a State in objecting to the reservation. Such is the rule of conduct which must guide every State in the appraisal which it must make, individually and from its own standpoint, of the admissibility of any reservation.

Any other view would lead either to the acceptance of reservations which frustrate the purposes which the General Assembly and the contracting parties had in mind, or to recognition that the parties to the Convention have the power of excluding from it the author of a reservation, even a minor one, which may be quite compatible with those purposes.

It has nevertheless been argued that any State entitled to become a party to the Genocide Convention may do so while making any reservation it chooses by virtue of its sovereignty. The Court cannot share this view. It is obvious that so extreme an application of the idea of State sovereignty could lead to a complete disregard of the object and purpose of the Convention.

On the other hand, it has been argued that there exists a rule of international law subjecting the effect of a reservation to the express or tacit assent of all the contracting parties. This theory rests essentially on a contractual conception of the absolute integrity of the convention as adopted. This view, however, cannot prevail if, having regard to the character of the convention, its purpose and its mode of adoption, it can be established that the parties intended to derogate from that rule by admitting the faculty to make reservations thereto.

It does not appear, moreover, that the conception of the absolute integrity of a convention has been transformed into a rule of international law. The considerable part which tacit assent has always played in estimating the effect which is to be given to reservations scarcely permits one to state that such a rule exists, determining with sufficient precision the effect of objections made to reservations. In fact, the examples of objections made to reservations appear to be too rare in international practice to have given rise to such a rule. It cannot be recognized that the report which was adopted on the subject by the Council of the League of Nations on June 17th, 1927, has had this effect. At best, the recommendation made on that date by the Council constitutes the point of departure of an administrative practice which, after being observed by the Secretariat of the League of Nations, imposed itself, so to speak, in the ordinary course of things on the Secretary-General of the United Nations in his capacity of depositary of conventions concluded under the auspices of the League. But it cannot be concluded that the legal problem of the effect of objections to reservations has in this way been solved. The opinion of the Secretary-General of the United Nations himself is embodied in the following passage of his report of September 21st, 1950: "While it is universally recognized that the consent of the other governments concerned must be sought before they can be bound by the terms of a reservation, there has not been unanimity either as to the procedure to be followed by a depositary in obtaining the necessary consent or as to the legal effect of a State's objecting to a reservation."

It may, however, be asked whether the General Assembly of the United Nations, in approving the Genocide Convention, had in mind the practice according to which the Secretary-General, in exercising his functions as a depositary, did not regard a reservation as definitively accepted until it had been established that none of the other contracting States objected to it. If this were the case, it might be argued that the implied intention of the contracting parties was to make the effectiveness of any reservation to the Genocide Convention conditional on the assent of all the parties.

The Court does not consider that this view corresponds to reality. It must be pointed out, first of all, that the existence of an administrative practice does not in itself constitute a decisive factor in ascertaining what views the contracting States to the Genocide Convention may have had concerning the rights and duties resulting therefrom. It must also be pointed out that there existed among the American States members both of the United Nations and of the Organization of American States, a different practice which goes so far as to permit a reserving State to become a party irrespective of the nature of the reservations or of the objections raised by other contracting States. The preparatory work of the Convention contains nothing to justify the statement that the contracting States implicitly had any definite practice in mind. Nor is there any such indication in the subsequent attitude of the contracting States: neither the reservations made by certain States nor the position adopted by other States towards those reservations permit the conclusion that assent to one or the other of these practices had been given. Finally, it is not without interest to note, in view of the preference generally said to attach to an established practice, that the debate on reservations to multilateral treaties which took place in the Sixth Committee at the fifth session of the General Assembly reveals a profound divergence of views, some delegations being attached to the idea of the absolute integrity of the Convention, others favouring a more flexible practice which would bring about the participation of as many States as possible.

It results from the foregoing considerations that Question I, on account of its abstract character, cannot be given an absolute answer. The appraisal of a reservation and the effect of objections that might be made to it depend upon the particular circumstances of each individual case.

Having replied to Question I, the Court will now examine Question II, which is framed as follows:

> "If the answer to Question I is in the affirmative, what is the effect of the reservation as between the reserving States and:
> (*a*) the parties which object to the reservation ?
> (*b*) those which accept it ?"

The considerations which form the basis of the Court's reply to Question I are to a large extent equally applicable here. As has been pointed out above, each State which is a party to the Convention is entitled to appraise the validity of the reservation, and it exercises this right individually and from its own standpoint. As no State can be bound by a reservation to which it has not consented, it necessarily follows that each State objecting to it will or will not, on the basis of its individual appraisal within the limits of the criterion of the object and purpose stated above, consider the reserving State to be a party to the Convention. In the ordinary course of events, such a decision will only affect the relationship between the State making the reservation and the objecting State; on the other hand, as will be pointed out later, such a decision might aim at the compete exclusion from the Convention in a case where it was expressed by the adoption of a position on the jurisdictional plane.

The disadvantages which result from this possible divergence of views— which an article concerning the making of reservations could have obviated— are real; they are mitigated by the common duty of the contracting States to be guided in their judgment by the compatibility or incompatibility of the reservation with the object and purpose of the Convention. It must clearly be assumed that the contracting States are desirous of preserving intact at least what is essential to the object of the Convention; should this desire be absent, it is quite clear that the Convention itself would be impaired both in its principle and in its application.

It may be that the divergence of views between parties as to the admissibility of a reservation will not in fact have any consequences. On the other hand, it may be that certain parties who consider that the assent given by other parties to a reservation is incompatible with the purpose of the Convention, will decide to adopt a position on the jurisdictional plane in respect of this divergence and to settle the dispute which thus arises either by special agreement or by the procedure laid down in Article IX of the Convention.

Finally, it may be that a State, whilst not claiming that a reservation is incompatible with the object and purpose of the Convention, will nevertheless object to it, but that an understanding between that State and the reserving State will have the effect that the Convention will enter into force between them, except for the clauses affected by the reservation.

Such being the situation, the task of the Secretary-General would be simplified and would be confined to receiving reservations and objections and notifying them.

Question III is framed in the following terms:

"What would be the legal effect as regards the answer to Question I if an objection to a reservation is made:

(a) By a signatory which has not yet ratified?

(b) By a State entitled to sign or accede but which has not yet done so?"

The Court notes that the terms of his question link it to Question I. This link is regarded by certain States as presupposing a negative reply to Question I.

The Court considers, however, that Question III could arise in any case. Even should the reply to Question I not tend to exclude, from being a party to the Convention, a State which has made a reservation to which another State has objected, the fact remains that the Convention does not enter into force as between the reserving State and the objecting State. Even if the objection has this reduced legal effect, the question would still arise whether the States mentioned under (a) and (b) of Question III are entitled to bring about such a result by their objection.

An extreme view of the right of such States would appear to be that these two categories of States have a *right to become* parties to the Convention, and that by virtue of this right they may object to reservations in the same way as any State which is a party to the Convention with full legal effect, *i.e.* the exclusion from the Convention of the reserving State. By denying them this right, it is said, they would be obliged either to renounce entirely their right of participating in the Convention, or to become a party to what is, in fact, a different convention. The dilemma does not correspond to reality, as the States concerned have always a right to be parties to the Convention in their relations with other contracting States.

From the date when the Genocide Convention was opened for signature, any Member of the United Nations and any non-member State to which an invitation to sign had been addressed by the General Assembly, had the *right to be a party* to the Convention. Two courses of action were possible to this end: either signature, from December 9th, 1948, until December 31st, 1949, followed by ratification, or accession as from January 1st, 1950 (Article XI of the Convention). The Court would point out that the right to become a party to the Convention does not express any very clear notion. It is inconceivable that a State, even if it has participated in the preparation of the Convention, could, before taking one or the other of the two courses of action provided for becoming a party to the Convention, exclude another State. Possessing no rights which derive from the Convention, that State cannot claim such a right from its status as a Member of the United Nations or from the invitation to sign which has been addressed to it by the General Assembly.

The case of a signatory State is different. Without going into the question of the legal effect of signing an international convention, which necessarily varies in individual cases, the Court considers that signature constitutes a first step to participation in the Convention.

It is evident that without ratification, signature does not make the signatory State a party to the Convention; nevertheless, it establishes a provisional status in favour of that State. This status may decrease in value and importance after the Convention enters into force. But, both before and after the entry into force, this status would justify more favourable treatment being meted out to signatory States in respect of objections than to States which have neither signed nor acceded.

As distinct from the latter States, signatory States have taken certain of the steps necessary for the exercise of the right of being a party. Pending ratification, the provisional status created by signature confers upon the signatory a right to formulate as a precautionary measure objections which have themselves a provisional character. These would disappear if the signature were not followed by ratification, or they would become effective on ratification.

Until this ratification is made, the objection of a signatory State can therefore not have an immediate legal effect in regard to the reserving State. It would merely express and proclaim the eventual attitude of the signatory State when it becomes a party to the Convention.

The legal interest of a signatory State in objecting to a reservation would thus be amply safeguarded. The reserving State would be given notice that as soon as the constitutional or other processes, which cause the lapse of time before ratification, have been completed, it would be confronted with a valid objection which carries full legal effect and consequently, it would have to decide, when the objection is stated, whether it wishes to maintain or withdraw its reservation. In the circumstances, it is of little importance whether the ratification occurs within a more or less long time-limit. The resulting situation will always be that of a ratification accompanied by an objection to the reservation. In the event of no ratification occurring, the notice would merely have been in vain.

For these reasons,

THE COURT IS OF OPINION,

In so far as concerns the Convention on the Prevention and Punishment of the Crime of Genocide, in the event of a State ratifying or acceding to the Convention subject to a reservation made either on ratification or on accession, or on signature followed by ratification,

On Question I:

by seven votes to five,

that a State which has made and maintained a reservation which has been objected to by one or more of the parties to the Convention but not by others, can be regarded as being a party to the Convention if the reservation is compatible with the object and purpose of the Convention; otherwise, that State cannot be regarded as being a party to the Convention.

On Question II:

by seven votes to five,

(*a*) that if a party to the Convention objects to a reservation which it considers to be incompatible with the object and purpose of the Convention, it can in fact consider that the reserving State is not a party to the Convention;

(*b*) that if, on the other hand, a party accepts the reservation as being compatible with the object and purpose of the Convention, it can in fact consider that the reserving State is a party to the Convention;

On Question III:

by seven votes to five,

(*a*) that an objection to a reservation made by a signatory State which has not yet ratified the Convention can have the legal effect indicated in the reply to Question I only upon ratification. Until that moment it merely serves as a notice to the other State of the eventual attitude of the signatory state;

(*b*) that an objection to a reservation made by a State which is entitled to sign or accede but which has not yet done so, is without legal effect.

Done in French and English, the French text being authoritative, at the Peace Palace, The Hague, this twenty-eighth day of May, one thousand nine hundred and fifty-one, in two copies, one of which will be placed in the archives of the Court and the other transmitted to the Secretary-General of the United Nations.

(*Signed*) BASDEVANT,
President.

(*Signed*) E. HAMBRO.
Registrar.

Treaties and Municipal Law

In determining whether treaties are valid, statesmen and students must consider that, although states in international law have the capacity to make formal agreements over wide fields of action, they may themselves limit their own capacity to act by their own constitutions. These limits are primarily matters of domestic law, but they may become inter-

national political problems when states with such constitutional limitations come to treat together.

In few states are the constitutional problems so complex as in the
United States, whose written constitution, federal form of government,
and separation of powers combine to make treaty making complicated
in the extreme and to raise many, varied legal arguments. Some of these
questions relate to the powers of the individual states in the American
union and the powers of United States federal government, and the
Supreme Court of the United States must settle the questions, as in the
two cases below.

IN THE SUPREME COURT OF THE UNITED STATES

October Term, 1964

———

No. 179

Stanley M. Corbett, Guardian of the Property of
Constantine Neonakis, a Minor, Appellant

v.

Viola Stergios, a/k/a Viola Steryiakis

———

ON APPEAL FROM THE SUPREME COURT OF THE STATE OF IOWA

———

MEMORANDUM FOR THE UNITED STATES

———

STATEMENT

By order of the Court dated October 12, 1964, the Solicitor General was
invited to express the views of the United States with respect to this case.
For the reasons stated below, we believe that it presents a substantial question
of federal law.

Appellant, the guardian of the property of Constantine Neonakis, a non-resident minor and citizen of the Kingdom of Greece, instituted this suit in
the District Court of Iowa in and for Woodbury County to reopen the estate
of Nicholas Stergios, who had died testate in 1958 while a resident of Iowa
(J. S. App. A19).[47] Stergios' will, executed in 1954, had made no provision
for Neonakis, his adopted son. Appellant alleged that under Iowa law[48]
Neonakis was entitled to a two-thirds share of the estate, consisting of realty
and personalty located in Iowa, because the adoption had taken place after
the execution of the will (J.S. App. A19–A21). The relief sought was an
order setting aside the final report in the estate proceedings and directing
that the minor recover two-thirds of the value of the estate (J.S. App. A21).

———

[47] "J.C. App." refers to the appendix to the Jurisdictional Statement.
[48] See Iowa Code Annotated, secs. 600.6, 633.13, 636.31.

The court dismissed the petition on the sole ground that appellant had not satisfied Section 567.8 of the Iowa Code, which provides that the right of a nonresident alien to take real or personal property located in Iowa by succession or testamentary disposition "upon the same terms and conditions as residents and citizens of the United States is dependent in each case upon the existence of a reciprocal right upon the part of citizens of the United States to take real [or personal] property upon the same terms and conditions as residents and citizens" of the country of which such alien is a resident. The court found that appellant had not met the statutory burden (Sec. 567.8 (2)) of establishing the existence of such a reciprocal right.

By a vote of five to four, the Supreme Court of Iowa affirmed. The majority rejected appellant's contention that the application of Section 567.8 to this case was limited by Article IX, section 2, of the 1951 Treaty of Friendship, Commerce and Navigation between the United States and the Kingdom of Greece 1954(2) U.S.T. & O.I.A. 1829, T.I.A.S. No. 3057, which provides:

Nationals and companies of either Party shall be permitted freely to dispose of property within the territories of the other Party with respect to the acquisition of which through testate or intestate succession their alienage has prevented them from receiving national treatment, and they shall be permitted a term of at least five years in which to effect such disposition.

The majority reasoned that this provision, construed together with other provisions of the treaty, did not prevent Iowa from imposing the conditions of a reciprocal right on the right of a non-resident Greek national to acquire property within the State (J.S. App. A8–A14). The dissenting Justices construed the treaty to provide that a non-resident Greek national who was prevented by State law from acquiring property by succession must be allowed at least five years within which to dipose of it, and ruled, as required by Article VI of the Constitution, that the treaty prevailed over the State statute (J.S. App. A15–A18).

DISCUSSION

The Iowa courts have held that State laws of inheritance may be applied so as to defeat the right of a non-resident Greek national to take by succession real and personal property located within the State. This holding depends on a construction of a treaty between the United States and Greece. That construction, in the view of both the Department of State and the Greek Government, is in error. Since the correct interpretation of the treaty is a matter of considerable importance to the United States in the conduct of its foreign relations,[49] we believe that review by this Court is warranted. Cf. *Kolovrat* v. *Oregon,* 366 U.S. 187, 191.

In letters to the Ambassador of the Kingdom of Greece (App. A, *infra,*

[49] The Greek Government called to the attention of the Department of State the decision of the Iowa trial court and the then pending appeal to the Supreme Court of Iowa. See App., *infra* . . . .

. . .) and the Department of Justice (App. B, C, *infra,•* . . .), the Department of State, which negotiated the 1951 Treaty on behalf of the United States, has expressed the view that, while the treaty does not guarantee "national treatment" with respect to rights of inheritance to nonresident Greek nationals, it does preclude the application of State law as a total bar to their inheritance of property located in the United States. In its opinion, the treaty guarantees that, irrespective of limitations imposed by State law, a Greek national shall enjoy the right, for a period of at least five years, freely to dispose of any property which he could have inherited if he were an American national.

The State Department's conclusion—which, on familiar principles, is entitled to great weight, *Kolovrat, supra,* at 194—is supported by the terms of the treaty. Article IX, section 1(a) (J.S. App. A29–A30) provides that Greek nationals shall be accorded "national treatment" with respect to the acquisition of "ownership rights in land, buildings, and other immovable property" within the United States, subject to the laws of the States in which such property is located.[50] Section 2 of Article IX, however, expressly provides that if a national of either party to the treaty, is prevented because of alienage from receiving national treatment with respect to the acquisition of property through testate or intestate succession, he shall have a period of at least five years within which "freely to dispose" of such property. This provision is applicable to the present case and limits the operation of the Iowa statute to bar the inheritance of appellant's ward. The reasoning of the Iowa Supreme Court (J.S. App. A8) that the second section applies only to the disposition of property which has been acquired in accordance with State law is contrary to the language and purpose of the treaty, which confers the right "freely to dispose of property * * * with respect to the *acquisition* of which * * * alienage has prevented * * * [a national] from receiving national treatment * * *." (Emphasis added.) See *Clark* v. *Allen,* 331 U.S. 508.[51]

For the reasons stated, it is the view of the United States that this case presents a substantial question of federal law.

Respectfully submitted.

ARCHIBALD COX,
Solicitor General.

DECEMBER 1964.

---

[50] Section 1(b) of Article IX permits the Greek Government to restrict in some respects the "national treatment" accorded American nationals.

[51] Contrary to the statement of the Iowa Supreme Court (J.S. App. A8), there is no provision in the Treaty which "supersedes" Article IX, section 2. The Court's reliance on Article XXIV, section 1 (J.S. App. A8) is misplaced; that section states only that "national treatment" shall not be taken to imply "immunity from the laws and regulations of a Party *which apply in a non-discriminatory manner to nationals * * * of both Parties*" (J.S. App. A31). (Emphasis added.)

APPENDIX A

DEPARTMENT OF STATE,
Washington, July 30, 1963.

His Excellency Alexander A. Matsas,
Ambassador of Greece.

DEAR MR. AMBASSADOR: I refer to a note No. 108/ST/5 dated January 17, 1963 from the Chargé d'Affairs ad interim of Greece, calling attention to a case pending before the Supreme Court of Iowa on appeal from the district court of Iowa in and for Woodbury County, entitled:

"*Stanley M. Corbett, Guardian of the property of Constantine Neonakis, a Minor, plaintiff-appellant,* v. *Viola Stergios a/k/a Viola Steryiakis, defendant-appellee.*"

The case concerns the question of the right of a resident of Greece to inherit property in the United States under an Iowa statute requiring existence of a reciprocal right of inheritance upon the part of residents and citizens of the United States to inherit real property in Greece.

The Chargé d'Affaires' note requests that the Department of State cause to be submitted to the Supreme Court of Iowa the view of the Chargé d'Affaires that aside from the fact that under the Civil Law of Greece aliens are entitled to reciprocal rights of inheritance, as communicated on March 20, 1945 to the Department by the (then) Ambassador of Greece, the Treaty of Friendship, Commerce and Navigation between the United States and the Kingdom of Greece, signed at Athens on March 3, 1951, makes it unnecessary to prove reciprocal rights as required under the Iowa Code.

The Department of State confirms that on March 20, 1945 the Ambassador of Greece at Washington communicated to the Department the following statement regarding the question of reciprocal rights of inheritance:

In the question as to whether Sections 259, 259.1 and 259.2 of the California Probate Code applies to heirs and legatees, residents and citizens of Greece, the Greek Ambassador begs to certify the reciprocity defined in the above Sections of the California Probate Code is accorded citizens and residents of the United States, for the reason that according to the Civil Law of Greece aliens enjoy the same civil rights without any exception to hereditary rights.

Article 4 of the Greek Civil Law of the old one and the newest published on March 15, 1940, reads as follows:

"An alien enjoys the same civil rights as our citizens."

The civil laws of Greece relating to inheritance where the citizens of other countries are involved, are inclusive and not exclusive. That is to say, practically all aliens, wherever they reside, are permitted to inherit from any person who leaves an estate there, and if there are alien heirs and non-residents of Greece, such heirs are expressly permitted to be represented by their Consuls and collect through them their distributive shares.

The Department is fully satisfied that reciprocal rights of inheritance exist under the laws of Greece.

With regard to the 1951 Treaty of Friendship, Commerce and Navigation, it is the view of the Department of State that the intent of Article IX (1) is to accord national treatment to Greek citizens in respect of acquisition of real property through inheritance, subject to local laws which may limit the rights of aliens to *hold* real property. Article IX (2) sets a limitation upon the exception for state laws prohibiting alien ownership of realty by requiring that the alien be allowed five years in which to dispose of real property he has acquired through inheritance.

Under this interpretation, the Department would agree with the statement that the Treaty eliminates any necessity of proving reciprocity of treatment where the property in question is realty and thus subject to Article IX.

It is suggested that the Embassy may wish to bring the foregoing to the attention of the Iowa Court, together with a statement from the Ambassador to clarify, to the extent desired by the Court, the rights of residents and citizens of the United States to inherit in estates in Greece. It is not intended, of course, that this note should be interpreted as passing upon the merits of the case presently before the Iowa Court.

I regret the delay in replying to the Chargé d'Affaires' note but trust that the foregoing may be helpful in connection with this case.

Sincerely yours,

ABRAM CHAYES,
The Legal Adviser
(For the Secretary of State).

APPENDIX B

DEPARTMENT OF STATE,
Washington, October 26, 1964.

The Honorable JOHN W. DOUGLAS,
Assistant Attorney General,
Civil Division,
Department of Justice.

DEAR MR. DOUGLAS: I refer to your letter of October 15, 1964, requesting the views of the Department of State on a question presented by the appeal from the Supreme Court of Iowa to the United States Supreme Court in the case of *Stanley M. Corbett, etc.* v. *Viola Stergios, a/k/a Viola Steryiakis* (Sup. Ct. No. 179). That question, as stated in appellant's jurisdictional statement is:

Whether the Treaty of Friendship, Commerce and Navigation between the United States of America and the Kingdom of Greece nullifies the requirement of Section 567.8 of Iowa, 1958, that Appellant nonresident Greek alien must prove the existence of reciprocal rights of succession before he may acquire an interest in Iowa real estate by intestate succession from his adopting father.

It is the view of the Department of State that the intent of Article IX (1) of the Treaty of Friendship, Commerce and Navigation between the United States and the Kingdom of Greece, signed at Athens on March 3, 1951, is to accord national treatment to Greek citizens in respect of the acquisition of real property through inheritance, subject to local laws which may limit the rights of aliens to *hold* real property. Article IX (2) sets a limitation upon this exception for state laws prohibiting alien ownership of realty by requiring that the alien be allowed five years in which to dispose of real property he has acquired through inheritance. The Department of State is of the opinion that the Treaty eliminates any necessity of proving reciprocity of treatment where the property in question is realty and thus subject to Article IX.

The Department of State has expressed this view in an official communication to the Ambassador of Greece dated July 30, 1963, the text of which is enclosed.

Sincerely yours,

ANDREAS F. LOWENFELD,
Acting Legal Adviser
(For the Secretary of State).

(Enclosure: Text of Official Communication of July 30, 1963.)

APPENDIX C

DEPARTMENT OF STATE,
Washington, December 7, 1964.

The Honorable JOHN W. DOUGLAS,
Assistant Attorney General,
Department of Justice.

DEAR MR. DOUGLAS: I refer to your letters of October 15 and October 29, 1964, in regard to a question presented by the appeal from the Supreme Court of Iowa to the United States Supreme Court in the case of *Stanley M. Corbett, etc.* v. *Viola Stergios, a/k/a Viola Steryiakis* (Sup. Ct. No. 179). In a subsequent telephone inquiry regarding this matter, you have requested the view of the Department of State as to the effect of Article IX of the Treaty of Friendship, Commerce and Navigation between the United States and the Kingdom of Greece, signed at Athens on March 3, 1951, on the acquisition of personal property by nationals of either country in the territory of the other.

Paragraph 2 of Article IX, although designed primarily to assure that aliens shall have the right to dispose of real property which they are not permitted to own under the law where the property is located, does not limit itself to real property. It relates to property in general. As applied to the question whether paragraph 2 accords any right with respect to the acquisition of property, the terminology of the paragraph is vague. It is, however, based upon the premise and intent that the aliens shall have the right, in cases where because of alienage they are prevented from enjoying all the benefits that a national would enjoy in regard to the taking of title to property through inheritance or succession, to receive the property and to effect a disposition of it within a period of five years.

Attention is directed to the use of the term "succession" in paragraph 2, in the light of customary references to inheritance of real property and succession to personal property. While paragraph 2 does not state specifically that the aliens shall have national treatment with respect to the right to succeed to personal property, it appears that the granting of a right to effect a disposition within a specified period of *any* property to which they would succeed on a national treatment basis except for their alienage is indicative of a general intent that so far as possible they should be allowed to take property, or the proceeds from the disposition thereof, through testate or intestate succession.

Sincerely yours,

RICHARD D. KEARNEY,
Deputy Legal Adviser.

[On May 3, 1965, the U.S. Supreme Court delivered the following opinion (381 U.S. 124):
"PER CURIAM, May 3, 1965:
"In light of our construction of the Treaty of Friendship, Commerce and Navigation between the United States and the Kingdom of Greece, a construction confirmed by representations of the signatories whose views were not available to the Supreme Court of Iowa, the judgment is reversed. *Clark* v. *Allen*, 331 U.S. 503."
[The opinion of the Supreme Court of Iowa of February 11, 1964, is reported 256 Iowa 12, 126, N.W. 2d 342 (1964).]

MISSOURI v. HOLLAND

UNITED STATES, SUPREME COURT, 1920

252 U.S. 416

HOLMES, J. This is a bill in equity brought by the State of Missouri to prevent a game warden of the United States from attempting to enforce the Migratory Bird Treaty Act of July 3, 1918, c. 128, 40 Stat. 755, and the regulations made by the Secretary of Agriculture in pursuance of the same. The ground of the bill is that the statute is an unconstitutional interference with the rights reserved to the States by the Tenth Amendment, and that the acts of the defendant done and threatened under that authority invade the sovereign right of the State and contravene its will manifested in statutes. The State also alleges a pecuniary interest, as owner of the wild birds within its borders and otherwise, admitted by the Government to be sufficient, but it is enough that the bill is a reasonable and a proper means to assert the alleged quasi sovereign rights of a State. . . .

On December 8, 1916, a treaty between the United States and Great Britain was proclaimed by the President. It recited that many species of birds in their annual migrations traversed many parts of the United States and of Canada, that they were of great value as a source of food and in destroying insects injurious to vegetation, but were in danger of extermination through lack of adequate protection. It therefore provided for specified closed seasons and protection in other forms, and agreed that the two powers would take or propose to their lawmaking bodies the necessary measures for carrying the treaty out. 39 Stat. 1702. The above mentioned act of July 3, 1918, entitled an act to give effect to the convention, prohibited the killing, capturing or selling any of the migratory birds included in the terms of the treaty except as permitted by regulations compatible with those terms, to be made by the Secretary of Agriculture. Regulations were proclaimed on July 31, and October 25, 1918. 40 Stat. 1812, 1863. It is unnecessary to go into any details, because, as we have said, the question raised is the general one whether the treaty and statute are void as an interference with the rights reserved to the States.

To answer this question it is not enough to refer to the Tenth Amendment, reserving the powers not delegated to the United States, because by Article 2, Section 2, the power to make treaties is delegated expressly, and by Article 6 treaties made under the authority of the United States, along with the Constitution and laws of the United States made in pursuance thereof, are declared the supreme law of the land. If the treaty is valid there can be no dispute about the validity of the statute under Article 1, Section 8, as a necessary and proper means to execute the powers of the Government. The language of the Constitution as to the supremacy of treaties being general, the question before us is narrowed to an inquiry into the ground upon which the present supposed exception is placed.

It is said that a treaty cannot be valid if it infringes the Constitution, that there are limits, therefore, to the treaty-making power, and that one such limit is that what an act of Congress could not do unaided, in derogation of the powers reserved to the States, a treaty cannot do. An earlier act of Congress that attempted by itself and not in pursuance of a treaty to regulate the killing of migratory birds within the States had been held bad in the District Court. *United States* v. *Shauver*, 214 F. 154; *United States* v. *McCullagh*, 221 F. 288. Those decisions were supported by arguments that migratory birds were owned by the States in their sovereign capacity for the benefit of their people, and that under cases like *Geer* v. *Connecticut*, 161 U.S. 519, 16 S. Ct. 600, this control was one that Congress had no power to displace. The same argument is supposed to apply now with equal force.

Whether the two cases cited were decided rightly or not they cannot be accepted as a test of the treaty power. Acts of Congress are the supreme law of the land only when made in pursuance of the Constitution, while treaties are declared to be so when made under the authority of the United States. It is open to question whether the authority of the United States means more than the formal acts prescribed to make the convention. We do not mean to imply that there are no qualifications to the treaty-making power; but they must be ascertained in a different way. It is obvious that there may be matters of the sharpest exigency for the national well being that an act of Congress could not deal with but that a treaty followed by such an act could, and it is not lightly to be assumed that, in matters requiring national action, "a power which must belong to and somewhere reside in every civilized government" is not to be found. *Andrews* v. *Andrews,* 188 U.S. 14, 33, 23, S. Ct. 237. What was said in that case with regard to the powers of the States applies with equal force to the powers of the nation in cases where the States individually are incompetent to act. We are not yet discussing the particular case before us but only are considering the validity of the test proposed. With regard to that we may add that when we are dealing with words that also are a constituent act, like the Constitution of the United States, we must realize that they have called into life a being the development of which could not have been foreseen completely by the most gifted of its begetters. It was enough for them to realize or to hope that they had created an organism; it has taken a century and has cost their successors much sweat and blood to prove that they created a nation. The case before us must be considered in the light of our whole experience and not merely in that of what was said a hundred years ago. The treaty in question does not contravene any prohibitory words to be found in the Constitution. The only question is whether it is forbidden by some invisible radiation from the general terms of the Tenth Amendment. We must consider what this country has become in deciding what that amendment has reserved.

The State as we have intimated founds its claim of exclusive authority upon an assertion of title to migratory birds, an assertion that is embodied in statute. No doubt it is true that as between a State and its inhabitants the State may regulate the killing and sale of such birds, but it does not follow that its authority is exclusive of paramount powers. To put the claim of the State upon title is to lean upon a slender reed. Wild birds are not in the possession of anyone; and possession is the beginning of ownership. The whole foundation of the State's rights is the presence within their jurisdiction of birds that yesterday had not arrived, tomorrow may be in another State and in a week a thousand miles away. If we are to be accurate we cannot put the case of the State upon higher ground than that the treaty deals with creatures that for the moment are within the state borders, that it must be carried out by officers of the United States within the same territory, and that but for the treaty the State would be free to regulate this subject itself.

As most of the laws of the United States are carried out within the States and as many of them deal with matters which in the silence of such laws the State might regulate, such general grounds are not enough to support Missouri's claim. Valid treaties of course "are as binding within the territorial limits of the States as they are elsewhere throughout the dominion of the United States." *Baldwin* v. *Franks,* 120 U.S. 678, 683, 7 S. Ct. 656, 657. No doubt the great body of private relations usually fall within the control of the State, but a treaty may override its power. We do not have to invoke the later developments of constitutional law for this proposition; it was recognized as early as *Hopkirk* v. *Bell,* 3 Cranch 454, with regard to statutes of limitation, and even earlier, as to confiscation, in *Ware* v. *Hylton,* 3 Dall. 199. It was assumed by Chief Justice Marshall with regard to the escheat of land to the State in *Chirac* v. *Chirac,* 2 Wheat. 259, 275; *Hauenstein* v. *Lynham,* 100 U.S. 483; *Geofroy* v. *Riggs,* 133 U.S. 258, 10 S. Ct. 295; *Blythe* v. *Hinckley,* 180 U.S. 333, 340, 21, S. Ct. 390. So as to a limited jurisdiction of foreign consuls within a State. *Wildenhus' Case,* 120 U.S. 1, 7 S. Ct. 385. See *Ross* v. *McIntyre,* 140 U.S. 453, 11 S. Ct. 897. Further illustration seems unnecessary, and it only remains to consider the application of established rules to the present case.

Here a national interest of very nearly the first magnitude is involved. It can be protected only by national action in concert with that of another power. The subject-matter is only transitorily within the State and has no permanent habitat therein. But for the treaty and the statute there soon might be no birds for any powers to deal with. We see nothing in the Constitution that compels the Government to sit by while a food supply is cut off and the protectors of our forests and our crops are destroyed. It is not sufficient to rely upon the States. The reliance is vain, and were it otherwise, the question is whether the United States is forbidden to act. We are of opinion that the treaty and statute must be upheld. *Carey* v. *South Dakota,* 250 U.S. 118, 39 S. Ct. 403.

Decree Affirmed.

VAN DEVANTER AND PITNEY, JJ., dissent.

The case of Missouri v. Holland has often been cited by those who oppose such treaties as the Genocide Convention and the United Nations Covenants on Human Rights. Opponents of these documents argue that because by using the treaty power, the United States government can do certain things which it cannot accomplish by legislative action, the treaty power itself is dangerous and should be limited. They conjure up frightening pictures of the dangers to states rights inherent in the treaty power. They seem to ignore the clear implications in Missouri v. Holland (which they are otherwise fond of citing) that the treaty-making power is not unlimited.

Thus those who argue that by treaty the United States might lower standards of human rights in this country ignore the clear indications that no treaty violating the first amendment to the Constitution would be constitutional.

In such cases as have arisen over the effect of treaties upon American

law, the courts have been very cautious. Thus, as noted in Chapter
I, when the California Court of Appeals invoked the United Nations
Charter to invalidate the Alien Land Laws in California in 1951, the
State Supreme Court, while invalidating the Alien Land Laws on other
grounds, denied that the United Nations Charter directly affected Cali-
fornia law:

> It is not disputed that the Charter is a treaty, and our Federal Constitution
> provides that treaties made under the authority of the United States are part
> of the supreme law of the land and that the judges in every state are bound
> thereby. A treaty, however, does not automatically supersede local laws which
> are inconsistent with it unless the treaty provisions are self-executing.[52]

A self-executing agreement is one that governmental authorities can
apply without any further legislation. A treaty that requires a state
to pay for certain land or services would not be self-executing if, as
is generally true, a legislature would still have to appropriate funds
to carry out the terms of the treaty. This divided responsibility in making
and executing treaties is, at the very least, awkward, for if a legislature
refused to carry out the terms of such a treaty, a state might be held
to be delinquent in international law.

In the United States, the problem arose during President Washington's
first administration. Secretary of State Jefferson had suggested to the
President in April 1792 that before affixing the Great Seal of the United
States to the proposed Algerian treaty, the President should be sure
that the two Houses of Congress had appropriated the funds the treaty
called for. Washington asked whether the House was not obliged, under
the Constitution, to appropriate the money once the Senate had consented to ratification and the President had ratified the document. Alexander Hamilton had no doubt on the point:

> . . . the House of Representatives have no moral power to refuse the
> execution of a treaty which is not contrary to the Constitution, because it
> pledges the public faith; and no legal power to refuse its execution because
> it is a law, until at least it ceases to be a law by a regular act of revocation
> of a competent authority.

Nor did Jefferson doubt the President's power. In his view, the treaty
"certainly" would be valid and

> . . . it would be the duty of the representatives to raise the money; but
> that they might decline to do what was their duty. . . . it might be incautious
> to commit himself by ratification with a foreign nation, where he might be
> left in the lurch in the execution; it was possible, too, to conceive a treaty
> which it would not be their duty to provide for.

[52] Sei Fujii v. California, 242 P. 2d 617.

Washington was not inclined to be so cautious and declared of the representatives that if they "would not do what the Constitution called on them to do, the government would be at an end, and must then assume another form."[53]

The legal and political stance of the United States as regards treaties has been in this uncomfortable position ever since 1792, for the House could in fact refuse to carry out a treaty commitment of which it disapproved, and the Executive and Senate must bear in mind its latent power in consenting to and ratifying treaties. In fact, some treaties have contained provisions making congressional action a condition of *ratification,* but these provisions are exceptions to the rule. Treaties, on the other hand, which require no further congressional action to come into effect—for instance, a treaty ending a state of war between the United States and Japan—are self-executing. There may, of course, be room for authorities to differ as to whether a given instrument is or is not self-executing.[54]

Although the Supreme Court of the United States has never found unconstitutional a treaty that the United States has ratified, there is no doubt that there are certain commitments that governmental authorities in the United States cannot constitutionally make. Judicial statements are quite clear on that point:

"Indeed a treaty which undertook to take away what the Constitution secured or to enlarge the Federal jurisdiction would be simply void."[55] "And a treaty cannot change the Constitution or be held valid if it be in violation of that instrument."[56] The nation "can enter into no stipulation calculated to change the character of the Government, or to do that which can only be done by the Constitution-making power, or which is inconsistent with the nature and structure of the Government."[57]

These statements record the generally held opinion that it would be unconstitutional, let us say, for the President and Senate to try to use their treaty-making power to incorporate the United States into the Commonwealth of Nations or to acknowledge England's sovereign as head

---

[53] Alexander Hamilton, *Works,* H. C. Lodge, ed. (New York, 1886), VII, 132, and *Writings of Jefferson,* P. L. Ford, ed. (New York, 1892–1891), I, 191.

[54] See Samuel B. Crandall, *Treaties: Their Making and Enforcement* (2d. ed., Washington, 1916), Chap. XIII, for examples.

[55] Fuller, C. J., in Downes v. Bidwell, 182 U.S. 244, 370 (1901).

[56] Swayne, J., in The Cherokee Tobacco, 78 U.S. (11 Wall) 616, 620 (1870).

[57] *Works of John C. Calhoun,* ed. by Richard K. Crolle (6 vols., Columbia, S. C., 1851), I, 204. Calhoun, incidentally, unlike Washington and Hamilton, looked upon "the right to withhold appropriations" as "an important control over the treaty-making power, whenever money is required to carry a treaty into effect." *Loc. cit.*

of state in the United States. But the questions which arise about the treaty-making power are more subtle than this. Some of them are not too difficult to deal with. For instance, because the Constitution of the United States grants to the Congress the power to declare war, the United States has never embarked upon war automatically in pursuit of a treaty obligation and, in entering into alliances, has employed formulae designed to be consistent with the powers granted in the Constitution. Thus Article 5 of the North Atlantic Treaty obligates the United States to "consult" with its allies and to "take such action as it deems necessary" after that consultation. Under the treaty, the United States has undertaken joint military planning with fourteen other member states in a common military command; it has made it clear politically that in the event of Soviet aggression in Europe, U.S. troops would undoubtedly come to the aid of the other NATO powers. But the treaty language was deliberately designed to meet U.S. constitutional limitations and leaves Congress free to decide how it would respond in case a situation should arise in which Article 5 of the treaty were ever to come into effect.

The United States Senate, at least, was left in no doubt about the matter.

> Article 5 is the heart of the treaty. . . . [It] is based upon the fundamental proposition that an armed attack against any one of us is to be considered an attack against all. . . . It is up to the signatories to determine whether an attack has occurred. . . . Once this original determination is made . . . then each party must forthwith take such action as it deems necessary. . . . How far each state will go and what action it will take to fulfill its obligations will be determined by each state in the light of existing circumstances. It is possible that a diplomatic protest may suffice. On the other hand, in the face of an all-out attack, it might be necessary to bring into full play the whole weight of the partnership and the ultimate decision of war. . . . The treaty does not involve any commitment to go to war nor does it change the relative authority of the President and the Congress with respect to the use of the armed forces. . . . Nothing in the treaty either increases or decreases the constitutional powers of either the President or the Congress with respect to the use of the armed forces. . . . The full authority of the Congress to declare war, with all the discretion that power implies, remains unimpaired.[58]

Similarly the veto which the United States enjoys (and sponsored) in the United Nations Security Council preserves the congressional perogatives under the Charter by preventing outside powers from com-

[58] Congressional Record, July 5, 1959, p. 8984 (speech by Senator Tom Connally); *D.S.B.*, XXI (July 18, 1949), 54–57.

mitting the United States to military action without its consent. On the other hand, it does not resolve the internal American constitutional problem: if the United States approves the use of force in the United Nations (as in Korea in 1950), the Executive branch of the government needs to be sure that it has the support of the legislature. Otherwise, it may find that it has committed the United States to action under a treaty which it is not in a position to carry out. The increasing disenchantment of the United States Congress with the Korean and Vietnamese conflicts illustrate both the legal and political problems the United States Constitution poses in carrying out treaty obligations involving the use of its armed forces.

CHAPTER VIII

Force and International Law

Introduction

Putting force behind the law and law behind the use of force is a
major and perennial problem for those who would strengthen international law. Natural law theorists once attempted to distinguish between
"just" (and, therefore, lawful) wars and "unjust" (and, therefore, unlawful) wars. The standards of justice involved were, however, far too
subjective to make the distinction useful in legal doctrine. Positivist
theorists dealt with war by ignoring the moral problem altogether and
classifying war as an extralegal fact to which legal consequences attached. By ignoring distinctions between right and wrong, the positivist
approach was, in its own way, unsatisfactory and could hardly support
a system whose purpose was to provide norms for the social use of
force.

The difficulties war poses for international law arise from the plain
fact that "it is not possible at one and the same time to base international
relations upon the independent existence of States and to concede to
each State the sovereign right to take up arms to attack or destroy
that independence."[1] Ideally, strong central international organizations
would regulate the use of force among states. But such thoroughgoing
reforms as would be necessary to bring so radical a new order about
"presuppose a radical change of mentality and postulate, in the last
analysis, the abolition of national sovereignties."[2] The political obstacles
to working such a revolution are only too plain to students of international relations and, for international law, the result has been an uneasy
compromise. It has specified certain circumstances under which war
is illegal. But it has also recognized that in the real world, such illegal

[1] Charles de Visscher, *Theory and Reality in International Public Law*, p. 286.
[2] *Ibid.*, p. 287. For an example of one such system, see Grenville Clark and Louis
B. Sohn, *World Peace through World Law* (3d ed., Cambridge: Harvard University
Press, 1966).

478

wars may occur. And given that fact, it has gone on to lay down certain rules that combatants are expected to obey, whether engaged in legal or illegal war. Some of the rules are archaic, like the declaration against launching projectiles from aircraft,[3] victims of technological developments over the years. What the rules are or should be raises problems not easy to solve at any time. But the paradox of a law attempting to regulate what the law itself has called illegal poses even more fundamental problems. An analogous situation would arise if municipal law attempted to prescribe rules for murder. The analogy is not perfect, of course, because domestic communities have the power to prevent murders and to punish murderers, whereas the international community is much less well organized to prevent war and to punish those who cause wars. Therefore, recognizing that illegal wars may occur, international law has traditionally taken the position that it is better to attempt to mitigate the horror of war wherever possible than to leave belligerents to their own devices:

> International Law . . . contains obligations limiting the right to resort to war and provides regulations with which belligerents have customarily, or by special conventions, agreed to comply in case war breaks out between them. Accordingly, although with the outbreak of war peaceful relations between the belligerents cease, there remain certain legal obligations and duties. Thus conceived, war is not inconsistent with, but a condition regulated by, International Law.[4]

In short, international law tries, like the common law, to "correspond with the actual feelings and demands of the community, whether right or wrong."[5]

International lawyers must concern themselves, then, with defining war and establishing "rules of war," while, at the same time, they try to eradicate it entirely. The materials they have to work with are contained in the decisions of several international tribunals, the Covenant of the League of Nations, the experience and doctrine of the Nuremberg Trials, and the United Nations Charter.

Use of Force Short of War

Sometimes, states employ force against one another without intending to go to war. This use of force short of war came about as states

---

[3] The First and Second Hague Conferences (1899, 1907) adopted such rules, but they were never binding in theory or practice because states did not ratify the relevant treaties.
[4] Oppenheim, II, 202; see also p. 557.
[5] Oliver Wendell Holmes, *The Common Law* (Boston: Little, Brown and Company, 1881), p. 41.

attempted to assert rights or impose penalties in ways which the international community could not successfully emulate, as in frontier societies, where every man and his gun were a law unto themselves. In national states, as central police and judicial systems came into being, individual attempts to impose law and order became illegal. A parallel development occurred in the international field: individuals once authorized by letters of mark and reprisal to obtain satisfaction from alien subjects had to surrender their rights to the governments of states. Strong central governments could safeguard their citizens without authorizing them to go on individual forays. Engaging in reprisals then became the prerogative of states and not of individuals.

Reprisals are injurious and otherwise internationally illegal acts that international law permits states to engage in on occasion to compel other states who have been delinquent in their duties to settle their differences satisfactorily.[6]

Rules governing states using reprisals are best set out in the *Naulilaa* Case.

NAULILAA CASE

ARBITRATION BETWEEN PORTUGAL AND GERMANY

RECUEIL DES DECISIONS DE TRIBUNAUX ARBITRAUX MIXTES, VIII, 409, 422–425 (TRANSLATION)

Arbitral decision of 31 July 1928 concerning the responsibility of Germany by reason of the damage caused in the Portuguese colonies of South Africa.

[In October and November 1914, several German officials were killed and others interned in Naulilaa, a Portuguese post in Angola. The Governor of the Germany colony of South-West Africa ordered German forces to attack and destroy certain Portuguese posts by way of reprisal. Portugal and Germany submitted the question of responsibility to arbitration.]

The Question of Reprisals

1. Most recent doctrine, notably German doctrine, defines a reprisal in these terms:

A reprisal is an act of self-help (*Selbsthilfehandlung*) of an injured state, retaliating—*after a demand for redress has elicited no response*—against an act of the offending state which is contrary to international law. It has the effect, in the relations between the two states, of momentarily suspending

[6] Oppenheim, II, 136.

the observance of such and such a rule of international law. It is limited by the rules of humanity and the rules of good faith applicable in the relations of state to state. *It would be illegal if a prior act, contrary to international law, had not furnished the motive.* It tends to impose, on the offending state, [the obligation to make] reparation for the offense or [to make] a return to legality, in order to avoid new offenses.

This definition does not require that the reprisal be *proportioned* to the offense. On this point authors, unanimous until a few years ago, are now divided in opinion. The majority see in a certain proportion between offense and reprisal a necessary condition of the legitimacy of the latter. . . . Other authors, among the more modern, no longer demand this condition. . . . As for international law, actually developing as a result of the experiences of the last war, it tends certainly to restrain the notion of legitimate reprisals and to prohibit excesses. . . .

2. The *German contentions* may be summarized as follows:

(a) The destruction or capture of the Schultze-Jena mission at Naulilaa constituted an act contrary to international law, an act giving to the Government of South-West Africa a just motive for engaging in reprisals.

(b) As soon as he was informed of the Naulilaa incident, Governor Seitz had for several nights openly broadcast to all German radio-telegraphic posts the news of the "assassination" of Dr. Schultze-Jena and his companions. This communication, which was also addressed to the government of Angola, was equivalent to a demand to the Portuguese authorities to furnish explanations and to surrender the two prisoners, Jensen and Kimmel. No reply having been made, "one was reduced, on the German side, to taking justice into one's own hands."

(c) Even if reprisals had been excessive, this excess, certainly excusable [in the circumstances], would not involve any responsibility for Germany. In fact, there was no excess. The death of Dr. Schultze-Jena and of his companions justified the attack on the Cuangar fort. Despite that warning, the Portuguese authorities not only did not free the two illegally interned prisoners, but they expelled the German vice-consul Schoess from Lubango.

(d) In consequence, the acts committed by the German troops at different points on the frontier of Angola do not involve German responsibility.

3. The arbitrators cannot admit this thesis for the following reasons:

(a) . . . The death of Dr. Schultze-Jena and the two officers who accompanied him was not the result of an act by the Portuguese authorities which was contrary to international law.

(b) A neutral state has the right [by the Hague Conventions of 1899, Art. 57; and of 1907, Art 11] to disarm and intern armed belligerents who penetrate its territory. The internment of the interpreter Jensen and the soldier Kimmel was then, in principle, authorized by positive international law. . . . The German authorities could have raised the question and insisted on a friendly adjustment of the question of internment. They could not, on the contrary, see in the internment itself, or in its continuance, an act contrary to international law, giving them sufficient reason for resorting to armed reprisals.

(c) Vice-consul Schoess was still on duty at Lubango, November 28, 1914. The attack on the fort of Cuangar, October 31, the destruction of the posts of lower Cumango from November 4 to 15, and the Franck expidition, decided upon October 28, cannot have been motivated by his expulsion. Moreover, the expulsion of a consular agent, against whom a state may wish to complain, may constitute an unfriendly act, leading to diplomatic representations, but there does not inhere, in such exercise of the sovereign rights of a neutral state, an act contrary to international law, justifying, by way of reprisal, an attack accompanied by all the rigors of war.

(d) The first condition—*sine qua non*—of the right of exercising reprisals is a motive furnished by a prior act contrary to international law. This condition, of which the German thesis recognizes the necessity, is lacking; which suffices to reject the means employed by the German government.

(e) Even if the arbitrators held the Portuguese authorities responsible for committing an act contrary to international law, providing, in principle, a motive for reprisals, the German contention would nevertheless be rejected for two other reasons, either of them decisive:

(1) A reprisal is only licit when it has been preceded by a request for redress which has been unavailing. Employing force is only justified in effect by necessity. . . . But it is impossible to consider as a demand by one state upon another the fact that the authorities of the offended state had communicated among themselves the news of the alleged offence. In fact, the messages sent from Windhoek to the German posts seem to have been ignored by the Portuguese authorities. Even if these messages had been intercepted, however, they would not have amounted to a demand [for redress]. According to Governor Seitz, the German authorities had to give up sending emissaries for fear they would be killed or imprisoned. The person of an emissary as such is inviolable. Furthermore, the events of Cuangar, to mention only them, show that it would have been very simple for the German frontier posts to escort and indeed obtain respect for an emissary bringing a message to one of the Portuguese posts. There has been, therefore, resort to force, by the authorities of South-West Africa without a prior attempt to obtain satisfaction by legal means—which again rules out the legitimacy of the reprisals employed.

(2) The necessity of a proportion between the reprisal and the offense appears to be recognized in the German reply. Even if one admits that international law does not require that reprisals be approximately proportionate to the offense, one must certainly consider as excessive, and consequently illicit, reprisals out of all proportion to the act which has motivated them. In the present case . . . there was an evident disproportion between the incident of Naulilaa and the six acts of reprisal which followed it.

The arbitrators thus arrive at the conclusion that the German aggressions of October, November, and December, 1914, on the Angolan frontier cannot be considered licit reprisals for the Naulilaa incident or for the latter acts of the Portuguese authorities, because of lack of sufficient justification, of previous request for redress, and of an admissible proportion between the alleged offense and the reprisals resorted to.

. . . .

[Germany must therefore make reparations for the damage caused by her aggressions.]

Presumably, a strong central international government would eliminate reprisals altogether, because reprisals vary inversely in importance with the strength of central governments.[7] If the League of Nations had been and the United Nations were now in fact able to impose law and order in the international community, reprisals would completely disappear. One can see, for instance, that up to the June war of 1967, the Arab states and Israel refrained from mutual reprisals only to the extent that they believed that the United Nations was enforcing law and order along the armistice lines in Palestine.

Reprisals of which the law has customarily taken account include such acts as establishing a blockade, an embargo, or a boycott; occupying territory; or seizing the property of aliens. Some recent examples of reprisals include the attempts by the United States in February 1962 to impose a nearly total embargo on Cuba to deprive the government there of $35 million in annual income and the occupation of northern Indian territory by the Communist Chinese in August and September 1959 in an effort to obtain certain political concessions.

The United Nations Charter does not entirely forbid states to use reprisals. Reprisals not involving the use of armed force would certainly conform to the Charter and, under Article 51, reprisals taken in self-defense would also seem to be valid. For instance, note the stress laid on self-defense by the United States in the 1964 Bay of Tonkin incident.

Attack by North Vietnamese torpedo boats on American naval vessels

A.J.I.L., LIX (1965), 112–113

On August 2, and again on August 4, 1964, U.S. naval vessels operating in international waters in the Gulf of Tonkin off the coast of North Viet-Nam were attacked by Communist North Vietnamese torpedo boats. The U.S. vessels took appropriate retaliatory action and, following the second attack, air units of the 7th Fleet fired on gunboats and on certain supporting facilities on the North Vietnamese shore. On August 7 the Congress, at the request

[7] De Visscher, pp. 286–288.

of the President, passed a joint resolution approving and supporting "the determination of the President . . . to take all necessary measures to repel any armed attack against the forces of the United States and to prevent further aggression."

The full texts of documents relating to the incident are reprinted in the *Department of State Bulletin* of August 24, 1964 (Vol. 51, No. 1313). The following items are of particular interest.

On August 3, the United States made the following protest to North Viet-Nam:

> The United States Government takes an extremely serious view of the unprovoked attack made by Communist North Vietnamese torpedo boats on an American naval vessel, the U.S.S. *Maddox,* operating on the high seas, in the Gulf of Tonkin, on August 2. United States ships have traditionally operated freely on the high seas, in accordance with the rights guaranteed by international law to vessels of all nations. They will continue to do so and will take whatever measures are appropriate for their defense. The United States Government expects that the authorities of the regime in North Viet-Nam will be under no misapprehension as to the grave consequences which would inevitably result from any further unprovoked offensive military action against United States forces.
>
> (As read to news correspondents on Aug. 4, 1964, by Department spokesman, Robert J. McCloskey.)

On August 5, Adlai E. Stevenson, United States Representative in the United Nations Security Council, made a statement in the Security Council regarding the North Vietnamese attacks. The statement included the following:

> I want to emphasize that the action we have taken is a limited and measured response, fitted precisely to the attack that produced it, and that the deployments of additional U.S. forces to Southeast Asia are designed solely to deter further aggression. This is a single action designed to make unmistakably clear that the United States cannot be diverted by military attack from its obligations to help its friends establish and protect their independence. Our naval units are continuing their routine patrolling on the high seas with orders to protect themselves with all appropriate means against any further aggression. As President Johnson said last night, "We still seek no wider war."
>
> Mr. President, let me repeat that the United States vessels were in international waters when they were attacked.
>
> Let me repeat that freedom of the seas is guaranteed under long-accepted international law applying to all nations alike.

Let me repeat that these vessels took no belligerent actions of any kind until they were subject to armed attack.

And let me say once more that the action they took in self-defense is the right of all nations and is fully within the provisions of the Charter of the United Nations.

(U.S. Mission to the United Nations, Press Release No. 4424, Aug. 5, 1964.)

Students of international law must still determine what self-defense is if the "new" law is to mean anything. Here again the Nuremberg Tribunal is helpful, because it had to adjudicate the German leaders' contention that Germany had invaded Norway in self-defense, to forestall a contemplated Allied landing. In dealing with this problem, the Tribunal relied strongly on the *Caroline* (1837) incident between Great Britain and the United States, which proclaimed the doctrine that "preventive action in foreign territory is justified only in case of 'an instant and overwhelming necessity for self-defense, leaving no choice of means and no moment of deliberation.' "[8]

Both the Germans and the Japanese argued that individual states were exclusively competent to decide upon the circumstances that required them to go to war in self-defense. The Tribunals in Nuremberg and at Tokyo both rejected this claim, on the ground that the London Charter had given the Tribunal, and not individual states, the right to determine this question; in other words, the right to interpret the Kellogg-Briand Pact no longer rested with the individual signatories. Moreover, the Nuremberg Tribunal stated, the international community had to assert the right to determine whether actions taken in the name of self-defense were legitimate, if international law was ever to be enforced. And the Tokyo Tribunal pointed out that any other interpretation would mean that the Kellogg-Briand Pact was absolutely meaningless. They did not believe "that the Powers in concluding the Pact intended to make an empty gesture."[9]

Pending such international determinations, states themselves must still decide, initially, what measures they can justify as self-defense. The United Nations Charter itself speaks in Article 51 of "individual and collective self-defense," and the United States has justified its actions in Viet-Nam in these terms.

---

[8] Moore, *Digest*, II, 409, 412.
[9] *Judgment of the International Military Tribunal for the Far East*, p. 68 (1948).

This legal memorandum was prepared by Leonard C. Meeker, Legal Adviser of the Department, and was submitted to the Senate Committee on Foreign Relations on March 8.

The Legality of United States Participation in the Defense of Viet-Nam

MARCH 4, 1966

I. THE UNITED STATES AND SOUTH VIET-NAM HAVE THE RIGHT UNDER INTERNATIONAL LAW TO PARTICIPATE IN THE COLLECTIVE DEFENSE OF SOUTH VIET-NAM AGAINST ARMED ATTACK

In response to requests from the Government of South Viet-Nam, the United States has been assisting that country in defending itself against armed attack from the Communist North. This attack has taken the forms of externally supported subversion, clandestine supply of arms, infiltration of armed personnel, and most recently the sending of regular units of the North Vietnamese army into the South.

International law has long recognized the right of individual and collective self-defense against armed attack. South Viet-Nam and the United States are engaging in such collective defense consistently with international law and with United States obligations under the United Nations Charter.

A. South Viet-Nam Is Being Subjected to Armed Attack by Communist North Viet-Nam

The Geneva accords of 1954 established a demarcation line between North Viet-Nam and South Viet-Nam.[1] They provided for withdrawals of military forces into the respective zones north and south of this line.

[1] For texts, see *American Foreign Policy, 1950-1955; Basic Documents*, vol. I, Department of State publication 6446, p. 750.

The accords prohibited the use of either zone for the resumption of hostilities or to "further an aggressive policy."

During the 5 years following the Geneva conference of 1954, the Hanoi regime developed a covert political-military organization in South Viet-Nam based on Communist cadres it had ordered to stay in the South, contrary to the provisions of the Geneva accords. The activities of this covert organization were directed toward the kidnaping and assassination of civilian officials—acts of terrorism that were perpetrated in increasing numbers.

In the 3-year period from 1959 to 1961, the North Viet-Nam regime infiltrated an estimated 10,000 men into the South. It is estimated that 13,000 additional personnel were infiltrated in 1962, and, by the end of 1964, North Viet-Nam may well have moved over 40,000 armed and unarmed guerrillas into South Viet-Nam.

The International Control Commission reported in 1962 the findings of its Legal Committee:

... there is evidence to show that arms, armed and unarmed personnel, munitions and other supplies have been sent from the Zone in the North to the Zone in the South with the objective of supporting, organizing and carrying out hostile activities, including armed attacks, directed against the Armed Forces and Administration of the Zone in the South.

... there is evidence that the PAVN [People's Army of Viet Nam] has allowed the Zone in the North to be used for inciting, encouraging and supporting hostile activities in the Zone in the

[Reproduced from 54 Department of State *Bulletin* 474-89 (March 28, 1966).]

486

South, aimed at the overthrow of the Administration in the South.

Beginning in 1964, the Communists apparently exhausted their reservoir of Southerners who had gone North. Since then the greater number of men infiltrated into the South have been native-born North Vietnamese. Most recently, Hanoi has begun to infiltrate elements of the North Vietnamese army in increasingly larger numbers. Today, there is evidence that nine regiments of regular North Vietnamese forces are fighting in organized units in the South.

In the guerrilla war in Viet-Nam, the external aggression from the North is the critical military element of the insurgency, although it is unacknowledged by North Viet-Nam. In these circumstances, an "armed attack" is not as easily fixed by date and hour as in the case of traditional warfare. However, the infiltration of thousands of armed men clearly constitutes an "armed attack" under any reasonable definition. There may be some question as to the exact date at which North Viet-Nam's aggression grew into an "armed attack," but there can be no doubt that it had occurred before February 1965.

B. International Law Recognizes the Right of Individual and Collective Self-Defense Against Armed Attack

International law has traditionally recognized the right of self-defense against armed attack. This proposition has been asserted by writers on international law through the several centuries in which the modern law of nations has developed. The proposition has been acted on numerous times by governments throughout modern history. Today the principle of self-defense against armed attack is universally recognized and accepted. [2]

The Charter of the United Nations, concluded at the end of World War II, imposed

---

[2] See, e.g., Jessup, A Modern Law of Nations, 163 ff. (1948); Oppenheim, International Law, 297 ff. (8th ed., Lauterpacht, 1955). And see, generally, Bowett, Self-Defense in International Law (1958). [Footnote in original.]

an important limitation on the use of force by United Nations members. Article 2, paragraph 4, provides:

All Members shall refrain in their international relations from the threat or use of force against the territorial integrity or political independence of any state, or in any other manner inconsistent with the Purposes of the United Nations.

In addition, the charter embodied a system of international peacekeeping through the organs of the United Nations. Article 24 summarizes these structural arrangements in stating that the United Nations members:

. . . confer on the Security Council primary responsibility for the maintenance of international peace and security, and agree that in carrying out its duties under this responsibility the Security Council acts on their behalf.

However, the charter expressly states in article 51 that the remaining provisions of the charter—including the limitation of article 2, paragraph 4, and the creation of United Nations machinery to keep the peace —in no way diminish the inherent right of self-defense against armed attack. Article 51 provides:

Nothing in the present Charter shall impair the inherent right of individual or collective self-defense if an armed attack occurs against a Member of the United Nations, until the Security Council has taken the measures necessary to maintain international peace and security. Measures taken by Members in the exercise of this right of self-defense shall be immediately reported to the Security Council and shall not in any way affect the authority and responsibility of the Security Council under the present Charter to take at any time such action as it deems necessary in order to maintain or restore international peace and security.

Thus, article 51 restates and preserves, for member states in the situations covered by the article, a long-recognized principle of international law. The article is a "saving clause" designed to make clear that no other provision in the charter shall be interpreted to impair the inherent right of self-defense referred to in article 51.

Three principal objections have been raised against the availability of the right of individual and collective self-defense in the case of Viet-Nam: (1) that this right applies only in the case of an armed attack on a United Nations member; (2) that it does not apply in the case of South Viet-Nam because the latter is not an independent sovereign state; and (3) that collective self-defense may be undertaken only by a regional organization operating under chapter VIII of the United Nations Charter. These objections will now be considered in turn.

C. The Right of Individual and Collective Self-Defense Applies in the Case of South Viet-Nam Whether or Not That Country Is a Member of the United Nations

1. South Viet-Nam enjoys the right of self-defense

The argument that the right of self-defense is available only to members of the United Nations mistakes the nature of the right of self-defense and the relationship of the United Nations Charter to international law in this respect. As already shown, the right of self-defense against armed attack is an inherent right under international law. The right is not conferred by the charter, and, indeed, article 51 expressly recognizes that the right is inherent.

The charter nowhere contains any provision designed to deprive nonmembers of the right of self-defense against armed attack.[3] Article 2, paragraph 6, does charge the United Nations with responsibility for insuring that nonmember states act in accordance with United Nations "Principles so far as may be necessary for the maintenance of

---

[3] While nonmembers, such as South Viet-Nam, have not formally undertaken the obligations of the United Nations Charter as their own treaty obligations, it should be recognized that much of the substantive law of the charter has become part of the general law of nations through a very wide acceptance by nations the world over. This is particularly true of the charter provisions bearing on the use of force. Moreover, in the case of South Viet-Nam, the South Vietnamese Government has expressed its ability and willingness to abide by the charter, in applying for United Nations membership. Thus it seems entirely appropriate to appraise the actions of South Viet-Nam in relation to the legal standards set forth in the United Nations Charter. [Footnote in original.]

international peace and security." Protection against aggression and self-defense against armed attack are important elements in the whole charter scheme for the maintenance of international peace and security. To deprive nonmembers of their inherent right of self-defense would not accord with the principles of the organization, but would instead be prejudicial to the maintenance of peace. Thus article 2, paragraph 6—and, indeed, the rest of the charter—should certainly not be construed to nullify or diminish the inherent defensive rights of nonmembers.

2. The United States has the right to assist in the defense of South Viet-Nam although the latter is not a United Nations member

The cooperation of two or more international entities in the defense of one or both against armed attack is generally referred to as collective self-defense. United States participation in the defense of South Viet-Nam at the latter's request is an example of collective self-defense.

The United States is entitled to exercise the right of individual or collective self-defense against armed attack, as that right exists in international law, subject only to treaty limitations and obligations undertaken by this country.

It has been urged that the United States has no right to participate in the collective defense of South Viet-Nam because article 51 of the United Nations Charter speaks only of the situation "if an armed attack occurs *against a Member of the United Nations*." This argument is without substance.

In the first place, article 51 does not impose restrictions or cut down the otherwise available rights of United Nations members. By its own terms, the article preserves an inherent right. It is, therefore, necessary to look elsewhere in the charter for any obligation of members restricting their participation in collective defense of an entity that is not a United Nations member.

Article 2, paragraph 4, is the principal provision of the charter imposing limitations on the use of force by members. It states that they:

488

... shall refrain in their international relations from the threat or use of force against the territorial integrity or political independence of any state, or in any other manner inconsistent with the Purposes of the United Nations.

Action taken in defense against armed attack cannot be characterized as falling within this proscription. The record of the San Francisco conference makes clear that article 2, paragraph 4, was not intended to restrict the right of self-defense against armed attack.[4]

One will search in vain for any other provision in the charter that would preclude United States participation in the collective defense of a nonmember. The fact that article 51 refers only to armed attack "against a Member of the United Nations" implies no intention to preclude members from participating in the defense of nonmembers. Any such result would have seriously detrimental consequences for international peace and security and would be inconsistent with the purposes of the United Nations as they are set forth in article 1 of the charter.[5] The right of members to participate in the defense of nonmembers is upheld by leading authorities on international law.[6]

D. The Right of Individual and Collective Self-Defense Applies Whether or Not South Viet-Nam Is Regarded as an Independent Sovereign State

1. South Viet-Nam enjoys the right of self-defense

It has been asserted that the conflict in Viet-Nam is "civil strife" in which foreign intervention is forbidden. Those who make this assertion have gone so far as to compare Ho Chi Minh's actions in Viet-Nam with the efforts of President Lincoln to preserve the Union during the American Civil War. Any such characterization is an entire fiction disregarding the actual situation in Viet-Nam. The Hanoi regime is anything but the legitimate government of a unified country in which the South is rebelling against lawful national authority.

The Geneva accords of 1954 provided for a division of Viet-Nam into two zones at the 17th parallel. Although this line of demarcation was intended to be temporary, it was established by international agreement, which specifically forbade aggression by one zone against the other.

The Republic of Viet-Nam in the South has been recognized as a separate international entity by approximately 60 governments the world over. It has been admitted as a member of a number of the specialized agencies of the United Nations. The United Nations General Assembly in 1957 voted to recommend South Viet-Nam for membership in the organization, and its admission was frustrated only by the veto of the Soviet Union in the Security Council.

In any event there is no warrant for the suggestion that one zone of a temporarily divided state—whether it be Germany, Korea, or Viet-Nam—can be legally overrun by armed forces from the other zone, crossing the internationally recognized line of demarcation between the two. Any such doctrine would subvert the international agreement establishing the line of demarcation, and would pose grave dangers to international peace.

The action of the United Nations in the Korean conflict of 1950 clearly established the principle that there is no greater license for one zone of a temporarily divided state to attack the other zone than there is for one state to attack another state. South

---

[4] See 6 UNCIO Documents 459. [Footnote in original.]

[5] In particular, the statement of the first purpose:
To maintain international peace and security, and to that end: to take effective collective measures for the prevention and removal of threats to the peace, and for the suppression of acts of aggression or other breaches of the peace, and to bring about by peaceful means, and in conformity with the principles of justice and international law, adjustment or settlement of international disputes or situations which might lead to a breach of the peace. . . . [Footnote in original.]

[6] Bowett, *Self-Defense in International Law*, 193–195 (1958); Goodhart, "The North Atlantic Treaty of 1949," 79 *Recueil Des Cours*, 183, 202-204 (1951, vol. II), quoted in 5 *Whiteman's Digest of International Law*, 1067–1068 (1965); Kelsen, *The Law of the United Nations*, 793 (1950); see Stone, *Aggression and World Order*, 44 (1958). [Footnote in original.]

Viet-Nam has the same right that South Korea had to defend itself and to organize collective defense against an armed attack from the North. A resolution of the Security Council dated June 25, 1950, noted "with grave concern the armed attack upon the Republic of Korea by forces from North Korea," and determined "that this action constitutes a breach of the peace."

2. The United States is entitled to participate in the collective defense of South Viet-Nam whether or not the latter is regarded as an independent sovereign state

As stated earlier, South Viet-Nam has been recognized as a separate international entity by approximately 60 governments. It has been admitted to membership in a number of the United Nations specialized agencies and has been excluded from the United Nations Organization only by the Soviet veto.

There is nothing in the charter to suggest that United Nations members are precluded from participating in the defense of a recognized international entity against armed attack merely because the entity may lack some of the attributes of an independent sovereign state. Any such result would have a destructive effect on the stability of international engagements such as the Geneva accords of 1954 and on internationally agreed lines of demarcation. Such a result, far from being in accord with the charter and the purposes of the United Nations, would undermine them and would create new dangers to international peace and security.

E. The United Nations Charter Does Not Limit the Right of Self-Defense to Regional Organizations

Some have argued that collective self-defense may be undertaken only by a regional arrangement or agency operating under chapter VIII of the United Nations Charter. Such an assertion ignores the structure of the charter and the practice followed in the more than 20 years since the founding of the United Nations.

The basic proposition that rights of self-defense are not impaired by the charter—as expressly stated in article 51—is not conditioned by any charter provision limiting the application of this proposition to collective defense by a regional arrangement or agency. The structure of the charter reinforces this conclusion. Article 51 appears in chapter VII of the charter, entitled "Action With Respect to Threats to the Peace, Breaches of the Peace, and Acts of Aggression," whereas chapter VIII, entitled "Regional Arrangements," begins with article 52 and embraces the two following articles. The records of the San Francisco conference show that article 51 was deliberately placed in chapter VII rather than chapter VIII, "where it would only have a bearing on the regional system."[7]

Under article 51, the right of self-defense is available against any armed attack, whether or not the country attacked is a member of a regional arrangement and regardless of the source of the attack. Chapter VIII, on the other hand, deals with relations among members of a regional arrangement or agency, and authorizes regional action as appropriate for dealing with "local disputes." This distinction has been recognized ever since the founding of the United Nations in 1945.

For example, the North Atlantic Treaty has operated as a collective security arrangement, designed to take common measures in preparation against the eventuality of an armed attack for which collective defense under article 51 would be required. Similarly, the Southeast Asia Treaty Organization was designed as a collective defense arrangement under article 51. Secretary of State Dulles emphasized this in his testimony before the Senate Foreign Relations Committee in 1954.

By contrast, article 1 of the Charter of Bogotá (1948), establishing the Organization of American States, expressly declares that the organization is a regional agency within

---

[7] 17 UNCIO Documents 288. [Footnote in original.]

490

the United Nations. Indeed, chapter VIII of the United Nations Charter was included primarily to take account of the functioning of the inter-American system.

In sum, there is no basis in the United Nations Charter for contending that the right of self-defense against armed attack is limited to collective defense by a regional organization.

F. The United States Has Fulfilled Its Obligations to the United Nations

A further argument has been made that the members of the United Nations have conferred on United Nations organs—and, in particular, on the Security Council—exclusive power to act against aggression. Again, the express language of article 51 contradicts that assertion. A victim of armed attack is not required to forgo individual or collective defense of its territory until such time as the United Nations organizes collective action and takes appropriate measures. To the contrary, article 51 clearly states that the right of self-defense may be exercised *"until* the Security Council has taken the measures necessary to maintain international peace and security."[8]

As indicated earlier, article 51 is not literally applicable to the Viet-Nam situation since South Viet-Nam is not a member. However, reasoning by analogy from article

---

[8] An argument has been made by some that the United States, by joining in the collective defense of South Viet-Nam, has violated the peaceful settlement obligation of article 33 in the charter. This argument overlooks the obvious proposition that a victim of armed aggression is not required to sustain the attack undefended while efforts are made to find a political solution with the aggressor. Article 51 of the charter illustrates this by making perfectly clear that the inherent right of self-defense is impaired by "Nothing in the present Charter," including the provisions of article 33. [Footnote in original.]

[9] For a statement made by U.S. Representative Adlai E. Stevenson in the Security Council on Aug. 5, 1964, see BULLETIN of Aug. 24, 1964, p. 272.

[10] For texts, see *ibid.*, Feb. 22, 1965, p. 240, and Mar. 22, 1965, p. 419.

[11] For background and text of draft resolution, see *ibid.*, Feb. 14, 1966, p. 231.

51 and adopting its provisions as an appropriate guide for the conduct of members in a case like Viet-Nam, one can only conclude that United States actions are fully in accord with this country's obligations as a member of the United Nations.

Article 51 requires that:

Measures taken by Members in the exercise of this right of self-defense shall be immediately reported to the Security Council and shall not in any way affect the authority and responsibility of the Security Council under the present Charter to take at any time such action as it deems necessary in order to maintain or restore international peace and security.

The United States has reported to the Security Council on measures it has taken in countering the Communist aggression in Viet-Nam. In August 1964 the United States asked the Council to consider the situation created by North Vietnamese attacks on United States destroyers in the Tonkin Gulf.[9] The Council thereafter met to debate the question, but adopted no resolutions. Twice in February 1965 the United States sent additional reports to the Security Council on the conflict in Viet-Nam and on the additional measures taken by the United States in the collective defense of South Viet-Nam.[10] In January 1966 the United States formally submitted the Viet-Nam question to the Security Council for its consideration and introduced a draft resolution calling for discussions looking toward a peaceful settlement on the basis of the Geneva accords.[11]

At no time has the Council taken any action to restore peace and security in Southeast Asia. The Council has not expressed criticism of United States actions. Indeed, since the United States submission of January 1966, members of the Council have been notably reluctant to proceed with any consideration of the Viet-Nam question.

The conclusion is clear that the United States has in no way acted to interfere with United Nations consideration of the conflict in Viet-Nam. On the contrary, the United States has requested United Nations consideration, and the Council has not seen fit to act.

G. International Law Does Not Require a Declaration of War as a Condition Precedent To Taking Measures of Self-Defense Against Armed Attack

The existence or absence of a formal declaration of war is not a factor in determining whether an international use of force is lawful as a matter of international law. The United Nations Charter's restrictions focus on the manner and purpose of its use and not on any formalities of announcement.

It should also be noted that a formal declaration of war would not place any obligations on either side in the conflict by which that side would not be bound in any event. The rules of international law concerning the conduct of hostilities in an international armed conflict apply regardless of any declaration of war.

H. Summary

The analysis set forth above shows that South Viet-Nam has the right in present circumstances to defend itself against armed attack from the North and to organize a collective self-defense with the participation of others. In response to requests from South Viet-Nam, the United States has been participating in that defense, both through military action within South Viet-Nam and actions taken directly against the aggressor in North Viet-Nam. This participation by the United States is in conformity with international law and is consistent with our obligations under the Charter of the United Nations.

II. THE UNITED STATES HAS UNDERTAKEN COMMITMENTS TO ASSIST SOUTH VIET-NAM IN DEFENDING ITSELF AGAINST COMMUNIST AGGRESSION FROM THE NORTH

The United States has made commitments and given assurances, in various forms and at different times, to assist in the defense of South Viet-Nam.

A. The United States Gave Undertakings at the End of the Geneva Conference in 1954

At the time of the signing of the Geneva accords in 1954, President Eisenhower warned "that any renewal of Communist aggression would be viewed by us as a matter of grave concern," at the same time giving assurance that the United States would "not use force to disturb the settlement." [12] And the formal declaration made by the United States Government at the conclusion of the Geneva conference stated that the United States "would view any renewal of the aggression in violation of the aforesaid agreements with grave concern and as seriously threatening international peace and security." [13]

B. The United States Undertook an International Obligation To Defend South Viet-Nam in the SEATO Treaty

Later in 1954 the United States negotiated with a number of other countries and signed the Southeast Asia Collective Defense Treaty.[14] The treaty contains in the first paragraph of article IV the following provision:

Each Party recognizes that aggression by means of armed attack in the treaty area against any of the Parties or against any State or territory which the Parties by unanimous agreement may hereafter designate, would endanger its own peace and safety, and agrees that it will in that event act to meet the common danger in accordance with its constitutional processes. Measures taken under this paragraph shall be immediately reported to the Security Council of the United Nations.

Annexed to the treaty was a protocol stating that:

The Parties to the Southeast Asia Collective Defense Treaty unanimously designate for the purposes of Article IV of the Treaty the States of Cambodia and Laos and the free territory under the jurisdiction of the State of Vietnam.

Thus, the obligations of article IV, paragraph 1, dealing with the eventuality of

---

[12] For a statement made by President Eisenhower on June 21, 1954, see *ibid.*, Aug. 2, 1954, p. 163.

[13] For text, see *ibid.*, p. 162.

[14] For text, see *ibid.*, Sept. 20, 1954, p. 393.

armed attack, have from the outset covered the territory of South Viet-Nam. The facts as to the North Vietnamese armed attack against the South have been summarized earlier, in the discussion of the right of self-defense under international law and the Charter of the United Nations. The term "armed attack" has the same meaning in the SEATO treaty as in the United Nations Charter.

Article IV, paragraph 1, places an obligation on each party to the SEATO treaty to "act to meet the common danger in accordance with its constitutional processes" in the event of an armed attack. The treaty does not require a collective determination that an armed attack has occurred in order that the obligation of article IV, paragraph 1, become operative. Nor does the provision require collective decision on actions to be taken to meet the common danger. As Secretary Dulles pointed out when transmitting the treaty to the President, the commitment in article IV, paragraph 1, "leaves to the judgment of each country the type of action to be taken in the event an armed attack occurs." [15]

The treaty was intended to deter armed aggression in Southeast Asia. To that end it created not only a multilateral alliance but also a series of bilateral relationships. The obligations are placed squarely on "each Party" in the event of armed attack in the treaty area—not upon "the Parties," a wording that might have implied a necessity for collective decision. The treaty was intended to give the assurance of United States assistance to any party or protocol state that might suffer a Communist armed attack, regardless of the views or actions of other parties. The fact that the obligations are individual, and may even to some extent differ among the parties to the treaty, is demonstrated by the United States understanding, expressed at the time of signature, that its obligations under article IV, paragraph 1, apply only in the event of *Commu-*

---

[15] For text, see *ibid.*, Nov. 29, 1954, p. 820.

nist aggression, whereas the other parties to the treaty were unwilling so to limit their obligations to each other.

Thus, the United States has a commitment under article IV, paragraph 1, in the event of armed attack, independent of the decision or action of other treaty parties. A joint statement issued by Secretary Rusk and Foreign Minister Thanat Khoman of Thailand on March 6, 1962,[16] reflected this understanding:

The Secretary of State assured the Foreign Minister that in the event of such aggression, the United States intends to give full effect to its obligations under the Treaty to act to meet the common danger in accordance with its constitutional processes. The Secretary of State reaffirmed that this obligation of the United States does not depend upon the prior agreement of all other parties to the Treaty, since this Treaty obligation is individual as well as collective.

Most of the SEATO countries have stated that they agreed with this interpretation. None has registered objection to it.

When the Senate Committee on Foreign Relations reported on the Southeast Asia Collective Defense Treaty, it noted that the treaty area was further defined so that the "Free Territory of Vietnam" was an area "which, if attacked, would fall under the protection of the instrument." In its conclusion the committee stated:

The committee is not impervious to the risks which this treaty entails. It fully appreciates that acceptance of these additional obligations commits the United States to a course of action over a vast expanse of the Pacific. Yet these risks are consistent with our own highest interests.

The Senate gave its advice and consent to the treaty by a vote of 82 to 1.

C. The United States Has Given Additional Assurances to the Government of South Viet-Nam

The United States has also given a series of additional assurances to the Government of South Viet-Nam. As early as October 1954 President Eisenhower undertook to provide direct assistance to help make South Viet-

---

[16] For text, see *ibid.*, Mar. 26, 1962, p. 498.

Nam "capable of resisting attempted subversion or aggression through military means." [17] On May 11, 1957, President Eisenhower and President Ngo Dinh Diem of the Republic of Viet-Nam issued a joint statement [18] which called attention to "the large build-up of Vietnamese Communist military forces in North Viet-Nam" and stated:

Noting that the Republic of Viet-Nam is covered by Article IV of the Southeast Asia Collective Defense Treaty, President Eisenhower and President Ngo Dinh Diem agreed that aggression or subversion threatening the political independence of the Republic of Viet-Nam would be considered as endangering peace and stability.

On August 2, 1961, President Kennedy declared that "the United States is determined that the Republic of Viet-Nam shall not be lost to the Communists for lack of any support which the United States Government can render." [19] On December 7 of that year President Diem appealed for additional support. In his reply of December 14, 1961, President Kennedy recalled the United States declaration made at the end of the Geneva conference in 1954, and reaffirmed that the United States was "prepared to help the Republic of Viet-Nam to protect its people and to preserve its independence." [20] This assurance has been reaffirmed many times since.

III. ACTIONS BY THE UNITED STATES AND SOUTH VIET-NAM ARE JUSTIFIED UNDER THE GENEVA ACCORDS OF 1954

A. Description of the Accords

The Geneva accords of 1954 [21] established the date and hour for a cease-fire in Viet-Nam, drew a "provisional military demarcation line" with a demilitarized zone on both sides, and required an exchange of prisoners and the phased regroupment of Viet Minh forces from the south to the north and of French Union forces from the north to the south. The introduction into Viet-Nam of troop reinforcements and new military equipment (except for replacement and repair) was prohibited. The armed forces of each party were required to respect the demilitarized zone and the territory of the other zone. The adherence of either zone to any military alliance, and the use of either zone for the resumption of hostilities or to "further an aggressive policy," were prohibited. The International Control Commission was established, composed of India, Canada and Poland, with India as chairman. The task of the Commission was to supervise the proper execution of the provisions of the cease-fire agreement. General elections that would result in reunification were required to be held in July 1956 under the supervision of the ICC.

B. North Viet-Nam Violated the Accords From the Beginning

From the very beginning, the North Vietnamese violated the 1954 Geneva accords. Communist military forces and supplies were left in the South in violation of the accords. Other Communist guerrillas were moved north for further training and then were infiltrated into the South in violation of the accords.

[17] For text of a message from President Eisenhower to President Ngo Dinh Diem, see *ibid.*, Nov. 15, 1954, p. 735.

[18] For text, see *ibid.*, May 27, 1957, p. 851.

[19] For text of a joint communique issued by President Kennedy and Vice President Chen Cheng of the Republic of China, see *ibid.*, Aug. 28, 1961, p. 372.

[20] For text of an exchange of messages between President Kennedy and President Diem, see *ibid.*, Jan. 1, 1962, p. 13.

[21] These accords were composed of a bilateral cease-fire agreement between the "Commander-in-Chief of the People's Army of Viet Nam" and the "Commander-in-Chief of the French Union forces in Indo-China," together with a Final Declaration of the Conference, to which France adhered. However, it is to be noted that the South Vietnamese Government was not a signatory of the cease-fire agreement and did not adhere to the Final Declaration. South Viet-Nam entered a series of reservations in a statement to the conference. This statement was noted by the conference, but by decision of the conference chairman it was not included or referred to in the Final Declaration. [Footnote in original.]

C. The Introduction of United States Military Personnel and Equipment Was Justified

The accords prohibited the reinforcement of foreign military forces in Viet-Nam and the introduction of new military equipment, but they allowed replacement of existing military personnel and equipment. Prior to late 1961 South Viet-Nam had received considerable military equipment and supplies from the United States, and the United States had gradually enlarged its Military Assistance Advisory Group to slightly less than 900 men. These actions were reported to the ICC and were justified as replacements for equipment in Viet-Nam in 1954 and for French training and advisory personnel who had been withdrawn after 1954.

As the Communist aggression intensified during 1961, with increased infiltration and a marked stepping up of Communist terrorism in the South, the United States found it necessary in late 1961 to increase substantially the numbers of our military personnel and the amounts and types of equipment introduced by this country into South Viet-Nam. These increases were justified by the international law principle that a material breach of an agreement by one party entitles the other at least to withhold compliance with an equivalent, corresponding, or related provision until the defaulting party is prepared to honor its obligations.[22]

In accordance with this principle, the systematic violation of the Geneva accords by North Viet-Nam justified South Viet-Nam in suspending compliance with the provision controlling entry of foreign military personnel and military equipment.

D. South Viet-Nam Was Justified in Refusing To Implement the Election Provisions of the Geneva Accords

The Geneva accords contemplated the reunification of the two parts of Viet-Nam. They contained a provision for general elections to be held in July 1956 in order to obtain a "free expression of the national will." The accords stated that "consultations will be held on this subject between the compe-

tent representative authorities of the two zones from 20 July 1955 onwards."

There may be some question whether South Viet-Nam was bound by these election provisions. As indicated earlier, South Viet-Nam did not sign the cease-fire agreement of 1954, nor did it adhere to the Final Declaration of the Geneva conference. The South Vietnamese Government at that time gave notice of its objection in particular to the election provisions of the accords.

However, even on the premise that these provisions were binding on South Viet-Nam, the South Vietnamese Government's failure to engage in consultations in 1955, with a view to holding elections in 1956, involved no breach of obligation. The conditions in North Viet-Nam during that period were such as to make impossible any free and meaningful expression of popular will.

Some of the facts about conditions in the North were admitted even by the Communist leadership in Hanoi. General Giap, currently Defense Minister of North Viet-Nam, in addressing the Tenth Congress of the North Vietnamese Communist Party in Oc-

---

[22] This principle of law and the circumstances in which it may be invoked are most fully discussed in the Fourth Report on the Law of Treaties by Sir Gerald Fitzmaurice, articles 18, 20 (U.N. doc. A/CN.4/120(1959)) II Yearbook of the International Law Commission 37 (U.N. doc. A/CN.4/SER.A/1959/Add.1) and in the later report by Sir Humphrey Waldock, article 20 (U.N. doc. A/CN.4/156 and Add. 1-3 (1963)) II Yearbook of the International Law Commission 36 (U.N. doc. A/CN.4/SER.A/1963/Add.1). Among the authorities cited by the fourth report for this proposition are: II Oppenheim, *International Law* 136, 137 (7th ed. Lauterpacht 1955); I Rousseau, *Principes généraux du droit international public* 365 (1944); II Hyde, *International Law* 1660 et seq. (2d ed. 1947); II Guggenheim, *Traité de droit international public* 84, 85 (1935); Spiropoulos, *Traité théorique et pratique de droit international public* 289 (1933); Verdross, *Völkerrecht,* 328 (1950); Hall, *Treatise* 21 (8th ed. Higgins 1924); 3 Accioly, *Tratado de Direito Internacional Publico* 82 (1956–57). See also draft articles 42 and 46 of the Law of Treaties by the International Law Commission, contained in the report on the work of its 15th session (General Assembly, Official Records, 18th Session, Supplement No. 9(A/5809)). [Footnote in original.]

tober 1956, publicly acknowledged that the Communist leaders were running a police state where executions, terror, and torture were commonplace. A nationwide election in these circumstances would have been a travesty. No one in the North would have dared to vote except as directed. With a substantial majority of the Vietnamese people living north of the 17th parallel, such an election would have meant turning the country over to the Communists without regard to the will of the people. The South Vietnamese Government realized these facts and quite properly took the position that consultations for elections in 1956 as contemplated by the accords would be a useless formality.[23]

IV. THE PRESIDENT HAS FULL AUTHORITY TO COMMIT UNITED STATES FORCES IN THE COLLECTIVE DEFENSE OF SOUTH VIET-NAM

There can be no question in present circumstances of the President's authority to commit United States forces to the defense of South Viet-Nam. The grant of authority to the President in article II of the Constitution extends to the actions of the United States currently undertaken in Viet-Nam. In fact, however, it is unnecessary to determine whether this grant standing alone is sufficient to authorize the actions taken in Viet-Nam. These actions rest not only on the exercise of Presidential powers under article II but on the SEATO treaty—a treaty advised and consented to by the Senate—and on actions of the Congress, particularly the joint resolution of August 10, 1964. When these sources of authority are taken together—article II of the Constitution, the SEATO treaty, and actions by the Congress —there can be no question of the legality

---

[23] In any event, if North Viet-Nam considered there had been a breach of obligation by the South, its remedies lay in discussion with Saigon, perhaps in an appeal to the cochairmen of the Geneva conference, or in a reconvening of the conference to consider the situation. Under international law, North Viet-Nam had no right to use force outside its own zone in order to secure its political objectives. [Footnote in original.]

under domestic law of United States actions in Viet-Nam.

A. The President's Power Under Article II of the Constitution Extends to the Actions Currently Undertaken in Viet-Nam

Under the Constitution, the President, in addition to being Chief Executive, is Commander in Chief of the Army and Navy. He holds the prime responsibility for the conduct of United States foreign relations. These duties carry very broad powers, including the power to deploy American forces abroad and commit them to military operations when the President deems such action necessary to maintain the security and defense of the United States.

At the Federal Constitutional Convention in 1787, it was originally proposed that Congress have the power "to make war." There were objections that legislative proceedings were too slow for this power to be vested in Congress; it was suggested that the Senate might be a better repository. Madison and Gerry then moved to substitute "to declare war" for "to make war," "leaving to the Executive the power to repel sudden attacks." It was objected that this might make it too easy for the Executive to involve the nation in war, but the motion carried with but one dissenting vote.

In 1787 the world was a far larger place, and the framers probably had in mind attacks upon the United States. In the 20th century, the world has grown much smaller. An attack on a country far from our shores can impinge directly on the nation's security. In the SEATO treaty, for example, it is formally declared that an armed attack against Viet-Nam would endanger the peace and safety of the United States.

Since the Constitution was adopted there have been at least 125 instances in which the President has ordered the armed forces to take action or maintain positions abroad without obtaining prior congressional authorization, starting with the "undeclared war" with France (1798–1800). For example, President Truman ordered 250,000 troops to Korea during the Korean war of the early

496

1950's. President Eisenhower dispatched 14,000 troops to Lebanon in 1958.

The Constitution leaves to the President the judgment to determine whether the circumstances of a particular armed attack are so urgent and the potential consequences so threatening to the security of the United States that he should act without formally consulting the Congress.

B. The Southeast Asia Collective Defense Treaty Authorizes the President's Actions

Under article VI of the United States Constitution, "all Treaties made, or which shall be made, under the Authority of the United States, shall be the supreme Law of the Land." Article IV, paragraph 1, of the SEATO treaty establishes as a matter of law that a Communist armed attack against South Viet-Nam endangers the peace and safety of the United States. In this same provision the United States has undertaken a commitment in the SEATO treaty to "act to meet the common danger in accordance with its constitutional processes" in the event of such an attack.

Under our Constitution it is the President who must decide when an armed attack has occurred. He has also the constitutional responsibility for determining what measures of defense are required when the peace and safety of the United States are endangered. If he considers that deployment of U. S. forces to South Viet-Nam is required, and that military measures against the source of Communist aggression in North Viet-Nam are necessary, he is constitutionally empowered to take those measures.

The SEATO treaty specifies that each party will act "in accordance with its constitutional processes."

It has recently been argued that the use of land forces in Asia is not authorized under the treaty because their use to deter armed attack was not contemplated at the time the treaty was considered by the Senate. Secretary Dulles testified at that time that we did not intend to establish (1) a land army in Southeast Asia capable of deterring Communist aggression, or (2) an integrated headquarters and military organization like that of NATO; instead, the United States would rely on "mobile striking power" against the sources of aggression. However, the treaty obligation in article IV, paragraph 1, to meet the common danger in the event of armed aggression, is not limited to particular modes of military action. What constitutes an adequate deterrent or an appropriate response, in terms of military strategy, may change; but the essence of our commitment to act to meet the common danger, as necessary at the time of an armed aggression, remains. In 1954 the forecast of military judgment might have been against the use of substantial United States ground forces in Viet-Nam. But that does not preclude the President from reaching a different military judgment in different circumstances, 12 years later.

C. The Joint Resolution of Congress of August 10, 1964, Authorizes United States Participation in the Collective Defense of South Viet-Nam

As stated earlier, the legality of United States participation in the defense of South Viet-Nam does not rest only on the constitutional power of the President under article II—or indeed on that power taken in conjunction with the SEATO treaty. In addition, the Congress has acted in unmistakable fashion to approve and authorize United States actions in Viet-Nam.

Following the North Vietnamese attacks in the Gulf of Tonkin against United States destroyers, Congress adopted, by a Senate vote of 88–2 and a House vote of 416–0, a joint resolution containing a series of important declarations and provisions of law.[24]

Section 1 resolved that "the Congress approves and supports the determination of the President, as Commander in Chief, to take all necessary measures to repel any armed attack against the forces of the United States and to prevent further aggression." Thus, the Congress gave its sanction to specific actions by the President

---

[24] For text, see BULLETIN of Aug. 24, 1964, p. 268.

to repel attacks against United States naval vessels in the Gulf of Tonkin and elsewhere in the western Pacific. Congress further approved the taking of "all necessary measures . . . to prevent further aggression." This authorization extended to those measures the President might consider necessary to ward off further attacks and to prevent further aggression by North Viet-Nam in Southeast Asia.

The joint resolution then went on to provide in section 2:

The United States regards as vital to its national interest and to world peace the maintenance of international peace and security in southeast Asia. Consonant with the Constitution of the United States and the Charter of the United Nations and in accordance with its obligations under the Southeast Asia Collective Defense Treaty, the United States is, therefore, prepared, as the President determines, to take all necessary steps, including the use of armed force, to assist any member or protocol state of the Southeast Asia Collective Defense Treaty requesting assistance in defense of its freedom.

Section 2 thus constitutes an authorization to the President, in his discretion, to act—using armed force if he determines that is required—to assist South Viet-Nam at its request in defense of its freedom. The identification of South Viet-Nam through the reference to "protocol state" in this section is unmistakable, and the grant of authority "as the President determines" is unequivocal.

It has been suggested that the legislative history of the joint resolution shows an intention to limit United States assistance to South Viet-Nam to aid, advice, and training. This suggestion is based on an amendment offered from the floor by Senator [Gaylord] Nelson which would have added the following to the text:

The Congress also approves and supports the efforts of the President to bring the problem of peace in Southeast Asia to the Security Council of the United Nations, and the President's declaration that the United States, seeking no extension of the present military conflict, will respond to provocation in a manner that is "limited and fitting." Our continuing policy is to limit our role to the provision of aid, training assistance, and military

advice, and it is the sense of Congress that, except when provoked to a greater response, we should continue to attempt to avoid a direct military involvement in the Southeast Asian conflict.[15]

Senator [J. W.] Fulbright, who had reported the joint resolution from the Foreign Relations Committee, spoke on the amendment as follows:

It states fairly accurately what the President has said would be our policy, and what I stated my understanding was as to our policy; also what other Senators have stated. In other words, it states that our response should be appropriate and limited to the provocation, which the Senator states as "respond to provocation in a manner that is limited and fitting," and so forth. We do not wish any political or military bases there. We are not seeking to gain a colony. We seek to insure the capacity of these people to develop along the lines of their own desires, independent of domination by communism.

The Senator has put into his amendment a statement of policy that is unobjectionable. However, I cannot accept the amendment under the circumstances. I do not believe it is contrary to the joint resolution, but it is an enlargement. I am informed that the House is now voting on this resolution. The House joint resolution is about to be presented to us. I cannot accept the amendment and go to conference with it, and thus take responsibility for delaying matters.

I do not object to it as a statement of policy. I believe it is an accurate reflection of what I believe is the President's policy, judging from his own statements. That does not mean that as a practical matter I can accept the amendment. It would delay matters to do so. It would cause confusion and require a conference, and present us with all the other difficulties that are involved in this kind of legislative action. I regret that I cannot do it, even though I do not at all disagree with the amendment as a general statement of policy.[16]

Senator Nelson's amendment related the degree and kind of U. S. response in Viet-Nam to "provocation" on the other side; the response should be "limited and fitting." The greater the provocation, the stronger are the measures that may be characterized as "limited and fitting." Bombing of North Vietnamese naval bases was a "limited and fitting" response to the attacks on U. S. destroyers in August 1964, and the subse-

---

[15] 110 *Cong. Rec.* 18459 (Aug. 7, 1964). [Footnote in original.]

[16] *Ibid.*

quent actions taken by the United States and South Viet-Nam have been an appropriate response to the increased war of aggression carried on by North Viet-Nam since that date. Moreover, Senator Nelson's proposed amendment did not purport to be a restriction on authority available to the President but merely a statement concerning what should be the continuing policy of the United States.

Congressional realization of the scope of authority being conferred by the joint resolution is shown by the legislative history of the measure as a whole. The following exchange between Senators Cooper and Fulbright is illuminating:

Mr. COOPER [John Sherman Cooper]. . . . The Senator will remember that the SEATO Treaty, in article IV, provides that in the event an armed attack is made upon a party to the Southeast Asia Collective Defense Treaty, or upon one of the protocol states such as South Vietnam, the parties to the treaty, one of whom is the United States, would then take such action as might be appropriate, after resorting to their constitutional processes. I assume that would mean, in the case of the United States, that Congress would be asked to grant the authority to act.
Does the Senator consider that in enacting this resolution we are satisfying that requirement of article IV of the Southeast Asia Collective Defense Treaty? In other words, are we now giving the President advance authority to take whatever action he may deem necessary respecting South Vietnam and its defense, or with respect to the defense of any other country included in the treaty?
Mr. FULBRIGHT. I think that is correct.
Mr. COOPER. Then, looking ahead, if the President decided that it was necessary to use such force as could lead into war, we will give that authority by this resolution?
Mr. FULBRIGHT. That is the way I would interpret it. If a situation later developed in which we thought the approval should be withdrawn it could be withdrawn by concurrent resolution.[37]

The August 1964 joint resolution continues in force today. Section 2 of the resolution provides that it shall expire "when the President shall determine that the peace and security of the area is reasonably assured by international conditions created by action of the United Nations or otherwise, except that it may be terminated earlier by concurrent resolution of the Congress." The

President has made no such determination, nor has Congress terminated the joint resolution.[28]

Instead, Congress in May 1965 approved an appropriation of $700 million to meet the expense of mounting military requirements in Viet-Nam. (Public Law 89–18, 79 Stat. 109.) The President's message asking for this appropriation stated that this was "not a routine appropriation. For each Member of Congress who supports this request is also voting to persist in our efforts to halt Communist aggression in South Vietnam."[29] The appropriation act constitutes a clear congressional endorsement and approval of the actions taken by the President.

On March 1, 1966, the Congress continued to express its support of the President's policy by approving a $4.8 billion supplemental military authorization by votes of

[37] 110 *Cong. Rec.* 18409 (Aug. 6, 1964). Senator [Wayne] Morse, who opposed the joint resolution, expressed the following view on August 6, 1964, concerning the scope of the proposed resolution:

Another Senator thought, in the early part of the debate, that this course would not broaden the power of the President to engage in a land war if he decided that he wanted to apply the resolution in that way.
That Senator was taking great consolation in the then held belief that, if he voted for the resolution, it would give no authority to the President to send many troops into Asia. I am sure he was quite disappointed to finally learn, because it took a little time to get the matter cleared, that the resolution places no restriction on the President in that respect. If he is still in doubt, let him read the language on page 2, lines 3 to 6, and page 2, lines 11 to 17. The first reads:

The Congress approves and supports the determination of the President, as Commander in Chief, to take all necessary measures to repel any armed attack against the forces of the United States and to prevent further aggression.

It does not say he is limited in regard to the sending of ground forces. It does not limit that authority. That is why I have called it a predated declaration of war, in clear violation of article I, section 8, of the Constitution, which vests the power to declare war in the Congress, and not in the President.
What is proposed is to authorize the President of the United States, without a declaration of war, to commit acts of war. (110 *Cong. Rec.* 18426-7 (Aug. 6, 1964)). [Footnote in original.]
[28] On March 1, 1966, the Senate voted, 92–5, to table an amendment that would have repealed the joint resolution. [Footnote in original.]
[29] For text, see BULLETIN of May 24, 1965, p. 822.

392–4 and 93–2. An amendment that would have limited the President's authority to commit forces to Viet-Nam was rejected in the Senate by a vote of 94–2.

D. No Declaration of War by the Congress Is Required To Authorize United States Participation in the Collective Defense of South Viet-Nam

No declaration of war is needed to authorize American actions in Viet-Nam. As shown in the preceding sections, the President has ample authority to order the participation of United States armed forces in the defense of South Viet-Nam.

Over a very long period in our history, practice and precedent have confirmed the constitutional authority to engage United States forces in hostilities without a declaration of war. This history extends from the undeclared war with France and the war against the Barbary pirates at the end of the 18th century to the Korean war of 1950–53.

James Madison, one of the leading framers of the Constitution, and Presidents John Adams and Jefferson all construed the Constitution, in their official actions during the early years of the Republic, as authorizing the United States to employ its armed forces abroad in hostilities in the absence of any congressional declaration of war. Their views and actions constitute highly persuasive evidence as to the meaning and effect of the Constitution. History has accepted the interpretation that was placed on the Constitution by the early Presidents and Congresses in regard to the lawfulness of hostilities without a declaration of war. The instances of such action in our history are numerous.

In the Korean conflict, where large-scale hostilities were conducted with an American troop participation of a quarter of a million men, no declaration of war was made by the Congress. The President acted on the basis of his constitutional responsibilities. While the Security Council, under a treaty of this country—the United Nations Charter—recommended assistance to the Republic of Korea against the Communist armed attack, the United States had no treaty commitment at that time obligating us to join in the defense of South Korea. In the case of South Viet-Nam we have the obligation of the SEATO treaty and clear expressions of congressional support. If the President could act in Korea without a declaration of war, *a fortiori* he is empowered to do so now in Viet-Nam.

It may be suggested that a declaration of war is the only available constitutional process by which congressional support can be made effective for the use of United States armed forces in combat abroad. But the Constitution does not insist on any rigid formalism. It gives Congress a choice of ways in which to exercise its powers. In the case of Viet-Nam the Congress has supported the determination of the President by the Senate's approval of the SEATO treaty, the adoption of the joint resolution of August 10, 1964, and the enactment of the necessary authorizations and appropriations.

V. CONCLUSION

South Viet-Nam is being subjected to armed attack by Communist North Viet-Nam, through the infiltration of armed personnel, military equipment, and regular combat units. International law recognizes the right of individual and collective self-defense against armed attack. South Viet-Nam, and the United States upon the request of South Viet-Nam, are engaged in such collective defense of the South. Their actions are in conformity with international law and with the Charter of the United Nations. The fact that South Viet-Nam has been precluded by Soviet veto from becoming a member of the United Nations and the fact that South Viet-Nam is a zone of a temporarily divided state in no way diminish the right of collective defense of South Viet-Nam.

The United States has commitments to assist South Viet-Nam in defending itself against Communist aggression from the North. The United States gave undertakings to this effect at the conclusion of the Geneva conference in 1954. Later that year the United States undertook an international obligation in the SEATO treaty to defend South Viet-Nam against Communist armed aggression. And during the past decade the United States has given additional assurances to the South Vietnamese Government.

The Geneva accords of 1954 provided for a cease-fire and regroupment of contending forces, a division of Viet-Nam into two zones, and a prohibition on the use of either zone for the resumption of hostilities or to "further an aggressive policy." From the beginning, North Viet-Nam violated the Geneva accords through a systematic effort to gain control of South Viet-Nam by force. In the light of these progressive North Vietnamese violations, the introduction into South Viet-Nam beginning in late 1961 of substantial United States military equipment and personnel, to assist in the defense of the South, was fully justified; substantial breach of an international agreement by one side permits the other side to suspend performance of corresponding obligations under the agreement. South Viet-Nam was justified in refusing to implement the provisions of the Geneva accords calling for reunification through free elections throughout Viet-Nam since the Communist regime in North Viet-Nam created conditions in the North that made free elections entirely impossible.

The President of the United States has full authority to commit United States forces in the collective defense of South Viet-Nam. This authority stems from the constitutional powers of the President. However, it is not necessary to rely on the Constitution alone as the source of the President's authority, since the SEATO treaty—advised and consented to by the Senate and forming part of the law of the land—sets forth a United States commitment to defend South Viet-Nam against armed attack, and since the Congress—in the joint resolution of August 10, 1964, and in authorization and appropriations acts for support of the U. S. military effort in Viet-Nam—has given its approval and support to the President's actions. United States actions in Viet-Nam, taken by the President and approved by the Congress, do not require any declaration of war, as shown by a long line of precedents for use of United States armed forces abroad the absence of any congressional declarat of war.

Senator YOUNG of North Dakota. Would you yield for one question?

Senator SMITH. Yes.

Senator YOUNG of North Dakota. This may be a bit unfair and not the proper place to ask it, but from the military point of view, what advantages or disadvantages would there be to a declaration of war? This question is often raised in my mail. Why don't we declare war on North Vietnam?

Secretary McNAMARA. Senator Young, this is a highly technical question with legal overtones. I wonder if I might answer that for the record. I would be very happy to do so.

Senator YOUNG of North Dakota. Thank you. Will you supply that?

Secretary McNAMARA. I will be very happy to supply it to you.

Senator MILLER. Mr. Chairman, I would like to receive a copy of that.

Chairman RUSSELL. I think you might offer it for the record, Mr. Secretary.

Secretary McNAMARA. I will do so.

Chairman RUSSELL. If there are any treaties that bind North Vietnam to Russia or China, that would bring Russia and China into the war automatically upon a declaration of war, I think you ought to state that. That to me is one very good reason.

Secretary McNAMARA. Yes.

(The information follows:)

The question has been raised whether it would be desirable for the President to seek a formal declaration of war against North Vietnam. This question should be considered with respect to both international and domestic considerations.

MILITARY AUTHORIZATIONS—DEFENSE APPROPRIATIONS   279

INTERNATIONAL CONSIDERATIONS

From the international standpoint it seems undesirable to request a declaration of war for the following reasons:

1. The policy of the United States in Vietnam is to assist the Government of the Republic of Vietnam, at the latter's request, in thwarting an armed aggression from North Vietnam and to achieve a workable settlement of the dispute among the principal parties involved. This policy is pursued with limited aims, seeking to end the aggression against South Vietnam without threatening the destruction of North Vietnam, allowing a miscalculation by the enemy as to our intentions, or unnecessarily enlarging the scope of the conflict. The United States believes that the struggle must be won primarily in South Vietnam and is in that context a defensive military effort.

2. To declare war would add a new psychological element to the international situation, since in this century declarations of war have come to imply dedication to the total destruction of the enemy. It would increase the danger of misunderstanding of our true objectives in the conflict by the various Communist states, and increase the chances of their expanded involvement in it. Such a declaration would question the continued validity of the President's statements concerning his desire for a peaceful settlement allowing the various nations of the area, including North Vietnam, to live together in economic cooperation, and his reiteration that we do not threaten the existence of North Vietnam.

3. On balance, a declaration of war—which would be the first since the signing

---

[Reproduced from Military Procurement Authorizations for Fiscal Year 1967: Hearings before the Committee on Armed Services and the Subcommittee on Department of Defense of the Committee on Appropriations on S.2950, U.S. Senate, 89th Congress, 2d Session, pp. 278-80. The excerpt reproduced here is from the testimony of Robert S. McNamara, Secretary of Defense, on February 25, 1966.]

of the United Nations Charter—would significantly reduce the flexibility of the United States to seek a solution among extremely complex factors and reduce the chances that our adversary will take a reasoned approach to a solution, when U.S. policy from the beginning has attempted to avoid closing off any possible avenue of resolution and to make the North Vietnamese more rather than less rational in the situation.

4. There is nothing in modern international law which requires a state to declare war before engaging in hostilities against another state; nor would a formal declaration of war impose any obligations on an enemy by which he would not otherwise be bound.

5. Absence of a formal declaration of war is not a factor which makes an international use of force unlawful. The only relevant legal question is whether the use of force is justified. Examples of hostilities begun without prior declaration of war abound in recent history. The fighting in Korea from 1950 to 1953, that in Indochina from 1947 to 1954, that in and around the Suez Canal in 1956, and that in West New Guinea between the Dutch and Indonesians in the spring and summer of 1962 all took place without benefit of declarations of war. We are not aware that the absence of declarations of war in these cases has been alleged to constitute a violation of international law.

6. The legal rules of international law concerning the conduct of armed conflicts apply to all armed conflicts without regard to the presence or absence of declarations of war. All that is required is armed conflict between two or more international entities. The 1949 Geneva Conventions for the Protection of War Victims were specifically made applicable to any "armed conflict of an international character" between two or more of the parties. The rules of war embodied in the Hague conventions formulated in the early years of this century are considered, in general, to be part of customary international law binding on all states, and their applicability is unrelated to declarations of war.

DOMESTIC CONSIDERATIONS

From the point of view of U.S. law it would be undesirable for the President to seek a declaration of war for the following reasons:

1. A declaration of war is not necessary either to authorize the actions that have been taken by the United States in Vietnam or to provide an expression of congressional intent on the Vietnamese situation. The President has power under article II, section 2, of the Constitution as Commander in Chief to deploy U.S. military forces to Vietnam for the purpose of assisting South Vietnam to defend itself from armed aggression by North Vietnam. Since the Constitution was adopted, there have been at least 125 instances in which the President, without congressional authority and in the absence of a declaration of war, has ordered the Armed Forces to take actions or to maintain positions abroad. Some of these historical instances have involved the use of U.S. forces in combat. Congressional intent is expressed by the joint resolution of Congress of August 10, 1964,

passed by a combined vote of 504 to 2, explicitly approving all necessary steps, including the use of armed force, in the defense of freedom in southeast Asia. A much fuller presentation of the views of the executive branch on the question of the President's constitutional authority was published in February 1951, as a joint committee print of the Senate Committees on Foreign Relations and Armed Services.

2. A declaration of war does not seem necessary in order to provide emergency authority to the executive branch. Many laws become operative in time of national emergency or in time of war. Most of these are operative today by virtue of the state of emergency proclaimed by President Truman in December 1950. These laws give the executive branch increased power to deal with the problems in Vietnam as well as other areas of the world. For example, they include special authority with respect to the movement of aliens in and out of the United States, the Armed Forces, Reserves, and the National Guard; procurement of material for the services; transactions in foreign exchange, Government contracts, security, and the protection of defense information; and defense transportation. A few emergency laws would not come into effect unless there were a declaration of national emergency or of war subsequent to the 1950 declaration of national emergency. However, there are only a few laws which can become operative only in time of war, and they have not been found necessary for the conduct of hostilities in Vietnam.

War

Armed hostility between states is called war. But wars can exist where states use no force; and states may use force without being at war, as recent history has shown in Korea and Vietnam.

Much confusion may be avoided by bearing in mind . . . that by the term war is meant not the mere employment of force, but the existence of the legal condition of things in which rights are or may be prosecuted by force. Thus, if two nations declare war one against the other, war exists, though no force whatever may as yet have been employed. On the other hand, force may be employed by one nation against another, as in the case of reprisals, and yet no state of war may arise. In such a case there may be said to be an act of war, but no state of war. The distinction is of the first importance, since, from the moment when a state of war supervenes third parties become subject to the performance of the duties of neutrality as well as to all the inconveniences that result from the exercise of belligerent rights.[10]

States are not always eager to clarify the international situation for the sake of international lawyers. Because a clear state of war does alter the legal obligations of belligerents and neutrals, states have tended in recent years to avoid using *war* to describe their uses of force. Japan described its hostilities in China in 1931 as an "incident"; Italy undertook a "civilizing mission" in Ethiopia in 1935; and both maintained that they had not violated the League of Nations Covenant, which spoke of *war*.

The United States, as we have seen, maintains that it is exercising the right of collective self-defense in South Vietnam, and it may be that declarations of war are now historical phenomena.

The United Nations Charter uses terms like "acts of aggression and other breaches of the peace" (Article 1), "threat or use of force" (Article 2), and "disputes" (Article 34), all in an effort to bring any use of force within its jurisdiction. It has logically attempted to give more precise content to *aggression,* as used in the United Nations Charter. Various attempts have been made, but few offer the international community as much security as is permitted under the provisions that allow the U.N. Security Council to determine whether there has been a breach of the peace or act of aggression merely by examining the facts at hand and applying common sense rather than a precise definition.

Those who argue in favor of defining *aggression* claim that a definition would serve to warn potential aggressors, guide U.N. organs responsible for maintaining international peace and security, and reduce international

[10] Moore, *Digest,* VII, 153–154.

tensions. The arguments against defining the word are equally compelling and almost the same, namely, that a definition would not promote peace because it could not possibly comprise all imaginable forms of aggression, the forms of which change constantly, and because it would restrict the flexibility of the principal U.N. organs and encourage premature censure of states. Moreover, opponents point out that treaties have not offered any real protection against aggression in the past and that the United Nations has not suffered without a definition. There is, in addition, some doubt that any definition could command the support it would require to be effective. Over the years, therefore, the United Nations has tended to gather the views of its members on the subject without coming to any conclusions.[11]

The United Nations Charter represents the most recent attempt by the "family of nations" to establish rules for preventing war. It provides ample rules and procedures in Chapter VI for settling disputes amicably, but if states choose in the future as in the past, to ignore the rules and not to use the procedures, they will have no recourse but to fall back upon those classical doctrines of the "law of war" which have developed out of the failure of international law to keep states from waging war for three hundred years.

Classical Doctrines

The "law of war" ignores the complete impotence of international law to prevent states from waging war and covers instead such subjects as permissible violence, sieges and bombardments, seizing and devastating enemy property; using expansive bullets, asphyxiating or deleterious gases, submarine mines, and torpedoes; the rights of neutrals; and the treatment of prisoners of war.

Many of these rules have fallen victim to technology. Rules that make it illegal for a belligerent "to employ arms, projectiles, or material calculated to cause unnecessary suffering," or "to destroy or seize the enemy's property, unless such destruction or seizure be imperatively demanded by the necessities of war,"[12] make very little sense in an age of atomic

---

[11] The United Nations has adopted several resolutions on defining *aggression:* 599 (VI) 31 January 1952; 688 (VII) 20 December 1952; 895 (IX) 4 December 1954; and 1181 (XII) 29 November 1957. The last resolution placed the matter in the hands of a committee charged with determining the appropriate time for the General Assembly to consider the question of defining aggression. The committee met in 1959 and 1962, deciding only to adjourn each time. After meeting in 1965 and 1967, it had at least got to the point of considering three possible draft resolutions.

[12] The Hague Convention (IV) Respecting the Laws and Customs of War on Land, Signed at the Hague, October 18, 1907, Annex: "Regulations Respecting the Laws

and hydrogen warfare. And the distinction between "combatants" and "noncombatants," widely accepted in 1914, has come to mean very little. "The principle . . . that the unarmed citizen is to be spared in person, property, and honor as much as the exigencies of war will admit,"[13] was hard to carry out from high-flying bombers in World War II and will be even more difficult for guided missiles. Significantly, no treaties exist which attempt to regulate warfare from or in the air, or to proscribe the use of atomic weapons. But the value of regulations affecting other forms of warfare is also open to question. For instance, in 1936, the following rule of submarine warfare was set forth:

> . . . except in the case of persistent refusal to stop on being duly summoned, or of active resistance to visit or search, a warship, whether surface vessel or submarine, may not sink or render incapable of navigation a merchant vessel without having first placed passengers, crew and ship's papers in a place of safety. For this purpose the ship's boats are not regarded as a place of safety unless the safety of the passengers and crew is assured, in the existing sea and weather conditions, by the proximity of land, or the presence of another vessel which is in a position to take them on board.[14]

In World War II, Germany waged unrestricted submarine warfare contrary to this Protocol. As a result, the Nuremberg Tribunal found German Admiral Doenitz guilty of violating the Protocol by ordering his submarines to sink merchant ships without warning when found within certain specified zones. The Tribunal argued that the Protocol was specific and that if a submarine commander could not rescue a crew, he should let it pass unharmed. The judges did not take the Admiral's guilt in these matters into account in sentencing him, however, because they noted that Britain had armed its merchant vessels and had ordered them to report the positions of German U-boats and to ram them, if possible, and that both Britain and the United States had also waged unrestricted submarine warfare at various times during the war.[15]

The failure of rules of war to keep up with technology and the failure of belligerents to observe all the rules does not mean that all of the treaties relating to warfare are useless. On the contrary, rules for handling prisoners of war, based as they are on a genuine reciprocal interest, have probably been more often honored than not.

---

and Customs of War on Land," Article 23 (e) and (g), in J. B. Scott, *The Hague Conventions and Declarations of 1899 and 1907,* (3d ed., New York: Oxford University Press, 1918), pp. 116–117.

[13] "Instructions for the Government of Armies of the United States in the Field," General Orders, No. 100 (Lieber's Code), Article 22; Moore, *Digest,* VII, 172–173.

[14] Hudson, *International Legislation,* VII, 491.

[15] International Military Tribunal, *Official Documents,* I, 311–313; *Trial of the Major War Criminals,* XVIII, 321–323.

GENEVA CONVENTION RELATIVE TO THE TREATMENT OF PRISONERS OF WAR OF AUGUST 12, 1949

U.S. DEPARTMENT OF STATE, GENERAL FOREIGN POLICY SERIES 34, p. 84

The undersigned Plenipotentiaries of the Governments represented at the Diplomatic Conference held at Geneva from April 21 to August 12, 1949, for the purpose of revising the Convention concluded at Geneva on July 27, 1929, relative to the Treatment of Prisoners of War, have agreed as follows:

Article 1. The High Contracting Parties undertake to respect and to ensure respect for the present Convention in all circumstances.

Article 2. In addition to the provisions which shall be implemented in peace time, the present Convention shall apply to all cases of declared war or of any other armed conflict which may arise between two or more of the High Contracting Parties, even if the state of war is not recognized by one of them.

The Convention shall also apply to all cases of partial or total occupation of the territory of a High Contracting Party, even if the said occupation meets with no armed resistance.

Although one of the Powers in conflict may not be a party to the present Convention, the Powers who are parties thereto shall remain bound by it in their mutual relations. They shall furthermore be bound by the Convention in relation to the said Power, if the latter accepts and applies the provisions thereof.

Article 3. In the case of armed conflict not of an international character occurring in the territory of one of the High Contracting Parties, each Party to the conflict shall be bound to apply, as a minimum, the following provisions:

(1) Persons taking no active part in the hostilities, including members of armed forces who have laid down their arms and those placed *hors de combat* by sickness, wounds, detention, or any other cause, shall in all circumstances be treated humanely, without any adverse distinction founded on race, colour, religion or faith, sex, birth or wealth, or any other similar criteria.

To this end the following acts are and shall remain prohibited at any time and in any place whatsoever with respect to the above-mentioned persons:

(a) violence to life and person, in particular murder of all kinds, mutilation, cruel treatment and torture;

(b) taking of hostages;

(c) outrages upon personal dignity, in particular, humiliating and degrading treatment;

(d) the passing of sentences and the carrying out of executions without previous judgment pronounced by a regularly constituted court affording all the judicial guarantees which are recognized as indispensable by civilized peoples.

(2) The wounded and sick shall be collected and cared for.

An impartial humanitarian body, such as the International Committee of the Red Cross, may offer its services to the Parties to the conflict.

The Parties to the conflict should further endeavour to bring into force, by means of special agreements, all or part of the other provisions of the present Convention.

The application of the preceding provisions shall not affect the legal status of the Parties to the conflict.

Article 4. A. Prisoners of war, in the sense of the present Convention, are persons belonging to one of the following categories, who have fallen into the power of the enemy:

(1) Members of the armed forces of a Party to the conflict, as well as members of militias or volunteer corps forming part of such armed forces.

(2) Members of other militias and members of other volunteer corps, including those of organized resistance movements, belonging to a Party to the conflict and operating in or outside their own territory, even if this territory is occupied, provided that such militias or volunteer corps, including such organized resistance movements, fulfil the following conditions:

(a) that of being commanded by a person responsible for his subordinates;

(b) that of having a fixed distinctive sign recognizable at a distance;

(c) that of carrying arms openly;

(d) that of conducting their operations in accordance with the laws and customs of war.

(3) Members of regular armed forces who profess allegiance to a government or an authority not recognized by the Detaining Power.

(4) Persons who accompany the armed forces without actually being members thereof, such as civilian members of military aircraft crews, war correspondents, supply contractors, members of labour units or of services responsible for the welfare of the armed forces, provided that they have received authorization from the armed forces which they accompany, who shall provide them for that purpose with an identity card similar to the annexed model.

(5) Members of crews, including masters, pilots and apprentices, of the merchant marine and the crews of civil aircraft of the Parties to the conflict, who do not benefit by more favourable treatment under any other provisions of international law.

(6) Inhabitants of a non-occupied territory, who on the approach of the enemy spontaneously take up arms to resist the invading forces, without having had time to form themselves into regular armed units, provided they carry arms openly and respect the laws and customs of war.

B. The following shall likewise be treated as prisoners of war under the present Convention:

(1) Persons belonging, or having belonged, to the armed forces of the occupied country, if the occupying Power considers it necessary by reason of such allegiance to intern them, even though it has originally liberated them while hostilities were going on outside the territory it occupies, in particular where such persons have made an unsuccessful attempt to rejoin the armed forces to which they belong and which are engaged in combat,

or where they fail to comply with a summons made to them with a view to internment.

(2) The persons belonging to one of the categories enumerated in the present Article, who have been received by neutral or non-belligerent Powers on their territory and whom these Powers are required to intern under international law, without prejudice to any more favourable treatment which these powers may choose to give and with the exception of Articles 8, 10, 15, 30, fifth paragraph, 58–67, 92, 126 and, where diplomatic relations exist between the Parties to the conflict and the neutral or non-belligerent Power concerned, those Articles concerning the Protecting Power. Where such diplomatic relations exist, the Parties to a conflict on whom these persons depend shall be allowed to perform towards them the functions of a Protecting Power as provided in the present Convention, without prejudice to the functions which these Parties normally exercise in conformity with diplomatic and consular usage and treaties.

C. This Article shall in no way affect the status of medical personnel and chaplains as provided for in Article 33 of the present Convention.

Article 5. The present Convention shall apply to the persons referred to in Article 4 from the time they fall into the power of the enemy and until their final release and repatriation.

Should any doubt arise as to whether persons, having committed a belligerent act and having fallen into the hands of the enemy, belong to any of the categories enumerated in Article 4, such persons shall enjoy the protection of the present Convention until such time as their status has been determined by a competent tribunal.

. . . .

Article 12. Prisoners of war are in the hands of the enemy Power, but not of the individuals or military units who have captured them. Irrespective of the individual responsibilities that may exist, the Detaining Power is responsible for the treatment given them.

Prisoners of war may only be transferred by the Detaining Power to a Power which is a party to the Convention and after the Detaining Power has satisfied itself of the willingness and ability of such transferee Power to apply the Convention. When prisoners of war are transferred under such circumstances, responsibility for the application of the Convention rests on the Power accepting them while they are in its custody.

Nevertheless, if that Power fails to carry out the provisions of the Convention in any important respect, the Power by whom the prisoners of war were transferred shall, upon being notified by the Protecting Power, take effective measures to correct the situation or shall request the return of the prisoners of war. Such requests must be complied with.

Article 13. Prisoners of war must at all times be humanely treated. Any unlawful act or omission by the Detaining Power causing death or seriously endangering the health of a prisoner of war in its custody is prohibited, and will be regarded as a serious breach of the present Convention. In particular, no prisoner of war may be subjected to physical mutilation or to medical or scientific experiments of any kind which are not justified by the medical, dental or hospital treatment of the prisoner concerned and carried out in his interest.

Likewise, prisoners of war must at all times be protected, particularly against acts of violence or intimidation and against insults and public curiosity.

Measures of reprisal against prisoners of war are prohibited.

Article 14. Prisoners of war are entitled in all circumstances to respect for their persons and their honour.

Women shall be treated with all the regard due to their sex and shall in all cases benefit by treatment as favourable as that granted to men.

Prisoners of war shall retain the full civil capacity which they enjoyed at the time of their capture. The Detaining Power may not restrict the exercise, either within or without its own territory, of the rights such capacity confers except in so far as the captivity requires.

Article 15. The Power detaining prisoners of war shall be bound to provide free of charge for their maintenance and for the medical attention required by their state of health.

Article 16. Taking into consideration the provisions of the present Convention relating to rank and sex, and subject to any privileged treatment which may be accorded to them by reason of their state of health, age or professional qualifications, all prisoners of war shall be treated alike by the Detaining Power, without any adverse distinction based on race, nationality, religious belief or political opinions, or any other distinction founded on similar criteria.

Article 17. Every prisoner of war, when questioned on the subject, is bound to give only his surname, first names and rank, date of birth, and army, regimental, personal or serial number, or failing this, equivalent information.

If he wilfully infringes this rule, he may render himself liable to a restriction of the privileges accorded to his rank or status. . . .

No physical or mental torture, nor any other form of coercion, may be inflicted on prisoners of war to secure from them information of any kind whatever. Prisoners of war who refuse to answer may not be threatened, insulted, or exposed to unpleasant or disadvantageous treatment of any kind. . . .

Article 18. All effects and articles of personal use, except arms, horses, military equipment and military documents, shall remain in the possession of prisoners of war, likewise their metal helmets and gas masks and like articles issued for personal protection. Effects and articles used for their clothing or feeding shall likewise remain in their possession, even if such effects and articles belong to their regulation military equipment.

At no time should prisoners of war be without identity documents. The Detaining Power shall supply such documents to prisoners of war who possess none.

Badges of rank and nationality, decorations and articles having above all a personal or sentimental value may not be taken from prisoners of war.

Sums of money carried by prisoners of war may not be taken away from them except by order of an officer, and after the amount and particulars of the owner have been recorded in a special register and an itemized receipt has been given, legibly inscribed with the name, rank and unit of the person issuing the said receipt. Sums in the currency of the Detaining Power, or which are changed into such currency at the prisoner's request, shall be placed to the credit of the prisoner's account as provided in Article 64.

The Detaining Power may withdraw articles of value from prisoners of war only for reasons of security; when such articles are withdrawn, the procedure laid down for sums of money impounded shall apply.

Such objects, likewise sums taken away in any currency other than that of the Detaining Power and the conversion of which has not been asked for by the owners, shall be kept in the custody of the Detaining Power and shall be returned in their initial shape to prisoners of war at the end of their captivity.

Article 19. Prisoners of war shall be evacuated, as soon as possible after their capture, to camps situated in an area far enough from the combat zone for them to be out of danger.

. . . .

Article 118. Prisoners of war shall be released and repatriated without delay after the cessation of active hostilities.

In the absence of stipulations to the above effect in any agreement concluded between the Parties to the conflict with a view to the cessation of hostilities, or failing any such agreement, each of the Detaining Powers shall itself establish and execute without delay a plan of repatriation in conformity with the principle laid down in the foregoing paragraph.

In either case, the measures adopted shall be brought to the knowledge of the prisoners of war.

The costs of repatriation of prisoners of war shall in all cases be equitably apportioned between the Detaining Power and the Power on which the prisoners depend. This apportionment shall be carried out on the following basis:

(*a*) If the two Powers are contiguous, the Power on which the prisoners of war depend shall bear the costs of repatriation from the frontiers of the Detaining Power.

(*b*) If the two Powers are not contiguous, the Detaining Power shall bear the costs of transport of prisoners of war over its own territory as far as its frontier or its port of embarkation nearest to the territory of the Power on which the prisoners of war depend. The Parties concerned shall agree between themselves as to the equitable apportionment of the remaining costs of the repatriation. The conclusion of this agreement shall in no circumstances justify any delay in the repatriation of the prisoners of war.

Article 119. Repatriation shall be effected in conditions similar to those laid down in Articles 46 to 48 inclusive of the present Convention for the transfer of prisoners of war, having regard to the provisions of Article 118 and to those of the following paragraphs.

On repatriation, any articles of value impounded from prisoners of war under Article 18, and any foreign currency which has not been converted into the currency of the Detaining Power, shall be restored to them. Articles of value and foreign currency which, for any reason whatever, are not restored to prisoners of war on repatriation, shall be despatched to the Information Bureau set up under Article 122.

Prisoners of war shall be allowed to take with them their personal effects, and any correspondence and parcels which have arrived for them. The weight of such baggage may be limited, if the conditions of repatriation so require, to what each prisoner can reasonably carry. Each prisoner shall in all cases be authorized to carry at least twenty-five kilograms.

The other personal effects of the repatriated prisoner shall be left in the charge of the Detaining Power which shall have them forwarded to him as soon as it has concluded an agreement to this effect, regulating the conditions of transport and the payment of the costs involved, with the Power on which the prisoner depends.

Prisoners of war against whom criminal proceedings for an indictable offence are pending may be detained until the end of such proceedings, and, if necessary, until the completion of the punishment. The same shall apply to prisoners of war already convicted for an indictable offence.

Parties to the conflict shall communicate to each other the names of any prisoners of war who are detained until the end of the proceedings or until punishment has been completed.

By agreement between the Parties to the conflict, commissions shall be established for the purpose of searching for dispersed prisoners of war and of assuring their repatriation with the least possible delay.

. . . .

Even in humanitarian matters related to war, time has worked changes in traditional rules. The 1949 Geneva Convention providing for belligerents to repatriate prisoners ran afoul of the desire of prisoners taken by the United Nations in Korea in 1950–1952 *not* to return to North Korea. The United Nations was confronted by ethical and humanitarian considerations that ran straight in the face of existing law. To resolve the dilemma, the U.N. Command arranged to give the prisoners the right to choose either to be repatriated or to be released. It also gave representatives of "the nations to which the prisoners of war belong" the opportunity to "explain to all the prisoners of war . . . their rights and to inform them of any matters relating to their return . . . , particularly of their full freedom to return home to lead a peaceful life. . . ."

AGREEMENT ON PRISONERS OF WAR[16]

SIGNED AT PANMUNJOM, JUNE 8, 1953

Within two months after the armistice agreement becomes effective, both sides shall, without offering any hindrance, directly repatriate and hand over in groups all those prisoners of war in its custody who insist on repatriation to the side to which they belonged at the time of capture. . . .

Both sides agree to hand over all those remaining prisoners of war who are not directly repatriated to the Neutral Nations Repatriation Commission for disposition in accordance with the following provisions:

Terms of Reference for Neutral Nations Repatriation Commission

I. GENERAL

1. In order to ensure that all prisoners of war have the opportunity to exercise their right to be repatriated following an armistice, Sweden, Switzerland, Poland, Czechoslovakia and India shall each be requested by both sides to appoint a member to a Neutral Nations Repatriations Commission which shall be established to take custody in Korea of those prisoners of war who, while in the custody of the detaining powers, have not exercised their right to be repatriated. . . .

. . . .

3. No force or threat of force shall be used against the prisoners of war specified in Paragraph 1 above to prevent or effect their repatriation, and no violence to their persons or affront to their dignity or self-respect shall be permitted in any manner for any purpose whatsoever. . . . This duty is enjoined on and entrusted to the Neutral Nations Repatriation Commission. This Commission shall ensure that prisoners of war shall at all times be treated humanely in accordance with the specific provisions of the Geneva Convention, and with the general spirit of that convention.

II. CUSTODY OF PRISONERS OF WAR

4. All prisoners of war who have not exercised their right of repatriation following the effective date of the Armistice Agreement shall be released from the military control and from the custody of the detaining side as soon as practicable, and, in all cases, within sixty (60) days subsequent to the effective date of the Armistice Agreement to the Neutral Nations Repatriation Commission at locations in Korea to be designated by the detaining side.

5. At the time the Neutral Nations Repatriation Commission assumes control of the prisoner of war installations, the military forces of the detaining side shall be withdrawn therefrom, so that the locations specified in the preceding Paragraph shall be taken over completely by the armed forces of India.

[16] *D.S.B.*, XXVIII (1953), 866.

6. Notwithstanding the provisions of Paragraph 5 above, the detaining side shall have the responsibility for maintaining and ensuring the security and order in the areas around the locations where the prisoners of war are in custody and for preventing and restraining any armed forces . . . in the area under its control from any acts of disturbance and intrusion against the locations where the prisoners of war are in custody.

. . . .

III. EXPLANATION

8. The Neutral Nations Repatriation Commission, after having received and taken into custody all those prisoners of war who have not exercised their right to be repatriated, shall immediately make arrangements so that within ninety (90) days after the Neutral Nations Repatriation Commission takes over the custody, the nations to which the prisoners of war belong shall have freedom and facilities to send representatives to the locations where such prisoners of war are in custody to explain to all the prisoners of war depending upon these nations their rights and to inform them of any matters relating to their return to their homelands, particularly of their full freedom to return home to lead a peaceful life.

. . . .

IV. DISPOSITION OF PRISONERS OF WAR

10. Any prisoner of war who, while in the custody of the Neutral Nations Repatriation Commission, decides to exercise the right of repatriation, shall make an application requesting repatriation to a body consisting of a representative of each member nation of the Neutral Nations Repatriation Commission. Once such an application is made, it shall be considered immediately by the Neutral Nations Repatriation Commission or one of its subordinate bodies so as to determine immediately by majority vote the validity of such application. Once such an application is made to and validated by the Commission or one of its subordinate bodies, the prisoner of war concerned shall immediately be transferred to and accommodated in the tents set up for those who are ready to be repatriated. . . .

11. At the expiration of ninety (90) days after the transfer of custody of the prisoners of war to the Neutral Nations Repatriation Commission, access of representatives to captured personnel as provided for in Paragraph 8 above, shall terminate, and the question of disposition of the prisoners of war who have not exercised their right to be repatriated shall be submitted to the Political Conference recommended to be convened in Paragraph 60, Draft Armistice Agreement, which shall endeavor to settle this question within thirty (30) days, during which period the Neutral Nations Repatriation Commission shall continue to retain custody of those prisoners of war. The Neutral Nations Repatriation Commission shall declare the relief from the prisoner of war status to civilian status of any prisoners of war who have not exercised their right to be repatriated and for whom no other disposition has been agreed by the Political Conference within one hundred and twenty (120)

days after the Neutral Nations Repatriation Commission has assumed their custody. Thereafter, according to the application of each individual, those who choose to go to neutral nations shall be assisted by the Neutral Nations Repatriation Commission and the Red Cross Society of India. This operation shall be completed within thirty (30) days, and upon its completion, the Neutral Nations Repatriation Commission shall immediately cease its functions and declare its dissolution. After the dissolution of the Neutral Nations Repatriation Commission, whenever and wherever any of those above-mentioned civilians who have been relieved from the prisoner of war status desire to return to their fatherlands, the authorities of the localities where they are shall be responsible for assisting them in returning to their fatherlands.

Neutrality

As already indicated (p. 504), Moore observes that "when a state of war supervenes third parties become subject to the performance of the duties of neutrality as well as to all the inconveniences that result from the exercise of belligerent rights."[17] The duties of neutrality, of which Moore speaks require that a state remain impartial and refrain from participating in armed conflict or abetting either side. To a large extent, doctrines of neutrality waxed with the determination of the United States after 1787 to remain aloof from European conflicts and to protect what the United States regarded as its right to carry on business as usual regardless of the international situation. These rights, often summed up in terms of "freedom of the seas," loomed large in American history throughout the 19th and early 20th centuries. They permitted the nationals of neutral states to trade with either belligerent and with one another, although neutrals had to cope with restrictions imposed by belligerents blockading enemy ports and designating as *contraband* certain articles which they would not permit to reach their enemies. All other trade was legal.

The law of neutrality received its most elaborate formulation at the Hague Conference of 1907, but the rules so carefully designed to protect both the territorial integrity of neutrals and the commercial relations of their nationals proved quite inadequate under the pressures generated in the first and second world wars. As war became more nearly "total," belligerents were willing to allow fewer and fewer goods to move into the enemy camp: they lengthened their lists of contraband; they invoked the "doctrine of continuous voyage," thereby proscribing from international trade any goods that a consignee might transship to a belligerent; and they ignored the distinction between "absolute" and "conditional" contraband, whereby they had once tried to distinguish between goods intended for civilians and those intended for the armed forces. Ulti-

[17] *Digest*, VII, 153–154.

mately, they asserted the right to seize "any article of enemy origin, ownership, or destination."[18] They also began to keep track of the volume of trade, so as to make sure that goods that neutrals produced or received did not find their way into enemy hands. Belligerents used "normal" trade statistics to justify seizing "surplus" goods, and they required the neutrals themselves to cooperate in carrying out the controls in order to salvage even a small portion of their trade. They thus involved the neutrals in economic warfare even against their inclination and interest.[19]

Neutrality owes much of its decline, as well as its rise, to the United States which, with other neutrals, tended to become increasingly chary of the law of neutrality. One lesson inhered in the results of the Italo-Ethiopian war of 1935, which was the last time that the traditional rules really operated. By keeping the Ethiopians from receiving aid, the law actually favored the stronger opponent, who happened also to be the aggressor. Although the law of neutrality had always favored the stronger enemy, the consequences were not serious in days of less-than-global combat. But the consequences were not to be borne in an age when aggressors had the technical capacity to make everyone suffer from their depredations.

Neutrality did not yield automatically to its opposite—the idea of collective security, for the leading neutral attempted first to try another approach to avoiding war by abandoning its neutral rights and isolating itself completely. The United States hoped thus not to run the risks of insisting that belligerents respect the traditional rights of neutrals to ply the seas and to engage freely in international commerce. By its neutrality legislation in the 1930's, the United States, ostrich-like, attempted to jettison the baggage of neutrality. Where Article 7 of Hague Convention XIII permitted individuals in neutral states to traffic freely with all belligerents, the United States in 1937 denied this opportunity to all U.S. nationals. And when the possibility of trading was reopened in 1939, the risk to democracy seemed so apparent that the administration made sure that the trade took place under conditions that guaranteed help for one side only and, even then, in ways that minimized the need for the United States to defend its commercial rights.[20] In Europe, only Switzerland and Sweden found it possible to maintain a neutral role in World War II—not so much as a matter of legal right, but merely out of expediency. Maintaining neutrality be-

[18] De Visscher, p. 301. See also Note of February 17, 1915, addressed by Sir Edward Grey to the Government of the United States, and the opinion of Sir Samuel Evans in the case of the "Kim" (1915), Privy Council, B. and C. Prize Cases, I, 405, and esp. 490–491.
[19] De Visscher, pp. 302–303.
[20] See de Visscher, pp. 299–300, 304–305.

came increasingly difficult, moreover, as the war progressed, and Sweden was forced in 1940 to permit German soldiers on leave and goods, including war material, to move by rail through the country. In 1941, Sweden had to grant Germany the right to move an entire armed division from Norway to Finland across its territory. These violations of Swedish neutrality continued until 1943, when Germany was far less strong and Sweden much better able to defend its rights as a neutral.

In the post-World War II world, military allegiances made the life of the neutral state difficult to maintain. Some seriously questioned the validity of neutrality in the contemporary world, where all states Members of the United Nations obligated themselves to support decisions of the Security Council by pledging armed forces or other assistance (*e.g.*, in Articles 43 and 49 of the Charter). These pledges were enough, for instance, to convince the government of Switzerland that, as a true and traditional neutral, it should not join the United Nations. Of those states that did join, some tried at least to stand aloof from the world's competing alliances, although they described their policies not in terms of neutrality, but of *neutralism*—the unwillingness to commit themselves in advance and in the abstract to either side in the "Cold War."

Even this limited aloofness was challenged, however, by some statesmen, like John Foster Dulles, sometime Secretary of State of the United States (1952–1959), who in 1955 described neutralism as immoral.[21] His views took little account of the strong desires of many new nations, to emulate the experiences of the young United States. But statesmen's views notwithstanding, it was obviously much more difficult in the late 20th century to apply policies that were entirely feasible in the late 18th century. Even after 1960, when the U.S. government was once again prepared to concede the right of a state not to associate itself with one of two Cold War camps, the chief exponent of neutralism, India, found that her aspirations to stand aloof did not prevent her from becoming the victim of Chinese aggression in 1962.

Contemporary Legal Doctrine

Students of international law in the 20th century now find themselves burdened with classical doctrines of dubious value and new institutions whose efficacy in preventing war is unproved. Even the legal status of war is today a matter of some dispute.

Under the League of Nations Covenant, war was not actually illegal. States Members of the League could resort to war legally once they had exhausted the League's mediation machinery and waited a specified three months after a arbitral or judicial decision:

[21] *D.S.B.*, XXXII (1955), 932.

COVENANT OF THE LEAGUE OF NATIONS (EXCERPTS)

(Amendments adopted in 1924 appear in italics.)

U.S. FOR. REL., PARIS PEACE CONFERENCE, 1919, XIII, 72 FF.

Article 10. The Members of the League undertake to respect and preserve as against external aggression the territorial integrity and existing political independence of all Members of the League. In case of any such aggression or in case of any threat or danger of such aggression the Council shall advise upon the means by which this obligation shall be fulfilled.

Article 11. 1. Any war or threat of war, whether immediately affecting any of the Members of the League or not, is hereby declared a matter of concern to the whole League, and the League shall take any action that may be deemed wise and effectual to safeguard the peace of nations. In case any such emergency should arise the Secretary General shall on the request of any Member of the League forthwith summon a meeting of the Council.

2. It is also declared to be the friendly right of each Member of the League to bring to the attention of the Assembly or of the Council any circumstance whatever affecting international relations which threatens to disturb international peace or the good understanding between nations upon which peace depends.

Article 12. 1. The Members of the League agree that, if there should arise between them any dispute likely to lead to a rupture, they will submit the matter either to arbitration *or judicial settlement* or to inquiry by the Council, and they agree in no case to resort to war until three months after the award by the arbitrators *or the judicial decision,* or the report by the Council.

2. In any case under this Article the award of the arbitrators *or the judicial decision* shall be made within a reasonable time, and the report of the Council shall be made within six months after the submission of the dispute.

Article 13. 1. The Members of the League agree that, whenever any dispute shall arise between them which they recognize to be suitable for submission to arbitration *or judicial settlement,* and which cannot be satisfactorily settled by diplomacy, they will submit the whole subject matter to arbitration *or judicial settlement.*

2. Disputes as to the interpretation of a treaty, as to any question of international law, as to the existence of any fact which, if established, would constitute a breach of any international obligation, or as to the extent and nature of the reparation to be made for any such breach, are declared to be among those which are generally suitable for submission to arbitration *or judicial settlement.*

3. *For the consideration of any such dispute, the court to which the case is referred shall be the Permanent Court of International Justice, established in accordance with Article 14, or any tribunal agreed on by the parties to the dispute or stipulated in any convention existing between them.*

4. The Members of the League agree that they will carry out in full good faith any award *or decision* that may be rendered, and that they will not resort to war against a Member of the League which complies therewith. In the event of any failure to carry out such an award *or decision,* the Council shall propose what steps should be taken to give effect thereto.

Article 14. The Council shall formulate and submit to the Members of the League for adoption plans for the establishment of a Permanent Court of International Justice. The Court shall be competent to hear and determine any dispute of an international character which the parties thereto submit to it. The Court may also give an advisory opinion upon any dispute or question referred to it by the Council or by the Assembly.

Article 15. 1. If there should arise between Members of the League any dispute likely to lead to a rupture, which is not submitted to arbitration *or judicial settlement* in accordance with Article 13, the Members of the League agree that they will submit the matter to the Council. Any party to the dispute may effect such submission by giving notice of the existence of the dispute to the Secretary General, who will make all necessary arrangements for a full investigation and consideration thereof.

2. For this purpose the parties to the dispute will communicate to the Secretary General, as promptly as possible, statements of their case with all the relevant facts and papers, and the Council may forthwith direct the publication thereof.

3. The Council shall endeavour to effect a settlement of the dispute, and if such efforts are successful, a statement shall be made public giving such facts and explanations regarding the dispute and the terms of settlement thereof as the Council may deem appropriate.

4. If the dispute is not thus settled, the Council either unanimously or by a majority vote shall make and publish a report containing a statement of the facts of the dispute and the recommendations which are deemed just and proper in regard thereto.

5. Any Member of the League represented on the Council may make public a statement of the facts of the dispute and of its conclusions regarding the same.

6. If a report by the Council is unanimously agreed to by the members thereof other than the Representatives of one or more of the parties to the dispute, the Members of the League agree that they will not go to war with any party to the dispute which complies with the recommendations of the report.

7. If the Council fails to reach a report which is unanimously agreed to by the members thereof, other than the Representatives of one or more of the parties to the dispute, the Members of the League reserve to themselves the right to take such action as they shall consider necessary for the maintenance of right and justice.

8. If the dispute between the parties is claimed by one of them, and is found by the Council, to arise out of a matter which by international law is solely within the domestic jurisdiction of that party, the Council shall so report, and shall make no recommendation as to its settlement.

9. The Council may in any case under this Article refer the dispute to the Assembly. The dispute shall be so referred at the request of either party to the dispute, provided that such request be made within fourteen days after the submission of the dispute to the Council.

10. In any case referred to the Assembly, all the provisions of this Article and of Article 12 relating to the action and powers of the Council shall apply to the action and powers of the Assembly, provided that a report made by the Assembly, if concurred in by the Representatives of those Members of the League represented on the Council and of a majority of the other Members of the League, exclusive in each case of the Representatives of the parties to the dispute, shall have the same force as a report by the Council concurred in by all the members thereof other than the Representatives of one or more of the parties to the dispute.

Article 16. 1. Should any Member of the League resort to war in disregard of its convenants under Articles 12, 13 or 15, it shall *ipso facto* be deemed to have committed an act of war against all other Members of the League, which hereby undertake immediately to subject it to the severance of all trade or financial relations, the prohibition of all intercourse between their nationals and the nationals of the covenant-breaking State, and the prevention of all financial, commercial or personal intercourse between the nationals of the covenant-breaking State and the nationals of any other State, whether a Member of the League or not.

2. It shall be the duty of the Council in such case to recommend to the several Governments concerned what effective military, naval or air force the Members of the League shall severally contribute to the armed forces to be used to protect the covenants of the League.

3. The Members of the League agree, further, that they will mutually support one another in the financial and economic measures which are taken under this Article, in order to minimise the loss and inconvenience resulting from the above measures, and that they will mutually support one another in resisting any special measures aimed at one of their number by the covenant-breaking State, and that they will take the necessary steps to afford passage through their territory to the forces of any of the Members of the League which are co-operating to protect the covenants of the League.

4. Any Member of the League which has violated any covenant of the League may be declared to be no longer a Member of the League by a vote of the Council concurred in by the Representatives of all the other Members of the League represented thereon.

Article 17. 1. In the event of a dispute between a Member of the League and a State which is not a Member of the League, or between States not Members of the League, the State or States not Members of the League shall be invited to accept the obligations of membership in the League for the purposes of such dispute, upon such conditions as the Council may deem just. If such invitation is accepted, the provisions of Articles 12 to 16 inclusive shall be applied with such modifications as may be deemed necessary by the Council.

2. Upon such invitation being given the Council shall immediately institute an inquiry into the circumstances of the dispute and recommend such action as may seem best and most effectual in the circumstances.

3. If a State so invited shall refuse to accept the obligations of membership in the League for the purposes of such dispute, and shall resort to war against a Member of the League, the provisions of Article 16 shall be applicable as against the State taking such action.

4. If both parties to the dispute when so invited refuse to accept the obligations of membership in the League for the purposes of such dispute, the Council may take such measures and make such recommendations as will prevent hostilities and will result in the settlement of the dispute.

The experience of the League of Nations shows that these provisions were adequate only for a few minor cases, such as the Greco-Bulgar border incident of 1925, but entirely inadequate in the face of the unlimited ambition of Imperial Japan (in Manchuria, 1931), Fascist Italy (in Ethiopia, 1935), or Nazi Germany (in central Europe in the late 'thirties).

Attempts to strengthen the League machinery by supplementary treaties and machinery also proved inadequate before the challenges of the second World War, but one of them, the Kellogg-Briand Pact of 1928, had considerable legal importance in later years. By the time World War II broke out, 63 states, including Italy, Germany, and Japan, had ratified the Kellogg Pact. To the Axis powers, the Pact was no more than a "scrap of paper," but it was to become important to the conduct of the Nuremberg Trials and the War Crime Trials in the Pacific.

TREATY FOR THE RENUNCIATION OF WAR
(KELLOGG-BRIAND PACT, 1928)

[The High Contracting Parties] . . . Convinced that all changes in their relations with one another should be sought only by pacific means and be the result of a peaceful and orderly process, and that any signatory Power which shall hereafter seek to promote its national interests by resort to war should be denied the benefits furnished by this Treaty . . . have agreed upon the following articles.

Article 1. The High Contracting Parties solemnly declare in the names of their respective peoples that they condemn recourse to war for the solution of international controversies, and renounce it as an instrument of national policy in their relations with one another.

Article 2. The High Contracting Parties agree that the settlement or solution of all disputes or conflicts of whatever nature or of whatever origin they may be, which may arise among them, shall never be sought except by pacific means.[22]

The legal basis for Nuremberg was the London Agreement of August 8, 1945, which established the Tribunal[23] of eight judges to try traditional war criminals, that is, persons who had violated the laws and customs of war, and also those who had committed "crimes against peace," and "crimes against humanity." As defined in Article 6 of the London Charter, crimes against peace included "planning, preparation, initiation or waging of a war of aggression, or a war in violation of international treaties, agreements or assurances, or participation in a common plan or conspiracy for the accomplishment of any of the foregoing." Crimes against humanity referred to "murder, extermination, enslavement, deportation, and other inhumane acts committed against any civilian population, before or during the war, or persecutions on political, racial, or religious grounds in execution of or in connection with any crime within the jurisdiction of the Tribunal, whether or not in violation of the domestic laws of the country where perpetrated."

The Charter made it clear that the responsibility for these crimes would lie not with the impersonal entity of "the State," but with "leaders, organizers, instigators, and accomplices, participating in the formulation or execution of a common plan or conspiracy to commit any of the foregoing crimes." By these provisions, the Charter sought to make international law bear directly on the individual.

. . . the very essence of the Charter is that individuals have international duties which transcend the national obligations of obedience imposed by the individual state. He who violates the laws of war cannot obtain immunity while acting in pursuance of the authority of the State if the State in authorizing action moves outside its competence under international law. . . . The Charter specifically provides in Article 8:

The fact that the Defendant acted pursuant to order of his Government or of a superior shall not free him from responsibility, but may be considered in mitigation of punishment [if the Tribunal determines that justice so requires].

The provisions of this article are in conformity with the law of all nations. That a soldier was ordered to kill or torture in violation of the international law of war has never been recognized as a defense to such acts of brutality, though, as the Charter here provides, the order may be urged in mitigation of the punishment. The true test, which is found in varying degrees in the

[22] *T.S.*, 796.
[23] *Nuremberg Trial of the Major War Criminals before the International Military Tribunal* (The Tribunal, 42 vols. 1947–1949).

criminal law of most nations, is not the existence of the order, but whether moral choice was in fact possible.[24]

These principles have also been accepted by the United Nations, which in 1946 approved the "Principles of International Law Recognized in the Charter and Judgment of the Nuremberg Tribunal."

PRINCIPLES OF INTERNATIONAL LAW RECOGNIZED IN THE CHARTER AND JUDGMENT OF THE NUREMBERG TRIBUNAL

Report of the International Law Commission, 2nd Session, 1950

U.N., G.A.O.R., 5th Session, Supp. No. 12 (A/1316), p. 11

Principle I. Any person who commits an act which constitutes a crime under international law is responsible therefor and liable to punishment.

Principle II. The fact that internal law does not impose a penalty for an act which constitutes a crime under international law does not relieve the person who committed the act from responsibility under international law.

Principle III. The fact that a person who committed an act which constitutes a crime under international law acted as Head of State or responsible Government official does not relieve him from responsibility under international law.

Principle IV. The fact that a person acted pursuant to order of his Government or of a superior does not relieve him from responsibility under international law, provided a moral choice was in fact possible to him.

Principle V. Any person charged with a crime under international law has the right to a fair trial on the facts and law.

Principle VI. The crimes hereinafter set out are punishable as crimes under international law:

a. Crimes against peace:

(i) Planning, preparation, initiation or waging of a war of aggression or a war in violation of international treaties, agreements or assurances;

(ii) Participation in a common plan or conspiracy for the accomplishment of any of the acts mentioned under (i).

b. War crimes:

Violations of the laws or customs of war which include, but are not limited to, murder, ill-treatment or deportation to slave-labour or for any other purpose of civilian population of or in occupied territory, murder or ill-treatment of prisoners of war or persons on the seas, killing of hostages, plunder of public or private property, wanton destruction of cities, towns, or villages, or devastation not justified by military necessity.

[24] International Military Tribunal, Nuremberg. *Official Documents,* I, 173, 23–224.

c. Crimes against humanity:

Murder, extermination, enslavement, deportation and other inhuman acts done against any civilian population, or persecutions on political, racial or religious grounds, when such acts are done or such persecutions are carried on in execution of or in connexion with any crime against peace or any war crime.

Principle VII. Complicity in the commission of a crime against peace, a war crime, or a crime against humanity as set forth in Principle VI is a crime under international law.

Questions have arisen quite naturally about the validity of the Nuremberg Trials, partly on the grounds that the Trial was an attempt by the victors to apply to the defeated powers doubtful international law *ex post facto.* The most effective answer to this charge was made by the U.S. Representative to the International Conference on Military Trials, Mr. Robert E. Jackson:[24]

The United States is vitally interested in recognizing the principle that treaties renouncing war have juridical as well as political meaning. We relied upon the Briand-Kellogg Pact and made it the cornerstone of our national policy. We neglected our armaments and our war machine in reliance upon it. All violations of it, wherever started, menace our peace as we now have good reason to know. An attack on the foundations of international relations cannot be regarded as anything less than a crime againt the international community, which may properly vindicate the integrity of its fundamental compacts by punishing aggressors. We therefore propose to charge that a war of aggression is a crime, and that modern International Law has abolished the defense that those who incite or wage it are engaged in legitimate business. Thus may the forces of the law be mobilized on the side of peace.

Any legal position asserted on behalf of the United States will have considerable significance in the future evolution of International Law. In untroubled times progress toward an effective rule of law in the international community is slow indeed. Inertia rests more heavily upon the society of nations than upon any other society. Now we stand at one of those rare moments when the thought and institutions and habits of the world have been shaken by the impact of world war on the lives of countless millions. Such occasions rarely come and quickly pass. We are put under a heavy responsibility to see that our behavior during this unsettled period will direct the world's thought toward a firmer enforcement of the laws of international conduct, so as to make war less attractive to those who have governments and the destinies of peoples in their power.

It is true, of course, that we have no judicial precedent for the Charter. But International Law is more than a scholarly collection of abstract and immutable principles. It is an outgrowth of treaties and agreements between

[24] International Military Tribunal, *Trial of the Major War Criminals,* II, 98.

nations and of accepted customs. Yet every custom has its origin in some single act, and every agreement has to be initiated by the action of some state. Unless we are prepared to abandon every principle of growth for International Law, we cannot deny that our own day has the right to institute customs and to conclude agreements that will themselves become sources of a newer and strengthened International Law. International Law is not capable of development by the normal processes of legislation for there is no continuing international legislative authority. Innovations and revisions in International Law are brought about by the action of governments designed to meet a change in circumstances. It grows, as did the Common Law, through decisions reached from time to time in adapting settled principles to new situations. The fact is that when the law evolves by the case method, as did the Common Law and as International Law must do if it is to advance at all, it advances at the expense of those who wrongly guessed the law and learned too late their error. The law, so far as International Law can be decreed, had been clearly pronounced when these acts took place. Hence, I am not disturbed by the lack of judicial precedent for the inquiry we propose to conduct.

There would thus seem to be ample grounds upon which to assert that under international law as it now stands, Members of the United Nations (and perhaps all states) are not entitled to use force except as prescribed in the United Nations Charter.

CHARTER OF THE UNITED NATIONS (EXCERPTS)

CHAPTER I

Purposes and Principles

[*Article* 2.] 3. All Members shall settle their international disputes by peaceful means in such a manner that international peace and security, and justice, are not endangered.

4. All Members shall refrain in their international relations from the threat or use of force against the territorial integrity or political independence of any state, or in any other manner inconsistent with the Purposes of the United Nations.

. . . .

CHAPTER VII

Action With Respect to Threats to the Peace, Breaches of the Peace, and Acts of Aggression

Article 39. The Security Council shall determine the existence of any threat to the peace, breach of the peace, or act of aggression and shall make recommendations, or decide what measures shall be taken in accordance with Articles 41 and 42, to maintain or restore international peace and security.

Article 40. In order to prevent an aggravation of the situation, the Security Council may, before making the recommendations or deciding upon the measures provided for in Article 39, call upon the parties concerned to comply with such provisional measures as it deems necessary or desirable. Such provisional measures shall be without prejudice to the rights, claims, or position of the parties concerned. The Security Council shall duly take account of failure to comply with such provisional measures.

Article 41. The Security Council may decide what measures not involving the use of armed force are to be employed to give effect to its decisions, and it may call upon the Members of the United Nations to apply such measures. These may include complete or partial interruption of economic relations and of rail, sea, air, postal, telegraphic, radio, and other means of communication, and the severance of diplomatic relations.

Article 42. Should the Security Council consider that measures provided for in Article 41 would be inadequate or have proved to be inadequate, it may take such action by air, sea, or land forces as may be necessary to maintain or restore international peace and security. Such action may include demonstrations, blockade, and other operations by air, sea, or land forces of Members of the United Nations.

Article 43. 1. All Members of the United Nations, in order to contribute to the maintenance of international peace and security, undertake to make available to the Security Council, on its call and in accordance with a special agreement or agreements, armed forces, assistance, and facilities, including rights of passage, necessary for the purpose of maintaining international peace and security.

2. Such agreement or agreements shall govern the numbers and types of forces, their degree of readiness and general location, and the nature of the facilities and assistance to be provided.

3. The agreement or agreements shall be negotiated as soon as possible on the initiative of the Security Council. They shall be concluded between the Security Council and Members or between the Security Council and groups of Members and shall be subject to ratification by the signatory states in accordance with their respective constitutional processes.

Article 44. When the Security Council has decided to use force it shall, before calling upon a Member not represented on it to provide armed forces in fulfillment of the obligations assumed under Article 43, invite that Member, if the Member so desires, to participate in the decisions of the Security Council concerning the employment of contingents of that Member's armed forces.

Article 45. In order to enable the United Nations to take urgent military measures, Members shall hold immediately available national air-force contingents for combined international enforcement action. The strength and degree of readiness of these contingents and plans for their combined action shall be determined, within the limits laid down in the special agreement or agreements referred to in Article 43, by the Security Council with the assistance of the Military Staff Committee.

Article 46. Plans for the application of armed force shall be made by the Security Council with the assistance of the Military Staff Committee.

Article 47. 1. There shall be established a Military Staff Committee to advise and assist the Security Council on all questions relating to the Security Council's military requirements for the maintenance of international peace and security, the employment and command of forces placed at its disposal, the regulation of armaments, and possible disarmament.

2. The Military Staff Committee shall consist of the Chiefs of Staff of the permanent members of the Security Council or their representatives. Any Member of the United Nations not permanently represented on the Committee shall be invited by the Committee to be associated with it when the efficient discharge of the Committee's responsibilities requires the participation of that Member in its work.

3. The Military Staff Committee shall be responsible under the Security Council for the strategic direction of any armed forces placed at the disposal of the Security Council. Questions relating to the command of such forces shall be worked out subsequently.

4. The Military Staff Committee, with the authorization of the Security Council and after consultation with appropriate regional agencies, may establish regional subcommittees.

Article 48. 1. The action required to carry out the decisions of the Security Council for the maintenance of international peace and security shall be taken by all the Members of the United Nations or by some of them, as the Security Council may determine.

2. Such decisions shall be carried out by the Members of the United Nations directly and through their action in the appropriate international agencies of which they are members.

Article 49. The Members of the United Nations shall join in affording mutual assistance in carrying out the measures decided upon by the Security Council.

Article 50. If preventive or enforcement measures against any state are taken by the Security Council, any other state, whether a Member of the United Nations or not, which finds itself confronted with special economic problems arising from the carrying out of those measures shall have the right to consult the Security Council with regard to a solution of those problems.

Article 51. Nothing in the present Charter shall impair the inherent right of individual or collective self-defense if an armed attack occurs against a Member of the United Nations, until the Security Council has taken the measures necessary to maintain international peace and security. Measures taken by Members in the exercise of this right of self-defense shall be immediately reported to the Security Council and shall not in any way affect the authority and responsibility of the Security Council under the present

Charter to take at any time such action as it deems necessary in order to maintain or restore international peace and security.

In other words, the Charter does not absolutely prohibit the threat or use of force, but it states the purposes and conditions under which states may resort to them. The Assembly has gone farther on several occasions in attempts to define these conditions, and in 1965 adopted a Declaration on the Inadmissibility of Intervention in the Domestic Affairs of States and the Protection of Their Independence and Sovereignty,[25] providing in part that:

1. No State has the right to intervene, directly or indirectly, in the internal or external affairs of any other State. Consequently, armed intervention and all other forms of interference or attempted threats against the personality of the State or against its political, economic and cultural elements, are condemned.

2. No State may use or encourage the use of economic, political or any other type of measures to coerce another State in order to obtain from it the subordination of the exercise of its sovereign rights or to secure from it advantage of any kind. Also no State shall organize, assist, foment, finance, incite or tolerate subversive, terrorist or armed activities directed towards the violent overthrow of another State, or interfere in civil strife in another State.

One year later, the Assembly reaffirmed this resolution and deemed it to be its "bounden duty":

(a) To urge the immediate cessation of intervention, in any form whatever, in the domestic or external affairs of States;

(b) To condemn all forms of intervention in the domestic or external affairs of States as a basic source of danger to the cause of world peace;

(c) To call upon all States to carry out faithfully their obligations under the Charter of the United Nations and the provisions of the Declaration on the Inadmissibility of Intervention in the Domestic Affairs of States and the Protection of Their Independence and Sovereignty, and to urge them to refrain from armed intervention or the promotion or organization of subversive terriorism or other indirect forms of intervention for the purpose of changing by violence the existing system of another State or interfering in civil strife in another State.[26]

Without any impartial body empowered to determine whether states have violated these resolutions, however, each state remains free to levy charges of intervention against any other. The Soviet Union has actually charged the United Nations itself with using force illegally, *e.g.*, in the Congo in 1960–1963.

[25] Resolution 2131 (XX), 21 December 1965.
[26] Resolution 2225 (XXI), 19 December 1966.

LEGAL ISSUES AT THE UNITED NATIONS

Oscar Schachter[27]

The Congo operation is significant, not only from the political and organizational standpoint, but also from the legal. This interest arises not simply because the Congo problem created unprecedented situations, but also because it demonstrated an extraordinary use of legal conceptions and principles in establishing the framework for United Nations actions, and in influencing the decisions taken by the organs and those responsible for administration.

The heart of the Congo operation was the use of force by an international organization. We all know that although the Charter provisions for using military force were elaborated in great detail at San Francisco and constitute the most comprehensive set of obligations in the Charter, they have remained a dead letter. The draftsmen of the Charter assumed that the United Nations would employ force as an enforcement measure, popularly called a sanction, in accordance with the agreement which the Security Council would conclude with Members providing armed forces and facilities. On the chance that these agreements might not come into effect, the founders also provided in Article 106 for the big powers to take joint action as may be necessary. But these articles have never been used. The troops in Korea acted on the basis of a recommendation under Article 39; the United States Government acted as the United Nations Command and only in a limited sense were the troops under U.N. direction. UNEF interposed a force, which was essentially an observers' corps, on a frontier line with the consent of the territorial state, Egypt, and the consent of the other state principally concerned, Israel.

The Congo situation differed from the previous cases in which the organization utilized military forces. The threat to peace was triggered by internal disorder rather than by a dispute between states. The Belgians, who had withdrawn from the Congo, returned, they claimed, to cope with the breakdown of law and order occasioned mainly by mutiny in the Congolese army. Other states considered the Belgian action a threat to international peace on the premise that if the Belgians remained, others would intervene. Thus internal disturbance and anarchy became the unprecedented basis for finding that international peace was threatened. Although the Council has never set forth in any authoritative way the precise legal basis for its intervention, it is apparent that there were two grounds. One was the request of the Central Government in the Congo for military troops to maintain law and order, so as to bring the Belgian troops to withdraw; the other was the finding of the Council that the United Nations might properly intervene because of the grave threat to international peace and security. The Secretary-

[27] *Annual Review of United Nations Affairs 1960–1961*, ed. by Richard N. Swift (Dobbs Ferry, N.Y.: Oceana Publications, 1962), pp. 142–148. In this article, Mr. Schachter refers to the United Nations Emergency Force (UNEF), which served in the Middle East from 1956 to 1967, and to the *Organisation des Nations Unies au Congo* (ONUC), 1960–1964.

General introduced the matter under article 99, the first time that Article had clearly been used.[28]

The Council made no specific finding under Article 39 that there was a threat to peace; its view was implicit in the statements delegates made. Some delegates, following the lead of the Secretary-General, referred subsequently to Article 40, which provides for provisional measures to prevent a situation from becoming aggravated. Nevertheless, out of the Council resolutions on July 13 and 22 and August 9, and the Assembly resolution of September 20, 1960, emerges the legal conclusion that the Council was exercising its peremptory authority under Chapter VII of the Charter. For the first time, the Council asserted Article 49 of Chapter VII, which is couched in obligatory language. It also referred, although not for the first time, to the application of Article 25, which stipulates that Council decisions must be carried out. On the other hand, the resolutions do not state that this operation was a use of sanctions in the specific sense of Article 42.

It is not uncharacteristic of the Security Council that throughout the discussions, the Members rarely referred to the specific articles of the Charter involved in the action taken. True, the resolution of August 9 did mention Articles 25 and 49, but these articles refer to the consequences rather than the legal basis of the action. The U.S.S.R. at a later stage reverted to the legal point in criticizing *ex post facto* what happened. They argued that Article 43 should have been followed, but this point was not raised at the time the resolutions were adopted.

One of the more significant legal aspects of the use of military force in the Congo relates to the view the Council took of Chapter VII. Most of the Members emphasized that the Council was employing its authority to require states, and particularly Belgium, to take certain action required in the interest of peace. But, at the same time, the Council's use of Chapter VII did not fall into the legal category of enforcement measures. While the Secretary-General referred to Article 40 as a basis and the Council later implied that it agreed with this view, no Member went beyond this position and claimed that Articles 41 and 42 were applicable. The United States, on February 20, 1961, explicitly said that those two Articles did not apply. Thus, the United Nations found itself using military force, but not employing such force in the sense of the enforcement measures or sanctions provided for in the Charter. The U.S.S.R. subsequently maintained that under the Charter, the United Nations could not use force except through agreements under Article 43 or under the temporary measures authorized in Article 106. They did not assert this view of the limits on United Nations authority, however, until April 1961; earlier they had gone ahead with the other Council members on the original resolution which simply asked the Secretary-General to provide military assistance to the Central Government of the Congo.

For the Council not to have invoked Articles 41 and 42 was not merely

---

[28] Trygvie Lie claimed he had used Article 99 in the Korean case, but that claim is not in fact borne out by the *Official Records*. See Trygvie Lie, *In the Cause of Peace* (New York: Macmillan Company, 1954), p. 328.

an oversight. The omission goes to the very heart of the matter. The Council chose not to invoke its maximum sanctioning authority because of the international and internal constitutional and political situations. The general principle which guided most of the delegates and certainly the Secretary-General, as the Council's chief agent, was that the organization was not using force as a sanction or enforcement measure against a government. Rather, it was attempting to maintain law and order and to eliminate the threat posed by Belgian troops in the country.

Many people said at the time that the United Nations was making a mistake in this situation. They argued that since there was no adequate governmental machinery in the country, and the idea of a Congo state or even a Central Government of the Congo was largely nominal, the United Nations could only have settled the matter by taking complete control of the Congo. The records show that in statement after statement, the Secretary-General found it necessary to oppose this view, to deny that he was seeking to substitute himself or the United Nations for the government of the Congo, to affirm that he considered it essential to adhere strictly to the limits that domestic jurisdiction and sovereignty impose on the United Nations. He reiterated that the United Nations could not interfere in a domestic, political, and constitutional conflict; at the same time, to maintain law and order, the United Nations had to assume responsibility for administrative and police action, which in many cases approached the exercise of governmental authority, but stopped short of imposing a political settlement on the country.

The reason for making this important distinction was in part the fact that early in the operation it was clear that the major powers disagreed about which of the competing groups should receive authority in the Congo. There were also substantial material limits on the United Nations capacity and capability, especially as the United Nations was using troops from states which were interested in one way or another in the constitutional conflict. The legal and constitutional principles of the organization were linked to these political and practical difficulties. In other words, the legal precepts both clarified the situation and provided guidance for the specific day-to-day action. Under these principles the United Nations was not using force against a state; it was not carrying out a traditional type of collective sanction against governmental authority; consequently it could not, for example, take the initiative in attacking garrisons where the Congolese army was entrenched in order to liberate political personalities.

Obviously, drawing a line between what the United Nations could and could not do was very difficult. The United Nations Force was trying to maintain law and order when national government in the Congo was entirely fictional, with little, if any, real authority. As there was practically no local administrative authority, the United Nations had as best it could to maintain order, to see that people did not kill one another, and to maintain civilian services. Performing these jobs inevitably brought the United Nations into conflict with the competing political groups, which always sought to use the United Nations forces or, alternatively, foreign governments to support their own particular ambitions. It was perhaps unrealistic to expect that major governments could resist these appeals for support. The whole situation became permeated, not only with local political leaders seeking United Nations support, but also with external foreign aid granted from time to time in varying degrees. Because the foreign governments were supporting different groups, the United Nations found it difficult to decide who were the legitimate authorities. The organization had to maintain law and order without the help of a local government and, at the same time, it had to deal impartially with several political factions which competed with one another.

The main problem the United Nations had was to walk the difficult and constantly changing line between the proper area in which the Congolese were to settle their own differences and the area where United Nations action was called for. Thus, the United Nations was told that maintaining law and order meant enforcing the Constitution, and that therefore it should act against the separatists of Katanga, who were in effect trying to alter the constitutional scheme. The United Nations also had all the problems of maintaining law in the more elementary sense of protecting lives and property. Then the United Nations had to determine how best to deal with various groups of official authorities, depending upon who was exercising reasonably effective authority within particular areas. Finally, the United Nations had the problem of coping with assertions of sovereignty by the government, which from time to time argued that it had invited the United Nations in and so could ask it to get out, an argument that brought into focus the fundamental bases of U.N. authority in the Congo. The Secretary-General pointed out that the U.N. was not operating entirely by consent, but primarily to maintain peace and security, and that therefore its forces could not leave merely at the request of the local government. The U.N. action was admittedly less than an enforcement measure in the sense of Chapter VII; and yet it was more than a purely technical assistance, contractual operation. It fell between the two and came closest to the provisional measures envisaged in Article 40, which were not supposed to prejudice the rights of the parties, and which were subject to Article 2(7), the spirit of which was reflected in the non-intervention provisions of the resolutions.

On February 21, 1961, the Congo situation took on a new dimension when the civil war there became more serious and the Council authorized the Secretary-General to use force "if necessary as a last resort." But even here in the opinion of the Secretary-General—he received little help from the Security Council in interpreting the resolution—the United Nations was operating in the same theoretical framework. It still was not using force against a state, nor was it replacing a government; it was just adding the new objective of preventing civil war to the mission of preserving law and order. The United Nations could therefore continue to apply the same basic ideas about using force which it had previously announced—namely, that it would use force essentially for self-defense. In this respect the United Nations position in the Congo was not really different from its position in the Gaza strip, where the United Nations had said that if anyone tried to force the United

Nations out of a position it was holding, it would respond with military force. In attempting to end the civil war, ONUC tried to arrange a cease-fire in neutralized truce zones and to supervise the truce by occupying certain places. Attempts to dislodge the United Nations were met by force if ONUC had the military capability to resist. In the port of Matadi and in certain other places, the United Nations did not have the capability, and withdrew. In other places, however, the United Nations used force effectively to maintain its positions. Special legal problems also rose over the power to arrest. The United Nations had been told to evacuate certain categories of foreign personnel, and it was pressed to arrest individuals in order to speed their departure. Despite this pressure, the United Nations refused to arrest persons except when ONUC captured them in repelling attacks against United Nations positions; in these cases of apprehension *in flagrante delicto* the United Nations Force did arrest and detain individuals and, under the authority of the new Central Government, evacuated them from the country.

This brief summary of the Congo situation should indicate that as the United Nations faced dilemmas about where to use force, when to arrest people, and when to deal with particular authorities, it did not resolve them arbitrarily. It decided each issue in terms of a set of reasonably consistent principles based on fundamental concepts of the Charter. Finding in some cases little guidance in the formal decisions of the organs, the Secretary-General followed a line supported by legal authority and principle in resolving the dilemmas which the organs, while calling for him to act, failed to resolve.

Perhaps I can illustrate how difficult a line the Secretary-General had to tread by referring to the problem he faced at the very beginning when the Council told him to send an army to the Congo. Since the Council had not defined the kind of army, the Secretary-General had to decide on its composition in the face of conflicting ideas. Some wanted only Africans in the ONUC; others a broader composition. The Secretary-General did not deal with this problem without considering basic principles. He refused to accede to the idea that ONUC should be an entirely African Army on the ground that the United Nations stood for principles of universality and nondiscrimination, and he could not select troops on the basis of race or color. The host state wanted to exclude states which it regarded as hostile, and the Secretary-General took its views into account, but he maintained the principle at all times that the organization itself would have to be the final judge.

Regardless of the extent to which the "laws of war" are obeyed, it seems hard to blink the fact that modern war and international law are incompatible. War is inherently lawless, and it would be far more constructive for international law to admit quite frankly that because war is a lawless phenomenon, the law has nothing to do with it. Law may still, without compromising itself, quite properly deal with means of averting war and with building international devices for the peaceful solution of problems. There certainly are no theoretical objections to having states use certain devices of international law, like treaties, to mitigate the horrors of modern conflict in the interests of civilians, the sick and wounded, and prisoners, but international law itself might properly exclude such matters from its ken. It would thus move along analogous lines with civilian law, which does not purport to regulate the conduct of persons engaged in gang warfare, but rather concentrates on eliminating the gangs themselves. International law could then free itself from the embarrassing doctrine that war is an element of the legal order and instead go about its business of attempting "to insure order by regulating the social use of force."[29]

[29] DeVisscher, p. 290.

CHAPTER IX

Future of International Law

If the state systems lasts, its future will depend on restraint and generosity among the constituent parts—restraint in not using nuclear weapons which might destroy the world physically, and generosity in respecting one another's rights while carrying out one's own duties. How to secure this balance of rights and duties is a central problem of international order.

In an effort to achieve the balance, lawyers and jurists have attempted from time to time to specify, sometimes in considerable detail, the "general rights and duties of states." They have also endorsed Declarations on the subject as, for instance, in the Convention on Rights and Duties of States adopted at a conference in Montevideo in 1933. The most recent attempt at formulating a comprehensive statement of rights and duties was made in 1949, when the United Nations General Assembly received and noted a Draft Declaration on the subject, prepared by the U.N. International Law Commission. The Assembly maintained that the draft contributed notably and substantially toward developing international law and referred it to the attention of member states and jurists.[1]

DRAFT DECLARATION ON RIGHTS AND DUTIES OF STATES PREPARED BY THE UNITED NATIONS INTERNATIONAL LAW COMMISSION

Annex to U.N. General Assembly Resolution 375 (IV), 6 December 1949

U.N. Doc. A/1251, p. 67

Whereas the States of the world form a community governed by international law,

[1] Resolution 375 (IV), December 6, 1949.

Whereas the progressive development of international law requires effective organization of the community of States,

Whereas a great majority of the States of the world have accordingly established a new international order under the Charter of the United Nations, and most of the other States of the world have declared their desire to live within this order,

Whereas a primary purpose of the United Nations is to maintain international peace and security, and the reign of law and justice is essential to the realization of this purpose, and

Whereas it is therefore desirable to formulate certain basic rights and duties of States in the light of new developments of international law and in harmony with the Charter of the United Nations,

The General Assembly of the United Nations adopts and proclaims this Declaration on Rights and Duties of States:

Article 1. Every State has the right to independence and hence to exercise freely, without dictation by any other State, all its legal powers, including the choice of its own form of government.

Article 2. Every State has the right to exercise jurisdiction over its territory and over all persons and things therein, subject to the immunities recognized by international law.

Article 3. Every State has the duty to refrain from intervention in the internal or external affairs of any other State.

Article 4. Every State has the duty to refrain from fomenting civil strife in the territory of another State, and to prevent the organization within its territory of activities calculated to foment such civil strife.

Article 5. Every State has the right to equality in law with every other State.

Article 6. Every State has the duty to treat all persons under its jurisdiction with respect for human rights and fundamental freedoms, without distinction as to race, sex, language, or religion.

Article 7. Every State has the duty to ensure that conditions prevailing in its territory do not menace international peace and order.

Article 8. Every State has the duty to settle its disputes with other States by peaceful means in such a manner that international peace and security, and justice, are not endangered.

Article 9. Every State has the duty to refrain from resorting to war as an instrument of national policy, and to refrain from the threat or use of force against the territorial integrity or political independence of another State, or in any other manner inconsistent with international law and order.

Article 10. Every State has the duty to refrain from giving assistance to any State which is acting in violation of article 9, or against which the United Nations is taking preventive or enforcement action.

Article 11. Every State has the duty to refrain from recognizing any territorial acquisition by another State acting in violation of article 9.

Article 12. Every State has the right of individual or collective self-defence against armed attack.

Article 13. Every State has the duty to carry out in good faith its obligations arising from treaties and other sources of international law, and it may not invoke provisions in its constitution or its laws as an excuse for failure to perform this duty.

Article 14. Every State has the duty to conduct its relations with other States in accordance with international law and with the principle that the sovereignty of each State is subject to the supremacy of international law.

Many of the rights and duties in this draft declaration refer to important topics of international law, which we have examined, *e.g.,* the use of force (Articles 3, 4, 9, 10, 12), settling disputes (Article 8), conducting foreign policy (Articles 13 and 14), and jurisdiction over persons (Article 6) and territory (Articles 2 and 7). The Draft Declaration is by no means the last word on these important subjects. Moreover, some of its articles are not universally accepted, which accounts for the General Assembly's not having acted more decisively upon them.

For instance, some critics would deny that independence (Article 1) is a right—they see it, rather, as a quality or precondition of statehood. Also, because all states have acquired territory by force and recognized such acquisitions by others, Article 11 calls into doubt every modern boundary and implicitly questions the validity of all treaties establishing or recognizing them. There is consequently little substance in that article.

One may also question the worth of Article 5, basic though it appears to be at first glance. What does it mean to say that a state has a "right to equality"? Interpreted literally, this article gives every state the right of equal treatment at the hand of every other state. Thus no state could make a treaty with another according it any privileges without granting the same rights to all others. To interpret the article in this manner would in effect introduce most-favored-nation clauses into all bilateral treaties. On the figurative plane, the article means only that states should treat one another according to international law. But this interpretation is tautological, because the idea of applying the law equally is inherent in the idea of law itself.

In more modest terms, to assert that states are equal before the law is to imply that the law cannot discriminate among them, that what one state claims, all may claim, and what one does, all may do. Thus all states presumably have the right to purchase and sell territory (and the duty to respect the purchases and sales of other states); the right freely to use the high seas (and the duty to respect others' use of the high seas); the right to send and to receive diplomatic agents (and the duty to respect the agents of others); the right to negotiate agreements (and the duty to respect agreements others make); the right to national security (and the duty to respect the security of others); and the right to independence, to determine policy without others interfering (with the corresponding duty to refrain from preventing others from exercising their independence).

As sound as such statements may be theoretically, they ignore the unequal physical capacities of different states, which give them diverse abilities to assert or to maintain their rights. In this regard, however, international law is no different from municipal law, which while asserting the equal rights of individuals to life, liberty, and property, recognizes that accidents of birth or economic and social conditions may make it possible for some persons to exercise their rights in far less significant ways than others. The physical incapacity of a subject is not necessarily incompatible with the equality of its legal status. Legal equality still has meaning if the law itself does not stand in the way of subjects' exercising powers which the law regards as belonging to all, if it provides equal protection of the laws for subjects and gives them an equal part in adopting new rules of law. Domestic law in democratic states is quite successful in doing all these things; international law is less so.

In permitting subjects to exercise their powers, international law is certainly as impartial as domestic law; in providing equal protection, some states (as George Orwell remarked in another context) are more equal than others. When it comes to adopting new rules, the balance also seems to favor the great powers: during the nineteenth and twentieth centuries, they made the major law-making treaties unrestrained by any considerations of abstract equality, *e.g.*, the treaties fashioned at the Congresses of Vienna (1815), Paris (1856), and Berlin (1878 and 1885), at the Conference of Algeciras (1906), or at the end of World Wars I and II. Ironically, when in 1899 and 1907, the Hague Conferences attempted to operate on the basis of equality, with the consent of all states needed for each convention, the results were negligible. The development of the law was even considerably retarded by the states' inability to agree on a Judicial Court of Arbitration. More recently, neither the League of Nations nor the United Nations has embraced full equality in its procedures.

What *equality* means must, in effect, be determined by the practice of states because (1) the specific fields in which equal rights are to apply must still be defined, (2) because the analogy between states and individuals may not be very apt, and (3) there are serious doubts about the merits of asserting the right in the first place.[2]

Aside from the Draft Declaration on Rights and Duties of States of 1949 quoted above, no precise statement of state responsibility exists, although some international lawyers have attempted to devise one. Such consensus as exists, however, is, not wide-ranging. Part of the difficulty in enlarging the consensus is in distinguishing the responsibility of *states* from the responsibility of *statesmen*. The problem is not easily resolved in theory and may well be impossible in both theory and practice.

Nonetheless, some formulations about state responsibility have attracted attention in recent years in matters relating to genocide, injuries incurred in the service of the United Nations, peace and security, the Nuremberg principles, outer space, atomic radiation, nuclear hazards, and sovereignty over natural resources.[3]

State responsibility for genocide is established in Article IX of the Genocide Convention:

Disputes between the Contracting Parties relating to the interpretation, application or fulfilment of the present Convention, including those relating to the responsibility of the State for genocide or any of the other acts enumerated in Article III, shall be submitted to the International Court of Justice at the request of any of the parties to the dispute.

Presumably, if the charge of genocide were raised among parties to the Convention, the Court would have the power to determine compensation for victims of genocide once it concluded that a State was responsible for the alleged acts.

States also have some responsibility for injuries to U.N. personnel. After the I.C.J. debate on the question, the General Assembly adopted a resolution (365 [IV]) authorizing the Secretary-General to bring an international claim against a government allegedly responsible for injuring a U.N. employee, with a view to getting reparations for the damage caused the U.N., the victim, or to persons benefiting from his estate. This responsibility is new in law, arising, obviously, only because the U.N. exists.

Lawyers have discussed state criminal responsibility in connection with the Draft Code of Offenses against the Peace and Security of

[2] For this and other cogent criticisms of the Declaration, see Hans Kelsen, "The Draft Declaration . . . " *A.J.I.L.*, XXXXIV (1950), 259–276.
[3] The paragraphs below on these subjects are based on the discussion of state responsibility in *Yearbook of the International Law Commission 1964*, II, 125–172.

Mankind, and in relation to the Nuremberg principles. In both cases, the idea of holding a state responsible as a criminal (as opposed to holding it responsible for civil and administrative faults) has been put aside. The consensus seems to be that states are obliged to punish those who commit crimes or to permit other states or an international tribunal to punish them, a doctrine which coincides with the views of the judges at the Nuremberg Tribunal that "crimes against international law are committed by men, not by abstract entities, and only by punishing individuals who commit such crimes can the provisions of international law be enforced."[4]

Responsibility of states in matters relating to outer space has been extensively studied by a General Assembly Committee on the Peaceful Uses of Outer Space, one of whose subcommittees dealt entirely with legal questions. The group's deliberations have now been incorporated in Articles VI and VII of the Outer Space Treaty (for text, see p. 183).

On other frontiers of modern science, formulations relating to state responsibility exist. Thus, in 1961, the General Assembly declared "that both concern for the future of mankind and the fundamental principles of international law impose a responsibility on all States concerning action which might have harmful biological consequences for the existing and future generations of peoples of other States, by increasing the levels of radioactive fall-out" [1629 (XVI)], and the International Atomic Energy Agency has prepared the Vienna Convention on Civil Liability for Nuclear Damage and a Convention on the Liability of Operators of Nuclear Ships.

The question of state responsibility has also arisen in the matter of sovereignty over natural resources, involving, as it does, issues of expropriation and compensation therefor. Reconciling the views of states on these subjects was not easy, for some wished to emphasize that nationalization should not be arbitrary; that expropriation should occur only for reasons of public utility; and that compensation was always required. Others maintained that requiring states to pay compensation actually restricted state sovereignty and would even make expropriation in some cases impossible.[5] The General Assembly finally formulated its views in the draft declaration on permanent sovereignty, of which paragraph 4 of the substantive part is the critical section, but one that leaves ample ground for states still disagree about rights and duties.

[4] *Yearbook of the International Law Commission*, 1950, II, p. 364, paras. 98–99.
[5] For further information on the subject of state responsibility, see *Yearbook of the International Law Commission*, II, 125–172 (1964).

UNITED NATIONS GENERAL ASSEMBLY RESOLUTIONS
ON PERMANENT SOVEREIGNTY OVER
NATURAL RESOURCES[6]

The General Assembly,

Recalling its resolutions 523 (VI) of 12 January 1952 and 626 (VII) of 21 December 1952,

Bearing in mind its resolution 1314 (XIII) of 12 December 1958, by which it established the Commission on Permanent Sovereignty over Natural Resources and instructed it to conduct a full survey of the status of permanent sovereignty over natural wealth and resources as a basic constituent of the right to self-determination, with recommendations, where necessary, for its strengthening, and decided further that, in the conduct of the full survey of the status of the permanent sovereignty of peoples and nations over their natural wealth and resources, due regard should be paid to the rights and duties of States under international law and to the importance of encouraging international co-operation in the economic development of developing countries,

Bearing in mind its resolution 1515 (XV) of 15 December 1960, in which it recommended that the sovereign right of every State to dispose of its wealth and its natural resources should be respected,

Considering that any measure in this respect must be based on the recognition of the inalienable right of all States freely to dispose of their natural wealth and resources in accordance with their national interests, and on respect for the economic independence of States,

Considering that nothing in paragraph 4 below in any way prejudices the position of any Member State on any aspect of the question of the rights and obligations of successor States and Governments in respect of property acquired before the accession to complete sovereignty of countries formerly under colonial rule,

Noting that the subject of succession of States and Governments is being examined as a matter of priority by the International Law Commission,

Considering that it is desirable to promote international co-operation for the economic development of developing countries, and that economic and financial agreements between the developed and the developing countries must be based on the principles of equality and of the right of peoples and nations to self-determination,

Considering that the provision of economic and technical assistance, loans and increased foreign investment must not be subject to conditions which conflict with the interests of the recipient State,

Considering the benefits to be derived from exchanges of technical and scientific information likely to promote the development and use of such

[6] The first of these resolutions, 1803 (XVII), was adopted on 19 December 1962; the second, 2158 (XXI), on 25 November 1966. Note that the later resolution, particularly, emphasizes rights rather more than duties.

resources and wealth, and the important part which the United Nations, and other international organizations are called upon to play in that connexion,

Attaching particular importance to the question of promoting the economic development of developing countries and securing their economic independence.

Noting that the creation and strengthening of the inalienable sovereignty of States over their natural wealth and resources reinforces their economic independence,

Desiring that there should be further consideration by the United Nations of the subject of permanent sovereignty over natural resources in the spirit of international co-operation in the field of economic development, particularly that of the developing countries,

I

Declares that:

1. The right of peoples and nations to permanent sovereignty over their natural wealth and resources must be exercised in the interest of their national development and of the well-being of the people of the State concerned.

2. The exploration, development and disposition of such resources, as well as the import of the foreign capital required for these purposes, should be in conformity with the rules and conditions which the peoples and nations freely consider to be necessary or desirable with regard to the authorization, restriction or prohibition of such activities.

3. In cases where authorization is granted, the capital imported and the earnings on that capital shall be governed by the terms thereof, by the national legislation in force, and by international law. The profits derived must be shared in the proportions freely agreed upon, in each case, between the investors and the recipient State, due care being taken to ensure that there is no impairment, for any reason, of that State's sovereignty over its natural wealth and resources.

4. Nationalization, expropriation or requisitioning shall be based on grounds or reasons of public utility, security or the national interest which are recognized as overriding purely individual or private interests, both domestic and foreign. In such cases the owner shall be paid appropriate compensation, in accordance with the rules in force in the State taking such measures in the exercise of its sovereignty and in accordance with international law. In any case, where the question of compensation gives rise to a controversy, the national jurisdiction of the State taking such measures shall be exhausted. However, upon agreement by sovereign States and other parties concerned, settlement of the dispute should be made through arbitration or international adjudication.

5. The free and beneficial exercise of the sovereignty of peoples and nations over their natural resources must be furthered by the mutual respect of States based on their sovereign equality.

6. International co-operation for the economic development of developing countries, whether in the form of public or private capital investments, exchange of goods and services, technical assistance, or exchange of scientific

information, shall be such as to further their independent national development and shall be based upon respect for their sovereignty over their natural wealth resources.

7. Violation of the rights of peoples and nations to sovereignty over their natural wealth and resources is contrary to the spirit and principles of the Charter of the United Nations and hinders the development of international co-operation and the maintenence of peace.

8. Foreign investment agreements freely entered into by, or between, sovereign States shall be observed in good faith; States and international organizations shall strictly and conscientiously respect the sovereignty of peoples and nations over their natural wealth and resources in accordance with the Charter and the principles set forth in the present resolution.

❋ ❋ ❋

The General Assembly,

Recalling its resolutions 523 (VI) of 12 January 1952, 626 (VII) of 21 December 1952 and 1515 (XV) of 15 December 1960,

Recalling further its resolution 1803 (XVII) of 14 December 1962 on permanent sovereignty over natural resources,

Recognizing that the natural resources of the developing countries constitute a basis of their economic development in general and of their industrial progress in particular,

Bearing in mind that natural resources are limited and in many cases exhaustible and that their proper exploitation determines the conditions of the economic development of the developing countries both at present and in the future,

Considering that, in order to safeguard the exercise of permanent sovereignty over natural resources, it is essential that their exploitation and marketing should be aimed at securing the highest possible rate of growth of the developing countries,

Considering further that this aim can better be achieved if the developing countries are in a position to undertake themselves the exploitation and marketing of their natural resources so that they may exercise their freedom of choice in the various fields related to the utilization of natural resources under the most favourable conditions.

Taking into account the fact that foreign capital, whether public or private, forthcoming at the request of the developing countries, can play an important role inasmuch as it supplements the efforts undertaken by them in the exploitation and development of their natural resources, provided that there is government supervision over the activity of foreign capital to ensure that it is used in the interests of national development,

I

1. *Reaffirms* the inalienable right of all countries to exercise permanent sovereignty over their natural resources in the interest of their national development, in conformity with the spirit and principles of the Charter of the

United Nations and as recognized in General Assembly resolution 1803 (XVII);

2. *Declares,* therefore, that the United Nations should undertake a maximum concerted effort to channel its activities so as to enable all countries to exercise that right fully;

3. *States* that such an effort should help in achieving the maximum possible development of the natural resources of the developing countries and in strengthening their ability to undertake this development themselves, so that they might effectively exercise their choice in deciding the manner in which the exploitation and marketing of their natural resources should be carried out;

4. *Confirms* that the exploitation of natural resources in each country shall always be conducted in accordance with its natural laws and regulations;

5. *Recognizes* the right of all countries, and in particular of the developing countries, to secure and increase their share in the administration of enterprises which are fully or partly operated by foreign capital and to have a greater share in the advantages and profits derived therefrom on an equitable basis, with due regard to the development needs and objectives of the peoples concerned and to mutually acceptable contractual practices, and calls upon the countries from which such capital originates to refrain from any action which would hinder the exercise of that right;

6. *Considers* that, when natural resources of the developing countries are exploited by foreign investors, the latter should undertake proper and accelerated training of national personnel at all levels and in all fields connected with such exploitation;

7. *Calls upon* the developed countries to make available to the developing countries, at their request, assistance, including capital goods and know-how, for the exploitation and marketing of their natural resources in order to accelerate their economic development, and to refrain from placing on the world market non-commercial reserves of primary commodities which may have an adverse effect on the foreign exchange earnings of the developing countries;

8. *Recognizes* that national and international organizations set up by the developing countries for the development and marketing of their natural resources play a significant role in ensuring the exercise of the permanent sovereignty of those countries in this field, and on that account should be encouraged;

. . . .

Ideas of independence and equality among states are, of course, sanctified by history and theory. They stem historically from the Peace of Westphalia in 1648 and theoretically from the natural law theorists. Emmerich de Vattel regarded them as "fundamental, essential, and absolute" rights along with *existence, respect,* and *territory* (although others regarded only existence as fundamental and derived the other rights from it alone). Vattel's classic statement equated men and states: "A dwarf is as much a man as a giant is," he argued; "a small Republic is no less a sovereign State than the most powerful Kingdom."[7] Attempting to protect the smaller states, he and others made an analogy between the "inalienable" rights of individuals and those of states. He regarded as sacred the corporate nature of a state, no less than the natural person of an individual human being. The analogy between equality for states and individuals obviously has a strong emotional appeal to have lasted, as it has, for over three hundred years. But there are serious questions to answer before one can rely upon the analogy.

Human equality rests on grounds that are either religious ("all men are endowed by their Creator with certain unalienable rights") or utilitarian (*i.e.*, only by assuming that men are equal, can one create a democratic society). But neither of these grounds will cover the state's claim to equality. The Creator could not endow states with rights because He did not create them; men did. Nor does state equality create a democratic international society (which we are here assuming to be a desirable goal). One cannot advance democracy by establishing mutually exclusive islands of authority where even totalitarianism may exist without let or hindrance, or from which governments may assert rights while denying duties. Moreover, the assumptions of human equality in successful democracies have never operated as theoretical or practical bars to effective government. Both John Locke and the authors of the Declaration of Independence recognized the need for instituting governments among men. However, the governments, in turn, have done all they can to remain aloof from superior authority and have been slow to recognize externally the common good which they profess to advance internally. The notion of the common good, for illogical (though allegedly patriotic) reasons, too often stops at the national frontier. In practice, states have tended to stress their own rights and the duties of others toward them.

The idea of rights and duties among states need not rest upon Vattel's notion of natural law. One may regard rights and duties as neither absolute nor inherent but merely part of international law—qualities, assumptions, or postulates, resting on custom, which are essential conditions for political entities coexisting in an international community. Positivists, for instance, traditionally look to the "facts" of international life and recognize only the rights which they believe that states themselves acknowledge as having been established by custom or treaty. Whether rights are or are not *fundamental* is a question with little meaning for them.

[7] E. de Vattel, *The Law of Nations or the Principles of Natural Law* (Washington: Carnegie Institution, 1916), III (transl. Charles G. Fenwick), Introduction, Sec. 18.

One could go one step farther, however, and assume that states enjoy these rights only as long as men express their sense of unity through states and employ them as devices for promoting common interests. The implication of this assumption is that international law is not forever fixed as a law of sovereign states and that one need not regard states as the final or absolute form of international community.

No dearth of new principles that might serve to strengthen the international legal system exists. Legal theorists and others can easily provide new doctrines for revised systems of law, or even full-blown constitutions for strengthened international organizations.[8] There is, however, little disposition on the part of existing states to surrender their authority or to modify it in favor of a stronger international law. And no stronger law can emerge unless states limit their own authority and acknowledge in law what they must often acknowledge in fact—that the state system as now constituted can no longer guarantee the security men need in a nuclear age.[9]

Even though states need not take at once all the steps required to achieve a stronger international legal system, they often resist moves for strengthening it even gradually. Sometimes, the very states that, on the one hand, argue strongly for law and order are, under other circumstances, just the ones which resist most strongly the required changes. The United States, for instance, has always had among its leaders champions of international courts. On the other hand, the United States has also weakened the International Court of Justice by accepting the Court's compulsory jurisdiction, but with conditions quite opposed to the Court's development. American reservations have also encouraged other states to be equally retrictive.

By its Statute, the Court's jurisdiction is modest enough, giving it compulsory jurisdiction over certain legal disputes between parties, when the parties have indicated that they were willing to accept the Court's jurisdiction. Under Article 36(2), the legal disputes involved relate to the interpretation of a treaty; any question of international law; the existence of any fact, which, if established, could constitute a breach of an international obligation; and the nature or extent of reparation to be made for such a breach.

When the United States agreed to accept the Court's compulsory jurisdiction it did so, however, only on condition that it could keep from the Court "disputes with regard to matters which are essentially within

---

[8] Grenville Clark and Louis B. Sohn, *World Peace Through World Law* (3d ed., Cambridge: Harvard University Press, 1966) is a good example.
[9] See John Herz, *International Politics in an Atomic Age* (New York: Columbia University Press, 1959).

the domestic jurisdiction of the United States as determined by the United States."[10] The fight to attach this reservation was led by Senator Tom Connally of Texas, and the Connally Amendment was adopted by the Senate.[11]

This reservation amounted to accepting and not accepting the Court's compulsory jurisdiction at the same time, because the United States could always invoke its reservation when it chose to do so in the future. At best, it was an excessively cautious step to take; at worst, an extremely hypocritical one. In either case, the reservation struck a severe blow at the Court. It was in fact a retrograde step because no state had ever adopted so crippling a reservation in its dealings, between the first and second World Wars, with the Permanent Court of International Justice. Following the United States example, however, seven other states adopted similar reservations.

Because the reservations are reciprocal in their effect, they actually affect all cases between these seven states and the forty other states which might appear before the Court. Thus, in the *Case of Certain Norwegian Loans (France v. Norway)*, the Norwegian government used the French reservation as a ground for not allowing the Court to hear the case on its merits. Norway argued that the French reservation of "disputes relating to matters . . . essentially within the national jurisdiction as understood by the Government of the French Republic"[12] was ample ground on which to decline to submit the question at issue to the Court since "by virtue of the principle of reciprocity . . . the Norwegian Government cannot be bound, vis-à-vis the French Government, by undertakings which are either broader or stricter than those given by the latter Government."[13] The Court upheld the Norwegian claim, because the Court could exercise jurisdiction only to the extent that the declarations by the two states coincided. Since the French Declaration defined the Court's jurisdiction more narrowly than the Norwegian, "the common will of the parties, which is the basis of the Court's jurisdiction, exists within these narrower limits indicated by the French Reservation."[14] France subsequently modified its reservation to permit the Court to determine such jurisdictional matters by excluding only "questions which, by international law, fall exclusively within the domes-

---

[10] 92 Cong. Rec. 10706; see Statement of Senator Connally, *ibid.*, pp. 10694–10695.
[11] *Ibid.*, p. 10697.
[12] *I.C.J. Reports*, 9 (1957); and *Hearings*, p. 362, n. 1 (1960).
[13] *I.C.J. Reports*, 63 (1957). The reciprocity principle has been upheld in other cases: *Phosphates in Morocco Case*, P.C.I.J., Ser. A/B No. 74, 22 (1938); *Electricity Co. of Sofia and Bulgaria Case*, P.C.I.J., Ser. A/B, No. 77, 81 (1939); *Anglo-Iranian Oil Co. Case* (U.K. v. Iran), *I.C.J. Reports*, 93, 103 (1952).
[14] *I.C.J. Reports*, 23 (1957).

tic jurisdiction."[15] Under these terms, the Court itself could determine whether a question was or was not a matter of international law.

Despite repeated attempts to start removing the Connally Amendment from the U.S. Declaration filed with the Court, it remains on the statute books.[16] The move to repeal it is not based on abstract legal principles or on the desires of "one-worlders" to strengthen international law. It rests on the hard realization that the reservation, because of the reciprocity principle, is actually more harmful than beneficial to the United States. It actually permits other states to invoke the reservation against the interest of the United States and its citizens.

For instance, the United States in concluding economic agreements with other states, requires recipient countries to agree to submit to the I.C.J. any case in which the United States asks for compensation for one of its nationals, as the result of any governmental measures which might affect contractual rights or concessions granted.[17] Under the reciprocity rule, however, there is nothing to stop any of these signatories legally from invoking the Connally Amendment to prevent any such dispute from going before the I.C.J.

The United States has in fact been quite circumspect in invoking the Connally Amendment and has in large part borne out Senator Connally's views that it would not adopt a subterfuge to block the judgment of the Court.[18] But there is no doubt that the reservation is inherently offensive to the Court and could be used extravagantly and arbitrarily. Good faith really requires a disputant to leave it to the Court to determine the legal question of whether an issue is a domestic or an international matter.[19] Some judges have even raised the question of the reservation's validity, arguing that since, by Article 36(6), the Statute gives

---

[15] *Hearings,* 362 (1960).

[16] U.S. Vice-President Nixon, in a speech before the Academy of Political Science in April 1959 urged states to elevate the I.C.J. to the status of a real Supreme Court of the world with the power to make binding decisions, especially in cases involving different interpretations of treaties. Earlier, in his 1959 State of the Union Message, President Eisenhower had indicated that he would ask Congress to modify the Connally Amendment. See also Herbert Briggs, "The United States and the International Court of Justice, a Re-Examination," *A.J.I.L.,* LIII (1959), 301–318, and Report of the American Bar Association Committee of International and Comparative Law, October 1959 (Chairman, Lyman F. Tondel, Jr.).

[17] Economic Cooperation Act of 1948, Section 115(b)10, 62 Stat. 152 (P.L. 452, 80th Cong.), and agreements concluded under it, *e.g.,* Economic Cooperation Agreement with Sweden, July 3, 1948, *T.I.A.S.* 1793; *Hearings,* 42, 58 (1960).

[18] For Connally's views on this point, see 92 Cong. Rec. 10695; for U.S. use of the Amendment, see Interhandel Case (*Switzerland* v. *United States*) [1959] *I.C.J. Reports,* 6 (Preliminary Objections).

[19] See statements by Judges Lauterpacht and Spender, Interhandel Case, *I.C.J. Reports,* 42–43, 52–53, 57–59 (1959).

the Court the right to determine its own jurisdiction, any reservation that runs counter to the Court's Statute could hardly be valid.[20]

The Amendment remains part of the U.S. Declaration because of misapprehensions that without it, the United States would find itself constantly subjected to arbitrary rulings by the Court that matters which the United States regards as domestic were in fact international. In actual fact, however, the Court would be bound by its own Statute to decide questions by the principles of international law, which has never claimed authority over domestic questions. While it is true that conceptions of what constitutes a domestic question change from time to time, the changes are not sudden or arbitrary, but stem from gradual changes in the international environment through treaties, customs, general principles, and judicial decisions, with which the United States would undoubtedly find itself in agreement. Proponents of the Connally Amendment who fear that the Court would interfere in U.S. immigration, tariff, and civil rights questions have no basis for their fears. Moreover, the United States could always withdraw its declaration under Article 36 of the Statute. The ultimate safeguard, of course, lies in the fact that the Court has no means for enforcing its judgments. The judges know that the future of the institution they serve depends on its reasonableness, and there is no reason to assume that they would act irresponsibly in drawing the line between domestic and international questions.[21] Quite the opposite objections, in fact, have been levied against the Court's reluctance to decide what seem to many legal observers actually to be international questions.[22]

Despite the slowness with which change comes to the international system, international law is not forever doomed to stand still because of inertia. Challenges are being posed to the law by the changed conditions of modern life: a suddenly enlarged "family" of nations, more international institutions than have existed ever before, and a growing social and economic interdependence among states.[23] From all these sources have come pressures to reconsider the adequacy of existing international law and international legal institutions.

The Soviet Union, with its radical notions about relations between

---

[20] Norwegian Loans Case, *I.C.J. Reports,* 45, 47 (1957).
[21] For a full discussion of the "Jurisdiction of the International Court of Justice and the Rule of Law," see address by J. Lee Rankin before the New York State Bar Association, June 24, 1960 (mimeographed).
[22] See, for instance, comment on the South West Africa Decision of 1966: Rosalyn Higgins, "The International Court and South West Africa: The Implications of the Judgment," *International Affairs,* XXXXII (1966), 573–599.
[23] Richard A. Falk, "On the Quasi-Legislative Competence of the General Assembly," *A.J.I.L.,* LX (1966), 782–791.

state and property was the first to challenge western conceptions of the need for states to pay "prompt, adequate, and effective" compensation for private property nationalized by a socialist state. Newer states of Asia and Africa have, particularly since the second World War, also attacked rules of law which, in the minds of their statesmen, tended to establish and preserve an earlier colonial order. They have therefore pressed to widen the limits of the territorial sea so as to protect indigenous fishing rights against states whose nationals were, because of superior technology, better able to exploit the sea's resources; they have called for changes in contractual arrangements made by colonial powers in order to guarantee to themselves control over their natural resources; and they have done their best to create in developed states a sense of obligation to assist them economically and socially.[24]

The pressure for change come, not only from the new states with new ideas, but also from international institutions. The two are related, of course, because the new states are members of the international organizations and, in fact, regard their membership as an important attribute of contemporary statehood, in itself an example of a change that may ultimately affect the law of recognition.[25] International institutions have long contributed to international law from the earliest regimes governing internationalized rivers in the nineteenth century to the elaborate institutions of the Council of Europe. Europe, despite its close association with the state system and international law, has gone so far as to breach the walls of state sovereignty with its regional organizations; the economic ones, like the High Authority of the European Coal and Steel Community, actually received authority to issue binding regulations to member governments. But even more significant for future developments are those institutions which have begun modestly to permit individuals to challenge state authority—as provided in the European Convention on Human Rights (see pp. 395 ff., *supra*).

The European experience will undoubtedly supply examples for other states, particularly for those which can function effectively in regional groups. In the meantime, all United Nations members are acquiring experience in the ways in which states may use international organizations. They will act in these forums, as everywhere, from self-interest. But with growing sophistication and better appreciation of the forces

[24] See Oliver J. Lissitzyn, "International Law in a Divided World," *International Conciliation* (New York: Carnegie Endowment for International Peace, No. 542, March 1963), pp. 37–62; Inis L. Claude, "Collective Legitimization as a Political Function of the United Nations," *International Organization*, XX (1966), 367–379.
[25] See Claude, pp. 375–376 and Rosalyn Higgins, *The Development of International Law Through the Political Organs of the United Nations* (London: Oxford University Press, 1963), pp. 1–57.

shaping our lives, they will come increasingly to realize what their true self-interest really is. As Wolfgang Friedmann has written: "not starry-eyed idealism, but the realization of the catastrophic consequences of the unrestrained use of the prerogatives of national sovereignty . . . led to the successive attempts of the League of Nations Covenant and the United Nations Charter to impose some restraints upon the use of force, and to lay the foundation for an international community of mankind."[26]

International politics and international law are certainly not on the verge of major and sudden transformations. The world has a long way to go to change the United Nations into the international government which has long been the goal of idealists. The United Nations does not legislate and, in fact, its founding members deliberately rejected the idea that it should do so.[27] None the less, U.N. resolutions may have a legal effect. They can provide evidence of an international consensus which tends to establish a rule, or they may act as a stimulus to move states in certain directions in developing law—as, for instance, the Assembly may have helped bring states to the point where they were willing to ban nuclear tests in the atmosphere.[28] General Assembly resolutions are not laws, but at some point, difficult to define, states may regard themselves as legally bound by practices in which they have long engaged, and new rules of law may emerge from these international transactions. The continuing efforts of states to formulate their views into resolutions, the records of U.N. debates, and the compiling of official votes thus build up more unremitting pressures on the international system than have existed before.

These pressures may destroy good order; they may, as one observer has suggested, "encourage behavior based upon calculation of what the political situation will permit rather than consideration of what the principles of order require," but one may hope that civilizing influences will help "collective legitimization . . . stimulate legal changes that will make international law more worthy of respect and more likely to be respected."[29]

Support for the more optimistic view comes from recalling the positive treaties that have already emerged from U.N. efforts, like the Covenants

---

[26] "United States Policy and the Crisis of International Law," *A.J.IL.*, LIX (1965), 857–871, 871.
[27] See the Philippine proposal in *U.N.C.I.O. Docs.*, IX (1945), 316.
[28] See Richard A. Falk, "On the Quasi-Legislative Competence of the General Assembly," *A.J.I.L.*, LX (1966), 782–791, and Rosalyn Higgins, *The Development of International Law through the Political Organs of the United Nations* (London: Oxford University Press, 1965).
[29] Inis L. Claude, "Collective Legitimization as a Political Function of the United Nations," *International Organization*, XX (1966), 367–379.

of Human Rights and the pact which rejoices in the name of the "Treaty Governing the Exploration and Use of Outer Space, including the Moon and Other Celestial Bodies." Moreover, there are other forces also at work, yielding constructive results year by year in matters of statehood, domestic jurisdiction, recognition, the use of force, and treaty law.[30] It may well be that students of international law will find that one of the most fruitful lines of development in the future lies in integrating the United Nations more and more into the law-making process, *e.g.,* by giving legal effect to General Assembly resolutions passed unanimously or with the substantial support of representatives from different legal systems.[31]

We should not delude ourselves that international law is a perfect system; it manifestly is not. Those interested in developing a more nearly perfect international order have much to do. Nonetheless, it is hopeful that international law has managed to survive and to profit from three epoch-making developments of the years since the second World War:

(1) It has, despite the nonwestern origins of many new states, incorporated them into the "family of nations."

(2) It has absorbed rules relating to modern economic development, coming to grips with the need to reconcile state and private trading systems and with new patterns of controlling natural resources. Much new law has developed at meetings like the U.N. Conference on Trade and Development in 1964 and through the workings of commodity agreements and the International Bank for Reconstruction and Development.

(3) International law has also been able to cope rather well with the ideological conflict that developed after the second World War, as seen in many treaties and in the work of many international organizations.[32]

Surely some hope for the future lies in these continuing efforts to substitute rules for anarchy and to develop institutions dedicated to preserving and glorifying human dignity in an increasingly complicated world.[33]

---

[30] See Higgins on these subjects.

[31] See Edward McWhinney, "The 'New' Countries and the 'New' International Law: The United Nations Special Conference on Friendly Relations and Co-operation Among States," *A.J.I.L.,* LX (1966), 1–33, esp. pp. 29–33.

[32] Wolfgang Friedmann, "United States Policy and the Crisis of International Law," *A.J.I.L.,* LIX (1965), 858–859.

[33] See Myres S. McDougal and Harold D. Lasswell, "The Identification and Appraisal of Diverse Systems of Public Order," *A.J.I.L.,* LIII (1959), 1–29.

Index

(For Table of Cases and Documents, *see* pages xiii–xx.)